THE IDENTITARIANS

THE IDENTITARIANS

THE MOVEMENT AGAINST GLOBALISM
AND ISLAM IN EUROPE

JOSÉ PEDRO ZÚQUETE

University of Notre Dame Press
Notre Dame, Indiana

University of Notre Dame Press
Notre Dame, Indiana 46556
undpress.nd.edu

Copyright © 2018 by the University of Notre Dame

Paperback edition published in 2021

All Rights Reserved

Published in the United States of America

Library of Congress Cataloging-in-Publication Data

Names: Zuquete, Jose Pedro, author.
Title: The Identitarians : the movement against globalism and Islam in Europe / Jose Pedro Zuquete.
Description: Notre Dame, Indiana : University of Notre Dame Press, 2018. | Includes bibliographical references and index. |
Identifiers: LCCN 2018036112 (print) | LCCN 2018055576 (ebook) | ISBN 9780268104238 (pdf) | ISBN 9780268104245 (epub) | ISBN 9780268104214 (hardback) | ISBN 0268104212 (hardback) | ISBN 9780268104221 (paperback) | ISBN 0268104220 (paperback)
Subjects: LCSH: Right-wing extremists—Europe. | Anti-globalization movement—Europe. | Social movements—Europe. | Identity politics—Europe. | Nationalism—Europe. | Islamophobia—Europe. | Europe—Politics and government—21st century.
Classification: LCC HN380.Z9 (ebook) | LCC HN380.Z9 Z97 2018 (print) | DDC 303.48/4094—dc23
LC record available at https://lccn.loc.gov/2018036112

This book is dedicated to my father and to the memory of my mother.

Europe is lying propped upon her elbows:
From East to West she lies, staring
Out, reminiscent—Greek eyes from the shelter
Of romantic hair.
                              —*Fernando Pessoa*

If the price of freedom is heavy, that of identity is doubly so.
The first can be given us by decree; the other is always up to us.
                              —*Miguel Torga*

CONTENTS

	Illustrations	ix
	Preface	xiii
	Acknowledgments	xv
	Abbreviations	xvii
	Introduction	1
ONE	Intellectual Foundations, Practices, and Networks	7
TWO	Identity against Globalism	105
THREE	Identity against Islam	168
FOUR	For a New Geopolitics of Europe	227
FIVE	Of Race and Identity	266
SIX	The Coming War?	320
	Postscript	364
	Notes	373
	Bibliography	407
	Index	459

ILLUSTRATIONS

FIGURE 1. Cover of *Terre et Peuple* magazine honoring Dominique Venner four years after his death (Summer 2017).   23

FIGURE 2. Poster for Polémia's second "Forum of Dissidence" (November 19, 2016). It reads, "Decrypt, Disobey, Act."   26

FIGURE 3. The logo of Génération Identitaire.   53

FIGURE 4. The logo of CasaPound Italia.   54

FIGURE 5. Image from the campaign *Visages de la Reconquête* (Faces of the Reconquest, launched in September 2016).   58

FIGURE 6. Logo, with the Spartan helmet in the middle, of the Identitarian boxing club/self-defense gym, The Agoge (founded in January 2017).   60

FIGURE 7. Logo of the "Identitarian and Patriotic" house La Citadelle in the city of Lille (open since 2016).   62

FIGURE 8. Image from the campaign "Show Your Face" showing Edwin, an Identitarian activist from Vienna.   80

FIGURE 9. Image from the campaign "Show Your Face" portraying Melanie, an Identitarian activist from Germany. It says, "Fights for our right to identity."   81

FIGURE 10. The logo of Arktos, a publishing house currently headquartered in Budapest, Hungary (founded in 2009).   99

FIGURE 11. Right On podcast dedicated to the European Generation Identity, and featuring Austria's Alexander Markovics as a guest (March 8, 2016).   101 x Illustrations

FIGURE 12. T-shirt declaring "Eat the universalists," from Austria's Identitarian label Phalanx Europa.   106

FIGURE 13. Poster for CasaPound's campaign of incentives to raise the birth rate of Italians of native stock (launched in January 2017) with the slogan "Fill the cradles, empty the welcoming centers [for refugees and migrants]."   136

FIGURE 14. Cover of the French Identitarians' magazine depicting their "defense" of Calais against the "invasion of immigrants" (May–June 2016).   140

FIGURE 15. Meme from the Austrian Identitarians depicting the Slovenian philosopher Slavoj Žižek and a quote from him: "The greatest hypocrites are those who call for open borders."   141

FIGURE 16. Identitarian propaganda material for the joint mission Defend Europe (June 2017).   143

FIGURE 17. Meme of the French writer Jean Raspail created by Martin Lichtmesz for a 2010 *Sezession* campaign showcasing its Hall of Heroes.   146

FIGURE 18. Cover of an issue of *Réfléchir & Agir* dedicated to the "crusade against the modern world" and including an interview with Renaud Camus.   149

FIGURE 19. Photo of a demonstration by the Austrian Identitarians in Vienna "against the Great Replacement" (June 6, 2015). Courtesy of IBÖ.   152

FIGURE 20. Poster of the German-speaking Identitarian movement alerting the people about the "Great Replacement."   154

FIGURE 21. Cover of *Terre et Peuple* magazine with the title "Crusade, Resistance, Reconquest" (Autumn 2005).   178

FIGURE 22. Poster/meme of Génération Identitaire: "Stop Islamization—We Are at Home!"   187

FIGURE 23. Meme created by the Austrian Identitarians depicting their stunt at the Turkish embassy in Vienna on March 22, 2017. Courtesy of IBÖ.   196

FIGURE 24. Meme created by the French Identitarians in support of their campaign to dissolve the Islamist organization UOIF (now French Muslims). It shows the words of the organization's former president, the Sheikh Ahmed Jaballah: "The UOIF consists of a two-stage process. The first one is democratic, the second will put in orbit an Islamic society."   206

FIGURE 25. Poster publicizing a Génération Identitaire demonstration in Paris (November 25, 2017) protesting the "terror" in Europe. "Against the Islamists let's defend Europe," it says. This demonstration was subsequently forbidden by the authorities, to the outrage of the group.   208

FIGURE 26. Poster from CasaPound's NGO Sol.Id. advertising a food drive for Syria.   218

FIGURE 27. Advertisement for the Academia Christiana annual summer conference held with the theme "Identity against the New Tower of Babel" (Summer 2016).   223

FIGURE 28. Meme or propaganda material from the German Identitarian movement. It reads, "Europe, Youth, Reconquista!"   238

FIGURE 29. Cover of the *Terre et Peuple* magazine with the title "Russia Is Back" (Autumn 2008).   245

FIGURE 30. T-shirt bearing the words "Europa Nostra," from Austria's Identitarian label Phalanx Europa.   254

FIGURE 31. Demonstration of CasaPound in Rome, in honor of Dominique Venner (May 23, 2016). The banner reads "Europe revolts against fatalism!," with the words surrounded by CasaPound flags, as well as Italian, French, and Spanish flags. Photo by Antonio Mele.   258

FIGURE 32. Meme created by the German Identitarian movement in January of 2017 in support of Donald Trump. The quote from Trump reads: "A nation without borders is not a nation."   261

FIGURE 33. White nationalism goes populist. Meme advertising the Unite the Right rally in Charlottesville, Virginia, with Richard Spencer center front (August 2017).   305

xii   Illustrations

FIGURE 34. German Identitarian street campaign in the northern state of Mecklenburg-Vorpommern, with an activist dressed as Pepe the Frog distributing propaganda leaflets.   311

FIGURE 35. Meme in support of the summer 2017 Identitarian Defend Europe mission depicting Pepe the Frog as the C-Star ship.   311

FIGURE 36. Meme from the German Identitarian movement advertising the need to rekindle the "fighting spirit" of Europeans. It reads: "Identity needs defense."   325

FIGURE 37. Meme from the early incarnation of Génération Identitaire (Une Autre Jeunesse) depicting an ancient Spartan warrior with the message "We are the youth that chooses Thermopylae rather than softening and renunciation."   325

FIGURE 38. T-shirt reading "Europa calling and I must go" sold by the German Identitarian movement shop. The bubble reads, "Oh my God, he is in love with his homeland."   327

FIGURE 39. T-shirt reading "Defender of Europe" from the French Génération Identitaire online shop. It shows the Lambda sign and the image of the Spartan King Leonidas.   327

FIGURE 40. Antifa sticker against Generation Identity. This is the German version. It reads "Hunt Nazi Hipsters—Smash the Identitarian Movement."   337

FIGURE 41. Covers of (*left*) Philippe Randa's book *Poitiers Demain* (orig. pub. 1986) and (*right*) Fenek Solère's *The Partisan* (orig. pub. 2014).   359

FIGURE 42. Cover of Modeste Lakrite's *L'Édit de Mantes*, originally published in 2016.   361

FIGURE 43. Poster by the French Identitarians of Lyon advertising a book talk by *Guerrilla*'s author, Laurent Obertone, at their Identitarian house, La Traboule (November 2016).   362

PREFACE

My purpose in writing *The Identitarians: The Movement against Globalism and Islam in Europe* is to inform readers of exactly what Identitarians have to say and how they imagine and present themselves. To accomplish this, it is vital to look at movements like this one from the inside out and not make hasty and uninformed assumptions about them. The type of knowledge that can be gained this way is necessary in order to gain a full understanding of the nature and appeal of Identitarian propaganda and social movements. With this premise in mind, it is crucial to bring home the point that the book is academic and ethnographic, not polemic, in nature. The attempt to understand and describe the Identitarian movement does not indicate approval or validation.

In today's world, it is vital for scholars, politicians, and media figures, right and left and in between, not to simplistically dismiss the Identitarian phenomenon—whose social media and activist youthful base have been growing in Europe since the turn of the millennium, although its theoretical foundations were laid much earlier—as a marginal movement. Many of the sociocultural trends that feed it—above all, the perception of an ongoing multicultural and multiethnic transformation of traditional European societies and the related "sense of threat" to traditional European values and identities that it provokes—are likely to continue in the coming decades. So, too, will the Identitarian ethnocultural backlash.

In the end, my intent was to employ an ethnographical and phenomenological methodology in presenting this multifaceted movement on its own terms as much as possible. As the reader will verify in the pages of the book, I undertook this inside look as exhaustively as possible, delving deep into the Identitarian literature and social media production, covering different geographic contexts, and drawing from a plethora of primary sources in different languages while simultaneously including many firsthand accounts, testimonies, and interviews with theorists, sympathizers, and activists. All of this was done in the hope that scholars and other readers can at least be well enough informed before drawing their own conclusions about the structure, history, beliefs, and moral perspectives of a movement that has made "Defend Europe" not just a distinctive hashtag but an overriding existential purpose.

ACKNOWLEDGMENTS

The making of *The Identitarians: The Movement against Globalism and Islam in Europe* took roughly three years, with intensive periods of research and writing that I engaged in mostly in the southernmost part of Portugal, in the village of Vilamoura. The whole time I've had the support of my institution, the Institute of Social Sciences at the University of Lisbon, as well as the financial support of the Foundation for Science and Technology. I want to thank, too, my colleagues and friends António Costa Pinto, Marina Costa Lobo, Bruno Cardoso Reis, Riccardo Marchi, and Filipe Nobre Faria for their overall support during this enterprise. The editor and poet Matt Stefon I thank for his help with the manuscript and for his continuous friendship and support. My friends Charles and Cherry Lindholm, Jeff Bristol, and George Michael offered, at different points, words of reassurance and wisdom. It was a privilege to have such an encouraging and diligent editor as Eli Bortz—I've greatly benefited from his tireless support. Also at Notre Dame Press I want to thank the managing editor, Matthew Dowd, as well as Wendy McMillen, the design and production manager. Marilyn Martin was a careful and judicious copyeditor, and I'm extremely pleased with her work. I am also grateful to the two anonymous reviewers who took time to read the manuscript. I believe that they have helped me to make the book more solid in terms of scholarship. Throughout, *Still in a Dream: 1988–1995—A Story of Shoegaze*, as well as the incredible discography of the Greek music label sound in silence—and its limited-edition releases—provided many, many hours of soundtrack for the writing of this book.

At the same time I want to express my gratitude to the various people who gave me interviews and/or assisted in other ways with the book project. In alphabetical order by first name, they are Adam Berčík,

Adriano Scianca, Alex Kurtagic, Alexander Markovics, Antonio Mele, Bo De Geyndt, Brittany Pettibone, Colin Liddell, Daniel Friberg, David Engels, Duarte Branquinho, Eli Mosley, Ernesto Milà Rodríguez, Fabrice Robert, Fenek Solère, Ferenc Almássy, Flávio Gonçalves, Georges Feltin-Tracol, Georges Hupin, Gergely Kőrössy, Götz Kubitschek, Greg Johnson, Jared Taylor, Jiri (Délský potápěč), Joachim Veliocas, João Franco, João Martins, John Lambton, John Morgan, Julian Langness, Julien Langella, Jurij Kofner, Kai Murros, Lucian Tudor, Manuel Ochsenreiter, Martin Lichtmesz, Martin Sellner, Martin van Creveld, Michael Francis Walker, Michael O'Meara, Patrick Casey, Pavel Tulaev, Philippe Randa, Piero San Giorgio, Pierre Krebs, Pierre Vial, Raivis Zeltīts, Rémi Tremblay, Richard Spencer, Robert Steuckers, Ruuben Kaalep, Tom Dupré, Tom Sunić, Tore Rasmussen, and Umberto Actis Perino.

Finally, and it couldn't be otherwise, I am grateful to my family, whose support never wavers; to my soccer team, Benfica, for the many moments of celebration they have given me; and to Ché, a pug like no other.

ABBREVIATIONS

4GW	Fourth-Generation Warfare
AfD	Alternative for Germany
CCC	Center for Continental Cooperation
CDU	Christian Democratic Union
CPI	CasaPound Italia
EDL	English Defense League
EU	European Union
FPÖ	Freedom Party
FQS	Fédération des Québécois de Souche, or Federation of the Quebecois of Stock
GI	Generation Identity
GRECE	Groupement de Recherche et d'Études pour la Civilisation Européenne, or Research and Study Group for European Civilization
GUD	Groupe Union Défense
IB	Identitäre Bewegung, or Identitarian Movement
IBD	Identitäre Bewegung Deutschland, or Identitarian Movement of Germany
IBÖ	Identitäre Bewegung Österreich, or Identitarian Movement of Austria
MAS	Mouvement d'Action Sociale, or Movement of Social Action
MPG	movement Giovani Padani
ND	Nouvelle Droite, or New Right
NPI	National Policy Institute
PD	Partito Democratico

PEGIDA	Patriotic Europeans against the Islamization of the Occident
RESF	Réseau Éducation sans Frontières, or Education without Borders
SIOE	Stop Islamization of Europe
Sol.Id.	*Solidarité–Identités*, or Solidarity–Identities
TAZ	temporary autonomy zone
UOIF	Union of Islamic Organizations of France
WIR	Wiens Identitäre Richtung, or Vienna's Identitarian Direction
WN	white nationalist

Introduction

This book is the chronicle of a rebellion. Against the backdrop of a once great civilization ravaged by a modern liberal capitalist world and under assault by a conquering foreign people, the writer and historian Dominique Venner preached a return to the sources of European identity, rediscovering the beauty, creativity, heroism, and uniqueness of its culture. He thought that, amid a world falling apart, Europeans loyal to the historical and cultural integrity of their civilization must engage in the struggle for Europe and resist, reconquering what has been lost. And much has been lost, because, "for the first time in their multi-millennial history, the European peoples do not prevail over their own space, neither spiritually, politically, nor ethnically."[1] It is, quite simply, a matter of survival. Either this Identitarian resistance succeeds or it fails, but it vows never to succumb to fatalism or to mindless indifference in the middle of the ruins.

A myth of identity lies at the root of this twenty-first century intellectual and activist rebellion: a myth not in the sense of truth or falsity but in that of a call to action, a vision that mobilizes, fueling the willingness to fight back and overturn, against all odds, a system of domination and an identity not thought out as an abstraction or a simple social construction but felt as something more profound, primordial, tied to space, territory, memory, and ethnicity, that *must* be revitalized today. At a regional, national—but, above all, continental, European—level this identity of "flesh and blood" has been defaced and disfigured, and the situation has deteriorated past the point at which only a radical change—political, economic, cultural, *and* spiritual—is conceivable. Europe has gone so far along the path of destruction that radicalism is the only available method and tool to save her.

The Identitarian indictment is a dark account of contemporary European life. Europe has been torn apart by the Western model of civilization that it helped to create, which today is synonymous with Americanization, and this dominant ideology—which in this new century bears the name of globalism—has diluted its distinctive character. Its communities, peoples, and cultures have suffered the onslaught of an abstract model that homogenizes all differences, and combats all natural attachments (to nations, regions, cultures, ethnicities), in an attempt to destroy all barriers to the free flow of markets, reducing human beings to a sorrowful condition in which the only identity that is allowed, and celebrated, is that of individual materialism and consumerism. At the same time, so goes the Identitarian accusation, European elites allowed the "opening of the gates," the decades-long policies of mass immigration, which softened and corrupted the relatively coherent and homogenous collective identity of European peoples, constituting a major dimension of the self-immolation of the continent. The more recent surge of immigration or invasion—whose participants the official line of thinking and its zealots labeled "migrants"—added extra fuel to this ongoing "Great Replacement" of peoples in European lands. Amid the degradation of its identity, the abjuration of its ancient Indo-European and Hellenic roots, feeling guilty about its own history, and awash in relativism, self-doubt, and self-loathing, Europe is on the verge of being conquered by Islam, a young, rooted, and spiritually strong civilization that is superior to an aging and frail Europe whose treacherous elites are behaving in a manner that is the greatest expression of a civilization in free fall.

Although the Identitarian network of resistance is diverse—it comprises a variety of figures and groups that may emphasize different aspects of this civilizational crisis, to the detriment of others—all of its participants share a calamitous diagnosis and a radical critique of the current state of Europe. They also share an avowed nonconformist ethos, abhor defeatism, and radiate, in their words and actions, a disposition of being the watchmen on the wall in a zero-sum struggle to keep alive what they perceive to be the real European identity. In this book Identitarians are viewed broadly, writ large. Since the late twentieth century they have been responsible for a vast literary production that has strengthened the depth of their philosophical and cultural critique of the status quo. This intellectual or cultural dimension—which supporters brand a true war of ideas in defense of Identitarianism—is, of course, important. But what has characterized the Identitarian struggle in the most recent times is the emergence of an activist, street-based, and Internet-savvy young militancy that has widened the repertoires of Identitarian combat beyond publications and conferences, emblematic of the Identitarian "old guard," to include disruptive street protests, flash mobs, occupations, media campaigns and stunts, vlogs, podcasts, livestreams, meme-making, and an intensified targeting of the perceived enemies of the collective identity—in this case, all those who conspire to bring about, or even actively work for, its destruction, from deracinated elites to sociocultural subversive groups and forces. This phenomenon has its epicenter in France and Italy, but it has spread, in different rhythms, to other European countries—particularly those of Germanic Central Europe—and it is viewed as an example of activism that is clean-shaven, appealing, with impact on the media and public opinion, and therefore worthy of imitation. Although not without rivalries and personal disputes, these two wings of combat—one more theoretical, the other galvanized by direct action—form the face of the Identitarian surge to regain the control of the destinies of European communities.

The Identitarians: The Movement Against Globalism and Islam in Europe charts and explores this territory of struggle. It begins with an excursion into its intellectual foundations, figures and groups of reference, dynamics of militancy, activism, and networking before proceeding with the movement's critique of globalization and its damning consequences, such as "immigration-colonization." It then analyzes the contemporary Identitarian battle against Islam, as well as the search for a new European geopolitics that safeguards its independence, shuns American tutelage, and looks in hope toward the East. Next it focuses on the ethnic-racial implications of this struggle for identity, which may imply formal or informal alliances with a wider, mostly US-based, white nationalist movement, and finally on the looming war (which for many Identitarians is already raging), along ethnic lines, that they believe will revitalize and awaken a wider European resistance. Throughout the book, and whenever necessary, other non-Identitarian groups, initiatives, and dynamics are described as a way of contextualizing the scenario in which Identitarians operate and in which they interact; this study always keeps in mind that Identitarians do not act in isolation and that they are also a mirror of the age and of its troubles.

In the most recent decades, political radicalism, particularly in its right-wing dimension, has become an important topic of study among scholars, law enforcement practitioners, and national security analysts. Although the aim of this book is not to go over familiar arguments and debates about ideological classification, it should be said that academia—and in this it has been followed by journalism and the activism of watchdog groups—conceptualizes most of the writers, activists, and groups present throughout this book as belonging to the radical—or even extreme—right. Generally, that is not how Identitarians see themselves. Within their vast and heterogeneous family, other self-descriptions are favored: from "patriots" to the "true Right," adherents to the "beyond Left and Right" line of thinking, or, simply, Identitarians. However, as will be shown in the pages and chapters that follow, at the heart of Identitarianism, in both its theoretical and activist dimensions, is the cleavage between Identity and globalism with all its ramifications and implications. This split is voiced and articulated in different ways, with some groups emphasizing more combating mass immigration or Islamization (as the most urgent thing to do), while others prioritize the consequences of an out-of-control capitalism that they conceive of as speculative and with no respect for any sort of boundaries and limits. Also, the gamut of defenses of ethnoidentity, within the broader arch of Europeism, fluctuates between regionalist leanings and more nationalist attachments. In all its expressions, it must be emphasized, it is not a strict attachment to rigid Left and Right categories that defines Identitarians. If there is an ideological "Other," it is what they denounce as the "left" or "liberal" establishment. They do not represent a "radicalization" of the mainstream liberal right—on the contrary, to a steady degree, they are its opposite, and they see that liberal right as their anathema—while the activism of their youth uses many ideas or tactics traditionally associated with left-wing groups or movements. They are not simply "conservatives" either. If they are "conservatives," they are radically so; they want a reset of the system, ultimately a change of the current globalist or liberal paradigm toward a rebooting of Europe's ethnocultural tradition for the twenty-first century.

Even though Identitarians give primacy to the noninstitutional dimension of politics, they also engage, directly or indirectly, in electoral and party politics, particularly with political parties viewed as sharing a like-minded disposition. These connections and bridges are of course part of this book's narrative. Yet its main focus is on the anti-systemic nature of Identitarians. The fact of the matter is that Identitarians of all stripes and in all locations are also much more far-reaching and sweeping—in their diagnosis of the evils that afflict Europe *and* in the solutions proposed—than are the right-wing populist political parties that they often defend. More than a simple attachment to the ideological spectrum, what defines Identitarians and invests them with both a sense of existential angst and an equal sense of existential purpose is the rejection of the system to which they impute the calamities that afflict Europe. They reject with the same fierce intensity the progressive Left and the neoliberal Right, guilty as both are in the process of defiling rooted European identities, as well as effectively complicit in advancing the marginalization and disempowerment of Europe's peoples. At the end of the day, it is this refusal to comply with a system charged with "destroying cultures and killing peoples" that fuels the European Identitarian uprising.

Douglas Murray, the conservative English author and commentator—and someone who, although very critical of the contemporary course of European politics and culture, is certainly not a European Identitarian—noted, in a podcast, that "the Identity of Europe—it's a very painful thing . . . people are not very good at talking about it . . . but I think it's just there underlying everything [the problems that afflict Europe]. What is this thing? What is it to be European? Who can be European? Can anyone be European? Is Europe the home for the peoples who've been living in Europe or is it the home for everyone in the world who wants to move and call it home? These are very, very big questions."[2] European Identitarians, in all their diversity, believe that they have indeed the answers for—and that is the theme of this book—these "very, very big questions."

ONE

Intellectual Foundations, Practices, and Networks

He who has grown wise concerning old origins, behold, he will at last seek after the fountains of the future and new origins.
—Nietzsche, *Thus Spoke Zarathustra*

INTRODUCTION: A EUROPEAN REVIVAL

The current Identitarian intellectual and activist movement that wants to transform Europe was not born in a vacuum. A major foundation has been on the rise since the late 1960s of a Francophone intellectual movement that, with the passage of time, became devoted to a guiding principle: striking down the hegemonic Western liberal-capitalist paradigm through cultural combat. Taking their cue from Marxist Italian Antonio Gramsci—especially his insistence on the power of ideas and the need for an organic intellectual vanguard to change mentalities—adherents to this movement saw a metapolitical drive for the conquest of minds and spirits as a priority in order for a regenerated and yet again powerful Europe to emerge from the ashes of a decadent West.[1] The subsequent labeling of this "école de pensée" (school of thought) by the French media as "Nouvelle Droite" (New Right, ND) was not without controversy: Although their original founders started their militancy on the French radical right, there has always been a tendency by many of its members to define their thought transversally, beyond political divisions and rigid dichotomies. In fact, the original aim of this school of thought was to create a "new culture." The fact of the matter is that the media label stuck. ND served to designate a wide rebel and heretical (owing to its self-proclaimed "anticonformist" and "antisystemic" ethos) network of thinkers, writers, publications, groups, and associations that have expanded well beyond its original borders.

Of course the rejection of this Western or liberal modernity was nothing new in the twentieth century. The ND, in fact, was particularly inspired by—and intellectually indebted to—what the Swiss-born German thinker Armin Mohler called the Conservative Revolution (CR), a movement that indeed aimed at creating a new culture, or a counterculture. Although heterogeneous, and with different thinkers and currents of thoughts, it basically consisted of a radical attempt by a cluster of German intellectuals in the interwar period to pull apart the new liberal foundations of the country (of which the Weimar Republic was a symbol), and it searched to overcome the loss of sacral, ethnic, and communal bonds with a holistic paradigm that—and this was the guiding idea of the CR's Young Conservative current gathered around Arthur Moeller van den Bruck—although rooted in tradition, would constitute not a restoration but a new revolutionary beginning. Above all, this movement represented a spiritual rejection of the modern world, and this is the reason that adventurous figures such as, especially, Ernst Jünger, but also Ernst von Salomon—the first a veteran and memorialist of World War I and an activist in the National-Revolutionary camp, and the other a member of the Freikorps active after that war, while plotting against the new order by making the rejection of the bourgeois civilization a modus vivendi—were a sort of existential (in heroic life and deeds) personification of the CR worldview.

Back (or forward) to France and to the ND, which for more than forty years, and with Alain de Benoist as its major intellectual reference, has produced a vast bibliographical output, always with the intent of spreading a counterhegemonic discourse, consolidating a cultural counterpower and, eventually, a new paradigm for European societies. The ancient philosophical schools of Greece served as the ideal for the ND, and its own cultural association is called, not coincidentally, Groupement de Recherche et d'Études pour la Civilisation Européenne (GRECE—Research and Study Group for European Civilization). Jean-Claude Valla, one of its founders, noted the importance of the name: "What counts is the abbreviation, the reference to Greece. 'The Greeks,' Nietzsche said, 'are for us what the saints are for Christians.'"[2] Indeed, a philosophical denunciation of Western modernity lies at the basis of the ND's cultural combat. Although the seeds of the evil that afflict human existence are traced back to the egalitarianism and universalism of Judeo-Christian monotheism (imposing the worship of one God on a plural and polytheistic world), modernity secularized this tradition. Its chief ideology, liberalism, and its radical philosophy of individualism, has had the devastating consequence of eradicating collective identities and traditional cultures, and thereby of putting an end to the integrated, organic, and holistic nature of communities across the earth. The advent of a capitalist civilization, on the back of liberalism's economic and political doctrines—and the submission of the world to the rationale of the markets, which does not recognize borders, limits, or historical and cultural differences—is only a continuation and exacerbation of the evil dynamics set in motion by Western modernity.

In opposition to the eradicating universalism of the West, the ND has for a long time upheld differentialism, or the Right to Difference. Individuals belong to humanity *only* through the mediation of a particular culture. Communities and cultures must be defended because they express the spirit of a specific context, a unique way of life, personality, and destiny. To reinforce this perspective, ND writings refer to romantic anthropological views, such as eighteenth-century theorist Johann Herder's assertion that each culture has its own integrity and metaphysical "creative genius," as well as evoking more recent theorizations, such as the anthropologist Claude Lévi-Strauss's sentiment that the prospect of the rule of one culture and one civilization would be a gateway for something ominous to mankind. The truth of the matter is that although the thematic focus of the ND has been multidimensional, and some of its positions have evolved, this insistence on singularity against sameness, on differentialism against homogenization, and on the defense of the plural against the single—of the group or community against the rootless individual, atomized and without a foundational culture—has remained at the heart of its worldview. Because the world is a "pluriversum," wrote Alain de Benoist and Charles Champetier in their *Manifesto for a European Renaissance*, "the West's pretense to make the world over in its own image" by imposing its model on all others in the name of progress is an existential threat to all cultures, obstructing their own unique path, has been happening for a long tortuous time in Europe.[3]

It is within this ideological context, and in the spirit of defense of the "cause of peoples" (and of preserving their diversity) that the ND—particularly but not exclusively in the writings of de Benoist—worked up its notion of identity. This reflection was gradual. As noted by Robert Steuckers (born in 1956)—a Flemish intellectual, close to the ND in the past but now philosophically closer to the Identitarians, and a specialist in the various currents of the Conservative Revolution, who sees himself as a *métapolitologue* (a metapolitical political scientist)—this school of thought initially did not directly address the "question of Identity." In its early years, the issues that put identity at the center of discussion in France and Europe (mass immigration, the mixing of cultures, and intensified globalization) were still not fully developed.[4] As they grew deeper, the ND adopted the position of calling for "clear and strong identities" against "indifferentiation and uprooting."[5] Neither the assimilation of the melting pot (which blends all differences into an undifferentiated whole) nor the exclusion of apartheid was the ideal. The ND focus, according to de Benoist, is on the "defense of identity in a positive and open way" and not as an excuse to "inspire the most aggressive xenophobia," which would only discredit the notion itself.[6] The French thinker disparages the "bad usages of identity" and its "pathologies," particularly essentialism, or the vision of identity as an intangible essence, as an attribute that does not change, something that is shared identically by all the members of the group. This is a shortcut to perceiving identity as a tool for exclusion, legitimizing ignorance, and keeping others apart. De Benoist is particularly critical of the notion of "biological identities," which, although propped up as *the* example of something that does not change, has only a relative value; the only specific existence of human beings, de Benoist says, is social-historical. Nevertheless, this notion is usually put at the service of ethnocentrism and racism.[7] What this means is that even though the ND calls for "strong identities" as an indispensable way out of the atomism and individualism of the modern era—a call that has moved it closer to communitarian thinkers such as the Canadian philosopher Charles Taylor (a recurrent reference in de Benoist's writings about the issue)—it sees identity in a dynamic and dialogical perspective (in interaction with the others) and, as it makes a point of honor in repeating, in a nonethnocentric fashion. In short, "for the ND, communities or collective identities are above all dialogical entities, and not ethnic entities."[8] In a conference given in Washington, DC, de Benoist stated that the biggest threat to collective identities of European and Western countries is not the phenomenon of immigration but "planetary homogenization," or the "ideology of the Same," which threatens the identity of all peoples.[9]

Actually, in the ND narrative, it is the modern era that has inaugurated and accelerated the destabilizing globalization that is at the root of an Identitarian "awakening," because if on one hand it erases identities, on the other hand it stimulates, as a reaction, all sorts of religious, linguistic, sexual, and ethnocultural demands. Above all, these constitute a desire for recognition in a magma of uniformity.[10] Thibault Isabel, the editor in chief of *Krisis*, the "revue of ideas and debates" of the ND, sees in the individual *and* communitarian Identitarian a resurgence—which takes the form of a desperate and aggressive search for authenticity (an out-and-out cult nowadays)—a consequence of the modern era's "reign of anonymity."[11]

Irrespective of the ND's excoriation of the excesses of Identitarianism—what de Benoist calls "Identitarian tribalism"[12]—the reality is that the ND has laid the theoretical ground for Identitarians, exercising a great influence on their preference for cultural combat, rejection of universalism, embrace of differentialism, and overall critique of a system captured by a disintegrating liberal capitalism. Many of the ND views are woven into the Identitarian narrative about the contemporary desolate condition of Europe. It could be argued that Identitarians—in both intellectual and more activist dimensions—pick and choose à la carte what serves them the best in the ND cultural production in order to carry on their combat for Europe.

THE IDENTITARIAN TURN

Although the ND, in truth, provided many of the intellectual munitions that are part of the Identitarian firepower, it is nevertheless distinct from Identitarianism. Because the driving force of the Identitarian Weltanschauung is ethnoculturalism—which has been largely abandoned by today's ND—Identitarianism has departed from the "mother house," constituting today a new ideological breed. The prologue to the twenty-first-century European Identitarian current of thought is the overriding emphasis on the group's ethnocultural worth, the urgency to preserve it, and the setting of boundaries between the in-group, those who belong to the people (ultimately ethnic Europeans), and those who do not belong to the people, the out-group (non-Europeans). Within Identitarianism this emphasis on ethnicity is not equal among all Identitarian thinkers and groups, existing on a continuum ranging from moderate to high-intensity, but nevertheless constitutes a distinguishing feature shared by today's European defenders of identity. What follows is a short description of the emergence of Identitarianism in France and its metapolitical strongholds.

Particularly since the turn of the century, a strain of thinking that emerged out of the ND developed into a dissident current to GRECE's metapolitical project. Sharing the same diagnosis regarding the sorrowful state of Europe, although not necessarily agreeing on the cure (or on the issues that should be prioritized), this rival wing has been expanding over time. In the words of the US writer Michael O'Meara, an "ethno-nationalist who sees Identitarianism as a kindred movement,"[13] in this day and age a "multiform Identitarian resistance,"[14] rose to put a stop to the plunge of Europe into a cultural abyss. The Identitarian intellectual uprising is indeed diverse, composed of a variety of writers, activists, and groups all over Europe. There is, however, no unifying center of Identitarianism, nor has there been a defining moment of creation or any sort of before-and-after event. From an intellectual standpoint, what happened was a gradual split from a group of intellectuals, initially belonging to the ND, that developed parallel interpretations in response to a series of emerging issues—primary among them the issue of mass immigration and its impact on the original communities' identity—and refocused the discourse on the endangered ethnic dimension of European peoples and cultures. In this process of separation and naissance of a new intellectual movement, truly Identitarian entrepreneurs played a foundational role.

Why We Fight

In 2001 a small Paris publisher put out the book *Why We Fight: Manifesto of the European Renaissance*. Its author was Guillaume Faye (born in 1949), a former intellectual of reference in the ND. As he later wrote, "In 1986, I decided to leave because I had said what I had to say. The ND was starting to go around in circles."[15] Faye, who has a PhD in political science and is given to many undertakings (including serving as a radio host and working as a scriptwriter) is a prolific polemicist and essayist, often delivering his thoughts in a provocative style, phrasing, and imagery. Ten years later, in its English-language edition, translated by Michael O'Meara, *Why We Fight* was praised in the following manner on its back cover: "As it was for the Nineteenth-century Left with Marx's *Communist Manifesto*, *Why We Fight* is destined to become the key work for Twenty-first century Identitarians." Although it was not mentioned, this description replicated that of Pierre Vial—a fellow traveler of Faye in many Identitarian battles—when the book first came out. In the foreword to the German edition, the Franco-German Pierre Krebs expressed his belief that the book was "predestined to become the reference work," a veritable "war book," all the more urgent "in order to counter the global deculturation of our people—the preliminary step towards its systematic genetic and Identitarian destruction."[16] Basically, all through the book, Faye champions ethnocentrism, and the need to stand up for it and shield it, if European civilization is to survive. Ethnocentrism "is the mobilizing conviction, distinct to all long-living peoples, that they belong to something superior and that they must conserve their ethnic identity, if they are to endure in history."[17] This is what today's Europeans lack the most: ethnic consciousness, or "the necessity to defend the biological and cultural identity of one's people," as "the indispensable condition for the longevity and autonomy of its civilization." In short, the destruction of the "biocultural identity" of European peoples settles the end of European civilization.

This view of identity as ethnic and biological clashes head to head with the ND reflections. De Benoist never misses an opportunity to distance himself and the ND from such views, repeating that Faye "left the ND more than thirty years ago."[18] He accuses Identitarians in general of "assigning ethnic factors the role that Karl Marx assigned to economic factors,"[19] while Michel Marmin, another founder of GRECE, objects when "the defense of national identity is in reality a pretext to express the most repugnant racism and the most stupid xenophobia, those old demons of the extreme-right."[20] Some Identitarians, above all Faye himself, do not spare any punches against such criticism. Against the ND motto of "cause of peoples," Faye posits the "cause of *our* people," accusing the "stargazing" ND intellectuals of being cut off from reality, minimizing threats such as mass immigration, and "howling with the wolves against racism," because of their obsession with respectability, to "'correctly protest' without ever crossing the cordon."[21] When Steuckers censures de Benoist for his "abstract" and "disembodied" view of History,[22] he adds force to this "stargazing" criticism, or the solipsistic inability to apprehend, and connect with, the real.

Identity is always contextualized, embedded, and rooted. But the Identitarian attachment to ethnocultural Identity is not felt as backward-looking in the sense of a return to a golden age in the past. Faye calls it a "vision of the world that is both traditional and Faustian" because it wants not to go back in time (like reactionaries) but to re-create the ancestral sources, virtues, and values of Europeans in modern times. It was in this sense that he coined the word "archeofuturism"—the title of his influential 1998 book—to stress that the sources of the future are already present in ancestral values (from its archaism it is possible to derive new creations). Tradition, therefore, must be continually re-created. This idea is connected to the view that identity is not frozen, but dynamic. It exists in a continuity, linked by a long memory—as if, notes Steuckers, "you're 'roped together' like alpinists with your fellow-citizens as the present-day philosopher Robert Redeker says"—and therefore tied with the destiny of a people. But it is in a permanent condition of being and becoming, and it can always survive and flourish—giving rise to new forms, new creations, new beginnings—as long as it is willed. This allows for a nonpessimistic, voluntaristic view of History, in which decline is never irreversible and a "renaissance" or "rebirth" is always possible (depending on the heroism of personalities and the audacity of peoples). In this Identitarians—and the ND, particularly de Benoist, who has always supported this view of historical time as a transition to new beginnings and dawns—are indebted to the refusal of a deterministic linear temporality, present in Nietzsche's and Heidegger's philosophies of history, and to the "forward-looking" tendency that existed within the German Conservative Revolution, which had Moeller van den Bruck as one of its main interpreters.[23]

Now in his late sixties, Faye, for whom the ND abandoned the Identitarian combat, has taken up the torch and is today one of the most blistering Identitarian voices in Europe. Faye is widely admired—even if he is also controversial within the Identitarian camp owing not only to his visceral style but also to his defense of ideological reorientations deemed necessary in view of the gravest threat to Europe, which for him is non-European, mostly Muslim, colonization. What is true is that Faye coined new words, developed concepts, and projected scenarios that are now an intrinsic part of the Identitarian language of combat for the battle of Europe.

The Völkisch Way

"The German word völkisch describes perfectly the doctrine of Terre et Peuple,"[24] notes the French Identitarian thinker Pierre Vial in the magazine *Terre et Peuple*, stressing in this way the importance given to the embeddedness of the volk, the people, in blood-and-soil ties and the sharing of a common destiny. Since the last decade of the twentieth century, a commanding supply of Identitarian thinking and cross-border interaction has been Pierre Vial's network. It gravitates around the cultural association Terre et Peuple, established in 1995, its magazine, annual roundtables, and countless appearances by its founder at conferences around France and Europe. Like all the founders of GRECE, Vial initiated his political militancy in the milieu of the French nationalist right, but he left the ND in the 1980s owing to disagreements over the rising issue of immigration and over the question of ethnicity. Vial would later join the Front national and was behind the launch of *Identité* (Identity), the revue of national studies of the party, before abandoning it also because of Vial's insistence on the need for a greater focus on the ethnic dimension of identity.[25] Vial has been the president of Terre et Peuple since its foundation, and in 1999 the first issue of its magazine was dedicated to the "clash of civilizations." In the editorial he announced as its core principle the "Identitarian cultural combat." Beyond the petty dichotomy of left and right, Vial claimed that the level of their challenge was much higher, focused on the ongoing civilizational clash, an all-out struggle between two communities whose coexistence in the same land generated unavoidable conflicts. "The quotidian accentuates, day after day, one truth: Ethnic conflicts, which have always existed, will always exist," he continued. The Identitarian task was to "arm our people for the resistance, and then for the war of liberation which will allow it to survive and take command of its destiny."[26] The idea that reality validates and reinforces the Identitarian worldview is recurrent in Vial's writings: "Our great strength lies in the fact that our conception of the world rests in taking account of realities. It is the same with ethnopolitics. Contrary to others, our conception of identity is based on the ethnic factor. The world progresses in such a way that it gives us reason everyday." Against wishy-washy conceptualizations of identity and compromises with "political correctness," Vial repeatedly states that the path taken by Terre et Peuple and its devotees is to not compromise with the system, even if the price they must pay is widespread demonization. "We are," he wrote, "we have *chosen*, to be in the camp of the damned. Forever."[27] Time, however, is on the side of the Identitarians, and Vial often expresses the belief that the twenty-first century will be the century of the "insurrection of the rooted identities" against the "zealots of the system," an insurrection characterized by the "refusal to get run over by the leveling of a uniformizing and cosmopolitan globalism, imposing the miscegenation and the *pensée unique* [single thought]."[28] This "cultural war," writes Jean-Patrick Arteault, is not "a banal conflict of ideas"; rather, "we need to understand it as a struggle to the death of two fundamentally hostile worldviews." What follows is that what is at stake is, very simply, the existence of "true Europeans" and the possibility of "prolonging in time their biological and cultural being." European Identitarians "may dream of being the pioneers of a new era and a true European renaissance" *if* they rise up to the challenge of our times.[29]

Terre et Peuple Identitarians, in their mission to defend and boost European identity, insist on a common ethnic root of Europe's peoples, which they trace back historically to the Indo-Europeans. This is their myth of origins. In this quest they intensify a path opened by the ND, whose metapolitical enterprise had as one of its founding themes the promotion of an Indo-European heritage. According to Jean-Claude Valla, "We gave new breath to Indo-European studies." In some validation of Valla's statement, the anthropologist Georges Dumézil (one of the major specialists in this field of study) collaborated briefly with the ND magazine *Nouvelle École*.[30] This Indo-European focus is still present in the ND, but not in the same intensity and breadth as in the Terre et Peuple network, whose magazine regularly features themes associated with the topic, as well as writings by professor of linguistics Jean Haudry, who also collaborated with *Nouvelle École*. Against the voices of "negationism," which deny the existence of Indo-Europeans as an ethnic group, and following on Dumézil teachings, Haudry affirms the existence of an "Indo-European tradition" that was characterized not just by language but also by a culture and an oral tradition. In the path of Dumézil's scholarly work, their communities are believed to have revolved around a specific ideology, a hierarchy of tripartite social functions—the priesthood, the warriors, and the producers—that put sacred values and warrior values ahead of merchant values. Likewise, Indo-European clans are regarded as having had an ethnic distinctiveness, a physical Nordic type, and therefore as having belonged to the white race.[31] In different phases they would eventually migrate all over Europe, populating it until the early Middle Ages. This Indo-European tradition—with its own mentality and religiosity—represents the most profound roots of the European peoples. It flowered in the pre-Christian heritage of Celts, Germans, Slavs, Greeks, and Roman peoples and societies. Many Terre et Peuple intellectuals favor a life-affirming paganism as the *real* European religiosity, rooted in and intertwined with nature and territory, in opposition to a universalist, detached—and Semitic—Judeo-Christianism.[32] Paganism, in short, is the cult of the real and not an abstraction. These views are shared by thinkers such as de Benoist and Faye, but Terre et Peuple takes it a step further, particularly in terms of ritualism, observing the cycle of the seasons, celebrating the solstices and equinoxes, and extolling folk traditions. No wonder that, in the obituaries of comrades, the hope for a future reencounter "in the Valhalla," the ultimate place of honor in Norse mythology, is often invoked in the pages of the magazine.

Pierre Vial is "the old warrior of European identity," says the magazine *Réfléchir & Agir*,[33] which described him on another occasion as "the undisputed leader of the European Identitarian revolutionaries."[34] Sharing affinities with *Terre et Peuple* and founded in 1993, initially as a fanzine, by Éric Lerouge (the pseudonym of Éric Rossi, a former skinhead), the magazine has been run for most of its existence by Éric Fornal (who uses the pseudonym Eugène Krampon), and Pierre Gillieth (also a pseudonym). This quarterly publication—which since 2007 has been sold at newsstands—promotes itself as "the autonomous magazine of ideological detox." Against political correctness, the self-proclaimed "national revolutionaries" who produce and read this magazine see themselves as "idealists who have political ideas," a far cry from the petty politics of the supporters of the system.[35] Their chosen path is "political radicalism," and they attack liberalism, miscegenation, Christian universalism (as the "first globalism of History"), and their biggest enemy, the "American-Zionist axis."[36] Although recognizing de Benoist's role as a crucial metapolitical thinker, they also criticize him for having given up on "biological realism" (which he first defended in the pages of *Europe-Action*), turning into the apologist of communitarianism and multiculturalism.[37] The magazine's writers uphold a racialist conception of the world. Their identity is "carnal and ethnic," and they define themselves and others like them in France in the following manner: "The peoples of France are the biological heirs of an old Indo-European people, whose source is found not in 1789, but in the Paleolithic, and this heritage has been magnified by the Nordic, Germanic, Celtic and Latin identity."[38] With a great emphasis on expressive culture and "everything that we think is beautiful and interesting," this publication wishes to be "the *Je suis partout* of the 21st century" (referring to the magazine run by, among others, the poet and fascist writer Brasillach in the 1930s and early 1940s).[39] *Réfléchir & Agir* pays close attention to the historical and present-day examples of intellectuals, authors, and militants who have promoted and remained loyal to the ancestral and foundational European cultures.

Venner's Founding Act

Identitarian entrepreneurs of all sorts function as dynamos for the community. Through their theoretical contributions *and* personal biographies they give legitimacy to the wider Identitarian struggle and its counteroffensive against the threats that menace and are poised to consume the continent. Hence the role ascribed within the vast and heterogeneous community to those viewed as truly "awakeners of peoples," as eternal examples of commitment to the Identitarian cause. In the new century, the French historian Dominique Venner is becoming the most prominent expression of such devotion as a man who willingly paid the ultimate price, with a final tragic gesture of loyalty to the identity of European civilization. First as a militant in nationalist combat and then as a writer and historian, Venner lived a life that fulfills the Identitarian ideals of uncompromising militancy. As an activist for the cause of French Algeria, one who in fact volunteered to fight in the war in Algeria, Venner was sentenced to prison for his involvement in the failed coup d'état known as "the General's Putsch" to overthrow the French president. This feverish period of militancy led him to establish a parallel with Ernst von Salomon's life. As he wrote: "You could say I felt a sort of kinship with him. The police were still hunting me down when I read his book *The Outlaws*. . . . I was truly living the rebellion and the furor that poured forth from those pages. Weapons, dreams, foiled conspiracies, prison."[40] While incarcerated, Venner anonymously wrote a Lenin-inspired *Pour une critique positive* as a guide for wannabe revolutionary nationalists, stimulated by his own militant failure.

After the fall of French Algeria, Venner continued his political combat for revolutionary nationalism (which had led him to join ultranationalist organizations in the 1950s), this time by founding Europe-Action, an organization that had a publication with the same name, in which many future founders of GRECE, such as Alain de Benoist, Jean-Claude Valla, and Pierre Vial collaborated. "Like the founder of the public school [Jules Ferry] and Kipling, *Europe-Action* believed in the civilizing mission of the white man, whose mission implied an idea of superiority," recalled Jean-Claude Valla.[41] In fact, Europe-Action is widely seen as reorienting the radical right toward transnationalism. But it did so by linking its Europeism with white racialism in terms of a defense of the Occident as a defense of the wide "White nation," including the United States and South Africa, and with allusions to an ongoing war of races.[42] The fact of the matter is that after this experience in more immediate political combat, Venner took a new path, dedicating his time to a career as a historian, publishing many books—especially, but far from exclusively, about political, social, and cultural dynamics associated with the European wars of the twentieth century, from the phenomena of Resistance and Collaboration to the struggles of the paramilitary Freikorps in the Baltics, for example—while founding publications about history promoted as fundamentally "different" from the mainstream narrative and "free" from ideological distortions. The first issue of *Enquête sur l'Histoire*, published in the early 1990s, had as its main theme "40 centuries of French Identity," while *Nouvelle Revue d'Histoire*, which began publication in 2000, dedicated its first volume to the "5000 years of European civilization." This focus expresses what was the overriding theme of Venner's historical reflections, mainly the question of the identity of the European homeland and civilization from its earliest expressions to its permanence over time.

The preeminence given to tradition, defined "not as the past, but that which does not pass away, our interior compass,"[43] pervades Venner's historiography. Accordingly, "if tradition crosses the times, it is because it is based on the hereditary dispositions of brother-peoples, but also on a spiritual heritage, whose origins reach back into prehistory, through the long maturation of the Indo-European peoples."[44] This quest for Europe's tradition is all the more important because of the "lost memory" of Europeans and the fall into absolute nihilism. Venner believed that Europeans have "forgotten what they are. This issue is not new. In reality it is very old. It is ancient. The thing is, when we were strong, powerful, and masters of the world, such a question was not put. It was enough to exist. But today in which we face new and mortal dangers, the question of our identity, of our own values, it imposes itself like never, at least since the times that the old Romanism collapsed."[45] As Venner wrote in his book *Histoire et Tradition des Européens: 30 000 ans d'identité*, in the face of the challenges that destiny poses to them, Europeans have "no other choice than to break with fatalism and fall back to their primordial [cultural and ethnic] sources."[46] This meant seeking respite, support, and inspiration in the "sacred book" of Europeans—constituted by the poems of Homer, the *Iliad*, and the *Odyssey*—which expresses a "multi-millennial" Indo-European heritage.[47] "Nature as our basis, excellence as our goal, beauty as our horizon"—these are the life principles in Homer that may mobilize Europeans, because these poems represent the "unique originality of our way of existence."[48] Such poems unveil the European soul and are the source of Europe's authenticity: "Even when we do not know it, we remain sons and daughters of Ulysses and Penelope, like others are the sons of Abraham or Buddha."[49]

Europe's crisis is therefore imminently spiritual and a major source of it was Europe's "civil war" between 1914 and 1945 (the "suicide" of Europe), which defeated it morally and opened the doors to an ominous culture of repentance and guilt that continues to this day. One of its consequences—and a symptom of this civilizational crisis—is the European elite's dismay at any sort of European manifestations of nativism. Europeans have gone from "arrogance to masochism, going out of their way to chase away their ancient ethnocentrism, while flattering [the ethnocentrism] of other races and cultures."[50] This belief led Venner to ask what was a recurring question in his criticism of the times: "Why is it that the desire for identity—to be conscious of what one is in all density of one's existence, amidst those who resemble us—yes, why is it that this desire is commendable in regard to Black Americans, to the Chinese, the Arabs, the Israelis, the Uighurs, the Turks or the Gabonese, but condemnable in the Europeans and the French?"[51] Venner, however, rejected declinism and believed that, even under critical circumstances (in fact because of them), Europeans would "find themselves again," and the notion of an inevitable European "renaissance" infused his writings.[52]

For him, the spiritual awakening of Europe entails the rediscovery of a system of values at odds with the materialistic and utilitarian ways of this day and age, as well as the revival of values such as heroism, honor, and sacrifice. It was in the light of such ancestral European values that Venner saw the theme of suicide in History. This was particularly the case in the Stoic Roman tradition—"Now I am my own master," said Cato, as recounted by Plutarch, moments before he ended his life with a sword as an act of freedom against Caesar—and in the Japanese Samurai tradition, as when the writer Yukio Mishima committed *seppuku* to protest the indignity to which his country had fallen. Whereas Judeo-Christian values denounced suicide as an ignoble, even sinful, curtailing of one's existence, Venner believed that voluntary death could be an exigency of honor; it affirms other values, and it may constitute a denial of nihilism, especially at a time "when people extol the value of life simply for the sake of living, regardless of its vacuity."[53] These words presaged Venner's last act on earth: In May of 2013, the 78-year-old shot himself at the altar of the Notre Dame cathedral in Paris. "I believe it necessary to sacrifice myself to break the lethargy that plagues us. I give up what life remains to me in order to protest and to found," his suicide note read; "while many men are slaves of their lives, my gesture embodies an ethic of will. I give myself over to death to awaken slumbering consciences. I rebel against fate." It was posthumously reported that Venner had suffered a terminal disease and had decided to end his life before it had run its course. The illness, therefore, provided the "setting" for Venner to make his final political statement.[54]

His choice of the place for his suicide was not random. The cathedral was built on top of ancient pagan temples and therefore is also linked with the most ancient Celtic sacrality. After Venner's suicide, his final book, a political-existential testament, was released: *A Samurai of the West: The Breviary of the Unvanquished*, which he said was "written by a European to Europeans," and read like a "neo-Stoic" guide to the "Europeans of the future."[55] After his death, many tributes were devoted to him, the first one shortly after, in Paris, with hundreds of admirers and friends, such as Alain de Benoist, who addressed the crowd saying that "the reasons to live and the reasons to die are often the same, such as has undeniably been the case for Dominique Venner, whose gesture sought to put in profound harmony his life and his death."[56] In the pages of *Réfléchir & Agir*, for example, Venner was apotheosized. Krampon wrote that Venner "died for us, as a martyr not of a religion but of an ethic, the [ethic] of an upright man," and he vowed to pursue the "combat for continental liberation" under Venner's "political and spiritual" stimulus and vision, saying that "the revolution has started on May 21 [2013], at 4PM . . . it will not stop from now on."[57] The title of a Spanish book published as a tribute to Venner five years after his death declares him "Dominique Venner—Homer's Messenger."[58]

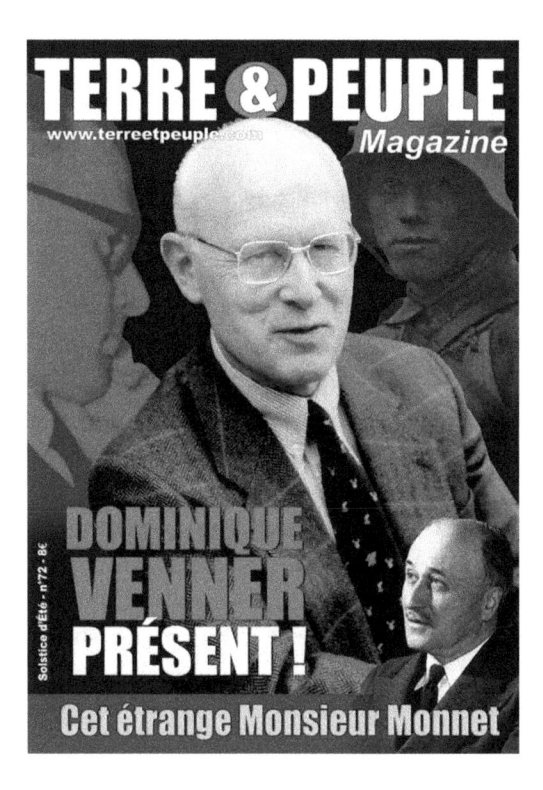

FIGURE 1. Cover of *Terre et Peuple* magazine honoring Dominique Venner four years after his death (Summer 2017).

To be sure—and this is tangible within the vast camp of Identitarians—Venner's martyrdom is ingrained in the collective memory not as an act of desperation but as a wake-up call for a slumbered Europe, as a deed to help precipitate the "awakening" of Europeans to the perils of the age, releasing them from their deadly torpor. In many narrations, the French writer has emerged as the cultural and political soldier who took his nonconformism to its very last corollary and chose the path of sacrifice as an act of honor for a higher purpose. In consequence, as a stoic figure who assumed from his early days the defense of the integrity and survival of his community and through the example of his life embodied the principle that, in his own words, truly defines a rebel ("It is to make yourself your own law, to find in yourself what counts"[59]), Venner appears as the personification of the watchman, whose voice, however, for many Identitarians, is no longer unheard.

Cognitive and Info Wars

The Institute Iliade (Iliad), dedicated to the "transmission of the long European memory" and the "awakening of European consciousness," was established in honor of the fallen historian Dominique Venner. With the historian and former member of GRECE, Philippe Conrad—Venner's friend and his successor as the helm of the bimonthly *Nouvelle Revue d'Histoire* (which ceased publication in 2017)—as its first president, the institute puts forth a program with pedagogical aims that is specifically directed at "the young generations of Europeans who will have to confront the tragic consequences" of current cultural and civilizational dynamics. Besides the formation of the consciousness of the young, it pursues cultural combat through meetings, writings, and visual communication, particularly through the Internet, with viral videos that focus on European identity. One of the founding events of Iliad was a conference with the theme "the aesthetic universe of Europeans," showcasing the uniqueness of the art that emerged in the "common heritage" of Europeans as the expression of a singular aesthetics and ethics (unlike the "contemporary art," currently hegemonic), and fundamentally different from that of all other civilizations.[60] "I refuse the great erasure of our identity, I want to act for the necessary European awakening," reads the customized banner of Iliad for online fundraising.

In the cultural field there are myriad "nonconformist," anti-system Identitarian forums at large that reject the ways that the French and other Europeans are bringing about their own demise and, in response, have engaged in the combat for identity. A major one has been Euro-Synergies—also the name of a website that functions as a platform of anti-system articles and essays—set up by Steuckers as a pan-European "informal gathering of nonconformists of all nationalities." This "forum of European resisters" sees itself as involved in a cognitive war against liberalism, globalism, and the media systems that support it while promoting alternative interpretations and projects (in geopolitics, law, economics, and so on), and always in defense of a rooted and independent Europe attentive to its roots, history, and longest memory. Jean-Yves Le Gallou, one of the co-founders of Iliad—he was a member of GRECE in its early days, and later an important official at the Front national (and one of its members in the European Parliament) in the 1990s—is also the man behind the launch in the early 2000s of the think tank Polémia. It takes its name from Greek mythology: Polemos was the daemon of war and battle and etymologically the root of the word "polemic." The think tank's motto is "Because *polemos*, conflict, is inseparable from life." Polémia's manifesto declares that "in a world preyed upon by chaos, and more and more dominated by the clash of civilizations, there must be the courage to identify the new dividing lines and perceive the coming conflicts in order to better prevent them." This was especially crucial at a time of "*normose*," the pathological pressure to look and think like the others in order to fit in and look normal. Against the "taboos imposed by political correctness, there is the need to reintroduce the free confrontation of ideas in the public debate."[61] Polémia has specialized in this communicational battle, fighting what it perceives to be the widespread disinformation coming in from the system and its acolytes. Its combat is for the "re-information" of the public about the real issues, trends, and dangers behind the official, sanitized discourse, whether pertaining to the miseries of globalism, mass immigration, and its ethnic conflicts, to creeping Islamization, or to Europe's geopolitical submission to America. Le Gallou also oversees the "daily bulletin of re-information" at the radio station Radio Courtoisie, which assembles and broadcasts many ND and Identitarian points of view. In 2015 Polémia published the *Dictionary of Newspeak*, an allusion to George Orwell's denunciation in his novel *1984* of a totalitarian system that subverts and controls language in order to maintain its rule. Today there reigns a system of true censorship, Identitarian dissidents believe, devotedly maintained by the mainstream media (the "media of propaganda"), that marginalizes and excludes all those that do not play by the rules of the game. The Internet, where Polémia carries on most of its "re-information," is the way out of this "media tyranny" and therefore the great hope for dissidence and rebellion. The annual "Forum of Dissidence" organized by Polémia is part of this Identitarian Info War. It is a gathering of rebellious voices against the distortion of reality by the powers that be.

Identitarians believe that, having lost its monopoly to alternative media and social media, the mainstream media has counteracted by

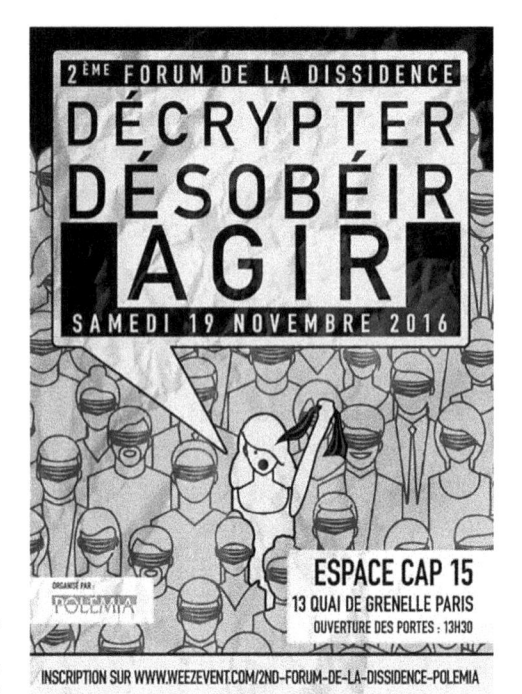

FIGURE 2. Poster for Polémia's second "Forum of Dissidence" (November 19, 2016). It reads, "Decrypt, Disobey, Act."

labeling as "fake news" what is often nothing more than the "uncomfortable" reality (the facts and analyses that upset and shake up the truisms of the dominant ideology) that the same media elite has tried for decades to hide. Le Gallou says that because these dissident media "make reality appear," the media "newspeak" tags such reality as post-truth; for him and many like-minded critics of the "media of the system," it is yet another "propaganda technique." No wonder that every year, in a public ceremony, Polémia attacks the mainstream media "Boboland"—from "Bourgeois Bohemians," or Bobos, as expression of left-wing, urban, wealthy and political-correct classes—awarding the satirical "Bobards d'Or" to the most "false and dishonest" journalist reporting, in the conviction that, as stated by Le Gallou, at the end of one such events, "laughter is the weapon of the dissidents."[62] In the end, and in all seriousness, Identitarians believe that the oligarchic-driven "war" against the "dissident" media will only get worse as the "rule of globalists" withers away.

THE NEW IDENTITARIAN ACTIVISM

In the 1920s, at a time when he was fully committed to the Revolutionary-Nationalist camp of the Conservative Revolution, Ernst Jünger paid tribute, in the magazine *Widerstand* (Resistance), to the revolutionary potential of youth: "Our hope rests in the young people, who can tolerate high temperatures, since in them, the fresh, festering sore of disgust is consumed."[63] This citation, in fact, is found in many youthful Identitarian activist circles across Europe. The Identitarian turn has not been restricted to the intellectual or theory-oriented field of Identitarianism; it has manifested itself in the more practical revolt of action-oriented Identitarian groups, mostly composed of young people in their twenties and thirties, who are "disgusted" with the dominant zeitgeist of the times, determined to create and experience a counterculture, and devoted to the defense of Europe's identity and civilization. These youth movements—which had their ignition in France and Italy before spreading elsewhere—represent the direct-action arm of Identitarianism.

French and Italian Beginnings

The Younger French Identitarians

The video clip went viral. The dramatic background music, the succession of faces of young militants, and the singleness of purpose of its message left no one in doubt. Bereft of true and wise guidance from its elders, watching as its country and Europe slid further into disarray and chaos, in the fall of 2012, Génération Identitaire, or Generation Identity, made public via the Internet its "Declaration of War":

> We are Generation Identity. . . . We are the generation of ethnic fracture, of the total failure of integration, the generation of forced crossbreeding. . . . We have closed your history books to find our own memory once again. We have stopped believing that Abdul is our brother, the planet our village and humanity our family. We have discovered that we have roots and ancestors—and thus a future. Our only inheritance is our blood, our soil, and our identity.

> We are the heirs of our destiny. . . . You will not convince us with a condescending glance, youth employment programs and a pat on the shoulder: for us, life is a struggle. . . . Don't deceive yourselves: this is not a mere manifesto, it's a declaration of war.[64]

Translated into many languages, and getting many hits, this YouTube video declaration helped to spread the message of this self-proclaimed "fighting community" across Europe and beyond. At its website Generation Identity introduced itself as "a generation that has been sacrificed, but not a lost generation, for we are launching a war against all who want to tear our roots from us and make us forget who we are." This generation is a "clan" that rose as the "first line of resistance," marching against what for them is a terrible, unbearable reality.[65]

The arrival of Generation Identity, however, was just one more stage in the history of the network that had first emerged in France in 2002 with the formation of Jeunesses Identitaires (Identitarian Youths) and been consolidated in 2003 with the creation of the Bloc Identitaire—Mouvement Social Européen (Identitarian Bloc—European Social Movement), which became the center—and from 2009 the official political party—of a new militant and activist web generically referred to as the Identitarian movement. In the summer of 2016 the Bloc Identitaire changed its status and was remodeled as an association named Les Identitaires (The Identitarians), which vowed to proceed as an Identitarian "center of agitation and formation" and as a "launching pad" of "Identitarian offensives" in the political and social landscape.[66] The Identitarian movement functions as a cluster of identity-driven groups across the Francophone world—but one whose effects, as will be shown, radiated beyond it and has gained the media spotlight because of its distinctive and youthful social and cultural activism. As a down-to-earth community it translates its Identitarian combat into an in-your-face and confrontational activism and intense street and audiovisual propaganda, all powered by a savvy use of the Internet. As a political organization, the Bloc Identitaire has been at the heart of a triangular Identitarian ensemble composed initially of a think tank called Les Identitaires (dedicated to the formation of militants) and a youth force, originally Jeunesses Identitaires (Identitarian Youths) but later replaced by Une Autre Jeunesse (Another Youth) and finally by Génération Identitaire. At the same time, since the early days, a number of local and regional associated groups and organizations have gravitated into the orbit of this Identitarian network. They are rooted and territorial: for example, in Nice there is Nissa Rebela (launched in 2007), in Paris Projet Apache (launched in 2009), and in Lyon the Rebeyne community (founded in 2010). Since 2012 and the rise of Génération Identitaire, these local branches have also added the name "Generation Identity" to their local designations, as has happened in the older groups such as Project Apache, Rebeyne, and Nissa Rebela (which also became known as, respectively, Generation Identity Paris, Generation Identity Lyon, and Generation Identity Nice), Vague Normande (Generation Identity Normandy), or in newer branches such as Generation Identity Flandre Artois Hainaut in the Flemish region. They all act through networking, in a sort of federation of entrenched local identities.[67] Even if this Identitarian collective operates as a flexible and relatively fluid network, it has its own hierarchy. Since its foundation, the Bloc Identitaire has had as its President Fabrice Robert (born in 1971), a political science graduate and multimedia consultant who is now national co-leader of Les Identitaires. A musical entrepreneur within French Identitarian Rock—with a ska-hardcore-metal band from Nice, Fraction, formed in 1994, and also the founder of the music label Alternative-s—and an early militant in the revolutionary-nationalist milieu with the political party Unité Radicale (Radical Unity), Robert embarked on a new course for political action after the dissolution of the party following the attempted murder of the French president Jacques Chirac by one of its militants. From then on the goal was to break away from a sectarian logic and outmoded models and create both a new language of activism and a renovated strategy of propaganda. Articulated no longer on nationalism and its demons, it was thought that this new paradigm should be one of the defense of identity and of the creation of "a new political force, turned to the future, Identitarian, social, and European."[68]

It was within this context of renovation and realignment that the Bloc Identitaire was born, casting itself as the protector of a triple identity: "regional (carnal), French (historical) and European (civilizational)."[69] This obviously entailed a self-assumed ethnocentrism. As Fabrice Robert explains, "To be an Identitarian it is therefore to have an ethnic conception of nations. Ethnic is not a swearword. It is not a war carrier per se." Consequently, "An Identitarian politics is the acceptance of ethnic determinism without which any cultural construction is impossible."[70] Instead of the alleged tragic and conflict-ridden mixing of peoples and cultures that Europe is currently undergoing, the Bloc Identitaire sees differentialism as the only sensible and realistic way out of ethnic chaos. As Robert writes, "For us identity is what distinguishes one people from the other. The diversity of peoples is also what makes the richness of humanity."[71] At the same time the defense of identity—at a time of "colonization" by non-European peoples—is a pan-European affair. "We are above all Europeans! . . . Through the happy or misfortunate days we are here to enrich and transmit, we are here to reinvent what does not pass, what will never pass: the identity of the European people, and its future. . . . We feel linked to the same origin and to the same destiny then as an Italian, a Polish, or an Irish."[72] Beyond holding Jacobin views of the nation, Identitarians look at Europe as a civilization, as their ultimate horizon, loosely united in ethnicity, culture, and destiny.

The chosen means of action is metapolitical, to be achieved through an occupation of thoughts and spirits, aiming for a cultural revolution. Influenced by the ND goal of waging a cultural and spiritual war as a requisite for attaining political power, the Bloc Identitaire has set out to promote and consolidate an Identitarian counterculture. According to Philippe Vardon, a co-founder of the Bloc Identitaire (and a former bandmate of Fabrice Robert as the lead singer of Fraction), this metapolitical strategy means "taking under assault the spirits, the language, the codes and fashions" as the only way to build a "real alternative, a real capacity of resistance."[73] However, this was to be an original creation, not a derivative product. The new Identitarians recognized that, although they were following a path opened up by the ND, they wanted, in the words of Vardon, "to get rid of the intellectualist tropism that has often been associated with their activity."[74] The rejection of scholastic and sterile erudition is also present in their refusal to embrace networks such as Terre et Peuple. Cultural combat, according to Fabrice Robert, "is not about preaching to the converts, but instead to convert those that are still not converted. That is the reason why I think it illusory to want to create a hermetic community, and sometimes disconnected from reality, when it is urgent, for the survival of our people, to reach a maximum of French."

He concluded: "To use culture to spread our theses in the popular masses, that is my conception of cultural combat."[75] And so the Bloc Identitaire's aim transcends the ambition of establishing a school of Identitarian thought. It wants to establish and affirm itself as a school of life.

This cultural combat must be taken on in a proper, effective, and consequent way, permeating and transforming the wider culture. The Bloc Identitaire was from the get-go promoted as "a lobby at the service of our identity." And this is all the more vital and demanding because what is involved is the survival of European peoples. Addressing an Identitarian convention, Philippe Vardon spelled out the defining issue of the age: "We cannot repeat it enough. If one of the major questions of the 20th century was the right of peoples to self-determination, THE [sic] central question of our century is the right of peoples to self-preservation."[76] At another meeting, Fabrice Robert reiterated the Identitarians' one-stop idea, saying "in the questions that we see as the most crucial—in brief: the disappearance of our people!—We are the only ones to 'do the job.'"[77] Arnaud Delrieux, the president of Génération Identitaire (from 2012 to 2017), professed that "the twenty-first century will be the age of identities, for it is the very essence of the European people that is threatened by the steamroller of globalism, the immigration invasion and multiculturalism."[78] As stated in one of the editorials of the magazine *Identitaires*, "The storm rages over our continent," and "in the face of the shock of History, the Europeans in slumber, as said by Dominique Venner, awake and organize themselves. Yes, some Europeans do not surrender."[79] And here lies a crucial idea that pervades Identitarians' self-understanding in this all-or-nothing combat: that they play the role of a vanguard, as pathfinders, taking the fight against the system and against the globalist aggression and its tragic consequences to where others do not dare to take it, which does not happen with political parties that are obliged to embrace political correctness and moderation. Therefore, as political actors they vow to be the "first line" of resistance, not an innocuous, romantic, isolated "last stand" as has been typical of the old revolutionary right.[80] In this pledge to widen the combat and to spread the war of culture and identity into the broader society, these French Identitarians are not alone in Europe.

The Fascists of the Third Millennium
When in 2002 a group of young Italian radical right activists squatted in a state-owned building on the periphery of Rome, replicating a tactic favored by radical left social movements, they named the building Casa-Montag, or the House of Montag, after Guy Montag, the main character of Ray Bradbury's science fiction classic *Fahrenheit 451*. The choice of name was no accident: As Montag sought refuge and redemption from a dystopian and authoritarian society in a community of resistance, so would these activists experience and profess their allegiance to a "nonconformist" society. No wonder that the group called it a "nonconformist occupation." The symbolism was also present the following year during a severe housing crisis in Rome, when the occupiers of another building, this time in Rome's Chinatown, named their refuge after the American poet and fascist dissident Ezra Pound. For Pound, usury (under which he included steep rent) was the greatest of evils and the symptom of an inhumane capitalism. With this "occupation for housing purposes," CasaPound was born. CasaPound Italia (CPI) was officially registered as an association for social promotion in 2008. Since then it has spread throughout Italian territory—with a greater emphasis on the Rome region—through occupations (both for cultural or political activities and for housing) and in "nonconformist spaces" (such as communal centers for activities ranging from lectures and debates to sports, music, or entertainment). CasaPound Italia is above all a community of militants who together demonstrate and are reinforced by a strong collective identity with repertoires of action traditionally not associated with the radical right, a hierarchical structure, and a sense of being invested with a mission to experience and achieve, beyond rigid and outdated dichotomies, a new politics. Neither a full social movement nor a political party, Casa-Pound presents itself, and operates, as a revolutionary hybrid.[81]

Members were labeled in the Italian press as "fascists of the third millennium"—a description that they accepted and joyously embraced. The more immediate roots of the political movement can be found in the "nonconformist" Italian music scene of the late 1990s. Probably the key event in the emergence of CasaPound Italia as a major Identitarian force was the formation of the hard-core Identitarian Roman band ZetaZeroAlfa (which toured with Fabrice Robert's Identitarian rock band Fraction), which is fronted by a journalist and radical right militant who looks as if he could be a character from a biker TV series, Gianluca Iannone. The band's anti-system nature, which is expressed through emotional lyrics that promote the vital need for rebellion, and the intense sense of communion and comradeship among its concertgoers, continue to serve as rallying points for many activists. Initially Casa-Pound and its activities were integrated within the radical right Fiamma Tricolore (Tricolor Flame), but Iannone and his group left the party because it lacked vitality and was captive to old-fashioned modes of political action. CasaPound Italia, however, chased and was an expression of politics-not-as-usual, so it has been following its own path since 2008, the year of its "official" debut in Italian politics.

In conformity with its hierarchical and leadership-oriented structure, there is a natural selection of cadres within the movement, which is based not on lineage but on condition, capability, and merit. Iannone, its president, is widely revered as the founder and leader, with Simone Di Stefano as the vice president. If Di Stefano leans more toward the "nationalist" side of CasaPound, Adriano Scianca is the more prominent voice on its "Europeist" side. Born in 1980, and holding a BA in philosophy, Scianca is the person in charge of CasaPound Italia's cultural activities and is its true *maître à penser*; he wrote *Riprendersi Tutto* (Retake Everything), which is one of the defining accounts of the movement and its concepts "for a revolution in the making."[82] Since the turn of the century Scianca has risen as a key contemporary thinker of Identitarianism. Although not formally involved with the movement, the longtime nationalist-revolutionary writer Gabriele Adinolfi—whose militancy during the 1970s' "years of lead" resulted in his prosecution by the Italian state for subversive activities and to his consequent exile and clandestinity, mostly in France—is an ideological mentor of CasaPound Italia and a recurring guest at its cultural activities and debates. The founder of myriad metapolitical forums and think tanks, Adinolfi has been driven by a long-standing idea: the need of the radical right for a meticulous metapolitical effort to create a civilian, social, and political counterpower. This drive toward a "cultural revolution" transcends a simple symbolism; it requires the formation of a multidimensional network—including cadres (new elites), research centers, and lobbying—operating synergistically, like guilds, at all levels of society.[83] From this emerges the need, for example, to pay attention to schools and universities; in fact, CasaPound has its own Blocco Studentesco (Student Bloc), a self-described "irreverent," "nonconformist" force that affirms a "new, diverse, way of being" against the "old" political correctness.[84] This student group has a strong presence in high schools and is very active in student unions, especially in the region of Rome. The new course of action that Adinolfi expounds entails, above all, taking charge, being on the offensive, not unlike that of historical fascism. The key concepts of this proactive strategy are "penetration" of the social fabric and "contamination," or radiating a new mentality through the formation of communities imbued by a new culture and a new value system. Only by following this strategy can the "radical Right" leave its current political and social dead end. The strategy CasaPound propounds "means to understand what power is, where it goes, and how to get there. [It means knowing] where the real fights are fought."[85] CasaPound has certainly taken this message and put it into action. Asked in *Réfléchir & Agir* about the movement, Iannone said he saw it as a "return to authentic politics after so many years of torpor and vassalage next to professional political parties." With the albatross of past politics now cut from their necks, CasaPound activists faced the imperative of "recover[ing] the time lost." CasaPound's president declared, "We need to open and to grow new structures, cooperatives, sport groups and be present in the streets and in the daily life of Italian politics."[86]

As expected, CasaPound activists view the question of identity in a revolutionary fashion and in clear opposition to the stagnant, backward-looking perspectives typical of the reactionary right. This comes to the fore in Scianca's definition, of the term, which echoes the original ND philosophy of history. Identity is based on an obvious "ethno-cultural *substrate*," but this "mass" is, above all, for the "new fascist consciousness," a source of creation and re-creation, something that is plastic and from which it is possible to experiment with new "spiritual and political regenerations" in the present. Scianca cites, approvingly, Heidegger's view that "the beginning still is. It does not lie *behind us*, as something that was long ago, but stands *before us*. . . . The beginning has invaded our future. There it stands as the distant command to us to catch up with its greatness."[87] The search for identity is thus a projection into the future. The contribution of the Paris-based Italian journalist Giorgio Locchi

(1923–92)—whom Scianca admires as a "genius" and who was an important intellectual reference in the first phase of the ND—clearly influenced this theorization. After all, Locchi, swayed by Nietzsche and with beliefs similar to those of Armin Mohler—as well as many conservative-revolutionaries that Mohler studied, above all Moeller van den Bruck—saw historical time not in a deterministic manner (as cyclical, like paganism, or linear, like Judeo-Christianity) but as "spherical," constantly returning but never in the same way and always open to decadence but also to regeneration. And this, for Locchi, was the real essence of fascist movements: a search for origins, a mythical past, but always projected into the future as a goal to reach. In this way, the fascist future is always the land of the children rather than of the parents. Although not cited by Scianca, Dominique Venner's notion of tradition (in the sense that tradition "still is"), tied with his anti-fatalist conception of history—decadence is not irreversible, a renaissance is *always* possible—also falls under this vitalistic philosophy. Most of all, in the case of CasaPound, the expression "returning to the future" is far from a paradox but is rather a logical consequence of its view of tradition, history, and identity.[88]

The ND differentialism is at the heart of CasaPound's stances on the dangerous consequences for identity of an out-of-control globalism. "We fight for a plural world," CasaPound states at its website in the "Frequently Asked Questions" section. "We want a world with a diversity of peoples, languages, cultures, religions, and foods." The forced mixing of peoples caused by massive waves of immigration is rejected on the basis that it "degenerates in confusion and in the disfiguration of the reciprocal identities." This true "infernal migratory mechanism" is "one of the main elements of loss of identity and social, cultural and existentialist impoverishment of all the populations involved in it whether hosts or guests," to the profit of both multicultural and capitalist fanatics."[89]

CasaPound's experience with total politics is categorized by its members not as neofascist or postfascist but simply as fascist. Asked about the "political models" of the movement, Iannone answered, "Italian fascism and its social dimension are an inexhaustible source of inspiration."[90] Certainly, both in words and in deeds, the movement sets itself against international capitalism and the power of plutocracies and banks, and the documents of reference most mentioned by militants are traced back to the social policies of the fascist regime (particularly, but not exclusively, its 1943 Manifesto of Verona, from the "social Republic" of Salò). Il Duce, too, is viewed in a reverential light. Scianca, for example, noted that "Mussolini, differently than any other politician in the history of Italy, towers in the collective imaginary even after 70 years," recalling that among his many facets he was "a socialist, a man of the people, the anti-bourgeois, and the anti-capitalist."[91]

At the same time, the direct-action tactics of CasaPound may involve physical confrontation with ideological enemies or with the police. Within CasaPound, violence is not a taboo. First, it is viewed as an inevitable form of self-defense: "CasaPound cannot allow anyone or anything to contest its legitimacy to act and to exist."[92] About opponents Iannone writes, "Since our foundation they have done nothing but to assault our sites, to set fire to our cars, to intimidate us. What would precisely our violence be? That of existence?"[93] "Philosophical 'nonviolence,'" wonders Scianca, "in a world that has not made the same choice—does that not simply imply passivity regarding the violence of the others?" Simultaneously, a violent ethos is part of CasaPound's community of militants, especially because it is felt to be a way of rejecting the dominant morality of safety and the mediocre conformity of modern times. The defiant, combative nature of fascist *squadrismo* (armed squads) is invoked as an inspirational model of action and a supreme example of nonconformism in many of the organization's manifestos and activities; this only serves to reaffirm CPI's rejection of a life drained of all vitality. On top of this, true violence, according to CasaPound, comes from the soulless ruling system, which imposes all forms of degradation on peoples and cultures and devalues human beings. "They have killed the soul of the world and they have the audacity to complain about a few slogans," wrote Scianca in his "Revolution in the Making."[94]

It has been argued that CasaPound's fascism is à la carte,[95] picking and choosing what from fascist ideology suits it best. But it has also been noted that this characteristic may be fully fascist itself,[96] because historical fascism did the same with myriad doctrines associated with socialism, syndicalism, nationalism, futurism, and other movements. This has added significance because it goes to the core of CasaPound's fascist project—in accordance with its "third-millennium" nature—of undertaking a synthesis of ideas as an exercise in re-creation that it is hoped will lead to a radical alternative to current political systems. That is why its members vaunt their refusal to be caged in neat ideological divisions: They are "neither Left nor Right," proclaiming that their ideology is *Estremo centro alto* ("extreme high center") and high above all conventional, classical definitions. That a motto of CasaPound is *Riprendersi Tutto* ("Retake Everything!") is not a surprise. It is as good as an announcement of the totalistic project that drives the group and the ushering in of a revolutionary, postliberal—but in their view still democratic or more so—new order of things.

Activism, Militancy, and Sociocultural Combat

Identitarians: Not the Same, Yet Comparable
The new French and Italian Identitarians—who gravitate toward the Bloc Identitaire and CasaPound—are not indistinct. They are, of course, heirs to different national traditions. In Italy, which had a historical fascist regime, it is more plausible for a group such as CasaPound to perceive itself and articulate its activism within a historical continuity with that regime. That is not the case in France. Furthermore, while the Bloc Identitaire extolls regional attachments and stays away from the semantics and imagery of nationalism, CasaPound casts itself as an Italy-wide nationalist movement. What is more, as will become clearer throughout the book, there are ideological differences between these Identitarian networks, particularly in terms of their choices of priorities in the struggle for culture and identity. With this in mind, we must remember that it is nevertheless true that their cultural combat for ethnoculturalism, ethos of action, repertoires, aesthetics, and youthful drive toward a countersociety, make them supreme representatives of the new twenty-first-century, Identitarian activism for both their own communities and, ultimately, for Europe.

Metapolitics with a Punch
It was at the dawn of the third millennium, and in an interview with *éléments pour la civilisation européenne*, the "magazine of ideas" of GRECE, that Dominique Venner sounded out a warning to would-be rebels: "To be a rebel is not to accumulate a library of subversive books or to dream of fantastic conspiracies or of taking to the hills."[97] Juxtaposing *both* the

imperative to combat the eradication driven by an oppressive system that poisons their peoples and cultures and *also* the need to evade old-style hermetic resistance, the Identitarians that emerged in the twenty-first century have given activism a cutting-edge, adrenaline-charged new face. Imbued with the belief that it is more harmful to the European cause to stay at the sidelines in polite protest or to reduce activism to the confines of conference halls, these new-century Identitarians see the streets as their headquarters, the Internet as a galvanizing weapon, and they rely on the hermeneutic power of shock to awaken the lethargic consciences of Europe's peoples.

Within this context, the new Identitarians' metapolitics rise above mere debates and ideological discussions and grow into a *way of life* in which the distance between the political and the nonpolitical is narrowed to the point at which everything is political. In his *Elements for an Identitarian Counter-Culture*, Philippe Vardon reminds his readers that "we are more loyal to an attitude than to ideas"—a phrase actually taken from *Gilles*, the 1939 novel by the French "nonconformist" and fascist sympathizer writer Pierre Drieu la Rochelle—and that "this counter-culture must be embodied and must authenticate itself in life, in action."[98] Faye sees in this development an essential condition for successful combat for Europe: "It's important to extend the field of ideas to include 'non-theoretical ideas,' that is, myths, artistic and aesthetic creations"—in short, "everything that electrifies the imagination."[99] "We must call for a rooted counter-culture," argued the editorial writers of *ID Magazine*, "not just to claim it, but to live it."[100] An all-inclusive view of politics is at the heart of CasaPound, because "politics for us is a community. It is a challenge, it is an affirmation. . . . That is why we are in the streets, on computers, in bookshops, in schools, in universities, at the top of the mountains or in newsstands. That is why we are in culture, social work, and sport."[101] For Identitarians, the maxim "Everything is political" means that, in the desert of a nonradical and conformist age, the beating heart of radicalism must pulse everywhere.

Above all, Identitarians wage this metapolitical combat based on the guiding idea that their communities and their continent have an essence, and the Identitarian mission is to rediscover and revitalize this essence, creating (or re-creating) a culture for this day and age through literature, art, music, sports, elements of popular culture, and also to expand its appeal—particularly with the youth. At the same time, Identitarians take in many mixed references and symbols not traditionally associated with radical-right environments but that nevertheless express values and "nonconformist" ways of being that they associate with their own existential combat.

An Ethos of Rebellion
It was also in the pages of *éléments pour la civilisation européenne* that the ND writer Pierre Bérard, in an article titled "Is Rebellion Still Possible?," postulated that to think today about the possibility of dissidence inside a ubiquitous system (one that absorbs all contestation) meant above all thinking *against*. For the moment, he concluded, "there are a lot of radical ideas without use and many revolts without ideas. Rebellion awaits."[102] Nonetheless, according to Venner, the "only contestation that the system cannot absorb" is the contestation of the "indomitable," the ones "attached to their city, their tribe, their culture or their nation, and that respect the Identitarian diversity."[103] Identitarians of all sorts elevate in their historical narratives those figures that through the course of time contributed decisively to the knowledge of their culture's roots and ancestry. At the same time, they also view History through the prism of those who fought for the independence and identity of their peoples, sometimes with personal sacrifice and against all kinds of oppression and subjugation.

The pages of Identitarian publications, as well as their imagery, are filled with reverential portraits of rebels. They are "Identitarian figures," awakeners of their communities, models of thought and life. The political action of CasaPound provides a striking example of such a propensity, starting with the name chosen for the movement. As Iannone has observed, Ezra's Pound vision was "so revolutionary" for the times that he was put in a mental institution by US authorities. Hence, "We see in Ezra Pound a free man who paid for his ideas."[104] CasaPound's symbol is a turtle, and such a choice is also a reference to Turtle Island, a seventeenth-century haven of piracy. Adinolfi identifies Turtle Island as "the example to follow," for "it teaches us how to be radically diverse, free, independent, dealing with intelligence or force with whoever wants to get rid of us."[105] On the island, Iannone says, "the last free men of the seas hid their treasures."[106] This allusion to pirates and buccaneers extends beyond CasaPound and is pervasive in Identitarians' narratives and symbolism, which often show their affinity with the misfits and heretics of History. Importantly, many historical rebels are lionized irrespective of where the prevailing narrative of the dominant culture places them ideologically. As long as they embodied the mindset of defiance and fought the powers of hegemony, they too are incorporated in the Identitarians' pantheon. One such example of "borrowing" for the Identitarian cause is the figure of Che Guevara, who has traditionally been associated with the left. "Che Guevara was a combatant, a man who put his own ideas on top of personal convenience," writes Iannone, who then asks, "He was a Marxist, but what prevents us from giving him military honors?"[107] Guevara was above all a rebel who had, in the words of Adinolfi, "an existential vision of revolution"; and CasaPound celebrated Guevara at an event advertised with the phrase "We Learned to Want You."[108] The appropriation of figures not immediately associated with the politics of CasaPound does not stop at Guevara. The Florentine section of CasaPound put up posters featuring the face of the Irish rebel Bobby Sands with the purpose of commemorating his death and that of one of his comrades during a hunger strike in protests against the British government. They focused on Sands for the example he conveyed and as a perennial symbol of a free man protesting against tyranny. Another example is the celebration, at the time of his death in 2013, of Hugo Chávez and his "Bolivarian revolution." CasaPound activists raised banners all over Italy honoring the deceased Venezuelan president, because, they said, "at a time in which the sovereignty and freedom of peoples are undermined we cannot but honor a staunch opponent of globalization" and a "fierce enemy of the same oligarchies that are putting Italy in its knees."[109] Of course not all these tributes have been without controversy: The daughter of Ezra Pound attempted to force CasaPound to drop his name—a contention ultimately settled in CasaPound's favor by an Italian court—while the Bobby Sands Trust called upon CasaPound Italia to "stop such misuse of Irish patriots."[110]

As expected, a similar attachment to the historical role of the rebel and the centrality of a dissident and renegade imaginary is also at the heart of the French Identitarian network. The 1871 experience of the Commune of Paris, which was severely repressed by the authorities, is hailed as a social and patriotic revolt in which the people and their aspiration for freedom—refusing capitulation to Prussia—were abandoned and betrayed by the elites of the time. The Identitarians' sympathies lie with figures such as Louis Rossel, the "hero of the Commune," a young military colonel who chose to stay at the side of the people and was executed for his decision. There have been regular pilgrimages to his tomb, and in one such moment the Bloc Identitaire drew an analogy with present times: "Then as now, the ruling bourgeoisie has never hesitated to cooperate with the foreigner in order to defend its own interests. The only difference is that today, the alien is already within our walls."[111] The example of the Commune is also very alive in Projet Apache, one of the local groups associated with the Bloc Identitaire. In fact, their own name is intended to establish a connection with the rebellious past of Paris, personified by the street gangs of the 1900s, which constituted an outcast and anti-bourgeois subculture. Viewed as savages, they were labeled Apaches. Projet Apache appropriated their rebellious and anti-establishment mystique. As Philippe Vardon wrote, the young Identitarian Parisians "recognize themselves in those indigenous Parisians. . . . Guilty of defending their identity, journalists make them their devils, and authorities their nightmare. A century later, they are really the apaches!"[112] The parallel between past and present is recurrent in these French Identitarian narratives. In one of their many activities to make Parisians "rediscover their local identity" and to celebrate the 140th anniversary of the Commune of Paris, they paid homage to the communards with a *banderole* on the steps of the Sacré-Cœur that said, "People of Paris, remember the blood spilled in 1871, for the [defense of] liberty!"[113] Like the Italians of CasaPound, the French Identitarians draw their models of rebellion from different contexts; for example, it is common to see laudatory narratives about the early twentieth-century Irish revolutionaries who fought and died combating British supremacy. The writer, poet, and resistance leader Patrick Pearse is widely praised as an example of the political soldier who made the ultimate sacrifice for the identity and freedom of his people. In short, Pearse strove to "awaken his people."[114]

In the twenty-first century, Venner is now part of the pantheon of "free men" in his dual condition as an unsubdued man and martyr for the Identitarian cause. Venner, who had titled his written testimony of his early revolutionary activism "Rebel Heart," is now, and especially since his tragic death, the recurring object of praise by the major Identitarian voices in Europe. In the preface to the Italian edition of *A Samurai of the West*, Scianca calls it a "manual of heroism" bereft of romanticism or lyricism but instead representing "a tough, severe recall to reality. . . . Reality: blood, soil, life, death, people, borders, wars, cultures, Gods." He sees it as in sheer contrast to a Western world "supposedly secular and disenchanted, living in a bubble of hedonistic mythology, in a rarefied and unreal dimension in which none of the roughness that make the real exists."[115] Iannone was present at Venner's tribute in Paris, and CasaPound was behind the planning of a European procession called "Fatherland" that was to be conducted simultaneously in several European cities (Rome, Paris, Athens, and Madrid) every May 21, the anniversary of Venner's sacrifice. "Venner was a European patriot who sacrificed himself for the renaissance of a millennarian culture," Iannone explained. "His 'suicide' was not a gesture of mere testimony but of mobilization. We intend to respond to his call."[116] What is sure is that, under the spiritual and ethical guidance of old and present-day rebels, the Identitarian resistance could be more accurately described as an Identitarian offensive that is energized with the goal of retaking territory and reconquering minds and souls. Their live-wired militancy is a reflection of that spirit.

The Live-Wired Militancy
A self-representation that makes of militancy a stirring story, a transformative experience, and a communitarian way of living pervades these Identitarian narratives. Above all, it is based on the premise that political activism is an adventure. "Militant engagement is one of the last adventures worth the trouble of experiencing it today," averred the spokesman of Génération Identitaire.[117] Asked about the formation of militants, Iannone replied, "It is done with adventure novels, the rest will come by itself."[118] Identitarians position themselves as the antithesis to the passionless and uninspiring way of contemporary politics, which they associate with conventional political parties, by promoting a different understanding of politics as daring, lively, and entertaining. The book *Nessun Dolore* (No Pain), a militant description of CasaPound, projects it as an epic performance put together by combative, idealistic, and imaginative militants who are joyfully committed to a cultural revolution. This

self-assurance is felt as a break with neofascism, because, as a female militant stated, "Neofascists are decadent, sad, [and] do not help to grow."[119] The suggestion that they are the "fascist pirates of the XXI century" only reinforces their understanding of politics as an adventure, coupled with the iconographic embrace of fictional characters from comics and animation that symbolize their own romanticized view of politics and of life as a whole. Such is the case with the Japanese anime legend Captain Harlock, a romantic space pirate who defends freedom against all sorts of totalitarianisms (Harlock was also the symbol of Cutty Sark, the Roman pub that served as a meeting and mobilizing place for the future activists of CasaPound), as well as the comic character and sailor-adventurer Corto Maltese, celebrated by CasaPound as a "comrade." French Identitarians have also praised these free spirits. Vardon included both Harlock and Maltese as necessary references for a twenty-first-century Identitarian counterculture.[120]

At the same time, the militancy of Identitarians is experienced as a full experience. As stated in an editorial of the French *ID Magazine*, a true Identitarian activism is necessarily at odds with what passes for militancy in a "relativist" society, which is just one choice among others.[121] Inversely, Identitarian militancy is not a transitory or partial choice but, at least as expressed in internal narratives, is a full-fledged existential engagement that demands a high level of commitment and an ethos of self-sacrifice that is at odds with the individualistic and hedonistic society at large. The equivalency of being an Identitarian militant and "entering into resistance"—with all the costs and hopes that come with it—is central in Vardon's book dedicated to stories of militants.[122] In practice, all this means is a return to the etymological origin of the word "militant," from the Latin *miles* (soldier). No wonder that the description of militants as "political soldiers" abounds in Identitarian circles. "Evidently, the militant is not a saint," wrote Pierre Chatov—whose real name is Thibaut Balladier—at the time editor in chief of the French Identitarian magazine (and today a writer and contributor to *éléments* using the name Xavier Eman). "The militant does not act 'uniquely' for the others but [rather acts] 'also' for the others, which by itself is a quasi-miracle nowadays."[123] In order not to let the levels of energy and devotion be drained dry by the outside world, the militant, in the words of

Fabrice Robert, and quoting the lyrics of a song by the French Identitarian rock band Île-de-France, must "kill the bourgeois within."[124] To be a militant today is therefore tantamount to a revolutionary act.

The vision of militancy as a "total experience" is of course bound to a holistic view of politics. "Politics for us is a community," Iannone reaffirms. "It is a challenge, it is an affirmation. That is why we say that if we don't see you, it is because you are not there."[125] At CasaPound "everyone respects the rules, but not because you're constrained to respect the rules, but because it comes natural to you, because you're part of it, part of something that moves like an organic entity," says a militant. There is "not a logic of punishment," only a natural "mechanism of self-exclusion."[126] Another states, "We have a very tight relationship between militants, it is not a hazard that we feel like brothers, regardless of whether someone is more or less friendly."[127] Hence the feeling of belonging to a "community of destiny," not in the sense of something in the future but as an "eternal present," a unifying "vital force" that gives sense to existence. "I could tell you that the program of CasaPound is revolutionary. . . . But no, it is CasaPound that is revolutionary," spoke a militant.[128] It is not surprising, then, that in CasaPound "the revolution is first of all personal and then political: you must kill the bourgeois that is in you."[129] The sense that its members express a "communitarian spirit" that subverts the dominant paradigm of individualism also emanates from the French Identitarians. Génération Identitaire expresses it this way: "Génération Identitaire is a fighting community. 'Community' because we are more than a political movement: we are a clan in which a spirit of mutual solidarity and solidarity reigns."[130] And in such a "clan," naturally, there is no room for political quiescence.

The emphasis on militant vitality and energy also owes much to the fact that these Identitarian movements—notwithstanding the fact that some cadres and officials in leadership roles (such as the founders) are older—are for the most part composed of young men and women who actively participate in the various activities. In fact, although women are far fewer in number among the Identitarians, they are no less active. Often—and this can be seen both in the French and in the wider French-influenced European Identitarian movement as well as in CasaPound—women activists are the ones leading the marches, holding banners, or featuring prominently in propaganda material. This has been the result of clearly a calculated effort to give the movement a more "feminine" look and to further accentuate the difference with "old-style," male-hegemonic, right-wing radical movements.

Time and again, these groups present the image of a cult of youth. Many cultural events, in the form of music concerts and sports activities, are also a way of extending their reach among youth. While the projection of a youthful image is, understandably, more prevalent in the youth sections, it seems that these groups as a whole keep close to their hearts Venner's principle that to be a true rebel "is to make sure that you're never 'cured' of your youth."[131] "More than a youth movement, we are the youth itself in movement," announced Génération Identitaire, with their declaration of war targeting older politicians: "We are tomorrow, you are yesterday."[132] "I'm seventeen forever," says a CasaPound slogan, in this way putting the emphasis on the young, dynamic, and optimistic cult of action that pervades the entire movement.[133] A prerequisite to participation in the annual French Identitarian Université d'Eté—summer camps, held from 2003 onward, dedicated to intellectual, moral, physical, and militant formation—is being younger than the camps' age limit, which since 2016 means to be under 25. This youth-driven spirit is also manifest in *"Failala": The Song Book of the Identitarian Youth*, which is used at the campfires held at these camps and is a classic marching hymn adopted by many European student and youth groups (of all sorts, but in France especially of a nationalist nature) in the twentieth century.

Importantly, this cult of youth also has a generational meaning: the overcoming of an older generation—which took power after the 1968 protests—and the rise of a European youth dedicated to expunging its evil and disruptive ideology. "The world of '68 is from now on the old world, and it is in agony," pronounced the president of Bloc Identitaire.[134] "We are the victims of the Generation of May '68—the one which claimed to liberate us from the weight of tradition, knowledge, and authority in the schools, but which first of all liberated itself from its own responsibilities," declared the younger Identitarians accusingly.[135] This indictment is also present in the student group of CasaPound, as a self-described "revolutionary movement of rupture with today's school . . . run by professors nostalgic for '68."[136] The revolt of the new Identitarian generation was more forcefully expressed by the Austrian university student Markus Willinger in his 2013 "declaration of war against the

'68ers." It reads like an accusation: "You've thrown us into this world, uprooted and disoriented, without telling us where to go, or where our path lies. . . . While you've chased utopias your entire lives, we want real values. . . . You've destroyed everything that could have offered us identity and refuge, yet you're shocked that we're unhappy." The indictment, however, is joined with the Identitarian hope that "there will come a day" when it will be "entirely natural for a student to be an Identitarian, just as it was to be a Leftist in '68 and a Rightist in '33."[137]

This rejection of utopias and ideologies as being detached from the real world is a centerpiece of Identitarian narratives about their own political activism. "I don't like the term 'Identitarianism' because it sends [us] back to an ideological concept," says Fabrice Robert, adding that "to be an Identitarian is not [to subscribe to] a dogma or [to embrace] an ideology; on the contrary, it is [to uphold] a principle based on the real, on what [human beings] are. The Identitarian engagement is born of rootedness and hence from the idea that we are the fruit of a land and of a lineage, a link in a chain."[138] It is common to find expressions such as "return to the real" or "to act on the real" used to describe Identitarian activities. *Hic et Nunc* (from the Latin Here and Now) is one of their mottos. At the same time, the word of choice is "idealism" (instead of utopianism). "Generation Identity is not a club for ideologues who fantasize about the 'bright future,'" French Identitarians make a point of saying. "But this does not keep us from having an ideal: we want to live in peace on our soil according to our identity, as is the right of every people."[139] "What we demand actually exists, and to possess it is our ancestral right," reiterates Willinger.[140]

Similarly, Iannone stresses CasaPound's visceral attachment to reality: "CasaPound does not recite from memory old sermons about what needs to be done, but acts."[141] This is tied to the way that CasaPound has always tried to engage in a dynamic dialogue with the realities of its own time, using the cultural codes, references, and expressions of today's youth in a vital rejection of ghettoization. In this sense they continue the "anthropological transformation" of right-wing radicalism that was attempted in the late 1970s by youth sections of the neofascist movement, particularly in the festival-like experiences (with music, theater, poetry, graphic arts, and so on) of the Hobbit camps (in a nod to J.R.R. Tolkien's saga and in an attempt to show a commitment to a world of tradition, fantasy, and myth against a soulless society).[142] This continuity is only reinforced by CasaPound's annual three-day militant national gathering—held since 2008 and titled Direction Revolution—featuring debates and conferences, as well as a mix of sport activities (especially involving combat sports, from Brazilian jiu-jitsu to Muay Thai and mixed martial arts), cultural, and musical events.

In any case, this relationship with the actual and the concrete—with society, social issues, and human beings *as they really are*—is the *élan vital* of the political activism of Identitarians in their war, as they see it, against a dogmatic and dangerously ideological system of domination.

The Communication War
In an interview with the blog Alternative Right, Iannone stated that the most important thing for CasaPound's activism was to "generate counterinformation and to occupy the territory."[143] The belief that it is crucial to build a counterculture based on a new language and a new political imaginary that is able to subvert the establishment's orthodoxy and its media gatekeepers is the fuel that drives the strategies of communication of all sort of Identitarians. This, of course, starts with language itself, in tandem with the view that vocabulary is at the service of—and is manipulated by—the dominant totalitarian ideology. "To advance our themes, our watchwords, and even our words: semantics is a war!" wrote Vardon.[144] In fact, these French activists relish the diffusion of the word "Identitarian" as representing a watershed moment. "But our main victory is semantic," said Robert in 2012. "Who eight years ago used the word 'identity'? Nobody. Today, almost everyone uses it. This word means something important in the present French and European political debate."[145] This is viewed as no small feat, especially because of the "tyranny of political correctness," or the all-powerful Orwellian reign of "Newspeak," whose function is dual, according to the Polémia writers of the "Dictionary of Newspeak": "To prevent the perception of reality, and to make impossible the emergence of any sort of deviant thought."[146] "All of the oligarchy," noted one of its authors, "uses newspeak fluently, and that is one of the reasons why the gap [between the oligarchy and] the real country never ceases to grow." In a world in which the establishment elites "talk about 'happy globalization,' 'immigration as a chance' or 'marriage for everyone,'" the author continued, "the rest of the

population talks about unemployment, precariousness, insecurity, or the crisis of the family."[147] In the case of France, the Bloc Identitaire, engaged in combat against a political correctness that functions as a thought police and hides or flat-out denies the real problems that affect the people, prides itself in calling things by their name, without taboos and euphemisms. They are engaged in what they call an "information war" and dedicate themselves to a "battle for the words" and "therefore for ideas." This dedication is a precondition to advance the political debate and for future "political victories."[148] Robert Steuckers sees in this speaking truth to power a "return" to the France of Rabelais (the Renaissance satirist) in the sense of both a defiance and a stigmatization of the faults and egotism of the elites.[149]

The Identitarian assault on the language, the spirit, the codes and fashions of the times—as the lifeblood of their "metapolitics with a punch"—takes on an unconventional and imaginative approach. Guerrilla media tactics—used to shock and create a buzz—abound in their political activism. In the case of the Bloc Identitaire, as its president states, "there is a mix between the GRECE metapolitical action and Greenpeace field operations."[150] Media stunts and provocative events are designed to break the censorship of the media and outsmart a system that silences any voices that speak against the dominant orthodoxy. The repertoire has a strong performative dimension. One major action that Identitarians perform is the occupation of buildings—places belonging to the ruling party or the European Union or future places of asylum for immigrants or Muslim worship—to protest the wrongheaded policies of the "political caste." Other more theatrical actions, particularly those that are directed toward Muslims, include the donning of pig masks in a halal-only fast-food restaurant, the distribution of pork-laden "Identitarian soups" to the homeless, or the attempt to hold pork sausage parties in heavily Muslim neighborhoods (where streets were regularly occupied for prayers). All of this theater is performed in order to provoke media and political debate (which has been quite successful so far) on the Islamization of the land. Each event is complemented by a social media blitz, with the viral diffusion of well-produced videos showing the performance of the activists.[151] Agitprop operations such as these, even though their success has varied, have been carried out under the spirit of setting the media agenda, entering the discussions of mainstream politicians, *and* influencing public opinion at large.

Squadrismo mediatico, or "media squads," is both the name of the method and the method itself employed by CasaPound militants to describe their strategies of communication. In order to make it known in the social and political landscape, its activists undertake actions meant to be spectacular and not easily dismissed by the media. With a keen eye to scenography and symbolism, they have performed actions such as hanging off of bridges, trees, and monuments mannequins representing the Italian victims of high mortgages and of the economic crisis in general, or wearing masks in the colors of the Italian flag in a demonstration against economic insecurity. At the same time, they intend to be at all times daring, as when they invaded a *Big Brother* set (whose "free residence" they saw as an insult to all Italians suffering due to the housing crisis), swarmed media outlets to protest unfair coverage, or disrupted rallies held by political opponents. Blocco Studentesco is also likely to carry out such actions, which may result in violent encounters with radical-left activists, such as a student demonstration in Rome (known as the "Piazza Navona clashes") in which militants projected a warrior image, and pushed back their opponents though they were far greater in numbers, in an event that got wide media coverage.[152] As in the case of the French Identitarians, many of these militant expeditions are filmed for posterity by activists—often turned into memes—and widely diffused in the social media.

These media guerrilla tactics—which, on a low budget, make the Identitarians' presence and causes much more visible—are intertwined with the tactics of their own alternative media networks, which, powered by the Internet, serve to intensify their communicational reach. The goal is not just to influence the news but, through their own media, to produce news content and rival the dominant interpretation of events and social dynamics transmitted by the mainstream media. CasaPound has a media arsenal of its own. Since 2007 its web radio network Radio Bandiera Nera (Radio Black Flag), with the motto "free, beautiful, and rebels," broadcasts from CasaPound headquarters in Rome, as does its web TV, known as "Turtle TV—a non-conformist television." Its website and social media presence, not only of those of the main headquarters but of all its local ramifications, besides spreading the group's themes and activities, are constant sources of recruitment, mobilization, and funding. Within CasaPound, Scianca is a major media entrepreneur, heading the newspaper *Primato Nazionale*—initially available online only, but now also with a monthly print edition sold in newsstands—as a vehicle of the "free press" and writing profusely on ideology and current affairs (Scianca is also an occasional contributor to the ND magazine *éléments pour la civilisation européenne*). In France, the Bloc Identitaire president is behind the creation of a news agency, Novopress, portrayed as "independent and iconoclastic" while giving voice to "alternative news, without taboos," in a logic of "cultural and technological combat."[153] The goal is to expand the cultural offensive online, interactively and through the heavy use of social media, in what has been described by academics as "digital Gramscianism."[154] Jean-Yves Le Gallou, the founder of Polémia, sees in this "technological Gramscianism" a crucial tool to use in combatting the dominant ideology.[155] All of this is done in the name of a systematic work of "re-information" (the motto of Novopress is "a weapon of mass re-information since 2005"), that in practice functions as a work of "deconstruction" of the dominant vocabulary while making visible what the media system tries to hide.[156] This media counterpower, which is possible only with the revolution of communications technology, is a result of what Identitarians call "Dissident 2.0," an interactive and increasingly autonomous web network in which every activist can become an Identitarian medium.[157] In this sense, the intensive and savvy use of the Internet by these activists in their communication war may also serve to "inflate"—in the virtual world—the actual force of Identitarians offline.[158] That, certainly, is one of the positive consequences of this electronic breed of guerrillas: their groupuscular nature is, if not overcome, radically diminished.

The Aesthetics of Rebellion
To interpret Identitarian activism as simply a matter of doctrine risks leaving aside a primal dimension made of images, symbols, and myths that is expressed by the deep-rooted sentiment that aesthetics *is* politics. The deeper meaning of this notion is that the society to come must be a poem, an epic—in sum, beauty made concrete. In the last pages of his book-testament Venner wrote, "It is a living antiquity we have to rein-

vent. So we set out to reconstruct our tradition into a myth of creation."[159] This "reconstruction" is holistic and must suffuse and nourish all spheres of life, as in a "total" work of art.

CasaPound calls its own metapolitical project Artecrazia (joining "art" and "cracy," or rule). "In all domains," said Iannone, "we try to restore the principle of *Artecrazia*."[160] As explained by Scianca, Artecrazia signifies the fusion of politics and art, or politics as a "sub-species of art." What this means is "to make of the community of reference a work of art to be built," implying boosting up a sensibility that "before being political, social, and cultural, must also, and above all, be aesthetic," based therefore on the senses and the feelings. Being nonrational, it must "seduce before convincing." Accordingly, in an "ugly world" that has been disenchanted by and is ruled by materialism and utilitarianism, "one who knows how to express experiences of beauty—that is the revolutionary."[161] It is only natural that CasaPound's politics of beauty corresponds to life in movement, a continuous embrace of vitalism, youthfulness, and also violence, *as* aesthetic forms and also *as part of* the wider work in progress: the creation of a new society. Such celebration is even more urgent owing to the decadence and the widespread inertia and mediocrity of modern life. This vision, of course, draws on a variety of influences and traditions, and it is only natural given CasaPound's acclaim of futurism's cry of revolt against the sterile bourgeois culture of the time and its heroic exaltation of a new dynamic mentality, in tune with a new, feverish era. Hence, the "artistic trend" *Turbodinamismo* (Turbodynamism) was launched as a sort of futurist manifesto, revisited for the third millennium. Contemptuous and mocking, like futurists of yore, CasaPound announces that "Turbodynamism is the glorification of the gratuitous, violent, and inconsiderate gesture, with deference and consideration towards dressing up smart." Further, "To those anesthetized by do-goodery we proclaim that we will systematically rip everything to shreds for the pure relish of doing so. We are well aware that always replying 'because it's funny' to who enquires for the reasons behind such intolerance only enlarges our halo of wickedness, but, hey, it *is* funny." The manifesto concludes with this: "We'll sip some good ol' whiskey while everything burns, we have decided that the world belongs to us."[162] Here again—in all its excess and bravado—is, nevertheless, the crucial rejection of conservative and bureaucratic political ways that overflows from Identitarian narratives: the sparking of a *new* golden age as a mobilizing myth, as an adventurous, daring, and ultimately aesthetic creation. This frame of mind—or, more appropriately, of spirit—is certainly shared by French Identitarians. They repeatedly call themselves an avant-garde, or front line. "Far from being the last expression of a world in its death throes, they are the first pangs of a new birth," writes Vardon. Among this avant-garde "are not those who are watching a dying flame, but rather are a thousand torches that light up in the night. Reach out your hands too, my friend—grab the torch and set it alight."[163]

More than other political programs, this "setting the torch alight" entails an aesthetic diffusion of an attitude toward life, codes of conduct—in sum, of a diffuse atmosphere, as an alluring portal into the world and political activism of Identitarians. Vitally, this metapolitical project must dance to the rhythms of the time. In the words of Scianca, "What is needed is to rethink the European identity, which cannot limit itself to the usual images of Stonehenge and the Greek Parthenon, but must speak to the youth of today, and above all the youth of tomorrow."[164] This need translates in practice into the primacy given to a type of visual communication in the political combat of Identitarians that is fresh and attuned to the times. In a modern life saturated with images, sounds, and advertising, Identitarians work to make identity (or their version of identity) marketable to the younger generations. To put it another way, they manufacture (again, like artists) a culture infused with Identitarian values and principles in order to appeal to a broader, younger environment. They attempt to create a "New Cool" that, however, is not based on self-gratification and consumerism but rather expresses the ethics and values that mirror an Identitarian worldview. Tradition, memory, roots, and communal bonds are therefore created, projected, and re-created in a rebellious, fun, "cool" fashion. This is done with the help of popular culture and, in particular, the ubiquitous American entertainment industry. Faye noted, "For better or worse, it's been the American cinema that has valorized European heroes. For example, films like *The 300 Spartans, Excalibur, Braveheart,* etc."[165]

Ancient Greece is a major foundation for this heroic, rooted, and holistic Identitarian worldview. The 2013 French Identitarian summer camp, for example, was titled On the Road to Ithaca and was devoted to Homer as "the prime narrator of the European soul."[166] The

Spartans were, from the outset, an ideal for Identitarians. Frank Miller's graphic novel *300*—which depicts the legendary last stand of the Spartan King Leonidas and his warriors in the fifth-century BC battle of Thermopylae against a far superior invading Persian army—was a source of inspiration for the Identitarian brand. One of their earlier summer camps was called Go Tell Sparta—a reference to the Greek poet Simonide of Ceos's epitaph to those who died at the battle: "Go, tell the Spartans, stranger passing by, that here, obedient to their laws, we lie." The movie *300* (adapted from the novel) became in time a central reference in the political message, marketing, and iconography of the French Identitarians. The release of this motion picture "was a beautiful occasion to illustrate the unity of Europeans in face of the absolute Other."[167]

Generation Identity adopted the Lambda symbol, which was on the Spartans' shields, as its own. It is the equivalent to the letter "L," for Lacedaemon, as the city-state of Sparta was known in Ancient Greece. "Don't you understand what it represents?" they asked in their declaration of war. "It means that we will not retreat, we will not give up! Weary of your cowardice, we shall not refuse any battle, any challenge!"[168] Immediately, one of the group's early shirts was adorned with the Lambda symbol and the inscription "Defend Europe."

FIGURE 3. The logo of Génération Identitaire.

In an editorial in the Bloc Identitaire magazine, the Identitaires' own perceived condition as the "front line" of combat for the people was compared to the one of "the Spartans at the battle of Thermopylae."[169] Vardon, for his part, sees the epic novel *Gates of Fire* by Steven Pressfield, which is a dramatization of that battle, as part of any authentic Identitarian counterculture. At the same time, in the Italian camp, Scianca lauds the same book as "by far the most read and praised romance in CasaPound." It is elevated to the level of an archetype, of an action that should be replicated, a once-and-for-all example of what "quiet strength" means, a proof that strength unites.[170] This emphasis on *esprit de corps* is very much present in the self-presentation imagery of CasaPound. Not only is the logo of its youth wing a circled flash, because "lightning is the strength that comes from being united,"[171] but also CasaPound's stylized turtle is made to recall the famous tortoise, or *testudo*, formation used by Roman legions in battles.[172]

The revolt against the modern world is also a decisive factor in the choice of movies that express the spirit of Identitarians. *Fight Club*, for example, is held up for reverence as a powerful celebration of the warrior over the trader through an inversion of the dominant materialist and utilitarian paradigm and its display of a heroic value system. Quotes from Tyler Durden, its fictional character, overflow into Identitarian

FIGURE 4. The logo of CasaPound Italia.

narratives and imagery. His dramatic monologue, for example—"We're the middle children of history, man. No purpose or place. We have no Great War. No Great Depression. Our Great War's a spiritual war. . . . our Great Depression is our lives"—is celebrated as a rejection of the sedated life that Identitarians pursue through their own political combat. *Fight Club!*, the website of Identitarians from Lyon, exclaims: "Here's a movie that, after watching it, we come out overwhelmed . . . a true hymn to the end of the bourgeois view of life!" A visual campaign of an earlier incarnation of the French Identitarians' youth wing featured an image of Tyler Durden (played in the movie by Brad Pitt) with the message "You're not what you possess." This is an evocation of this Durden speech: "You're not your job. You're not how much money you have in the bank. You're not the car you drive." Projet Apache took its name from "Project Mayhem," the name given in the movie to the project of destroying the current society.[173] *Fight Club* is also, for CasaPound, an example of "nonconformist" art. Circolo Futurista (Futurist Circle), which is part of the ensemble of CasaPound's universe and collaborates in many of its social and media campaigns, calls its members the "heirs" of Roman legionaries, the *arditi* (shock troops) of Fiume, the futurist fascists, and "of Tyler Durden," and stresses as it proudly proclaims this heritage that "we are the ones who live splendidly, in a world of dead."[174] "What is the youth seeking in CasaPound?" Iannone replied: "They are looking for life. CasaPound is life in a world of dead."[175] In CasaPound narratives there is a constant evocation and re-creation of vitalism: a vigorous way of life at the antipodes of how so-called "life" is experienced today in a zombielike senseless and consumerist inferno. From this ethos results the acceptance of violence as *part* of the human experience and the creation of a virtue and morality that are at odds with the bourgeois ethics of comfort and devitalized living. No wonder that movies such as *Fight Club* are revered. The performance during the concerts of ZetaZeroAlfa of the ritual dance of *Cinghiamattanza*, in which male youths fight shirtless with belt straps, is also experienced as a shot of life against the anaesthetized experience of today. Iannone calls it an "extreme version of pogo [an ecstatic dance also associated with punk]," that is "hilarious to watch" and a "shock for the weak."[176] "If in doubt, fight and you will see that you will live longer," say the lyrics of one of the band's songs exalting the role of fighting (in order to feel alive, in typical

Fight Club fashion) in the formation of the character and comradeship of the young fascists of the third millennium.

The aestheticization of politics and the significance of visual communication go hand in hand with the development of an innovative political marketing. Identitarians are overwhelmingly brand conscious, and that becomes immediately apparent in their logos, which provide instant recognition and attempt to establish a brand that carries and projects an image of rootedness, unity, and strength. Here again is the attention to the real, to today's society, and an awareness of the pervasiveness of advertising. This is, of course, reflected in CasaPound's self-presentation, particularly in their clothing and other apparel. It is reinforced in their cultural-political campaigns, on posters, stickers, banners, and in their overall iconography that circulates in the streets and on the Internet. The design creativity of the French Identitarians, for example, has even been dubbed by a graphic arts specialist as a "graphic revolution."[177] With a strong emphasis on the traditions of each region (with its linguistic and cultural codes), French Identitarian visual communication juxtaposes an immense variety of colorful images (taken from cartoons, movies, statues, and monuments; from militants, real and stylized; or from immigrants and Muslims, for example) with themes of defense and revolt against specific groups, policies, and overall dangers that threaten France and Europe. In these the self-portrayal of the group is invariably heroic and defiant (again, as the "front line"). The seduction of would-be recruits takes place through a vibrant design that mixes strong colors with vintage, or other striking, visual elements.

Naturally, without the Internet and all the online networks directly or loosely associated with the Identitarians, this visual offensive would fall flat. Since the mid-2000s, the blog Zentropa—which takes its name from the Lars von Trier movie and was founded by, among others, Pierre Chatov, then editor in chief of the Identitarian magazine *ID*—has been at the forefront of the aesthetic combat for a transformation of the European spirit. It is a major producer of the Identitarian New Cool. "Love, Absinthe, and Revolution," the title of a song by the Identitarian French rock band *Hôtel Stella*, was its original motto. In time it developed into the so-called Zentropa clan, a community of associated blogs and sites dedicated to the poetics of dissidence against the modern world through the diffusion of audio-visual content related to Identitarians but also to "anticonformists" at large. It presents itself as a "phalange of comrades spread through several continents, but irremediably united through a series of common values, those of the European spirit and culture."[178] It is very closely linked to the metapolitical project of CasaPound—as it is with the Italian blog Badabing—and its aim, through the messianic power of images, is to re-create and update the aesthetics of identity for modern times and for the youth of today.

The Marking of the Territory
As Fabrice Robert has claimed, "I often say that the street and computer networks are our offices."[179] In fact, Identitarians are territorial. Their struggle for identity, therefore, transcends the virtual battlefield and expresses itself in physical territory, in autonomous spaces, in urban areas, in the streets at large. They assert their presence, and often reclaim lost territory (abandoned to neglect, to insecurity, to criminality, and so on). "The street must be seen as our permanent political office," said a spokesman for Generation Identity. "The street remains and will remain the principal place where we express ourselves. . . . By extension, we must radiate over the whole public square: secondary schools, universities, concert halls."[180] Iannone's view that the goal of CasaPound, at all times and through a wide variety of means, is to affirm its presence and "occupy the territory," is a prevalent Identitarian disposition.

This comprehensive action of reclamation is, ultimately, a work of Reconquest. As Guillaume Faye noted, in his Manifesto of the European Resistance, "Every resistance not arising on a foundation of *Reconquista* is destined to fail."[181] The newer generations of French Identitarians use such a word, which, in its original Portuguese and Spanish context, referred to reconquering the territory that had been lost to the Arabs. It carries a meaning that, according to the Identitarians, is well applied to contemporary times. *Reconquista* (also the title of one of the albums of the French Identitarian band Fraction) is a "mobilizing myth," declares Vardon.[182] Besides the larger, metaphorical meaning of expulsion of the invaders, this *Reconquista* is also felt as something very concrete that starts in the streets and in fact all public spaces where the presence of a disruptive, threatening, and ultimately non-European population is felt. This territorial takeover—this daily fighting back—is a precondition for a wider retaking of European identity. No wonder

FIGURE 5. Image from the campaign *Visages de la Reconquête* (Faces of the Reconquest, launched in September 2016).

that one of the self-promotion campaigns of Génération Identitaire, launched in the fall of 2016, was called Faces of the Reconquest. It consisted of the portrayal on posters and stickers across France of the images of militants in proud and confident poses, with calls for youths to join the movement.

It was also in this state of mind that, years before, Génération Identitaire had launched the campaign Génération Anti-racailles. Nicolas Sarkozy, who used it to name the rioters who shook France in 2005, had made the pejorative word *racaille* (rabble) famous. Generation Anti-rabble directly targets the second and third generations of immigrants (sub-Saharan and North African), mostly living in suburbs, who are accused of being the source of the daily intimidation and insecurity suffered by the native (European) French, especially the young. This new campaign only reinforced a long-running theme. For a long time, noted Fabrice Robert, "we had wanted to show that to keep our eyes down in the street hadn't become something compulsory."[183] "On public transportation, in the schools, in the neighborhoods, when French people go out, they have to live with this reality: at every moment the worse can happen. . . . In face of the hateful groups, the young Frenchmen and Frenchwoman are too often isolated, scared. . . . Generation Identity wants to break this isolation," the group announced. "From now on the rabble will be confronted by a vigilant youth."[184] This was illustrated by the launch of "security tours" in different cities, in which militants, wearing K-way jackets in yellow—the main color of Generation Identity—patrol the subways as a dissuasion force, under the conviction that "the predators are only strong because of our own weakness."[185] These tours created a controversy, and participants were viewed by opponents as dangerous militias. "But we haven't invented anything," argued Damien Rieu (a pseudonym), at the time spokesman of the group, establishing a comparison with the 1980s Guardian Angels that "eradicated the violence in the subway system of New York City," emphasizing further that if the authorities fail the people, the people must act by themselves.[186] These security tours, with the passage of years, were further expanded to include, for example, city areas often targeted by the "rabble" (such as the area surrounding Lyon's railway station) or offered protection to small businesses against North African rioters, as in the Normand city of Rouen: "If the police does not answer, contact us and we'll send a team of 'yellow K-way' militants," read a leaflet distributed in the city center.[187] Other initiatives, launched in order to counter the emasculation of the people, who had been made a "docile prey" to attackers, included the offering of self-defense courses to men and women. "To teach the youth to defend itself, if it is necessary, is it a crime?" the French Identitarians asked.[188] As a reflection of the influence that the world of the ancient Spartans wields in the Identitarians' imagery, when they established the first Identitarian combat sports facility in the city of Lyon—marketed as the first of its kind that was "100 percent reserved to the patriotic and Identitarian youth"—they called it Agoge, the name of the educational program in which the boys of Sparta were enrolled.

French Identitarian youths have also hung silhouettes in public squares, each representing a victim of a deadly crime committed by the "rabble." The propaganda materials, posters, stickers, and sweatshirts all disseminate the notion that the best defense weapon is the communitarian spirit. "They have their gang, join your clan," reads one leaflet; "Against the rabble, you're not alone anymore" and "Against the rabble, we are the first line of defense," read two more. This emphasis on

FIGURE 6. Logo, with the Spartan helmet in the middle, of the Identitarian boxing club/self-defense gym, The Agoge (founded in January 2017).

self-defense—as displayed by the quasi-instruction "We are at home, defend yourself!," which has become prominent in the political marketing of the group—can also be seen, for example, in the Identitarian summer camps, with boxing and martial arts available to participants, that are part of the formation of new Identitarian cadres. The Bloc Identitaire even launched a campaign called "Yes to Self-Defense" against the inaction of the state in defense of the "little people," who have the right to defend their businesses, families, and homes.[189]

All in all, what emerges from the struggle for territory is the need to impose an Identitarian spatiality in a hostile environment. Crucially, such a spatial dimension constitutes the DNA of CasaPound, with its network of occupied houses, associations, and concert halls all over its territory, especially in central Italy. These are spaces of freedom outside the dominant left-wing and liberal hegemonic system of domination. Writing about CasaPound, Colin Liddell, the co-editor of the online magazine *Alternative Right*, noted its "visibility" and "strong image" in the "neighborhoods that it regards as its own. This street profile often means using posters and street art to visually 'claim' areas they believe are theirs. It is as if they 'tag' their 'hoods' and warn other gangs off."[190] This spatial imagination—this delimitation of borders and reclaiming of a territory that exudes a different approach to life and a different value system—fuels the creative myth of these spaces as self-perceived locations of rebellion, freedom, and beauty. Far from achieving hermetic, or sealed spaces, however, the goal is to have centers of social aggregation, especially for the youth, through which an alternative paradigm of existence is lived and experienced. Or, as Iannone put it, in an allusion to this territorial, rooted perspective, it is as if these spaces were "the marble that is defeating the swamp."[191] For example, Area 19, an abandoned Roman subway station (occupied by CasaPound from 2008 to 2015) that promoted musical and sports events associated with the group, was a space they named an "enemy post," symbolically separating, and celebrating, the dissidence of this "nonconformist" area. Without a doubt, the fact that there have also been in these localities clashes and physical confrontations with anti-fascist militants (the "other gangs"), only serves to reinforce their sense of territorial assertion and protectiveness. All things considered, this social philosophy of occupation, coupled with a heavy street activism through marches, parades, sit-ins, and even actions such as clean-ups of degraded streets, public parks, and urban areas "abandoned" by public authorities, are all part of CasaPound's desire to entrench itself, systematically, all over the territory.

Importantly, the local branches of the French Identitarian movement have founded their own communitarian "Identity Houses," heralded as "places of freedom" and dedicated to intellectual, cultural, and sports activities. In these areas—which Fabrice Robert calls "rebel zones" and Vardon views as "the places where we remake a people"[192]—the autochthonous culture, under attack by globalization and Immigration-Islamization, finds a place to be experienced and celebrated. Each Identity House—and part of the effort to boost the community network development—is viewed as a "home" for local Identitarians. For example, in Paris Identitarians have La Barricade (The Barricade), in Nice Lou Bastioun (The Bastion, in local dialect), and in Lyon's Renaissance neighborhood La Traboule. In Lille, the capital of Flanders, activists set up the "patriotic and Identitarian house" La Citadelle (the Citadel)— named in reference to the city's tag as "Queen of Citadels." Its local leader, Aurélien Verhassel, said that it is open only to "sincere patriots, Hellenic-Christians and Europeans of stock."[193] These self-managed spaces have multiple uses. They often are composed of pubs, libraries,

62   THE IDENTITARIANS

FIGURE 7. Logo of the "Identitarian and Patriotic" house La Citadelle in the city of Lille (open since 2016).

and conference halls—for example, both Alain de Benoist and Guillaume Faye have spoken at the Lyonnais House[194]—and offer expositions, sports (often with courses on combat sports), and music events, functioning as communal and alternative spaces for today's Identitarians in the hope that many more will flourish across the territory.

Finding That Ballots Are Not Enough
While grappling to prevent their societies from being torn apart by a multitude of forces arrayed against them, Identitarians have adopted a "total" model of political action in the sense that, while they have the dynamics of a privileged social movement, they have not completely neglected the arena of institutional politics. Whether in France or in Italy, Identitarians operate through hybrid organizations that mix social movement imaginaries and repertoires with ventures in electoral politics. This has been done both autonomously, especially at a local and regional level, but also, and increasingly, by throwing their support to major po-

litical "classical" parties that share at least some of their grievances, enemies, and goals.

Speaking about the Bloc Identitaire, Fabrice Robert said that "it is better defined as a network rather than a conventional political party." Further, in typical metapolitical fashion, he contends that "in order to take the political power in a country a preliminary and successful conquest of the minds is still necessary." This of course requires extending political activism beyond the electoral process, which is a means and not an end in itself.[195] The most important thing, consequently, has been to "impose the terms of the debate on the political and media class," in the words of Arnaud Delrieux.[196] This attitude, however, has not prevented the French Identitarians, at a local and regional level, from engaging in electoral politics. Nissa Rebela, in the city of Nice, when it was led—from 2007 to 2013—by Philippe Vardon, was the most electorally active branch of French Identitarians. Alone or supporting like-minded candidates, it has run on a pro-local, anti-immigration, anti-Islamization platform. In one of the elections in which it was active, writing in *Identità*, the "journal of the *niçoise* resistance," Vardon alerted readers that the choice given by the Identitarian candidates was clear: "either being masters at home or preparing to live on reservations like the last Indians."[197] Bloc Identitaire even attempted to run with their own candidate in the presidential elections of 2012, but fell short for logistical and financial reasons, and, after an internal referendum, decided to support the candidate of the Front national, Marine Le Pen. The relationship between these French Identitarians and the largest radical-right party in France was initially, for the most part, one of love and suspicion. If on one hand the Front national was praised for its anti-system nature and its combat against immigration and Islamization, on the other hand it was seen as promoting a hegemonic and centralized view of the French state to the detriment of its regions, and it was believed to be against European ideals and to be too moderate (or politically correct) in the defense of ethnic identity. Nevertheless, in regard to Marine Le Pen, Fabrice Robert says, "I do not want to insult the future."[198]

What is certain is that, with the passage of time, the Identitarians' relationship with the Front national increasingly—from the viewpoint of Identitarians—began to be defined by a logic of complementation instead of rivalry or competition. This is usually framed, for pragmatic reasons, as a process of providing mutual aid, synergistically, between Identitarians and "Patriots." As Fabrice Robert stated, in a speech to militants, "We are not the right wing of the patriotic movement, we are its spearhead. . . . The patriot is the masses, the Identitarian is the first line of the masses. . . . The Identitarian movement aims at awakening the consciences, and to agitate the energies. The Identitarian does not act to reach consensus, but to go further, always further." In the long run, "The ideal would be a transubstantiation of the patriotic movement into an Identitarian movement. In any case, there is currently a complementarity between us." It was also in the name of this avowed complementarity that the Bloc Identitaire ceased to be a political party and returned, in 2016, to its original, associative condition, in the form of Les Identitaires. For these French Identitarian activists it is as if they are special forces behind enemy lines, advancing the lines of combat and opening the way for the future political victories of the army.[199] It is not surprising that Vardon, one of the major Identitarian entrepreneurs in the city of Nice and nationally, has openly campaigned regionally for the Front national's candidate, Marion Maréchal-Le Pen, and subsequently he was elected, in late 2015, as a party's candidate for a seat in the legislative body of the PACA (Provence-Alpes-Côte d'Azur) region. Marion's passion in defending the French people's identity has been much closer to what Identitarians prefer than has her aunt and party leader, Marine Le Pen, and throughout the years she has been the main gate within the Front national for the ideological entry of Identitarians. Damien Rieu, for example, a key figure of the early days of Génération Identitaire as its spokesperson, has been a member of Marion's coterie, and since 2015 has been responsible for the Office of Communications of the Front national mayor of the Southern village of Beaucaire. Vardon, in his new situation as "unofficially" associated with the Identitarian movement, referred to the Front national, as the "central pillar" in the defense of the "identity of the people." Emphasizing, however, that "around the Front national there must be initiatives in the terrain, targeting the formation of the youth, and the intellectual, media, associative, social, and sport fields. It must be the ensemble of society that must be irrigated."[200] No wonder that, tongue in cheek, some Front national representatives call Identitarian activists "our Trotskyists."[201] The fact of the matter is that Vardon has been moving up within the Front national. In early 2018, as Marine Le Pen was beginning her third term at the helm, the former Identitarian leader entered the party's national bureau. In any case, Identitarians feel that their metapolitical, complementary work is a necessary and required step in the preparation and, eventually, future consolidation of the victories of the patriotic camp.

Like the French Identitarians, but more steadfastly, CasaPound has engaged in electoral politics, initially by throwing their support in local elections to parties of the radical right, but also by running autonomously for local and national elections. They have had some degree of success locally, electing candidates to city councils in a few regions. Such electoral engagement, however has been constantly viewed as only a small part of a much wider metapolitical groundwork. As CasaPound's president, Gianluca Iannone, stated in an interview with Novopress, "To some, elections are everything, the only thing that counts, the only goal of politics and even, maybe, of life itself." But efforts to make politics in a single form are foredoomed: "You need to be everywhere, in the streets, in the media, etc. . . . and also in the ballots." The emphasis is on elections as "no more than a stage—the important thing is that they are a means, and not the end of political action."[202] This also means that electoral failures are not entirely dispiriting or catastrophic, because the "building of the revolution" is not dependent on the voting booth.

At the same time, and in order to reinvigorate its status within the conventional political world, CasaPound found its "own" natural ally in the field of Italian politics in the form of a direct collaboration with the Lega Nord (Northern League)—a successful right-wing populist political party that, under the leadership of Matteo Salvini, attempted to expand its reach to the central south of the country. This culminated in the creation of Sovranità (Sovereignty), a political-cultural association that functioned as a CasaPound movement of support for Lega Nord. "There is not a blood pact but a convergence on the themes of rejection of the Euro, an end to immigration, and priority for Italians," explained Iannone. "These are battles that we have always fought, therefore for us to look at Salvini was a natural thing to do."[203] The goal, as made clear by Simone Di Stefano, the vice president of CasaPound, was to envision a future of strength for an "Identitarian political actor," with Salvini as the candidate for prime minister of Italy.[204] In this way, Salvini could be, as Scianca hoped, the spear of a wider cultural charge (of rootedness and community) against the "established" civilization of the power elite.[205] But, as Iannone made clear, there was no "blood pact" indeed, and the alliance faltered at the time of the 2016 mayoral elections in Rome, when the ally supported a center-right candidate from the establishment—which was viewed as a concession to the same, worn-out political system—with CasaPound breaking ties and running independently with its vice president, Di Stefano. If anything, the frustrated hopes of the "Salvini revolution" served to show how tortuous—especially because until now the group has often fared badly in national elections—the electoral path was for CasaPound's goal of "taking back" the country. And this notwithstanding Di Stefano's conviction that "one CasaPound member of parliament would do more for Italy than four center-right governments."[206] To date, however, they have not managed any breakthroughs in national elections, and they have been unable to reach the threshold level (3 percent) to get into parliament.

Asking "Which Way for Revolution?"
Viscerally attached to tradition—as re-created, reinvented, and adapted to modern times—Identitarians aim for a complete reversal of the dominant deracinated paradigm of European societies. Identitarians tend to reject the label "conservative" because they associate it with maintaining a status quo that, they believe, should be revolutionized. Even when it is labeled "conservative" it should be hyphenated with "revolution." Lucian Tudor, a Romanian-American Identitarian, sees the movement as "revolutionary to the extent that it aims to displace the *current system*—with its liberal ideological hegemony, multiculturalism, false democracy, etc.—and replace it with a new social, political, economic, and cultural order," but it is "also conservative" because the new order is founded on a regenerated tradition.[207] What is evident is that, in their self-understanding, Identitarians are at war with the "current system." As Scianca articulates the situation: "I think that to affirm a strong identity is the most revolutionary thing that is, also because everything today combines to demolish the numerous bonds and ties. So cosmopolitanism certainly cannot be revolutionary, because it goes exactly in the direction

of the current."[208] Identitarians, thus, are moving upstream, against the hegemonic flow of the times.

Reflecting on the "revolutionary potential" of the Identitarians' struggle, Michael O'Meara sees it in terms not of "revolution" (which is "a category more appropriate to modern rather than postmodern societies"), but of an "anti-system tendency." "Given that the prevailing American-centric system rejects historic, multi-generational, linguistic, religious, and ethnic identities," O'Meara writes, "Identitarianism is necessarily anti-system."[209] This revelatory statement echoes the idea, pervasive in the narratives and practices of the new Identitarians, that—at a time of intensified globalization, with multiple forces eroding the traditional nation-state from below and above, and where it is increasingly difficult to locate the sources of power, which are often ubiquitous, deterritorialized, and impersonal—the revolutionary path must be calibrated to the new times. In an article titled "What Is Rupture?" Eugène Krampon called for an "adaptation" of revolutionary combat. "To take power is certainly a noble idea that we are obsessed with," Krampon wrote. "But it is not a linear path from theory to reality. . . . To try to create a climate of tension in society and hope for a convergence of catastrophes to take power, as a sort of Identitarian coup that would put in the palace a providential man . . . it seems to us obsolete today." Instead of a full frontal assault that would ultimately be doomed to failure, Krampon advocated the strategy promoted by the Irish libertarian-Marxist philosopher John Holloway of "changing the world without taking power."[210] Holloway said that the development of alternative forms of doing *is* the revolution, and resistance implies a "constant moving against-and-beyond"—both against the world as it is and beyond, toward the world as it should be. This autonomist ethos of "not waiting for the future" and "living now the world we want to create" has deep roots in anarchist theory—the notion of "planting the seeds of the new society within the shell of the old"—and has been rejuvenated in the twenty-first century, especially through the spreading of "do-it-yourself" tactics of direct action and the movement of occupations.[211] Within a similar strategic mindset, Guillaume Faye postulates that the first imperative of the struggle for European civilization is to construct a "real counter-society, an embryo of the coming society," in line with the biblical precept of "being in the world but not of it."[212] Ultimately, what this means is that this prefigurative strategy is not exclusive to any ideology, in the sense that it can be practiced by very distinct groups with opposite value systems. What matters is the drive to carve out communities of resistance and build the world they want to live in now, through a joyful communitarian fusion of the means and ends of political action.

Crucially, this "revolt of doing" is at the center of the activism of the newer Identitarians. For one, it fits solidly within their emphasis on acting on the real, on the concrete, in the case of French Identitarians—and also in the case of other Lambda groups across Europe, as the next pages will document—as well as on the dynamism and vitalism embraced by CasaPound. Further, the philosophy of direct action, the drive to confront issues directly, has taken root—in nonauthorized protests, in spectacular and courageous actions, in blockades, sit-ins, and die-ins, in confronting the police if necessary, in challenging what they call the "rabble" without intermediaries, in the occupation of roofs and buildings, and of course in the creation of autonomous spaces free from an oppressive system. This last dimension comes to the fore in the "nonconformist" occupations of CasaPound, but also in the creation of "Identity Houses" by the French Identitarians. These are communal experiments of "the world as it should be." When Robert, the co-leader of Les Identitaires, says that the goal "is to develop zones of liberation, identity areas that enable us to show that another society is possible,"[213] he is only reaffirming such a prefigurative praxis. It is no wonder that Vardon included the notion of TAZ—or temporary autonomy zones, a concept from the anarchist thinker Hakim Bey—as one of the principles to guide the building of an Identitarian counterculture. "Alter-globalists have their own TAZ," wrote Vardon. "We need to have our permanent autonomous zones."[214]

Which way for revolution? In the case of Identitarians, it is surely in the direction of an alternative politics that subverts the current order from within, opening cracks to freedom. Such a vision, as noted, goes beyond the strict Identitarian camp but also finds common ground with one of their earliest metapolitical references. "When a global change is impossible, it is first of all necessary to recreate spaces of freedom and social life which are, as it were, 'territories' removed as much as possible from the ruling controls," once wrote Alain de Benoist. This means that "those who are employed in this task can only be revolutionaries."[215]

EUROPEAN NETWORKS AND BEYOND

As the twenty-first century was dawning, Guillaume Faye argued that, in the long term, "the birth of a revolutionary European-identitarian party" was "indispensable." Time had not brought to fruition, at least not yet, what he saw as an "imperative" to the "fight for Europe."[216] Be that as it may, the formation and mobilization of a wider transnational Identitarian counterculture, heavily active on the World Wide Web, and with many entrenched outposts in Europe and beyond, is seen by Identitarians, or by those who see the Identitarian movement with sympathy, as not only needed, but also as natural. John Morgan, a lit major and the former American director and editor in chief of the publishing company Arktos, which has published and translated many New Right and Identitarian works, is optimistic: "The great thing about the Identitarian idea is that it can be transplanted almost anywhere, not only within Europe but anywhere in the world where a people is rooted in a particular culture and historical tradition."[217] Lucian Tudor believes that Identitarians are "naturally aware of the benefits of international alliances," because "all Identitarians are aware of being everywhere in the 'West' a repressed group whose members and beliefs are attacked and demonized by the ruling political systems (usually liberal of some sort)."[218] A linked idea is that the Identitarian cooperation across borders has just begun, which leads the Croatian intellectual Tomislav Sunić—who has a doctorate in political science from the University of California, Santa Barbara; has propped up Nouvelle Droite themes, especially in the Anglo-American world; and has also been close to the Terre et Peuple network—to argue that "for the time being [Identitarianism] is still a new romantic would-be movement with no clear cut trans-European political agenda."[219] What is more, in the view of Colin Liddell, even though "[Identitarianism] has enormous revolutionary potential," it will also "be quite easy to set one group of Identitarians against other." This may have a crippling effect on the overall movement, and "unless we can counter such tendencies, it will remain less revolutionary than class consciousness was in the early 20th century."[220] What is undeniable is that Identitarians of all dispositions, whether combating through ideas or actions, have been drawn to band together across regions and countries. After all, within their own diversity, they see themselves as belonging to the same threatened European civilization.

Terre et Peuple Expanded

Critically, the choice of the words "Identity" and "Identitarian," and the focus on the shared "ethnocultural identity" of Europeans facilitates at least theoretically the networking of activists across borders, owing to the fact that through this conceptual process they are primarily or exclusively defined no longer by national attachments but by membership in, and loyalty to, a wider ethnic community of a greater Europe. Pierre Vial has for a long time reiterated this view. "The primary reason of our engagement is the combat for the identity of our peoples, all the brother-peoples of the Great Europe," read his editorial, "The Identitarian Movement," in the second issue of the magazine *Terre et Peuple*. Since the inception of his Terre et Peuple network, Vial has pressed on for the constitution of a Europewide Identitarian front, or network. This engagement has taken many forms. Throughout his activist career, Vial has crisscrossed Europe, including Russia, participating in a vast number of conferences, promoting magazines of "resistance," and establishing overall ties with like-minded groups and regional associations in the spirit of Identitarian entrepreneurship. The annual meetings of its association have served as gatherings of European defenders of the Identitarian cause and have been held under such themes as "Europe Our Great Motherland" and "From Sparta to the Conquest of the Stars: The Destiny of the European Man." Vial was also behind Europe-Identité, a political organization with no "electoral ambition" but with the sole purpose of "awakening the members of our community," in the conviction that "European peoples are united by a common cultural identity that goes back many millenniums and has been forged by history: from Homer to Solzhenitsyn this filiation has never been interrupted."[221] Vial's network has also been a staunch supporter of political parties viewed as "rooted" and "Identitarian," especially, but not exclusively, those with strong regional roots, such as Lega Nord, or the Flemish Vlaams Blok (later renamed Vlaams Belang), whose founder, Karel Dillen, was lionized at the time of his death as the "awakener of a people" by Jean-Yves Le Gallou, in the pages of *Terre et Peuple*.[222] But other parties, such as Greece's

Golden Dawn, or even the Front national, have also been praised because "they fight the good fight." Vial wrote, "I have as a principle only retaining what unites us (Identitarians of all countries, unite!), leaving aside a few divergences, because what is important is to face up to the enemy."[223] In defense of the "European motherland," Vial has actively collaborated in myriad initiatives, both fleeting and more durable, aimed at establishing such a Europe-wide line of Identitarian defense. Pierre Krebs, the founder of the German *völkisch* think-tank Thule Seminar and a proponent of a "new culture" in radical opposition to the Western system that has "defaced" Europe, has been a longtime traveling companion of Vial. Together they were present at events such as the Action Européenne (European Action)–sponsored conference dedicated to establishing a "European Identitarian combat front," at which Krebs advocated an "Identitarian revolution" in order to win the "war of the planetarians against the Identitarians."[224]

At the same time, autonomous Terre et Peuple branches have emerged outside France. In this case, too, the work of Identitarian entrepreneurs was crucial. In Belgium, Georges Hupin, who had previously been involved in the foundation of GRECE-Belgique, was the main promoter behind the local Terre et Peuple, devoted to the Identitarian cause of the mostly French-speaking Walloon region, in particular in the long-running magazine *Renaissance Européenne* (European Renaissance). In Portugal, especially through the ethno-cultural intellectual contributions of Miguel Jardim (heavily influenced by Guillaume Faye) and the activism of João Martins—who, won over by the new, younger Identitarian French activism, as well as by Faye, "who had a tremendous impact on [his] ideological revolution," founded Causa Identitária (Identitarian Cause), the first Identitarian Portuguese group, which existed from 2005 to 2009[225]—as well as the metapolitical action of Duarte Branquinho, the Identitarian offensive was meant to revitalize the nationalist movement, which had been moribund since the post-authoritarian era. It was Branquinho who, after being president of Causa Identitária, set up the Portuguese section of Vial's network (Terra e Povo) and, besides speaking at Terre et Peuple roundtables, organized conferences in Lisbon in which Vial, but also Faye and Gabriele Adinolfi, participated. Branquinho's goal was to diffuse Identitarian symbols, practices, and ideas while inserting the Portuguese struggle for identity into a wider,

French-inspired but fundamentally European, network.[226] In a later period, when he was director of the right-wing weekly newspaper *O Diabo* (The Devil) from 2011 to 2016, Branquinho spoke at the first Iliade conference, The Aesthetic Universe of Europeans, which he praised as a sign of the "renaissance of European culture."[227]

In Spain, Enrique Ravello played a similar role. Greatly involved in the blogosphere, Ravello also led the Spanish Tierra y Pueblo (the Spanish section of Vial's network) and its magazine (of the same name) and was the director of the magazine *IdentidaD* (which ran from 2006 to 2009), whose international collaborators included, among others, Pierre Vial, Pierre Krebs, and Guillaume Faye. In true Identitarian fashion, Ravello later engaged in the fight for regional, rooted peoples and identities, first playing a role in the Catalan party Plataforma per Catalunya and subsequently creating his own Identitarian party, the separatist SOM Catalans (We Are Catalans), for the "identity of Catalonia" against "Spanish colonialism and the immigrant invasion,"[228] as well as the threat of "Islamization." The combat against the "Islamization" of Europe—but not the fight for the separatism of Catalonia—is certainly at the forefront of the mindset of the former editor in chief of *IdentidaD*, the Catalan Ernesto Milà. A neofascist and "revolutionary nationalist" militant until the turn of the century, and founder and editor of the Spanish magazine *Revista de Historia del Fascismo* (since 2010), he sees himself today as more invested in the "Identitarian cultural combat" through writings, translations of authors such as Guillaume Faye and Dominique Venner (of whom he translated three books into Spanish), a personal blog called Info/Krisis, and speaking engagements. In a theorization that is common among Identitarians, Milà professes his attachment to "three levels of identity (a) the national, from the nation-state, b) that of the native birthplace, c) and the European level)," even if, unlike Terre et Peuple, he is a strong supporter of the nation-state as the "only defense" against globalization and its "evils."[229]

The Identitarian Lambda Movement

Extolling the merits of the Identitarian vision and practices of Génération Identitaire and its affiliates, the Welsh author who uses the nom de plume Fenek Solère—who has said, "I would describe myself as a European writer with Celtic origins"—said that their "clarion call" of renewal of identity "echoes through the towns and cities as far apart as Lviv and Derry. Through the winding valleys of the ancient villages of the Pyrenees. Across the valleys and wide flat steppe to the suburbs of the cities of the East."[230] This lyrical portrayal may be caught up in hyperbole, even if it is true that the example of Identitarian activism of the newer French militants has inspired a phenomenon of informal franchising in which groups of mostly young people across Europe have indeed adopted its imagery, themes, and repertoires of action. Developments such as these, of course, are welcomed by Fabrice Robert—especially because "we will not win alone." He continues, "Our struggle must be waged across Europe with the movements that share our values and civilizational consciousness."[231] Likewise, Arnaud Delrieux declares, "since we have the same identity and are encountering the same problems (mass immigration from the countries of the Global South, pressure from the Islamic world, American hegemony, and pauperization due to globalism), we must adopt a common front."[232]

This search for convergence meant, for one thing, the establishment of ties with political parties that are viewed as expressions of "popular and rooted movements," such as Lega Nord, the Vlaams Belang, or the Austrian FPÖ. This has also been done through the youth sections affiliated with the Bloc Identitaire, as through the relationship developed with the movement Giovani Padani (MGP), the youths of Lega Nord. "The combat against immigration and Islamization, the defense of our cultural and ethnic identities, a federal vision of the State: Identitarian and Padani youth have one more time realized how close and tied their combats are," asserted *ID Magazine* about the presence of French activists in an MGP congress.[233] Throughout the years, Lega Nord's Mario Borghezio, a long term member of the European Parliament, has risen to the status of a true Identitarian sponsor across Europe and has always supported the Bloc Identitaire and its local affiliates (such as Nissa Rebela), also speaking at the movement's national meetings (the Identitarian Conventions) in France. "His determination and character have conferred on him a lot of popularity among Identitarian militants," wrote Philippe Vardon.[234] These conventions, with featured speakers, roundtables, and music concerts, have served, during the initial phase of the movement, as gatherings of myriad French and European Identitarian activists.

The cross-border adoption of Identitarian activism and practices, especially associated with Génération Identitaire (as a sort of franchisor), is also a major dimension of this internationalization. This has been evident in the Francophone world, especially in French-speaking Switzerland, initially with the activities of the Swiss offshoot of Jeunesses Identitaires and afterward with Génération Identitaire Genève (Generation Identity Geneva). One of leaders of the Swiss Identitarian youth movement, Jean-David Cattin, became a member of the Bloc Identitaire executive bureau and now runs Les Identitaires, together with Fabrice Robert.

Die Identitäre Bewegung

The copycat phenomenon has taken off at full speed, especially after Génération Identitaire's "declaration of war" and movements modeled on the French group gathered up steam—especially in Austria and Germany. In fact, within the Identitarian Lambda movement, the activists from Germanic Central Europe have managed—through both intense street and online activism—to establish themselves as a force in protest politics. "Respect My Identity!" shouts the character Cartman from the adult TV cartoon *South Park*—recalling his catchphrase "Respect My Authoritah!"[235]—in an image produced and circulated over the Internet by the Vienna-based group WIR (Wiens Identitäre Richtung, or Vienna's Identitarian Direction), founded in early 2012 by university students. By the end of the year, on December 12, 2012, a triumvirate formed by Martin Sellner, a philosophy major, Alexander Markovics (a History graduate and, together with Sellner, a former member of WIR), and Patrick Lenart (a philosophy and history student), created the IBÖ (Identitäre Bewegung Österreich, or Identitarian Movement of Austria). Roughly a month before, as representatives of WIR, Sellner and Markovics attended the French Identitarian convention in the city of Orange. "It was important since we met the French Identitarians there for the first time," notes Markovics.[236] "Generation Identity is about the defense of our cultural identity, which means ethnicity on one hand and culture on the other," he said about the new Identitarian creation.[237] Almost simultaneously, the German chapter Identitäre Bewegung Deutschland was created, initially led by the civil engineer Nils Altmieks. Although they are separate organizations both groups are intertwined, and most militants are in their twenties or early thirties. Under the heading IB (Identitäre Bewegung, or Identitarian Movement), these German-speaking activists released the video *Future for Europe*, addressed to the ruling powers and elites, as a sort of Germanic equivalent to the French Identitarians' Declaration of War. Against somber background music, a succession of young men and women, including Sellner and Altmieks, declared:

> You do politics which sacrifice our values and traditions for a multi-cultural utopia. . . . Our Europe is dying. Our future is being threatened. What is normal in other countries is being endangered by our government. Identity is valuable. We are becoming aware of it again. . . . We are connected by over 1,000 years of German and European history. We are continuing this chain. . . . Our goal is not taking part in the discourse but its end as a consensus. We do not want to join the conversation, we want a new language. . . . We are the youth without a migratory background which wants to live and still has not given up on its country. . . . We are the European youth, we are the Identitarian movement.[238]

With a lively presence on the Internet, social media, podcasts, blogs, and vlogs, presenting themselves as "Europe's youth," IB activists use elements of popular culture in order to prop up the theme of an ethnocultural identity threatened due to globalism, mass immigration, and especially Islamization. "And we will show the Sky People . . . that they cannot take whatever they want! And that this . . . this is our land!" said the character Jake Sully in James Cameron's *Avatar*. In Austria the imagery of this movie was used by Identitarian activists to establish a comparison between the Na'vi people's nativist defense of the moon Pandora against humans (the "Sky People" above) with their *own* rejection of threatening and corrosive threats to their identity.[239] "This film is about the struggle of an ethnocultural community for the preservation of its homeland, its customs and tradition, against a foreign mass immigration that would radically 'change' all that," wrote Sellner in an article posted to Identitaere—generation.info—the initial online intellectual and cultural platform of the IB. From 2015 to 2017 Markovics was the editor in chief of this theoretical forum before parting ways with IBÖ in order to focus on his studies (as a master's student in history at the University of Vienna) and dedicate himself to his career as an independent Identitarian political analyst, as well as lecturing different groups on topics from political theory to geopolitics and writing in his blog and in other publications.[240]

Like their French counterparts, IB activists have distinguished themselves and attracted media attention through unconventional, spectacular, direct actions. The first emblematic act of IBÖ, for example, which put them in the media spotlight, came in 2013, when they occupied the Votive Church in Vienna in protest against the church's occupation by asylum seekers. Likewise, on Federal Government Open Day, the annual state holiday on which the government opens its doors to the public, IBD militants pulled a stunt at Berlin's landmark Brandenburg Gate. They scaled the neoclassical monument, lit pyrotechnics, waved black-and-yellow Lambda flags, and unfurled a gigantic banner reading "Secure Borders—Secure Future" in protest of the "Open" borders paradigm—all in broad daylight and before the stunned crowd of onlookers below. The next day, the *Berliner Kurier* ran the irate headline "Fools Desecrate the Brandenburg Gate."[241] "These young men were not alone on the gate, but together with the fate of all peoples of Europe," the group said on its Facebook page.[242] The "courageous patriotic youth, uninterested in doctored lives and a conformist middle-class existence stood on the Brandenburg Gate," the Facebook post further said, proclaiming that actions as "peaceful, symbolic and decisive" as these are what is needed in order to "revive the lost spirit of Europe."[243] Here, too, much as in the French and Italian milieus, a vision emerged of Identitarian youth militancy as risky, adventurous, and in direct opposition to the dominant "bourgeois" resignation of society at large. It is only natural that these militants often see themselves as in continuity with the "nonconformist" path of earlier figures, such as Ernst von Salomon, who wrote in *The Outlaws* of his yearning in the interwar period for something "more. . . . I want some aim which will engross my life. I want to savor life whole. I want to know that this has been worthwhile."[244] This idea of a life "with a purpose" pervades the Germanic Identitarian youth narratives. A 2016 Facebook post declares that "Generation Identity will not have a career, but a destiny."[245] In their eyes this ethos is more than justified owning to the dire ethnocultural condition of German and other European peoples; from this stems the moral belief that "we are the last generation" that still has time to reverse the downfall of European culture. "We are already the last generation who will be able to change something about this development," Altmieks said in an interview with *Sezession* (Secession).[246] In the same magazine Sellner, who was born in 1989, maintains that the "last generation" is more than an "age group"; it refers to all those who "share the fate of German and European presence in the territory." Instead of waiting for their own D-Day, for the "right moment," Sellner said, the "revolution" should be launched with daily acts because "we ride the last wave, the last breath of life of our ethnocultural traditions." Hence, "Each of us is called as a member of the 'last generation' to become involved, to support, to network, to gather, to politicize, and to act," because "to do nothing would be much riskier."[247] This last-chance, running-against-time spirit is a sort of Identitarian trademark.

"If I were twenty years old, you would find me on the Brandenburg Gate!" says Götz Kubitschek, a man in his forties.[248] A key figure of today's German Neue Rechte (New Right), which emerged in the 1970s, borrowing many themes from the French ND, as well as its Gramscian strategy of achieving cultural hegemony, Kubitschek is a major supporter of the IB and is seen by many of its activists as an important spiritual and intellectual influence. In fact, particularly since the turn of the century, this German intellectual has run a network of forums and publications—with emphasis on the magazine *Sezession*, the publishing house Antaios (where his wife, Ellen Kositza, plays a prominent role), and the Institut für Staatspolitik (Institute for State Politics)—through which he has not only pursued the metapolitical work of delegitimation of the liberal capitalist order (and all its 'isms,' from consumerism to immigrationism and postgenderism, for example) but also provided intellectual, logistic, and, when warranted, especially in legal matters, financial support for the Germanic Identitarian movement. He sees it as an action-oriented energy boost to the metapolitical combat: "The Identitarian Movement is the activist wing of the New Right. It features a few new notions and links in the matter of theory, but its paramount input is its active, in-your-face potential. So it is not quite an heir to the New Right, but an addition: a vigorous, youthful addition."[249] It is only fitting, then, that many Identitarian youths attend the academies organized by the Institute for State Politics, held twice a year, in the small village of Schnellroda, the place of residence of Kubitschek and the focal point of his network of cultural combat. The age limit is 35, and year after year, at least since the early 2000s, many intellectuals and academics have discussed a variety of themes, often around an issue covered by *Sezession*. By saying that "Schnellroda is for us something like a spiritual center,"[250] Sellner only emphasizes this dynamic relationship between Kubitschek's New Right and its "vigorous, youthful addition." Naturally, *Sezession* and Antaios are major outlets for the ideas and writings of the young Identitarians, and in the autumn of 2017—when Antaios was invited, for the first time, to the world's largest publishing gathering, the Frankfurt Book Fair—Sellner was scheduled to give a reading of his first book, *Identitär!* (Identitarian!), an event that was cut short due to the protests of left-wing activists whistling and chanting, "Nazis out," to which many people in the audience answered back with the cry "Everybody hates antifa."

Another Antaios author whose presentation at the Frankfurt Book Fair was disturbed by protests was the Austrian political essayist Martin Lichtmesz (the pen name of Martin Semlitsch), a film-school graduate, former journalist for the weekly paper *Junge Freiheit* (Young Freedom, with which Kubitschek collaborated as well), writer for *Sezession*, translator of many ND and Identitarian works, and author of several books. Lichtmesz is a known advocate of the IB and close to its leadership. His role as a social critic of left-wing sociocultural hegemony, especially in his writings and social-media activism, is widely acknowledged. The Identitarian movement, Lichtmesz says, is a vital "call back to the spiritual and historical roots of Europe which is sorely needed in a time of cultural decay, demographic decline, democratic disenfranchisement and ethnic self-hatred."[251] According to Sellner, while "Alain de Benoist and Guillaume Faye have been very important figures in the development of our ideas, writers like Götz Kubitschek and Martin Lichtmesz deserve the credit for clearing a lane through the ideological dichotomy for a new Identitarian idea" in Germany.[252]

In *The Art of War*, Niccolo Machiavelli informed his readers that "every nation has made its men train in the discipline of war, or rather its army as the principal part," and that "the number of men involved varied little, as all have comprised six to eight thousand men. This number was called a Legion by the Romans, a Phalanx by the Greeks, and a Caterna by the Gauls."[253] IBD activists declare that "we are in the front row, we are the patriotic phalanx!"[254] Phalanx Europa is also the name of the online Identitarian store created by IBÖ activists that supplies Identitarian New Cool items in several categories. As Sellner explained, "Phillip Vardon, one of the head figures of the Identitarian idea, once said: 'We have to create a counter culture. Whether you become a singer, a tattoo artist or a T-shirt designer. Everyone needs to take advantage of all his skills to help build it,'" and "because Patrick Lenart and myself are not the best singers, we've created an Identitarian label, to reinforce our counter-culture. Since 2012 Phalanx Europa has become the favorite brand for Identitarian activists and is seen in every manifestation and action."[255] Their shirts, hoodies, posters, stickers, and other merchandise mix style and social criticism, showcasing traditional themes and historical events (from the Spartans to the *Reconquista*) or revered heroic figures (Nietzsche, Mishima, and Ernst Jünger, for example), but always with a provocative, quirky, defiant, and sarcastic attitude. "We, Identitarians, patriots, conservatives, traditionalists, simple folks, are the last bastion to defend European values. In 500 BC we had to fend off enemies from the outside; today the enemy is in our own country. We are the last battalion. That's too 'radical,' too 'political,' and too 'extreme' for you? That's 'madness'? No: this is Europe!" reads the catalogue description of their "European Spirit" shirt, emblazoned with the ancient Spartan helmet and the inscription "Defending the homeland since 500 BC."[256]

The Identitarian counterculture has also rooted itself in the technological realm. Tech-savvy and social media–savvy, Identitarian activists use the Internet extensively, and Sellner, for example, has become a sort of Identitarian YouTube personality with his vlogs. The creation by IBÖ of a social media networking app—in order to build communication between like-minded Identitarians—was also a way, in the minds of activists, of both "defending the homeland" and propagating the Identitarian New Cool through technology. Although Kickstarter, invoking "hate speech," banned the initial funding campaign, Sellner found an alternative online funding platform, and Patriot Peer was created as "an app for the silent majority." Austrian Identitarians have also created a professional film studio—Studio.ID—in order to give a more professional look to their visual communication, particularly in regard to video production. The marketing of Identitarianism—and making ideas such as homeland, tradition, freedom, and "defense of Europe" look "fashionable" and "cool"—has also picked up within IBD, and this is especially evident in their online shop (IB-Laden), which sells stickers, pamphlets, clothing accessories, carry-on bags, and Lambda buttons. Backed by Identitarians, the online Berlin-based brand Cuneus flaunts a similar philosophy, aimed at "patriots and activists in Germany and Europe," and yet again reinforcing the idea that "there is nothing wrong in looking proudly at the past of one's culture and recognizing its achievements" while doing it in "style."[257] This notion that "there is nothing wrong" in showing pride in the history and identity of the homeland and Europe is also what drives the "Show Your Face" campaigns of Identitarians in Germany and elsewhere in Europe. In fact, inspired by the French Identitarians' Faces of Reconquest marketing operation, IB militants in Austria and Germany also launched their own meet-the-Identitarians recruitment campaign with posters and memes showing activists' photos, ages, and professions, proudly showing their commitment to the Identi-

FIGURE 8. Image from the campaign "Show Your Face" showing Edwin, an Identitarian activist from Vienna.

tarian cause. IBD's Stefan Lüdtke's comment that "it has always been our firm conviction that we must fight openly and honestly for what we love and want" epitomizes this spirit.[258]

Following in the footsteps of their French counterparts, and in order to keep boosting their "European Spirit," the movement in Austria also developed a network of "Identitarian houses," or centers, in major Austrian cities to serve as starting points of Identitarian counterculture: communitarian spaces dedicated to the formation of militants, to sports activities, and to overall Identitarian activism. The city of Halle, in east-central Germany, was the first place to host an IBD "Identitarian center"—named Kontrakultur Halle and located a stone's throw from Martin Luther University—which was presented as a "patriotic space for culture, life and political work" and a "flagship project" for the movement. Likewise, the goal of IB's "activist weekends" and "summer camps"—of which the group makes memes and videos that become part

FIGURE 9. Image from the campaign "Show Your Face" portraying Melanie, an Identitarian activist from Germany. It says, "Fights for our right to identity."

of its marketing—are geared toward ideological formation, sports (especially combat sports), and outdoor activities such as mountain hiking and even gatherings around bonfires. These in fact demonstrate an ethos similar to the "back-to-nature" ethos of the Wandervogel, the German youth groups that began in the early twentieth century—and always in the spirit of furthering comradeship among activists. Sometimes they are held as celebrations of major Identitarian figures, as in the case of an IBÖ training camp dedicated to the "ethics of action" of Dominique Venner on the fourth anniversary of his death.

This focus on promoting and experiencing a counterculture is, of course, part of the DNA of the Identitarian Lambda movement as a whole, and IB activists, too, tend to see their cultural combat through a logic of complementarity with the electoral/political process and with political parties that they see as sharing a common spirit. This means that political forces such as the Freedom Party (FPÖ) in Austria and the Alternative for Germany (AfD) are supported and viewed as allies in the greater scheme of the ethnocultural defense of European civilization. "Yes, we see the Freedom Party, just like the Front national and the AfD, as an important factor in a European renaissance," Sellner says. He then adds, "We as a metapolitical movement have no direct links or ties to parties, but of course we are influencing them like the whole political scene with our actions and ideas. We think that a vote for the FPÖ is in fact an Identitarian vote. Our job is to turn coming electoral successes into metapolitical victories."[259] Daniel Fiß, the head of IBD in the north German state of Mecklenburg-Vorpommern and a major coordinator of Identitarian activism in Germany, is clear about the aims of the group: "In a few years we want to be an established NGO, so to speak, the Greenpeace of the right-wing scene. In the Bundestag the AfD could become our extended parliamentary arm."[260] According, therefore, to the snowballing logic that the metapolitics "with a kick" of the Identitarian youth and the "patriotic-minded political parties" ultimately roll together, getting simultaneously stronger and bigger, "On you, friends!" exulted Robert Timm—the Berlin leader of the Identitarians—on Twitter over a Leonardo DiCaprio toast meme after the AfD Bundestag breakthrough in 2017. When, at the end of the same year, the FPÖ entered the Austrian government in a coalition with conservatives, which lasted in principle until 2022, Sellner took some of the credit for his group: "It is also, of course, our success . . . but it's not the end, because power corrupts. . . . We as Generation Identity will watch over whether they are actually doing what the people voted for them for." He concluded, "What we are doing is actually working, it is having an effect—in changing society . . . everything [political changes] comes upstream from metapolitics."[261]

Particularly in Germanic territories, the Identitarian youth movement often finds itself in defensive mode, especially in regard to accusations against the movement for political extremism, and even for ideological ties with National Socialism. In short, Identitarian youths find themselves collectively portrayed as a potential threat to democracy. For example, the regional German newspaper *Schwarzwälder Bote* ran an article titled "What Can Be Done to Protect Young People from Radicalization and Extremism" and specifically mentioned Identitäre Bewegung as a prime example of such a nefarious influence, adding, "They consciously use names from the time of National Socialism. The grouping is unambiguously classified as extreme-right." German Identitarians immediately reacted against this "slander." In a nighttime operation, they "locked" the entrance to the newspaper headquarters in the town of Oberndorf am Neckar, stringing red crime-scene barrier tape around it and leaving behind a banner with words from the German actor Oliver Hassencamp: "The one who lies knows the truth after all."[262] An accusation of having Nazi ties, of course, has stringent, far-reaching consequences in a country whose jurisprudence on militant democracy is highly developed and became so precisely as a *response* to its Nazi past and whose Basic Law is oriented toward the protection of the liberal democratic constitutional order against enemies of democracy. In a press statement, the group reserved the right to take legal action against what they saw as defamation and insisted both on their ideological separation from "overhauled ideologies" and on the "nonviolent democratic" nature of the Identitarian movement, which was, in fact creating a peaceful activist escape for "patriotic youths" that would ultimately "protec[t] them from extremism and radicalization."[263]

This is an argument often heard in Germanic Identitarian narratives. Martin Sellner gives his own history of political activism—in his teen years he was a member of Nationaler Widerstand (National Resistance), a German National Socialist subculture—as an example of such a transcendence of "overhauled ideologies" presumably represented by the Identitarian movement. In "Confessions of a Mask" (a nod to Mishima's autobiographical work), which he posted online, Sellner explained his gradual intellectual-spiritual break with such a fringe culture. Especially influenced by the readings of Conservative Revolution and Nouvelle Droite authors (around whom he organized a reading group at the University of Vienna, as well as the blog Der Funke), Sellner described his and his colleagues' adoption of an Identitarian Third Way beyond the Nazi scene and the multicultural order. "Above all," he wrote, "what we want to make clear to them [the people] is what we have become so deeply aware of: the struggle for one's own identity does not mean the struggle for the Nazis, and there is an Identitarian third path between the national-socialist scene and the liberal system, no matter what the media claim." Here the idea that Identitarian militancy actually protects militant youths and society itself *against* the "wrong/extremist" kind of political activism is further articulated:

> We are concerned about the youth "without a migration background," which no longer has a voice, and which is categorized by the media altogether into the discarded "Old Europeans." We will not allow this generation of young patriots to be pushed into the right-wing extremist scene, and thus into a devil's circle of violence, hate, and extremism, through the prohibition of thought and speech, exclusion and incitement. To give these young people a meaningful and positive way of expressing their legitimate anger beyond senseless violence and ideological madness has become a central concern for me, especially for reasons of my own youth. A strong identity movement is the best and only means against an extremist, totalitarian and violent Nazi scene, which is recruited from the legitimate wrath of our youth. However, with our message of diversity and freedom, we Identitarians are also the most effective force against the immigration lobby, against the culture of guilt, multiculturalism and egalitarianism. No wonder the representatives of both camps are attacking us with feverish hysteria. The Nazis and multiculturalists know their time is over.[264]

This idea that the break with Nazism is not tactical but foundational—and Sellner in his letter aimed at showing this break as life-changing and transformative—courses through all accounts of Identitarian activists. IBD's Daniel Fiß, previously affiliated with the youth section of the National Democrats—a political party that Germany's constitutional court argued "demonstrates an affinity . . . with the mindset of National Socialism"[265]—says that new members formerly associated with extremist movements must show that they have overcome such a phase and have moved on.[266] Mario Müller, the head of German Identitarians in Halle—who, in a line of tradition started by the Frenchman Philippe Vardon, wrote *Kontrakultur*, a German A-to-Z dictionary of Identitarian culture (published by Antaios)—noted that in previous times "I was something like a Nazi," seeing this phase like a "sin of youth."[267] Asked about the former connections with the neo-Nazi scene of some militants, IBÖ's Markovics said that they have "made peace with their past" and that "everyone has earned the chance to change," with the conviction that the Identitarian movement "wants to finally end neo-Nazism by giving young people a patriotic, democratic alternative."[268]

Irrespective of this line of reasoning, the fact of the matter is that the suspicion of "extremism" hangs over the movement, and this is the reason that the German and Austrian States have taken vigilant, even repressive, measures against them—measures that, according to activists, serve to overwhelm and stifle the growth of the movement. "It is clear to us that the state is seeking means to intimidate us," said the leadership of IB Bayern. "There are some people who would like to join us but are afraid of getting into professional troubles. Many guys are therefore afraid to join us. We also had a few older ones who have retired because they are civil servants and are afraid to come into conflict with the state. This mechanism has already worked at other times and, in our opinion, it is used deliberately." They further defend themselves: "We do not want another state, as we are accused [of wanting]. We also do not want a revolution, and we are not anti-constitutional—quite the opposite. And [the keepers of the status quo] know that too. They would like to get rid of us because we are uncomfortable, because they know we are spreading the truth, because we are a thorn in their sides."[269]

In the end, in the eyes of Identitarians, the indictments of "extremism" and "threat to democracy" fall flat because of the rising popular—

and therefore inherently democratic—appeal of Identitarianism itself not only in Germany but also in Europe. In a context marked by the news that the Federal Agency for Protection of the Constitution placed the group under surveillance, with the argument that IB activists may be a potential threat to the free, democratic constitutional order, Götz Kubitschek, in the aftermath of the occupation of the Brandenburg Gate, told them that the only solution was to hold the line. "Guys, this is it, never forget: What we want is the obvious, and, thirty years ago, you would have shrugged and in good German asked, 'So what?'" In his view, it is the establishment that is "excessive" and increasingly "out of tune" with what people want—whether it be ethnocultural identity, tradition, borders, security, or whatever. To Kubitschek, and to those who agree with him, the Identitarian movement, as well as populist/Identitarian parties, are "not the stress test of democracy but its litmus test."[270] In fact, again and again German Identitarians reiterate not only their democratic credentials but call for an expansion of democracy to include "patriotic arguments" such as theirs; when the IBD filed an injunction against the domestic intelligence service of the Federal Republic of Germany calling for the discontinuation of the "unlawful state surveillance of the Identitarian movement" and an end to the labeling of the movement as "extremist," they insisted, "You do not have to like us and our positions. But the fact that we are being watched for the protection of the homeland and patriotism is an unspeakable stain on democracy."[271]

Likewise, when authorities in Austria decided to prosecute the IBÖ as a "criminal organization (in a development that involved raiding activists' homes and the confiscation of funds), they saw it as a "scandalous" political repression against the right to "patriotic activism"—"We demand what is enshrined in our Constitution: A policy of love for one's own." No wonder that the motto of their successful crowdfunding campaign to raise money to fight the accusation in court was "Patriotism is not a crime!"[272] They subsequently received a not-guilty verdict.

Other European "Generations Identity"
While Identitäre Bewegung is the most established and solid Identitarian Lambda group outside the French hexagon—even matching, in terms of initiatives, campaigns, and public impact, their French counterparts—the movement has spread to other countries, though not

as strongly. The French "franchisors," understandably, encourage all of these Identitarian undertakings, pointing them out in their own publications and social media. "Europe! *There* is not the least of our success. In Italy, Switzerland, Austria, the Czech Republic, Germany, we have diffused our political direction, our methods of action, giving rise also to local Identitarian movements," French activists rejoiced in their magazine *Identitaires*.[273]

The youth movement moved into East Central Europe. In the summer of 2013, activists from the Czech Republic—mostly students, some of whom had previously been involved in the network of Autonomous Nationalists—founded Generace Identity. In the following year, representatives of the French Identitarians—Philippe Vardon and Jean-David Cattin—traveled to the country to tighten the relationship and "introduce the 'original' Identitarian movement, in its ideological and methodological foundations."[274] The group distances itself from "petty" nationalist thinking—"We are of course patriots, but we refuse nationalist resentments (while we appreciate positive aspects of it, such as national solidarity) and chauvinism," says its spokesman, Adam Berčík—while adhering to the typical Identitarian Europeist ethnocultural outlook: "European identity consists of ethnicity, culture, history, and a shared destiny. You do not become a European just because you receive a German, French or Czech passport."[275] "Or a Hungarian passport," he could have added. In fact, in 2016 a group of Hungarians officially established Identitás Generáció—Magyarország, the country's Generation Identity, aimed at protecting the "white, European identity and culture in an increasingly hostile environment" that "attacks everything that is ours, traditional, and European."[276] Gergely Kőrössy, one of its main coordinators, says that "the average age [of activists] is circa 20–24 year olds, our youngest activist is 15 years old, the oldest is 35, this is a young movement," adding that "our biggest influence were the French Identitarians, their success and the [example they provide] that this movement can go beyond national borders and can connect Europeans in a different way." In the light of this, "We can say that we're nationalists but only . . . in a 'Europe-compatible' sense, because we think that every European ethnical, historical, local minority is valuable and they are important 'building blocks' of the organic and real European diversity."[277] At the first press conference of the group, Ábel Bódi, the head of the Hungarian Identitarians, stood beside Jean-David Cattin, from Les Identitaires, and Ingrid Weiss, on behalf of IBÖ, who had traveled to Budapest to show the support of the wider Identitarian youth movement.[278] The idea of connecting European nationalists in a "different" pro-European way is also present within Generacija Identitete Slovenija (Generation Identity Slovenia), another chapter of the movement that emerged in the Central European region, presenting themselves as "harbingers of the new European reality, which must, if Europe wants to survive, stand up like a phoenix from the ashes of modernity."[279] By and large these Identitarian chapters in Central and Eastern Europe are still minor in terms of both activists and activities, especially in comparison with their more successful Western European Identitarian "brothers."

For example, the Italians. In Italy, in 2012, strongly inspired by the French Identitarians' "Declaration of War," a group of five activists from Piedmont's capital city, Turin, founded Generazione Identitaria. Umberto Actis Perino, a computer engineer and co-founder of the Italian movement, says that "at the time none of us had any political experience: our core curriculum was our enthusiasm and drive to do something to change the severe situation of immigration in Italy."[280] Aiming at "defending our people, culture and tradition against globalization, capitalism, uncontrolled immigration and cultural standardization," they mimicked the style and adopted the themes and guerrilla-type actions of the wider European movement, which to an increasing degree they network with.[281] Although geographically the group is, for the most part, concentrated in the northern part of the country, it also aspires to expand southward, as attested by the opening of Generazione Identitaria Roma five years after the foundation of the Italian Lambda movement. At the same time, it has also expanded to the Mediterranean Sea with the creation of Generazione Identitaria Sardegna on the isle of Sardinia.[282]

The branch-centric expansion of Generation Identity continued—especially fueled by the increased visibility of Lambda activists in other European countries—and that notoriety (in terms of press coverage and social media conspicuousness) was a powerful factor in the opening of branches. It was certainly a reason for the opening of the first Belgian/Flemish Identitarian group—Generatie Identiteit—which was officially founded in September 2017. Here, too, the more experienced European

Identitarian activists helped in the formation of activists. Jean-David Cattin, the co-leader of the French Les Identitaires, traveled to the Belgian city of Ghent to give a presentation of the European Identitarian movement to the new Flemish Identitarians and "to tell us," according to the new branch of the movement, "what it's all about to be Identitarian, about how our European identity has evolved over the centuries, about specific historical events and why it's important to engage ourselves in preserving our European Identity."[283] Bo De Geyndt, one of the leaders of the new group, described this conference as the "kick-off" event of Generatie Identiteit. "We have attracted a lot of young people with our first conference and the average age would be around 23. . . . Most people we attract are people completely new to activism," says De Geyndt, a former member of the Flemish Catholic nationalist students' society, representing this group at the 2012 French Identitarian convention in Orange and very involved overall with the French Lambda movement, including as a participant in their annual summer camps. "The movement was created because we felt the time was right to form a movement that transcends the typical nationalistic movements," De Geyndt argues, adding, "a movement whose main focus is Europe and its people, a movement that fights not only the minarets of the local mosques but also the modern mosques of McDonald's or modern tea houses like Starbucks, a movement that understands that we as Europeans have failed at maintaining our self-respect and the values of our own culture." They are not separatists, saying that squabbles between fellow Europeans are ultimately "secondary," which in this case means that "the Walloon part of Belgium consists of fellow Europeans" and that "nonetheless all of the problems there may exist between the North and the South we consider Europe, her people and her culture, as the primary objective."[284]

Around the same time, Scandinavia witnessed the birth of the first Generation Identity–influenced youth group—Identitær, in Denmark, led by the Lithuanian-born 29-year-old Aurelija Aniulyte—as a "strong patriotic community." They started, typically, with online activity (a Facebook page) before proceeding to the "real world" with activities such as banner droppings, pamphleteering, and stunts in public places. Their goal is to "defend Europe," in the conviction that they have the "responsibility to ensure that Danish culture and our common European culture exist for the next generation." And, in the words of Aniulyte, "We are in a battle against time. . . . If we do not turn the demographic trend out, it's too late." Fittingly, then—as a symbol of this running-against-time spirit—one of their first initiatives was to hang on the statue of the Danish poet Adam Oehlenschläger, in Copenhagen, a cardboard sign with words both from his poem "The Gold Horns": "Storm-winds bellow, blackens heaven! Comes the hour of melancholy" and their own caption "Defend Europe."[285]

The expansion of the Identitarian movement did not stop there. It continued to the northwestern coast of continental Europe—the British Isles and Ireland. Initially, of course, it was carried there only by a handful of activists and almost exclusively through an online presence rather than heavy street activism (at a maximum posting stickers in public spaces). It was in this way that in the late summer or early autumn of 2017 that Generation Identity Great Britain and Republic of Ireland saw the light of day—comprised of groups focusing on England, Alba/Scotland, Wales, and Ireland—and presenting itself as "the newest branch of the pan-European Identitarian movement or Generation Identity sweeping Europe that originated in France." Naturally it vowed to dedicate itself to the "preservation of our ethno-cultural heritage," which has "characterized our countries and the continent of Europe over many thousands of years. We do not want to break this chain."[286] In this case, too, they received the help of more seasoned European activists, and the Austrian leader Martin Sellner traveled to the British Isles to help set up the network of Generation Identity there. Also, the fact that Tore Rasmussen—a Norwegian, holder of a master's degree in business management and a freelance contributor to the "alternative news" site Ekte Nyheter—played an important role in the development of the Generation Identity branch in the United Kingdom is further evidence of the Europeanization of the movement's organization. Another activist, Tom Dupré, who has an experimental psychology degree from Bristol University and is a former member of the Conservative Party ("though not an active one"), describes his enlisting in the British Identitarian movement in the following manner: "My activism with GI started after I followed the group's activism online, decided to get involved, and applied to join. After going through the vetting process I was invited to a study circle before attending leafleting actions in London. All prospective activists go through a similar process, to ensure they are both who they say they are and, equally important, sufficiently committed." He adds: "After a few weeks of this, I became more heavily involved with GI's work. Since then me and all the British activists have been kept very busy!"[287] In 2018, during the year following its official creation, the Identitarian Lambda activism became "very busy" indeed, notwithstanding the hostility of some of the mainstream press and of watchdog groups. While the gathering under the Lambda flag of English and Irish may look odd owing to the notorious historical rivalries, a 30-year-old Belfast native, a woman named Damhnait McKenna, co-founder of the Irish branch (together with two female friends), explains that at this present and perilous juncture those animosities inevitably shrank: "Being an Irish I never thought I'd be saying this . . . a lot of Irish people have been saying the same thing . . . but we never thought we would ever pity the English, but now we do because we realize we have far more in common with them than anything else, you know? We can't lose that."[288] This idea, recurring in many, many narratives—"We can't lose that"—with "that" understood to be a wider civilizational bond, fuels the transnationalism of this twenty-first-century Identitarian activism. Finally, the French Identitarian summer training camps have increasingly become annual ritualized get-togethers of European Identitarians who "do not want to break this [ethnocultural civilizational] chain." Their range of activities has widened to include not just intellectual formation and sports but also rope and rappel training (which come in handy for many of the occupations of buildings and rooftops, as well as the climbing of monuments, carried out by Identitarians), along with workshops dedicated to issues such as "how to make a banner" and "pamphleteering and its details" and fast courses on web design, video and photo editing, and even media training. Campfires with singing are also held in order to fortify the communitarian spirit. Throughout the years these camps have been attended by French and non-French European youth—sometimes with more than two hundred participants—from numerous places, such as Austria, Flanders, Germany, Italy, the Netherlands, Slovenia, Hungary, and Sweden, for example, in a development that the "original" French Identitarians have dubbed a European rendezvous that is leading to the "emergence and reinforcement of a European brotherhood."[289]

CasaPound across Borders

An Italian Thing?

In 2015 CasaPound set up a Facebook page under the name CasaPound Italia—International. Its description, translated into many languages, said that its purpose was to "provide multilingual documents to the audience following CPI's activities outside the borders of Italy." Its aim was "purely informative," with no intention to "compete with any political movement abroad."[290] Initially, the Italians showed a marked reluctance to engage in transnationalist cooperation—because, they said, there is "almost no movement in Europe that is really fascist,"[291] which prevented them from forming solid links with other groups. This Italian idiosyncrasy—their claim of continuity with Italian fascism—kept at bay the French Identitarian youth movement. "I am very familiar with the leaders of CasaPound, whom I started to meet well before they became a source of inspiration for various currents of the radical right in France," says Fabrice Robert in a reference to his musical connections with Iannone's ZetaZeroAlfa. However, "CasaPound remains a phenomenon linked to Italy, and its positioning is not identitarian but rather 'post-fascist.' There is therefore no political connection between les Identitaires and CasaPound,"[292] says the founder of the Bloc Identitaire and now co-leader of the group that replaced it, Les Identitaires.

Speaking about CasaPound, Umberto Perino, from Generazione Identitaria, says, "We do not have official relationships with CasaPound, although some of our members maintain cordial relationships, esteem and friendship with members of this important reality." Although recognizing that many of their battles are alike, the Italian Lambda Identitarians also distinguish their belief system from that of their compatriots: "The ideology behind CasaPound, though it has many commonalities with our Identitarian thought, is not one hundred percent the same thing. We differ a lot, for example, in our discourse of local identities, of a more decentralized state, and of a break with a certain kind of past." Such dissociation from "a certain kind of past" is in fact the reason that the wider Identitarian Lambda youth movement prefers to keep its official distance from CasaPound. Martin Lichtmesz, who wrote in 2010 in the pages of *Sezession* the first major introduction of CasaPound's philosophy and activities to a German audience—in an article that was subsequently translated into English and widely circulated on the web—also sees this throwback to fascist times as an idiosyncrasy, even if many of the methods of action and goals of the two groups are common:

> Yes, there is quite an overlap between them and the Identitarian movement as far as political ideas and aims are concerned, also partly the aesthetics. They have been quite influential in demonstrating how to create a sub-cultural network of one's own, adopting pop culture icons, developing a sort of "branding" and a movement corporate identity, undogmatically connecting leftist and rightist ideas, etc. However, they see themselves firmly rooted in the tradition of Italian fascism and worship all the usual suspects: D'Annunzio, Evola, Pound obviously, Il Duce, Italo Balbo, Decima Flottiglia MAS, the fighters of the R.S.I., the "cuori neri" [black hearts, or neofascists] of the 1970s "years of lead.". . . They draw a lot of motivation from this kind of nostalgia.

So, he continues, "I wouldn't call them post-fascist, but rather neo-fascist, or simply 'fascists of the 21st century,' as they themselves do."[293] Similarly, Martin Sellner, who was a visitor to CasaPound in the years that preceded the foundation of IBÖ, sees it as "a very Italian thing, an Italian 'sonderweg' [special path]."[294] This conviction, however, has not prevented *Sezession* from showing a continuous interest in "CasaPoundism"—to use Lichtmesz's expression—as testified by the inclusion in one of its issues of an article by Scianca explaining CasaPound to its German readers. CasaPound is not a "product of exportation"? Gabriele Adinolfi does not see it as a problem: "Each country has its culture, its mentality and its ways," he writes, adding, "Each one is or will be of value to the extent that it is able to model itself on the template of his country, his generation, and, above all, on the original archetype."[295]

The Spread of CasaPoundism
CasaPound's "sonderweg," its originality, which is well established in the minds of its activists, has not stopped it, however, and to an increasing degree, from calling for a Europe-wide synchronization of struggles. In an interview published by Zentropa, Iannone was adamant about the

need, in the face of growing Europe-wide threats and trials, for an all-out defense, creating a "European front, with common topics, and the same battle cry."[296] This state of mind has led to a tightening relationship with political movements from abroad, that, like CasaPound, promote their own brand of national originality, their own "special path." Naturally, these are groups that are much more likely to vaunt a nationalist symbology and mystique. What this means is that the network of movements that have a closer bond with CasaPound have, like the Italian group, a more laid-back and easy relationship with each national tradition of political radicalism; that is why, like CasaPound, they are less worried about showing how detached they are from maligned political traditions. What this also means is that these are groups that, as a rule, the Identitarian Lambda movement would not associate with owing to its own methodic effort to separate its activism from "toxic" historical references.

One such group with which CasaPound associates is the Greek Golden Dawn, whose roots and practices have been associated with a Greek version of National Socialism. "We have been the first ones in Italy to welcome and give voice to them, who have been ostracized like other European nationalist movements," declared Scianca.[297] Golden Dawn representatives have been present at CasaPound's annual meetings, and the two movements launched joint campaigns of food distribution in Athens for needy Greeks. Such initiatives are viewed as examples of the "real Europe of solidarity, of brother-peoples who have made common front to escape the speculation and crisis."[298] "Manolis e Giorgos Immortals," read CasaPound's banner put up in numerous Italian cities in the winter of 2015 honoring the two Golden Dawn militants gunned down in the streets of Athens in a still-unsolved murder—the proof, according to Iannone, that some people "still believe that to kill a fascist is not a crime." The culprit is clearly identified; it is "antifascism, not just the militant one, but also the [antifascist] in suit and tie who does not accept the consensus picked up by Golden Dawn in Greece and by the Identitarian movements that advance in the rest of Europe."[299]

CasaPound has been a source of inspiration for the Greek political party but also for many extraparliamentary movements across Europe, even if none has achieved its success. "A terrible beauty is born," a line from William Butler Yeats's poem about the Irish 1916 insurrection—

often invoked in CasaPound narratives about its own birth—is also the title of the French translation of Scianca's book about the Italian movement. The fascination with the Italian creation seen as unconventional and innovative by anti-system individuals and groups—has also helped to spread the range of influence of CasaPound's web radio station, with affiliated stations across Europe. The most popular station has been, in France, Radio Méridien Zéro, "the voice of freemen, combatants of the new century," operated for a while by the Mouvement d'Action Sociale (MAS, or Movement of Social Action). Since 2008, MAS has tried to emulate CasaPound, aiming at opposing "the System with organic ways of being and acting, [both] communitarian and autonomous." As Arnaud de Robert, its leader, explained, "Following the example of what our friends of CasaPound managed to do, we want to create and develop places which give us the possibility of thinking differently and freely." In sum, MAS aspired to create autonomous free spaces where the counter society can be experienced. Are they "just like [left-wing] alterglobalists?" its spokesperson was asked. He responded, "Maybe not everything from them needs to be thrown out, even if they remain prisoners of the ghost of planetarian 'happiness.'" And, repeating a phrase made famous by Ernst von Salomon, he said, "We don't want happiness, we want a destiny."[300] The destiny of MAS, however, was short-lived, and after eight years, it ended its activities. Time will tell, but a more enduring example of the power of attraction of CasaPound in France may well be the mutation of the Groupe Union Défense (GUD)—initially a neofascist student movement from the late 1960s and afterward a "revolutionary nationalist" youth group—into the self-described "political, social, and rooted movement" Bastion Social, which emerged in mid-2017. Bastion Social—born in the city of Lyon but with the ambition of becoming a national movement—is the closest that there is to a French version of CasaPound. Its founding moment, like that of CasaPound, was the occupation of an empty house, around the time of the fourth anniversary of Venner's death and as a way of marking the event, with the squatters announcing their goals with banners that read "Bastion social" and "A home for the French." Even though, and unlike what happened to CasaPound, authorities ended up expelling the activists, this occupation marked the symbolic launching of a movement that closely follows CasaPound's model of activism in terms of its defense of occupations as a response to the housing crisis that affects the autochthonous population, as well as its direct-action tactics, slogans, and the furthering of a counterculture and autonomous way of life. The movement has since expanded to other cities and calls its local sites (in Lyon, Le Pavillon Noir, or the Black House) "places of autonomy and freedom" for nationalists. Its key propaganda words are "identity, autonomy, and social justice," and in an interview with Adriano Scianca, Steven Bissuel, its 23-year-old president, said, "Taking inspiration from our European friends," Bastion Social was "the most innovative French political adventure of the 21st century, no doubt."[301] Or so it hoped.

In recent years, CasaPound has also developed a close relationship with a small Spanish movement of "anti-conformist patriotic occupations," also clearly modeled on the Italian experience. Since 2014, these "cultural and social centers," branded as NGOs exclusively for Spanish people in need, have been called Hogar Social (Social Place). Groups associated with, among others, the youth wing of the Movimiento Social Republicano, a self-described "national-revolutionary" political party, but also with the ultra supporters of Real Madrid, have given birth to Hogar Social Madrid, calling the first vacant building they occupied in a multicultural district of the capital Hogar Social Ramiro Ledesma in honor of the national syndicalist who attempted to initiate Spanish fascism and was executed by the republicans at the time of the Spanish civil war. The building was decorated with flags of Spain and CasaPound banners.[302] The group is led by Melisa Ruiz, whom the national newspaper *El Mundo*, in a nod to the character Queen Daenerys, Mother of Dragons, in the TV series *Game of Thrones*, calls "the Khaleesi of the new homeland fascism."[303] Its activities have been fraught with tension with both the authorities (they have been expelled from different buildings that they have occupied) and antifascist protesters, even if they deny the accusations that they are linked with fascism and Nazism, declaring, "We are patriots who fight for the social rights of our people."[304] They have subsequently established two other delegations in the cities of Granada (Hogar Social Granada) and Toledo (Hogar Social Toledo).

Hogar Social has had close relationships with Golden Dawn, and especially CasaPound, which launched a campaign of solidarity all over Italy in support of the Spanish experience. "In this difficult time for

European peoples, all the national forces that react to the crisis and legalized usury with action and concrete activities will be strenuously supported," declared CasaPound at its site.[305] Together with CasaPound and Golden Dawn, but also MAS and GUD (before its transformation into Bastion Social), Hogar Social Madrid participated in the second "European Congress," held in Paris in late 2015, and hundreds of activists marched in Madrid—while CasaPound and Golden Dawn held simultaneous rallies in Rome and Athens—in honor of Dominique Venner on the third anniversary of the death of the French thinker, to "revive the cause for which he gave his life: to awaken the dormant souls of a decadent Europe."[306] In early 2017 the ties between CasaPound and Hogar Social were tightened in a ceremony in Madrid that established the "Official Brotherhood" of the two groups. Finally Melisa Ruiz, together with the president of Bastion Social, attended the tenth "national party" of CasaPound, and they spoke about the political and social activism of their respective groups.

Beyond "decadent" Europe, CasaPound has gained high praise from nationalists and Identitarians alike, such as the independentist North American Fédération des Québécois de Souche (Federation of the Quebecois of [Quebecois] Stock, or FQS), which, since 2005, has cast itself as the "active resistance" of French Canadians for the "preservation of our people, our culture, and our identity above everything else." This ethnocultural organization—whose members are mostly "students and young parents"[307]—believe that the survival of the European peoples of Quebec is threatened by multiculturalism and massive non-European immigration. FQS has had contacts with the French Lambda movement but has also featured CasaPound prominently in their magazine *Le Harfang* (The Snowy Owl), which has included interviews with Adinolfi and Scianca, while members of CasaPound and Blocco Studentesco have been invited to a conference in Montreal organized by the group as representatives of a "remarkable nationalist movement in Italy," with groundbreaking activism.[308] As Rémi Tremblay, its founder and spokesman, has stated, "Although the setting somehow differs, a North American group with enough dedicated members ready to put their career, safety and freedom in jeopardy could use media squadrismo in order to build an organization that would have to be reckoned with."[309] FQS often collaborates with Atalante Québec, an activist youth organization dedicated to "the Identitarian renaissance of the Québec peoples," which, since 2014, has constituted yet another expression of CasaPoundism, but this time across the Atlantic. "A few of us were reading Venner, Jünger and Evola, and others visited Rome and returned very motivated after going to CasaPound," says Alexandre Peugeot, a co-founder of Atalante Québec, about the beginnings of the group. The importance of these visits and their experience at CasaPound's headquarters in Italy is recurring in the movements that follow its model of activism. In the case of Atalante Québec, which is especially active in Québec city, this influence is seen in their drive to create an alternative, countercultural communitarian ethos; a related focus on cultural dynamics (with the creation of a nationalist bookshop, conferences, events of ideological formation with invited guests, etc.), and combat sports; the adoption of a "neither Left nor Right ideology"; the defense of national preference; slogans (e.g., "Ours before the others!"); a vitalistic philosophy (with mottos such as "To exist is to defy what represses me," taken from Dominique Venner); an emphasis on social work (with regular food assistance to the homeless of Quebec stock); street activism (with the regular putting up of banners that are aesthetically very similar to the one of the Italian activists); and their overall self-understanding as a "revolutionary and Identitarian nationalist movement for the new millennium."[310] All of this, for supporters, means, to use CasaPound's symbology, the birth of another "terrible beauty."

Making Identitarianism Global

The circulation of the themes and practices associated with Identitarians, facilitating the movement's internationalization and also its attraction of a wider audience beyond the frontiers of their territory and continent, has certainly been accelerated by the Internet, social media, and vlogging and blogging platforms. But it has also been greatly enhanced by the more "old-school" translation into many languages of relevant works and authors. The publishers of these works extensively use crowdfunding sites and online funding platforms in order to raise money to finance many of their publishing projects. In regard to the English-speaking world, the Budapest-based UK media company Arktos has played a major role since 2009 in bolstering Nouvelle Droite and Identitarian works—translating for the first time works by Alain de Benoist, many books by Guillaume Faye, and a compilation of interviews with Dominique Venner—filling a gap in the market because for many years the vast majority of works, especially those in French, had remained untranslated. "We are open to publishing works that come from any perspective, provided that they fit into our general areas of interest, which I've described as 'alternatives to modernity.' That being said, we consider Identitarianism to be extremely relevant to what we're doing," explained the co-founder and former chief editor (from 2009 through 2017) of Arktos, the American publicist John Morgan.[311]

Arktos, in fact, is part of a northern Europe/Scandinavian network that since the 2000s has contributed both to the Identitarian strain of thinking and to discussions of Identitarianism, and also to the promotion of the Identitarian pan-European youth movement. At the center of this network stands the former CEO of a Swedish mining company, Daniel Friberg (born in 1978). Associated in his early youth with the Swedish neo-Nazi subculture, with the passage of time Friberg, who holds an MBA from Gothenburg University, devoted himself to the "war of ideas," launching the right-wing/nationalist Metapedia and becoming a founding member of the Nouvelle Droite–inspired metapolitical think tank Motpol (in Swedish, "the opposite pole"), before cofounding Arktos, of which he has been the CEO since its origin. From 2015 Friberg ran the website Right On (no longer active), which was

FIGURE 10. The logo of Arktos, a publishing house currently headquartered in Budapest, Hungary (founded in 2009).

created because, "among the ruins of European culture, the need for an alternative has never been greater. . . . Right On is an online resource for the rising True Right of Europe."[312] Right On would later be merged into a transatlantic site called Alt Right. This "True Right"—alluding to the title of Friberg's book-manifesto, translated into many languages, *The Real Right Returns*—is culturally protectionist and ethnicity-conscious. It is at the opposite end of the spectrum, therefore, from the liberal pseudo-right that, together with the Left, the Swedish writer believes to be irreversibly collapsing, paving a way for a return to power of the Identitarian Right and a chance to save European civilization. "During the coming years, they [people on the mainstream Left and Right] will become painfully aware that the peoples of Europe have had their fill of their deranged work of destruction. Europe rises!" said Friberg in a speech broadcast by Right On TV.[313] The Identitarian Lambda movement participates in this rising, or uprising, and Friberg thinks that "they are doing an excellent job promoting our ideas, and [are] a good example of how important marketing and aesthetics is for any political movement. Their terminology, name, symbolism, colors, and especially tactics when it comes to their choice of activism is new and fresh, which helps attract scores of young people to their ranks."[314]

No wonder that the activism of Identitarian youth is showcased throughout the network. According to its former editor in chief, Arktos's interest in the "fresh" activism of the newer Identitarians is justified because "publishing books, running Websites, and holding conferences are indeed important, but if this doesn't eventually lead to activity in the real world, we will remain nothing more than a cult on the margins of society."[315] The works of Austrian Markus Willinger—whose writings have focused on the revolutionary potential of the rising "generation identity," even if he has never been affiliated with the Austrian Lambda movement or taken part in its activism—are featured in the Arktos catalogue, which has translated and released in several languages two of his book-manifestos. In addition, the publishing house introduced the French Génération Identitaire to an English-speaking audience, releasing a compilation of seminal texts and interviews—while the activities of the wider movement, as well as interviews with leading figures, were also highlighted in Right On texts and podcasts. At the same time, the Motpol-organized Identitarian Ideas, a conference that takes place every

Right On Radio:
#6 - Generation Identity: Reconquering Europe

◎ March 8, 2016 ▭ Right On Radio

FIGURE 11. Right On podcast dedicated to the European Generation Identity, and featuring Austria's Alexander Markovics as a guest (March 8, 2016).

year in Stockholm, in addition to inviting established authors such as Guillaume Faye or Tomislav Sunić, for example, has also featured speeches by figures deemed representative of the new Identitarian wave, such as Markus Willinger, Philippe Vardon, and the IBÖ co-founder Alexander Markovics.

Another guest of Motpol's Identitarian Ideas has been Greg Johnson, the co-founder (together with Michael Polignano) of the US–based Counter-Currents publishing house and webzine—and the place where John Morgan started to work as a book editor after leaving Arktos—which has been a major sponsor of Nouvelle Droite and Identitarian themes and thinkers in North America. Besides carrying Arktos titles, the website puts up translated articles, excerpts of books, and reviews and speeches by Alain de Benoist, Guillaume Faye, Dominique Venner, and many others while also covering the activities of the Identitarian youth movement, especially in its French expression, through the writings of its contributor Patrick le Brun. The site has also offered very favorable coverage of CasaPound's philosophy and activism. As Johnson explains, "Counter-Currents, particularly in our webzine, has given a great deal of coverage to Identitarianism in Europe because we wish to encourage an Identitarian movement adapted to North American conditions, in which our population is largely of mixed European ancestry, and our national identities are abstract, propositional, and raceless," adding, "Even though the groundwork of Identitarianism was laid through decades of deep metapolitical thinking, writing, and teaching, the movement itself is ideologically minimalist, blunt, and plain-spoken. Europe belongs entirely to Europeans. The goal is to make that a reality once more."[316] As to the German branch of the Identitarian movement, it has been more extensively covered by the Breitbart News Network via its London office, which has often reported on developments related to the activities of what it calls the "hipster-right Identitarians."[317] The responsiveness is reciprocal. For instance, on Twitter Martin Lichtmesz and Martin Sellner shared a picture in which they were holding copies of "Righteous Indignation," written by Andrew Breitbart, the news website founder, in which he describes his combat against the US left-wing media system. "An important work on metapolitics," tweeted Lichtmesz.

Together with more traditional publishers as well as online sites, the European Identitarian movement has been widely covered by citizen-journalists (who often describe themselves as "independent journalists"), meaning people sympathetic to the cause who operate as social media influencers. Among them are young and attractive female activists with a large number of followers, and also prominent YouTubers such as the Canadian Lauren Southern. "Europe's Culture: Is It Dying? Is the 'Identitarian' Movement the Cure?" (from 2016) was the title of her first foray into the coverage of the European Identitarian youth movement, which included an interview with Martin Sellner, at a time when she worked for the Canadian right-wing online site Rebel Media.[318] Roughly a year later, Southern posted a widely seen video on YouTube, "Generation Identity: Europe's Youth Reconquista," documenting her trip to France, where the Canadian freelance journalist had interviewed Jean-David Cattin and visited the Identitarian's headquarters in Lyon (la Traboulle), as well as their boxing studio (l'Agoge).[319] Like Southern, the American Brittany Pettibone has been vocal in her support and promotion of the activities of the Identitarian youth. According to Pettibone, "A growing number of European youths are admitting to and coming to terms with the fact that the mass and uncontrolled migration to Europe has been disastrous for their respective countries. But I believe that many of them feel that they can do nothing to resolve the problem on their own. This is why Generation Identity is so important," she continues, adding, "It's the perfect outlet where youths concerned for the fate of their countries can get involved in activism. No one fights alone."[320] In fact, especially after entering into a relationship with Martin Sellner in 2017, Pettibone became even more involved with the European Identitarian Lambda movement—particularly, but not exclusively, in its German-speaking form (accompanying Sellner and covering his activities, as well as interviewing activists and intellectual leaders for her YouTube channel)—and it is safe to say that Pettibone became the major promoter of European Identitarian youth, particularly of the "Generation Identity" kind, on English-speaking alternative or dissident media platforms.

Beyond the English-speaking world, while Arktos has taken the early lead in spreading Identitarian writings in English, it has also translated many of these works into non-English languages. All over the web, myriad other sites/groups/publishing companies contribute similarly to such internationalization of Identitarian writings, even if they make much less of an impact. The Czech website Délský Potápěč, for example, whose name means Delian Diver—referring to the ancient skilled fishermen from the Greek island of Delos who were able to dive successfully into murky depth—a name chosen for the need to "revive critical thinking" to find ways "out of the profound sociocultural crisis" of today.[321] Founded in 2007, originally as a blog, it operates now as a collective, also active on Twitter, and open to many contributions. Besides constituting a sort of metapolitical companion to Generace Identity—"We occasionally cooperate with them but we are not part of it," says Jiri, one of its founders—it posts, links, and translates all sort of articles related to the Nouvelle Droite, Identitarianism, traditionalism, and anti-globalism in general. One of its long-standing featured books is the Czech translation of Guillaume Faye's *Why We Fight*, released by its own publishing company (Metanoia) because it "represents one of the earliest and best coherent expressions of 'why we fight.'"[322] *Finis Mundi*, a magazine of "dissident thought" whose current director, João Franco, is a former member of Causa Identitária, has also promoted, since 2010, many authors and translated their writings—especially authors related to the ND—and aims at being a cultural counterforce in a Portuguese-speaking sphere in which "cultural Marxism and political correctness reign supreme."[323] In the southern hemisphere, in Latin America, the Chilean group Identitas or Círculo de Investigaciones PanCriollistas has diffused in Spanish the work of many authors, including Alain de Benoist, Guillaume Faye, Tomislav Sunić, Lucian Tudor, and Dominique Venner. If Arktos's motto is "Making anti-globalism global," the work of all these diffuse networks—and many others not cited, regardless of size, language, and impact—is aimed at making Identitarianism, at least in connection with ethnocultural European peoples, a global phenomenon.

TWO

Identity against Globalism

> Where is America heading, where are we all heading in this reign of universal bureaucracy? The robot man, the ant man, scurries from assembly line to card table.
> —Antoine de Saint-Exupéry, Letter to General "X"

IN THE BEGINNING... THERE WAS ANTI-UNIVERSALISM

The Identitarian revolt against the present-day ideology of globalism as an expansionist one-world amalgamation of peoples, cultures, and ethnicities ultimately draws from a philosophical critique of modernity that was first developed by the Nouvelle Droite. In this sense, globalism is viewed as just the current manifestation of a much older evil that has plagued European thought for roughly two thousand years, specifically the universalism and egalitarianism disseminated by Judeo-Christianity. In his proposal for a European resistance and renaissance, Guillaume Faye calls both of these dogmas "totalitarian" (the "parent of all totalitarianisms" in the case of universalism and "the source of all modern totalitarianisms" in the case of egalitarianism).[1] This monotheistic belief system imposed the absolute primacy of one absolute and uncreated being (God) ruling over an abstract humanity composed of individuals who are in essence equal before that God as a single metaphysical family. This equality ultimately overrides all other distinctions, attachments, and, obviously, inequalities. Such a universalist and egalitarian theological narrative, which gained an intense fervor during the Enlightenment, went through a process of secularization, and this secularized view of the world constitutes the political and philosophical basis of modernity. Although in the post-1989 world liberalism reigns as the victor in its battle with Marxism, it shares with it the status of "ideologies of modernity" because ultimately they belong to the same mental universe. As the ND's "Manifesto for a European Renaissance" states, both ideologies possess "the same individualism, even the same universal egalitarianism, the same rationalism, the same primacy of economics, the same stress on the emancipatory value of labor, the same faith in progress, the same idea of an end of history."[2] In the end, according to this interpretation, liberalism only perfected the Marxist goal of the eradication of human attachment to territories and collective identities.

The "Westernization" of the planet, a term often used interchangeably with "Americanization," is yet another manifestation of homogenizing universalism, aiming at, in the words of Faye, "universalizing the

FIGURE 12. T-shirt declaring "Eat the universalists," from Austria's Identitarian label Phalanx Europa.

absolute primacy of market society and egalitarian individualism—one of whose consequences is to cause Europeans to forget their own destiny."[3] And this imposition of a world civilization based on an abstract model of a free-market order (the monotheism of the market), which destroys all otherness, is presented as "progress" (which is exclusively viewed in terms of a linear materialistic and economic path). A radical philosophy of individualism also fuels the ideology of the rights of man, or human rights, which treats humans as abstract and isolated atoms and has become a novel civil religion, functioning as a powerful ally in the "colonizing" Westernizing project. Above all, for the ND as well as for Identitarians, an anthropological falsehood is at the core of this totalitarian new order because it is blind to the realities of life and peoples—turning its back on the variety and diversity of life—because actual human beings' interaction with the universal is mediated though the particular, such as a location, a heritage, and a culture. The denial of human nature, or of the way that individuals are rooted in a *context*, can thus only lead to all sorts of social and cultural pathologies and to an abnormal human condition.

AWAY FROM NATIONALISM?

Anti-universalism, thus, takes its strength from the guiding idea of the *singularity* of cultures and peoples against the ideology of sameness that is fueled by a global system hell-bent on worldwide standardization. In the case of Identitarians, the defense of the particular against the universal is framed in ethnocultural terms; with more or less sophistication, and with some variation in the way that this combat is waged, this great narrative transcends the differences among Identitarian groups and pervades the Identitarians' self-understanding of their role in contemporary Europe.

In the view of French Identitarians, of both older and younger generations, this battle to wrest control of their communal destiny away from an evil civilization is not waged in the name of nationalism. "The revolution of the 21st century will result from the insurrection of rooted identities," wrote Pierre Vial.[4] Fabrice Robert says that "the 21st century will be [the century] of awakening of identities. And we have to confront the extremists of Progress, which will do everything to gag us in the name of human rights, of 'living together,' and of forced homogenization."[5] Owing to the political and social history of the twentieth century, the word "nationalism," for the most part, still has a precarious standing and a harmful reputation. Polémia's *Dictionary of Newspeak* entry on "Nation" says that it is a "taboo word in Europe: a construction reputed to be arbitrary, the source of all conflicts in Europe, and an obstacle to the total efficacy of the market, according to the dominant ideology."[6] Tomislav Sunić, for example, sees this as a major factor in the semantic option for identity, because "it sounds more neutral than nationalism for the time being and does not leave a bad aftertaste as does the word nationalism. . . . Identitarianism sounds more politically correct and better for mainstream ears."[7] In this way, the seductive power of the neologism emerges from its commonsensical nature, associating the defense of land, heritage, and self-determination with an reflexive, spontaneous, and almost expected mechanism that is naturally inherent to all peoples. "What is interesting: if you travel in other countries and cultures you won't find something like 'identitarians.' That has an easy reason: because these cultures are 'identitarian' by themselves,"[8] says the German journalist Manuel Ochsenreiter.

Importantly, nationalism is not rejected *tout court*. In the French context, what is repelled is Jacobin nationalism and its centripetal drive, homogenizing the population and vernacular practices according to what the powers that be establish as the "universal." This is connected with the tendency to look beyond the political-geographical division of nation-states and into units of reference that are viewed primarily in an ethnic matter. The first consequence is the attachment to regional identities that are celebrated as nations in their own right, but not simply as civic or political-legal communities, but, above all, as "carnal," according to an ethnic conception. The second consequence is a transboundary push to encompass the struggle for identity to the whole of Europe, not because of a political link, but as the place of a shared ethnos, and hence of a European nation. In any case, as far as the wider European Identitarian Lambda movement goes, the self-identification with "nationalism" is rare, while "patriotism" is favored as *the* word for activism and metapolitical combat.[9]

CasaPound instead, and in line with its reclaiming of the historical experience of fascism as a vital inspiration, does not steer away from the word "nationalism"—in fact, it welcomes it. The purpose of its multifaceted political, social, and cultural action is both to protect and to revive the national community as a whole. Its work of "national reconquest," as stated by its political program, is geared toward shielding the sovereignty and independence of the Italian state. Here too, the combat is against a putative totalitarian global system that wrought fundamental challenges to Italy, and also to Europe. Mirroring the anti-universalist narrative that shapes the Identitarian offensive across Europe, CasaPound says, "Our enemy is a thought that for two thousand years has inflicted egalitarianism and standardization, it is a one-dimensional world, it is the global massification, it is a mind dominated by the monoculture, the ubiquitous logos, and progressive cosmopolitanism. In sum, it is all of this that expresses actual 'hatred for what is diverse.'"[10] Importantly, the Italian nation is viewed in a holistic way; CasaPound believes that it must "become again an organism" superior to the individuals that are part of it and must give form to an "economic, political, and moral unity" accomplished within the state.[11] It must become a bounded community, therefore, and at the antipodes of what Identitarians at large see as, ultimately, the hallmark of the liberal theory of life: a nonorganic, abstract society of free-floating individuals.

A CARNAL EUROPE

For Identitarians against the steamroller of globalism, communities and cultures must be forcefully defended: they express the spirit of a specific context, a unique way of life, personality, and destiny. In the eighteenth century, the German philosopher Johann Herder helped establish the foundations of this intellectual defense of each culture's integrity and creative genius. The Identitarian conception and defense of organic communities finds its roots in what Robert Steuckers called, at a Terre et Peuple conference, the "other Enlightenment," to which Herder was a major reference.[12] It was Herder who put forward an ethnocentric and genealogical paradigm of a nation (as a people, or *Volk*, in a mystical unity), each of which was diverse and different and had a fundamental authenticity that was corrupted by the mixing of cultures, a process that was inevitably destructive of their cultural essence. Hence the importance given, in order to face the challenges of the time, to the quest, which is both archeological and genealogical, for the cultural sources and primordial origins of nations.[13]

In France the concept of *patrie charnelle*, or carnal homeland, is at the forefront of Identitarian narratives of resistance against the evils of globalism. This concept, for which we are indebted to Herder, was first introduced by the French writer Saint-Loup, the pseudonym of Marc Augier, who dedicated a series of romances to the regional, carnal homelands of France. Earlier he had been an officer of the French Waffen-SS, and later he became a novelist of the military engagements of the Charlemagne Division. "His trilogy about the French combatants of the Eastern front," recalled Jean-Claude Valla, "exerted a certain fascination over the 1960's nationalists, in the same way that the International Brigades, or the guerrillas of South America, have fascinated the young Marxists of the same generation."[14] In his writings Saint-Loup emphasized the pan-Europeanism of the SS. At the end of the war, Saint-Loup claimed in a more doctrinal text, the Waffen SS "was no longer German in the narrow nationalist sense of the term. It was European and wished to revive the basic values of blood and soil. . . . It was a racially based and denationalized Europe. I consider it perfectly valid today."[15] This postnationalist vision—in terms of an attachment to ethnogeographical entities intimately tied to a wider ethnic Europe—is found in all of Saint-Loup's writings, grounded in the conviction that only "small carnal fatherlands" have the ultimate force (nourished by blood and soil) to preserve their identities and survive.

The magazine *Réfléchir & Agir* calls Saint-Loup one of its "evangelists."[16] One of the other evangelists is Jean Mabire, a Norman writer who is widely viewed as a sort of spiritual father of an Identitarian Europe. An early defender of the ancestral, pre-Christian roots of peoples and cultures—promoting, for example, in the case of Normandy, its Nordic roots in the 1950s magazine *Viking*—Mabire was also, for a short period, editor in chief of Dominique Venner's *Europe Action*, where he framed "our combat" as "the defense of the individual against the robots, and of the homelands against universalism." Influenced by Saint-Loup, Mabire helped disseminate—within the network of Terre et

Peuple, for example, to which he was particularly close—the concept of "carnal homelands" as a basis for a remapping of Europe that counters the abstract and technocratic constructions of the dominant elites. Pierre Vial, who in the mid-1970s co-wrote with him a guide to the organization of solstice festivals (published by GRECE), views Mabire as an ethnologist, "in the better sense of the term, which means, someone who does not make the study of peoples an academic subject, but instead a tool for action."[17] This is connected with the way that Mabire embraced what has been described as the "ethnic conception of the nation," in which the nation is understood as "first and foremost a community of descent" and *the* "place of vernacular culture." Mabire gave a supreme role, therefore, to "the role of philologists, folklorists and lexicographers."[18] He was committed to the creation of an awareness of the vital and ancestral sources of the French and European peoples—their languages, customs, arts, festivals, myths, and popular traditions—in order to unearth and reengage the link with its deepest roots. From this also derived Mabire's interest in and promotion of those throughout history who succeeded as "awakeners of peoples," in the sense of playing individual roles in the revitalization of the primal and communal sources. He wrote, for example, a biography (published by Terre et Peuple) of Patrick Pearse, who believed that an "enslaved nation" like Ireland could not die as long as its ancient spiritual tradition, expressed in language, folklore, literature, music, art, and social customs, "lived in the heart of one faithful man or woman." To Mabire, Pearse's political and cultural combat for the liberation of the Irish nation was inherently Identitarian.[19] Throughout his life, he viewed the carnal homelands, as rooted and living entities, as the best ramparts against the universalism of the times. Hence Mabire's defense of a Europe of regions, decentralized, respectful of their organic communities, contrary to the abstract and oppressive technocracy of the European Union. In this defense, he was hardly alone. The Breton Yann Fouéré, for example, in his *Europe of a Hundred Flags*, claimed such an alternative and regionally based project for Europe that valued the respective natural communities to which Europeans belong. At the same time, as was noted at the time of Mabire's death, in 2006, this engagement for a Europe of Regions bears a close resemblance within the French Identitarian milieu to a "Europe of Ethnicities, Europe of Peoples, or Europe of carnal homelands, all very similar."[20] This is true because all are based on a rooted, fundamentally ethnic view that, when expanded to all of Europe, translates into the common ethnohistorical destiny of the European peoples.

The concept of a carnal homeland—as a perennial force of distinction amid the wave of indifferentiation that crosses the world—is dominant within the Terre et Peuple network. "The carnal homeland is the real country," affirms Pierre Vial, "the organic union of soil and blood, of a Land and of a People. That is why the simple mentioning of carnal homeland bristles all those who preach the religion of cosmopolitanism and generalized crossbreeding as the unsurpassable future of humanity." Further, "The gap between partisans and enemies of carnal homelands constitutes the real cleavage of today's world."[21] The rise of micronationalisms within nation-states is often praised as a sign of vitality and viewed as an "awakening of European peoples." Beyond the "globalist" European Union and the self-centered nation-state, Alain Cagnat writes, Europeans must "gain consciousness of belonging to a larger community, that of the heritage of Indo-Europeans." In any case, "We must not delude ourselves, the path that takes one to the *Europe of a Hundred Flags* of Yann Fouéré and to the old dream of unity of Jean Mabire and Saint-Loup is still long. It is not a reason to despair."[22] The notion of a carnal homeland in these Identitarian narratives is always projected as an alternative vision for Europe as a liberated land, with its peoples as masters, once again, of the continent's destiny. After September 11, Pierre Vial refused the "obligation" to choose between "Jihad and McWorld." "Our response is clear," the president of Terre et Peuple wrote. "We choose the third European way, the way of freedom. . . . Europe has been since Athens and Sparta (the spirit and the sword) a land of freedom. Not, of course, the official Europe, vassalized, humiliated by the United States. But the Europe of peoples, the Europe of carnal homelands, our Europe, the Great Motherland."[23] The *Occident* (West), which is viewed today as nothing more than a totalitarian "American-centric system," is the antithesis of such a "real" Europe. No wonder that the phrase "Against the West, for the carnal homelands of Europe" is commonly evoked by Terre et Peuple.[24] Europe as the "Great Motherland" is often viewed in imperial terms as a decentralized ethnocultural federation of European peoples. Interviewed by the magazine *Terre et Peuple* on the occasion of the release of his book-manifesto

Fighting for the Essence, Pierre Krebs denounced the "superficial frontiers" and "small chauvinisms" while reaffirming the need to "re-root ourselves, from Ireland to the Ural," on a foundation of "carnal homelands," within the "imperial motherland [defended] by the good Europeans, Nietzsche, Drieu [la Rochelle], and [Julius] Evola."[25]

The defense of a Europe of regions, as part of the "contestation of the established, artificial order, in the name of carnal realities, concrete, and anchored in time and space," in the words of Steuckers,[26] resonates widely in the Identitarian camp. "For a revolutionary European Identitarian, the more a man is rooted in his land the more perfect he is. We know that there is a mysterious alchemy between a man and his soil," wrote Krampon in *Réfléchir & Agir*. "This enrootment only a small carnal homeland can achieve to perfection."[27] Consequently, the nation, or at least the "real" nation, is not an "ideological" notion (based on a contract to abstract values) but something deeper, genealogical, in sum "a rootedness in territory since time immemorial."[28] Although less invested in theoretical and erudite work, at least compared to Terre et Peuple, the network that gravitates around the Bloc Identitaire, now Les Identitaires, also sees the concept of a carnal homeland as a cornerstone of its worldview. The attachment to the regional identity (defined as "carnal") is the very first, basic level, of their "triple identity" (the others being "historical" and "civilizational"). "The notion of an incorporeal citizenship—with no relation to filiation," the group explains, "is in total opposition to our vision of a rooted and carnal identity. To the concept of the 'France of the Enlightenment' we prefer the living reality of the identities and diversity of the world."[29] When Mabire died, these Identitarians eulogized him by saying that "after him, we will continue to keep vigil under the star that watches over our destinies." This could well be an allusion to Mabire's book *Thule, the Recovered Sun of the Hyperboreans*, about the mythic Northern origins of Indo-Europeans.

THE GLOBALIST TSUNAMI

Dedicated to the "Globalist Tsunami over Europe," the issue of *Réfléchir & Agir* displayed on its cover the superhero character Captain America, with his shield engraved with the dollar sign and the text "Enjoy capitalism."[30] The indictment of global capitalism, which is a cornerstone of the Identitarian metanarrative, was laid down by the Nouvelle Droite. In the early 1980s, when he was still an active member of GRECE, Faye released *The System That Kills Peoples*, denouncing the West as a soulless technoeconomic world system that is the opposite of a true civilization: "A civilization remains humane. A system, on the contrary, is mechanical and a-temporal. . . . It lacks an inner life."[31] The solution, for Europe, would be to renounce the West. The rejection of the Anglo-American universalist and imperialist imposition of a planetary market—not founded on any sort of spirituality but wholly on materialistic and economic relations—was a precondition for Europe to rediscover itself. "Then one day our Europe will emerge, her heroic values transfigured and resplendent, hailing the new dawn,"[32] hoped Faye in a subsequent article.

Twenty-first-century globalization—driven by the ideology of globalism—is nothing, then, but an intensified form of Westernization as a planetary extension of a deracinated liberal model of society and its radical individualism, which functions as the perfect companion of free trade and boundless markets. From this derives the attempted commodification of all social life, or the transformation of everything into merchandise, and the absolute primacy of commerce-engendered values in social and human relations. Writing about Europe, Dominique Venner saw this historical regression as the triumph of the myth of "sweet commerce" promoted by, among others, the British economist Adam Smith, who believed that personal self-interest not only drives the economy but guarantees social peace. The expansion of this bourgeois theory of utility to all spheres of social life through liberal capitalism is, however, far from "gentle" but constitutes instead a "new violence" that is inherently totalitarian. "In order to change the world," like Communism in the past, the Western-American system "must also change humans, fabricate the *homo oeconomicus* of the future, the zombie, the new man, homogenous, empty of content, possessed by the spirit of the universal and unlimited market." "The zombie is happy," Venner concluded. "It is whispered to him that happiness is to satisfy all his desires, because his desires are those produced by the market."[33]

At the core of the Identitarian visceral rejection of the "globalist tsunami" is an attack on the anthropology of capitalism as a "total system" that remodels humans and minds through deculturation, alienation, and massive propaganda. It is a work of decolonization that must be done, and this combat must be waged in all spheres of life. As early as the 1970s, Jean Cau, who collaborated with GRECE and lamented Europe's decadence, said that its culture was facing the onslaught of "Coca Cola," a code term for the "moral barbarism from the West."[34] Writing in the 1980s, Faye warned, "The human masses we see milling in the streets are more than just deculturalized and denationalized: they are the ambassadors of what Konrad Lorenz [the founder of Ethology who had ties with GRECE] aptly called a tepid death."[35] With time, the ND developed a wide-ranging critique of the anthropology of "capitalist civilization," with de Benoist, in a later period, even rehabilitating Marx because of his understanding that capitalism was much more than a purely economic system but a reification of human relationships. Hence, "there is an anthropology of capitalism, a type of capitalist man, a capitalist imagination, a capitalist 'civilization,' a capitalist lifestyle and, as long as one has not broken with capitalism as a 'total social fact,' . . . it will be futile to claim to be fighting capital."[36]

For these critics, it is as if in the atomist West humans have been deactivated, "living" in a state of alienated meaninglessness; hence, narratives of robotization and self-enslavement abound. This is viewed as the consequence of the perfect achievement of the kingdom of the individual. Individualism, according to Polémia's *Dictionary of Newspeak*, is a "liberal euphemism that means selfishness."[37] Karl Hauffen, in an article titled "Why We Are Identitarians" published in the Bloc Identitaire magazine, asserted that the ideal of individual autonomy and emancipation is the central dogma of modern societies, constituting a subversive force that carries with it the "frontal opposition to," as well as the negation of, "the individual's community of origin, group of belonging, or family."[38] Adriano Scianca, for example, denounces the "aberrant" anthropology behind liberalism. "The liberal idea of the self is poor, unreal, and de-historicized," he wrote. "In reality, the individuals as they are conceived by liberalism—without memory, immune to causality and out of History, moral agents that 'during their lives are perfectly rational beings . . . ,' have never existed."[39] This is a common view, and Identitarians often focus on the origins, magnitude, and effects of this evil idea, referring to writers and scholars of all sorts who have made a genealogy of modern individualism, such as the French sociologist Louis Dumont, with his analyses of the differences between traditional, holistic societies and modern ones, or the American historian and social critic Christopher Lasch, with his portrayal of the modern culture of narcissism.[40] The guiding idea of this Identitarian critique is that Europe is living through the terminal, and decadent, phase of the historical evolution of modern individualism. "For more than a thousand years," wrote Steuckers, "the West has reasoned in terms of individual salvation, during the religious phase of its development [and afterward] in terms of individual profit, during its bourgeois and materialistic phase, and now in terms of hedonistic narcissism, during its current phase of total deliquescence."[41]

Following this logic, mass narcissism is at the center of a disenchanted modern world that knows only the "divine twins of money and market."[42] Impelled by the ideology of desire, which perpetually creates the need for consumerism (functioning as a capitalism of seduction), the human condition has been lowered to primitive and slavish urges of material consumption. This is the era of "mass men," wrote Faye, "who are neither citizens, nor actors, nor responsible individuals, but rather passive, domesticated beings." This condition—this immersion in what the French traditionalist René Guénon called the "reign of quantity"—is often associated with nihilism. To Venner, "In the world of nihilism, everything is submitted to the utilitarian and to desire, or, to put it another way, to what is qualitatively inferior."[43] It represents a devaluation of the human being, reduced to a market dimension and deprived, or indifferent to, his cultural, or ethnic, ties. This one-dimensional man (an expression taken from Herbert Marcuse) is thus cut off from his natural roots, lives uniquely for the present, and exists in an ever-increasing virtual world that the society of the spectacle (as a modern version of the Roman bread and circuses) provides in order to keep humans domesticated and under control. It is common to find comparisons between this pitiful human condition and the "Last Man" announced by Nietzsche. "This appeal to the lowest pulsions of the human being," wrote Vial in a text about globalism's destructive effects, "it is the world of the 'Last Man' denounced by Nietzsche: 'What is love? What is creation? What is longing? What is a star?—so asks the Last Man, and blinks."[44] A market society founded on the idea that everything has a price but nothing is of value and that happiness corresponds to consumerism—while in practice consumerism spurs loneliness and spiritual misery—is viewed as a real-world application of Nietzsche's nightmarish vision. A world where "whoever wants soul instead of gold," wrote Hermann Hesse, depicting the lower condition of bourgeois life, "finds no home in this trivial world of ours."[45]

"For the egalitarians of all confessions," writes Scianca in his *Revolution in the Making*, "Identity is, simply, the *bête noire*, a nightmare. In fact, they are characterized by a certain 'ontophobia,' a 'fear of being' and a longing for the indistinct, the indeterminate, and the generic . . . with the rootless nomad as the end-goal, with no origin or destiny."[46] In fact, the denial of limits is widely viewed by these critics as a founding principle of the capitalist world system. This means that, on the homogenizing path, there are no limits, whether physical (such as borders or nature) or even biological. The pervasive gender ideology, for example, that sees gender as a cultural and social construction and not as a biological attachment, is also understood as part of this process of the destruction of natural attachments and massification of human beings. Distinction is diluted, and the different is reduced to the same. Through gender theory and its corollaries (such as transgenderism and gender fluidity), not only are human beings indistinct; they are also replaceable and reversible, with no core foundations (not even biological ones). In an article in the ND magazine, François Bousquet says that "our neoliberal century" carries the name of the French philosopher Michel Foucault as the "dark angel" who heralded, through his theories, including gender theory, the "post-Identitarian and post-humanist future." Foucault thus preached a "mutant future" and a "hybrid bricolage" as a supposed identity: "'I is another.' Arthur Rimbaud's formula takes here an unexpected development. The other is trans, queer, schizo. A little bit man, a little bit woman, a little bit Minotaur."[47] The emancipation of human beings from any determinism (ethnic, cultural, or biological), following the logic of these enemies of the system, is viewed as grotesquely inhuman; it vitiates the natural and celebrates the inauthentic.

In their indictment of Western civilization, Identitarians make use of the work of authors who are viewed as dissidents against the dominant culture, even if they are not formally affiliated with their respective milieus, provided that, in one way or another, they give legitimacy to their own critiques of the excesses, miseries, and pathologies of liberal capitalism. The economist and essayist Hervé Juvin, for example, is widely quoted in French Identitarian circles. His denunciation of the "great separation"—perpetrated by the West, which eradicates humans from territories, identities, and origins while celebrating the man from nowhere, the perpetual migrant, without identity, without membership, and without ties, in short, "the man without soil"—is naturally interpreted as yet another confirmation of the diagnosis of a world gone mad. It is also his view that "globalization, which was thought out as a homogenization of the world, is about to lead to its opposite: the return of Identitarian particularisms, singularities, and, more generally, a return of an 'us.'"[48] The Bloc Identitaire, for example, has praised and promoted Juvin's views both on the Internet and at conferences. But in Italy "nonconformists" at large draw special inspiration from CasaPound. Diego Fusaro, for example, is a neo-Marxist philosopher who calls for a rehabilitation of Marx and Gramsci at a time of totalitarian "absolute capitalism" or "globalitarianism"—a neologism, by the way, first used by the French cultural theorist Paul Virilio to describe the unprecedented, worldwide, potentially totalitarian character of globalization.[49] Interviewed by Scianca for the ND magazine *éléments*, Fusaro lamented the "present misery, the age of the last man, the feverish consumer willing to do everything to obtain on credit the last smartphone."[50] The young philosopher, however, was forced to decline to participate in a debate at CasaPound owing to threats from antifascists, which goes to show that the meeting of "nonconformists" against a common foe still faces entrenched, and historical, hostilities.[51]

REBOOTING THE ANTI-CAPITALIST AND SOCIAL TRADITION

An Identitarian Socialism

For Identitarians, at a time of turbocapitalism, of an all-embracing capitalist system that subverts all spheres of life, the only possible reaction must be totalistic. It is within this anti-systemic consciousness that, in the twenty-first century, Identitarians have called upon socialism—in its original, antagonistic, anti-capitalist dimension—to come to the rescue.

What they invoke is "real socialism," not its current version, which is subjugated by liberal capitalism. In the mid-1990s Robert Steuckers had already asserted that, at the beginning of its historical trajectory, socialism was "fundamentally protective of organic freedoms and communal goods." Despite its subsequent deviations, "Socialism, whether we want [to admit] it or not, remains a communitarian impulse and aspiration."[52] Writing in an issue of *Réfléchir & Agir* dedicated to "Our Identitarian Socialism," Georges Feltin-Tracol—a French author, born in 1970, very active in the "combat of ideas" for the ethnocultural defense of Europe in books and magazines (since 2010 regularly in *Réfléchir & Agir*), at conferences, and at the site Europe Maxima, which he founded—said that the time had come to "rediscover our socialism, a socialism rooted in the people and hostile to the repeated treasons of partitocracy, [which is nothing but a] happy back-up of global liberalism." In his defense of an "Identitarian revolutionary socialism," Eugène Krampon wrote that what was needed was to deny the politicians of the establishment "the right to call themselves European and socialists, because they are nothing but *Europe*-ists at the service of international finance."[53] This rediscovery and rehabilitation of socialism through the adoption of a particular reading has had as a major proponent the Nouvelle Droite—and this emerges in the writings of de Benoist. Interviewed by *Réfléchir & Agir*, de Benoist reiterated the fundamentally oppositional nature of socialism: Its anthropology is holistic rather than individualistic (prioritizing therefore the social and not the economic), popular and anti-elitist, and "against the mobility, flexibility, and deracination of capitalism, which dissolves all the ties in the war of all against all that characterizes absolute competition." "Every true socialism is rooted,"[54] he added. The fact that Ken Loach—whose movies celebrate the popular working-class fighting spirit against liberal capitalist societies—is one of de Benoist's favorite filmmakers fits into his apology of "real" socialism.

This return to the sources of "true socialism"—as communal, solidaristic, holistic, and popular because [it exists] in moral and spiritual harmony with workers and peasants—is viewed by many Identitarians as revolutionary because it clashes with a contemporary system, supported by the Right and the Left, that celebrates capitalism (and its inbuilt dynamic of destruction) as the only possible horizon. This leads to a reappraisal of early nineteenth-century theorists of socialism who took into account the communitarian foundations of society, such as Pierre-Joseph Proudhon with his economic system of mutualism and with cooperatives and interest-free loans against the power that usury wields. A major reference in this work of genealogical digging up of "authentic socialism" has been the radical philosophy of Jean-Claude Michéa—who comes from the anti-capitalist Left—and his insistence on the fundamental mismatch between original socialism and what today is called the "Left." The founders of socialism shared with the anti-liberal Right of the past the same anthropological vision, in which the individual, contrary to what postulated the liberalism that emerged out of the Enlightenment, was not a sovereign self but a "political animal" attached to a historical community. According to Michéa, what has happened today is that the official Left has accepted the liberal anthropology while jettisoning its anti-capitalist compass; even if it criticizes the excesses of the market, it extols, in practice, its cultural and moral consequences. *In practice* it contributes to the liberal project with its cultural liberalism and its overriding emphasis on personal fulfillment, individual self-expression, and civil rights instead of social and anti-capitalistic struggles. The weight given to individual narcissism—seeing all popular, communitarian, and rooted traditions and mentalities as atavisms that need to be overcome—has cut off the Left from the lived experience of the masses and the "common decency" (a term taken from George Orwell) of the ordinary people.[55] It was in this sense that, in *La Gauche du Capital* (The Left of Capital)—a book that *Réfléchir & Agir* calls "essential"—Charles Robin, a student of Michéa, reinforced the view that the "libertarian" left, while protesting against capitalism, worked at the same time to legitimate the conditions of its acceptance. Libertarian liberalism is thus a pleonasm.[56] This challenge to traditional, conventional political categories and to the division between Left and Right is, of course, in the DNA of the Nouvelle Droite (always in the quest for a new synthesis), and it is simultaneously or subsequently transferred to Identitarian narratives against the established order.

Among the "political roots" of the Bloc Identitaire, its president mentions the "French socialism of a Proudhon, or a Sorel."[57] The reference to George Sorel is indicative, because revolutionary syndicalism is viewed by these Identitarians as one of the important sources of the recovery of the "lost" socialist tradition. Any socialism worthy of the name—especially at a time of unrestrained liberal capitalism—must be on the offensive, disparaging reformism and being as radically antisystem as syndicalist revolutionaries were at the beginning of the twentieth century. Here again, the influence of the Nouvelle Droite emerges, and de Benoist—who wrote a biography of Sorel's disciple Édouard Berth and his "heroic socialism"—sees in their uncompromising stance in regard to bourgeois society and its decadent values (at odds with warrior and proletarian values) an inspiring example of the anti-reformist ethos that needs to be re-created today in the "war" against the capitalist system. This stems from de Benoist's conviction that, regardless of differences, history shows that "the revolutionaries of all stripes will always be closer to one another than they will ever be to the reformists of their camps."[58]

"Are we in 1788?" asked Eugène Krampon in *Réfléchir & Agir*, alluding to the current troubled, potentially pre-revolutionary times that may be fomenting the "great front of labor—workers, employees, small traders, artisans, small entrepreneurs—against the liberal and globalist capitalist oppression," or the birth of Identitarian socialism.[59] This, of course, entails protectionism, national preference—"an idea of good sense, practiced by all peoples on Earth, except by sick Western societies," says Faye[60]—in the job market and in social benefits, for example, along with a widespread nationalization program (of banks and major industries). The Terre et Peuple network has also served as an outlet of diffusion of this concept, often in close partnership with Krampon's magazine, as well as in his emissions in *Meridien Zero*. Interviewed by the magazine of the Fédération des Québécois de Souche, Roberto Fiorini, the general secretary of Terre et Peuple, who has been active in French syndicalism, defended Identitarian socialism against the "financial and merchant dictatorship" and an organic union between work and capital because socialism must be understood "as the need for everyone to be at the service of a higher interest, the preservation of our identity, of our blood."[61] Protectionism is thus viewed as unavoidable: "The official way of thinking would like us to believe that protectionism is war! Instead it is the economy that it is the war! Only Europe is open to all the winds," Fiorini declared in an interview with *Réfléchir & Agir*.[62]

Community and Solidarity

The symbol of the Bloc Identitaire is the *sanglier gaulois*, or the wild boar, as a "symbol of the force, freedom, family solidarity and immemorial companionship of our European peoples."[63] It is also a symbol of attachment to the roots, to the earth, and to a particular territory. No wonder, therefore, that, in its rejection of the globalist steamroller, the socioeconomic views of the network uphold the bastions of community and earth-based localism. The newer Identitarians see themselves as pioneers in the struggle against globalization and its evils; they advocate "deglobalization" and have chosen as one of their battle-cries "Anti-Global/Pro-Local." That is also the title of a book published by their publishing house Éditions IDées. The book states, "While globalism, as the ideology to which all our governments of the right and of the left adhered, does not know but the search for maximum profitability, localism revives the notions of rootedness and equilibrium."[64] At the same time, their idea of an "Identitarian economy" is geared both against the unlimited power of deterritorialized multinational corporations and the defense of the "little producers and independent artisans," aiming at a "relocalized economy, at a human scale, and integrated into a protected European market."[65] The Identitarians have also been active in the denunciation of transnational capitalism, with its outsourcing and delocalization, which is always in search of reducing production costs by using cheap labor (whether immigrant or non-European) and leads to a devastating deindustrialization, the lowering of salaries, and overall job and human insecurity. They have adopted confrontational tactics against the "madness of the global money system" that strangles nations and communities, which included the invasion of the Goldman Sachs Parisian headquarters (with a slogan of "From Paris to Athens: Stop the banksters!") and the occupation of H&M stores to protest that company's policy of delocalization to zones of cheap labor, berated as a "modern form of slavery."[66] Under the motto of "Ours before the Others," young Identitarians have also been involved in voluntary service to homeless people, provided they are "indigenous" or full-blooded French. It was in this spirit, and against the perceived "foreign preference" of official social agencies, that "Generation Solidarity" emerged, launching regular campaigns of providing clothing and food, as well as "comfort," to those French who were "abandoned." "In the face of the dereliction of public officials . . . we will never let our compatriots fall," they announced during one of their solidarity tours.[67] In these social work initiatives, French Identitarians have been followed, although to a lesser extent, by German-speaking Identitarians who have also started to engage in such campaigns of donating food for the homeless. Finally, it should be noted that the target is capitalist "civilization," a world system viewed as totalitarian and as creating a new human type. The combat is against the reduction of everything to the economic. Ultimately, however, there is a place for markets and private initiatives as long as they are limited, proportional, and *part of* the community (not above it, like finance capitalism)—contributing to the welfare of the many and not solely the enrichment of the few. Another idea formulated by de Benoist is this: "There is a big difference between a market society and a society with a market."[68]

CasaPound's "Social Question"

Not surprisingly, in tandem with the view of the nation as an organic community of destiny, the idea that the economy is dependent on the political pervades CasaPound's "One Nation" political program. The idea of a strong, free Italy demands a "reconquest" of the sovereignty and autonomy lost to private and international powers. This, of course, implies a full stop to the privatization and the nationalization of crucial and strategic industries. Most importantly, the critique of financial capitalism and the power of banks is at the heart of CasaPound's worldview. Advanced capitalism and the autonomization of finance, with deregulated economies constituting an easy prey to rapacious transnational oligarchies, only exacerbate the evil.

The European sovereign debt crisis (which began in 2009)—and the concomitant submission of nations to global capital markets, lenders, investors, and speculators—is therefore one more phase in the descent of Europe, as a whole, into the darkness of usury. As Scianca has written, usury is "perhaps, the only true 'absolute evil.' In any case, it is the main enemy of CasaPound,"[69] and "the head of the octopus," as Iannone says.[70] CasaPound's fight against usury has a dual dimension: It is both a search for new policies and, more profoundly, an indictment of usury as a telltale sign of the spiritual malaise of modern civilization. Following Ezra Pound—and his use of the image of ancient Eleusis and its mysteries as the source of the lost connection with the sacred and with a more balanced and fulfilling life—Scianca notes the "eternal" metaphysical conflict between usury and Eleusis. Between "fecundity and sterility, life and death, construction and dissolution," or spirituality and materialism, in a world cut off from beauty and the numinous, where to an increasing degree money alone serves as a measure of one's worth.

According to Scianca, "The art, the house, and work are the three victims of usury."[71] And, in a context of acute economic crisis marked by austerity measures that affected mostly the working and middle classes, CasaPound put forth its solutions to the problems faced by Italian families. No wonder that—and in line with the Poundian canto "With usura hath no man a house of good stone"—the combat for housing has been a major priority of CasaPound. It was also one of the reasons that the group chose the turtle as its symbol; "it is one of the very few living creatures fortunate enough to have its home, so for us it represents our main struggle, the right to ownership of the house."[72] Influenced by the Manifesto of Verona of later-period fascism, CasaPound advocates the "right to the property of the house," launching the *Mutuo Sociale* (Social Mortgage) campaign with the goal that the state would construct houses that it would then sell at production cost, interest-free, with no intermediaries, to Italian families. This would free families from the speculation of constructers and the usury of banks. A related campaign is Ferma Equitalia (Stop Equitalia [Italy's tax collection agency]), aiming at putting an end to that agency's coercive practices. A "stylized black man with a briefcase and vampire teeth symbolized the campaign," accompanied by shocking images (often suicidal) of despair and hopelessness.[73] True to their motto, "Against all forms of usury," CasaPound also launched a free service of providing assistance to citizens in matters regarding banks and credit institutions and the verification of interest rates and loan practices, as a watchdog against "illicit banking," in an initiative called Nemica Banca, or Enemy Bank. It has often unfolded banners outside banking agencies to protest their "treason" against the people.

The priority of the social question within CasaPound—the way that it sees itself as the defender of the national community and "shield" of the people—takes for its major inspiration the fascist experience, especially its dimension as a "social revolution," in the words of Scianca, which are tied to its original "intersecting strands of the immense and red fascism [in the expression of Brasillach], its Sorelian, syndicalist, and popular roots."[74] "The dictatorship of the free market, [and] the short-sighted and servile policies of various governments so far," reads its political platform, "succeeded in dismantling the welfare state created during Fascism, forcing Italians to suffer unemployment, job insecurity, forced proletarianization and uncontrolled immigration."[75] Within this logic, CasaPound's policy of national preference—"Italians first" in matters of housing, work, school and the welfare state—is to be expected. This protection of the national community and desire to "give hope, dignity, strength, will, to a population that has been exhausted and tired"[76] also translates into campaigns of poverty alleviation for low-income Italian families, collecting and distributing basic provisions and nonperishable items, or giving clothes and toys to children during the Christmas season. For example, one of the group's food drives, in Milan, was addressed to "the Italian [in bold type] families that do not make ends meet at the end of the month."[77] On another occasion, in Ostia, in the district of Rome, CasaPound ran an extended food drive to help poor Italians and, when the locals were asked by journalists about the ideology of the group, they answered, "They are fascists? Well, they give us food," which became a motto that was immediately replicated on the group's social media platforms.[78]

CasaPound's social activism also encompasses disaster relief. The group's volunteers were present to provide aid to the populations affected by the 2009 earthquake in the Abruzzo region, and this event was a stimulus to the subsequent creation of La Salamandra (the Salamander). With its headquarters in Rome and local branches throughout Italy, it presents itself as a "volunteer group of civilian protection," providing disaster response to floods or earthquakes, for example, but also food and services to the homeless. When other earthquakes hit central Italy in the summer of 2016, Salamandra volunteers rushed to the disaster areas, participating in search-and-rescue operations, helping in the emergency camps, and providing food and medical aid to the populations. Casa-Pound, as noted in the first chapter, has also organized food banks outside Italy, giving, in conjunction with Golden Dawn, humanitarian aid to Greeks affected by their economic crisis. This was promoted as an example of the "real Europe of solidarity."[79] This emphasis also comes to light in CasaPound's defense of protectionism, which they believe must be done at a European level. "We believe in a strong Europe, self-sufficient," states its political program, "which does not expose European workers to competition from countries whose populations do not have the same protection, working hours and wages as European workers. In short, a sort of commercial State closed on a continental scale."[80] It is hoped that this Europe-wide autarchic space, in which the economy is proportional and controlled by the political will of Europeans, will constitute, to the extent possible, a plutocratic and usury-free zone.

To the People's Defense

In his tribute to CasaPound, the Portuguese Identitarian Duarte Branquinho said, "The most important thing is that CasaPound showed that it is possible to reach the people, to defend it, and to create an alternative."[81] This idea goes to the heart of the self-perception of Identitarians, of all stripes, as defenders of the people, particularly of ordinary citizens, who have been left behind by the political establishment and the ruling elites. For a start, the idea of "abandonment" of the people has been a mainstay of the Nouvelle Droite. "Whereas the Right has renounced the nation and the critique of money, the Left renounces socialism and every radical critique of the influence of capital. Both, in doing so, cut themselves off in like manner from the people," argues de Benoist.[82] According to this logic, the liberal Right and progressive Left are part of the system, upholding the market society that homogenizes cultures, and therefore the new class war of the twenty-first century, the real cleavage and antagonistic struggle, is, and will be, between the people (still territorialized, still attached to traditions) and the globalist (and therefore rootless) elites, as a cosmopolitan hyperclass at the center of a cosmocracy. Reflecting on the "elite's hatred for the people," Scianca concluded by noting that in today's Europe, "the real excluded, the real voiceless, are those who belong to the indigenous popular classes," because "those wretched who come from other continents always find a politician, a director, an editorialist, an artist from the trans-vanguard, a philosopher, ready to be their spokesperson. We, instead, are alone, surrounded by the hatred from the elites."[83] Because of the hollowing out of popular sovereignty, CasaPound's program states that, until now, democracy has been a "fraud" that has served only to perpetuate both the system and the power of a usurper caste. In its entry on democracy, the *Dictionary of Newspeak* calls it a "misnomer" that "does not mean 'the government of the people, by the people, and for the people' anymore, but only the submission of voters and governments to political correctness and to the interests of the big corporations and financial institutions."[84] The elites are thus fundamentally "anti-democratic," according to Guillaume Faye, and they are characterized by "anti-populism," a disposition that marks "the final triumph of the isolated, pseudo-humanist, and privileged political-media classes—which have confiscated the democratic tradition for their own profit."[85]

This means that the word "populism," as opposed to what happens in mainstream politics, is highly valued in Identitarian milieus. "The do-gooders call him arrogant, xenophobe, and populist," read Simone di Stefano's Facebook banner during the 2016 campaign for the city of Rome's mayoral elections. This is "only because he has always been on the side of Italians." Vial wrote in a *Terre et Peuple* editorial, "Populisms. The word gives the hives to the zealots of the system, scared of losing their sinecures." Further, "What those imbeciles call populism (a word that, of course, we claim) is the Identitarian awareness of peoples who want to remain what they are."[86] Against the "treason of the elites," being a populist is "the defense of one's people," said Fabrice Robert in an interview, "and to defend one's people is to defend one's identity."[87] In fact, books, scholarly and nonscholarly, that view populism in a positive light circulate in Identitarian media. The philosopher Vincent Coussedière's definition of populism, in his *Éloge du Populisme* (Praise of Populism), as "the ensemble of signals sent out by the people to indicate that it is still alive"[88]—even though in his view the people's attachment is to a shared sociability and not to an identity—certainly finds overwhelming acceptance and agreement in the Identitarian insurgent camp.

If the Identitarian "defense of the people" (from the "evil" political class) is unconditional, the same cannot be said, however, about their defense of right-wing populist parties. Generally these parties are supported, but they are sometimes also criticized for a "limited view" of long-term goals and for a the lack of enthusiasm or willingness to wage a wider cultural, metapolitical war against liberalism and globalism. Such criticism is very much present in CasaPound's Adriano Scianca, as well as voices from the Identitarian Lambda movement, like Alexander Markovics, who believes that "the Right in Europe needs to develop think thanks and develop theories in order to present alternatives to the current liberal society in every aspect"; otherwise it risks playing along with the liberal capitalist system that has created the "threats" that afflict Europe (like mass immigration and Islamization). Without such an alternative Weltanschauung, critics like Markovics believe that right-wing populism will be more of an illusion than a true solution to Europe's tribulations.[89]

IMMIGRATION AND SURVIVAL

The Looming Demographic Disaster

Writing in *ID*, the Bloc Identitaire magazine, about the ancient Scythes, the mounted warriors of the steppes of Eurasia who were described as "invincible" and "unassailable" by Herodotus, Philippe Lambert noted that, nevertheless, "we know today that it is possible to disappear without being defeated [in battle], and that the unassailable can be submerged." This served as a reminder that "we are the children of ethnic islands engulfed [by] demographics."[90] "To paraphrase a comrade," said Roberto Fiorini, tongue in cheek, at the end of an interview, "if you want to be Identitarian revolutionaries, make babies!"[91] Daniel Friberg is even more explicit in his breeding call: "Get married as early as possible in life, and have four children or more, so that we ensure that future Europeans are our descendants rather than those of colonizing minorities or deranged political opponents."[92] For Identitarians, the seriousness of the demographic challenge currently faced by flesh-and-blood Europeans, in fact—a combination of falling birth rates, a rapidly aging population, a rising age at first marriage, delayed childbearing, and a massive decades-long influx of non-European peoples—is of such magnitude as to generate a pervasive, existential despair. This arises from the belief—which to Identitarians is a matter of fact—that the iron law of demography determines the survival or downfall of civilizations. This is all the more factual because, for Identitarians, a people is not made of abstract human beings, interchangeable and replaceable, but is an ethnic ensemble that shares a common biocultural destiny in time and space.

The current unprecedented demographic crisis is at the center of many Identitarian debates. Demographers often play the role of Cassandras warning about what Gérard-François Dumont, in an interview with the *Nouvelle Revue d'Histoire*, called Europe's "demographic Winter," which has been occurring since the 1970s, setting off a "historical rupture," for the reason that "in the 21st century Europe loses its ancient position of being the third center of population of the globe, after East Asia and the Indian sub-continent."[93] Also, in the same magazine, at a time when Dominique Venner was its director, the geopolitical thinker (and for a short period a political heavyweight of the Front national) Aymeric Chauprade noted that the "catastrophic collapse of European demography" was just the translation of the "collapse of the will to power of Europeans," visible in their "negation of the idea of a European civilization, permanent repentance over the History of the West, a culture of death (the nihilism of the youth, sexual deviations, abortion, drugs), and the feminization of the main values." The combined effects of this civilizational regression and the vast settlement of peoples from extra-European regions led Chauprade to conclude that, if nothing is done to reverse the current trends, "at the end of the century Europeans will be a minority in the European part of the Eurasian continent."[94] The narrative of a youthful society to the south, with time on its side, and with the will to put down roots in the aging continent to the north, is viewed as the sword of Damocles hanging over Europe. In Faye's view, "demography is the only exact human science." The lesson to draw from demography is that "the demographic weakness of a people causes a settlement immigration in its territory, as well as its global decline of power, influence, and prosperity. In time, it causes its disappearance. It is the physical problem of high and low pressures."[95] Identitarians believe that this is exactly what has happened, and the result is that Europe, as an ethnohistorical organism, has lost its vitalistic drive. Scianca writes of "the cradle, [as] the most powerful weapon." He writes further, "Rulers for centuries . . . Europeans are on the brink of the abyss, because of spontaneous combustion, and of a spirit of abdication. The baby cots are empty, civilization dies."[96]

The deactivation of Europe, however, is attributed to the market civilization and its cultural and moral zeitgeist. The rise of radical individualism and the dissolution of community and family ties, coupled with the pro-immigration policies of both the Right and the Left—in an unholy union of progressive activists, supranational NGOs, religious campaigners, and businessmen—within the space of a borderless European Union (which has adapted to the needs of the global markets), have gravely endangered the future of ethnocultural Europeans. Scianca refers to "financial, cultural, and religious internationalism" as the triad that drives the "process of destruction of Europe."[97] According to this logic, if on one hand profit-obsessed capitalists have always pushed for immigration flows in search of a less demanding, docile, and cheaper workforce, the multicultural left, on the other hand, has made immigrants, both legal and illegal, the new subjects to identify with (instead of the "old" proletariat)—using charges of anti-racism as the weapon of choice against all those who criticize immigration, whether for its pressure on infrastructures or its social and cultural impact on the host population, especially in working-class neighborhoods. Combined with the ecumenical social activism of the churches and charities—always preaching tolerance and combating all sorts of perceived exclusions against the newcomers—the consequence is that the "process of destruction" of Europe has steadily marched forward in the past few decades until it reached, in many countries, an explosive sociocultural stage. What happened, therefore, was the transformation of *work* immigration into *settlement* immigration—facilitated by lenient policies of naturalization, and especially "catastrophic" family reunification laws (known as chain migration)—leading to the swelling of communities of immigrants *and* their European-born descendants, all attached to their own traditions and cultural practices. Over the years this development made the concepts of immigrant "assimilation," or the mainstream politicians' much-vaunted "integration"—because of the sheer number of non-European peoples *already* established in Europe—simply unachievable. Referring to the situation in France, the president of Bloc Identitaire asks, "When the first name of newborns in [the Parisian department] of Seine-Saint-Denis is Mohammed, where is the integration?" Additionally, "Where is the integration when entire cities are populated by non-Europeans? When there are trains whose only occupants are Africans? When, in some neighborhoods, we think that we are in Algiers, or Bamako. . . . What is the conclusion we should reach?"[98] Integration has failed to such an extent that, according to the *Dictionary of Newspeak*, it became in practice its reversal, or "the adoption by the majority of practices from the [as of yet] minorities."[99]

Colonization, Ethnomasochism, and Xenophilia as a "Mortal" Triad

The decades-long mass immigration into Europe is thus perceived by Identitarians as a process of colonization. "The term 'immigration' ought to be criticized as insufficient," asserts Faye, "and replaced with the term 'colonization,'" which is "the gravest historical phenomenon to beset Europeans since the fall of the Roman empire."[100] Immigrants should therefore be referred to as "alien peoples" who are undertaking a "colonization from below" that is fueled by "porous borders" and "maternity wards."[101] The current trends are akin to an "ethnocide" of European peoples. "Immigration-invasion," writes Pierre Vial in an editorial, "is, and it will be more and more, a mortal menace for the peoples of Europe," notwithstanding the "lies of the System" and the smokescreen it puts up to cover the true extent of the problem.[102] The colonization of European peoples, however, advances only because of what Dominique Venner calls their "zombification." Their mass consciousness has been thoroughly numbed: "In order to zombify Europeans, once so rebellious, mass immigration came to the rescue. It allowed the import of cheap labor, and the destructuring of national identities," while the system inculcated at the same time in the masses a guilt complex about their own history.[103] Faye calls this "collective psychopathology," or the instillation of shame and self-hatred, of "ethnomasochism"—the "concerted propaganda campaign to make Europeans feel guilty about how they've treated other peoples and to make them see themselves as 'oppressors.'"[104] In the often-lauded 1973 novel on the demise of the West, *The Camp of the Saints*, by the French writer Jean Raspail, this Western mentality of self-hatred is depicted as "The Beast" (as the narrator states, "Nothing can stop The Beast").[105] For Identitarians, a major consequence of this omnipotent "Beast" has been, therefore, Europeans' unwillingness to fight for their own survival. The Austrian Identitarian Markus Willinger writes of this pervasive unwillingness: "Never before in human history have foreign peoples invaded to such an extent into a populated region without encountering any resistance from its indigenous residents."[106] Ethnomasochism has been compounded with the European elites' xenophilia, which, according to Faye, "systematically overestimates the value of the alien, which it sees as a victim, as it unconsciously devalues the 'Same,'" Anti-racism is only its "pathological expression."[107] No wonder that Identitarian narratives often refer to these elites as accomplices in the destruction of the ethnocultural essence of Europeans. In an entry on "xenophilia," Philippe Vardon, for example, adds in parenthesis the word "collabo" (collaborator).[108] The "Identitarian anticorps have been neutralized by an incessant propaganda" that extols "diversity" as a moral obligation of Europeans, said Fabrice Robert during a speech. "They must be reactivated." What does such "reactivation" mean for Europeans? "Be ourselves," Robert said, "and become ourselves," because "European peoples have the same rights as the tribes of the Amazon. A society without memory and roots, is the same as [a society that is] dead."[109]

Unsurprisingly, what became known as the 2015–16 migrant crisis—which, in one way or another, continued after that—or the record numbers of people, mostly from the Middle East and Africa, crossing the Mediterranean Sea or infiltrating Europe's southeast borders in order to reach it, are widely viewed as yet one more phase in the ongoing colonization of the continent. The promises by Western European leaders to accommodate a rising tide of people seeking asylum and refugee status, the creation of a European quota system to distribute "migrants" (a word that Identitarians say is a euphemism for "illegal immigrants"), the setting up across Europe of reception centers and free access to public housing and benefits, and an overall mainstream media coverage of the whole affair that has been viewed by critics as lachrymose and dishonest because it omitted the fact that a vast number of the arrivals were not genuine refugees but economic migrants and for the most part young and male—all of this was viewed by Identitarians as added confirmation of their own narrative about an "invasion" of the continent. In Lawrence Osborne's novel *Beautiful Animals*, the father tells his "good Samaritan" daughter that "apparently, they [migrants] have other reasons for throwing themselves into the sea. They seem to like what we have," to which she replied, "I don't think it's that at all. It's just survival." "No, it's not survival. You don't have to go to Sweden to survive," he observed.[110] This fictional dialogue could well encapsulate the divide between European Identitarians and pro-migrant Europeans.

In a way, for Identitarians, the whole "refugee crisis" was the perfect storm that allowed an inside look at Europe's ethnomasochism at work in its relationship with the supposed wretched of the earth. "The European marines every day *assist* the boat people ([according to the] humanitarian ideology), instead of *repressing* them, [and this help] acts as a suction pump," wrote Faye in his blog. "They are an aid to the invasion and not a protection. Unprecedented in history: armed forces who give *assistance* to the invader. Dementia."[111] In an editorial in *Réfléchir & Agir*, Eugène Krampon said that the survival of ethnic Europeans demanded drastic measures at the antipodes of the dominant and suicidal ideology of "human rightsism." Therefore, "the order must be given [to the naval forces] to open fire on boats of refugees or at land crossings. When a few dozens fall in the water or on the ground, that will soon be known in Africa and in the East! Yes to Fortress Europe!"[112] According to Faye, the immigrants' "demand" to establish themselves in Europe, with some resultant episodes of rioting and clashes with European law enforcement agents, has been caused by the "pathological [European] humanitarianism" that "persuaded 'migrants' that they have an imprescriptible right to seek 'refuge' in our house, to install themselves, and be supported." He concluded, "They would not dare to reason in the same manner with Israel, Russia, Australia, or the United States!"[113] The notion that Europe, as the continent of Europeans, is being torn apart by the immigrant tide is also behind the Iliad Institute–released video, subtitled in several languages and posted at many Identitarian and nationalist sites, about "what it means" to be a European. Its first line reads: "Europe is not Lampedusa [the Italian island that has since the turn of the century been a major entry point for African immigrants into Europe], it is our civilization!"[114] Lampedusa has in fact become the symbol of an ominous future. The Austrian Identitarians, for example, sell T-shirts in their online shop with "Lampedusa Coastguard" logos.[115]

The widespread feeling is that while the native population is abandoned, xenophilia predominates. It was in this sense that, in response to Matteo Renzi, the Italian prime minister from 2014 to 2016, who in the heat of the migrant crisis said that the welcoming of immigrants was a showing of humanity against the "beasts," CasaPound's vice president,

Simone Di Stefano, said, "We *are* beasts. We are those who remain on the waiting lists of kindergartens and social housing, we are those who died while waiting for medical help, a job, a social service, that you cannot guarantee to YOUR PEOPLE (capitals in original), but want to guarantee to foreigners."[116] From the outset, in its "defense of the abandoned people," CasaPound has been against immigration, which it has attacked as destructive of both the host and immigrant population. "The infernal migratory mechanism is one of the main elements of loss of identity, and of the social, cultural, and existential impoverishment of all the populations involved in it," states its political program. "In this system designed to kill peoples [an allusion to Faye's early 1980s book], winners do not exist, but only an elite of a few private groups with their own ideological prejudices and an anti-national group with its own economic interests."[117] CasaPound has often emphasized that the enemy is not immigrants per se, but the phenomenon of immigration, which it views as an invasion that is sustained by the activism of Catholics and subsidized by the state and the progressive left—in a joint effort often denounced as "cathocommunism"—and by unions (whose numbers are boosted by immigrants). In the end, immigrants are used as foreign labor by capitalist employers to satisfy their desire for cheap labor. These groups are all viewed as lobbies for which "immigration is a resource," says Iannone. Yet "for us" immigration "is a poison" that leads to a "war among the poor."[118] Far from profiting only people-traffickers, the Italian activists believe that immigration is an all-around business for many individuals and groups. When the Italian government launched the EU-funded Mare Nostrum (Our Sea) as an emergency search-and-rescue naval and air operation in the Mediterranean Sea, which lasted roughly a year (2013–14), it was understood as yet another example of the encouragement of the immigrant invasion. "Mare nostrum: Importing slaves, producing unemployed," was the slogan of CasaPound in its combat against the enterprise. When in 2017 the UN Refugee Agency launched a new plan to respond to the situation of refugees and migrants in Europe, a plan aimed at supporting "long-term solutions and orderly and dignified migration management," Scianca asked: "Is it a strategy to avoid the departures, and to attack a system that requires some to leave their homelands and others to see their own homelands invaded? Nah.

The priority of these benefactors is obviously 'complementing and reinforcing Governments' efforts to ensure safe access to asylum and the protection of refugees and migrants.' In short, we must organize ourselves better so that we can be invaded more efficiently." Reacting to the financial cost of the plan, Scianca wrote, "Only 691 million USD to replace us as a people," then asked his readers, "Did you perhaps think that you would be extinguished for free?"[119]

The "infernal migratory mechanism" and its multiple consequences must, then, be counteracted at various levels. CasaPound launched a vigorous campaign against changes in Italy's citizenship law that would allow for the passage from *Jus Sanguinis*, the right of blood, to *Jus Soli*, or the award of citizenship on the basis of birth in a territory (instead of hereditary ties). It has unfurled banners across Italy with the slogan "No to Jus Soli—citizenship is not a gift" while defending a popular referendum on the issue against those "who want to erase Italy from history," with the reminder that "there are still some Italians who do not surrender."[120] Turkish President Recep Tayyip Erdoğan called on his compatriots living in Europe to "make not three, but five children. Because you are the future of Europe. That will be the best response to the injustices against you." Afterward, Simone Di Stefano commented on his Facebook page that Erdoğan had explained with those words the menacing nature of *Jus Soli*: "This is why citizenship should not be given, but in many cases revoked."[121] In the end, as Scianca argued, in the current European context characterized by a "convergence of three emergencies: immigratory, terroristic and demographic," *Jus Soli* becomes a "suicidal and criminal" mechanism.[122] At the same time, and against the "demographic death of Italy and Europe," CasaPound pushes for a pro-natalist policy with incentives for childbearing, tax concessions to large families, and generous benefits for motherhood, which in the law it has proposed, *Tempo di essere madri* (It's time to be mothers), means granting part-time work schedules for working mothers, with full pay.[123] CPI also started a campaign for the enactment of a new pro-natalist bill—called national income for birth rate—allocating 500 euros monthly for children born of Italian parents for the duration of sixteen years. They say that money spent financing pro-immigrant policies and infrastructures should be spent on what the country "really" needs, Italian newborns.[124]

FIGURE 13. Poster for CasaPound's campaign of incentives to raise the birth rate of Italians of native stock (launched in January 2017) with the slogan "Fill the cradles, empty the welcoming centers [for refugees and migrants]."

All the while, CasaPound has engaged in a series of direct actions against immigration in myriad Italian cities and villages, whether by staging protests at reception centers or refugees centers (with battle cries that often equate immigration with an illicit "business" that needs to be shut down); by joining the struggles of local communities, mostly on the outskirts of big cities, against the setting up of such infrastructures; or by blockading roads and engaging in clashes with the police (some of its members have received jail sentences because of these actions). CPI also organizes sit-ins against Roma camps. All these initiatives are undertaken in "defense" of the peoples' will against the "criminal pro-immigration policies" of the power holders. As Davide Di Stefano declared at a rally against an immigration center, "Our infrastructures and money must be used for *our* services, *our* schools, and *our* elderly." This, of course, is in line with CasaPound's motto, "Italians first!," which aims to avoid the fate of Italians' becoming "strangers in their own home."[125] In fact, both of their political slogans, "Sovereignty" and "Italians first!" were trademarked by CasaPound. This direct-action approach also translates into the defense of Italian women against the "ravages" of mass immigration. This was done, for example, in Naples, where Casa-Pound offered self-defense courses and close-combat training for women after reports of harassment and sexual assaults perpetrated by immigrants in the area surrounding the city's central train station. "Yet again CasaPound acts" against the "total silence" of authorities, they declared in a communiqué.[126]

At the peak of the migrant crisis, Scianca showed its stupefaction at the "paradox of an age" that shows compassion and sympathy only for foreigners. "Those who have for decades attacked any sense of communitarian belonging, and any sort of shared ethic between co-nationals, today show themselves to be in solidarity with perfect strangers, coming from all over the globe," he wrote, seeing in this the sway of cosmopolitanism, the ideology of human rights, and "ethical emotionalism."[127] It is in this sense that Alex Kurtagic—a UK-based "radical traditionalist"—believes that the future of the Identitarian movement is dependent on whether it is capable of justifying itself "morally in the eyes of the wider society." The rejection of the influx of extra-European immigrants cannot be done solely in "arguments based on trends, statistics, and ideas of existential threat, because it is easy to dismiss them as the product of 'fear' and 'prejudice,' even if such arguments are valid and need to be made." It must be crucially complemented at the level of moral philosophy and through "radical critique of the ethics of egalitarianism" and its "fundamentally unfair, undesirable, intolerable consequences."[128] What is true is that Identitarians see "Scianca's paradox"—grounded in what Raspail called, in a new preface to his influential book, the modern-day religion of the "Big Other"—as one of such "intolerable" outcomes.

The "No Way" Spirit of Calais

In his foreword to Markus Willinger's book, Philippe Vardon avowed, "I too shall shout out loud and clear that 'immigration is an opportunity'" before clarifying that "I see immigration as an opportunity because it has enabled the reawakening of our people—of our peoples. For it is in the face of the Other that the notion of 'we' acquires meaning."[129] The network of the Bloc Identitaire puts at its center the motto "0 percent racism, 100 percent identity," which, in the words of Arnaud Delrieux, means that "it is not hatred of others which motivates our politics, but love of our own. With a fighting love, if necessary."[130] This "fighting love" triggers their activism against immigration, which, in the case of French Identitarians, is often hyphenated with Islamization. One of the main battles of the Bloc Identitaire is for the abrogation of *Jus Soli* citizenship, which in France dates to the mid-1800s. "We cannot be Identitarian and not [also] want to abandon the right of soil in France and in Europe," its President states.[131] The French Identitarians associated with the Bloc Identitaire have fought mass immigration, especially from the Maghreb and Africa—whether originating from family reunification or done illegally—and all the public and private networks that have supported it. For example, a major target has been Réseau Éducation sans Frontières (RESF), or Education without Borders, an organization that protects refugees and immigrants from deportation. The Identitarians launched an anti-RESF group called Collectif Expulsion sans Frontières, or Expulsion without Borders. Agitprop operations against this pro-immigration group included the organization of "circles of noise" to disturb the RESF "circles of silence" held to protest the plight of immigrants. The expression *sans-papier* (undocumented) is viewed as a ruse to mask the illegal conditions of a vast number of immigrants, and these Identitarian activists have denounced the squatting in buildings of those immigrants, as well as businesses that have employed them.

Naturally the eruption of the migrant crisis only amplified the Identitarians' fears about the civilizational demise of Europe, as well as their own activism to stop it. When Génération Identitaire occupied the European Commission office in Paris, they unfurled a banner stating, "Immigration kills Africa, immigration kills Europe." The communiqué of their action read, "The passivity of the fight against illegal immigration, the systematic welcoming of the boats of illegals, the mad policy of quotas, only reinforce the ghost of an Eldorado that does not exist." This is because "the future of Africans is not found in Europe, in the same way that the future of Europe is not to become Africa! To each people its identity, its land, and its future to build."[132] When the Syrian boy Alan Kurdi drowned in the Mediterranean Sea and his body washed up on a beach in Turkey, as recorded in an image that made global headlines, Fabrice Robert wrote on his Facebook page that "he died because they have done nothing to stop the immigration. Now they exploit his death to favor even more the invasion."[133] The imposition of quotas of immigrants by the European Union—on top of the already vast illegal and legal immigration—was viewed by the French Identitarians as a form of treason "not just democratic or political, but more profound, symbolic, philosophical, civilizational. . . . This massive immigration is on the way to precipitating the death of our civilization."[134] Against what is perceived as the "mad politics" of the EU—which are opposite to the tough and dissuading stances of Hungary and Australia—French activists have launched a series of protests against immigrant centers and encampments, with slogans such as "Illegals, Europe is not your destiny!" and "Go back home!"

Drawing inspiration from the slogan "No Way! You will not make Australia home," which was part of that country's advertising campaign to deter asylum seekers, over a hundred French militants, many wearing blue helmets with the Lambda symbol and carrying banners stating "No Way" and "Go Home," blocked roads and bridges—"As long as there are no borders, we will put up barricades!" read the front cover of the magazine *Identitaires*—to stop migrants from entering Calais. Particularly since 2000, this French port city has been a gathering point for those seeking to enter the United Kingdom illegally. According to a Génération Identitaire communiqué, "For months Calais has become the symbol of the true invasion confronting our continent. . . . Calais to the *Calaisiens*, Europe to the Europeans." This was a communiqué about an action that was forcefully disbanded by the police and led to jail sentences for some of the activists, who were accused of "acts of rebellion."[135] This high-profile action was part of the Génération Identitaire campaign On est chez nous! (We are at home!), launched as an affirmation of their refusal "of chaos, immigration, and Islamization, and of merchant, economic, and cultural globalization."[136]

"Storming" Multiculturalism

In Austria, as noted in chapter 1, the founding moment of IBÖ, the Austrian chapter of Generation Identity, came after Austrian militants attempted, in February of 2013, to counteroccupy the Votive Church in Vienna. This church had been taken over by a group of asylum seekers staging a hunger strike to protest the government's refugee policy. The IBÖ has since then consistently protested against the new wave of immigrants, blocking border crossings (for example, at the Austrian-Slovenian border) and even building a border fence on the border with Hungary. Their feeling is similar to that of their French counterparts,

FIGURE 14. Cover of the French Identitarians' magazine depicting their "defense" of Calais against the "invasion of immigrants" (May–June 2016).

FIGURE 15. Meme from the Austrian Identitarians depicting the Slovenian philosopher Slavoj Žižek and a quote from him: "The greatest hypocrites are those who call for open borders."

and its former spokesman, Alexander Markovics, has said that mass immigration and multiculturalism "make the preservation of ethno-cultural identities impossible" and will inexorably lead to a "non-European Europe."[137] Typically these Identitarians, in their active production of memes against open borders and multiculturalism, use phrases by myriad authors with whom they agree, even if they are not traditionally associated with the patriotic/Identitarian camp. One of these, for example, was the Slovenian philosopher Slavoj Žižek.

In what became a media event, IBÖ militants stormed the pro-refugee play *The Suppliants* by the Austrian writer Elfriede Jelinek—held at the main auditorium of the University of Vienna and featuring actual refugees—unfurling a banner reading "Hypocrites! Our resistance to your decadence!" and subsequently throwing fake blood into the audience while warning that 'multiculturalism kills!'"[138] All of these and other actions are recorded and then circulated online in promotional videos, doubling down on the message that the flock of "so-called refugees" constitutes a dual threat to Europe's culture and the security of its native peoples.

Defending Europe: "We Shall Fight Them on the Sea," in the Mountains, and All Over

On its website, at the start of the summer of 2017, the Italian online communist newspaper *Contropiano* spoke angrily of a "vile fascist provocation" against an NGO ship operating on the Mediterranean in a mission for the search and rescue of migrants and refugees. The "provocation" referred to a small boat, displaying the Lambda symbol, that blocked one such humanitarian ship at the port of the Sicilian city of Catania. In fact, this action was the opening salvo of Defend Europe—a joint mission of Identitarians from Italy, Austria, Germany, and France—dedicated to stopping the "criminal NGOs" from providing a sort of "taxi service" to Europe and, by doing this, boosting the international human trafficking ring and the migrant business. "We are preparing a big rescue mission on the Mediterranean. It's a mission to rescue Europe by stopping illegal immigration," the group's mission statement read. "We want to gather a crew, equip a boat and set sail on the Mediterranean to chase down the trafficking ships. We want to protect our borders from illegal immigration and want to face the enemies of Europe on the sea." A donation campaign was launched, with an accompanying video featuring appeals from Identitarians in different languages, because, as these activists argued, "The immigration lobby is funded with hundred thousands of Euros by the government and by big donors. We, on the other hand, depend solely on you to fund this mission and to defend Europe. Let's work together for our future."[139]

Even though initially, under pressure from left-wing activists and online petitions launched by watchdog groups like Hope Not Hate and the online NGO SumOfUs, the bank accounts of the groups involved were shut down and the payment site PayPal blocked the Defend Europe account, invoking its rejection of "activities [that] promote hatred, violence or racial intolerance," the project went ahead. The money was easily raised—much more than the initial target—through another crowdfunding campaign at the American site WeSearchr. For their mission the Identitarians raised more than US$220 thousand from roughly four thousand donors. They were able to charter a ship—the C-Star—and for a short time they managed to operate on the Mediterranean; this

FIGURE 16. Identitarian propaganda material for the joint mission Defend Europe (June 2017).

coincided with a tougher approach by both the Italian government and the Libyan coast guard to the activities of the NGOs, which for the most part stopped their search-and-rescue operations.

When the mission ended, the Identitarians announced its "undisputable success" in terms not just of activism but also of media coverage. "Given that a key objective of 'Identitarians' is getting media attention, this boat thing is going very well so far," tweeted the radical right scholar Cas Mudde at the outset of the Defend Europe project.[140] It is true that this project managed to put the Identitarians at the very center of a mainstream media frenzy, particularly in Italy but with ramifications across Europe and even into Australia, where their goal of replicating the "No Way" policy was duly noted. Throughout, sympathetic alternative media personalities—like Brittany Pettibone and Lauren Southern, who both flew into Catania—reported on every step of Defend Europe and interviewed members of its team, like Martin Sellner, as well as other activists. On a political level, their efforts were applauded by right-wing populist politicians such as Vlaams Belang's Filip Dewinter—"Don't talk about it, DO something and follow @DefendEuropeID," tweeted the Flemish politician—while Nigel Farage posted on Facebook a photo of the C-Star, a news clip about the sharp decline of migrant crossings to Italy, and the comment "This says a lot about how little effort Europe's nations are putting into patrolling their seas."[141] The fact of the matter is that the activists behind the mission were able to overcome tremendous opposition (including refusal of access to some ports) and succeeded in increasing the media spotlight not just on their Identitarian "brand" but also on their criticism of NGOs and overall open-border policies. The mission also served as a magnet for recruitment to and expansion of the movement to other European countries. "After DE we got many, many messages and we want to use the rise in popularity to establish new sections," noted Sellner. "The UK will be the first case where we want to build it up."[142] In the months that followed, across Europe, the Identitarians involved in "Defend Europe" gave presentations—to other activists and to the interested public—about the mission. The Italian Gian Marco Concas, a former naval officer and the writer of *Ri-Generazione Identitaria* (Identitarian Re-Generation), a book of "support and diffusion of the 'Identitarian Spirit,'" was even invited to the European Parliament (by the political group "Europe of Nations and Freedom" under the initiative of Lega Nord's Mario Borghezio) and held a press conference in Brussels with the title "Immigration in the Mediterranean, Alternative Information."[143]

What is more, the Defend Europe initiatives did not stop at sea. They continued inland, specifically to the 1,762-meters-high Col de l'Échelle mountain pass in the French Alps, which in recent years has become a key entry point for illegal migrants into the country. It was there that, in the spring of 2018, Identitarians began the "Defend Europe Alps Mission." Wearing blue down jackets with the logo "Defend Europe," riding 4 × 4 vehicles, and flying rented helicopters, around 100 activists, mostly French—but also with activists from Austria, Germany, Denmark, Hungary, and Italy—performed a highly symbolic and media-grabbing mission. For a few days they erected a makeshift barrier along the Franco-Italian border crossing, built temporary checkpoints, and patrolled the area in vehicles, planes, and afoot, acting like vigilant protectors of the nation's borders. Their avowed goal was to show the authorities that even with limited resources it was possible to shut down illegal immigration.

This action provoked a media frenzy (especially in France), a social media storm (on Twitter the hashtag #StopMigrantsAlpes was trending high, to which many critics opposed the hashtag #StopfachosAlpes), and the indignant reaction of many mainstream journalists and left-wing politicians, while it was praised by Front national notables (such as Marine Le Pen). Brittany Pettibone and Lauren Southern, always loyal to Identitarian causes, were also present and made celebratory videos and livestreams of the mission. Many of the Who's Who of Lambda Identitarian activism participated in the planning and execution of the mission, including Jean-David Cattin, the co-leader of Les Identitaires, and the leaders of Generation Identity chapters in Austria, Italy, and Hungary. When the French interior minister, in response to the action, pledged to increase the patrolling and security of the country's Alpine borders, the Identitarians reacted joyously ("Victory!" exulted the Identitarian leader of Lille Aurélien Verhassel on Twitter).[144] In all, Mission Alps bore all the marks of Identitarian activism—direct-action tactics that were "bold" and "daring," brandishing the message that it is possible to take the destiny of Europe into one's hands ("If our rulers don't protect our borders, we will"), while attempting to have an impact on public debate. The chances are very good that similar actions at other entry points for illegal non-Europeans into Europe will take place in the future.[145]

THE GREAT REPLACEMENT

"Carpet-like, the great migration was beginning to unroll. Not the first time, either, if we pore over history," wrote Jean Raspail in his dystopian novel. "Many a civilization, victim of the selfsame fate, sits tucked in our museums, under glass, neatly labeled. But man seldom profits from the lessons of his past."[146] In the opinion of Aymeric Chauprade, "In the decades to come the migrant pressure is going to increase, fulfilling the prophecy" of Raspail's novel.[147] Indeed, the French writer's blistering satirical description of the end of a Western civilization immersed in self-loathing and unable to defend itself and counter the descent of the Third World upon it is widely viewed as much more than a novel. It is a "prophecy," a stunning, grotesque portrayal of the future that finds its perfect accomplishment in Europe's present. Although Raspail's clarion

FIGURE 17. Meme of the French writer Jean Raspail created by Martin Lichtmesz for a 2010 *Sezession* campaign showcasing its Hall of Heroes.

call was not heeded, his role in the Identitarian camp remains that of the bearer of truth. The First Forum of Dissidence, for example, organized by Polémia, had Raspail, together with Edward Snowden and Alexandr Solzhenitsyn, as sources of inspiration.

Renaud Camus: "Believe in Your Eyes"

In his "Reasons for a Voluntary Death," Dominique Venner said, "While I defend the identity of all peoples in their homes, I also rebel against the crime of the replacement of our people." In this way Venner touched on the metanarrative that has taken hold of Identitarian discourses about the impact of immigration on the European continent. There is a "Grand Remplacement" (Great Replacement) currently occurring in Europe, a change of its cultural and ethnic makeup and therefore of its people and civilization. The French writer Renaud Camus, in his eulogy of Venner in a speech given at the Notre Dame cathedral in Paris, compared his sacrifice to the self-immolations of Jean Palach (the Czech student who lit himself afire to protest the military invasion of his country during the Cold War) and the Tibetan monks who protested Chinese control over Tibet; his departure was a "sign, a cry, a call, a founding act," and a gesture of "horror" at the Great Replacement.[148]

The left-wing *Libération* newspaper calls this "literary expression," forged by Camus himself—laid out in a series of conferences that were published in 2011 with the title "The Great Replacement"—as the new "totem" of the political "fringes." However, such "expression" is viewed by Identitarians not as a concept, but instead as an accurate, ideology-free description of everyday reality. "In order to be convinced it is enough to take to the streets, the metro, the schools, the real life," says Camus. "Believe in your eyes, that's my message."[149] Against the "big lie" promoted by the media-political powers that "in changing the people we can still have the same history, the same culture, the same civilization, the same country, the same eternal nation, the same France, the same Europe, the same identity"—that "if we change the handle, and then the blade, we can still have the same knife"[150]—Camus launched the NON (NO) organization (NO to the replacement of people and civilization). According to Camus, the two major tools driving this replacement of peoples are demographic trends and what he calls "nocence"—the daily practice of delinquency and violent acts committed against the indigenous population by a significant number of the non-natives, which is akin, Camus says, to a strategy of territorial imposition and, ultimately, of conquest. Nocence is the opposite of innocence, and that is the reason that Camus created a political party named Parti de l'IN-nocence. For this comparison—between non-natives and conquerors—he was condemned for "incitement of racial hatred." A similar justification was given by YouTube for removing the video of Camus's public address at the village where General de Gaulle is buried, in which he announced the foundation of the Conseil National de la Résistance Européenne (National Council of European Resistance) and asked for a collective European commitment: "All the European nations are invited to lead by our side the fight for the salvation of our common civilization, Celtic, Slavic, Greco-Latin, Judeo-Christian and free-thinking."[151]

More generally, what happens in Europe is just one facet of what Camus calls the universal ideology of "replacism," a nefarious, insidious ideology anchored by the dogma of anti-racism and the alleged "nonexistence of races." Replacism is the creation of the "replaceable man," the man "exchangeable, decultivated, decivilised, denationalized, and uprooted, such as needed by and for generalized exchange." The struggle of the times, therefore, as Camus said in an interview with the website Right On, is "between replacists, the champions and promoters of the Great Replacement, and anti-replacists, those who are prepared to do anything to prevent it. Inside the anti-replacist camp, we should all stick together and be united."[152] As the French writer said in an interview with *Réfléchir & Agir*, today anti-replacists must bear witness to the example of Plato's Cratylus and his naturalistic commitment to the sources, the essence of things, and the sense of origins.[153]

By and large, Identitarians have adopted the narrative of the "Great Replacement," the "term-shock," in the opinion of Steuckers, that constitutes "one of the current avatars of the famous *The Camp of the Saints*."[154] Terre et Peuple took note of the call for unity in its roundtable In the Face of the Great Replacement: A Patriotic and Revolutionary Identitarian Front. In his quest for an Identitarian socialism, Robert Fiorini is under no illusion about the attachment of businesses to the native population, because "in Europe, they look at the substitution of the population with a different angle from the Identitarian resisters that we are. They will simply adapt their commercial offer. . . . Europeans are replaced, and others convert to Islam? They will sell halal food instead of pig. . . . They do not feel attached anymore to our destinies. It is up to us to carry the torch."[155] Grégoire Gambier, the spokesperson for the Iliad Institute, says that the institute is open "to all of those who, conscious that the 'Great Erasure' of our memory allows and accelerates the 'Great Replacement,' are committed to the 'Great Ressourcement': a rediscovery of our peoples in their singular tradition, over the soil of their ancestors."[156] At the same time, the Great Replacement is at the very heart of the Bloc Identitaire's anti-immigration outlook, and they have worked closely with Renaud Camus, who sees its network as composed of "courageous and ingenious, well-formed, and deeply European [militants], and they have a very good sense for the emblematic and non-violent gesture. I certainly do think their efforts are a step in the right direction, and

FIGURE 18. Cover of an issue of *Réfléchir & Agir* dedicated to the "crusade against the modern world" and including an interview with Renaud Camus.

I have great admiration and sympathy for them."[157] They created an Observatory of the Great Replacement (sponsored by Camus) that works closely with their Observatory of Islamization and pays close attention to all the trends, dynamics, and statistics that in their view are telltale signs of the ongoing replacement of peoples. When a French medical report showed, for example, that the genetic disease sickle-cell anemia, which is predominant in people of African descent, was rapidly increasing among French newborns, this was taken as yet one more proof of the Africanization of the country and the steady substitution of peoples.[158] In fact, increasingly, statistics about newborn screening for sickle-cell disease circulate in the French Identitarian social media, showing what for Identitarians is a demographic ticking time bomb. A few months before the French presidential elections of 2017, Arnaud Delrieux tweeted a graphic of the screening for sickle-cell anemia across France and wrote: "The focus of the elections should be this one: 74% per cent of births in IDF [Île de France, the Paris region] are coming from non-European immigration."[159] One of the French Identitarians' campaigns to denounce the Great Replacement was named "Smile, you're being replaced!"

Beyond the strict Identitarian camp, the "Great Replacement" is not consensual. As a case in point, in the ND Alain de Benoist, although "not surprised" by the success of the expression "Great Replacement," which he sees as "very good for striking people's minds," does not see it as accurate: "In France, today, this is true only in well-circumscribed places, for example, when a peripheral area is completely emptied of the population of European origin to be replaced by a population of foreign origin. But even in this case, the population hit by the 'white flight' does not disappear, it goes away to go and live elsewhere. In the country there is no substitution in the strict sense." Instead, he prefers to focus on the "Great Transformation" of the population of European origin, provoked by globalism and its evils, that "modifies its genetic heritage, its social habits, its lifestyle, its way of conceiving the world, its specific values, etc."[160]

At the same time, the Great Replacement has made some inroads into the Front national, even if it has not been adopted as the official position of the party. Marine Le Pen disavows it because of its "conspiratorial vision." Truth be told, the Great Replacement is—at least as a rule—denounced by Identitarians not necessarily as a conspiracy but as a policy, one even suggested by the United Nations itself. Throughout the years the UN series of reports about the need to facilitate human mobility and enhanced international cooperation for safe, orderly, and regular migration—and even a 2000 report by the UN Population Division about "replacement migration" as a possible way to offset the population decline and aging in developed countries—have been taken as proof of such a UN-driven agenda.[161] Be that as it may, Le Pen's senior advisor, Florian Philippot, who was quite involved in the task of "de-demonizing" the party (until he let the party shortly after the electoral disappointments of 2017), sees the Great Replacement, further, as a "racialist conception that we do not share."[162] Other voices within the party, however, particularly in the circle of the young Marion Maréchal-Le Pen, share the assumptions of the Great Replacement. For example, Aymeric Chauprade, who was close to Marion when he was a high-ranking official of the Front national—said in an interview with Fabrice Robert's NovoPress that "it [the Great Replacement] is not an illusion . . . but a mathematical equation."[163] In fact, for French Identitarians at large, as noted in chapter 1, Marine Le Pen's niece is viewed as a sort of last best hope. "What if the future of Identitarian populism is called Marion? A new Eva Peron?," wrote Pierre Vial at the end of an article on the deep historical roots of populism in France.[164] Faye, another admirer, sees 2022 (the year of the next presidential election) as the moment in time when Marion may fulfill her "national destiny" as long as "she is not discouraged and continues to be in politics."[165] A few months after Faye wrote those words, in the spring of 2017, Marion, in fact, quit politics, even if temporarily, in order to gain life experience. What is certain is that many intellectual French Identitarians are very disparaging toward the leader of the Front national, especially since her heavy loss in the 2017 presidential elections to the "candidate of the globalists," Emmanuel Macron, which they impute to her refusal to focus her campaign on Identitarian issues and on the threat of capitalism and immigration to the way of life of the rooted French. "The real cleavage" and the only one that "matters" is between "those who accept and those who refuse the civilizational and demographic Great Replacement," Jean-Yves Le Gallou declared soon after the defeat. Everything else, according to this logic, pales in comparison.

Mobilized against Der Große Austausch

Beyond France, the Identity movement in German-speaking countries has also taken up the torch of the Great Replacement. In an interview, Markovics said, "Mass immigration and Islamization are only symptoms of a wider process: the substitution of the European population with Middle Eastern and African peoples. . . . In 50 or 100 years, there will not be any more indigenous Europeans as we know them."[166] When militants invaded the European Union's Vienna headquarters in the spring of 2015, they did it to demand an "end to the Great Replacement." In one of their protests in Austria's capital, they marched with their Lambda flags, holding a banner that said, "Soon we will be a minority in our own land. Stop the replacement!" As they declared in a follow-up communiqué, "Everyone sees, hears, and feels it. We are going to be strangers in our neighborhood, our own city, and our own country. The Great Replacement is going to happen!"[167]

FIGURE 19. Photo of a demonstration by the Austrian Identitarians in Vienna "against the Great Replacement" (June 6, 2015). Courtesy of IBÖ.

Translated by Martin Lichtmesz, the writings of Camus were described by the German publisher Antaios in the following manner: "Renaud Camus has called the foreign infiltration of Europe the 'Great Replacement' and this notion is already beginning to be asserted!"[168] In a post about the Great Replacement, the Germans IBD noted, "It is the vague feeling that creeps over you when you are sitting in the subway and around you only foreign languages are spoken." Further, "It is the same strange feeling when you go through a neighborhood of your city and the people and the shops resemble more a metropolis of the Middle East rather than the place where you grew up." Although the feeling is overwhelming that "something is violently out of hand," in the media "you will not read anything about your impressions" except that "we need more immigration or [learn] about the new tattoo on the ass of Lady Gaga. The only impression that you get is the one that you obviously live in a parallel world." As a result, in different parts of the country, activists hung posters and distributed leaflets warning about the coming minority status of Germans and Europeans, denouncing the Great Replacement as "the most famous mystery of our time. Everybody knows about it, but nobody dares to talk about it openly." Because "the numbers do not lie," each European is enjoined to "inform yourself and become active against the Great Replacement, before it's too late!"[169] There has also been a sort of German equivalent to Camus's writings, with the publication by Antaios of Akif Pirinçci's corrosive *Umvolkung: As the Germans Are Replaced Quietly*, in which the Turkish-born German writer applies the Nazi-era term "umvolkung" (meaning the change of the ethnic composition of the population pursued by Nazis in Eastern Europe) to describe the current ethnic replacement in Germany. Pirinçci "uses this word for shock value and provocation, arguing that the multiculturalist 'replacement migration' politics are essentially the same as that aspect of Nazi [ethno]politics," says Martin Lichtmesz.[170]

In an article about the German-speaking Identitarian movement in the weekly news magazine *Stern*, the journalist linked its extremism with "the past of many members, the campaigning against minorities, especially Muslims, and the right-wing conspiracy theory of the Great Replacement."[171] Activists, however, fight off the view that the Great Replacement is a "theory"; they see it as a reality caused by processes set in motion by misguided elites, one that can be reversed by a radical change

FIGURE 20. Poster of the German-speaking Identitarian movement alerting the people about the "Great Replacement."

in policies. Daniel Fiß, one of the leading activists of IBD, gives a typical, matter-of-fact, explanation: "If immigration continues as in previous years, a billion migrants will have come to Europe by 2050. This is a purely mathematical replacement process."[172]

Critically, this sentiment—that demographic changes *are* leading to a replacement of peoples—is widely shared in the Identitarian youth movement across Europe. When, for example, the Irish government unveiled its plan, Project Ireland 2040, aimed at preparing the country to deal with the predictable population increase due to mass immigration, Generation Identity Éire/Ireland and Northern Ireland reacted as expected: "They can't pull the wool over our eyes. Do the politicians of our country think we haven't noticed what is happening in France, Sweden, Germany, and England? . . . The English are a minority in London, the Germans a minority in Frankfurt, is Dublin next?" The banner that Irish activists unfurled on the iconic Ha'penny Bridge in Dublin read, "Generation Identity. Defend Ireland. Stop the Great Replacement."[173]

In Europe this narrative of the Great Replacement (and the related Islamization) finds a strong advocate in the studies and publications of the New York–based Gatestone Institute and its European project, Gatestone Europe. It presents itself as a "non-partisan, not-for-profit international policy council and think tank dedicated to educating the public about what the mainstream media fails to report," and its projections, for example, that Germany will have twelve million immigrants by 2060, or that the population of Muslim origin in France will reach between fifteen and seventeen million in 2025, have been shared, retweeted, blogged about, and commented on widely, under the flag of the Great Replacement, by Identitarian activists.[174] As a rule, the idea that, given the current demographic and sociocultural trends, Europe will be unrecognizable in the near future is featured heavily in the analyses not only of the Institute's fellows but also of its guest columnists.

CasaPound's Fighting Back against La Grande Sostituzione

In the very first pages of his book *Sacred Identity: Gods, Peoples, and Places at the Time of the Great Replacement*, Scianca asked *the* question that haunts European Identitarians of all ages: "Let's think about the world in twenty, fifty, one hundred years. Whatever happens, whatever transformation occurs at every level, we know today that there will still exist Arabs and their culture, or the Chinese and their culture. But what about Europeans? Do we really manage to imagine that there will still be Europeans in one hundred years' time without an epochal epiphany?"[175]

Maybe, the Italians hope, there are signs of "awakening" to the problem. A 2016 CPI Facebook entry read as follows: "A must-see event at CasaPound: on the 25th of February Renaud Camus—the French writer who has revolutionized how we think about immigration and has imprinted [upon our minds] the formula of the 'Great Replacement of Peoples,' influencing the nationalist parties of half of Europe—arrives."[176] This event became one of the most popular podcasts of CasaPound's web radio station. Scianca says that the French writer hit the spot with the "crucial operational concept" of the Grande Sostituzione (the Great Replacement). It allows the "ontological rejection of immigration" and makes "obsolete" the debate over the integration of foreign peoples. "In a neighborhood populated by 90 percent of allogenous, who must integrate with whom?" Scianca asks before pointing out that "the scenario in which Europeans are a minority in their own home makes all the discourses about the reasons, costs and impact of immigration relative and secondary. . . . Immigration is rejected as a whole, beyond all other considerations." Furthermore, there is no conspiracy behind it, a sort of "diabolic plan," but it constitutes instead "an actual historical dynamic." In fact, "the Great Replacement has already some explicit supporters (UN studies, some declarations from Pope Francis, or some proposals from the Democratic Party [Italy's Partito Democratico, or PD]), which make useless any sort of allusion to a dark scheme."[177]

The Great Replacement was easily integrated into the anti-system narrative of CasaPound. In the discussion about changes to Italy's citizenship law, CasaPound issued this statement: "After having destroyed the State and chewed the economy, they now want to replace the Italian people with other peoples."[178] Practical examples of the Great Replacement are invariably denounced—for example, when the small Sicilian village of Sutera decided to receive refugees as a way to stop its depopulation. "What to do now, when the residents do not make babies, or when they immigrate in search of better fortune?" Scianca asked derisively. "Youth policies? Family policies? Create wealth locally? Nah, it is much easier to replace the people." He then added, "How clever, how come no one thought about it first: to become an African city! That's what will revive the village. How fortunate Sutera is. As long as it still exists, that is."[179] The insistence by some European leaders, policy makers, and opinion makers that the influx of immigrants will serve to "save" the welfare state is met with scorn. "It serves to pay the pensions, they say," writes Scianca. "To destroy a civilization in order to pay the pensions: it is a little like those who have a headache and solve the issue with a gun to the temple."[180] Camus sees in the pro-pensions argument a defining sign of decadence: "At any other time the issue of pensions would have seemed perfectly ridiculous, insignificant, unworthy, with regard to national independence and identity of the people."[181]

Ultimately, as the head of cultural affairs at CasaPound stated when he interviewed Camus for the online edition of *Il Primato Nazionale*, the Great Replacement provides a look at what is *really* at stake with mass immigration. "It is not just a question of public order and degradation, abuse [of social benefits], or religious conflicts," he writes. "There is something more profound, and more dangerous, in what we are heading toward. It is the idea that we are not 'at home' anymore, that no one is, and that the peoples are replaceable."[182] The Great Replacement has also become part of the vocabulary of CasaPound's former political ally, Lega Nord. In the discussion about the adoption by Italy of a new Citizenship Law, Matteo Salvini said, "I do not accept the *Jus Soli* in Italy, it is a substitution of peoples."[183] In a context in which the Italians are the ones who must be protected under "anti-discrimination laws," Salvini responded: "An operation of ethnic substitution is underway, and Europe is coordinating this operation." He declared in an interview with the party's radio station, Radio Padania, that in their ancestral land "Italians are discriminated against, victims of ethnic cleansing, ethnic substitution—call it whatever you want it."[184]

Planning the Great Return

Because, for Identitarians, any cursory look into European societies shows that the Great Replacement is a reality, the ultimate solution for many thinkers and activists is the "Great Return." In order to counter the substitution of peoples in progress, the apology for what they call "Remigration"—or "Exigration" in the words of Colin Liddell—has gained momentum in the Identitarian camp. One of the reasons for the schism between the Nouvelle Droite and Identitarians relates to what the solution is in face of a massive number of immigrants and their descendants who are *already* living in Europe. De Benoist believes that, instead of blocking out an uncomfortable reality, it is necessary to deal with things as they are. In the face of an immigration that has been too vast and too concentrated over a short period of time, this coming to terms with reality involves the acceptance of a degree of communitarianism, with enough space for particular groups and traditions, coexisting under a common law.[185] Identitarians believe, instead, that communitarianism is not a solution for the failure of assimilation and integration because it only gives further strength to the cultural and ethnic demands of foreign peoples and facilitates their territorial rootedness and conquest. Ultimately, it smoothes the expansion of peoples that do not belong to Europe. Yes, they should hold onto their own identities, but not on a continent that is not their own. Such is the message, for example, of Markus Willinger: "Muslims and Africans! Take down your tents and leave this continent. Entire regions of the world belong to you. . . . Even more so than European help, Africa and the Global East need you and your strength. Return to your home countries, for they belong to you. Europe, however, will never belong to you. Europe belongs to us."[186]

One of the mottos of the Bloc Identitaire is "In order for Europe remain European, we demand Remigration." The "peaceful and organized return of a great part of immigrants and their descendants" is viewed as the only viable solution to provide a peaceful future for France and for Europe overall. These French Identitarians, in fact, organized a day-long conference in 2014 that was dedicated to Remigration, with appearances by, among others, Guillaume Faye, Iliad's Philippe Conrad, Polémia's Jean-Yves Le Gallou, and Renaud Camus. Remigration is "the most realistic option and the only one that avoids the descent into chaos engendered by multiculturalism," the organizers asserted.[187] The Bloc Identitaire's "Blueprint for a Politics of Identity and Remigration"—endorsing measures such as ending birthright citizenship and chain migration (family reunification), placing a moratorium on naturalizations, as well as forming partnerships with immigrants' countries of origin aimed at helping them control their populations—includes the creation of an "Aid Fund for Return" to encourage immigrants to go home and a "High Commissioner" of Remigration. The Bloc further believes that if Remigration sounds "radical" or "impossible" today, the passing of time will make it both possible and necessary tomorrow.[188] There should be no surrender to fatalism or to the idea "that is somehow mystically impossible to do anything about the large number of immigrants already within our borders." At least that is the belief declared by Motpol's Daniel Friberg in his defense of a "humane, non-violent programme of repatriation" that should include incentive measures such as a "re-establishing subsidy" for those who return to their homelands. "Since this remigration program would entail taking away those welfare benefits that brought the migrants across the globe to our countries in the first place, it is unrealistic to assume that the majority of migrants would like to stay after removing those financial incentives—and on the contrary offering financial incentives for remigration. I just can't see that scenario happening," the Swedish author argues. Moreover, "Repatriation is often portrayed as something 'impossible,' but that is just simple propaganda. Repatriation is easy, fun and humane, and as soon as the political will exists, relocating at least 90% of the non-European migrants will be as easy as a walk in the park."[189] Regardless, there is an overriding sentiment that the "inevitable" unfolding of chaos—already happening and getting worse by the day—will engender its own antidote in the form of policies aimed at the departure of the peoples of non-European ethnic origin.

Remigration apologists reject the notion that "remigration" is just a euphemism for the "ethnic cleansing" of the European continent. Sellner calls the analogy "insane" because "Remigration means the turn of the influx of mass migration and consists of many different policies. It doesn't mean to create an ethnostate and kick out everyone who fails a 'race test.'" In the end, according to the Austrian Identitarian, it means both "a change of the demographic tendency by legal, financial, and cultural measures" combined with the adoption of a *leitkultur*, a strong leading culture, which neutralizes the establishment of cultural or ethnic separatisms and parallel societies within European countries.[190] Adam Berčík, the spokesman of Generace Identity in the Czech Republic, believes that the concept of Remigration suggests a radically "different" climate than does ethnic cleansing. "The term 'ethnic cleansing' evokes violence and injustice," he says, adding, "We want a peaceful and lawful process, when people of non-European descent will be deported in humane conditions, they will probably receive financial compensation (of course only if they weren't convicted as criminals or illegal intruders) and remigration will begin after the introduction of relevant laws."[191] João Franco, the Portuguese author of *Identitarian Foundations for the Post-Modernity*, in his explanation of the merits of Remigration, makes the historical comparison with the processes of decolonization after 1945, in which Europeans left Asian and African territories on a large scale.[192] "How did European academics, and the media, see those remigrations?" Franco asked, then answered: "They saw them in a normal manner, and using terms such as decolonization, independence, self-determination and justice. The peoples of Europe also have the same right, which the peoples of Africa and Asia have demanded and which I recognize all the legitimacy to do so, and [therefore] it is the most elementary justice, the self-determination of the European peoples and the decolonization of Europe."[193] In the end, for Identitarians, the "moralistic" and "judgmental" academic and mainstream media's disparaging of Remigration will not stop the "reality of things" and the development of a process that they see, sooner or later, as bound to happen.

Freedom from Strife

For Identitarians, what is at stake is social peace. The theme of the inherent violence of multicultural societies is dominant in Identitarian anti-immigration narratives. They are often viewed as "multiconflictual" and "multiracist" and as incubators of intolerance and conflict. "The irenic and comforting idea of a 'multicolored' society, with red, yellow, and white children who make a circle [of hands]," writes Scianca, "is in fact short-circuited and brought back to reality by a significant neologism: 'multiracist society.'"[194] Fabrice Robert, for his part, in a speech to militants, said that "ethnic nations sometimes make war against their neighbors. Multiethnic nations make war on themselves."[195] The *Dictionary of Newspeak* asserts that "the oligarchy sings the virtues of the multicultural society in order to hide that multicultural societies are hopelessly multiconflictual and implosive."[196] When a British newspaper reported that in early 2018, for the first time in modern history, London had overtaken New York in the number of murders, Charlie Roberts, a top activist from Generation Identity UK, tweeted, "Proof that multiculturalism is a complete and utter failure."[197]

Often, the image of a "Lebanization" of European countries—of a situation in which multiple groups are brought together into a singular political entity, with all the conflicts that inevitably ensue—is invoked as the likely result if the current demographic, immigration, and multicultural trends are not put in reverse mode. Multinational Brazil is also invoked as an example of an ethnically heterogeneous nation whose fate is anything but desirable. "First of all, we believe that the ethnic and cultural homogeneity of a people is a precondition for social peace: look at Lebanon, Brazil, South Africa," declared the spokesman for Génération Identitaire.[198] Fabrice Roberts talks about the possibility of France becoming a "mini-Brazil, or a mega-Lebanon."[199] According to this line of thought, episodes of ethnic rioting are nothing but signs, opening salvos of a potentially broader conflict—and the "natural" consequence of multicultural society's growth. "It would be wiser to read [the Greek historian] Polybius more often, and what he said about the expected decline of the ancient powers," wrote Dominique Venner in his opening words about the suburban riots in heavily immigrant communities in the fall of 2005. As long as nothing is done to reverse the migratory tide, "we only widen the chasm that leads to the inescapable catastrophe," he concluded.[200] When Frans Timmermans, the Dutch vice president of the European Commission, said in a speech that "diversity is humanity's destiny" and that European societies should not give up "our values to refuse diversity" or else "Europe will not remain a place of peace and freedom, for very long," it only corroborated what had already been viewed as the gap between the current dangerous utopias of elites and hard reality. In his essay "Great Replacement as 'Manifest Destiny,'" for the German magazine *Sezession*, Martin Lichtmesz portrayed Timmermans's statement as another example of a "dishonest, criminal," and "Orwellian" rationalization. As if "'our society' would 'disintegrate' by the refusal of 'diversity' and risk its inner peace, when it is obvious to everyone that the case is the exact opposite," Lichtmesz indignantly wrote. Even though the "enforcers of progress cling to this ideological opium," it is increasingly hard to hide the truth: European societies risk disintegration, and their peace, *because* of the "beatific," elite-driven diversity.[201] The only way to prevent the scenario of a "Brazilization" of Europe, declared the IBÖ leader Martin Sellner, is "to stop massive immigration and start Remigration within the next 5–10 years. . . . If you stop immigration, send back all illegals and criminals, ban Islam as a political religion, and create financial stimulations for [re]emigration, this number will go down significantly. [Therefore,] this dangerous process could be slowed down, stopped, and eventually reversed during the next centuries."[202]

Identitarians of all sorts associate multiracial societies with tribalism and neo-tribalism. That is how they see American society, whose racial violence of the early twenty-first century—as evidenced by the perceived out-of-control rate of black violent crime; the Ferguson, Baltimore, and Milwaukee riots; and the high level of racial tension between law enforcement and black communities—only serves as added confirmation of the danger lurking within multicultural societies. "That's American society: a world divided into communities that are close together but separated by waterproof barriers,"[203] Pierre Vial wrote after the chaos that followed Hurricane Katrina in an editorial titled "The Colossus with Feet of Clay." In the summer of 2016, in the aftermath of a series of killings of black people and white officers, Génération Identitaire Damien Rieu tweeted that "the only thing that must be concluded from the events in the USA is that a diverse society is one where everybody hates everybody," spreading misery equally among everyone.[204]

CLASH OR NO CLASH, A CIVILIZATIONAL STRUGGLE

In the twenty-first century "civilization" was transformed into a "taboo word," according to the *Dictionary of Newspeak*. This was because Europeans "do not know anymore how to define themselves positively in relation to other civilizations, and because they do not want to recognize the logic of the clash of civilizations."[205] The default position for Identitarians is not only that civilizations exist but also that current dynamics and events are interpreted in terms of a civilizational defense of the European space and its peoples—which have a specific, unique civilization—against corroding influences and forces. Dominique Venner frequently invoked the Annales school of History, particularly the work of Fernand Braudel, to emphasize the prime importance of the longevity of civilizations and their material, intellectual, and spiritual persistence throughout the ages. The long-term reality and viability of European civilization in particular—neglected today because of "presentism," the cult of the moment, and the compression of historical time into "real [present] time"—is viewed by Identitarians, instead, as the key to a more complete understanding of events in progress. "Realities of long duration, they survive religious, economic, and political upheavals. They exceed in longevity the other collective realities," Venner wrote in an editorial for his magazine. "They have eternity on their side. This is true of European civilization, in spite of what disfigures it today, and the threats that assail it."[206]

This emphasis on a broader view of History is complemented by the conviction that clashes of civilizations have *always* existed across the centuries. In his *Chronicle of the Clash of Civilizations*, Aymeric Chauprade is adamant about the fact that "even if history is not reduced to the clash of civilizations, the clash of civilizations is at the heart of history." In fact, "the theme of the clash of civilizations is very ancient" and has in fact "haunt[ed] Europe since the beginning of times."[207] Likewise, in an issue covering "the clash of civilizations throughout history," the *Nouvelle Revue d'Histoire* asserts that "there have always been civilizational conflicts, both frontal, visible, evident and others less so." Furthermore, these conflicts "may reveal [themselves] to be salutary if the organism is in good health," but "on the contrary they are mortal for an organism that is weak or dilapidated,"[208] unable to give rise to an Identitarian awakening. The mounting of an "Identitarian awakening" against the clash of civilizations has always been at the center of *Terre et Peuple*. The first issue of its magazine was dedicated precisely to "the clash of civilizations: today in France?" Here, too, the theme is viewed through the lens of its long duration, because, as Vial asserted, "the clash of civilizations is a reality as old as human societies.... When Cato the Elder repeatedly said in the Roman Senate that 'Delenda Cartago est' ['Carthage must be destroyed'], he displayed an awareness of the clash of civilizations between an Indo-European Rome and a Punic, which means Semitic, Carthage." Or, "when the Spanish and the Portuguese of the Middle Ages engaged in the Reconquista against the Muslim invaders, they drew the conclusion of a clash of civilizations, refusing to submit to a Law that contradicted their cultural heritage."[209]

If the historical reality of civilizations and its clashes is well-recognized in Identitarian narratives this is not, however, interpreted as support for what they see as the "America-driven" clash of civilizations politics—in the wake of Samuel Huntington's re-actualization in the 1990s of the concept and its posterior "confirmation" in the Islamist attacks at the dawn of the new century. This vision only serves to implement and justify Western imperialism over all the world. For one, a distinction is made between the America-centric West and European civilization. "The interest of their civilization—Europe, and not the American West—should push Europeans to think about the three great challenges they face: the violent awakening of Islam, the American globalist utopia, and the desire for revenge of Asia," avows Chauprade.[210] The totalitarian West as the "new Omega of Humanity,"[211] in the words of Alain Cagnat, is fundamentally different from, and constitutes the nemesis of, the "Europe of carnal homelands" that Vial foretold.[212] "If, once upon a time, Europe was confused with the West, today Europe has returned," says Fabrice Robert. "Europe is not an 'idea' but a carnal reality that refers to history, peoples, a cultural and religious heritage and also specific popular traditions."[213] "The European empire that we want to build is not the West," asserts *Réfléchir & Agir* in an editorial titled "Clash of Civilizations: Watch Out with the Words." In it, Identitarians are warned about the dangers of overusing the expression in an anti-Islamic manner, because it ultimately implies an adherence to US-driven geopolitics. Therefore, the editorial stated, "the clash of civilizations is, indeed, a reality. On one side the forces of chaos of capitalism, on the other side the peoples of the world who refuse the domination of the market. The only enemy is capitalism!"[214] It is in this sense that the French publisher and writer Philippe Randa sees the clash of civilizations as a "good theory to fuel a jingoist foreign policy," because al-Qaeda and Daesh are nothing but "modern Golems," or "creatures that have escaped their creators."[215] The journalist Manuel Ochsenreiter sees a wider mechanism at work with the operationalization of the clash of civilizations. "The general problem with the 'clash of civilizations' is that many of those who promote the concept see the Western liberal civilization as the superior role model for the world," he says. "In their eyes all the other civilizations are types of inferior models that will move more and more toward the Western liberal civilization model." The consequences, therefore, are well known: "This 'moving' includes 'helpful measures' by the West: the work of NGOs, open markets, LGBT propaganda—and if this all doesn't work well enough, even wars. And there we have the 'clash' of civilizations."[216]

Nevertheless, even with its supposed appropriation by an imperialist West, many Identitarians do not wholly discard Huntington's theory. According to Bloc Identitaire's president, "To limit the expression 'clash of civilizations' to an imperialist manifesto of American neoconservatives—to justify their interventionist policies—would be a grave mistake."[217] Obviously, Huntington's attention to long-term historical-civilizational dynamics and the importance he has given to particular and rooted realities—not to mention the increasing role of cultural, ethnic, and religious issues and conflicts, which collide with the dominant ideology of the triumph of liberal capitalism and the alleged universalism of Western values (as a "world civilization")—could be viewed only favorably by Identitarians. "[Huntington's] essay does not have the breadth (not even close), or the style, of the writings of [Oswald] Spengler, [and] we are dealing here with another level of thought," declares the *Nouvelle Revue d'Histoire*. "Nevertheless," the editorialist included as a caveat, "it must be recognized that the author [displays] original and vigorous intuitions—especially coming from an American." As expected, the American political scientist is criticized for joining Europe with the West, ignoring "what distinguishes, historically and spiritually, Europe from the United States."[218] Writing in the magazine *Terre et Peuple*, Alain Cagnat recognized Huntington's merit in undermining the postulate that only a common "human civilization" existed, saying that "the 20 years that passed since the publication of his book show that History instead gave him reason." Nevertheless, the great "weakness" of the book remains Huntington's omission of the "gangrene" of immigration and its corollary clash of civilization *within* Europe, probably because of his "America-centrism" and the fact that "multiculturalism impregnates the United States to its core."[219] Jean-David Cattin of the (at the time) Bloc Identitaire praised Huntington's thesis as a whole, particularly his insight that Identitarian questions will only increase in importance. "This is not to rejoice or to despair," Cattin writes, "it is simply about not denying it. It is up to the ideologues, especially those on the left, to deny the real."[220] In his enthusiastic review of Huntington's book, IBÖ's Patrick Lenart wrote: "It provides a great framework for understanding current developments in Europe, Islam and geopolitics. A required reading!"[221]

Will the real enemy please stand up? The priority given to or the secundarization of the narrative of the "clash of civilizations" is directly proportional to what Identitarian groups see as the biggest danger in the ranking of threats to European civilization. In the wake of the German philosopher Carl Schmitt, Guillaume Faye makes a distinction between adversaries and enemies. "America is our principal adversary, not our *principal enemy* (italics in original). The latter is the mass of alien colonizers, the collaborators (foreign states and fifth columnists), and Islam," he postulated in *Why We Fight*. "The enemy," he wrote years later, "is the one who threatens you and wants your loss, your death, short or long term, even if he does not confess it; the adversary only wants to weaken you and win the game."[222] CasaPound, on the contrary, is closer to the

Nouvelle Droite and the analysis of de Benoist, for whom the "clash of civilizations" plays the "classic role of a diversion in relation to class conflicts."[223] CasaPound, as Scianca states, "does not adhere to this conceptual scheme and believes that it is a trap to divert to the wrong tracks the well-grounded Identitarian frustration of European peoples."[224] Identitarians, therefore, according to this view, should not lose sight of the target, which is the liberal capitalist plutocracy, in order to avert the risk of ending up fighting on the wrong side, aligned with the "real enemies" of Europe, in the name of a lure called the clash of civilizations. If there is an obvious problem with mass immigration, its root cause, following this train of thought, is the America-centric Western system of domination. "It is up to the peoples of Europe," writes Eugène Krampon, "who must now unite to literally besiege the liberal order, provoke a political rupture, and support a desperate struggle against the only enemy: globalism!"[225] The nemesis, therefore, is what Tomislav Sunić calls "Homo Americanus and his system," a subspecies that is no longer confined to the United States of America. Today they thrive in all corners of the globe."[226] As Dominique Venner stated, "We do not confuse the 'Western-American system' with individual Americans, who are often its victims."[227] This is also related to the view that the triumph of the American materialistic system was the triumph of a "particular" dimension of America—Yankee, mercantilist, and northerner—fundamentally distinct from the Old South. In *The White Sun of the Vanquished*, the history of "the Southern epic and the War of Secession," originally published in 1975 and reissued forty years later with a preface by de Benoist, Venner wrote about what he saw not as "civil war" but as a conflict between two distinct nations: an imperialistic "democratic" war of conquest launched by the North against a demonized South, subsequently occupied and vitiated. Later he established a parallel with Europe: "If one of my first books was dedicated to the history of Southerners, it is because I intuitively felt the 'Old South's' defeat as the first act of what was done to us in the second half of the twentieth century."[228] This view of a "good" America that, although historically defeated, lives on spiritually, if only in a diffuse manner, also reverberates in Sunić's statement, in an interview with *Réfléchir & Agir*: "Regarding America's famed heartland, including the antebellum South, which still persists in some parts, and which I like much—that's something else, and has nothing to do with today's Americanism."[229] Remembering the anti-American turn of the Nouvelle Droite, which occurred in the mid-1970s, Jean-Claude Valla said that, at the time, a significant number of individuals were against it because of their belief in the American "Southern spirit" that was invoked by Maurice Bardèche."[230] After all, it was Bardèche—a French writer and art critic who declared himself a "Fascist" after World War II and the execution of his brother-in-law Robert Brasillach—who designated, using the name of Southerners, "anyone, at any time, who felt a profound contradiction between the way of life and purpose that an ideology intended to impose upon them *and* their temperament, their instinct, their commitment to a certain way of being that they deem consistent with the nature of things." They are the "'white guards' that do not capitulate to the sense of history, that do not believe in a sense of history."[231] The Rebel South, therefore, is a perennial symbol both of resistance and of attachment to a rooted, organic way of life.

In the end, according to Identitarians as a group, what matters is that, at this historical moment, the stakes have never been so high for Europe's civilization. Not since, according to Faye, the wars of the Greeks against the Persians and the Romans against Carthage.[232] Even though Europe's forefathers emerged as the victors of those clashes, nothing guarantees, today, the same result. Not even the supposed "eternity" of civilizations serves as a consolation, because the widespread feeling is that European civilization may *indeed* collapse under the weight of the multilayered forces arrayed against it. At an Identitarian convention, the spokesman for the French Generation Identity rendered into words this sense of a turning point: "Globalism will kill identity, or identity will kill globalism." This is because, in the struggle against the global system of death, "There is no other possible outcome."[233]

THREE

Identity against Islam

Perhaps the interpretation of the Qur'an would now be taught in the schools of Oxford, and her pulpits might demonstrate to a circumcised people the sanctity and truth of the revelation of Mahomet. From such calamities was Christendom delivered by the genius and fortune of one man.
—Edward Gibbon, *History of the Decline and Fall of the Roman Empire*

THE "'DESPICABLE WEAKNESS'"

The tone was somber. "In the year of 1995, three days before Midsummer Day, was inaugurated in Rome the most imposing mosque ever built in Europe," wrote Dominique Venner the following year in an editorial for an issue of *Enquête sur l'Histoire* covering the perennial conflict between Europe and Islam. The symbolism could not be greater. "After Brussels, Lyon, and Madrid, the city of Caesars and popes, the *Urbs*, the spiritual center of pagan and Christian Europe, sees itself imposing a minaret whose significance is obvious," noted the French historian, who added that "the event was hailed in all intellectual, religious and political milieus." Because of his certainty that "a people condemns itself to die (if it is not already dead) when it does not throw itself at the throat of the foreigner who, in provocation, taunts his gods in their own sanctuaries," Venner believed that the episode, more than being about the reach of Islam into Europe, revealed the pitiful state of Europe itself and provided a chance to reflect upon what is fundamentally wrong with it.[1] The consent to and tolerance of the building of mosques was yet another flagrant example of what the British writer Michael Walker—who was one of the early advocates within the anglosphere of ND ideas, especially in his publication *Scorpion*, and who has reemerged in the 2010s as a contributor to the webzine CounterCurrents—calls Europe's "despicable weakness" in dealing with Islam domestically, which contrasts with all sorts of prohibitions endured by Christians in Muslim countries. "The failure to draw a clear line for Muslims living in non-Muslim countries is not respected at all," he said, further noting that "it is embarrassing and despicable in the eyes of most Muslims." What is more, "I strongly believe that a demand, for example, for the rights of Christians to build churches in Saudi Arabia would [paradoxically] earn Europeans respect."[2] The widespread Identitarian belief, however, is that the postcolonial fall of Europe into pathological self-flagellation hinders any sort of assertion of self-belief or demand for "respect," something particularly evident in the most recent decades in the European confrontation *within its own borders* with a vigorous, self-assured, supremacist, and entrenched Islamic civilization.

When Venner wrote his editorial, what is now known as the ideology of counter-jihadism was still nonexistent. It was only after the turn of the century and the Islamic terrorist attacks in Western countries that a broader, transatlantic counter-jihadist movement—constituted of Internet activists, pressure groups, and some political parties—developed. What defines counter-jihadism is not simply the denunciation of Islamic terrorism on European, North American, or even Australasian soil. Nor is it characterized mainly by the rejection of practices that may well collide with the pluralism of a civil society or with entrenched traditions such as the separation of church and state, freedom of speech, and gender equality. Counter-jihadism, instead, is defined by its apocalypticism.

Islam is viewed by counter-jihadists not as a religion but as a worldview that constitutes an *existential threat* to Western civilization. Therefore, *all Muslims*, because they adhere to this worldview, together constitute a potential threat, especially when they are *already* living within Western boundaries.[3]

This is the prologue to any counter-jihadist script. Their combat, crucially, is waged in the name of Western liberalism, which of course is at odds with Identitarian anti-globalism, which is often associated with a malicious ideology of Western origin that destroys cultures, nations, and identities the world over. If by and large Identitarians adhere to the counter-jihadist diagnosis of the dangers of "green totalitarianism" (green is the color traditionally associated with Islam), they stay clear of its solutions while waging the battle *for* Europe and its authentic identity. A contributor to the Counter-Currents website called counter-jihad the "false friend" of Identitarians and nationalists because it fights Islam in the name of a "system of abstract values (personal freedom, free markets, tolerance, yada, yada)," the supposed "pillars of our civilization."[4]

Identitarians, therefore, should know better than to sleep with the enemy and let themselves be confused with a purely liberal anti-Islam movement. Venner, too, was conscious of the danger, especially because counter-jihadism propels and is propelled by what he calls the "universalist belief" that lies at the heart of the West and that "denies and destroys other cultures and civilizations, specifically those that threaten the universalist values said to be 'Western,' which in reality exist simply for the benefit of globalizing markets and 'democracy,' summed up in the triptych: *fun, sex, and money*."[5] This belief "rallies against it the revolt by peoples—including those from Islamic countries—who rightfully refuse it."[6] Such carefulness, however, has not prevented the occasional joining of forces against the common enemy. The margins between Identitarians and counter-jihadists are not clear-cut in the sense that—and this is particularly visible within the younger Francophone and Germanophone activism—there have been collaborations and networking, online and offline, in the mobilization against the presence and perceived ravages of Islam in Europe.

What is true is that the questions "What is wrong with Europe?" and "Who or what is fundamentally to blame for it?" run throughout the Identitarian camp, and the answers to them help to establish the precedence given, or not, to the combat against Islam. In one of his books Renaud Camus amusingly recalls a cartoon depicting a McDonald's restaurant selling halal meat, with the caption "No to the Islamization of our Americanization!"[7] Jeans, that all-American creation, have also served as a metaphoric weapon of combat in the debate. True to his vision that Western civilization *is* the "most decadent of all civilizations," Alain de Benoist has noted, "Symbol for symbol, I think we should rather exclude those who wear jeans [instead of the women who wear the Islamic veil]."[8] In contrast, Guillaume Faye proclaimed that even though "cultural Americanization is indeed detestable," one "can always get rid of McDonalds more readily than a mosque, or abolish jeans with greater ease than a *chador*."[9] De Benoist's "Islamophilia" is often commented on by Identitarians such as Faye, who has observed, for example, that against the Western ideology "certain unseeing philosophers (on the intellectual Right) imagine that a 'spiritual' alliance with Islam is desirable. That would be like falling between Charybdis and Scylla [the two monsters of Greek mythology, reflecting the adage 'being caught between a rock and a hard place']."[10] The editorial line of *Réfléchir & Agir* is immovable about the fact that Europe is indeed "caught" between "two globalisms," Islamism and Westernism, and if the first "threatens our European vision of the world," the other's "cosmopolitan, feminist, and metrosexual values are hardly suitable to us."[11] Regardless, from the Nouvelle Droite to the vast Identitarian camp, the conviction is that the root cause of the rise of Islam in Europe—whether targeted hyperbolically (according to de Benoist) or not—is immigration. Writing in *Terre et Peuple*, Robert Dragan presents this view as a matter of fact: "In Europe, Islam is present only because the globalist governments have forcibly imported millions of immigrants for 40 years."[12] As Damien Rieu stated at a meeting of Generation Identity, "We do not forget that at the beginning there was immigration. Without massive immigration there wouldn't be massive Islamization."[13] Islamization is the nasty tip of the iceberg. "Integration or assimilation failed completely and so this process leads to a Great Replacement of the European peoples," notes the head of Austria's Generation Identity, Martin Sellner. "Islamization is a 'side-effect' of this process, making it quicker, deadlier, more aggressive and more visible."[14] What differs among European Identitarians is the *primacy* given to the specter of a Muslim Europe, as well as the *intensity* of the fight specifically against Islamization.

FROM TIME IMMEMORIAL

A Religion Like No Other

A sympathetic writer wrote that counter-jihadists, "like modern day Jeremiahs," are "unloved for issuing a warning of what could eventuate by acquiescing to the demands of the virtual Caliphate."[15] The depiction of counter-jihadists as "modern day Jeremiahs" could also account for a number of anti-Islamic thinkers whose narratives and prophetic warnings circulate widely in Identitarian circles. The French former journalist René Marchand—praised by the Identitarian news agency Novopress as "one of the last great experts about Islam"[16]—shines especially brightly in the anti-Islamic pantheon. As Marchand makes clear in the foreword of his book *Reconquista or the Death of Europe*, the premise of any understanding of the current relationship between Europe and Islam is that this is an existential civilizational struggle with roots stretching deep into the past, across centuries. And so

> [i]n less than fifty years, Europeans have let settle by the millions, within their territory, nationals of a foreigner community against which they have been at war since its formation for centuries. A community whose religion, ideology, law, customs and practices . . . make it a sacred duty to its members to fight [Europeans] and destroy their religion and civilization. These enemies have not come [today], as [they have] often in the past, with weapons in hand, but most of all, following the appeal of Europeans themselves, and then with their tolerance. . . . Europe—European civilization—must now look its death in the face.[17]

Europeans should never forget that "Islam" means "submission" and that Islamic scholarship divides the world into Dar al-Islam (the House of

Islam) and Dar al-Harb (the House of War), where Europe belongs, as a place of ignorance, unbelief, and darkness—a *Jâhiliyya* (ignorant) society (as was pre-Islamic Arabia)—because it has not submitted (yet) to Allah. As he wrote in a text titled "The Europeans, Their Enemies" in Venner's *La Nouvelle Revue d'Histoire*, Marchand has little doubt that Europeans play the role of "perpetual enemy" in the eyes of Islam, as the "hereditary enemy of Islam *sub specie aeternitatis*."[18]

Guillaume Faye has written extensively, particularly since the turn of the century, about the Islamization of Europe, its ongoing transformation into a *Dar al-Islam*. Widely heard and read, particularly among Identitarians but also beyond the Identitarian movement, Faye is unyielding in his denunciation of the primordial intentions of "millenarian Islam" regarding the European civilization with which it has been locked in conflict since the eighth century. Unlike Europe's "amnesic population," who disregard the historical forces and especially conflicts that have shaped it, Muslims are an expression of "long-living peoples" that "never forget their past and possess tenacious memories. . . . [They] haven't lost the memory of their *Qur'an* and from this comes their force."[19] Jean-Yves Le Gallou, in his defense of the right to a civilizational preference ("European and Christian") for Europeans, wrote: "Islam is a civilization that has opposed our [civilization] since the Hijri [the Islamic calendar]," wrote. While writing against the surge of mosques in French and European landscapes, Le Gallou ends up touching on an issue that is vital in all anti-Islamic narratives: "Islam is not only a religion, regulating the relations of man and the sacred, but also, and especially, a civilization contrary to ours, which has continued to oppose it for thirteen centuries."[20]

Here is the overriding idea: The "Islam as a religion" mantra is a fiction. Islam is not just a faith, but a social and political doctrine, a full worldview, and hence a totalitarianism seeking to provide a totalizing narrative and total framework for human life without regard to national borders and ethnocultural distinctions. With this in mind, Marchand believes that "the greatest success of the Muslim conquerors is to have planted the idea that Islam was a religion, and that it was only a religion among others." Behind "the smoke and mirrors of Islam-as-religion is Islam in its entirety: a controlling, expansionist, warrior totalitarianism, killer of civilizations. The trap is fatal in the long term. It has functioned perfectly until now."[21] Faye similarly asks, "Is Islam a religion like the others?" before answering, "No, it is a *political-religious totalitarian doctrine with a superstitious dimension.*" Its power derives from its brutal dogmatism and simplicity: "Barring a few exceptions in the variations of Islam, like Sufism, which is not very representative, the Muslim is totally subjected to its dogma, simple and clear: Salvation, that is to say, the Paradise of Allah, will be obtained only if we do jihad ('struggle for God'), each in his own way and according to his capabilities, but, if possible, by the sacrifice of the martyr-murderer."[22]

Bound up with the falsehood of the exclusively religious character of Islam is the rejection of any sort of "moderation" attached to it or the existence of a mild and restrained Islam in opposition to "Islamism." This latter, more radical Islam is often portrayed in the West as a "deviation" from the "true and peaceful" Islam and identified with Salafism or Wahhabism. Writing in *Terre et Peuple* and using the work of the Arab expert Hamid Zanaz, a former professor of philosophy at the University of Algiers, as a source (who therefore "cannot be seen as suspect"), Alain Cagnat notes that "all Muslims that live on our continent wish an Islamized Europe." He quotes Zanaz's view that "the majority of Muslims are, in fact, Islamists, but gradualists, that is to say, [they] intend to achieve the same goal: to install Sharia law in two or three generations, through preaching, school, psychological pressure, the veil, democratism. . . . The difference is that Islamist activists are in a hurry." In the end, Cagnat reaffirms his belief that "the notion of Islamism [as a movement distinct from the more "tolerant" remainder of Islam] is an invention of Westerners who are afraid to call a spade a spade."[23] In his battle against political correctness as the twenty-first-century version of Newspeak, Polémia's Michel Geoffroy says that "Islamism" is a "concept used to present Islam as a soothing form that is distinguished from" extremism. Just an anesthetic used to numb people to the reality."[24] "Only the ignorant believe that there is a difference of nature between Islamism and Islam," Faye writes in *Understanding Islam*. "It is simply a matter of degree, phase, strategy of the place and time in the battle of conquest, the Jihad, which can take all forms. Islam is a bloc." Using the old fairy tale of Little Red Riding Hood and the Big Bad Wolf as an analogy, Faye adds, "Moderate or secular Islam, or [Islam] 'corrected by an updating,' is an impossibility and corresponds to a naive western sheep-like fantasy that falls into the trap, like the Little Red Riding Hood [trapped] by the wolf disguised as nice."[25]

The Historical "Other"

The absolute "otherness" of Islam to European civilization is at the center of all of these anti-Islamic narratives. Early medieval confrontations with Islam serve as a focal point to assert this narrative of distinctiveness. The culture of knighthood and chivalry, the epic poems of heroic deeds as well as courtly love, troubadours, and the relationship with femininity, expressed in art, iconography, and literature, are all part of what Venner calls manifestations of the "European spirit"—deeply rooted in Greco-Roman antiquity—that are at the antipodes of a dogmatic and repressive Islam. When he writes that "together with the figure of the knight, the idea of love differentiates the spirit of the Europeans,"[26] Venner reaffirms this view of a fundamental apartness that defines the histories of both civilizations. "When have we seen, in history or in Muslim fiction, a couple like Hector and Andromache, Ulysses and Penelope?" wondered Marchand, adding that "the couple does not exist in Islam: a woman is the mother of the children or the object of the sexual pleasure of the male."[27] The romantic ideal—immortalized by the lady and the knight, which has roots stretching all the way back to the ancient Greek poet Homer and to the Roman poet Ovid's *Ars Amatoria*—is a full-blown European affair. Europe is "the civilization that honors the woman: goddess, mother, or warrior," claims the video of the Iliad Institute that tells the viewer what European civilization is all about.[28]

To those who argue that in the Middle Ages Islam set foot in Europe and that *there was* an Islamic Spain—making the argument of the otherness of Islam more ambiguous—anti-Islamic thinkers view this episode as yet another confirmation that Islam's place is not in Europe, focusing on the subjugation that all sort of minorities suffered at the hands of their Muslim masters. The denunciation of the myth of al-Andaluz as a multicultural haven of tolerance—a vision often found in contemporary political and media storylines—is pervasive. Above all, this idea not only ignores the violent conquest of Visigoth Spain but, more importantly, passes over the status of inferiority of the non-Muslims. The conquered "People of the Book" (such as Christians and Jews) were subjected to the *dhimma*, a treaty of protection that established the superiority of Islam and the religious, political, legal, and economic submission of the infidel. As told by Philippe Conrad, writing in a special issue of *La Nouvelle Revue d'Histoire* addressing the theme of "being a minority in the land of Islam," the *dhimmi* were obliged to pay a poll tax (the *jizya*) in order to remain nominally free and were subjected to all sorts of discriminatory rules, such as, for example, prohibition from building places of worship, exclusion from public offices, a requirement to possess houses lower in height than those of Muslims, the need to wear specific clothing to distinguish them as non-Muslims, and prohibition from riding horses or camels (noble animals)—with *dhimmi* limited to riding donkeys—in what amounted to "an adoption of a general attitude of servitude."[29] At the same time, the "tolerance"—which also at times included pogroms against Jewish communities, the martyrdom of Christians (like the ninth-century priest Eulogius and his companions in Cordoba), and kidnappings of Christian women in order to make up for the lack of Muslim women—ended in the first half of the twelfth century with the arrival of the Moorish dynasties of the Almoravids and Almohads and the subsequent forced conversion and deportation to Africa of the Mozarabs (Iberian Christians) and Jews. Arnaud Imatz, also writing in *La Nouvelle Revue d'Histoire* and using as a source the work of the Spanish medievalist Serafín Fanjul, a fierce critic of the current mass media–driven "idealized interpretation of seven centuries of Muslim presence in the Iberian Peninsula"[30]—says that the promotion of al-Andaluz as an example of tolerance is nothing but a gross manipulation of history aimed at justifying the ideology of multiculturalism. At the same time, Faye argues, the much-vaunted intellectual and scientific contribution of al-Andaluz is in large part indebted to "converted Christians and Jews who have changed their names."[31]

For these critics, the persecution and dhimmitude of non-Muslims in Islamic Spain is not the only reality that has been hidden by the dominant ideology. Additionally, the slave raids on Europe by North African pirates between the sixteenth and eighteenth centuries—in which

Muslims abducted, by some estimates, close to a million southern but also northern Europeans—is underresearched and minimized because, in the eyes of Identitarians, it does not fit the contemporary official script of "evil" Europe. For them this is nothing but yet another bit of evidence of the historical war of Muslims against Europeans.[32] At the same time, the occupation of the Balkans by the Ottoman Empire (in the fourteenth century and lasting for five centuries) is viewed similarly to the occupation of Spain, as a period of the imposition of submission and dhimmitude on non-Muslims—of which the conscription (*devchirme*, or "gathering") and conversion of Christian boys taken from their families to form a special militia, the Janissaries, at the service of the empire, remains a powerful symbol—and was a far cry from any sort of "model of coexistence" between different religions and cultures, often expressed in terms of a "multicultural" Ottoman Sarajevo.[33]

The condemnation of Islamic Spain is countered with the exaltation of their destruction through the *Reconquista* (literally, "the Reconquest"). Its personalities, symbolic places, and significant episodes and battles are at the very center of anti-Islamic narratives and constitute perennial sources of inspiration. Although it only gained full steam in the twelfth and thirteenth centuries (and lasted until the final expulsion of the Moors from Granada in 1492), the first phase of the *Reconquista* in the Cantabrian mountains, with the victory of the Visigoth nobleman Pelagius soon after the Muslim invasion of the peninsula at the Battle of Covadonga in the heart of the Asturias region, is widely revered as a foundational moment of Identitarian resistance to the Islamic Other. And so is, from a much later phase of the Christian conquest of Muslim Iberia, the Battle of Navas de Tolosa, in which, in 1212, a decisive blow was struck against the Muslim (Almohad) forces by a united army of Iberian kingdoms with the help of French forces, which, according to Pierre Vial, "answered the appeal of the Papal bull of Innocent III, a sign that the Reconquista was a crusade, in the same way as that of the East."[34]

In the treatise *The Loyal Counselor*, the fifteenth-century Portuguese King Duarte wrote: "The war against the Moors, let us agree that it is well to wage, because the Holy Church so determines it," adding, "and it should be waged without weakness of the heart, unduly tormented with scruples."[35] More than five centuries later, many European Identitarians have no doubt that in order to counter the Muslim threat, such "weakness of the heart"—which they see rampant in the halls of power—is suicidal and imperils the future of the continent. Therefore, *Reconquista*, more than a mere description of a historical episode, has become a rallying cry for twenty-first-century Europeans amid the "new" Muslim invasion. In tune with the importance given to the "long memory" of peoples, Terre et Peuple's belief system is anchored on the premise that Europeans are living through a new phase of a long war. Today's context is regularly linked with historical clashes between Europe and Islam, with a special role given to the medieval Crusades and the *Reconquista*. As Vial wrote: "Crusade, resistance, and *Reconquista*, words that had a strong meaning, for many centuries, to Europeans. And that today find again a heavy significance. Today more than ever, more tragically than ever."[36] No wonder, then, that one of the group's annual roundtables was dedicated to the theme of "Reconquista: Yesterday, Today, Tomorrow."

FIGURE 21. Cover of *Terre et Peuple* magazine with the title "Crusade, Resistance, Reconquest" (Autumn 2005).

Remember Martel

"The Arabs never resumed the conquest of Gaul, and they were soon driven beyond the Pyrenees by Charles Martel and his valiant race," wrote the English historian Edward Gibbon about the "defeat of the Saracens" in AD 732.[37] In fact, the Battle of Poitiers of that year, also known as the Battle of Tours—in which the Frankish army led by Charles Martel halted the advance of Islam in Europe on the plains of Moussais, between Poitiers and Tours—is at the center stage of all Identitarian narratives about the return of an ancient enemy of European civilization and lends itself to various comparisons, analogies, and interplays between past and present and their shared dangers. De Benoist's *éléments* may argue that the Battle of Toulouse (in 721)—in which the Aquitanian army of Duke Odo defeated the army of the governor of Al-Andalus, which was besieging the French city—was *the* battle that "brought the most serious setback to the Muslim conquest of Gaul."[38] Regardless, it is impossible to dethrone Poitiers (and Martel) from the collective imaginary of Identitarians across Europe. And knowing that the crypt of Charles Martel lies in the Gothic Basilica of Saint-Denis, in a heavily immigrant, and Islamic, northern suburban part of Paris that is widely viewed by Identitarians as a symbol of what is wrong with France and Europe, adds an ironic twist to the circumstance. Nor is the symbolism of Martel lost in Michel Houellebecq's novel *Submission*, a romanticized account of France's slow descent into Dar al-Islam, whose protagonist and narrator sought temporary refuge amid the turmoil in the small medieval village of Martel, which, legend has it, was the place where the defeated emir of the Battle of Poitiers died at the hands of the Frank warriors. In any case, the Battle of Poitiers—which the Arabs have called "The Battle of the Court of Martyrs"—is etched in the Identitarian vision as an eternal testament of the clash of two separate civilizations. "Charles Martel, a hero for our time," reads the title of an article in *Réfléchir & Agir* by Pierre Gillieth, quoting the French romantic writer Chateaubriand, who said, "Without the bravery of Charles Martel, we would wear the turban today."[39] Martel is in every listing of the heroic figures and deeds of the European past in its civilizational struggles.

"Europe is the heroes who defended it over the centuries. It is Leonidas and his 300 Spartans saving Greece from Asia. It is [the Roman General] Scipio, the African preserving Rome from Carthage. It was Charles Martel pushing back the Arab invasion," pronounces the Iliad Institute video.[40] Marchand laments that for now, "One has not seen rising any [politician such as the great Athenian] Themistocles, any Charles Martel or [Byzantine emperor] Leo III, the Isaurian, committed to blocking the invasion and able to gather and energize men and means for a liberating counterattack."[41]

Naturally the Battle of Poitiers has a place of honor in Terre et Peuple's epic narrative of European anti-Islam clashes. One of its roundtables, for example, was named "For the Reconquest, Come Back Charles Martel!" In 2015 its founder spoke at the first in a series of meetings—Charles Martel near Poitiers, which was organized by a local Identitarian association and was attended by a delegation of Génération Identitaire who, as "sons of Charles Martel," vowed to "sacrifice their youth," and "reconquer our land from the biggest threat that our multimillennial civilization has ever faced."[42] For his part, Vial assigned the Battle of Poitiers a "fundamental place in our long memory," declaring that what is needed today is a "Battle of Poitiers at great scale," which will have to exclude compromises and petty political calculations.[43] In a summary of the event, the magazine noted: "Today Charles Martel is removed from curricula [because] what is important, in fact, is not to let settle in the minds of young Gauls bad ideas, such as the need to fight and drive out the invaders if we want to safeguard our identity and remain masters in our country."[44] The "appropriation" of the symbolism of Poitiers and Martel is not, of course, exclusive to Identitarians. A counter-jihad calendar, for example, circulates in the counter-jihad blogosphere, showing as days of celebration October 7, which is "Victory on the Seas Day" (commemorating the Battle of Lepanto, or the defeat of the Ottoman fleet by Christian forces); October 10, as "Charles Martel Day (Battle of Tours)"; and October 18, as "Eurabia Day," in honor of a speech given by Bat Ye'or—the pen name of the Egypt-born British essayist responsible for the prominence of the overriding concept of "Eurabia" (as well as of dhimmitude) in counter-jihadist circles—at a counter-jihad summit.[45]

There seems to be no doubt among Identitarians that Europe is once again a battlefield. "Islam has been trying to invade Europe for 1,300 years. On two previous occasions it failed, but it keeps returning obstinately to the assault and is never discouraged," Faye declares.[46] What this means is that the need to heed the warning call of History is widespread. It is urgent to extract lessons from the past and apply them to the present. Philippe de Villiers, a prominent anti-Islam French politician who has become a reference in the Identitarian camp—and who believes that "we have imported to our territory, to the very heart of our nation, another nation, the Muslim nation, the *umma*"—touched on this urgency to regain a historical outlook when he said, in an interview with the former spokesman of Generation Identity, Damien Rieu, in the webzine *France*: "To have had Islam implanted at home has been a serious mistake that we owe to the ignorance, negligence, incompetence, and the stupidity of all our cultural and spiritual authorities. If we know the history of Christendom and Islam we know that in the places where Islam established itself, the Reconquista took six centuries."[47] Alain Cagnat reminds us, "Spain didn't liberate itself but in 1492, and Europe had to fight against the Ottoman Empire until the nineteenth century," before making this appeal: "May we remember this at a time when the traitors who govern us let enter again the City more Islamo-alien multitudes!"[48] In the early seventeenth century, the expulsion by the Habsburg king Philip III of 300,000 Mouriscos, the Muslim population of Iberia, due to fears of sedition and for reasons of religious homogeneity, leads Philippe Conrad to comment: "We can draw from this episode a general lesson." This deportation significantly "demonstrates the impossibility of assimilating a large human group, rooted in its own culture, supported by a perennial religious belief. When this culture and religion appear too distant from the context into which we attempt to 'integrate' them— what the kings of Spain tried to do—we reach a crisis situation that will inevitably worsen."[49] The message regarding the present-day situation of France and Europe is unmistakable. So is the thrust of Conrad's words in introducing the special "Being a Minority in the Land of Islam" issue of *La Nouvelle Revue d'Histoire*, about the status of non-Muslims, the *dhimmi*, in the land of Islam: "By proposing this special issue . . . we thought mainly about the threatened Eastern Christians. But Europeans would be wrong to think that the current tragedy will remain restricted to this geographical area. More than ever, the use of history should contribute to [raising] the necessary awareness."[50] Such "awareness" for sure, infuses the activism of the younger generations of French and European Identitarians.

GENERATION "ISLAM OUT OF EUROPE": GALLIC STRATEGIES

Together with their video "declaration of war" against the system, the early morning of October 20, 2012, witnessed the other founding act of Génération Identitaire. On that day, about eighty activists climbed to the roof of the construction site of the future Grand Mosque of Poitiers and unfurled their Identitarian banner reading "732 Generation Identity." The reference, of course, was to the year that Charles Martel defeated the Moors. While the building was still occupied they released a press statement that made the connection clear: "It will soon be 1,300 years since Charles Martel stopped the Arabs at Poitiers following a heroic battle that saved our country from Muslim invasion. Today, we have reached 2012 and the choice is still the same: live free or die." They further demanded a national referendum on immigration and Islamization, ending their declaration with the exhortation to "let all Europe hear our call: here and now, RECONQUEST!"[51] The occupation succeeded in getting media attention, and many public condemnations followed—even prosecution by the French authorities, spurring solidarity campaigns with the militants against what the magazine *Identitaires* called "judicial harassment."[52] In an open letter to the prime minister, Génération Identitaire said, "'Incitement to racial hatred' for having chanted, among other slogans, 'Charles Martel!' Is this your republic?" they asked.[53] For all that, the Identitarians took great pride in what they saw as a powerful publicity coup with a greater impact on people's minds than yet another tired street protest. Five years later, speaking in court during the trial of five of its activists, Arnaud Delrieux, the group's president, said that the court had the "responsibility to reaffirm that it was still possible in France to freely oppose mass immigration, and that it has not become a forbidden debate." The Poitiers court "failed" the putative test, and the Identitarian activists were given a suspended one-year jail sentence and a heavy fine.[54] In all, the occupation of the Poitiers mosque certainly fits the description offered by Filip Dewinter—a longtime notable of Vlaams Belang (Flemish Interest), widely praised in the Identitarian camp as a like-minded political force—of Generation Identity as the "Greenpeace of radical movements" because of their "actions, always very well prepared and altogether spectacular."[55] Most of all, to the question posed by René Marchand of whether "facing the Muslim pride of belonging that challenges them . . . Europeans [will] claim a pride of European belonging?," the answer of the French and European branches of Generation Identity—through actions such as the 2012 occupation—has been a loud and confrontational *Yes!*

In fact, the Identitarian network that revolves around the Bloc Identitaire, now known as Les Identitaires—to which Génération Identitaire belongs as the newest expression of its youth wing—has, since its earliest days, developed a full array of "spectacular" strategies. These are heavily promoted afterward on the Internet and often covered by mainstream media in order to stigmatize the Muslim presence and to denounce the "Islamization" of the country. They are in tune with what Fabrice Robert calls the movement's "hallmark" of "permanent action, the agitation of ideas."[56] The pig—the meat of which is contrary to Islamic *halal* dietary laws—has been adopted as a cultural weapon and tied to many of these strategies: "These are funny times . . . times where this little pink animal becomes a symbol of resistance!"[57] One of the first operations was the distribution of "Identitarian soups" (containing pork) to homeless people. As giving this soup in practice excluded Muslims, it was labeled "racist" and banned by the state. "In our own land, in our own capital, giving pork to hungry persons from our own people is forbidden as a so-called 'discrimination,'" the Bloc Identitaire president declared in slamming the government policy prohibiting the soup.[58] This initiative, however, caught on and would be replicated in the wider European Lambda movement. Years later, in the streets of London, activists from Generation Identity UK began handing out warm pork suppers to the homeless—with the Lambda sign on the lids of the soup containers—arguing in their social media, "That the government can find money and sponsor programs for 'refugees' whilst the country has such a high rate of homelessness is a disgrace."[59]

"It is five in the morning when you are gradually awakened by what you thought was an ugly nightmare. . . . But you are not dreaming, it is a call to Muslim prayer that you hear echoing in the street,"[60] writes Philippe Vardon, describing one of the strategies used by Identitarian activists to alert the population to the impending Islamization and to shake them out of their torpor. In the early hours of the day they have imitated the *muezzin* call to prayer to denounce the approval of Islamic centers or mosques by local councils: "Allah Akbar, the companion to breakfast."[61] Or, in order to criticize plans to construct a mosque, militants, under the cover of night, have modified the name of a village (Saint-Martin-le-Vinoux became Saint-Martin-la-Mosquée, for example), as well as the names of its streets ("Sharia Street," "Infidels Street," etc.).[62] The continuous Identitarian offensive against the construction of mosques—a defining trait of their anti-Islamic activism—is in line with the argument that Islam is not "simply" a religion. "Mosques are not mere places of worship but cultural centers, places for strengthening the community, embassies of Islam, and bases for conquest," Génération Identitaire reminds us.[63] Also, in what could be seen as an ironic nod to the "No to the Islamization of our Americanization" motto mentioned by Camus, when a franchise of the fast-food chain Quick decided to turn *halal*, activists wearing pig masks invaded it, uploading on the Internet the video of the operation, which "quickly" went viral, with the motto: "If you don't want pigs, pigs will come to you."[64] "Marches of the Pigs," with protesters in pig masks, were also held to protest *halal* food and Islamization. Identitarians have also been successful in putting before the public eye the issue of Muslim prayers in the streets, in the cities of Paris and Nice, for example, with videos denouncing the blocking of entire streets while calling, together with other groups, for "pork and wine buffets" in those Muslim-dominated neighborhoods—with Facebook used as a tool of mobilization. Although banned by the police due to "public order" concerns, these actions sparked political debate, and open-air calls to prayer were ultimately banned by the French government in 2011. Identitarians hardly miss an opportunity to denounce the "ominous" trends. In Rouen, for example, activists even joined a "Zombie Walk," mingling with participants dressed up in zombie costumes and subsequently unfurling a banner depicting the undead and the caption "Islamization, Immigration, Globalization: We have voted Macron."[65]

A recurring theme of the Identitarian activists has been the protection of European women against the advances of Islam. Because "European women" and "especially the young ones" are the "first victims [through verbal and physical attacks] of the Islamization of our society" (owing to the sexism and gender discrimination that Identitarians and other anti-Islamic groups claim are inherent to Islam), in 2006 the Identitarian Youth launched the campaign "Neither veiled, nor raped! Do not touch my sister!," which involved covering the faces of many female statues all over France with veils. This is felt as one of the issues where the abyss between Europe and Islam is manifest. As explained by the text that launched the campaign, "From ancient deities to the Virgin Mary, through the tradition of courtly love and the women who have marked history (as Catherine de' Medici, Joan of Arc, or the revolutionary Irish women of 1916), women have always been respected and protected in Europe." In the face of rampant Islamization, "because we do not want to see European women veiled tomorrow, because we had enough of collective rapes and physical and verbal aggressions against our young women," the protesters raised the cry "DO NOT TOUCH MY SISTER!" (capital letters in original).[66] Ten years later, in 2016, in the aftermath of the New Year's Eve attacks on women in Germany, mostly by men of North African descent—in which, according to the police, close to 1,200 women were attacked in Cologne and other cities—the slogan resurfaced amid the denunciation of the immigrant hordes and "rapefugees" that do not belong to Europe. "From Cologne to Paris, do not touch my sister. Illegals out!" read the banner held by activists of Generation Identity–Paris in front of the French Ministry of Women's Rights. Young female Identitarian activists made an "appeal to revolt":

> We are the generation that has seen the importation to our streets of the submission of the woman, through the veil, the niqab, the burqa. We are the generation that saw [victims of] the most horrific mass rapes renamed *tournantes* ["pass-arounds," teenage girl victims of gang rape in the suburbs] in order to underestimate them and ignore them. . . . We are the generation of [women] who are afraid

when they go out at night, who hide their shapes not to be harassed, who are insulted or beaten for a phone number refused. . . . We are the European female youth of Cologne, Zürich, Stockholm, Brussels, or Paris, assaulted and raped by illegal immigrants. We decided that fear has to change sides! . . . We do not need your ministry of women's rights, to live our femininity according to our traditions is our right. You [feminists] think to speak in our name? You have usurped our word, your cause is not ours. You say "neither whores nor submissives," we reply "neither veiled nor raped"![67]

In a public address, Anaïs Lignier, a female Generation Identity militant from Montpellier and founder of the collective Never Again Cologne, said, "If European states are not capable of protecting us, then we hand it over to our friends, our husbands, our brothers. We refuse to suffer rapes because our leaders have lost their honor and political courage."[68] Not surprisingly, Generation Identity decided to intensify its self-defense courses, particularly addressed to women, across France.[69] More traditional rallies and demonstrations have also been part of the repertoire of protest of the younger Identitarians. *"On est chez nous!"* (We are at home!) chanted hundreds of Generation Identity militants at a protest in the streets of Paris, together with "Islam out of Europe!" On this occasion, Pierre Larti, the Generation Identity spokesman, addressed the crowd, "You, the defenders of 'This is our home,'" as having the "same spirit 'This is our home' that energized the troops of Charles Martel in Poitiers, or the Christian fleet at Lepanto."[70] Once again, hammering home the rallying idea that his predecessor Damien Rieu once noted, "We are the generation of confrontation with the Islamic Other."[71]

Aware of the truism that language is power, Identitarians praise their own role in putting the issue of "Islamization" at the center of political debate. The urgency to counter Islamization demands, above all, action, not sterile discussions and endless debates. The president of the Identitarian network has always been clear about the path ahead: "In the face of the offensive of the bearded and the undermining job of Islam's useful idiots, we have to act, we have to occupy the territory, to create synergies, to obtain successes."[72] For the Bloc it is a sign of the *success* of their metapolitical strategy that the focus is on the "Islamization" of the country, because "this term is far from being neutral, it reveals the trans-

FIGURE 22. Poster/meme of Génération Identitaire: "Stop Islamization—We Are at Home!"

formation of our society by Islam."[73] After all, this conviction is at the heart of Identitarians' "clash of civilizations" narrative; it is not a fear of what could happen, but a reality that is already happening *within* European civilization. Together with the "appropriation" of language and the attempt to set up the terms of public debate through aggressive campaigns, this network of Identitarians pays careful attention to the ideological formation of its militants through countless workshops and conferences in their "Identity Houses," as well as in their summer camps. Although exclusively focused on fighting the Islamic presence in the daily life of their community, Identitarians pay attention to History—and its messages for the present. Viewed as a "school of formation of the cadres of the Reconquest," their summer camps have been held with themes such as "From Excalibur to the Grail, a myth for a new knighthood" or "From Charles Martel to Charles de Gaulle, the French rebelliousness!" The fourteenth encounter, held in the region of Rhône-Alpes and titled "European Reconquests: From Covadonga to Calais," evoked the figure of Pelagius and the start of the *Reconquista*. This back-and-forth between the past and the present is always present in the Identitarians' indoctrination and in their street activism. As when Identitarians from Nissa Rebela, in the southeastern city of Nice, hold a yearly March of the Torches to honor Catherine Ségurane—a sixteenth-century heroine who, as the story goes, played a decisive role in repelling the Ottoman siege of Nice in 1543. This is one more way that Identitarians connect the past resistance to Islam (particularly with 1543 as the symbolic sacred date) with the need for a reawakened, resurgent resistance in the present.[74]

The Anti-Islamic Front

Anti-Islamic networking, both nationally and internationally, has always been critical to these French Identitarians. The Observatory on Islamization, founded in 2007 by the essayist and activist Joachim Veliocas with the goal of "re-informing public opinion" about the true nature of Islam, has given its support to the Identitarians' opposition to the establishment of Dar al-Islam in France. "I have given lectures for these organizations," said Veliocas, "and I welcomed the action of Génération Identitaire on the roof of the Poitiers mosque, which belongs to the French Muslim Brotherhood of the UOIF [Union of Islamic Organizations of France]. It was a peaceful action to generate media interest. We fight the same fight to denounce the mass immigration of Muslims with very low education." He noted, "They do not come to visit the Louvre, but to enjoy the right of soil. In the Paris region, 40% of births are non-European. The French population with a low birth rate is about to be replaced—it is factual."[75] In light of this, Veliocas has accepted "right away" a partnership with the Identitarians' Observatory on the Great Replacement, which "is not a 'conspiracy theory' but a statistical reality that is confirmed in the figures from the National Institute of Demographic Studies."[76]

Other allies of the Bloc Identitaire network have been groups originating from the Left, such as Riposte Laïque (Secular Response, founded in 2007) and Résistance Républicaine (Republican Resistance, founded in 2010), strongly attached to the traditional French republican model and its secularity, which they believe is critically threatened by the advance of Islam. On many occasions, and in the name of a united fight against Islamization, they have collaborated and joined forces. Riposte Laïque, originally an online journal before becoming an association, was founded by Pierre Cassen, who says that his lifelong militancy has been defined by his refusal of the three totalitarianisms: Stalinism, Fascism, and Islam. Cassen sees "separation" between France and Islam, "to the delight of lovers of freedom and Arab-Muslim apostates," as the only feasible solution.[77] Riposte Laïque—whose publishing house has put out many books, including Marchand's *Reconquista, or the Death of Europe*—collaborated with the Bloc Identitaire in the call for "sausage and booze" parties in Muslim-dominated urban areas of Paris, and together with Résistance Républicaine (led by Christine Tasin), in 2010 organized an international conference on Islamization—Assises Internationals sur l'Islamisation de Nos Pays—which featured such speakers as, among others, René Marchand and Renaud Camus. Importantly, notable counter-jihadist activists, such as the Danish Anders Gravers, one of the founders of the SIOE (Stop Islamization of Europe) movement, were present. "We will never be dhimmis!" he proclaimed. And a message from Bat Ye'Or was read to the participants, the "dear friends of freedom, human rights, and democracy," against Islam's "obscurantist fanaticism." A manifesto was adopted in the end: "We launch on this day a movement of European resistance grounded on the defense of our civilization against a new totalitarianism."[78]

At the same time, French Identitarians have interacted with a number of groups—broadly included in the counter-jihadist movement—which, particularly since the late 2000s, and in a context of perceived dereliction and betrayal of popular sovereignty, have been taking to the streets by the hundreds, sometimes the thousands, to protest the creeping Islamization of their region, country, or continent. The English Defense League (EDL), founded in 2009, was the first major visible sign of this type of anti-Islamic street activism, and also an object of major media coverage.[79] The formation of a common platform for the rejection of Islamization—the feeling that there is a common enemy—was the reason that, at least for an initial period, there were many contacts between the EDL and the Bloc Identitaire. French Identitarians have participated in EDL protests and vice versa, while the co-founder and former leader of the EDL from 2009 through 2013, Tommy Robinson (aka Stephen Yaxley-Lennon), was invited to the Paris conference. Although unable to attend, his text was read: "Europe! The time of resistance has come because Jihad advances under many guises. . . . *Je suis English Defense League*, and I will never submit!"[80] Overall the rise of anti-Islamic street politics in Europe through marches and demonstrations—in the form of "Islamo-vigilant" groups—has been well received by French Identitarians, and such an appraisal is not limited to the Bloc Identitaire (now Les Identitaires) network.

The German movement PEGIDA (Patriotic Europeans against the Islamization of the Occident) is a case in point, as it rocked the headlines of the international media in the winter of 2014–15 when it held massive rallies in Dresden, the capital of Saxony, which were attended by thousands of people—many of whom held signs such as "Against Religious Fanaticism," "United against a Holy War on German Soil," and "Mrs. Merkel: This Is the People" (under an image showing a veiled chancellor). Beyond German cities, other PEGIDAs emerged, such as in Scandinavia and the United Kingdom (with Tommy Robinson initially involved in its creation). In France, a PEGIDA-like movement has not picked up steam among Identitarians. "We support evidently all the initiatives that combat Islamism and Islamization," said Fabrice Robert, even if "we think that in France it is better to privilege other forms of action. I think, for example, that the occupation of the roof of the mosque in Poitiers in 2012 has left a much deeper impression in the [people's] spirits than a demonstration bringing together 300 people in Paris."[81] Renaud Camus says that "for us [PEGIDA] is not an obsession. We have a different political orientation, because they are more oriented toward challenging Islam while our focus is on the rejection of the Replacement, by whatever people, of our Civilization."[82] In any case, Pierre Vial, for example, sees the PEGIDA phenomenon as a sign of the changing times, leading him to wonder whether "new forms of political and social action, based on Identitarian socio-economic, political, and cultural solidarities (the refusal of Islamization as a reflexive defense of a European conception of life, of the man . . . and of the woman!) [are] arising."[83] Le Gallou and Antoine Ormain, a royalist and former Front national candidate in local elections, believe that the times are ripe for a "civilizational alliance," a conjugation of forces comprising "populist parties in the West, Eastern European governments (especially the Visegrad

Group [the alliance of the Czech Republic, Hungary, Poland, and Slovakia] and the Baltic countries), conscious of having to defend the identity of their people, [and] movements of defense of peoples, like the Identitarians in France, PEGIDA in Germany, the English Defense League, and the innumerable local vigilant groups."[84]

The Germanophone "Defense of Europe"

In Germanic central Europe Identitarians are no less outspoken in their anti-Islam stance. "Today, the youth, the other youth (not the Antifa) arises, and it occupies mosques, streets, theatres, and no one can stop it. I think that the Reconquest has started, from Paris to Vienna," Martin Sellner, the co-founder of Austria's Generation Identity, announced to the crowd assembled at the Identitarian demonstration "This is our home" in Paris.[85] Sellner has also been close to the PEGIDA movement, speaking at its rallies in the city of Dresden, much like the German mentor of the group, Götz Kubitschek, who addressed the PEGIDA offshoot LEGIDA (located in the city of Leipzig) against the politician-driven "replacement" of the people.

Like Sellner, the English anti-Islamic activist Tommy Robinson also appeared onstage at PEGIDA's third anniversary. In his post-EDL career, as a reporter, first for Rebel Media and afterward as an independent, Robinson has been a supporter of the emerging UK branch of Generation Identity and has shown his admiration for the Identitarian Lambda movement: "I grew up in a town where English people are a minority. . . . I don't have an identity. . . . We were sort of like made to feel that our history, culture, identity, it was something we should be ashamed of . . . . That is why it is interesting to see in the Generation Identitarian movement [that] they know who they are . . . those youth know their identity."[86] Importantly, Robinson has also increasingly reported on the activities of the Austrian and German branches. In fact, in 2018, when the Austrian Identitarian leader and his girlfriend, Brittany Pettibone, were temporarily detained and barred from entering the United Kingdom on the grounds that, inter alia, their presence and activities could "incite tensions between local communities," Robinson became their biggest advocate, berating the UK authorities: "We live in a post–free speech era, if you criticize Islam the government will come down on you."[87] Not only was Robinson the first to interview the power couple of Lambda Identitarian activism on their return to Austria, but he also delivered a speech written by Martin Sellner at the Speakers' Corner in London's Hyde Park (which was what Sellner initially intended to do)—an event that made international news.[88] Sellner asked for his social media followers to support Robinson's projects, saying, "This man is authentic. He has sacrificed a lot and he has a vision," in a show of both gratitude and admiration for Robinson's life and activism.[89]

In fact, the combat against Islamization—a consequence of multiculturalism and the "Great Replacement"—is at the center of the Austrian Identitarians' goal of reconquering the German world and Europe. *Defend Europe* (from mass immigration and Islamization) was, for example, the name of one of their demonstrations in Vienna that was violently met by extreme-left counter-protestors. "We are the future of Europe! We went out for you to the streets and had stones, firecrackers, pepper spray and glass bottles thrown at us," they announced on their Facebook page.[90] Occupations and street theater go hand in hand as the Identitarians' preferred methods of action, for example, the staging of mock beheadings of Austrians (such as "Welcome refugees" activists) by Muslim terrorists on the streets of Vienna and proclaiming that "the people who now shout 'Welcome refugees' have also invited terrorists. They talk about diversity but what we see is foreign infiltration and Islamization."[91] The Identitarians also invaded a lecture on asylum policy at the University of Klagenfurt, dressed up in burqas and staging a 'stoning' of one of their members, her head and hands trapped in stocks, symbolizing an "Austrian patriot."[92]

For Identitarians, "Defend Europe" means also—crucially—"Defend European women." Women of European stock are invariably presented as the first victims of the twin evils of non-European mass immigration and Islamization. The New Year's Eve sex attacks in Cologne played a central role in this narrative; a year after those events, German Identitarians occupied the roof of the city's railway station, staging a protest at "the place of shame" and hoisting a big banner with the Lambda logo and the words "Never Again Cologne—Remigration." Pepper spray has become a sort of Identitarian symbol of the (new) dangerousness of times for women. Activists in Austria and Germany have recurrently distributed self-defense pepper spray in the streets. Annika

Franziska—a German IBD member and student at the University of Tübingen who in 2017 co-founded Radikal Feminin, a traditional blog whose intention is to "show that the classic role models of man and woman are anything but obsolete!"—makes this connection clear: "When I started studying in Tübingen there was nothing like that. . . . Now at a normal store where you get your makeup there's a pepper spray [nearby]. . . . [Women] are walking around with them and if you ask them 'Are you scared or something?' they are like, 'I don't know' . . . but they know why. . . . and it's not because of some German guys waiting for them in the park or something."[93]

When Alexander Van der Bellen, the former leader of Austria's Green Party—who was sworn in for a six-year term as the country's president in 2017—said that "if this real and rampant Islamophobia continues, there will come a day where we must ask all women to wear a headscarf—all—out of solidarity with those who do it for religious reasons,"[94] Austrian Identitarians launched an online petition calling for his resignation and organized a social media campaign encouraging women to take photos of themselves holding signs saying "Not with me!" Their fellow German Identitarians saw Bellen's remark as yet another sign of the ongoing "submission" of the European political class to Islam.[95] In solidarity with their Austrian counterparts, Italian members of Le Identitarie—the female group of Generazione Identitaria—also posted photos with the message "Dear Van der Bellen, Not in Europe!"[96]

"We were silent for too long. Now starts our resistance. Mothers, women, sisters, daughters of Europa, this state will not protect you, nobody knows who will be next; You need to stand up for yourselves! 'Cause your name is Mia, your name is Maria, your name is Ebba, they could be you, and you could be them." Thus started the video that, in early 2018, launched the "120 Decibels" campaign of German and Austrian Identitarian women, with Annika Franziska as a major promoter, against the abuse and violence perpetrated against European women by migrants (Mia, Maria, and Ebba were the names of two German and one Swedish girls who were killed, in different circumstances, by migrants). Named after 120-decibel self-defense pocket alarms that many women carry and taking its inspiration from the #MeToo movement—in which women denounced in mainstream and social media episodes of sexual harassment and assault—#120dB vowed to be the "true #MeToo," encouraging European women to "tell in social media with the hashtag #120db about your experiences with imported violence." In one of the first actions of a movement that pledges to "be loud" and confrontational toward multiculturalist politicians and elites, activists crashed the Berlin International Film Festival and—before being expelled with shouts of "Nazis out" by some members of the audience—displayed a banner onstage that read, "The voices of the forgotten women #120dB."[97]

The group's activists have also begun interacting crossnationally with the broader European anti-Islamic movement. One of them, Aline Morars (a native German with Romanian parents) addressed, in Birmingham, a demonstration of the Football Lads Alliance, a self-described "anti-extremism," mostly working-class, street movement that emerged in the United Kingdom following the 2017 Islamic terror attacks. "Women of England, women of Europe . . . ," Morars began. "Violent misogyny is not some minor aspect of Islam, it is central. If you care about your daughters and granddaughters, you have no excuse for not resisting it with everything you've got," she said to the applause of the attendees, in a speech covered by Tommy Robinson on YouTube.[98] "There were many people who were waiting for this . . . who were actually waiting for someone to address this problem," said Ariane, an 18-year-old German finance and business student, in "#120dB: The Documentary" (2018), which was presented by Ábel Bódi, the Hungarian Identitarian leader, and produced by Studio.ID, the professional film studio of the Austrian Identitarians.[99]

Like participants in the wider Identitarian movement, German-speaking Identitarians retrieve historical episodes and figures and employ them as sources of inspiration for their present-day struggle. There is heavy use of symbolism. For example, Identitäre Bewegung activists from the southwestern German city of Karlsruhe established in public places figures representing hoplites (members of the ancient Greece infantry) labeled with the dates and names of the famous battles of the *Reconquista* and the Ottoman Wars. The activists proclaimed that this was done in the spirit of "remembering that more than once Europe succeeded in defending itself from the invaders!"[100] The catalogue description of one of the T-shirts sold at Phalanx Europa, the Austrian Identitarians' online shop, read: "We simply have no desire for an Islamist mass immigration to Europe under the guise of the 'right to asylum.'" The shirt showed a knight chasing away armed Muslims, with the inscription "Against jihadists, Islamists and other 'cultural enrichers,' we recall the old European tradition of 'Reconquista.'" The description of another shirt, showing the image of Leopold of Austria (future Saint Leopold III) holding the Lambda sign, says, "As a bastion of Europe, Vienna has always been the last stronghold against the storms from south and east. Its unconquered walls were the starting point for Prince Eugene's mission of reclaiming the Balkans and liberating them from the reign of terror of the Turks. All this is absolutely Identitarian and ultimately originates from the spirit of men like Leopold."[101] At the beginning of 2017, attendees of the IBÖ congress in the city of Graz witnessed the first awarding of the Prince Eugene Prize for "outstanding achievement in Identitarian activism."[102] Eugene of Savoy—"the noble knight" who, in the service of the Austrian Holy Roman emperor, made himself known by such military feats against the Ottoman Turks as the defense of Vienna and the recapture of the fortress city of Belgrade—was also invoked at a rally organized by the Austrian Identitarians in the city of Klagenfurt. It was there, in downtown Klagenfurt, that Tomislav Sunić invoked Eugene in a speech against the "multicultural madness" in Europe: "In retrospect, the question arises as to why our Prince Eugene conducted such long wars against the Turkish invaders. Fortunately, however, history is always open and it is up to us to reshape it anew."[103] In the Identitarian mindset, "reshaping history anew" means showing that Eugene, and others like him, did not fight in vain. Months later, on Kahlenberg Mountain—where John III Sobieski, King of Poland, led the cavalry charge that ended the Turkish siege of Vienna in 1683— roughly two hundred Identitarian activists (mostly from Austria but including delegations from other European countries), many holding torches, celebrated the "liberation of Vienna/Defense of Europe." The Facebook post of the Austrian movement read, "The fight against mass immigration, islamisation and a treasonous policy is the battle of our generation.... We must fight with the same power, the same energy and the same destiny as the defenders and liberators of Vienna did it in 1683!," and there was an accompanying video of the event produced by Studio.ID.[104]

This back-and-forth between the past and the present is evident in the constant equivalence that Identitarians draw between the Ottomans of yore and the Turks of today—specifically in regard to Europe's

Turkish diaspora communities. It is as if yet another siege of Vienna (and consequently of Europe) is ongoing and Identitarians must rescue the anti-Ottoman examples of the past. This is especially the case every time ethnic Turks living in Europe engage in violent protests, whether in support of the Turkish government or in confrontations with other ethnic communities, such as Kurds. In the aftermath of one of such event in Vienna, Identitarian activists protested in the streets, holding a huge banner that portrayed a "remigration airline" ticket with the document number "1529-1683-2016" (the dates of earlier Ottoman sieges of Vienna) and flight number 732 (yet another reference to Charles Martel's Battle of Poitiers).

The periodic accusations made by Turkey's president, Recep Tayyip Erdogan, against Europeans for xenophobia—especially strident in the aftermath of the 2017 refusal by some European governments of Turkish politicians' plans to hold rallies in European countries, and accusations

FIGURE 23. Meme created by the Austrian Identitarians depicting their stunt at the Turkish embassy in Vienna on March 22, 2017. Courtesy of IBÖ.

that they have "commenced a struggle between the Cross and the Crescent," only serve to rile up Identitarians and "confirm" their view that the Turks of today, confident in their rising numbers and empowerment, have declared a war on Europe. Identitarian street performers in Graz organized a fake Erdogan rally, with the audience wearing burqas and the fake Turkish leader defending, in regard to Europe, a simple formula: "Strength through numbers! We are the grandsons of Kara Mustafa [the defeated Turkish vizier of the 1683 siege of Vienna]. Europe can choose whether to have a peaceful conquest or a religious war!"[105] In a militant action whose video and iconic picture were widely shared in social media, Identitarian activists accessed the roof of Turkey's embassy in Vienna and displayed a huge banner with the slogan "Erdogan, get your Turks home!," accompanied by a silhouette of the Identitarian hero Prince Eugene. "If you liked the action, support us with a donation!" Austrian Identitarians said on their Facebook page.[106]

THE CONQUEST

Anti-Islamic Identitarians of all generations *know* that Europe is experiencing settlement and colonization from mostly Muslim masses—in what translates into an actual conquest whose end result will be Islam's domination of Europe. This historical development, they insist, is not new in itself. Marchand reiterates this when he writes, "Contemporary Muslims, like their ancestors throughout fourteen centuries, consider that one of their most sacred duties is to never stop trying to extend their domination, which can be translated, ideologically, as spreading Islam."[107] *What is new*, according to the Identitarians, is Europe's weakness, making this development a particularly dangerous phase of its centuries-long struggle against Islam.

The Islamization from Below

For Identitarians, the escalation of Islamic terrorism on European soil shows, in all its ghastliness, that Islam is a threat to European security. But that is only a part—and ultimately a secondary part—of a wider challenge, which is the *existential* threat that Islam poses to Europe's civilization. In the end, it is the *Islamization from below* that may turn out to be Europe's death knell. This driving force of Islamization comes naturally to Muslim communities because Islam (according to Identitarians) is naturally, ontologically, a conquering power. It is only through the lens of this conquest, which is consubstantial with Islam, that one can understand the full measure of the terrifying situation in which Europe finds itself. This idea is at the center of Faye's grim tale about the future of France and Europe. Terrorism is a "wasp sting," but "there is something much more serious than terrorist Islamism, which is Islamization from below, like moisture corroding walls."[108] What is needed is to put together the pieces of the puzzle called "Islamization" and sound the alarm on every occasion—and in this, Faye and others in the Identitarian camp, excel. The signs are everywhere. As Faye writes, Islamic head coverings, for example, have "nothing to do with tradition, but [constitute] a militant act, a symbolic act of affirmation of invasion, of *our* invasion," and are a manifestation of an "ethno-political logic of intimidation."[109] In a text titled "Islamization of France—Prophecy," Faye predicts upcoming events: the suppression of Christian holidays in favor of Muslim holidays, the compulsory designation of prayer rooms in businesses, the abolition of the ban on face coverings, changes in student textbooks to suppress everything (in history and the sciences) that is anti-Qur'an, the undermining of same-sex marriages and gender equality ("which is rather ironic," Faye thinks, owing to the Left's progressive defense of the "benefits" and "enrichment" brought by non-European immigration), and, finally, further pro-Islamic redirection of French foreign policy. "You can imagine the rest," Faye writes, but "all of this has already started. I do nothing more than to anticipate the trajectory of a curve."[110]

There are, therefore, many mechanisms of Muslim conquest. Marchand explicitly calls the present conflict a war that is waged in myriad ways. Above all, it is an asymmetric kind of war that is conducted through the religion-sanctioned doctrine of *taqiyyah*, of dissimulation, and the deliberate deception of the infidels, hiding from Europeans the true intention of the Islamizing zealots. Far from being a "religion of Peace," as the popular mantra goes, Islam, as it has historically been, is a religion that requires the submission of the others to Islam, as commanded by Allah. *Taqiyyah* is used provisionally by its "soldiers," while Islam is still not capable of imposing its will but instead is obliged to co-habit with non-Muslims—though this is just a temporary tactic of biding time in the spirit of the Arab proverb "When you cannot bite a hand, kiss it." Islam is the "great deceiver," and Europeans are woefully ignorant of its devious might. What has been happening in the last few decades has been the manipulation of European civil society—including its current dogmas of religious freedom, pluralism, tolerance, equality, and openness to others, and, in short, the use of democracy, its institutions and values—in order to expand Islam's hold and power in Europe. This will, in the long run, ironically mean the end of democracy itself. "Confronted with the blindness of some Europeans before the current offensive of Islam on their territory, we can retain an explanation that may serve as an excuse for the most honest of them (I want to believe that they are the majority)," Marchand writes, adding that, in their blindness to the Islamist threat, such Europeans "do not see that a war is being waged against them, because it is a war of a kind that they do not know and that they do not know exists."[111] *When they do* realize it, the war will be over, and they will see that they have lost, warns Faye. This is the equivalent of a "soft conquest," accomplished in stages and following a "skin-of-the-leopard" strategy (little by little, spot by spot) that is fueled by radicals, whether explicitly or in the form of "false" moderates, imams, and Muslim intellectuals who are specialists in double talk. The strategy is to "occupy the society . . . the social space before advancing toward the gradual takeover of local and state powers, institutions, and the State itself, due to the law of numbers [the greater the number, the greater the power]. It is the logic of the *fait accompli*: too late, we are here."[112]

Another driving idea is that—and this is a testament to the increasing weight of Islam in some European societies—there are all-too-evident symptoms that "submission" to the will of global Islam has already started. The conversion of autochthonous Europeans is prime among them. Taking as an example the protagonist of the French writer Vladimir Volkoff's "premonitory novel" *L'Enlèvement* (The Kidnapping), which describes a French youth's conversion to Islam, Venner diagnosed the phenomenon's cause as a lack of "Identitarian consciousness" of the contemporary generation of Europeans: "Heir to . . . a broken society, a destroyed civilization, a defunct religion"—a void that Islam fills—the indigenous European convert is a "son of his time."[113] Faye has no doubt that this submission portends the end not only of France but also of Europe as we know it: "It is exactly like the Balkans during Ottoman domination. The conversion to Islam falls under the 'Stockholm syndrome,' a desire for submission and protection." In the end, there will be a much-vaunted integration and assimilation, "but backwards."[114] Pierre Vial is less charitable when he writes, in *Terre et Peuple*, "It is also in the name of the right of blood that we consider as traitors the European converts to Islam, and it is as such that they will be accountable to the justice of the community of the people." As "useful idiots," they "do not want to understand that, from the perspective of the invaders, religion is but a pious pretext to seize our European land."[115] Submission, of course, shows itself in many shapes. A full array of the ignorant, of dupes, of opportunists, and of double agents are all exposed in Identitarian narratives as "collaborators" with Islam, facilitating its slow capture of society and its institutions. "Every occupation has its collaborators: the politicians and the intellectual media class make up the backbone of the pro-immigration party. . . . They are well supported by the Catholic, Jewish, and Protestant religious hierarchies, none of whom suspect how much they are at risk of being devoured whole," wrote Faye in the introduction to his 2000 volume *The Colonization of Europe*.[116] Politics-as-usual is also to blame. Joachim Veliocas, who denounced "those mayors who pander to Islamism," believes that at the root of this treacherous behavior lies "political opportunism [oriented toward] obtain[ing] the votes of the Muslim electorate which represent a significant portion of the electorate. French politicians have no other job, they live off politics."[117] In any case, because collaboration is widely seen as a major tool for the invasion and Islamization of European lands, it must be denounced and combated at all costs. Especially because "without the collaborators," writes Marchand, "the opportunities they provide to Muslims for funding from abroad, for building their sites of propaganda, [and] the place they give them in our media, our armies, our prisons, the license they grant them in schools, hospitals, public places . . . the occupation army collapses."[118] The "occupation army" also has at its disposal, in order to disallow all opposition to its march, the accusation of Islamophobia. The suffix "phobia" itself is a shock term used "to turn dissident opinions into mental diseases, as in the USSR," says the *Dictionary of*

Newspeak.[119] From the Identitarian perspective it stigmatizes them and their supporters as being somehow "disordered" in their opposition to Islamization. But most of all, it is employed as a weapon of war. "Muslims and Islamo-leftists, but not only them (treason is also in good shape at the center and on the right), have developed an unstoppable war machine: any refutation of Islam is an attack against Muslims, which amounts to an "incitement to racial hatred,"[120] says Alain Cagnat. And this happens, for example, in France, a country that does not officially recognize the existence of races. The stigmatization of Islamophobia as a hate crime, criminalizing any tough questioning of Islam, leads in practice to self-censorship and clears the way for Dar al-Islam. According to the dominant ideology, "Islamophobia is to defend itself from Islamization," says Faye, calling it a "fantastic gift" offered to the Islamic conquerors "because it virtually prohibits the conquered from protesting against the conquerors." It feeds the victimhood narrative of the invaders—again, using "democracy" and liberal dogmas as a protective shield—while masking the fact that *they* are the actual aggressors. *Taqiyyah*, which Identitarians identify as the art of Islamic ruse, in all its splendor.[121]

Finally, according to the Identitarian mindset, at the root of the creeping Islamization of Europe is the Great Replacement—driving it, fueling it, because the vast majority of the non-Europeans "invading" Europe, whether Africans, Arabs, or Asians, are Muslims. Vial writes, "The tree of Islam must not hide the forest of the Great Replacement, which is not a phantasm but a crushing reality."[122] In the end, the conversion phenomenon, the collaboration, the persecution of dissidents and resisters—all are features of the ongoing process of Islamization and testify to the force and momentum of the Great Replacement. The rise of Muslim politics in Europe and the gradual ascension of Muslim politicians is but another feature of this process. When, in the spring of 2016, Sadiq Khan, the son of Pakistani immigrants, was elected mayor of London until 2020, this was viewed as a confirmation of demographic and social trends that are opening the door for a dark and foreboding age for Europe. "The election of Sadiq Khan will surely please the cosmopolitan bobos. It is mostly a sign of a disturbing demographic shift," tweeted Generation Identity's Arnaud Delrieux. "There is no Great

Replacement in England," says Le Gallou, "but the new mayor of London is called Sadiq Khan. This Pakistani Muslim was elected as a result of the departure, in ten years, of 600,000 of British stock, cockneys, from the east of the city."[123] When, as 2017 was drawing to an end, the British media reported that, with all different spellings accounted for, Muhammad had become the most popular boys' name in England and Wales, it just fit to perfection the Identitarian narrative.[124] Things such as these are widely seen as "just the beginning," as the "first dominoes" to fall, as the Islamization—and the Great Replacement that boosts it—advances unabated.

The Terror

In many Identitarian narratives, Islamic terrorism is a *companion* to Islamization in the sense that it is part of the comprehensive strategy of Islamic conquest of the continent. In "A religion sure of itself and domineering," an editorial in *La Nouvelle Revue d'Histoire*, Philippe Conrad makes this point clear when he says that the terrorist attacks "are part of a project of conquest that is based on the demographic dynamism of Muslim societies, on the proselytism implemented by the monarchies of the Arabian Peninsula, and on the blindness of the Western elites beholden to the 'Great Replacement' announced by the writer Renaud Camus."[125] Islamization takes many forms, guarantees Le Gallou in an interview with *éléments*. "Between the *Taqiyyah* of so-called 'moderate' imams and the territorial takeover by the rabble, themselves a pool of Islamists and terrorists, there is a continuum."[126] It is not that, in the end, there is no "positive" fallout from Islamic terrorism, in all its manifestations and geographic settings. Its carnage destroys the propaganda of the alleged peacefulness of Islam. "The widely circulated videos showing the beheading, with a long blade, of hostages of jihadists, are much more eloquent than the rhetoric of people wanting to explain to us that Islam is a religion of peace, tolerance and love," says Vial.[127] This is the reason why Faye believes that the proponents of "soft" Islamization, the "intelligent and deceitful Arab-Muslims," see as "premature and counterproductive" these violent excesses of Islam in its current phase of conquest: by showing the true nature of Islam they may awake Europeans to the dangers of Islamization.[128]

From the Identitarian perspective, radical Islamism is, despite its ominous and insidious nature, in some sense a sort of tragic gift that keeps on giving: It serves the purpose of awakening Europeans to the true nature of an enemy that constitutes a real threat to Europe's existence. This "awakening" is what Identitarians are after. And in the wake of every terrorist attack, Identitarians remind their fellow Europeans that Europe is on the front line of the war that Dar al-Islam has declared upon Dar al-Harb, the world that has not submitted itself to the will of Allah and lives in supposed "rebellion" against it. *That* is the true face of Islam. Naturally these attacks are viewed as nothing more than proof that the Identitarian side is the side of truth and one more confirmation, if it is needed, of the righteousness of their mission. When the intention of Forsane Alizza (Knights of Pride), a French Islamist radical group, to target Fabrice Robert, the Bloc Identitaire president, was unveiled, the Identitarian wore it as a badge of honor: "It is the tribute of vice to virtue, these plans have the merit of showing that for Islamists, the major obstacle to their success is above all the Identitarian movement."[129] Finally, Islamic terror serves as a way to further undermine the establishment, to "break" the official taboos and disrupt the official script focused on immigration and diversity as a "source of enrichment" or as the joys of "*vivre ensemble*," when the reality is that they fuel terrorism. One particular campaign launched in 2014 by the Bloc Identitaire displayed photos of French criminals and terrorists of Muslim descent—such as the French-Algerians' Mohamed Merah, the man behind the 2012 killings in the cities of Montauban and Toulouse, and Mehdi Nemmouche, the 2014 Brussels Jewish museum shooter—with the heading "A chance for France?" In the same year, they also tied the Jihadist war in Syria with the potential explosion of terrorism in the homeland with posters such as "Today Jihadists in Syria, Tomorrow terrorists in France! Demand the withdrawal of French nationality and the prohibition to return to France for the 'French' engaged in jihad in Syria."[130]

The succession of terrorist acts of violence in subsequent years—including the January 2015 Île-de-France attacks (such as that on the satirical paper *Charlie Hebdo*'s headquarters), the shootings in Copenhagen in February of the same year, the foiled attack on board a train from Amsterdam to Paris in the summer, the November 2015 Paris attacks, the 2016 Brussels bombings, the Nice terrorist attack on Bastille Day, the 2017 Las Ramblas attack in Barcelona, and a string of attacks in Germany, Russia, Sweden, and England, as well as targeted single assassinations by Islamists throughout Europe—has reinforced the Identitarian narrative that Islam and Europe do not mix and that the former must be resisted, not abetted by the suicidal poison of political correctness.[131] "This [the 2015 *Charlie Hebdo* and Copenhagen terror attacks] is just the beginning," declared Guillaume Faye in a video interview.[132] In a communiqué from Terre et Peuple, Pierre Vial saw in the *Charlie Hebdo* attacks a vindication of many warnings and predictions: "If this isn't war, it sure does look like one, as we have said for some time now. . . . But damn! When will they [the elites] understand that we are already in war and that we still haven't seen anything?"[133] The Bloc Identitaire, in the aftermath of the January 2015 slayings, put the blame on the political establishment: "The parade of political leaders calling, one after the other, for 'national unity' is something abhorrent. Abhorrent because it is precisely they who are responsible for the terrible situation into which our country is now plunged!"[134] Soon after, Generation Identity launched the campaign—through stickers, posters, and a social media hashtag—"I Am Charlie Martel" (another allusion to the victor of the Battle of Poitiers and a parody of the "I am Charlie" hashtag established for those mourning the *Charlie Hebdo* attack) because, "instead of the alleged spirit of January 11 [the date of the "republican marches" for unity] we prefer the spirit of 732."[135] The January 2015 attack showed yet again the failure of "integration" and immigration policies, "but today the facade is crumbling," Fabrice Robert proclaimed. "We have seen it when the many minutes of silence for *Charlie Hebdo* were interrupted with cries of 'Allah Akbar.'"[136] *Réfléchir & Agir* saw the call for national unity under the banner "I am Charlie" as an unprecedented, totalitarian manipulation of the masses at the service of the dominant ideology, intended to put on the same level, as one common enemy, all those that did not support the values of the Republic—from Islamists to nationalists and Identitarians.[137] The idea that those in power persecute those who are nonaligned with the official way of thinking and acting, such as Identitarians, is widespread. It was seen when Génération Identitaire militants were taken into custody after they climbed to the roof of the TGV station, where a Moroccan terrorist was apprehended, holding a banner saying "Expulsion to Islamists" and the images of a plane, a boat, and an alien spaceship. "This must be a joke, the Socialist government does not expel the Islamists, but instead puts in custody those who demand it," they lamented.[138]

The November 2015 Paris attacks were portrayed as another tragic proof of the impossibility of cohabitation with an expansionist Islam. "It is our youth that pays for decades of irresponsible immigration policies. It is our youth that pays for the laxness, and sometimes even the complicity, of our governments regarding the development of Islamism in our soil," read the communiqué of Génération Identitaire.[139] The Bloc Identitaire insisted on urgent measures, from the freezing of legal immigration, to the reestablishment of borders, stopping the construction of new mosques, and outlawing all sort of Islamist organizations. When the socialists in power, in the aftermath of the attacks, vowed to strip away the nationality of jihadists, an old demand of Identitarians, this was viewed as a victory, albeit only temporarily; not only did the proposal target only convicted terrorists of dual nationality, but it was subsequently dropped by the French president. In response, the Identitarian magazine showed a picture of French President (2012–17) François Hollande holding a sign saying "I am weak."[140] "Chase away the Islamists" was the name that Génération Identitaire gave to another of its campaigns (waged in the streets and social media) against the Islamic presence in the country, and the call for the banning of Islamist organizations has been a major part of the Identitarians' efforts. In "10 Urgent Measures to Defend the Security and the Identity of France," Les Identitaires (the successor to the Bloc Identitaire) included their outlawing as crucial, "whether they are Salafist" or "connected to the Muslim Brotherhood like the UOIF."[141] In fact, a permanent target has been the UOIF (renamed, in 2017, Musulmans de France, or French Muslims). Activists occupied the building where one of its congresses was held, with a huge banner at its entrance bearing the slogan "Let's stop the Islamization of Europe," and Génération Identitaire conducted anti-UOIF social media memetic warfare campaign—using the hashtag #UOIFdissolution—with citations from past and current Muslim Brotherhood ideologues against France and the Jews and in favor of jihad.

> **AHMED JABALLAH**
> ex-président de l'UOIF
>
> « L'UOIF est une fusée à deux étages. Le premier étage est démocratique, le second mettra en orbite une société islamique. »
>
> *L'Express, 02/05/2005*
>
> #UOIFdissolution   GÉNÉRATION **IDENTITAIRE**

FIGURE 24. Meme created by the French Identitarians in support of their campaign to dissolve the Islamist organization UOIF (now French Muslims). It shows the words of the organization's former president, the Sheikh Ahmed Jaballah: "The UOIF consists of a two-stage process. The first one is democratic, the second will put in orbit an Islamic society."

The neighborhood of Molenbeek in Brussels—and its role as a logistic center for the French and Belgian terror actions—was taken by Identitarians as a perfect example of all that is wrong with contemporary Europe. Its symbolism is heavily used in Identitarian campaigns. "If this suburb is unfortunately not the only one in this situation in Europe, it is a symbol of the war that is not being played out in Palmyra or Mosul, but inside our walls," stated the French Generation Identity in its call to the "European youth" to join in a rally in Molenbeek under the rallying cry "Expel the Islamists!" The local mayor banned it, and Génération Identitaire responded by saying that "the authorities prefer to stay locked up by their blindness and in their guilty cowardice, hunting down those who alert [against the dangers] and denying any popular manifestation of reconquest."[142] Molenbeek was also used in a series of images that circulated on social media and showed, for example, the shadow of Identitarian militants or a militant wearing the V-mask in front of a graffitied wall with the following dates and words: "732—Poitiers; 1571—Lepanto; 2016—Molenbeek." For a while the hashtag #decolonizonsmolenbeek trended high on social media. The Identitarians also launched the campaign Certified Molenbeek, which caustically called attention to the "homegrown" terrorist threat by adopting the terminology of the official certification of organic vegetables. The modus operandi was as follows: Under the cover of night the militants were to put up posters in suburbs and villages that they saw as havens of Islamism in French territory. "Bravo to the village of Sevran, certified 'French Molenbeek.' Sevran is an important center of Islamism in France: co-management with Imams, Jihadist associations recognized, Islamist mosques tolerated by the municipality . . . and 14 Sevran youths gone to Syria to make the Jihad! Sevran, a village where one lives well. . . . Like an Islamist." French Molenbeek is above all "the guarantee of a terrorism of controlled origin: from the first prayer to the death as a martyr, all the way through radicalization and exportation to Syria, you know that the terrorist was produced and grown locally!"[143] Finally, the image of a doll lying next to a dead body following the terrorist truck attack in the city of Nice was used by Pierre Larti to emphasize that the time had come to deal drastically with the root of the problem: "Neither forgetfulness, nor forgiveness: stop islamization, #IslamOutOf Europe."[144] The same image circulated in the Austrian and German Generation Identity movements' social media with the caption "Multiculturalism kills. In memory of the victims of Nice." Again and again Identitarians reveal what they see as the "unspoken" (by the mainstream media–political establishment) link: "Let us continue to disconnect the dramas of Islamization from the problem of immigration and we will only reap blood and tears," tweeted Larti after the Manchester Arena terror attack.

In Hildesheim, a city in Lower Saxony, IBD activists lit candles and wrote in chalk on the sidewalk the Lambda logo and the cities of recent terrorist attacks in Europe—"Paris, Nice, Berlin, London, Stockholm," followed by "Soon also here." On their Facebook page they stated that these were "victims of Islamic terrorism, but also the victims of a wrong policy," adding, "We know that the terror does not fall from the sky, that it is not a law of nature, and that it is not normal."[145] In fact, in recent years, in German-speaking countries, Identitarian activists have taken to the streets and protested, often engaging in flashmobs and street theater in order to make the connection clear between terrorism on their soil and "mad" open-border policies—of which the welcome of massive numbers of mostly Muslim migrants by the German chancellor Angela

FIGURE 25. Poster publicizing a Génération Identitaire demonstration in Paris (November 25, 2017) protesting the "terror" in Europe. "Against the Islamists let's defend Europe," it says. This demonstration was subsequently forbidden by the authorities, to the outrage of the group.

Merkel (who said, "We can manage this, we can do it," as the country opened its borders in 2015) is seen as a perfect and dangerous symbol. When activists from Berlin-Brandenburg occupied the rooftop of the city hall of Cottbus (the region's second largest city), unfurling banners saying, "Protect borders—save lives," they did it to protest their government's alleged attempt to "sell" terror, and a general rise in violence, as a "new normal."[146] Stunts such as these are sometimes performed in broad daylight, with activists using cranes, dressed up as construction workers, in order not to raise suspicions and to allow the operation (e.g., unfurling banners from the top of a building) to go smoothly. Occasionally, Identitarian "fake workers" have even printed on their uniforms references to major intellectual influences, for example, from the ND (like de Benoist) or the Conservative Revolution (like Oswald Spengler).

Over and over again, the Identitarians vow to fight against submission to the idea that terror is now the "new normal" in Germany and Europe. Austrian activists, for example, have performed protest guerrilla theater actions in front of the headquarters of the establishment parties, pretending to fall dead to a soundtrack of explosions and cries of terror, while blaming those parties and their multicultural policies for the blood spilled in Europe.[147] German activists have also engaged in these die-in protests against the consequences of open borders and multiculturalism. On one such occasion, in the city of Stuttgart, Identitarian protesters, female and male, laid down on the ground, pretending to be dead, in front of black cardboard tombstones with inscriptions such as "Raped and murdered," "Overrun by a truck," and "Thank you Merkel."[148] Activists are thus public space performers, often using parody as their mode of protest. Militants have also engaged in overnight raids on the headquarters of political parties deemed complicit, because of their open-border policies, with rising insecurity and terrorist attacks. This happened to the Austrian Green Party; for example, the entrance to one of its locations was bricked up and painted with the words "Pro border" and "Your Fault!," and the area in front of another was crammed with cardboard coffins labeled with the names of European victims of terror attacks in what was described by the mainstream media as a "macabre action."[149] In Germany, activists from the Identitarian movement drew chalk outlines of bodies, with fake blood in them, in several prominent places—such as around the Frankfurt Cathedral and the Goethe Monument—in order to protest the "irresponsible policies" that are leading to "waves of terror" in Europe.[150] After the Berlin Christmas market truck attack, IBD tweeted, "We do not forget anything! Make sure you close the borders immediately. Stop praying, start defending! #defendberlin." A day later, activists blockaded the entrance of the ruling party's—the Christian Democratic Union's (CDU's)—headquarters, an action that could be followed in real time on the movement's Facebook and social media platforms, which offered live streams, videos, and memes. Before the police evacuated the protest, a spokesperson said on a megaphone: "The government says we can't stay here. But the truth is that it is the hundreds of thousands of illegal immigrants that should not be in Germany and Europe."[151]

German militants have also satirized the welcome culture (symbolized by crowds greeting refugees at train stations) by engaging in mock campaigns at railway stations that involved fake naïf refugee-greeters, "We love open borders" ISIS flags, activists dressed in mock

Islamic dress holding the names of Muslim terrorists, and banners declaring, "NO WAY—you will not make Europe home"—all of this to the bewilderment of the public and intended to awake them from their "multicultural daydreaming."[152] Another common campaign involved the performance in a public place of three female activists symbolizing the ongoing Islamization of their countries and Europe: one looking happy ("Europe 2006"), another bruised and with her clothes torn ("Europe 2016"), and one wearing a burqa ("Europe 2030"). Around them is a banner with a computer loading icon, "Please wait," showing that the time to stop Islamization is running out.[153]

"An iconic picture. This is what our politicians are doing with the legacy of Maria Theresa," said the official Twitter of IBÖ in referring to the giant burqa with which its activists—with the help of a crane—covered the large bronze statue of the Habsburg Empress Maria Theresa in Vienna's imperial surroundings of Maria-Theresien-Platz. A sign was laid at the location reading: "Islamization—No Thanks!" "If we do nothing this is our future," the Austrian Identitarians added in a subsequent tweet.[154] Inspired by actions such as this, Italian activists of Generazione Identitaria scaled the monument to the opera composer Donizetti—displayed prominently in the Lombard city of Bergamo—and stuck a poster to the statue with the inscription "Islam in Europe—2050," then covered the muse of lyrical poetry with a niqab. This "symbolic act" was intended to "show what will happen to our daughters and wives, and to our culture, as long as the blindness toward the way that Islam acts in our Europe and in our cities continues," they announced in a communiqué headlined "Islam won't be our future."[155] This sense of urgency is prevalent in all these campaigns across Europe. It was not by chance, therefore, that the kick-off event for Generation Identity in the United Kingdom was the dropping of a large banner on Westminster Bridge with the slogan "Defend London, Stop Islamisation." Martin Sellner, one of organizers of the stunt, instagrammed, "UK starting to fight back islamization."[156]

And when Germany's domestic security agency decided to put the Identitarian movement "under surveillance" as a possible "threat" to the "democratic constitutional order," even though they saw this measure of the state as a sign of a despotic order (the "intimidation of dissent")—decrying it as baseless and starting a legal battle against it—they also downplayed such "political warfare." In the greater scheme of things, the consequences to activists of being put on a watch-list are irrelevant. To them, "All these defamation attempts and scare tactics will not work in view of the dramatic developments in Europe and in our country. What does the official repression and the possible loss of reputation, traineeships and jobs, matter, in view of a future of displacement, with social disruption and ethnic conflicts on the daily agenda and when terrorism is declared to be the normal state?"[157] That is why, to them, and in the greater scheme of things, it all comes down to requiem, or *Reconquista*.

Remigration as *Reconquista*

The picture soon became an IB meme: the yellow banner with the Lambda symbol, unfurled by German Identitarian activists of Swabia, on one of the gates (the Blaubeurer Tor) of the nineteenth-century fortification of the town of Ulm had on it the words, in black, "Reconquista," with "youth of Europe" just above it.[158] "*Reconquista*" is, in fact, a term that is at the center of Identitarian narratives and imagery and a part of the Identitarian New Cool, which is often invoked as an answer to the ongoing Muslim conquest of the continent. "Remigration against Islamization" read the banner that Generazione Identitaria activists flaunted as they invaded the stage of the movie theater of Borgosesia, a commune in the Piedmont region, which was hosting the Islamic-promoted cultural event "I am Italy too."[159] "Remigration" of Muslim immigrants and even of Muslim citizens of European countries is widely viewed as an unavoidable element of the much-needed *Reconquista*. In their presentation of René Marchand's participation in the Bloc Identitaire conference on remigration, the French Identitarians said that "he could not but be receptive to the will of peaceful 'Reconquista' represented by remigration."[160] In fact, a defining issue behind the realization of such a conference was explained by Pierre Cassen in a positive review of the meeting: "Can we pretend to save France, its culture, its identity and its civilization without launching a massive remigration of the supporters of Sharia law (among others) as the only solution to save our country from an ineluctable Islamization?"[161] The Bloc Identitaire "delivers a clear message to those who want to 'niquer la France' [fuck France] or who claim another homeland, those who intend to impose their culture or religion among us: leave our country! Or it will be the country that will leave you. . . . the 'Hijrah' [voluntary emigration of the faithful] now, or remigration tomorrow," the group said, at the start of their campaign "France: We Love It When They Leave It!"—which consisted of a number of images showing "the rabble," or Islamized populations in daily urban French life, and the call for them to leave. Although it may be viewed as unworkable and infeasible, many Identitarians believe that remigration is bound to happen. With the passing of time and the deepening of the social and cultural pathologies associated with immigration and Islamization, it is inescapable. "Even though it is a taboo today, the return to the country will end up to impose itself on everyone as the only solution to escape the catastrophic consequences of immigration-invasion," stated a Génération Identitaire militant, stressing remigration's contribution to peace in Europe, because "ending the massive presence of Muslims means to limit the Islamist propaganda and therefore the risk of Jihad."[162] In its official communiqué after the Christmas terror attack in Berlin, Génération Identitaire reiterated, "Today more than ever, we want to remind you that here or in Germany, it will be the halt of immigration and a politics of remigration, that is, incentives for the return of non-European populations, which will allow peace and security in our continent."[163] It is unavoidable, believes Alexander Markovics, because "every terrorist attack, every rape, every act of 'nocence' (harassment of autochthonous Europeans by immigrants, in the language of Renaud Camus), brings many Europeans to the realization that the only way to prevent future attacks is to allow no more *Willkommenskultur* [the culture of welcome], no more clapping at the station [in applause at the arrival of refugees], no more mosques and benefits to immigrants, but the closure of European borders and remigration of those people who have come to Europe illegally and without ever asking Europeans [for permission to immigrate]."[164] Joachim Veliocas, for his part, believes that, although total remigration of Muslims is "impossible and undesirable," a phased, gradual remigration is feasible, which must include in the first wave illegals, unemployed foreigners, and Islamists, from Salafists to groups such as the French UOIF, associated with the Muslim Brotherhood. At the same time, for those who cannot be expelled, return to their ancestral countries may be achieved in an alternative manner—that is, through a toughening of the policies regarding Muslim traditions and practices, stamping out any favorable treatment: "We must stop the halal menus in public canteens, give an opportunity for employers to interdict the *hijab* in companies, ban halal slaughter that increases the pathogenic risk of dangerous germs. There are food poisonings related to halal meat in France, [and] if we prohibit this practice condemned by all veterinarians, Muslims would leave by themselves in order to respect this Islamic duty." All told, "Each retreat on our part is felt as a victorious advance for them. There cannot be any further retreat," which means that a newfound assertiveness by French and European authorities will also boost remigration.[165]

Le Gallou—a staunch defender of returning a great number of immigrants to their countries of origin, starting with all the illegals—also believes that making it difficult, if not impossible, for Muslims to live as "good Muslims" in France and Europe will turn out to be a driving force of remigration. When officials in Slovakia refused Muslim migrants with the argument that "we don't have any mosques in Slovakia, so how can Muslims be integrated if they are not going to like it here?," Le Gallou saw it as a humorous quip containing a "deep truth." This deep truth, Le Gallou further said, also holds a message that Europeans should send all over the continent, the message that Muslims have the right to live as "good Muslims . . . but in a Muslim country."[166] Ultimately, as defended by René Marchand, the solution to the Islamic threat in the face of the "current offensive of Islam against its territory and its peoples" will have to entail the "interdiction of Islam in Europe," a return to the situation "before the invasion . . . before the putting in place of the strategy of Islamization that we suffer. That cannot be but the Liberation, the Reconquest, the *Reconquista*."[167]

AN IDENTITARIAN ALTERNATIVE: CASAPOUND AND THE "GOOD ISLAM"

The mourners gathered. Outside the Bataclan concert hall, the scene of deadly Islamic terrorist attacks, the grand piano sounded the notes of John Lennon's "Imagine," which instantly invoked the classic invitation to "imagine there's no countries / it isn't hard to do / nothing to kill or die for / and no religion too." Adriano Scianca noted the tragic irony: "In

Paris they thought fit to play [Lennon's] hymn of abolition of borders [while it is] the soundtrack for the ideology that led us into this situation."[168] Within European Identitarian circles, if there is no unanimity about the place that the theme of "anti-Islam" should have in political and cultural combat, there is agreement on who and what are to blame for Europe's vulnerability to Islamic terrorism: the establishment and its disastrous immigration policy. "The idea that we can still continue with uncontrolled immigration and then with the building in the European capitals of Islamic ghettoes, I think is now erased from history," declared Simone Di Stefano soon after the Bataclan attacks, noting the role of such ghettoes as "the breeding ground in which terrorists can be born and develop, as we have seen in Molenbeek in Belgium." Mass immigration and lenient citizenship laws have teamed up to shake the security of European peoples at its very roots. This ended the Schengen agreement in practice: "And this failure occurred not because of the ugly, dirty, and evil Fascists and Nationalists, but because someone thought to 'give away' nationality by *jus soli* to persons who do not have any intention to integrate and become European."[169] Or, as Scianca wrote after the bombings of Brussels, the terrorists are the "children of a model of society" put in place "with all the best intention," which became an "open sky ghetto" symbolizing the failure of a multicultural archetype that was supposed to serve as a source of inspiration for a radiant future.[170]

These Italians, however, believe that the anti-Islamic impetus should not be prioritized in the Identitarian European struggle. Even though a certain amount of "Islamization" may be happening in a few European places, the real and ultimate root cause of this process is uncontrolled immigration. An exclusive focus on Islamization is, according to Scianca, simplistic and reductive: "I do not deny that the problem exists, but I think it is wrong to think in religious terms, about a problem that is [primarily] demographic, ethnic, and social."[171] He continues, "Unless it is believed that the defense of our identity is done in a tough way against Moroccans, Syrians, and Kosovars, while it is possible to happily accept the arrival of Christian Filipinos, Congolese, or Ecuadorians, it is obvious that the frontier between what is acceptable and what is not acceptable does not go through religion," in his criticism of overemphasizing religion thus obscuring the "crucial dimension of the phenomenon, which is ethno-demographic."[172] This concern is shared, of course, by other dissident voices. For instance, the former editor in chief of Arktos, John Morgan, asks, "So, in brief, do I think large numbers of Muslims belong in Europe? No, but neither do I think large numbers of people from any non-European group belong in Europe." Then he asks: "Do I think Islam is the problem? No."[173] The Identitarian writer Lucian Tudor thinks that "the Muslim population in Europe is still a growing, ethnically foreign group which threatens the ethno-cultural makeup and identity of native Europeans *just as any other large non-European immigrant group.*"[174] At the same time, we should keep in mind that the centrality of "Islamization" in some Identitarian narratives (such as in France, for example) is context dependent in the sense that the visibility and cultural assertion of the religion is much more perceptible in some areas and countries than in others.

At any rate, in the case of CasaPound, the shifting of the focus away from Islam and toward immigration is also a way of distancing themselves from the deadly kiss of counter-jihadism. After every terrorist attack, a call is sent out to avoid the impulse to establish "easy" alliances. "Yes, we are at war. Terrorism is not only at the door of our house, but we now know that it has also crossed it," Scianca wrote. "We are at war, then. But against *whom*? And in the name of *what*? To defend *which* values? . . . And what shall we defend, maybe that idea of a 'multicolor' and multiracial society that now is imploding in all the suburbs of Europe." So he notes that "the crucial point is to not mistake the fronts"[175]—even if it means that Europeans must disown the increasingly "seductive" figure of the late Italian journalist and polemicist Oriana Fallaci, whose trilogy about the existential threat of Islam to the West is heavily referenced in counter-jihadist circles. In the current war, the urgency is not to engage in "abstract lucubrations about the true and false Islam, but [rather to] take note that the Muslim world is going through a very deep fracture. And that a part of [such world] is on our side of the fence." The "Americans and the West, understood as an ideological category," meaning "the defenders of multiculturalism, of uncontrolled immigration, the exporters of democracy that are allied with the most antidemocratic and obscurantist Arab states, the creators of armed militias that, if one wants to be generous, always escape from control, the destroyers of secular Arab states, the assassins of Saddam, Gaddafi, the enemies of Assad"—the "evil" lies in these forces, "and not only on the clouded minds of fanaticism." And so this is not "our side of the barricade."[176]

Here is the crucial insight: At the barricades against Islamic terrorism and against the destructive forces of what passes for "The West," CasaPound stands together with secular Arab nationalism. They are not alone in this stand. Always with an eye on geopolitics, Robert Steuckers, for example, believes that, in the face of a chaotic Middle East, a true, nonaligned French and European position would "refuse to participate in the cleansing of the Levant and Iraq" demanded by "the Americans and their petro-monarchist allies" and would pursue instead, as the only sound policy, "a return to the *status quo ante* in the region, because the *status quo ante* avoided the belligerent presence of uncontrollable fundamentalist elements and created civil peace by imposing a modern and syncretic military-political system, the only one able to manage the effervescent diversities and differences of this key zone of international geostrategy."[177] CasaPound, for its part, translated its position, as stated on one of the group's banners, into full support of "the sovereign, secular and socialist Syria" of Bashar al-Assad against *both* the Western allies and the Persian Gulf states intent on removing the Baathist leader from power and against Islamic extremism. Scianca wrote in an appeal for support for "sovereign Syria": "The war on terrorism, the *real* one, is being made by a single man and a single people in the world. It is Bashar al-Assad. It is the Syrian people" who are the truly brave warriors against Islamic extremism, and "whoever yaps against terrorism and opposes Assad is stupid or is in bad faith [and] in any case [is] an objective accomplice of the terrorists."[178] After the US strike on a Syrian air base, CasaPound hoisted the flag of a "free and sovereign Syria" on its Roman headquarters in a symbolic rejection of the "American aggression" against the "government of Assad, [which is] the only guarantee against terrorism and for a stabilization of the Middle East."[179] "For Syria! For Assad," sing Iannone's ZetaZeroAlfa in their 2017 album *Morimondo*.

There has been more than verbal (or chanting) support for the cause: Since 2013 CasaPound has launched a full campaign of assistance to Syria through its NGO Sol.Id. (*Solidarité–Identités*, or Solidarity–Identities), dispatching volunteers and providing humanitarian and food aid to the country. With its stated goal of providing "assistance and support to peoples struggling for their own survival, the preservation of their culture and the defense of their own identity," Sol.Id. works in close partnership with the European Front of Solidarity with Syria, which presents itself as "open to all those who love Syria, support the positions of President Assad, in solidarity with the Syrian nation and its army."[180] Together with medical and food distribution, another initiative of Sol.Id. has been to contribute—in partnership with the Syrian community in Italy and with the sponsorship of the Syrian Ministry of Tourism—to the efforts to reconstruct such treasures of Syria's archeological heritage—including its shared Greco-Roman heritage, such as that of the ancient city of Palmyra and its Roman monumental arch— damaged or destroyed by Islamic State extremists. From the beginning, Sol.Id. has been highly active in the mission of "reinforming" public opinion—through volunteers' accounts of their trips, debates, videos released on the Internet, and photo expositions—about the reality of the country, in conscious contrast to the perceived manipulations and falsifications of Western media. Ada Oppedisano, the female president of Sol.Id., sees in Syria an "age-old example of coexistence among different religious faiths. Perhaps that is why today is under attack."[181]

Sol.Id.'s range of action in the Middle East extends beyond Syria. It also launched a campaign of solidarity with Lebanon. In Beirut, together with the European Front for Syria, its members established ties with Hezbollah, participated in the group's Resistance and Liberation Day (celebrating Israel's withdrawal from southern Lebanon in 2000), and paid homage, in the Martyrs' Mausoleum, to its combatants fallen in the war of Lebanon and in the Syrian Front's actions against ISIS. All of this has been done, as argued by CasaPound member Alberto Palladino in an interview to Hezbollah's al-Ahed News, under the conviction that "all the people in the Mediterranean zone, every free people, have the right to defend their homes from invasion," from the perspective of rebuilding "the relationship between Europe—specially the countries that are in contact with the Mediterranean Sea—and the Close East, that is, the Middle Eastern countries on the Mediterranean Sea."[182] In fact, Sol.Id.'s First International Congress, held in September 2015, was dedicated to the theme of *Mediterraneo Solidale* (Mediterranean Solidarity), with the attendance of many Syrians and Lebanese. One attendee of particular note was Sayyed Ammar Al Moussaw, who was introduced as the head of Hezbollah's international relations, which led the Lazio region

FIGURE 26. Poster from CasaPound's NGO Sol.Id. advertising a food drive for Syria.

to withdraw its support of the event owing to the classification of Hezbollah by the European Parliament, in 2005, as an international terrorist organization.[183] Oppedisano stated that the event was "very important to [Sol.Id.] because it allowed us to shed light on questions of high interest regarding the Mare Nostrum [from the Latin "Our Sea"]" as a "basin of civilization that involves all of us, with guests that, for the first time in Italy, had the opportunity, through this conference, to freely express their thoughts, their own truth and their own being."[184] In the end, CasaPound's emphasis on the Mediterranean Sea displays, above all, a geopolitical purpose that is an alternative to Europe's current Atlanticism. This concept of Mare Nostrum is consequently bound to the view that the Mediterranean has been the center for millennia of encounters of civilizations, a place of trade, of the utterances of many languages, and the arena for cultural exchanges, and it epitomizes the rooted "diversity" of peoples that is being steamrolled by the imperialism of "McWorld."

A CHRISTIAN COMEBACK?

It may be called the paradox of a purely negative identity. Alain de Benoist sees it in many discourses against immigration and Islamization: "the complaint of a culture that has *already* lost its identity and that panics when it sees itself brutally confronted with another, that has remained alive. Such complaint does not express identity, but reveals its loss."[185] Manuel Ochsenreiter touches on it when, referring to "the counter-jihadism of some right wing circles and Identitarians," he says, "They will sooner or later discover that one will not rescue his own religious or cultural identity by fighting against other traditional identities. Or in other words: They do right now the job of the liberals. If I want to save my 'Christian identity,' I should go to church on Sunday instead of protesting against a mosque."[186] Of course, in regard to Christian practices, this is easier said than done. In Europe, and especially in Western Europe, the Church's impact on the public sphere is low; it declined both institutionally, with fading church attendance and a steep decline in the ordinations of priests, and individually, in terms of the diminishing importance of its codes of behavior and values in people's personal lives. The phenomenon of abandoned churches is a ubiquitous symbol of today's Europe.

Many Identitarians are longtime enemies of Judaeo-Christian universalism and egalitarianism and its subsequent secularization; this abstract, ontological conception of human beings plagues human societies the world over and is the root of the Western "evil." However, Identitarians also view favorably the heritage of Christianity—as it has been lived and expressed in actual experience—as an important component of Europe's identity. Starting with the historical fact that Christianity itself is indebted to the heritage of pagan antiquity (expressed, for example, in the cult of saints) and that, in the words of Venner, in Europe "[Christianity] was often experienced as a transposition of ancient Pagan worship," lived through the centuries as a *de facto* "Pagano-Christianity," a "particular religious variety, far removed from its biblical origins."[187] Beyond this, medieval Christendom is highly respected in many Identitarian settings; Faye, for example, sees it as proud, combatant, chivalrous, sacral, and aesthetic at the antipodes of the current effete Christianity, desacralized and soft. "Contemporary churches resemble post offices, having retained nothing of the cathedral," Faye lamented, blaming this development on the post-Conciliar Church that has opened the way for its "'ecumenical' tolerance of the Islamic offensive, the systematic alignment of its prelates along neo-Trotskyist lines, its encouragement of ethnomasochism, its almost perfect accord with the politically correct intellectual-media classes." Traditional Christianity, whether Catholic or Orthodox, which still retains a "Pagan-Christian sense of the sacred," is an important ally in the defense of Europe.[188]

While mentioning the lack of impact of massive street protests in actually altering the dreadful course of events, Philippe Randa gave as an example of the futility of such mass gatherings the La Manif Pour Tous (the Manifestation [or Protest] for Everyone) series of rallies in 2012–14 against same-sex marriage: "The repeated demonstrations of the Manif Pour Tous were unexpected, impressive . . . and perfectly sterile."[189] Beyond the actual failure (the "Marriage for Everyone" law was not revoked), its significance is seen by many Identitarians as much deeper and as the sign of a paradigm shift in mentalities—a sort of May '68 for traditional activists, and even a spiritual and Christian sort of revival in the form of a "Christian populism," in the words of the conservative thinker Patrick Buisson. "It is still difficult to assess what will be the impact in the long term of this reaction, but it clearly demonstrates the renewed spiritual aspirations identified with a very strong traditional Catholicism at the margin of the official church, largely adherent to the dominant system," said Philippe Conrad. He called it an "Identitarian Catholicism" that, "fueled by rising Islamism," should "take its place in the slow and patient conquest of minds and souls that is in progress today."[190] In fact, this "Identitarian Catholicism" is very much present in the younger generation of Identitarians. In their case it is an attachment to Christianity not just in terms of belonging (to a distinct Christian Europe) but in terms of belief. "Europe is a civilization with an immense spirituality; whether from the wisdom of the elders of Antiquity or from the message carried by Christ, it is impossible to engage in our battle without spirituality," says Arnaud Delrieux. This attachment, therefore, goes beyond the mere inclusion of the Christian heritage as part of Europe's identity and in fact translates, especially because "many militants of Generation Identity are fervent Christians,"[191] into actual activism through initiatives and networking. The annual Identitarian march in honor of Saint Genevieve, the patron saint of Paris, collapses the reverence of Saint Genevieve's cult with the residents' attachment to the city and its history into a single activist rite. The cult of the Virgin Mary is also present, and Identitarians from Lyon hold a march every year in her honor. "Celebrate Mary, let us show that the Lyonnaise identity is alive, let us show that the cultural and spiritual roots of our people are not dead," read their communiqué in response to the city mayor's decision to cancel the procession, which was also supposed to honor the victims of the Paris attacks, on the grounds that the organizers were inciting hatred against part of the population. "No one will deny the Lyonnaise youth the celebration of Mary!"[192] This Catholic activism is driven by the sense that Christianity is under attack by Islamization.

Instances of vandalism of Christian cemeteries and churches on European soil, in the eyes of Identitarians, are concrete, in-your-face signals of this. "Degradation is the euphemism used to designate the profanation of Christian graveyards; when it refers to any other burial grounds then the term *profanation* is used," says Polémia's dictionary.[193] "A beautiful allegory of the Great Replacement, isn't' it?," asked the writer of the editorial of the Identitarians' magazine, commenting on the suggestion by the rector of the Grand Mosque of Paris, Dalil Boubakeur, that abandoned churches be transformed into mosques because "it's the same God, these are neighboring rites, fraternal, and I think that Muslims and Christians can coexist and live together," he said.[194] This suggestion was viewed favorably by the bishop of Évry, a suburban Parisian commune that already has one of the largest mosques in Europe, who said, "As a principle, I prefer that churches become mosques rather than restaurants." Yet while the bishop expressed his favor, in the words of Faye, in "the most incredible way," Faye and other Identitarians view the rector's suggestion as a typical example of an Islamic ruse.[195] When the cathedral of Bourgoin-Jallieu was graffitied with anti-Catholic and Islamic writings, local Identitarians stood on its steps with a banner bearing the message "Do not touch my church."[196] Their motto became "Defend your church!" after the jihadist slaying of an elderly priest in Normandy, which triggered a mobilization of activists for weeks in front of French churches protecting churchgoers: "We will protect our churches from Islamists, with or without the government." The heavy symbolism of the church attack was not lost on Identitarians: "It was a long time since there were Christian martyrs in Europe. History always comes back, always!" wrote Arnaud Delrieux. This was also felt widely as a warning sign for the Church to regain its foothold and renew its combative spirit. "To all Christians: Chase away your lousy cardinals and bishops and do something! #remigration," Martin Sellner tweeted from Vienna, posting an image of the late eleventh-century Pope Urban II with the captions "Defend Europe" and "Deus Vult," or God Wills it, the rallying cry of the First Crusade.[197]

The Identitarian activism shows itself, too, in the initiatives to heighten the Catholic formation of militants. When Zentropa posted an announcement of the 2016 Catholic workshop/summer school of Academia Christiana (Christian Academy) in Normandy, with the theme Identity against the New Tower of Babel, it was promoting that sort of Identitarian Catholicism that Identitarians hope is on the rise. Its mission is geared toward the city. "The tidal wave of the Manif pour tous and the creative explosion that accompanied it revealed the existence of a youth that is rebellious, combative . . . and Catholic," wrote its founder, Julien Langella.[198]

A former militant and spokesperson for Generation Identity, Langella says, "Following [Pope] Leo III we believe that 'Christians are born for combat,' and as [the French Roman Catholic diplomat, poet, and playwright] Paul Claudel used to say, 'Youth is not made for fun, it is made for heroism.' A new Catholic youth must stand up to defend and propagate the faith, the love of country and social justice." Including a defense of "deep ecology" in the "love for the homeland," he notes, "Indeed, biodiversity, ethnodiversity: same struggle! As Benedict XVI said at Lourdes in 2008, 'Nations must never accept seeing disappear what makes their own identity unique.'"[199] In short, the de-Christianization of the continent has made possible, and easier, the current Muslim conquest, and a reinvigorated Christian Europe is *the* way out of the ongoing collapse:

> The immigration-invasion of Europe and its corollary, the Islamic conquest, are certainly a shock for the peoples of the Old Continent. It must be understood that to brandish the miserable Western "freedoms" of getting laid with anyone and drinking until vomiting

FIGURE 27. Advertisement for the Academia Christiana annual summer conference held with the theme "Identity against the New Tower of Babel" (Summer 2016).

the guts is not an act of resistance to Islamist fanaticism, but a way of offering our country on a platter. The slavery to impulses, the addiction to consumerism and lack of self-control are all signals to Islam that "this land is to be taken!" The de-Christianization of Europe has left the field open to all false merchants of hopes, because the thirst for the absolute is a vital need of the human soul that modernity has proved incapable of feeding: nature abhors a vacuum, the secularization of Western societies has created an irresistible suction effect for the foreigner, confident and determined to prevail where the sum of our cowardice prepared him a comfortable place. Our Lord warned us: "And if a house is divided against itself, that house will not be able to stand" (Gospel of Mark), and also: "For false Christs and false prophets will arise and will show great signs and wonders, so as to mislead, if possible, even the elect" (Gospel of Matthew). No nation is invaded from the outside without first having collapsed from within.[200]

For this new Christian militantism to assert itself, according to Langella, "You have to be everywhere: on the street, in high schools, universities, sports clubs, political parties, associations, etc. It is here and now, in patience and determination, that is built the counter-society destined to take the place of the rotten anti-civilization we see collapsing around us."[201] And, because "you have to be everywhere," together with Generation Identity; they too marched in the streets of Paris at the "This is our home!" demonstration.

The Vatican's "This is everyone's home" philosophy—even more obvious, from the standpoint of Identitarians, since the beginning of the mandate of Pope Francis in 2013 and his unconditional welcome of all immigrants and refugees—has been nothing but an aiding and abetting of the foreign conquest of "home." That is certainly the view of Tom Sunić. "Surely, one can blame George Soros [a Hungarian-American financier] and a host of murky NGO's for flooding the West with African and Asian migrants," he wrote. "Yet the fact remains that these migrants follow first and foremost the unilateral invitation calls from EU high-ranking politicians seconded by the Pope and the high Catholic clergy."[202] Speaking about Pope Francis, Philippe de Villiers—a right-wing politician, as well as a writer, who permanently alerts others to the "islamization" of France—calls him "the Pope of the Camp of the Saints," probably recalling Jean Raspail's words about the "His Holiness" of his chronicle of the end of the West: "A pope in tune with the times, congenial to the press. What a fine front-page story!"[203] The vast majority of the Catholic clergy is no different, and when the Archbishop of Cologne celebrated a Corpus Christi Mass in front of the city's cathedral with a refugee boat serving as the altar, Martin Lichtmesz saw this "macabre theatre" as a scene that could have come from "The Camp of the Saints" and a defining symbol of the "perversion of the Christian religion." It is now impossible to deny that "mainstream Catholicism—with the Pope at the helm—is unlocking, with increasing speed, the globalist religion of humanity, open borders, and hyper moral ethics."[204]

Langella, although critical, is benevolent toward the pope. "The Church is not a political party, it is a family," he says, adding, "To me, when the Pope speaks of immigration, I somehow seem to hear an old uncle who goes off the rails. I do not listen to everything he says and I have a profound affection for him."[205] But Faye, in this most perilous hour, instead spares no words in speaking of the pope. In all his pronouncements ("We are all migrants" or "It is hypocritical to call oneself a Christian and send away a refugee") and gestures (from "washing the feet of Arab and African illegal immigrants in front of TV cameras" to bringing Muslim families to Rome, to the detriment of persecuted Middle Eastern Christians), Francis is the pontiff of submission to Islam: "His signals have heavy international consequences: an open door for the Muslim invasion is being recommended by the Pope himself, it's a real 'miracle of God!' For the Pope, Europe is a 'homeland for human rights' and not the home of a people and a civilization."[206] Is the man who is seen by many as the Holy Father "a deluded naïve utopian or a cynic destructive of European identity? . . . In any case, the message to Christianity and Europeans is clear: do not resist the Islamization, you risk nothing. Does the Pope himself believe in this lie?"[207] And when the Pope asked the refugees for "forgiveness" because of Europe's "closure" and "indifference," Adriano Scianca responded with "Of course, forgive us. Forgive the endless stream of non-refundable money thrown into the business of welcoming what enriches the few and impoverishes the world; forgive us if we gave entire neighborhoods and entire cities to newcomers; forgive us if we stopped defending ourselves, our land and our family; forgive us if we want to offer, in addition to sustenance, also citizenship; forgive the movies, the conferences, the editorials glorifying immigrants and insulting the locals." All of this, for the pope, "is still not enough," even though it is "much more than any other people in history has ever done to abet its own invasion." Scianca then follows with the question: "Pope Francis, beyond any assessment about his religion, is he today the number one enemy of Europe?"[208] The same pope who, in a private audience with French Catholics, accepted that "we can speak today of an Arab invasion [as] a social fact," but then, nevertheless, de-dramatize it by remarking, "How many invasions Europe has known throughout its history!" Europe "has always known how to overcome itself, moving forward to find itself as if made greater by the exchange between cultures."[209] But Identitarians see only a mix of delusion and capitulation in his words. "Pope Francis speaks about an 'Arab invasion' of Europe. But then, for him, it is not a Great Replacement but an enrichment," tweeted the president of the Bloc Identitaire. Jean Raspail, a royalist and Roman Catholic who is a longtime disbeliever in such "enrichment," deems instead that, in the face of the influx of non-European populations to the continent and in order to avoid the "submersion" of "our countries," Christian charity needs to take a backseat, and the faithful, if they are able, need to "harden their heart and remove from it any kind of compassion."[210] When all is said and done, maybe a "kind of reconquest" is *possible*, "undoubtedly different from the [*Reconquista* of the] Spanish but taking as a starting point the same reasons." It will be a "perilous story to write about," and "its author has probably not yet been born, but it is a book that will see the light of day at the appointed time, I am sure," Raspail prophesied more than thirty years after he had his "vision" of the suicide of the "decadent lot" known as Westerners.[211]

FOUR

For a New Geopolitics of Europe

> Europe cannot live without its homelands . . . but the homelands cannot live anymore without Europe. Born of Europe, they must return to Europe.
> —Pierre Drieu la Rochelle, *L'Europe contre les Patries*

A CONTINENTAL LIBERATION

Seeking a pathway to Europe's liberation from the "death-grip of globalism" and all its putative evils, Identitarians often look back at that moment in time when the decline of a once dominant continent began. "The Summer of 1914: Why Did Europe Commit Suicide?," questioned the cover of a special issue of *La Nouvelle Revue d'Histoire* precisely one hundred years later. "Patiently built over a long time, 'the most precious part of the terrestrial universe' evoked by [Paul] Valéry came out ruined and helpless from the 'Thirty Years' War' caused by the assassination at Sarajevo," editorialized Philippe Conrad.[1] The two world wars and the interwar period—Europe's second Thirty Years' War—in fact, is the tragedy that occupies a founding role in Dominique Venner's narrative about the continent's present-day decadence. Europe lost the "confidence in its civilization and destiny," and from this protracted civil war, which was nothing less than a "suicide," it emerged "politically defeated, socially shattered, and morally broken down."[2] Geopolitically, Europe was cast from the driver's seat of history, with the Yalta agreements demoting it to a pawn between "two messianic systems [Americanism and Communism] whose geostrategic interests were opposed to each other, but which nevertheless remained united in their aversion to old Europe and her civilization, and by the desire to make men homogenous economic agents."[3] It was Europe as a whole that was shaken by the destructive wars of the twentieth century, and that is why Venner repeatedly sent out a call for a European "awakening" that would transcend its nation-states in the name of a wider, historically, physically, and spiritually connected "European homeland." This emphasis on pan-Europeism is far from novel and in fact manifested itself in the interwar and postwar periods in various ideological settings, including in the nonconformist and fascist-inspired movements and the writings of intellectuals—such as the French writer Pierre Drieu la Rochelle, a veteran of World War I, who throughout his life was a passionate defender of a united Europe, or a "United States of Europe," as the only way to achieve a viable future for the continent.[4] Europe's liberation demanded more than what "petty nationalisms" could offer.

It was in this spirit that in the early 1960s, in the context of the Cold War and within the camp of the defense of a continent-wide "nationalism," the Belgian optometrist and geopolitical theorist Jean Thiriart launched the movement Jeune Europe (Young Europe), which became active in many countries. Based on the refusal to accept a weak Europe stuck between two antagonistic power blocs, it vowed to find a third way whereby "real Europe" (as a "European nation") could regain its status, power, and destiny. Later, while the Cold War was coming to its end, in order to free Europe from America's "golden slavery," Thiriart defended a tightening of the relationship between Europe and the Eastern superpower, the Soviet Union, as a way of promoting a sort of anti-American "Euro-Soviet empire." Ultimately, what matters is that the twin notions of Europe as a *great motherland* and of *European patriotism* as the way forward for Europe's emancipation—which in the post–Cold War years indicated emancipation from US tutelage *and* from the US-approved model of European unity in the form of the European Union (EU)—have resounded across the years and reverberate today, in various fashions, throughout the European Identitarian camp. These ideas fuel the search of many groups, intellectuals, and activists for a new geopolitics that, after the trauma of the European civil war, will at long last free "old" Europe and honor its legacy and identity.

THE GEOPOLITICS OF DISSIDENCE

The Input of the Nouvelle Droite

The European Nouvelle Droite (ND) helped to establish the geopolitical master frame through which the Identitarians of today view and interpret international events, processes, and dynamics. No doubt Europeism was *the* driving concept behind the ND's intellectual enterprise. As did the Europeism advocated, for example, by Thiriart, it also became a factor of distinction in regard to traditional, more conventional, nationalist formations still too attached to a nation-state-centered way of thinking about international affairs. Jean-Claude Valla, one of the founders of GRECE, described the cultural milieu from which this ND think tank emerged as "viscerally European."[5] And so the title of its long-running magazine—*éléments pour la civilisation européenne* (elements for European civilization)—is by itself a manifesto of these intellectuals' intention: ideological combat for Europe.

The defense of an autonomous, independent, and powerful Europe was at the forefront of the ND's self-proclaimed mission. "Neither slaves, nor robots," wrote Alain de Benoist, rejecting in this manner both the "military colonization" of Europe by the Soviet Union and the "moral colonization" by the United States.[6] In fact, since the mid-1970s, under the influence of the Italian intellectual Giorgio Locchi, the ND started to bear as its hallmark both a vociferous condemnation of the United States and the defense of an indissoluble separation between *l'Amérique* and Europe. "As so often happens," recalls Guillaume Faye, "the most important and the most groundbreaking people remain little known: it was the case of Giorgio Locchi, who did not come from the right at all but was on the Italian [political] chessboard in the center-left. However, his philosophical reflection was very powerful and he had the vision of a decoupling Europe–West and Europe–United States."[7] Valla sees in his own "anti-Americanism" and in that of his colleagues one of the most important themes of the metapolitical action of GRECE.[8] "Neither by history, culture, geopolitics, philosophy, nor fundamental affinities is Europe tied to the United States," proclaimed de Benoist in an editorial.[9] With the end of the Cold War there remained only one choice: resistance to a US-dominated new world order. In the face of American hegemony, "one may collaborate with it, or [one may] find ways of resisting it," said de Benoist at a seminar organized by GRECE dedicated to the topic United States Danger. "We chose resistance."[10]

This ND focus on protecting Europe's civilizational space from the forces arrayed against its historical and cultural integrity is grounded in geopolitics; the group has constantly taken a spatial approach to international relations and given a geographic interpretation to both domestic and foreign issues, with special attention paid to the exercises and modalities of power. From this premise derived its depiction of the West as an ever-expanding US project of world domination. The post–Cold War *Pax Americana*, in the mind of de Benoist, was nothing more than the imposition of a global leadership that took advantage of "the misery of the Third World, the Soviet collapse, and the European mess."[11] To challenge the destructive designs of the "American hyperpower," ND theorists have consistently called for the establishment of an international multipolar order. The model for this order is taken from German political philosopher Carl Schmitt's defense of a "new *nomos* of the earth": a united but pluralistic community that guarantees world equilibrium and generates a new, balanced international law. Following Schmitt's suggestion that the new nomos be constituted by an equilibrium of several independent geopolitical, cultural, and civilizational blocs (each with its own Monroe Doctrine), the ND theorists have defended a multipolar system—also described as a *pluriverse*, as opposed to the *universum* of the West—in which Europe would be a united and autonomous power committed to its *own* project of civilization.[12] Thus the geopolitical focus of the ND is on a politics of great spaces—on a continental scale—which is viewed as being much more consequential for the future of Europe, particularly in times of increased globalization, than the model of the nation-states that has been superseded and long been in decline. No wonder, then, that de Benoist poses the question, "Which European country by itself, even if one of the big ones, can regulate the financial system . . . or confront the migratory wave? The challenges of a changing climate? Or the coming pandemics, and all sorts of trafficking that are expanding on a global scale?"[13] All of these challenges can be faced up to only at a European, continental scale.

Instead of the current EU, which, according to this logic, has been molded by Western liberal capitalism and is intrinsically authoritarian, a truly federalized, decentralized Europe will respect local and regional diversities. ND theorists favor a reversion to an imperial model because empire, according to de Benoist, "always sought to establish an equilibrium between center and periphery, between sameness and diversity, unity and multiplicity."[14] The federalist dynamic is an "extension of the old idea of a supranational empire."[15] In describing in this way the path that should be pursued by a new united Europe, de Benoist is consciously invoking the memory of the Austro-Hungarian Empire. Only within such an imperialistic federal setting is Europe capable of defending the integrity of its civilization, carving out an independent path for itself, escaping decline and a destiny of insignificance in the world. The choice that Europeans will have to make is between "Europe as a Market"—with a "geopolitics of impotence"—and "Europe as a Power"—with a *newfound geopolitics* based on the collective will to matter again in the world stage.[16]

Such a coming new geopolitics demands a reconfiguration of alliances because, in the words of de Benoist, "World War IV" is being waged by "the United States against the world."[17] Picking up on a tenet of classical geopolitics—the principle of "Land and Sea," or that the history of the world is the history of the conflict between maritime and continental powers—he writes that in the twenty-first century "the Land and Sea are the United States against the world—above all against the continental Eurasian bloc."[18] This belief provides the opening for sustained—and quite often passionate—support for a closer relationship, collaboration, and ultimate alliance between Europe and Russia. In an editorial titled "Russia, Europe: The Same Struggle!," de Benoist states that Europe needs a strong Russia, particularly now that Russia under Vladimir Putin has recovered its former status as a great power, in order to safeguard its own independence and escape all forms of external (read: American) "supervision and interference." Their destinies are connected: "Europe must completely disengage from the West and turn to the East. If Russia declines, it will be [Europe's] decline that will follow."[19] Another variation on this theme is the defense of a Paris-Berlin-Moscow axis in order to counteract the US strategies to divide and weaken the continent.[20] "Tomorrow the Russians! In face of American imperialism, Russia with its power restored becomes again a major actor of multipolarism," announced the "magazine of ideas" published by GRECE.[21]

Dugin's Eurasianism

It is within this post–Cold War context that the European New Right established an intellectual and cultural bridge with the Russian political geographer/philosopher Alexander Dugin. The Russian thinker, a major proponent of neo-Eurasianism, had close ties to GRECE in the early 1990s (Dugin named his journal *Elementy* to honor his French counterpart), and, after a period of detachment, the relationship has, if anything, intensified in recent years, with Dugin seeing in his French equivalent "the greatest European thinker of our time."[22] De Benoist, in turn, praises Dugin for his "original thinking" and anticonformist ideology.[23] Dugin, in fact, highly values political imagination, and, particularly since his time as the head of the Center for Conservative Research of the Department of Sociology at Moscow State University (from 2008 to 2014), he has attempted to design a new ideology, a Fourth Political Theory, as an alternative to the failed ideologies of fascism, communism, and liberalism (the only one that still survives).[24] In this sense, neo-Eurasianism, according to Dugin, "may be well regarded as one of the preliminary versions of such a fourth political theory."[25] In fact, Dugin has been an especially attractive thinker to the ND because of his attempt, through his version of the doctrine of neo-Eurasianism, to provide an ideological justification both for a reassertion of the status of Russia as a great power and also for a revolt against the purportedly US-driven New World Order. Dugin believes that Eurasianism, being an anti-Western ideology, has the potential to attract all those movements that challenge the status quo of liberalism, atlanticism, and the global oligarchy associated with them. Also, in a view that finds wide agreement in ND and Identitarian settings, Dugin separates Europe ("I love real Europe," with its "traditional spirit and heroic values") from the West because "Anglo-Saxon liberalism is not Europe, but Anti-Europe."

As Dugin wrote for the website of Katehon, a Russian think tank "whose contributors hold firm to the main principles of the continentalist school of geopolitics": "The West is the sunset, the fall, the descent, which is precisely the etymology that the word has in Russian. I am against the West and for the East, for ascent."[26] From this derives Dugin's defense of a world order based on *multipolarism*, composed of distinct civilizational blocs, each with its own characteristic identity, instead of the unipolar globalism that is hell-bent on imposing a "universal" Western model on the planet. Eurasia—with Russia as its center—would be one of such Great Spaces in a world constituted by multiple regional and distinctive empires. In tandem with the revival of geopolitics in post-Soviet Russia,[27] Dugin understands international relations in geopolitical terms and sees the present situation as the continuation of the historical duel between homogenizing sea-based powers ("thalassocracies") and distinctive land-based civilizations ("tellurocracies"). Amid this he calls out for a "network war" waged by the multipolar world against the Atlanticist hyperpower attempt at global hegemony.[28] It is not surprising that this set of beliefs resonates with the ND ideology, especially with the urgency of counterweighting US hegemony and reversing the onslaught by the disintegrating forces of Western liberalism in the world. In a world freed from the universalizing claims of the West, Europe could follow its own sovereign path, perhaps as part of a Eurasian bloc (a Eurasian federation), or at least in close partnership and communion with Russia, knowing that its own distinctiveness would be respected and fulfilled.

At least that is the hope. The assumption that underlies the ND view of international relations is that the United States is the mastermind of all the tensions between the West, particularly the EU, and Russia. This, too, is a mainstay of the thought of Dugin, who never tires of warning against the war—the instigation of chaos and disorder—to be waged by the unipolar, Atlanticist forces to prevent the reassertion of the European continent and of a Eurasian alternative. According to the theorists of this geopolitics of dissidence, the Cold War never ended, and Americans have waged a proxy war against Russia's geopolitical interests, whether by supporting the "color revolutions" (in Serbia, Georgia, Ukraine, and Kyrgyzstan),[29] allowing Georgia's war against breakaway provinces, expanding the reach of NATO close to Russia's borders, or backing the Eastern enlargement of the EU. The 2014 Crimea crisis, the deposition of the Ukrainian President Viktor Yanukovych, and the conflict in eastern Ukraine are all part of a larger geopolitical picture. They are new episodes of a long historical drama of Western/American promotion of popular unrest in Russia's neighborhood. The overriding goal is to prevent the formation of a "continental bloc" uniting Europe and Russia, a great heartland power that could become a geopolitical challenge to the United States and put an end to Europe's servitude to Washington.[30] Since the rise of Putin the confrontation has intensified, owing to the rescue by the Russian leader (who, de Benoist wrote, is "evidently a great statesman, much superior to his American and European counterparts") of Russia's great historical power and his decision to advance toward a multipolar reorientation of the world against American interests, if need be.[31] The demonization of the Russian president by the Western media is thus expected, "revealing their degree of submission" to the American hyperpower.[32] There should be no wonder, therefore, at the strengthening of ties between GRECE thinkers and Russian neo-Eurasianists. Russia has emerged as a vital ally to the ND search of a great "collective project" for Europe—the dreamed European "imperium"[33]—rooted in a Eurasian continental logic.

THE IDENTITARIANS AND THE SEARCH FOR AN ALTER-EUROPE

The European Union against Europe

Venner could have written these words in the name of all Identitarians, old and young, who militate for another Europe: "Europe was not born of the Treaties of the late twentieth century. She has come from brother-peoples, who have, between the Baltic Sea and the Aegean Sea, and over thousands of years, given rise to an unparalleled community of culture."[34] Indeed, a common thread that crosses the Identitarian field is a fervent Europeism, coupled with a rejection of the current so-called European Union, whose liberal and merchant nature sullies, for Identitarians, what a *real* European unity ought to be. Such materialism is, obviously, at the antipode of the fallen "old Europe," which has been subjugated to the worst of the tyrannies—the tyranny that, in the interwar period, Ernst von Salomon invoked in *The Outlaws*: "There is one tyranny to which we can never submit—economic tyranny; it is entirely foreign to our being, and we cannot develop under it. Its pressure would be unbearable, for it is too narrow and contemptible."[35] Although a continent-wide assertion is imperative in order for the Identitarians to stand their ground against the multiple dangers that corrode its nations, for them the EU is indeed "unbearable" and is actively working to destroy the authentic European identity.

The EU—whose initial configuration had been rebuked in the political manifesto of Thiriart's Young Europe as "legal Europe" as opposed to "real Europe, Europe of the peoples, our Europe"—not only is not the embodiment of European civilization but also is viewed as an Atlanticist, pro-American weapon against the real interests of European peoples. Many Identitarians believe that one of the celebrated architects of the EU, the French diplomat and political economist Jean Monnet, played a decisive role in this development as a lifelong influence-peddler for Anglo-Saxon geopolitical and geoeconomic interests. The EU became both an element in and a stage in the advancement of a liberal-capitalist, "Westerner," world order. The belief expressed by Monnet at the end of his 1976 *Memoirs*—that "the sovereign nations of the past can no longer solve the problems of the present; they cannot ensure their own progress or control their own future. And the Community itself is only a stage on the way to the organized world of tomorrow"[36]—is presented in many Identitarian narratives as a confirmation of the "American mission." Guillaume Faye believes that Monnet was instrumental in establishing the EU as a solid building block of the "America-sphere." Monnet's ideological project prevailed over the Carolingianesque Europe envisioned at the beginning, giving rise to "a purely mercantile European Union, technocratic and rootless, enlarged to almost thirty countries and led by an antidemocratic Commission." This actual, existing EU is, "in reality, an anti-Europe."[37] The idea that the project of European unity was not even at the outset a noble enterprise but from the get-go part of a grander scheme at work is also present in some Identitarian narratives. Sometimes it is even traced to the project initiated by nineteenth-century politician/businessman Cecil Rhodes and executed through a secret society initially entrusted to the British diplomat Alfred Milner of creating a world government that would ensure Anglo-American domination. Writing in *Terre et Peuple* about "the hidden defects of the European construction," Alain Cagnat concluded by saying that "the European Union has achieved the dream of the pioneers Rhodes and Milner: a political union compliant to the Anglo-Saxon New World Order, a liberal economic community tied to Wall Street and the *City*, a single currency subordinated to the dollar and a defense taking orders from the Pentagon and the State Department."[38] No wonder that Cecil Rhodes is one of the "princes of globalism," wrote Eugène Krampon in *Réfléchir & Agir*.[39]

"Transatlantic," the *Dictionary of Newspeak* alerts us, is a "misleading word designating the unequal relations between Europe and the United States," which should in fact be translated as "submission."[40] The US/EU attempt (as of yet unachieved) to create the world's largest free trade market—known as the Transatlantic Trade and Investment Partnership—is viewed as yet another step toward this "submission" of Europe, exploited by and sold to the dictates of Big Business. This "merchant putsch," wrote Georges Feltin-Tracol, sets up the "final dissolution of the Old World in a Western pandemonium *made in Hollywood*."[41] "After seventy years of brainwashing through the media, movies, and music, Europe as a whole is about to forget what it once was, to finally become the great outstretched hand between oligarchs of both sides of the Atlantic,"[42] argued Krampon, echoing the widespread sentiment that agreements such as these—or similar ones in the future—will only result in the final vassalization of Europe.

Brexit as a Good Omen

With each EU crisis, Identitarians of all stripes believe that the project as a whole is nearing its end. Daniel Friberg, an advocate of the return of the "real" Identitarian Right, regards today's EU as a "failed project, dominated by liberalism and subservience to globalist interests."[43] The EU desecrates European civilization, and most of all, as argued by Duarte Branquinho in the Portuguese weekly *O Diabo*, "It is not the European Union, den of bureaucrats and a political abstraction based on economics, that makes us Europeans. The path of Europe is our common History, and it is we who make it."[44] Viewed as a symbol that indeed it is "we," the European peoples, who determine Europe's destination, Brexit, the 2016 British exit from the EU after a popular referendum, was met with widespread acclaim. Its "surprise victory" was a "magnificent kick to the globalist oligarchies," says Feltin-Tracol, even if it may not be a mortal blow, given that the "Brussels Organization will continue to remain an apolitical machine until the moment when men of power gather together and relaunch the beautiful European idea, establishing a European Confederation of states."[45] Writing from Italy on the eve of the referendum, CasaPound's Adriano Scianca remarked that it was an enlightening sign that "all of the oligarchy of the continent mobilized against Brexit," and therefore, "We root for Brexit."[46] Brexit was a lesson for political scientists, noted Faye, because it showed that it was not materialism that was the prime mover of the popular vote, "contrary to the cosmopolitan bourgeoisie, the rooted people does not think in terms of 'money first,' but 'identity first.'"[47]

Within the Identitarian youth movement, from France to Germanic countries and beyond, Brexit was viewed as a harbinger of good and better things to come. This position is coherent with a movement whose adherents, two years earlier, in 2014, for example, marched in the streets of Vienna under the motto "Our Europe is not your Union!" In a follow-up communiqué, the French Génération Identitaire, whose members took part in the demonstration, reiterated that "the European Union is not the European civilization! More than ever, and seeing ourselves as Alter-Europeans, we defend a European Europe, free, strong and united."[48] On the day of the British referendum, Pierre Larti, the spokesman for the French Generation Identity, tweeted that the choice at the polls was between "the EU at the service of the powerful and wealthy of globalization [and] the Identity at the service of peoples! #LeaveEU." The German activists of Identitäre Bewegung celebrated the referendum outcome with "[a tip of the] chapeau to the British." The IB activists cheered: "May this be an incentive for all other countries that they have to put an end to the current European dictatorship," and concluded with the rallying-cry, "Because our Europe is not their Union!"[49] Brexit also helped to breed a new type of Identitarian activist. Such was the case with Generation Identity's Tom Dupré, whose involvement with the Leave campaign was his first experience with political activism and for whom "this seemed to me to be the first time issues around identity had been discussed at the national level in England, and it was a pivotal moment. The campaign highlighted the gulf between accepted and popular opinion and called into question the 'democratic' nature of a lot of the changes and decisions made in Britain over the last decades."[50] The Austrian Martin Sellner, one of the leading members of the movement in Europe, believes that, ultimately, Brexit is "the beginning of the removal of the internationalist utopia that the EU was. . . . They thought that they were building 'the first non-imperial empire' (in the words of the former EU Commission President Durão Barroso) that would last and expand forever. In fact, they have just built a frail festival stage for the end of an era. Now the festival of multiculturalism is over and the European people are faced with a rough and inevitable decision. Reconquista or requiem. Either way this Union has no future."[51]

As a sign that for most Identitarians the EU indeed "has no future," Czech Republic activists from Generace Identity performed a "funeral"

FIGURE 28. Meme or propaganda material from the German Identitarian movement. It reads, "Europe, Youth, Reconquista!"

to "bury" the EU, marching in the streets of Prague carrying a mock coffin draped in an EU flag with the procession, led by a fake priest, ending in a burial ceremony in front of the government buildings. "*Identitáři* reject the European Union because it is not regarded as a representation of Europe and its people, but as an exponent of the interests of the US and international globalist elites," they later announced on their website. This comment appeared under the headline "We Buried the European Union."[52]

If across the Identitarian intellectual and activist spectrum the commitment to the idea of Another Europe is total, the primacy given to geopolitics, or to geopolitical debates, varies, ranging from very high in older publications and networks associated with the Identitarian school of thought—more invested in the theoretical side of the war of ideas—to flimsy within the more praxis-driven younger Identitarian Lambda movement and CasaPoundism. In general, on the activist side, the sentiment is that there are other, more urgent daily things to fight about, such as the ravages of multiculturalism across European nations. The same variation occurs regarding the time and attention paid to the role of Russia across the geopolitical board, or about the levels of Russophilia, which, although prevalent, is not uniform.

THE SUN RISES IN THE EAST

Dwarfed by America

For people on the more theory-oriented side of the Identitarian network, geopolitics has always been the heart of their understanding of international politics. Starting from the premise that Europe is a vast space that is delimited by geography and contains a unique civilization, Identitarians have held firmly to the geopolitical driving idea that Europe's future must be dissociated from that of "the West," which is nothing more than an imperialist projection of America.

A long-standing intellectual contributor to geopolitics and geostrategy—and a reference in dissident and Identitarian circles in all matters pertaining the geopolitical state of Europe—has been the Brussels native Robert Steuckers, who regularly addresses these issues in publications, at conferences, in interviews with alternative/dissident media sites, and in online writings, especially in his blog and Euro-Synergies network.[53] The reason for this commitment, as he explains in the final pages of the first volume of *Europa*, subtitled *The Values and Deep Roots of Europe*, lies in his specific interpretation of Europe as a "community of combat," meaning, he says, "Yes, I belong to the community of combat that wants, despite all the vicissitudes and all the neglect, to keep our civilization and its peoples out of any foreign stranglehold, to remove them from any geopolitics or geostrategy aimed at their suffocation and submersion."[54] Above all, and consistently throughout his interventions, Steuckers has denounced what he calls the "Americano-centric globalist system" and the various instruments that it uses in order to keep Europe subordinated, as a "dwarf," always dependent on the will and whims of the geopolitical hegemon across the Atlantic. Accordingly, if the history of Europe has been characterized by attempts at "de-enclaving," projecting itself and its power outside its original medieval space, the plan by American strategists has been to "re-enclave" Europe, blocking any independent efforts to establish relations and alliances that would better serve its own self-interest. The strategy of destabilization serves this geopolitical purpose: "One can see it," Steuckers writes: "The enemy is Europe, which must be re-enclaved and which must be imploded from inside by delivering it permanently to scatterbrained politicians and by constantly discharging into it heterogeneous and inassimilable populations."[55] At the same time, America instigates turmoil in crucial transit zones, or gateway regions, such as Eastern Europe and the Middle East, transforming them into shattered belts, or zones of endemic instability, which block the points of entry into the heartlandic Eurasian region.

This is done in accordance with the geopolitical imperative announced by the late US geostrategist Zbigniew Brzezinski in *The Great Chessboard*: because "America's global primacy is directly dependent on how long and how effectively its preponderance on the Eurasian continent is sustained," for America, "the chief geopolitical prize is Eurasia."[56] In the view of Steuckers, the fronts of the Donbass region in eastern Ukraine and in Syria are two theaters of the same war—both are "'gateway areas' over 'rimlands' surrounding the 'heartland' middle earth, dominated by Russia," which heightened the strategic need to artificially create conflicts in these portal regions so they can no longer play their role as an interface between large regions of Eurasia. This led to the creation of "permanent turbulence or long-term wars and indirect support to intermediaries, 'proxies,' whose ideology is always crazy, delusional, criminal and fanatic." For decades, these portal regions will be unusable, and can no longer be used to construct alternative "continental" projects, which, of course, is the goal of the great "thalassocratic power of the New World."[57] Steuckers believes that a crucial step for Europe to develop a "strategy of power" to combat the American strategy is to reappropriate its own history and invest in the humanities, which is contrary to what the current mercantile Europe has recently been doing: "Without historians and philologists, without geopolitical offices and institutes, one falls into muck and mediocrity. That in which we are actually wallowing."[58] Such intellectual investment should be the "ground zero" of Europe's geopolitical liberation.

The Euro-Slav Embrace

Writing about Russia's first Emperor, Peter I the Great, as the "Czar who looked to Europe," the Spanish Identitarian Enrique Ravello said that throughout its history the country, like the double-headed eagle on Russia's coat of arms, experienced the tension between facing the East or the West; this tension could be sublimated by a "Euro-Slav Russia, as an axis of continental unification of all the peoples of boreal origin, from Reykjavík to Uelen: once again, our Eurosiberia."[59] In fact, this concept of Eurosiberia, which was introduced and promoted by Faye and became the geopolitical mobilizing myth of many Identitarians, entails, in his words, "the decoupling of Western Europe from the American West, and Europe's solidarity and alliance with Russia," as a sort of "destined space in which European peoples will finally regroup."[60] The notion is dominant in the Terre et Peuple network, which defends a pan-European continent that includes Russia (and excludes Turkey and Israel)—a sort of "pan-European boreal arc of nations that goes from Brest to Vladivostok," the seaport city located on the far eastern side of Russia.[61] This historical and cultural community constitutes a "homogenous ensemble, without ruptures, from Lisbon to Vladivostok, and from Reykjavík to Yerevan," and its union in an imperial confederation, which should bear the name of Eurosiberia, is "the only hope of survival for Europeans."[62] The coming Eurosiberia, or the new European empire, claims Alain Cagnat, "European and white, strong with its 700 million people, will be the most powerful ensemble of the planet and the leader of future geopolitical blocs: the Jewish-Anglo-American world, China, India, the Arab-Muslim world."[63]

The project of Eurosiberia, viewed as a "positive utopia,"[64] embraces Russia as a vital partner, a brother of civilization and history. Consequently, Faye announced at the turn of the century, "It is not toward New York that would be the intelligent turn in order to confront our millenarian enemies but toward Moscow. *There* is our true alliance . . . *there* is our empire, our fortress, our vital space. We are one and the same people, alone in front of the destiny, today under siege."[65] In more recent years, especially under the influence of Russian Identitarians such as Pavel Tulaev, the concept of "Euro-Russia" has also been used as a substitute for Eurosiberia in order to recognize the role of Russia as an actor in the Eurasian space. As Steuckers explains, "Tulaev believed, rightly—and Faye recognized it—that Siberia was not a player of history. The player of history in the Eurasian and Eurosiberian space has been Russia, from Ivan the Terrible to Putin. That is why we talk of Euro-Russia in our regions, instead of Eurasianism."[66] In favor of such a project, Tulaev says, "I would be happy if the authentic Europe would be free from American globalism . . . 'Americanization,' 'Westernization,' I call it 'Honey Hell.' Russians are ready to help our European brothers in many ways. We have even started the project of the Euro-Russian Confederation or the Continental Empire, if you would like. My good friend Kris Roman is coordinating the Euro-Russian geopolitical center in Belgium."[67] Advertised as an independent think tank, this "Euro-Rus" center proposes "a future, from Gibraltar to Vladivostok!" as another motto for the coveted Great Europe.[68]

The combat against US-driven globalism, warns Krampon, is titanic and requires "novel alliances" and the creation of a "united Europe from Dublin to Vladivostok to take down the filthy hydra which is, in fact, the real cancer of the planet."[69] Whether called Eurosiberia, Euro-Russia, or another neologism, this space is looked at as an ethnosphere, or a bloc of ethnically related peoples. "No globalist barbarism," wrote Pierre Krebs in *Terre et Peuple*, "will stop in the long run the birth of a Europe-Russia ethno-socialist empire."⁷⁰ It is only natural that Identitarians do not identify with neo-Eurasianism as described by Dugin, owing to the fact that it implies the formation of an empire that is multiethnic and multiracial, extending way beyond the frontiers of Europe and far from the ethnocentric European project that they envision.⁷¹ Says Faye, "Dugin has interpreted anti-Westernism in a simplistic way: We are Asians! But his theories are dangerous because they distance Russia from its true roots."⁷² Because Atlanticist liberal capitalism *is* the enemy, Dugin goes as far as defending a broader "revolutionary" alliance of all peoples, including Islamic movements: "If Identitarians really love their identity," he wrote, "they should ally themselves with Eurasianists, alongside traditionalists and the enemies of capitalism belonging to any people, religion, culture or political camp."⁷³ In the end, as Dugin said in an interview with John Morgan and Daniel Friberg of Arktos, for tactical reasons, "all those who oppose liberal hegemony are our friends for the moment. This is not morality, it is strategy."⁷⁴ The supposed benefits of such a strategy, however, are not strong enough to cause these Identitarians to deviate from their own ethno-spiritual attachment to Europe.

Russia as the Last Best Hope

What is Europe? Europe is its "high places," says the Iliad Institute video: "The Parthenon, the Place Saint-Marc, Saint Peter of Rome, the Belém Tower, Saint-James of Compostela, the Mont-Saint-Michel, the Tower of London, the Brandenburg Gate, and the Kremlin Towers."⁷⁵ *European* Russia is often looked at as the last best Identitarian hope of the continent. At the very heart of the Identitarian embrace of Russia is its perceived role as the guardian of Europe's tradition. Amid the crumbling of ancient European traditions—in religion, family, and values—caused by an out-of-control liberalism and the risk of substitution by the cultural assertiveness of non-European peoples, Russia is viewed as the remaining stronghold of the "original" European culture.

"'Liberal—is that a dirty word?' Bezletov asked. . . . 'In Russia, it's worse than the plague,' Sasha answered simply." Thus wrote Zakhar Prilepin in his novel *Sankya*, an account of the post–Cold War Russian nationalist revolt.⁷⁶ Announcing a new term that is "all the rage" in Moscow—*Liberast*, or one who is totally subjugated to the Western liberal model—*Réfléchir & Agir* exults: "A beautiful definition to be used in abundance."[77] Identitarians include the struggle against something that they also view as "worse than the plague" in a wider framework. Aymeric Chauprade sees the struggle between "materialism" and "tradition" as the ideological combat of our times. When he was still influencing the geopolitical doctrine of the Front National (from 2013 to 2015), in a speech at the Duma (Russian parliament) he called for the establishment of an "International identity" against "Western globalism," the "totalitarianism" that "destroys simultaneously the family and the nation, reducing the human being to a consumer enslaved to merchandising and sexual instincts" and declared that instead "the time has come to create, around Russia, and with the patriots of all countries, the International of all those who love their identity, and their family."[78] Not only is Russia widely viewed as the reservoir of assailed European values; it is also viewed as a possible protective shield of Europe against the imperialist advance of the American superpower. By and large, international affairs are viewed through a default position of Russophilism.

This Russia-oriented geopolitical path is now possible because, after the "dark times" of Westernization immediately after the Cold War, Russia managed to regain its identity and assertiveness on the world stage. In the mid-1990s, Dominique Venner predicted that "in one way or another, Russia would reemerge as a great power" and as an "empire," replicating what has happened before in Russian history after similar periods of decline.[79] Later Venner saw Putin's speech at the Munich security conference of 2007, in which the Russian president denounced the pernicious role of the United States in international relations, as a watershed. Putin's defense of sovereignty was a return to an "ancient European tradition" and was in direct opposition to imperialistic inroads under pseudo-humanitarian pretexts.[80]

"Russia Is Back," announced one of the issues of *Terre et Peuple* containing a long article by Jean-Patrick Arteault about the 2008 Georgia-Russia conflict that was viewed as a striking example of the idea that Russia "is the only remaining European state with the will to oppose the West. Maybe the last chance for the West to crash, allowing in its fall our liberation."[81] The presidency of Putin is seen by Identitarians as a globe-shaking circumstance that may lead to the salvation of Europe. Sometimes Putin is regarded as a quasi-providential figure. "At the end

FIGURE 29. Cover of the *Terre et Peuple* magazine with the title "Russia Is Back" (Autumn 2008).

of the 20th century Russia's situation was almost desperate. . . . But Russia never dies," proclaimed Alain Cagnat. "An obscure KGB colonel manages to save her from disaster. . . . Slowly he gives back to Russia its status of great power and to the Russian people its pride. The fifteen years of his reign allow the new Czar to accomplish a series of successes at the expense of the West."[82] Writes Pierre Vial, "Today, we see Westerners falling in the trap to besiege Russia." Washington, in particular, "fears and refuses all Identitarian assertiveness, thinking that it may threaten its hegemony—which is true."[83] Faye, in a speech in Moscow, reinforced a similar credo: "Without Russia Europe does not exist. And even if all European peoples have been sickened by the Americanization of culture, the replacement of a population by immigration, and the phenomenon of decadence, nevertheless Russia is the country that, in spite of all, has still preserved and kept its sanity."[84] Russia is a "shocking word," says the *Dictionary of Newspeak*, "a sort of mafia hell always opposed to the liberal paradise of the multiracial and globalist society."[85] Identitarians' Russophilia, then, is proportional to their perception of the rampant US-instigated Russophobia in the West.

Not that the demonization of Russia is by itself a new phenomenon, argues Steuckers. It has a long history, from the times of the czars to the times of Sovietism, and today the anti-Russian propaganda has as its overriding goal to "prevent the development of an alternative geopolitical thought that is non-Atlantist."[86] This pervasive Russophobia in the ruling historiography and in the media is part and parcel of a larger geostrategy. "Russia's renaissance," under Putin, Faye alleges, led to a vicious campaign by the "three sisters"—the US Pentagon, the CIA, and the military-industrial complex—who are hell-bent on "reconstituting the Iron Curtain: a second Cold War."[87] The NATO encroachment on Russia's borders, the support given to rebellions in regions under Russia's sphere of influence, the sanctions against Russia, the deployment of NATO military forces in Eastern Europe under the pretext of deterrence (Faye believes that a military confrontation pursued by the powerful transatlantic lobbies may happen in the Russian enclave of Kaliningrad on the Baltic Sea, which borders two NATO members, Poland and Lithuania), and the manufacture through constant disinformation of the image of so-called "Putinland" as a menace to peace and world security are all components of a strategy of "provocation" aimed at overthrowing the hated regime of Putin, stopping Russia's comeback as a great power, and preventing a Euro-Russian alliance.[88] By this logic, Identitarians' providing support to Russian ventures—whether in foreign policy or national affairs, such as in regard to traditional family values—is almost a foregone conclusion. In the end, what matters, according to Pierre Vial, whose Terre et Peuple network is dominated by high levels of Russophilia, is that "all those in Europe who wage the combat of Identitarian resistance, salute the flag of 'Great Russia.'"[89]

Although Russia has never lived up to the status of "Third Rome" envisioned by the monk Filofei in his epistles of the early sixteenth-century—after Rome and the "New Rome," as Constantinople was known—many Identitarians hope that Russia may yet accomplish, in strong communion with the rest of Europe, the historical mission of challenging and overcoming the Western hegemon. This Eastern reorientation of European politics—very much present already in Moeller van den Bruck's defense of a "community of destiny" between Germany and Russia instead of their subjugation to the decadence of the West—often translates into a defense of a Paris-Berlin-Moscow axis as a touchstone for such a geopolitical regeneration. No easy task, of course, owing to the multitude of forces amassed against it. "The budget from the United States for spying on Russia has surpassed that of the Cold War," announced the Russian television network RT (and immediately retweeted by Steuckers) in September 2016.[90] The news that the US intelligence agencies vastly increased their spying operations against Russia was just another confirmation of the challenges faced by any would-be rivalries to American hegemony.

The US National Security Agency's clandestine data surveillance programs—from the earlier system known as ECHELON to the twenty-first-century PRISM, whose existence was leaked by Edward Snowden—show the extent to which the Western hegemon goes in order to strategically control foes and allies alike. "No diplomatic secret, no freedom of action is possible," contends Steuckers. What is more, Europe is unable and unwilling to shake off its serfdom: "Europe does not respond as it should, with a sensational exit from the American sphere, but on the contrary she shows servility, in the name of an alliance without object and based on old fantasies of WWII [that is, of Europe's closeness to the United States because of the latter's saving Europe in the war]; this does not prevent the United States from seeing Europe in practice as a group of 'suspicious' countries, as enemy nations to be monitored so that they do not have any autonomous initiative." If one adds to this US method of "unconventional warfare" the ever-increasing influence of the "new superpowers," the Internet companies that collaborate with surveillance programs and feed on the insatiable human need for exhibitionism, Steuckers thinks that the world is approaching the situation not of Orwell's *1984* but of Ismail Kadaré's novel *The Palace of Dreams*, in which total transparency and the ascendancy of the ruling power over society are achieved through voluntary collaboration by its subjects.[91]

In the end, according to Steuckers, in a world where "Americans, Russians, Indians and Chinese clearly affirm their national—and even subcontinental and civilizational—sovereignty," Europe stands alone in its renunciation of *Realpolitik*.[92] In this frame of mind, Steuckers is not the least shocked by the accusations that Russia—particularly since 2016—has used the Internet and social media to influence electoral results in the United States and Western Europe: "It is obvious that this back-and-forth accusing each other of using the new means of communication for the purpose of propaganda is a normal accusation between powers that clash in all areas."[93] This is what great powers do; therefore, the allegations that Russia meddled in Western liberal democracies—through influence operations—is added confirmation that, under Putin, and against the American hegemon, Russia has regained its central role in international affairs.

East Central Europe as a Precious "Vault"

An eastward-looking geopolitical orientation as a "salvation" from the West is not solely focused on Russia. There is also in many Identitarian settings an emphasis on East Central Europe as a whole, as a sane, healthy, commonsensical space that has been preserved from Westernism and within which the roots of an alternative Europe may emerge. "While communism did a lot of irreparable damage to the nations of the Soviet bloc, it was not nearly as efficient in eroding national and cultural identities as liberalism has been," notes Friberg, whose Arktos publishing house is based in Budapest, expressing in this way the hope that what has happened in the Western half of Europe may "serve as a warning to Eastern Europe of how bad things can get when you adopt ethnomasochistic principles and allow the mass immigration of non-Europeans into your countries."[94]

By the same token, the French-Hungarian Ferenc Almássy, an active voice in the anti-Atlanticist network, upholds the idea that the rooted, Identitarian European spirit still blows strong in East Central Europe because the "former communist countries were like stuck in the ice for a half century, keeping most of their traditional values and a traditional ethnic composition," while "Western countries got rotten by liberalism, consumerism and nihilism." In an interview with *Réfléchir & Agir*, Almássy pointed out that "the awareness that Christianity, as moribund as it is, remains the basis, with Greek ethics and Roman law, of our civilization, and that the European ethnicities—which the bravest dare to call the European white race—are the only legitimate [peoples] of Europe, [these] are now dominant ideas in Hungary, Poland, and other countries in the region." Engaged in the communicational battle against the Western "liberal media"—he was a featured speaker of Polémia's second Forum of Dissidence, for example—Almássy founded the online *Visegrad Post* (in 2016), promoted as an unbiased news source about Central Europe and the Balkans. In fact, the Visegrad Four (V4), a group that encompasses Hungary, Poland, Slovakia, and the Czech Republic, is viewed as "the rock on which rests the European resistance," a springboard for "an alternative Europe [that] is designing itself right now, and this is happening in Central Europe, with the V4 as the key of this 'anti-liberal counter-revolution.'"[95]

The winds of such "counter-revolution" are spreading through the Carpathian Basin, and for many Identitarians, Hungary—especially under the leadership, since 2010, of Viktor Orbán—is an inspiration and an example to follow in terms of *what it means* to defend Europe's identity. Tongue-in-cheek, in a video interview with Ábel Bódi, the leader of Hungary's Generation Identity, Sellner said that "Austria needs to become Orbanized."[96] In fact, he could have said that about the whole of Europe. After all, Identitarians can only agree with the Hungarian prime minister's policies—known as Orbanism—of establishing stricter border controls and rejecting non-European immigration, as well as his recurring warnings that, under attack by liberalism and globalism, Europe's fate hangs in the balance and that the defining question of modern times, as he told the newspaper *Magyar Idők*, is "whether the character of European nations will be determined by the same spirit, civilization, culture and mentality as in our parents' and grandparents' time, or by something completely different."[97] In a show of support for protectionist policies viewed by Identitarians as "life-saving" not just for Hungary but for Europe itself, a handful of Generation Identity activists from Germany, Austria, and Slovenia joined their Hungarian fellow Identitarians in the donation of boxes of luxury goods to Hungarian border guards, whom they praised as the ones standing at the forefront of "Europe's defense." They vowed to repeat this initiative on a regular basis.[98]

Often, in Identitarian literature, the roots of Hungary's current "resistance" to the "dictates" of globalism are searched for and found in the country's own history. In an issue of *La Nouvelle Revue d'Histoire* dedicated to "Indomitable Hungary," Philippe Conrad praised the "spirit of resistance and resilience demonstrated by the Hungarians in their millennial history" and said that their historical memory proves to be the "indispensable source of maintaining their identity, and the best defense against the deadly leveling generated by liberal globalism."[99] Writing in *Réfléchir & Agir*, Eugène Krampon ended the review of a book about the 1956 Hungarian Revolution by saying, "1956–2016, Hungarians are always between the best combatants for freedom . . . yesterday against communism, today against globalism."[100] The fact that the billionaire George Soros—infamous in many Identitarian circles for bankrolling allegedly subversive pro-globalist NGOs and a myriad of other groups under the cover of philanthropy, destabilizing in this way the ethnocultural foundations of Europe—is Hungarian-born, adds a touch of (unwanted) irony to this blissful view of the Magyar country. Even if, of course, it is "Orbán's country" that Identitarians have in mind when they think of Hungary as the bedrock of an alternative Europe.

Such an alternative Europe will have to pass through the northeastern part of the continent and through the Baltic Sea; at least that is the hope of Ruuben Kaalep, an ethnonationalist member of the Conservative People's Party of Estonia, who sees himself, too, as a "European Identitarian." Kaalep says, "This sense of being European is important especially in the current demographic crisis which is faced by all European nations and can be handled only by European nationalists [working] together."[101] Here too, Eastern Europe is viewed as "something of a vault" for European peoples, because "what survives in Eastern Europe and has to be rekindled in the West is the principle of ethnonationalism: protection of the true diversity of mankind in both the biological and cultural sense." From this principle, "after the fall of the current liberal system," a "new Europe" may emerge.[102] In fact, Baltic ethnonationalists tend to believe that Identitarianism is fundamentally a "Western European thing." Such is indeed the view of Raivis Zeltīts, the secretary general of Latvia's National Alliance and a former speaker at the Swedish conference Identitarian Ideas, for whom "[Identitarianism] is in a way a step back—the idea is that Europeans are some kind of 'natives' in a multicultural society, where they have to compete with other ethnic groups that could in the future become the dominant ones. . . . Therefore, Identitarianism is a way to be ethnonationalist in Western European context. For us, nation and national state are closely linked. The nation state secures the existence of the nation with a certain ethnic core."[103] Here again the idea that what European Identitarians fight to maintain—and to a large extent to recover (their ethnocultural roots and ties)—has not yet been lost in Eastern Europe because of its different historical evolution, particularly since World War II.

Europe, On Its Feet Again

In the end, the common threads that run through the various Identitarian geopolitical narratives on Europe are the attachment to Europe as a civilizational space and the desire to see it on its feet again, liberated from the destructive Western/globalist domination. Also, although a Russia-oriented geopolitical course is widely seen as a better alternative to the current Western submission, it does not necessarily follow, at least in some Identitarian circles, that it is the ideal alternative. In Germany, Götz Kubitschek echoes this sentiment, saying that "Europe should detach from the United States as far as necessary and follow Russia as closely as necessary," cautioning, however, against "a brotherly kiss between Europe and Russia—following the three-foot rule in any direction is essential. Europe, Russia, the US—just three out of a dozen *Großräume* (greater spaces) in a multipolar world."[104] Perhaps the idea of an "imperial Europe from Reykjavík to Vladivostok" should be seen essentially, says Feltin-Tracol, as a "mobilizing myth," while a more adjusted solution would be a "Confederation of European States, which would correspond to the current pseudo-EU without Britain or Russia, which would still be our main ally." The "destiny of Europe is neither in the East nor in the West and even less in the South: it is in itself."[105] What counts is that Europe should no longer be an occupied continent. "Ideally, I would like to see an independent European geopolitical alliance," argues Friberg. "Europe has been divided and occupied by the Atlanticist liberals in the West and the Soviet socialists in the East since WWII. It is time for Europe to unite and assert itself, and stop allowing foreign powers to rule her."[106] The imperialism of Russia may reveal itself to be detrimental to an Identitarian Europe. "I see no chance that Russia would sacrifice its geopolitical ambitions and imperial mindset for one that would value the diverse European nations and European ethnic-self-preservation above all," contends the Estonian Kaalep, almost certainly recalling the recent history of his country.[107] From this derives a certain mistrust of Dugin, and neo-Eurasianist ventures, because, in the words of Feltin-Tracol, although it is "a brilliant reformulation of the Pan-Russian nationalism," Dugin's Eurasianism "answers the call of the Tundra, the steppes and the Taiga, in the same way that liberalism corresponds to an Anglo-Saxon worldview."[108] As Martin Lichtmesz has pointed out, "I think what Dugin is doing is to sort of create a 'Reichs-ideologie,' an Imperial ideology or even theology for a new Russian Empire. . . . So I think Dugin suits his ideas to fit Russian geopolitical interests, and that would naturally not work with Identitarianism."[109] In the long run, for Identitarians, true Europeanism, even if decidedly Eastern-looking, can flourish only by respecting and preserving the spatial memory and integrity of historically and ethnically related peoples and communities.

THE IDENTITARIAN YOUTH MOVEMENT

Getting the Priorities Straight

A recurring historical anecdote has it that as Constantinople was falling to the Ottoman Turks in 1453, Byzantines were entangled in serious discussions about the sexuality of the angels. This unfair portrayal of the last days of "New Rome"—especially because the Romans of Byzantium *did* try to defend their Queen of Cities from the Sultan Mehmet's invasion—most likely originated from fact that the Byzantine Empire was characterized by complex theological discussions and controversies. This is, in fact, the reason that today "Byzantine" stands for "complicated and difficult to understand" in many languages.

This prelude to Byzantine history, or to the end of Byzantine history, serves to illustrate the sentiment that fills many of the younger activists of the European Identitarian front when confronted with "Byzantine" discussions about geopolitical assumptions and speculations regarding the state of their continent. For them, as Europe faces *another* invasion, as it is being turned upside down and conquered by *new* invaders, its priority should be to wage battle and set up barricades instead of making intellectual incursions into interesting but ultimately secondary-at-best issues that may end up functioning as pointless diversions from *the* Identitarian battle of our times. This latter way of thinking is seen as prosaic and, as the leading Austrian activist, Martin Sellner, argues, "At the moment we are losing our very own countries and everywhere in Europe patriots have lost any control or influence in the states in which they live. So I always considered the magniloquent geopolitical projects of some right-wing writers as an escape from reality." Geopolitical conjectures "will become completely irrelevant if the Islamization of Europe continues in the way it does."[110] As in the fall of Constantinople in the past, what is at stake today is the survival of a people and a civilization, and *this* puts *all other issues* into perspective. "A nation can recover from economic and cultural crisis. The worst mistakes and defeats can be fixed already in the next generation. The process of the Great Replacement, however, is irreversible. It goes to the substance. All debates about forms of government, economic systems, religious and environmental issues, will be useless if the 'subject' of these questions, the people, no longer exists," reiterated Sellner when presenting his movement to the readers of the German sovereigntist magazine *Compact*.[111] In order to avoid the fate of the Byzantines, debating into oblivion is the last choice the youthful frontline of European Identitarians should make.

Low-Intensity Geopolitics

The program of Les Identitaires—which in July 2016 became the new name for the Bloc Identitaire—for example, makes clear that "*Reconquista*," the retaking of the territory and the culture lost to Muslims, is its "mobilizing myth," its leitmotif, reaffirming the overriding priority of the Identitarian movement mentioned by Sellner.[112] At the same time, even if the interest in geopolitics is low and does not occupy center stage, it is far from absent, because there still lies within the activism of the Identitarian movement a geopolitical vision, as well as a diffuse pro-Russian outlook, in opposition to Europe's ongoing "submission" to America's geostrategic hegemony. Fabrice Robert, the national director of Les Identitaires, asserts, "I think that Europe and France have vis-à-vis Russia"—and in their desire to better align themselves with Washington—"a catastrophic foreign policy. But the goal of the United States is quite clear: to cut Western Europe from Russia in order to better subjugate the first." A geopolitical revamping of Europe must include, he believes, "a strong alliance with Russia," while Putin is flaunted as the type of leader who is sorely lacking in Europe because "he is not willing to renounce his sovereignty and his national independence, representing an example against the European leaders who have abdicated to Washington. A Euro-Russian alliance can only be beneficial to Europe."[113] Here, too, the notion that the emergence of a new, "powerful Europe" entails a tighter communion with Russia is extensive, despite all the perceived Russophobia in progress. When a political scientist wrote in the newspaper *Le Monde* that Russia, not terrorism, is the "first threat to Europe," the president of Generation Identity called it "an article from another planet" and a product of ideological blindness.[114] The new Europe, on the contrary, will be realized "in friendship with our Slavic brethren and Russia," and "we must affirm clearly: neither Allah nor the USA: *Europa Nostra*! [Our Europe!]."[115]

While selling shirts and hoodies emblazoned with the slogan *Europa Nostra* encircling the helmets of the ancient Spartan warriors, the Austrian Identitarian online shop Phalanx Europa explains that this Latin expression means "that Europe belongs to us" and vows to "reclaim our heritage" amid the "ongoing invasion of Europe."[116] In the German-speaking world, too, the Identitarian youth activism for "Our Europe" is

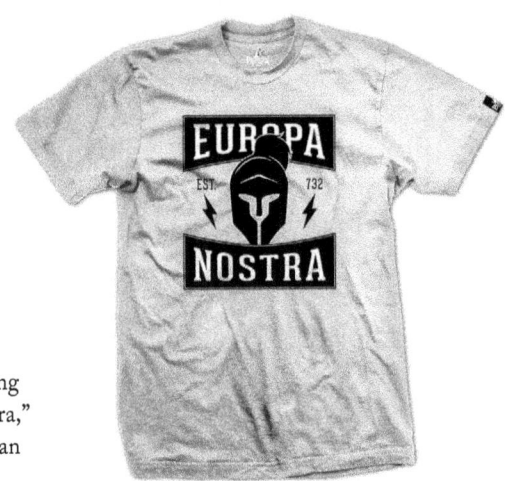

FIGURE 30. T-shirt bearing the words "Europa Nostra," from Austria's Identitarian label Phalanx Europa.

not insusceptible to geopolitical considerations. Identitarians denounce on every occasion European manifestations of Russophobia. For example, after the Saint Petersburg subway terrorist attack—and the refusal of the German authorities to illuminate the Brandenburg Gate in the colors of the Russian flag, as they had done in the past when other countries had been attacked—German Identitarians saw it as yet another instance of the "Russia-bashing" rampant in Europe.[117]

In fact, the concept of continentalism, as opposed to the current Atlanticism of the EU, has become a sort of inspiration, especially in the years following 2014 and the escalating diplomatic and political conflict between Western powers and Russia. An alternative to the current stranglehold of America on Europe, continentalism has been promoted by thinkers such as the Lithuanian Algis Klimaitis, whose book *The European Continentalism: Where Does Europe Stand in the Now Questionable Transatlanticism?*—a book in which Klimaitis denounces the current "Cold War II" as the fault of America and its policy of provocation and encirclement of Russia, especially through NATO—was enthusiastically reviewed by Alexander Markovics. Klimaitis wrote that, liberated from America's yoke, Europe should stand up as an independent bloc in a multipolar world and in close association with Russia as the basis of a continental economic, cultural, and social space—in short, a "Europe from Lisbon to Vladivostok," or the geopolitical nightmare of Americans. Writing at the identitaere-generation.info website, Markovics sees this anti-EU vision of European continentalism as a "ray of light," adding, of Klimaitis, "You show us the way to freedom."[118] Alexander Dugin, who was interviewed by Markovics for the Identitarian site, is also viewed as an important reference, not only because of his similar focus on multipolarity against American hegemony—a geopolitical construction that fits much better the Identitarian defense of ethnopluralism—but especially because of Dugin's quest to transcend the global hegemony of liberalism and forge a new political/ideological path, as displayed in his book *The Fourth Political Theory*.[119] *Europa Nostra*, many hope, will only benefit from Dugin's open project, which is circulating widely in European Eurasianist networks, such as in that of Manuel Ochsenreiter's German Center for Eurasian Studies, a Berlin-based NGO that has close ties to the Russian thinker because of his "alternative concept to EU-Europe,"[120] which is not unlike that of the center director's defense of a "real Europe," a "European Europe," as a replacement for "American Europe."[121]

Although, as Martin Sellner has pointed out, the Identitarian youth movement has, officially, "at the moment no link to Russian or Eurasian groups," there have been exchanges and contacts with pro-Russia Eurasianist networks in Europe, which in itself is normal owing to their defense of similar geopolitical and Identitarian goals. This was particularly evident in regard to the Munich-based think tank the Center for Continental Cooperation (CCC), founded in December 2015. Led by the German-Russian Jurij Kofner (born in 1988), at the time also the chairman of the Eurasian Movement of the Russian Federation, the CCC was highly active in conducting lectures, seminars, conferences, surveys, and the writing of research papers. Algis Klimaitis was a member in his capacity as a geopolitical "expert." The "About us" page of the center's website reads like an Identitarian manifesto, saying that the center aims, inter alia, at "the liberation of Europe from the US hegemony in all sectors of society," the "resurgence of traditional European identity and culture, "the end of the Great Replacement of the European autochthonous population," and the "creation of a continental European economic, social, and cultural space that includes Russia as a basis for security, peace, and prosperity in Europe and as a real contribution to peace in the world."[122] In an interview that Kofner did with Sellner and posted at the CCC website, the director of the center declared, "I personally see the Identitarian movement as the new force for Europe's rescue," extolling its similarities with Eurasianism and hoping for "further cooperation" in the future.[123] Kofner—an admirer of Dugin's Fourth Political Theory, even if critical of his exclusion of the importance of "true, original, Christian liberalism"—was also behind the creation of the blog and website European Identity, a joint effort of "European Identitarians (Generation Identity–Munich) and Russian Eurasianists." European Identity defends the "building of a Greater Europe from Lisbon to Vladivostok" and also promotes, in its images, an aesthetic view of Europe's tradition, in typical Identitarian New Cool fashion.[124] The CCC, however, had a short existence, and roughly a year after its foundation Kofner terminated its activities. Kofner justified it on the basis of external forces—"the black PR in the German and Austrian mainstream media," a form of "McCarthyism" that "made me conclude that at this point in time it was impossible to raise a respectable conservative think tank"—and also due to the fact that he had joined HSE, Moscow's Higher School of Economics, as the head of the university's newly formed Eurasian sector—while the home page of the CCC was transformed into that of the more exclusively Eurasian-oriented Center for Eurasian Studies. In the meantime, Kofner says that he grew distant from the Austrian Identitarian movement, owing especially to "their lack of understanding of the fact that mass immigration was not the root problem of Europe, but only a symptom of the main problem: US imperialism in the Middle East and Africa and US-American hegemony over Europe."[125]

Another member of the CCC was the Austrian Patrick Poppel, chairman of the Vienna-based Suvorov Institute, which was founded in 2014 and named after Alexander Suvorov, a famous eighteenth-century Russian military leader and the commander of the Austro-Russian army during the French Revolutionary Wars. The institute published the book by Klimaitis and is "committed to an honest dialogue with Russia. All activities of the Institute are aligned in terms of broadening and deepening this dialogue." Activities include lectures—Markovics gave one on the Identitarian movement, while Poppel gave a video interview to Markovics as a "Russian expert" that was posted at the identitaere-generation.info site—as well as Russian courses (one of them advertised with the words "Putin speaks German! Do you speak Russian?") and opportunities for networking with Russian and pro-Russia cultural milieus.[126] Subsequently, Markovics's relationship with the institute has only deepened as he has joined its managing board, become its spokesperson, and, together with Poppel, presented the "Geopolitical Weekly Review" on the Suvorov Institute's YouTube channel. The activities and goals of the institute are very much in tandem with the title of a Moscow workshop held jointly with the CCC, "Prospects for an Eastern Shift of European Foreign Policy and a Common Space from Lisbon to Vladivostok," in which Poppel praised Russia as the "new global bastion of traditional values" and the Identitarian movement for its role in "resisting transatlanticism" and "protecting the interests of the Europeans more than the current parliamentary parties."[127] In "Why We Love Putin," Poppel wrote, "Putin stands for faith, people and tradition. And that is exactly what the politicians of the West hate about him."[128]

CasaPound's Revolt against the "Fatalism" of Europe's Submission

In Italy, when CasaPound activists marched in the streets of Rome behind a banner showing the image of Dominique Venner and the words "Europe revolts against fatalism!"—as a tribute to the French icon on the third anniversary of his death—they marched in the name of a "European Front" for the defense of "borders, traditions, and identity." They marched, therefore, in opposition to the current EU and for an alternative Europe. When CasaPound activists, wearing masks painted with the Italian tricolor, raised a ladder, and its vice president climbed the EU's Rome offices and tore down the EU flag—for which Simone Di Stefano was condemned to a brief prison sentence—they did so precisely to send out the message that the globalist-run EU does not represent the Italian people or the other peoples of Europe.

FIGURE 31. Demonstration of CasaPound in Rome, in honor of Dominique Venner (May 23, 2016). The banner reads "Europe revolts against fatalism!," with the words surrounded by CasaPound flags, as well as Italian, French, and Spanish flags. Photo by Antonio Mele.

The attachment to an alternative Europe triggers, of course, geopolitical considerations, even if they do not occupy the center stage of CasaPound's activism. Adriano Scianca, as usual the more theory-inclined figure of CasaPound's community, reiterates that it is important to think about the format of an alternative Europe, provided that such thinking does not lose itself in the far-out land of abstraction. "Federation? Empire? Alliance of sovereign states? I'll be honest," Scianca writes: "I find this level of the debate for the most part dull, at least in respect to the future geographical boundaries of the coming Empire: will it stretch to the Urals? Up to Vladivostok?" Even if this discussion "is not necessarily useless," it goes "without saying that the making of Europe will not depend on those discussions. The reality is that Europe will be built through political willpower, now unseen and following concrete, not abstract, designs."[129] In terms of concrete stands, then, CasaPound's defense of Europe's liberation from transatlanticism translates into a diffuse pro-Russia sentiment in international relations and a preference for most of Russia's positions in the West–East diplomatic conflict of recent years. The exception was CasaPound's support for the ouster of Ukraine's pro-Russian president by Ukranian nationalists, even if it immediately alerted followers to the danger of substituting one oligarchy for another, this time EU-sanctioned, globalist, and pro-NATO.[130] But Europe's incremental alignment with the United States regarding Russia—of which the punitive sanctions on Moscow over Ukraine, which hurt the European economy, constitute a tell-tale indication—is consistently understood as "geopolitical suicide" because of Russia's historical condition as a "natural" and "crucial" strategic partner for Europe. There is indubitably admiration of Putin's leadership qualities and his personification of a type of leader that contrasts starkly with the political elite of Western Europe—independent of the globalist "sirens"—and a defender of the national interest and well-being of his people above all else, but ultimately CasaPound's Russia predilection rests on geopolitical grounds, that is, on the Russian president's avowed resistance to the iron grip of US unipolarism.[131]

And the hope is that perhaps in a new multipolar world with different centers of power and geopolitical spaces, Europe may reassert itself as an autonomous and powerful player; this expectation fuels

Scianca's proclamation that what is needed is "the creation of a contemporary European imaginary, a European form, a European discourse projected towards the future," in sum, a "revolutionary Europeism"[132] that allows Europe to put behind it the "existing fatalism" against which Venner summoned an insurgence.

Make Europe Great Again

It was the morning after the 2016 US presidential election. Wearing a "Make America Great Again" cap, Martin Sellner took a selfie in the streets of Vienna, posted it on Instagram, and declared, "We are making history, folks. #maga #trump."[133] The Austrian Identitarian leader's reaction to the against-all-odds election of Donald J. Trump as America's forty-fifth president reflected, for the most part, the exhilaration felt across the European Identitarian camp. This was only to be expected. As a candidate Trump ran on a platform of economic and cultural protectionism, against the furor of the "progressive orthodoxy" (*vulgo* political correctness) of the liberal media while vowing to set the country on a new path of noninterventionist foreign policy; in truth, his call to "no longer surrender this country, or its people, to the false song of globalism" could have been taken from an Identitarian manifesto.[134] If for Germany's foreign minister (and, since 2017, the twelfth president of the Federal Republic of Germany), Frank-Walter Steimeier, Trump's taking office meant that "the old world of the 20th century is over for good," Identitarians saw it not as reason to mourn but to revel; the disbelief and fear of the "globalist political class" in the face of what seemed like a Trumpocalypse was only, in fact, an added reason to press ahead with the celebrations.[135]

And so they did. After all, as the head of Les Identitaires, Fabrice Robert, tweeted, "The election of Donald Trump gives a spectacular slap [in the face] to the Establishment. The people have spoken!"[136] It was, indeed, the first time "one [in the Identitiarian movement] could really endorse an American President," recognized Sellner. "His idea of American isolationism fits our idea of a multipolar world. His mixture of socialist and conservative principles is a European style of right-wing policies. He doesn't have the neoconservative, universalistic mindset," while "his honesty [in proclaiming] 'America First!' sounds much more likeable than the 'false song of globalism' and humanism that the other Presidents were preaching."[137] The youths of the German Identitarian movement were no less aflame over the "outrage" that the new American president stirred up with "globalists, left-liberal and multicultural utopians."[138] Trump's pledge to protect his land was an example to be followed far and wide—especially in Europe.

Trump was thus viewed as an inspiration for the replication of sound policies in European lands, with Identitarians applauding his executive orders aiming at the construction of a border wall and boosting the deportations of irregular immigrants. But the importance ascribed to his victory did not stop there. Trump's election also meant for Identitarians the *possibility* of a wider geopolitical shift that might "free" Europe. Prevalent throughout European Identitarians' postelection narratives is the idea that a "new chance" for Europe—unconstrained by globalism and US imperialism—has arisen and that a "historical opportunity" to abate the liberal international order had been opened. In "Donald Trump, a Chance for Europe?," Alexander Markovics wrote about the hope that "Make America Great Again" was more than a campaign

FIGURE 32. Meme created by the German Identitarian movement in January of 2017 in support of Donald Trump. The quote from Trump reads: "A nation without borders is not a nation."

slogan and that it actually meant "the end of American imperialism," generating a new geopolitical chessboard where "the European freedom of movement will grow, and thus the possibility of launching patriotic politics—and the emergence of a free and sovereign Europe in the multipolar world of the future." In this way Europeans should follow the example of "European-born Americans who are capable of resisting the will of the most powerful military-industrial complex in the world, the largest and most repugnant media conglomerate on earth and its murderous political correctness, in order to take their freedom back." After "America makes the US 'Great Again,' it is now up to us Europeans to do the same with our continent" in order to "Make Europe Great Again!"[139] Writing on the web portal of Les Identitaries, Jean-David Cattin expressed the same sentiment: "In any case, the new US president will not save Europe; his isolationism, if confirmed, can instead provide sufficient space for the Old Continent to regain its independence and the tools to defend its identity. This will depend on the will and the work of those who are committed to protecting their own and their civilization."[140] In sum, Identitarians proclaimed, Trump's victory may have created the right conditions for a historical reversal. Yet Europe, and especially identity-minded Europeans, still had their work cut out for them.

"American Miracle or Mirage," read the front cover of the Belgian Identitarian magazine *Renaissance Européenne* over Trump's image in its first postelection issue. Noting that "the system of domination that claims to govern the world and, with it, to reform our European civilization, is in a state of commotion," the accompanying text alerted readers that "by logic, the very powerful system should at all costs prevent [the miracle] from happening."[141] Guillaume Faye, for his part, titled his three-part analysis of Trump's arrival at the White House—seen as an "additional proof" of the twenty-first-century "revolt against the cosmopolitan oligarchy"—"Trump: Revolution or Simulacrum?" The French theorist noted that "the system admits to only a temporary setback" and that "after Brexit and Trump's election, the System will do everything to neutralize one and the other." The most important thing was to prevent at all costs the "failure of Trump," especially because "he has crystallized an enormous energy of hope." Faye's advice that "Trump will have to be careful not to cause a huge disappointment after the considerable expectations that he aroused, not only in the autochthonous American people but also in Europe," was joined with his apprehension that "in the event of failure by retreat and lack of will, the sovereignist, populist and Identitarian ideas would be discouraged and discredited."[142] Writing from Italy, CasaPound's Adriano Scianca rejoiced in Trump's victory. "Give all the geopolitical analysis that you want," he posted to Facebook, "but the fact that in every recent election pictures of rich progressive idiots crying sprang up everywhere, is not the least of the cool things." He did, however, raise a cautionary flag about any misplaced euphoria. "That Trump is absorbed, if not openly used, is likely. In politics it is not difficult to be the outsider in the election especially if you are a billionaire (see Berlusconi)," Scianca warned, adding, "It is difficult to be free when elected (idem)." This happens not only "because of the encircling maneuvers of lobbies, strong powers and all sort of masonries," but also "[because of] the web of the official power, which immediately enwraps the rulers, normalizing with technicalities and bureaucracies every heterodox desire."[143]

Not a man to be carried away excessively by anything American, Alain de Benoist, the chief theorist of the Nouvelle Droite, nevertheless, in the aftermath of the triumph of an "anti-establishment candidate" such as Trump, made a historical comparison: "November 9, 1989: fall of the Berlin Wall. November 9, 2016: election of Donald Trump. In both cases, it means the end of a world. Our recent Nobel Prize for literature, Bob Dylan, has finally revealed himself a good prophet: *The times they are a-changing!*"[144] Months later, in an editorial in *éléments*, de Benoist noted that "the strange personality of Donald Trump makes him, in truth, unpredictable, and it is too early to know what his politics really are." Yet, geopolitically speaking, de Benoist was relatively confident that "his break with all-out interventionism, equivalent to an acceptance of the principle of multipolarity, seems nevertheless probable. The United States remains the main power of the world but no longer wants to participate in the treatment of all crises or to be the perpetual global policeman."[145] In fact, the notion that a reversal of traditional US foreign policy tenets was somewhat likely under a Trump Administration became recurrent in dissident geopolitical thinkers, even if few of them rose to the level of enthusiasm showed by Alexander Dugin, for whom a geopolitical paradigm shift was at hand because "Trump's ascent first and foremost puts a decisive end to the unipolar world. Trump has directly rejected US hegemony in both its mild form, which the CFR [Council on Foreign Relations] insists on, and in its harsh form, as the neocons call for." Not all Identitarians were necessarily ready, with the advent of Trump's presidency, to proclaim with Dugin that "the peoples and states of the world can finally take a deep breath [because the] expansion of globalism has been stopped at its very center." Nor did they universally agree that even anti-Americanism was "over" and that it should be abandoned.[146]

Still, Trump's election and inauguration invigorated the Identitarian movement with the fresh hope of new possibility. At the end of the first hundred days of Trump's presidency, however, suspicion grew within the wider Identitarian camp that the rebel president had been swallowed up by the status quo. For European Identitarians, this "neutralization" of Trump was most obvious in the field of foreign policy and geopolitics. The April 2017 US cruise missile strike on a Syrian airfield in response to an alleged lethal chemical weapons attack on civilians by Bashar al-Assad's forces drew a big "Here we go again" sigh from many Identitarians in a reaction that mixed both concern over a possible Trump deception and anger at the "deep state," the supposed shadowy de facto government of civil servants that had forced Trump's hand and reoriented his policies toward conventional American interventionist/meddling courses of action in foreign policy. The suspicion grew further when the president who had once declared the North Atlantic Treaty Organization (widely viewed by Identitarians as the military arm of globalist/imperialistic designs) "obsolete" did a volte-face and, like his White House predecessors, expressed his strong support for the organization—all of this while adopting the "traditional" hostile US stance toward Russia (and Putin), ignoring, in this way, his own promise to restore friendlier ties between Washington and Moscow. Months later, and well into Trump's first year in office, Alexander Markovics—in view of the American president's softening of his anti-immigration stance as well as his increasingly fiery rhetoric regarding foreign affairs—noted, despondently, that "he's now collaborating with the same swamp that he promised to drain."[147]

Developments such as these boded ill for Identitarian hopes of helping to free Europe from what they see as a nefarious liberal international order. But regardless of what the future will bring—hopes nurtured or dashed—it is true that the elation that Trump's anti-establishment victory brought to Identitarians will probably remain as a symbol of the idea that the "impossible" (defeating the "globalist" establishment) is indeed "possible." In the hope, therefore, that the sentiment that led to statements such as "We are making history, folks" can be multiplied in the future all over a Europe "made great again."

FIVE

Of Race and Identity

> In two hundred years someone will look at a statue of a white man and ask if such a strange thing ever existed. . . . Someone will answer, "No, it must have been painted on." That is the answer!
> —Louis-Ferdinand Céline, *Evergreen Review*

"TO HELL WITH ANTI-RACISM"

To celebrate the International Day for the Elimination of Racial Discrimination, the Italian minister for constitutional reforms, Maria Elena Boschi (2014–2016), tweeted that "to be against a multiethnic society is like living in Alaska and being against the snow." This phrase, in fact, was a reference to a quote from the twentieth-century American novelist William Faulkner, who declared in a speech to the Southern Historical Association that "to live anywhere in the world of A.D. 1955 and be against equality because of race and color, is like living in Alaska and being against the snow."[1] Adriano Scianca could not let the admonishment pass without comment, and most of all without denouncing it as yet another demonstration of the *doxa*, the unquestioned truth, not open to discussion, of the ruling European elite. "The multiethnic society is like the snow: a thing that, therefore, simply 'is,'" Scianca said. "A natural phenomenon that does not have anyone responsible or culpable. Well, this way of thinking has a name: it is called fetishism."[2] The attribution of an inherent, uncontrollable inevitability to the ascent of societies of multiple, or even mixed, ethnicities is a way of obfuscating the idea that "only in Europe and in a few other Western countries is the imperative of ethnic self-destruction," as a matter of fact, striven for by those who hold political, economic, and cultural authority. With this strong belief in mind, Scianca then said that the proper name of the International Day against racism should be "Western Day" against racism, "because the rest of the world does not give a damn about these obsessions imposed upon our lands by cultural minorities bloated with self-hatred."[3]

"The ideology of anti-racism is a tool of the 'Great Replacement' described by Renaud Camus," observed Dominique Venner in the pages of his *Nouvelle Revue d'Histoire*.[4] Anti-anti-racism is diffused throughout the Identitarian camp. A major reason for this is the fact that a dogmatic and inquisitional anti-racism—which stigmatizes and persecutes all those opposed to the official line of thinking regarding the dogma of diversity and the benefits (or at least the inevitability) of multicultural ways of living—is understood by Identitarians to be *part and parcel* of the globalist assault on identity (see chapter 2). In this indictment of contemporary anti-racism, the Nouvelle Droite has provided major intellectual munitions. Anti-racism is the "surveillance system" of the totalitarian Big Other, functioning as a "tribunal of the conscience," stated François Bousquet.[5] Universalist and egalitarian anti-racism, as de Benoist never fails to point out, is intrinsically racist, and more perversely so because it does not value differences and reduces the Other, devoid of its heterogeneity, to the Same, which becomes in this way the one and only criterion for defining what a human being truly is. That is why the ND advocates a "differential and heterophile anti-racism" that holds differences as "intrinsic values" and defines racism as the will to make them disappear. Although ethnic and cultural differences are neither nonexistent nor unimportant, at the same time, the categorization as "racism" of the notion of "the existence of human groups genetically differentiated, which can be designated or not by 'races,'" is simply erroneous.[6] The term "racism" should be altogether discarded, argues Götz Kubitschek. "I agree with Benoist," and his defense of a "differential anti-racism," but "I prefer a different titling: When you look at the term 'ethnopluralism,' you find distinctness by the side of equality, and you do not have to use the word 'racism,' which is scorched beyond repair."[7] It is with this mindset that Polémia's Michel Geoffroy, in a talk about the need to engage in a "battle for vocabulary" against the system, views the term racism as used by the "dominant ideology" as a misleading term that has been forcibly divorced from its real meaning: "In the past [racism] was the doctrine that affirmed the inequality of human races; nowadays, a racist is someone who states that human races *exist* or who is troubled with immigration (and this is according to the judicial system)."[8] Race is thus the "supreme taboo" of the times, writes Jean-Yves Le Gallou. "It is a taboo, which means that it does not have any rational justification, and the anti-racist discourse that aims at justifying it, does not have logical or scientific consistency. If it is idiotic to explain everything according to the race factor, it is absurd to deny differences of origin," the co-founder of Polémia concluded.[9]

What is more, according to the French theorist, the doctrine of miscegenation, which goes hand in hand with anti-racism, is ultimately a driver as well as an effect of the globalist ideology of the "Great Mixing" aggressively pushed by the entertainment industry and advertising. Le Gallou calls it the "imposition of the Benetton ideology," and it extends beyond cultures and races, and its ultimate goal, in the words of de Benoist, is the "worldwide extension of the ideology of the Same." In all domains, the goal is to erase all distinctions, all limits, all borders. Advertising, says Le Gallou, replicates such a world, "in which everything would be more beautiful if alterity and ethnocultural differences were at last destroyed, allowing the advent of the sovereign world market."[10] Identitarians can argue, then, that this normative "mixophilia," which they perceive as an attempt to create a world that is uniformly miscegenized, is one more (crucial) step in the direction of a new human type, one that Robert Redeker called "the indifferent," the last resident of the kingdom of absolute liberalism; a being that is a "negation of nature" because it does not belong to any race, in the same way that, postgenderism *oblige*, it does not belong to any sex.[11] "Instead of mixing and standardization, we want to preserve difference," reiterated the Austrian Identitarian Markus Willinger in a statement that by now sounds familiar: "We want different peoples, cultures, and identities. Our own included!"[12]

The struggle for "our own" identity demands, therefore, a radical reframing of the question of anti-racism and its dialectics. This being so, the further we advance into the exploration of the role of race in the Identitarian cosmology, the more pressing will be the need to differentiate and tell apart different approaches, and the significance of the issue, in each collective. This is particularly important because the emphasis that Identitarians place on the biocultural identity of Europe—and the relationship between culture and race—is not viewed with the same intensity, for ideological or strategic reasons, across the Identitarian spectrum. In his description of the core principles of "Identitarianism," the Identitarian thinker Lucian Tudor asserts that "'Identitarians advocate the idea that European peoples as a whole, due to their close biological relatedness, form primarily a general 'White' or European race." Further, "To deny the racial relatedness of European peoples is akin to and just as incorrect as denying the existence of a general European culture and type."[13] This interpretation of what Identitarians believe is not incorrect per se. Identitarians of all strands would agree, for example, with the founder of human ethology (the field of study of the biology of behavior applied to humans), Irenäus Eibl-Eibesfeldt, for whom "Humanity (as an abstract definition) is an invention of the European mind. . . . Humanity as a biological unit does not exist."[14] Accordingly, they follow Europe not as an "idea," but as a rooted biocultural entity, with its peoples as heirs, transmitters, and re-creators of an ancient lineage. However, Tudor's interpretation is too broad, because not all Identitarians categorize their fight for Europe unequivocally in terms of a defense of racial identity or of a white race. It could be said that, on this matter, there is a generational gap between older and younger Identitarians, for example, in France (even if, in different ways, there is a common emphasis on a white racial consciousness), but also a geographic gap; in Italy and Germanic Central Europe, for example, this emphasis on whites *as such* is for the most part absent. Ultimately, and in regard to race, Identitarians are better seen in two camps—of racialism and pragmatism[15]—certainly not necessarily opposed to each other but showing a different way of expressing a racial consciousness, whether *explicitly*, as in the defense of whites, or *implicitly*, in terms of ethnoculturalism.

THE RACIALISTS

Life Sciences to the Rescue

"Public discourse is rapidly drifting away from the discourse of the life-sciences—a striking sign of these confusing times," wrote Pierre Krebs in *Fighting for the Essence*.[16] This emphasis on the life sciences was dominant in the early years of the Nouvelle Droite—to such an extent, actually, that its theoretical approach to the human condition was decidedly racialist. Looking back, de Benoist said that at the time "I accepted the notion that race was a strong explanatory key of universal history."[17] In order to counteract the belief, which originated in the Enlightenment and has been at the root of Western philosophical anthropology (studies of human nature), that man was born in a blank slate, ND theorists emphasized race with the overriding goal of embedding the study of humans in the scheme of evolutionary development and hereditarianism. The life sciences, particularly sociobiology, evolutionary biology, and evolutionary psychology, and their quest for the biological basis of behavior, were central to the ND worldview. Inegalitarian biologism was thus prevalent, as was an emphasis on human racial differences, particularly those believed to affect intelligence and educational achievement. ND theorists extolled scholarly works that stressed the genetic basis of people's abilities, such as those of psychologists, as Hans Eysenck—whose book *The Inequality of Man* was translated and published under the supervision of de Benoist in 1977—and Arthur Jensen, who featured prominently in the early days of GRECE's magazine *Nouvelle École*. Gradually the ND racialist paradigm gave way to the paradigm of cultural differentialism, which still dominates today. Clearly the role of evolutionarily derived biological diversity is still very much present in the ND narratives about the human condition—*éléments*, the ND magazine features in each issue a section dedicated to the latest research on genetics and genomics, covers paleoanthropological findings, and gives special emphasis, for example, to new theories about the multi-regional origin of Homo Sapiens, in light of DNA genealogy, which debunk the Out of Africa theory.[18] Genetic determinism, however, is viewed as insufficient in providing an understanding of the human condition. "It is not insignificant if one belongs to one race rather than another," de Benoist noted in an interview with the *Occidental Quarterly*, "but to privilege racial factors to the detriment of all others [social-historical] is one of the innumerable ways of being ideologically hemiplegic."[19]

At the same time—and this is increasingly touched on by the latest intellectual endeavors of the ND—the advances of biotechnology in the third millennium may well one day surpass those that fueled "old" debates about human ethnicities and races. Transhumanism and the creation of designer humans, or posthumans, who are enhanced beyond the biological limitations of the species, may even attempt to show that death itself, the ultimate biological frontier, is no longer inevitable—sending into oblivion, too, in this way, the modernist dogma of egalitarianism. Humans would be endowed with a new nature. The elixir of life would then cease to be a mythical tale.[20] In his writings de Benoist recurrently warns about the "posthuman" plans that are being designed in the "extreme West" of Silicon Valley.[21]

Racialists as the "Real" Identitarians

Identitarians, of course, and among them racialists, do not live in such futuristic times. In fact, it can be argued that Identitarian racialists took up where the ND left off in regard to the role of race. After all, the Identitarian dissidents distanced themselves from the ND because of the ideological schism regarding the weight and implications of ethnicity and race.[22] As a descriptive and explanatory theory of history and society, racialism is viewed as an attachment to the "real"—race, according to this view, is *obviously* the biological constituent of ethnicity—and, in this sense, the defense of racialism is the defense of life as it really is, without the mystifications imposed by the dominant ideology of the times. Against the premise of an abstract universal man, racialists oppose actual men, localized within a specific ethnicity *and* race. As explained by

Pierre Vial, "Biological belonging conditions numerous human characteristics, both at the individual and collective levels. The man on the street, still possessing a bit of common sense despite the media's ceaseless brainwashing, knows very well that there's a difference between a Senegalese and someone from the Auvergne." Vial says this is true even if "difference here doesn't necessarily imply inferiority or superiority."[23] The Identitarian organic and carnal conception of Europe and its homelands, as shown in the case of the Terre et Peuple and *Réfléchir & Agir* networks, obviously feeds, and at the same time is nurtured by, this original racialism and their view of Europe as, naturally, the land of whites. Commenting on the "awakening of the carnal homelands," Vial says, "The time of the right of blood will come as many eyes and ears open themselves to our racialist worldview, making the zealots of globalism full of rage."[24] Similarly, in his article "Toward the Great Europe of Ethnicities," Eugène Krampon says that "to defend an identity is therefore to defend a race and a soil." Krampon continues, "We know it, the great combat of the twenty-first century is for the existence of the white race, quite simply." Nevertheless, he says further, "We do not fight for the generic 'white man.' . . . For us, the issue of race cannot be separated from the crucial question of rootedness."[25] Racialism is also central to the German Thule seminar and its founder, Pierre Krebs. It serves, too, as a way of distinguishing between that group and other Identitarians. According to Krebs:

> If being "Identitarian" means being aware of one's ethno-cultural roots, I am obviously an Identititarian. But a consequential Identitarian—a racialist Identitarian—you will have to excuse me the tautology that I am obliged to sacrifice to, in order to differentiate myself from the "Identitarian movement." Indeed, whether by tactic or by conformity to the spirit of the times, these Identitarians evacuate from their speech the fundamental parameter of biology: the "race" is excluded for the exclusive benefit of culture. This exclusion serves neither the tactics nor the intelligence because everyone knows that cultures do not fall from heaven, that they all possess an identity: a people, a group of peoples . . . a race. The taboo word par excellence![26]

According to the German thinker, the "insidious daily terrorism of political correctness" has made of race the ultimate taboo. But there is a reason. It constitutes an obstacle to the "eradication of territories and peoples." Because "this word, beyond its strictly scientific connotations, alone contains a metaphysics of blood and soil that, beyond the endophysic instincts of the body, speaks to the great secrets of life and destiny, to the questions of the spirit."[27] Guillaume Faye, for whom at the core of a people's or civilization's rests a biological root—a *germen*—"gravely threatened" in Europe, says that the denial of biological factors is "as intelligent and effective as denying the Earth's roundness, the circulation of blood, heliocentrism, or the evolution of the species—as the spiritual and intellectual ancestors of the present dominant ideology once did." Faye also says, echoing a view that is diffused within racialists, that what is really at stake when it comes to race is more than just phenotypic differences (such as color) but essentially genotypic variations that effect temperament and mental abilities. Being "white" thus constitutes a way of being, conceptualizing, and acting in the world. In sum, it is an expression of a full-fledged mentality.[28] It is attached, therefore, to the "spirit" and "destiny" referred to by Krebs.

A "Borean" Alliance

The source of such racial and spiritual destiny, at least as Identitarian racialists believe, can be traced down to the Hyperboreans. This name for this group is rooted in the name of Boreas, the personification of the north wind in Greek mythology. That is, they were a people that lived in the extreme north, beyond the north wind, and are associated in racialist narratives with the early/proto Indo-Europeans. "Forget about Game of Thrones," announced the left-wing French news website Rue 89, "the Identitarians have crazier theories," because they "fantasize about an ancestor from the north, a prehistoric Aryan founder of a supposed 'European race.'"[29]

The circumpolar origins of Indo-Europeans, however, is far from a fantasy to them; it is a deeply held belief that they believe is reinforced by ancient narratives, such as those of the Greek geographer and explorer Pytheas of Massalia, who thought he had discovered the ultima Thule, another name for the farthest-away land of the "peoples of the north."

This *ex septentrione lux* (light that comes from the north), the Nordic-polar thesis, explicitly gives Europeans a common ancestry that distinguishes them from other peoples.[30] These are the deepest roots of the Indo-European Arctic tradition, theorized by, among others, the linguist Jean Haudry, a tradition that, as I noted in chapter I, includes not just a particular worldview but a physical Nordic type. In "Thule, the recovered sun of the Hyperboreans," Jean Mabire says, "the real secret of Thule is the conservation of the blood, which means, ultimately, of the spirit."[31] The ethnogenesis of Indo-Europeans is the reason that Dominique Venner argues that they should more appropriately be called "Boreans" in order to distinguish between the Indo-European languages and the original Boreal ethnicity.[32] As the racialist Bruno Favrit tells it, Thule is the "sacred original land" of autochthonous Europeans even if, in these "anti-Thulean" times, this ancestral source is denied, forgotten, and repressed, for "despite the prevailing discourse peddled by the followers of panmixia and relativism, there are specificities, there are sensitivities deeply rooted, [there is] a conscience of blood more or less acute, which marks the obvious differences, and inherent genius forms. The race originated from the Hyperboreans is characterized by the love of freedom, courage, fidelity to tradition, the sense of honor, of the real, and of tragedy . . . features that are not obviously taught in schools and universities."[33] In any case, it is the feeling of acute racial consciousness—of inhabiting and embodying a unique, authentic, and endangered ethnosphere—that boosts the notion, theorized earlier, in the 1960s, by Venner's *Europe Action*, of racial unity. This magazine, after all, attempted to reframe nationalism with a wider, supranational, white foundation. In geopolitical and ethnopolitical, terms, the defense of the "white world" today translates into the constitution of a sort of "Borean alliance," a union of the white peoples of Europe and, eventually, of the whites of the northern hemisphere. *Réfléchir & Agir* calls it an "imperial vision of White Europe."[34] As Jean-Patrick Arteault has argued, "Real" Europe and "true" Europeans—which, when they are aware of the interaction of race and spirit, may be described as "Albo-Europeans" (from the Latin *albus*, "white"), a sort of aristocracy of the white world in general, or "those who represent, self-consciously, the White race laid out by the European spirit, and whose essence is found in the Indo-European matrix"[35]—justify the construction of a new, alternative, identity-based

European project. Georges Feltin-Tracol, who sees himself as a "racialist in the Evolian sense of the term"—from Julius Evola, who saw race not just in terms of the body but as a carrier of a specific heritage and spirit—believes that "Albo-European," although a "redundant expression," has the "merit of making clear that Europeans are historically whites." And, to him, this is particularly important at a time like this, when historical truths are being ideologically deconstrued: "Soon they will try to 'prove' that Julius Caesar was black, Charlemagne an Inuk and Louis XIV an aborigine from Australia."[36] In any case, an "identity-based European project," wrote Vial in an article titled "White Europe," rests on a racialist basis, on "a racialism that makes clear that the identity of peoples is rooted primarily, but non exclusively, in racial belonging; the recognition of this reality allows us to recognize that each people has the right to its own identity."[37]

This undertaking, however, as mentioned previously in the book, is a far cry from Alexander Dugin's multiracial Eurasia: "We, racialists, cannot accept the project of Eurasia, which would become, by legitimizing miscegenation, another way of justifying the end of White identity. That is why we have adopted as a mobilizing myth of the awakening of White peoples, [the concept of] Eurosiberia."[38] Guillaume Faye, who first came up with the notion, wrote that "if it should ever be constructed, Eurosiberia would regroup all White, Indo-European peoples in the great regions into which they have spread," becoming "the first hyper-power in history."[39] Attempts to fuel White Europeanist solidarity have not been lacking, either. As in the case of the 2007 "Chart of Moscow" that emerged from an international meeting of thinkers organized by the Russian association Ateney (Athenaeum) and dedicated to "the future of the White world." Signed by, among others, Guillaume Faye, Pierre Vial, Pierre Krebs, Enrique Ravello, and Duarte Branquinho, the document called for the defense of the "biocultural heritage" of Europeans, the need for White unity in the world ("Whites of the world, unite!" it entreated), and the creation of an Organization of Identitarian Nations.[40] Its host, the pan-Slavist Pavel Tulaev—whose compilation of writings and interviews in the West was released with the title "The White World in My Heart"—published Faye's books in Russia, and throughout the years has been close to Robert Steuckers's European Synergies network, as well as Terre et Peuple. Tulaev, as became clear in his speech at the conference, is a major voice in support of the constitution of Euro-Russia, a geopolitical entity rooted in historical and racial connections and a future stalwart against the "degradation of the White world": "We do not want Eurasia (a mixture of Asia and Europe) . . . and we proclaim the fundamental principles: 'Blood before Soil!' Biopolitics versus Geopolitics!"[41]

The justification for racial solidarity—in this case of Whites—is established on a purported scientific basis. "The racial roots of Europe are well known. They are described precisely, and [have been] for a long time, in innumerable works by anthropologists," notes Vial. Following the criteria established by physical anthropologists of the nineteenth and twentieth centuries, the classification of the races of Europe is divided among the Nordic, Dalic, Dinaric, Alpine, East Baltic, and Mediterranean races. This is the "racial stock" of the peoples who have forged, "since the Bronze Age," the culture and civilization of Europe: "Greeks and Latins, Iberians, Ligures, Celts, Germans and Slavs." With this in mind, Vial says that "it is by having a clear consciousness of the racial kinship of these peoples that we can develop a European spirit capable of overcoming the divergences that have, throughout history, caused Europeans be opposed to each other."[42] "The Races of Europe: What Is Your Race Type?" asked the title of Eugène Krampon's article in an issue of *Réfléchir & Agir* dedicated to "Our Racial Origins." "With their qualities and their faults, these are all European races to be defended and to illustrate the Empire of tomorrow," Krampon writes in the last paragraph. "We will persist in saying and writing that it is in the interest of the whole of humanity to protect these White races, to develop them all in general, *and particularly the Nordic*, because it has been [the Nordic racial type] that has written the History of the world."[43] In fact, Nordicism has a central place in Identitarian racialism. The work of racial anthropologists of yore plays a continuous role in such centrality of the Nordic paradigm. Eugène Krampon, for example, includes the late nineteenth- and early twentieth-century racial eugenics French theorist Vacher de Lapouge—who divided humans into two basic racial groups, the superior Aryan dolichocephalic (long-headed) and the mediocre brachycephalic (short-headed) types, and who defended racial selection—among those who have warned against "racial decadence" and tried to "open the eyes" of the public.[44]

Above all, it is the German anthropologist-raciologist Hans Günther who stands at the top of the canon of Identitarian racialists. Günther, who was celebrated as the "pride of the NSDAP," the Nazi Party, for his research into race, and was strong in his belief about the qualitative superiority of the Nordic race, was a major proponent of the process of the "Nordification" of the German people through eugenics and racial hygiene, both as a university professor and a popularizer in best-selling books. His treatise on the raciology of the European peoples that classified the European races attributed to each phenotypical, psychological, and ethic features. When, in the early twenty-first century, it was republished by the Identitarian publishing house Les éditions du Lore, *Terre et Peuple*, in a review, noted that the work of Günther was "indispensable to those who want to understand, serenely, what is the human reality of Europe. It is better to rather say, what [the human reality of Europe] was, because these past decades have transformed the biocultural face of Europe." Thus, "It is with a certain nostalgia that we read today, in its French translation, Günther's book (initially released in 1924) . . . [for] it describes a world that, if it is not yet dead, is dying. Unless . . . unless there are sufficiently strong souls to survive the coming chaos."[45] Also, Günther's work on the ancient spirituality of the Indo-Europeans, which had its own rooted and noble ethic that was fundamentally opposed to "oriental" Christianism, is a reference in Identitarian circles. Originally published as "Nordic Religiosity," its French translation by Robert Steuckers was released with the title "The Religiosity of Indo-Europeans."[46]

The Racial "Degradation" of Europe

Races are seen, in essence, as evolutionary competitors. "The engine of humanity has been, and will always be, not the war of classes, but the war of races for survival," wrote Krampon in a text about the early theorists of the "cursed" science of raciology.[47] The question of racial survival and decadence pervades, in fact, the narratives of many Identitarian racialists. According to them, decades-long trends endanger the hierarchy of racial intelligence, dynamism, creativity, and achievement, with Europe at the forefront of this battle for survival. "We need to be conscious of the fact that, as demonstrated by professors Jansen and Eysenck, with the abundance of exotic races, our societies of high intellectual quotient are driven toward a model of society that is nonqualified, sliding toward the Third World," states *Réfléchir & Agir*.[48] According to Michel Alain, writing in *Terre et Peuple*, because the society of today does not debate taboo subjects, such as racial IQ differentials, it persists in enacting the wrong policies in Africa (ignoring, he says, the warning by the geneticist Nobel Prize–winner James Watson that these policies are "based on the fact that their intelligence is the same as ours—whereas all the testing says not really") *and* in Europe, where "the immigration-settlement that we are undergoing is, and will be, a factor of intellectual," and ultimately "civilizational impoverishment."[49] If the twentieth century saw a general rise in IQ scores (what is known as the Flynn Effect, after the New Zealander social scientist James Flynn), the fact that some studies have shown a decline in more recent times in Europe—in a country such as France, for example, in what has been dubbed a "negative Flynn Effect" also attributed, among other factors, to replacement migration—it has only increased the conviction of racialists, and overall critics of immigration, of the ongoing "civilizational impoverishment."[50] The urgency to protect the hereditary traits of Europeans led, Krampon's magazine, for example—in a review of the French release of Günther's 1959 *The Decline of Talent in Europe*—to defend racial selection as a solution to the impending demise of European peoples:

> Today we shudder when we see the degree of decay that egalitarian policies got us into. They have systematically denied the hereditary factor, eugenics, and racial, genetic and cultural selection, providing the same assistance to parents who would give life to children well born as to degenerates, knowing in advance what kind of offspring they will be able to breed, unfortunately. Can one be surprised, then, at the increase in crime, the vertiginous fall of the intellectual and cultural level, the lack of substance of modern man?[51]

In the book under review, which was written by the "great German raciologist," the reader "will find the solutions defended by the professor" that "should have found echo at the highest summits of the State, if our rulers were willing to open their eyes."[52]

Miscegenation or the "End" of European Whites

A guiding principle of Krampon's "strategy of combat" for a "White Ethnonationalism" in France and Europe is the "interdiction of miscegenation."[53] In fact, the opposition to miscegenation—as both a telltale cause and a symptom of the European people's degeneration—is widespread among racialists. The mission, according to Vial, is to awaken the racial identity of Europeans, "submersed by a mental conditioning that incites them to forget or to betray their origins, and to accept, even to seek, the death of their biological identity through miscegenation, the logical follow-up to the implantation of exotic populations that experience this settlement as [an act of] conquest."[54] Instead of a "community of destiny," Europe is nothing more than a suburb of a multiethnic America, "which it wants to resemble," by allowing the settlement of "millions of allogenic destined to miscegenate it and destroy from within," laments Alain Cagnat.[55] This process of the self-destruction of Europe through mixing with other, non-European, peoples is often denounced in terms of a dialectic between ethnocide and ethnomasochism, as is a recurrent theme in the writings of Guillaume Faye. This ethnocide is underway because "with the replacement population that comes with Third World colonization, miscegenation threatens to destroy our *germen*, i.e., the roots of European civilization." This ethnocide is fueled by ethnomasochism, which "promotes a systematic apology for race-mixing and cosmopolitanism." European elites have already "succumbed to this collective disease, which explains their indifference to the present colonization and their idea that we should welcome it."[56] Venner sees this mentality of self-hatred as akin to a death-wish: "In the last decades of the 20th century this plague of the spirit spread to the whole of the White world to the point of reaching self-destruction through generalized mixing" and the adoption of "miscegenation as the horizon."[57] What hangs over Europeans is the "impending threat of complete disappearance into the great void of the universal melting pot and 'Brasilization.'"[58] As if confirming, therefore, Jean Raspail's suspicion that "it must have been written in the Book of Fate, in the chapter on the White man, that . . . simple reflexes of self-preservation were destined to remain rare exceptions, hidden or deformed, never able to add up to a meaningful whole."[59]

In any case, many racialists, fully devoted to such "self-preservation," see behind this process of the racial deterioration of the European stocks an ultimate ambition: the "production" of "new" humans, mixed-raced individuals (or *métis*) with no defined roots, but perfectly fit to the globalist new era of interchangeable individuals. "Differently from a colonized people that can return to its roots as soon as it liberates itself from a foreigner's yoke, a *mestizo* people is a genetically manipulated people lacking any root," Krebs declared in an interview with the Spanish *IdentidaD*.[60] Anti-racist ideologues, editorialized *Réfléchir & Agir*, have set their goal on a Humanity *café au lait*, acting under the assumption that "the *métis*, a product of the encounter of two hereditarianisms, is a more malleable being, more amorphous . . . a universal man, without roots, traditions, or culture."[61] At the same time, massive immigration drives onward this ethnocidal wave; in practice it is the same as race-replacing, while escalating the ongoing clash of civilizations within Europe. This is because Identitarians believe that multiracial societies are not "harmonious" but inherently disharmonious and multiracist (fueling racial hatred), a lesson that should have been grasped if History had served as a guide: "The clash of civilizations is a racial clash," writes Vial. "In the face of the invaders, the Greeks of the V century BC were able to forget their divisions and form a bloc, conscious of defending a civilization, their conception of the world . . . and therefore their race."[62] In the twenty-first century the ultimate racial nature of the clash is no different, with the added danger that the Others are already settled in Europe. The fact that Faye sees also a "racial motivation" associated with Islamic terrorist attacks against Europeans—in which "Islamic radicalization" goes hand in hand with "dissimulated racial combat"—also fits this narrative of the "ultimate racial nature" of the clash.[63] No wonder that, in its defense of remigration, *Réfléchir & Agir* proposes as a fundamental measure in the French case stripping the nationality "of all those that are not of white stock (with the exception of the former soldiers of the French colonial empire)."[64]

Above all, most Identitarian racialists believe that the word "genocide" is a description of the current "extermination" of Europe's indigenous populations. After all, *genos* is the Greek word for race. "The multiracial project leads directly to the 'soft genocide' of which the biologist Erlung Kohl speaks. It is the expression of a 'society that despises races insofar as it destroys them,'" writes Pierre Krebs.[65] This genocide is unique, Faye points out, in the sense that it comes not from an external enemy but is pushed, in several ways, from inside the European nations. These "are victims of a surreptitious attempt at genocide, demographic and cultural elimination, driven by their own ethnomasochist and xenophile elites. A first in history."[66] Voluntary and nihilistic, soft or hard, this genocide—the ethnic cleansing of Europeans—is a matter of fact for Identitarian racialists.

THE PRAGMATISTS

The pragmatists differ from the more racialist Identitarians in a number of ways, as this chapter will show. According to Martin Lichtmesz, the political essayist close to Austria's Generation Identity, "Culture and ethnicity form a cluster/synthesis that cannot be separated and applied like Lego pieces. Of course Europe is the historical homeland of White people (which are by now, globally speaking, a minority on this planet) and should be defended as such."[67] In general, the pragmatic defense of European whites is best encapsulated by the expression "It goes without saying," without the need to overly racialize the discourse. What is more, there is no use in doing it explicitly when the goal is to reach out to a wider public. If something needs to be overemphasized, it is the notion of ethnicity. This approach clearly transpires in Martin Sellner's view: "In Europe everyone understands that terms like 'Italian,' 'French,' 'German' intrinsically describe a cultural and an ethnic reality. That's why the so-called 'Integration' of millions of non-European immigrants into those narratives was a complete failure." The Austrian Identitarian leader adds: "A people isn't something that is 'racially pure' or completely static, but it clearly has clear limits of assimilation and integration and an ethnic continuity that is fundamental to its identity."[68] If the racialists' approach is "heavy," Identitarian pragmatists adopt a "lighter" approach, even if, as is the case of France, they sometimes openly frame their combat *as* the defense of whites. Unlike the racialists discussed in the first section of this chapter, the pragmatist case is made not in connection with the life sciences or with biogenetics but rather in interaction with current sociocultural dynamics deemed threatening, unfair, and discriminatory against the native populations.

Racial Discrimination against Whites

French Lambda Identitarians see themselves at war with a putative system that is hell-bent on redefining the identity of the autochthonous French, even attempting to cancel—through political correctness and the "religion" of anti-racism, for example—its most widely perceived commonsensical and lasting attributes. For them, what was supposed to be consensual regarding the identity of the people has become a source of contention, subversion, and even outright stigmatization of those who fail to conform to the dominant multiracial paradigm. The fact that in 2013 the French legislators, as an initiative of the socialists in power, struck the word "race" from all legislation ("There is no place in the Republic for race," said President François Hollande at the time), only reinforced this view. A further case in point, and one that was much explored by Identitarians, occurred when Nadine Morano, a center-right politician of the Republicans, said in a televised interview, "We are a Judeo-Christian country of White race that welcomes foreigners." These words triggered an outcry even though she insisted she was quoting Charles de Gaulle. In fact, as the general said to his biographer, "It is very good that there are yellow French, black French, brown French. They show that France is open to all races and has a universal vocation. But [it is good] on condition that they remain a small minority. Otherwise, France would no longer be France." De Gaulle reiterated, "We are still primarily a European people of the White race, Greek and Latin culture, and the Christian religion." In the wake of the affair, Jean-Yves Le Gallou declared that "dissidence" today meant to "recognize, in the wake of General De Gaulle, echoed by Nadine Morano, that 'the French are still primarily a European people of the White race, Greek and Latin culture, and the Christian religion.'"[69] Likewise, the Belgian writer Christopher Gérard, a defender of a modern pagan spirituality with Ancient Greece as its model, addressing Iliad's 2016 annual conference—

which was held under the name, In the Face of the Migratory Assault, the Awakening of European Consciousness—noted that "with this philosophical tale [*The Camp of the Saints*], Jean Raspail launched with panache a terrifying challenge: do we truly want to remain, and I quote, the great 'racist' that was Charles de Gaulle, 'a European people of the White race, Greek and Latin culture, and the Christian religion'?"[70] The quote, and the polemic associated with it, reverberated through the Identitarian social media, and Aurélien Verhassel, from the French Flanders Generation Identity, commented in a tweet about it that "although it goes without saying, it is even clearer when it is said."[71] For these Identitarians, even the "what goes without saying" is under attack as a target of a totalitarian deconstruction of what it *means* to be French and, consequently, European.

Together with national legislation, EU treaties have set forth a common framework for fighting racial discrimination and intolerance across Europe—but Identitarians see this widespread "racial correctness" as a new form of Inquisition with double standards. The accusation is as follows: The official anti-racism line of thinking, while postulating the existence of only one type of racism (that of Europeans born and bred), ignores the issue of "reverse racism," or of racism on the part of minorities against the majority, and in the case of France, the widespread anti-French racism prevalent in Afro-Maghrebin populations. Since its foundation, the Bloc Identitaire (and its new version, Les Identitaires) and the youth groups that are in its orbit have made of this issue—the racial discrimination suffered by the *français de souche*, or French of French stock—a major mobilizing force in their political, social, and cultural activism. This issue of the racism against French that is alleged to be taking hold of society expands, of course, the camp of Identitarians. It has been the subject since the 2000s of heated debate in the public sphere, with the engagement of public intellectuals such as Alain Finkielkraut, for whom the entrance of Europe into a new cosmopolitan "post-Identitarian age" is marked by *oikophobia*, or the hatred of its roots and heritage—of which the ideology of anti-racism and its "bitter combat against reality and its emissaries" (and the reality is the "deep crisis" of the society of "diversity") is a mainstay. According to this paradigm, postcolonial penitence and expiation have provided a fertile terrain for the development of Francophobia.[72] Within this wider discussion, the

Identitarians have engaged in systematic combat against what they term anti-French racism by framing it as explicitly anti-white racism. Fabrice Robert reclaims for his network the role of precursor, for they were the ones to put the spotlight on the issue, while the others (the politicians and the media) have followed their path: "We were the very first to talk about it in France. . . . We showed the way. Sarkozy's party, the UMP [the Union for a Popular Movement, the earlier designation of the Republicans] made anti-White racism one of its themes during its 2012 internal election. Suddenly, the media started talking about anti-White racism. They minimized it, they denied it, but they talked about it. And it liberated the debate on this issue."[73]

Throughout the years, this Identitarian theme expressed itself in several ways. A major example was the launch by Jeunesses Identitaires (the first youth section of the Bloc Identitaire) of a campaign against the North African Parisian rap group Sniper and its perceived anti-France lyrics, declaring: "Sniper wants to *nique* [slang word for fuck] France? Let's fuck Sniper!" Soon protest stickers with "Explicit Lyrics: Anti-White Racism" appeared on the band's CDs, and the Identitarians organized themselves as an anti-Sniper pressure group, targeting concert organizers and mayors and succeeding in cancelling many of its concerts. Philippe Vardon saw in this activism "the instinctive reflex of young people who are proud of their roots and do not accept that little thugs could make of the hatred of their country and their people a blossoming business."[74] At the same time, the dominant idea driving the Identitarian anti-white racism narrative is that whites are the most vulnerable ethnic group, and they are targeted by other non-European ethnic groups— through assaults, robberies, and even murder—*because* of their whiteness. This conviction is reinforced by episodes such as when in 2005 and 2006 high school students protesting against school reforms were assaulted and robbed by North and West African youths—events that were heavily covered by the media. In order to further alert the populace to anti-white racism "that kills," the Bloc Identitaire has, for example, engaged in street theater, with a number of activists dressed in white and holding signs with the names of white victims of ethnic violence, reenacting their deaths.[75] In the Identitarians' view, white youth suffer the most color-based stigmatization, since they are the ones at the forefront of the failure of multiculturalism and the ethnic fracture of the country. Martin

Lichtmesz sees this failure, in the "sense of a lost future" when "their fate is to become strangers in their own homeland," as the driving force for joining Identitarian movements. They experience firsthand the "new Europe," meaning that "many in their early twenties have already experienced dysfunctional school classes or immigrant tribalism or have been ethnic minorities in their classes."[76] Julien Langella, one of the cofounders of Génération Identitaire, says that "today the most dangerous place for a White is the high school. Or the bus. Or coming out of a nightclub. It has never been this difficult to be a young native French." The parents "have not known this barbarian France of ours. . . . With their sub-loser morality that disguises cowardice with Tibetan wisdom, they have thrown us hand-and-foot-bound to urban predators, whose imported morality confuses tolerance with cowardice, and respect with submissiveness. This clash of civilizations down the block they cannot understand. They have not known it." Against the "descendants of immigrants" who have a "very assertive ethnic consciousness that takes precedence over any other consideration," the "young White" as a "deracinated being" is disarmed, the product of a "devirilized era" reigned by "family decomposition, individualism and indifference." Standing "alone in the face of the rabble" the young white lives in a "state of revolt."[77] Recalling his experience as a youngster in the suburbs of the north of Paris, Generation Identity's Pierre Larti says, "Sometimes there was violence, I was beaten because I was the only French on public transport or on the streets."[78] The personal experience of having been the targets of immigrant violence, therefore, has also served as a spark for Identitarian activism, a way of channeling the "state of revolt."

The campaign against anti-white racism has featured prominently in propaganda materials of the young Identitarians. Stickers displaying provocative questions such as "Is it because I'm White that you assault me?" and "Is it because I'm White that you insult me?," followed by the phrase "STOP Anti-White racism!," have been distributed by Jeunesses Identitaires in order to rebel against the taboo that stipulates that racism has only one face and that it is unidirectional (from whites in the direction of all other minorities). This is because, in their eyes, even though whites are the major victims of interracial acts of violence, everything is done to deny them the status of victims. For the oligarchy, says the *Dictionary of Newspeak*, anti-white racism is "an oxymoron, a non-existent phenomenon, or, at the extreme, something completely isolated."[79] In *Sale Blanc!* (White Bastard!), the "chronicle of a hatred that does not exist," the Identitarian Gérald Pichon writes that these are "strange times where Whites, this invisible majority, undergo daily a veritable racial hatred in the streets. A hatred, they tell us, in addition, that does not exist." At the root of the problem, according to Pichon, is the "anti-European ideology," the ideology of the "hatred of France and of the native French that leads to self-hatred by Whites, and to the hatred of Whites from non-European communities." Pichon concludes, "Let's repeat, anti-white racism is above all a problem of Whites!," requiring therefore for its solution a process of "Identitarian reappropriation" of the European peoples.[80] "The weakness of character is the *mal du siècle* [evil of the century] of the White youth," reaffirms Langella. "The immigrant rabble knows it too well. And takes advantage." Only a "new education" aiming at *mens sana in corpore sano* (a sound mind in a sound body) may start to change things.[81] This diagnosis is similar to that of Julian Langness, an American traditionalist and a defender of masculinity both in his writings and, for a brief period, on his YouTube Channel Conquering Modernity. An admirer of Generation Identity, which he calls the "White Identitarians" of France, Langness, after traveling to Europe, had a sort of Identitarian awakening, of which he said, "It changed me profoundly." As Langness recalled, "I ended up feeling an intense shame regarding my native European contemporaries, and abhorrence of their ideology of self-hatred (what I now call "ethno-suicidalism"). At the same time, I developed great respect for the Muslims in Europe as a result of their focus on honor, strength, and community. They would never allow their women to be raped, they would never suffer insults without fighting back, and they cared about the future of their people. These were all traits lacking in 95% of native Europeans."[82] Nevertheless, it is because of youth movements like Generation Identity that Langness is optimistic about the future of ethnic Europeans, as portrayed in the fast-paced, epic narrative of his self-published book *Identity Rising: How Nationalist Millenials Will Retake Europe, Save America, and Become the New 'Greatest Generation.'*[83]

If, according to the American author, "95%" of Europeans of European stock lack virtuous and manly qualities, certainly these Identitarians want to be part of the remaining 5%. One of the stickers distributed by the young Identitarians showed a group of stylized figures with a number of names that ethnic minorities call native French, such as "*Toubabs* [Senegalese slang for 'white persons'], *culs* blancs ['white asses'], Gauls, *faces de craie* ['crackers']," and the message, in capital letters, "AND PROUD OF BEING!" This example, like the subsequent campaign of the young French Identitarians in which they call themselves "Generation Anti-Rabble," shows their goal of ethnic reassertion and confrontation. From this perspective, they are no longer part of a cowed white populace (albeit one that still constitutes the majority); they want to defy the spirit of a civilization that, unlike that of the "alien colonizers," is too weary to fight and that, adding insult to injury, physically and morally disarms their sons and daughters with an ideology of endless tolerance, openness, and humanitarianism and consequently facilitates and legitimizes their submission.

As noted before, a common motto of these French Identitarians—which was taken up by related movements across Europe—is "0 percent racism, 100 percent identity." This means, according to Arnaud Delrieux, "that it is not hatred of others that motivates our politics but love of our own."[84] To João Martins, the founder of the Portuguese Causa Identitária (Identitarian Cause), "We use this slogan" to say that "the recognition of the existence of human races and the exaltation of ethnic differences does not make us hateful and xenophobes." On the contrary, "It allows us to appreciate the specificities of other peoples and exhort them to defend what makes them unique, i.e. their identity. Having said that, in the same way that many designate Africa as the Black Continent, we have the reciprocal right to state that Europe is the White Continent."[85] At the same time, they frame their rejection of the doctrine of miscegenation in terms of a wider rejection of the globalist erasure of ethnocultural distinctions. "Contrary to what some people think, the Identitarians are not supporters of racial purity or of the thesis of the superiority of the white race over the others," said the Bloc Identitaire president. "But, at the same time, we refuse the propaganda extolling the merits of miscegenation and the model of the world citizen, undifferentiated and without roots, which incidentally may be the result of a certain French Jacobinism, negating the differences."[86] As Joseph-Marie Joly wrote in *ID Magazine*, "The new man of the future must be a miscegenated man," and that is viewed by these Identitarians as an essential part of the universalist dream (which is nothing but a nightmare for them) of a uniform humanity.[87] Miscegenation, however, is an unlikely scenario, according to Langella, for whom, as he stated in an interview with *Réfléchir & Agir*, "the reality looks [instead] like apartheid: The Whites leave the Africanized suburbs, no one believes anymore in '*vivre-ensemble*' [living together]."[88] Similarly, Jean-Yves Le Gallou believes that the most apt comparison to the current collapse of Europe is "with the US states, where the 'minorities' are a majority, or with today's South Africa and Rhodesia." It is "eye-opening" and shows that "the same causes have the same effects," among which is included "the escape of Whites when they can."[89]

When state-funded or academic sociological studies defend the belief that minority racism is marginal, that is, a "racism of reaction"; does not reflect a "mass experience"; and is not a "system" or a producer of "social inequalities" (unlike majority racism), the Identitarian reaction is one of derision.[90] Fundamentally, Identitarians laugh at the notion, as promoted by the Left and anti-racist groups, of "white privilege"—in which racism becomes something structural and institutional, a system of discrimination. For them, this type of thinking not only amalgamates all kinds of whites in a monolithic bloc (regardless of social classes and standard of living) but also does not reflect the reality of the daily lives of millions of whites, especially if they live in working-class neighborhoods or in suburbia. Contrary to the official line of thinking, these whites are the "real excluded." As Philippe Vardon stated in a speech in the southern city of Béziers, "We, Identitarians, are the Union of the people, the Union of the little whites that no one else defends."[91] Fabrice Robert says that although anti-racist groups, aided by media, academic, and political elites, complain about racial profiling against ethnic minorities, they never focus on the "racial profiling that the Whites are victims in some neighborhoods, in which they have become a minority. The '*faces de craies*' [chalk faces] or '*babtous*' [whites] are regularly the targets of gangs of the rabble that think that France has become an African colony." Accordingly, in face of the "Great Replacement," the time has come, says Robert, to defend the interests and address the grievances of white citizens, through similar anti-discrimination associations, because they are "victims of discrimination in the land of their ancestors."[92]

What is more, the notion that this racism is one of "reaction" against the perceived "dominant class or race" is rejected by Identitarians as delusional; this racism does not derive from "victimization" but from triumphalism, territorial conquest, and subjugation of the indigenous palefaces, of the "Little Whites," to the new masters. "The 'Little Whites' killed, raped, or mutilated are viewed by successive governments as collateral damage of the replacement of population that is happening throughout Europe," says Gérald Pichon.[93] When in the United Kingdom the scandal broke about the decades-long sexual exploitation of mostly working-class white girls by "grooming gangs" of Muslim men of Pakistani and Bangladeshi backgrounds—in the English cities of Rotherham and Telford, for example—the French Identitarians blamed it on the ideology of anti-racism, which allowed the organized abuse to happen by making it taboo, with the authorities failing to confront it for fear of the "racist" charge. In a communiqué, Génération Identitaire demanded a country-wide investigation because "in France the same anti-racist taboos exist, and the same rapes of European women happen."[94] Another indictment of the "blindness" of power-holders to the reality of whites came in the spring of 2016, when the French government launched the anti-racist campaign called All against Hatred. This campaign consisted of a series of videos showing episodes of violence against ethnic and religious minorities, ending with the message "Racism begins with words. It ends with spit, blows, and blood"—but it did not include anti-white racism. Anti-racism, therefore, is still officially viewed as a one-way street. "In which infernal logic are [French politicians] locked to deny with such an arrogance a reality that it is not possible not to come across?," asked the essayist Didier Beauregard at Polémia's site. For the "dominant caste," the ordinary French have "no official existence," the daily aggressions they suffer are not part of the statistics; "we are non-beings."[95] In response, Génération Identitaire posted its own anti-white racism video online, illustrating it with the text "Anti-White racism begins with words. It ends with spit, blows, and blood."[96]

CasaPound Italia and the "Error" of Racialism

In contrast to the situation in France, in Italy CasaPound's struggle for ethnodifferentialism is not categorized in a racial, or pro-white, fashion.

In fact, the group's public rejection of xenophobia or racism is self-interpreted as part of their wider rejection of the "misguided" clash-of-civilizations narrative, which is promoted by other voices and collectives in Europe. Because, as Scianca has said, "Phobias are by their own definitions for all those of weak intellects and fearful hearts," on every occasion CasaPound leaders state that their refusal of immigration is a positive effort to protect Italy's identity and not, negatively, a "racist" rejection of the immigrant population, who are also "victims" of the plutocratic globalist system. Asked if the future of "White Europeans" was endangered, Scianca replied, "I believe so, even if the question is deceiving because [it] explicitly evokes Anglo-Saxon or American subcultural models that are distant from our own political tradition and our historical models."[97]

This "historical model" is, of course, the fascist experience. Casa-Pound argues that the relation of Italian fascism to cultural, ethnic, or racial diversity was much more open and considerate than was postulated by antifascist propaganda. A case in point was the "colonial fascist adventure." As Gianluca Iannone believes, "Fascism is associated with a racism that is non-existent." What is overlooked is that "fascism, for example, abolished slavery [by the Italian colonial government in Ethiopia], while apartheid remained in the United States until 1976. This must be told because otherwise a distorted reality is often promoted."[98] Italo Balbo, the fascist governor general of Libya in the 1930s, is praised by Scianca as a major example of a leader whose fascist administration was respectful of cultural and religious diversity, even giving special Italian citizenship rights to indigenous Libyans.[99] The fascist regime, of course, promulgated in 1938 the racial laws that especially targeted the Jewish population. This, however, is viewed as a "historical error," one that is fundamentally at odds with the true nature of fascism. It was a measure taken for geopolitical (and, in the case of 1930s Italy, an approximation of the National Socialist regime in Germany) rather than ideological reasons. "The racial laws alienated the Hebrews from the Fascist revolution, of which they had been among the protagonists since the [1922] march on Rome. In the government of Mussolini in 1932 [until 1935] the Minister of Finance, Guido Jung, was a Hebrew. And it couldn't be otherwise, because our Mediterranean culture has always been a conglomeration of different cultures," stated its president, Gianluca

Iannone.[100] CasaPound insists time and again that the "reality [that is] well known to Historians but very much ignored by the wider public because it is incompatible with the demonization of fascism"[101] is that anti-Semitism was not practiced in Fascist Italy. "We are not racists, we are not anti-Semitic, we do not have problems with Israel," said Simone Di Stefano, CasaPound's vice president, when its then-political ally Matteo Salvini was denied entry into Israel on the purported basis of his CasaPound connection. Di Stefano recognized that "to some this will sound strange," but then reiterated that fascism "in its doctrine has not been racist or anti-Semitic."[102] The moment when CasaPound found itself at its most defensive occurred in the aftermath of the killing and injury of Senegalese vendors in the streets of Florence by one of its supporters in what was described as a type of lone-wolf attack. The group immediately condemned it, attributing the act to a "mental imbalance" in one individual rather than to any sort of ideological validation provided by CasaPound.[103] "We are against immigration, but we are not racists," Di Stefano said to the media. Then, in order to further accentuate the organization's distance from racialism, he said, "We have young Italians who are second-generation [immigrants] as militants."[104] Even when, or if, the rank and file stray from the official line, CasaPound's leadership maintains a persistent line of denunciation of racism as a weakness of character and as ill-advised activity because it scapegoats and attacks the wrong targets.

As a general rule, a strictly blood-and-soil definition of national identity is not found in CasaPound's vocabulary—nor are any sort of verbal or intellectual incursions into the white race. This is also evident in the theorizations put forth by Scianca. In tandem with his revolutionary view of ethnocultural identity as a source of demiurgic shaping and modeling, the Italian thinker rescues Oswald Spengler's definition of race, which the revolutionary-conservative German defined not solely and reductively in terms of genetics but as a strong-willed vital-creative-Faustian force. "What is needed is not a pure race, but a *strong* one, which has a nation within it," Spengler wrote in *Hour of Decision*.[105] Not that the contribution of the life sciences is not welcome; in fact, it is needed in order to counter the "attack" on human nature of the globalist juggernaut—based on the dogma of egalitarianism, which itself is rooted in an abstract conception of human beings. When the University of

Salzburg revoked the honorary doctorate of Konrad Lorenz, the founder of ethology (a subdiscipline of zoology that studies animal behavior through comparing species and contributes to the comparative behavioral study of humans and other animals), decades after his death, for his "Nazi past," Scianca saw it as a posthumous punishment of a true dissident. Lorenz's claim regarding the inherited nature of human behavior challenged "many egalitarian dogmas: whether about the supposed naturally good condition of man, or about its endless cultural malleability."[106] At the same time, evolutionary psychology, particularly earlier writings of a popularizer such as the playwright-turned-anthropologist Robert Ardrey—who emphasized the role in human development of innate/instinctive traits of human nature, such as those toward territorial defense—have been marshaled in order both to undermine the blank-slate orthodoxy *and* to give legitimacy to the refusal of the immigrant "invasion" of Italian and European lands as something inscribed in human nature as a territorial imperative.[107]

THE AMERICAN IDENTITARIANS

Fighting the "Dispossession"

"Do you see yourself as an Identitarian?" I asked the American dissident racialist thinker, author, and pro-white entrepreneur Jared Taylor. His reply was unequivocal: "Yes. The word does not exist in English but more and more English-speakers are using it. Soon it will be an accepted part of our language."[108] A Yale graduate in philosophy, Taylor—who welcomed the label "Identitarian" at a time (early 2015) when it was not a word of choice in America—is the founder of the Virginia-based think tank American Renaissance. Taylor's think tank maintains a race-realist website that, since the 1990s, has promoted a white racial consciousness and has vowed to advance the collective interests of whites against the "dark reality" behind the reigning multiculturalist paradigm. Taylor's definition of identity as "the recognition that culture and identity can be carried forward in a meaningful way only by the biological heirs to the people who created them" could well stand as the default position of North American Identitarians.[109] Often viewed in the media and by anti-racist groups as bearers of "white supremacy"—a label that Taylor rejects "because that implies that White people want to rule over other people, while most of White people today just want to be left alone,"[110]—activists more commonly use the term "white nationalism" (WN) even if it is not applied uniformly across the white racialist spectrum. Taylor himself favors "white advocacy," because "it sounds less scary but says what we want to say," instead of the "pretty stern"-sounding WN.[111] At the same time, particularly since the middle of this decade, "Identitarian" has really picked up steam as another word of choice for many American defenders of white identity politics.

The blunt defense of white nationalism is certainly the driving force behind the project of Greg Johnson—who has a doctorate in philosophy and is a former editor of the *Occidental Quarterly* and co-founder and editor in chief of the San Francisco–based Counter-Currents Publishing—in creating a North American version of the European Nouvelle Droite. Although thematically much more in tune with the dissident Identitarian wave (which means closer to the *early* intellectual production of the ND), this New Right enterprise makes every effort to set in motion a metapolitical counterhegemony to what it sees as the dominant liberal, universalist, and fundamentally anti-European and anti-white orthodoxy of the times. What this means is that throughout North America and Europe, and wherever European peoples have settled, they are threatened with cultural and, especially, biological extinction. What is at stake, therefore, is an existential struggle for the survival of ethnic white Europeans against, as Johnson argues in *New Right versus Old Right*, the "present regime," which "is a form of soft totalitarianism, which is enacting the genocide of the White race in slow motion. But the point is that this regime was not imposed upon our people through a violent revolution. They accepted it because of the transformation of their consciousness. They can be saved the same way."[112] The carrying out of this redemptive "transformation" through propaganda, however, must be conducted while simultaneously creating an alternative community as a galvanizing vision *and* experience of the new society to come. Alex Kurtagic, a racialist social critic, musician, and founder of the publisher Wermod and Wermod, in a conference speech that was subsequently posted at the Counter-Currents website, proposed that a "winning formula" for white politics "means acting *as if*. Acting as if we are already there. Which implies operating like an alternative society, offering access to a parallel universe, physical and metaphysical." Access, "to a different cosmology, a different system of symbols, a different way of understanding life. The new nationalism looks like an establishment in waiting."[113] At websites and in blogs, message boards, podcasts, vlogs, and many publications and conferences, this "new nationalism" presents itself as the only possible way to thwart the passing of the white race. This should be the foundation of the new secessionist "White Republic" envisioned by Michael O'Meara as the mobilizing Sorelian myth of white nationalists, implying "an all-white national community, which in turn, would mean a total rejection of the existing blood-sucking system of cultural-racial chaos that shames us and causes us to hate the world in which we have to live."[114]

The guiding idea of white liberation from a system of dispossession is central to the pro-white activism of Richard Spencer. A former doctoral student of history at Duke University "before dropping out to pursue a life of thought-crime," Spencer has promoted "white consciousness" in several magazines and online publications, and, since 2012, as the president and director of the Montana-based National Policy Institute (NPI). This organization has been associated from its founding in 2005 with William Regnery of the publishing family—who is also the founder of the Charles Martel Society, which publishes the racialist quarterly journal the *Occidental Quarterly*. The text of one of NPI's videos, about white identity, titled "Who Are We?," subsequently disseminated, for example, by the Zentropa community, sums up the overall philosophy of the organization: "We aren't just white, white is a checkbox on a census form, but we are part of the peoples, history, spirit, and civilization of Europe. So long as we deny our identities at a time when every other people is asserting its own, we will have no chance to resist our dispossession."[115] Spencer views "Identitarian" as an accurate description of his outlook: "Yes, in the sense that my American colleagues and I share a great deal of intellectual common ground with Identitarians in Europe, particularly regarding the importance of the French New Right [the ND], the thinkers of the Conservative Revolution, and German idealism."[116]

Instead of white nationalism, increasingly the semantic focus has been on an Alternative Right (a term coined by Spencer), later abbreviated and diffused online as "Alt Right" and propagated as a sort of "new creation" labeling a right that is free from the shackles of the "universalist liberal system," its dogmas, and the political correctness that defines the conventional and conservative right (which has been overwhelmingly represented in the Republican Party). The rejection of traditional conservatism (often identified with William F. Buckley) is common in racialist circles. To Johnson, "Buckley's description of conservatism as 'Standing athwart the tracks of history yelling stop' pretty much captures this mentality.... We White Nationalists, however, want to be in the engine of history, steering it toward our goal, and cheerfully pouring on the steam when the Buckleys of the world try to get in our way."[117] Kurtagic makes a similar statement: "I make a distinction between conservatism and tradition, the former being an effort to freeze the flame, the latter being an effort to keep the flame burning. In this later conception, futuristic visions are not incompatible with tradition—on the contrary, they are necessary."[118] From this position derives the self-description of many activists as "radical traditionalists," echoing, as discussed earlier in the book, Guillaume Faye's Nietzschean "archeofuturist" concept, in which the future is approached in terms of primordial, ancestral values, revitalized and regenerated. The purported origins are the source of new beginnings. It is in this ultimate sense that Spencer sees identity: "I also think that the term Identitarian is quite powerful [because] Identity is a search for something much deeper: the European spirit, the European race and people, the European historical experience. It is also something much broader than the borders of the European and American nation-states."[119] According to this line of reasoning, outside the territory of Americans of European descent the struggle for the white race means, ultimately, reawakening, beyond national borders, the primordial historical, cultural, and biological heritage of Europeans. NPI also owns and produces the Radix network—of which Spencer is the editor and founder—which, besides producing an online magazine issues a biannual print journal. *Radix* is Latin for "root" and is the source of the English word "radical." The mission of the network is portrayed as radical in the true sense of the word, since "the radical" seeks to uncover the heart of the matter; he searches out the source.[120] Here again, the image is one of a search for origins as the pathway for the future.

A TRANSATLANTIC NETWORK

The presentation of American Renaissance at one of its annual conferences stated: "The West faces many crises, but the greatest is the crisis of race. In virtually every Western country, the European majority is threatened with dispossession by non-white immigrants." As a consequence, "Unless whites rekindle their consciousness of race and act in their own interests, they will be pushed aside by others."[121] The overriding sentiment is that European white peoples are, consciously or unconsciously, on the same barricade in a struggle over life and death, even if, by necessity and context, this combat is expressed in different ways.

The need to emphasize race at a time when the word "race" is radioactive is not felt with the same urgency in Europe as in the United States. In fact, the European "goes-without-saying" trope is viewed by American racialists as a potent weapon. "In this respect Europeans have an advantage over Americans," Jared Taylor notes, for "Americans have no choice but to speak in terms of race as our unifying factor, whereas European nationalists can emphasize language, history, and culture without specifically talking about race. Anti-identitarians are especially provoked by expressions of white racial solidarity, so it may be useful for Europeans to avoid speaking of explicitly racial appeals."[122] It is in this sense that the editor in chief of Counter-Currents says that "because of the blending of European stocks and breakdown of more compact European national identities in North America, we are forced to stress the deeper roots of common European identity, including racial identity."[123] No wonder that O'Meara sees "Identitarianism (as an ideological/political stance)" as a "brilliant ploy to defend European identities and culture. Particularly in disarming the inquisitional exclusion that comes with liberal charges of 'fascism' and 'racism.'"[124]

The inorganic character of white nationalism, or of the white advocacy subculture, in America, however, is its deepest flaw, according to skeptical voices within the movement, for the American context is unlike that in Europe with its dense cultures, territories, myths, and ancient folkways always "available" to serve as "anchors" to Identitarian groups. The Croatian-American Tomislav Sunić—heavily involved in US racialist networks and, together with Jared Taylor, part of the board of directors of the American Freedom Party, which fights against "the dispossession of America's founding stock"—shares such skepticism. In "Which Way White Man?" Sunić says, "However similar the scenario White Europeans and White Americans are facing today regarding the continuing danger of non-European immigration, nationalists in Europe have an advantage of being always able to fall back [on their territorial imperative]. . . . No amount of racial pride can be exhibited in abstract talks about Whiteness, unless backed up by a solid earth-bound notion of nation and state."[125] A British contributor to Right On, John Lambton, declared, "Saying 'whites' to me is an American idea." "Europeans are diverse ethnically not just 'white,' they are Germans, Gallic, Alpine, Italian, Celtic, etc."[126] In the end, according to John Morgan, this fundamental difference blocks any sort of filiation of the American white subculture with a broader pan-European Identitarian movement because "as an attempt at identity politics it is completely rootless and cosmopolitan, contrary to the Identitarian vision." The reality is that "the concept of 'whiteness' is an American invention which has no reality outside of ideology. Nobody can define what it is, outside of 'I know it when I see it.'" As Morgan says of the idea that there is a single characteristic, ethnic or cultural, that unites Europe, "It's a fantasy and another manifestation of the American drive to homogenize and level everything in its path—another form of the famous 'melting pot' that is the American ideal." Those who dream of exporting the idea of a white identity to Europe, "are in for a rude awakening."[127] At a later stage, especially after the rise of Donald Trump, thanks to whom "white identity politics has become an issue in the US on a scale that hasn't been seen for decades," Morgan contended that WN makes sense in an American context—"It is very clear that Americans of European descent as a whole remain a distinct group, and have their own particular needs and interests"—while still not seeing it as "possible" or "desirable" to export White Nationalism to Europe.[128]

With a "rude awakening" in sight, or not, the fact of the matter is that the idea of a natural encounter between Americans of European descent and autochthonous Europeans resonates on both sides of the

Atlantic, fueling attempts to boost a transatlantic network. Lucian Tudor says that the "instability" of white nationalism (in terms of its "tendencies toward hostility and alienation toward other races") makes it "unclear if relations [with Identitarians] will always remain friendly."[129] Until now, in the WN (or white advocacy) settings, the truth remains that the intellectual contributions of the ND—particularly its undermining of the philosophical and anthropological roots of modernity—and the defense of the biological and cultural identity of Europeans of Identitarian authors such as Guillaume Faye are viewed as absolute intellectual pillars, and their texts are often translated, commented on, and disseminated. The surge of interest in the figure of Dominique Venner, for example, whose writings have started to be translated and are getting wider recognition since his death, are also part of this intellectual porosity. In a post titled "Frenchman, European, White Man," Jared Taylor began his review of Venner's *The Shock of History* by claiming: "On May 21, 2013, a Frenchman virtually unknown outside of Europe suddenly burst into the consciousness of racially aware Americans."[130] In the past few years, Arktos Media, through its releases and translations, caused many of the crucial works of the ND and the Identitarian camps to travel into North America, opening them to a wider audience. It has, for example, acquired the English-language rights to all of Guillaume Faye's works that have been written over the past twenty years. Counter-Currents also plays an important role in this intellectual propagation, and its co-founder—who was the one who translated and posted online Venner's suicide note—says that the North American New Right as a new movement does "not have any thinkers of the caliber of Alain de Benoist, Guillaume Faye, and many others. We are deeply indebted to the decades of work they have done."[131] They have established a relationship as well with Robert Steuckers's blog *Euro-Synergies*, which republishes many Counter-Currents articles and posts. But the more recent Identitarian wave—whether in the form of Generation Identity movements or that of CasaPoundism—are no less praised, and sympathetic reports about their activities and also interviews abound in the part of the web devoted to white identity. "Just as guerrilla fighters arm light to maximize mobility, Identitarian ideological minimalism allows them to nimbly step over the clichés of the mainstream's defenders and stay on the attack," wrote Johnson in tribute to European Generation Identity groups. Presenting in the Counter-Currents webzine an introduction to the English-speaking world of the French Generation Identity (published by Arktos), its translator, Roger Devlin, urged readers to "read for yourself what its own representatives have to say. You will find it admirably forthright and uncompromising: the kind of movement desperately needed in these United States."[132]

Richard Spencer has made clear his intellectual debt to the ND, which he views as essential in his intellectual formation while helping him move toward a "real Right," away from conservatism. The 2013 NPI conference, with the theme After the Fall: The Future of Identity, had de Benoist as a featured speaker. In Washington, DC, de Benoist spoke on the subject of identity. The French thinker, however—years later, when the Alt Right had become the center of attention (and was receiving much criticism for its intolerance and racism) in the American and European presses—attempted to disavow any links he had with it, even distancing himself from the event he was attending, arguing, "Obviously I never endorse the views of those who invite me. On that occasion, at a time when no one was talking about the Alt Right, I immediately realized that the audience was completely foreign to me."[133] Spencer, however, sees no "foreignness" in regard to European Identitarians and has been a major supporter of a broader Identitarian network. "There are so many powerful forces bringing us [American and European Identitarians] together," he states. "The Internet is one; English as a lingua franca is another. Also, we share an historical experience of the mass immigration of foreign peoples and our coming minority status. In the eyes of the 'Other,' we already share a White Identity, whether we are American, Swedish, Australian, etc. As time goes on, we will grasp this as well."[134] The Scotsman Colin Liddell—the co-editor of the site Alternative Right, originally founded by Spencer in 2010 (who subsequently closed it down before Liddell and Andy Nowicki relaunched it), which Liddell describes as a "space for modern-day heretics, who don't necessarily agree with each other"—thinks that "if Europe awakens, we will see this resonate in America. A transatlantic alliance would be natural and healthy."[135]

Beyond projections about the near and distant futures, what is clear is that there have been many exchanges, transmissions of knowledge, speaking engagements, and overall back-and-forth between the Identitarian camps. Guillaume Faye—whose work has been translated and extensively commented upon by Michael O'Meara—is credited as a leading voice of the European resistance to decline. Introducing Faye, as the keynote speaker of NPI's 2015 conference Become Who We Are, held in Washington, DC, Richard Spencer said: "No one has better articulated the ideal of our movement, of an ethno-state ... in a more provocative fashion. Guillaume Faye has given us something to dream about."[136] Recalling his first meeting with Faye—who has also been a speaker at American Renaissance conferences—Jared Taylor noted, "When it came to an understanding of race, of the biological foundations of European civilization, we were immediately old comrades."[137] In his review of Faye's *Why We Fight*, Taylor emphasized that "racially conscious Americans invariably see European identitarians as allies in a world-wide struggle."[138] It was with this target in mind that the president of the Bloc Identitaire was invited to the eleventh American Renaissance conference. In his talk, "Europe Awakes," Fabrice Robert spoke about the importance of strengthening a White European front:

> We may be separated by an ocean, by two centuries of hostility, of rivalry, but we agree on a fundamental reality: we are Whites, with common problems in the 21st century, such as so-called "anti-racism," which is a code-word for anti-white racism, our demographic decline and our substitution on our ancestral lands by Third-World people. We might differ on solutions to these problems, on goals, but we are confronted with the same hatred for what we are: Europeans. And whether we are Europeans from France, America or New Zealand, what the people who attack us want is our extinction.

Accordingly, "We, European Identitarians, want to emphasize what brings us together with you. ... We are sons of the same matrix: Europe. We are brothers of the same people, the European people."[139] A few years later, as an invited speaker at the fifteenth American Renaissance conference, Martin Lichtmesz gave a presentation about the German-speaking Identitarian youth movement—with many moments of laughter when the Austrian speaker showed slides of the Identitarians' provocations and "pranks"—calling it "the first right-wing international youth movement ever" and stressing the need for further networking and collaboration: "My very presence here, in the US, is a sign of the internationalization of patriotic and right-wing ideas. . . . I hope it continues because most countries in the West share similar problems and conflicts."[140]

The founder of American Renaissance, for his part, has been a frequent speaker on the international circuit, always manifesting his "deep faith in the solidarity of all Europeans, whether on the home continent or overseas in North America, Australia, New Zealand, or South Africa. We speak many languages and have many cultures, but we are one people with a common origin and a common destiny." In his view, "Identitarianism will succeed at different rates in different countries. It will be natural for those who have made more progress to help those who have made less. It is important for us to share with each other our experiences and insights."[141] Taylor advocates what he calls a "world brotherhood of Europeans." In the fall of 2014 he did so, in an NPI conference in Budapest dedicated to "The Future of Europe"—a conference that was held even though not in its original format because of a prohibition by the Hungarian authorities and a series of repressive measures against participants, including the arrest and deportation of Richard Spencer. Taylor addressed the participants by indicting the "poisonous ideology of diversity that my country wants to force upon you," of which "Western Europe has already swallowed an enormous dose." He said prophetically, "Perhaps the healthier Central European nations will support Western Identitarians and save all of Europe." Today "the lines are not so clearly drawn, the crisis is not so sharp, but for our generation, this is Thermopylae, this is Poitiers, this is the Siege of Malta, this is [Enoch Powell's] Blood River."[142] According to Taylor, speaking to a forum of politicians and activists in Saint Petersburg, in the face of the onslaught of the "insanity of diversity" (which is the "new religion of America"), Europeans must stand together to preserve their priceless cultural and genetic heritage, or, in one way or another, perish.[143] The geopolitical implications of the necessary and urgent convergence of white peoples led Michael O'Meara, writing in the *Occidental Quarterly*, to advocate a "Borean alliance" as a sort of "Northern imperium of white peoples." Like many European Identitarians, O'Meara pays high tribute to the future role of

Russia in this project; he believes that when the Paris-Berlin-Moscow axis is firmly established, White Americans "in alliance with their kinsmen in Europe and Russia . . . will have no choice but to accept that they are made not in the multihued images of a deracinated humanity, but in that of the luminous Boreans." As the new aurora of "Boreas" rises, so will end the present-day downfall of whites.[144]

Alt Right: The Franchise?

In tandem with the drive toward teamwork, in early 2017, in what was viewed by its creators as a decisive step toward a viable Identitarian transatlanticism, Richard Spencer and Daniel Friberg joined forces and, together with other activists, founded the AltRight Corporation as a joint Euro-American venture. In the first podcast of AltRight Radio they aimed at making of the project an agenda setter for the Alt Right from the outset and, eventually, a key instrument of "policy making for the Alt Right in the coming years." Buoyed by electoral events—such as Brexit, but most of all, the election of Donald Trump—the project was created in the conviction that "Alt Right and Identitarian ideas are becoming more mainstream than ever."[145]

Soon afterward, Nordisk Alternativhöger—the Nordic Alt Right—emerged. Basically, it represents an expansion of the Alt Right into the Nordic European countries. Founded by, among others, Friberg and Christoffer Dulny, a law graduate who worked in the Swedish parliament for the nationalist party Sweden Democrats before committing to this project as its editor in chief and president, it is presented as a metapolitical organization—with a website, podcasts, videos, and the organization of conferences—and a place where the "true Nords" can gather and experience a real "counter-culture." It replicates the themes of the American Alt Right—even the websites are alike—and, in the same way as its "mother ship," operates as an open advocate of white identity politics in European, in this case Scandinavian, territory. It vows to not be antagonistic toward other pro-white groups. In an interview with Nordic Frontier, the English podcast of the National Socialist Nordic Resistance Movement (which operates in Sweden, Finland, and Norway), Dulny speaks about some sort of "tribal" solidarity: "Let's be honest, the situation is so dire that we need all the people we can have on our side. . . .

I do believe we belong to the same tribe, we have maybe different strategies, different backgrounds, different ideology in some way . . . but we are on the same side."[146] On another occasion he said, "We're part of the Altright.com franchise, so to speak—I hope we have a lot of altright .com platforms in the future."[147] In fact, this creation of a sort of Alt Right "international"—operating synergistically to advance white interests on both sides of the Atlantic—is a long-term objective of Alt Right Inc. The Nordic Alt Right became the first of its kind in European lands.

Alt Right Troubles

The idea that the "tide is turning" boosted the Alt Right joint venture and, at least for a short while, one of the new slogans of Friberg's publisher Arktos became "Influencing the White House since 2017"—a reference to the anti-globalist campaign promises of the new US president, as well as his choice as his chief strategist of former Breitbart News chair Stephen Bannon, who was viewed as traditionalist/Identitarian friendly. This affiliation with the Alt Right was far from consensual, however. It became a factor, among others, in the departure of Arktos's long-time editor John Morgan. "Regarding the editorial line, I am very skeptical of Arktos becoming so closely associated with the Alt Right," Morgan argued. "I always wanted Arktos to remain aloof from day-to-day politics, and definitely not get so involved in specifically American politics, and also I'm not sure it's wise to piggyback on a 'movement' (if you can even call it that, which is debatable) that may or may not fizzle out before long."[148] In truth, especially after the postelectoral euphoria, the movement found itself engaged in a sort of tug-of-war. Movement people grappled with each other over a variety of topics—as was the case in the clash of Richard Spencer and Daniel Friberg with Counter-Currents' Greg Johnson about "character issues."

Also, a wider point of contention is ingrained in the US white nationalist subculture itself in terms of the tension between a strictly metapolitical path and a more overtly political, street-based approach to the "plight of Whites." This has become even more apparent after Donald Trump's election to the US presidency. Asked in the early months of 2015 if he thought Identitarianism was revolutionary, Spencer replied: "Yes, though not directly so (in other words, we're not going to take to the barricades next Tuesday)." Two years later, if not exactly "taking to the barricades," Spencer began taking part in the movement "to the streets."[149] In fact, one side of the white nationalist (WN) camp, exemplified by Richard Spencer—which until then had been more invested in scholarly and intellectual networking—adopted a more populist, out-in-the-open approach to the cause, with demonstrations, marches, torchlit rallies, agitation in the streets, media-grabbing tactics, speaking tours of college campuses, and so forth. The opening salvo of this new direction, at least from a symbolic standpoint, could well be traced to what became known as "Hailgate," when Spencer closed an NPI conference by exclaiming, "Hail Trump! Hail our people! Hail Victory!" and raised his glass. This gesture—which Spencer later called "provocative" and "outlandish"—was met by Nazi salutes from some of the people in the audience and promptly went viral. Many Alt Right figures (white nationalists or not) saw it as a moment of self-sabotage that provided the media with the "perfect" image with which to "vilify" the entire movement, and distanced themselves from Spencer and even the Alt Right label, as if it was something forever damaged.

A second moment that further antagonized the resistance to Spencer's activities came in the aftermath of the Unite the Right rally in Charlottesville, Virginia—where Spencer was to be a keynote speaker—organized to show support for white heritage and to protest the removal of the statue of the Confederate general Robert E. Lee from a Charlottesville public park initially named after him (which was renamed Emancipation Park). On the night before the event, hundreds of WN's, holding torches, marched on the campus of the University of Virginia in a visual spectacle that brought a broad sense of accomplishment to the activists and organizers. The next day, the presence of militias, Klansmen, and Nazi imagery among the participants—as well as the violent confrontations with antifas (antifascists) and the death of a counterprotester—took over the headlines and made national and worldwide news, turning what was supposed to be a "positive" symbol of white identity politics into a "negative" throwback to times and symbols long rejected and maligned by the wider public. These words, directed by a Twitter user writing under the name of Ruben to Richard Spencer and Evan McLaren (a lawyer and the executive director of the NPI), illus-

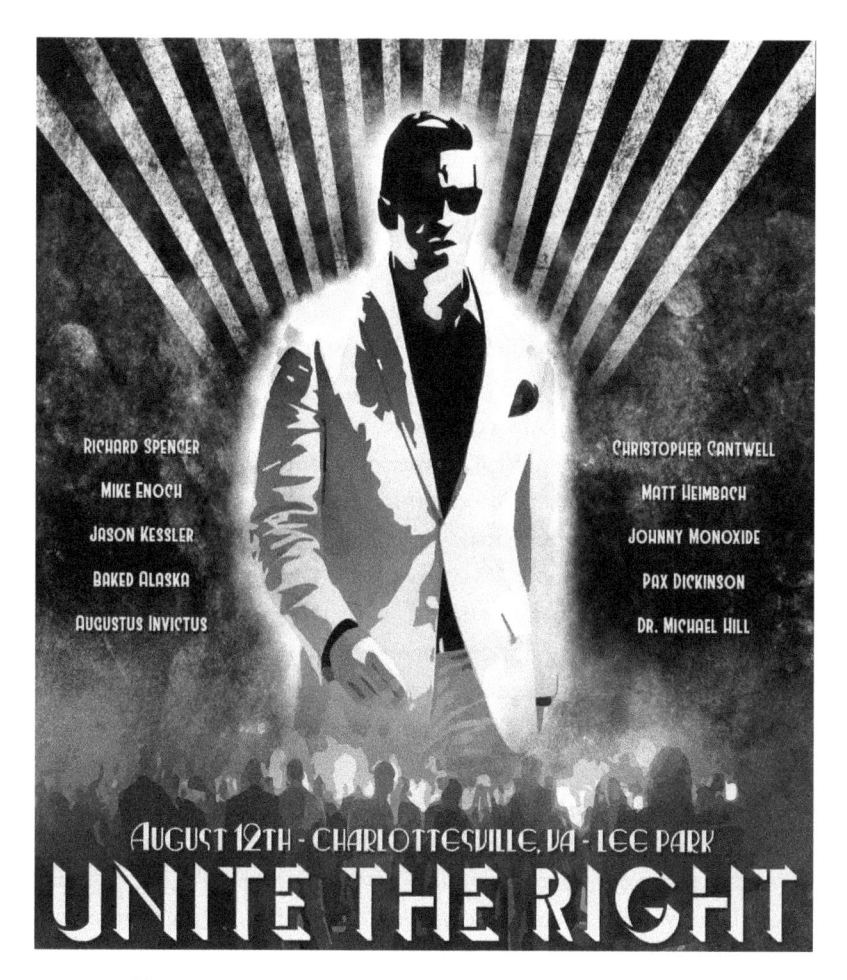

FIGURE 33. White nationalism goes populist. Meme advertising the Unite the Right rally in Charlottesville, Virginia, with Richard Spencer center front (August 2017).

trate well the sentiments of anger and despondency shared by many white nationalists: "You and Spencer took the best new political brand in a generation ("alt right") and drove it into a ditch by playing footsie with Nazi larpers."[150] Not surprisingly, more infighting ensued in the aftermath of Charlottesville, aggravated by a deplatforming offensive of WN groups by tech and webhosting companies, many lawsuits against those involved in the rally, and an overall hostile environment for the Alt

Right that lingered for many months afterward and also had a negative impact on transnational networking, especially because of travel bans. Christoffer Dulny and Daniel Friberg, European fellow travelers who attended the rally at Charlottesville, were afterward banned from traveling to the United States, while Spencer (who was already forbidden to travel to the United Kingdom) was barred from travel to Poland to speak at a nationalist conference. Even the annual Identitarian Ideas conference, organized by Friberg in Stockholm, did not take place owing to pressure from political opponents and indications that Swedish authorities would deny admission to Spencer.

At the same time, and consistently, there is another side of the WN camp—epitomized by Counter-Currents and also American Renaissance—a side that is lower-profile and that continues to be fundamentally attached to an elitist/academic approach that is constituted by a sometimes anonymous (as many people conceal their identities by using pseudonyms) "battle of ideas," with writings, conferences, and private invitation-only gatherings across the United States but also in Europe—with vetting procedures in place to keep infiltrators and doxers at bay, not always successfully.[151] They prioritize comradeship and networking, while WN populists are seeking a more direct route to the masses, a strategy that is often met with violence by opponents and antifa groups that are energized by anti-Trump fervor. Greg Johnson believes that in the end there is nothing "new" about this split, arguing that "there has always been an elitist vs. populist split in White Nationalist thinking about strategy. This split roughly maps out of the distinction between those who believe that metapolitical foundations need to be laid before political action can be successful, and those who think that we need to do something, anything, right now."[152] What for some is passivity (defending whites exclusively in lecture halls) is for others daydreaming because the overall population is still "not ready" to openly join pro-white activism. Hence the need, according to these activists, for intellectual/cultural groundwork. Regardless, these conflicts—personal and strategic—may have helped to weaken the movement at the exact moment when, at least in the hopes of activists and sympathetic observers, it was strengthening and positioning itself for (some degree) of success.

"Bound to Happen"

Whether the Alt Right, and all its tendencies, will endure and grow or become a footnote in the twenty-first-century history of political activism remains uncertain. What is certain, however, is the belief among these groups and the various individuals who join them that there is a powerful logic at work that will gain sufficient momentum to ensure the inevitability of wider fellowship and solidarity between Europeans with the passing of time. Such movement activists hope that the worse the situation gets in Europe, especially in terms of increasing mass immigration, the faster the sociopolitical reality will be divided along ethnic and racial lines—accelerating Europe's awakening and increasing the chances of a strong transatlantic Identitarian alliance between the "brother-peoples" of Europe and white America. The much-talked-about issue of the Islamization of the continent is, ultimately, only a symptom, a consequence, of a deeper process of the displacement of peoples. It is in this sense that Greg Johnson says that the fight against Islamization—which is often used as a proxy term for non-white demographic replacement—is understandably necessary and useful, and "if some Europeans are awakened by Islamization to our demographic and cultural peril, that is something to welcome." However, "Islamization is an incomplete account of the problem, so merely solving the Islamic problem will not save Europe. But it is a start, and identitarians should regard Counter-Jihadism as an opportunity to more fully educate our people about the real problem and the real solution, namely the demographic and cultural displacement of whites by non-whites, which can only be solved by the creation of homogeneously white homelands. Non-whites have no business in Europe. Europe should be for Europeans only."[153] As stated by the Englishman Bain Dewitt (a pen name)—a Counter-Currents contributor and former editor of the (now defunct) British site/group "Identity Forum," which is committed to "revitalizing European ethnic consciousness"[154]—even though "love for the white race is the real love that dare not speak its name lest one be interred as a dissenter and institutionalized," the reality is that "the removal of 'Islam' is just a proxy issue that will make the racial conflict of Europeans ever more apparent."[155] This, in turn, according to this logic, will only cause them to be even more allied with the Americans of European descent.

Generation Identity Made in USA?

It started by advertising itself as "a generation of awakened Europeans who have discovered that we are part of the great peoples, history, and civilization that flowed from the European continent." Alongside the Dragon's Eye symbol the caption for the online video read "Identity Evropa" (pronounced with a "v" sound). In fact, Identity Evropa is the closest there is to a US-based Identitarian activist movement—even if in this case it is strictly white nationalist and undeveloped in comparison with the original European movements. Since 2016, and initially run by Nathan Damigo, an Iraq War veteran, this action-oriented group—or "fraternity," as its founder sees it—which started in Northern California, spread to the East Coast while aspiring to develop into a full-fledged national network. It brands itself as an "American based identitarian organization dedicated to promoting the interests of People of European Heritage."[156] Intellectually indebted to Guillaume Faye—whose book *Why We Fight* is advertised at their site as "the Identitarian Manifesto" (and a book that Damigo read while serving time for assault)[157]—the group was initially closely aligned with Richard Spencer's activities and public engagements, including in the look of their members, who are typically clean-cut, like Spencer, and sport undercut hairstyles.

Identity Evropa's role models of activism, as Damigo acknowledged, were the Bloc Identitaire and the French Lambda movement. Their "professional" defense of native Europeans impressed him: "They have mastered this branding, this aesthetic. They've really done an amazing job with it."[158] Identity Evropa—first under the leadership of Damigo and subsequently headed by Eli Mosley (the pseudonym of the Pennsylvanian WN activist Elliott Kline) and, since the end of 2017, Patrick Casey—has taken the fight for "white identity" to "cultural Marxist-dominated" US campuses (but also targets densely populated areas) with campaigns of promulgating flyers, posters, and stickers depicting classical sculptures with slogans such as "Protect Your Heritage," "Let's Become Great Again," and "Only We Can Be Us." Guillaume Faye's Arktos books have often featured in their propaganda, especially that targeting schools and universities; "So radical your professors will blush" reads one of the posters showing an image of the English translation of

Understanding Islam, while another says "Neoliberalism can't stop what's coming" above the cover of Faye's *Convergence of Catastrophes*, and "Yeah, we called it what it is" above Faye's *The Colonization of Europe*.

A running theme is the fight against non-European immigration and the associated theme of ongoing racial replacement, and the slogan "You Will Not Replace Us" (in a nod to Camus's "Great Replacement" claim) features prominently in Identity Evropa's protests and demonstrations. When they unfurled a banner with such a slogan at a bridge in Atlanta, their press release asked for an "end to immigration" under the justification that "the American people are being replaced in the nation their European ancestors founded and built. We refuse to be replaced by policies that exploit people from impoverished, non-European nations as cheap labor for globalist greed."[159] Still incipient—and committed especially in this first phase to increasing its name recognition while developing into a brand of political activism—Identity Evropa stands as an example of a group attempting to transfer to US soil the methods and direct-action tactics of the European Identitarian youth movement. This attempt has intensified, particularly since the rise to leadership of Patrick Casey, but with an American twist; the combat is specifically against (and is framed as such) what they see as the anti-white agenda of the political, economic media and the cultural establishment.

And Then Identitarians Met the Frog

The Alt Right began as a *specific phenomenon*—as a way of billing a dissident, and for the most part white nationalist right,[160] as opposed to progressivism, traditional conservatism, and neo-conservatism. At a later time, the term "Alt Right" also developed into a broader label for anti–political correctness in online activism. What characterized this offensive—which came to the attention of mainstream media owing to its incessant activism in support of the "anti-establishment" Donald Trump in the 2016 US presidential campaign—was a Rabelaisian and iconoclastic spirit fueled by social media activism, Internet forums and image-boards, which crudely torpedoed—by trolling and conducting memetic warfare—the "egalitarian orthodoxies" of the times. Although white nationalism was still present as a key tendency, there were other non–white nationalist tendencies within the umbrella of this activism.

One of them was subsequently labeled by Alt Righters as Alt Light because it is defined not by racial nationalism but by civic nationalism instead while still vocally opposed to establishment conservatism. It was from within the "Alt Light" that some of the most blistering attacks on Spencer's Hailgate came—and these only intensified after the Charlottesville episode—and that led to the decision of many of its figures to disavow not only the Alt Right label but also the Alt expression altogether in favor of such designations as "New Right."[161] It can be argued, in fact, that this split helped to move the Alt Right as a whole closer to its white nationalist origins.

If, by and large, Nouvelle Droite and Identitarian theorists have been the ones who have influenced American Identitarians ideologically, it must be said that in terms of Metapolitics 2.0, American activists have been the ones influencing the youths of European Identitarian activism. The incessant sabotage and mocking of the "correct" political discourse that are features of Alt Right activism, while pushing the boundaries of what is allowed to be said in a liberal democratic society that is allegedly dominated by the thought control of cultural Marxism, is often praised by European Identitarians as a clever way of breaking long-standing taboos while further exploring and accentuating the limitless power of images—or "meme magic"—for political, social, and cultural combat. Alt Right memes have become a part of the virtual arsenal of European Identitarians; prominent among them is the cartoon character Pepe the Frog, which, although included in the Anti-Defamation League's official list of hate symbols, is nevertheless viewed by Identitarians as *the* symbol of free-spiritedness and mockery of the established "liberal/progressive" wisdom. Alt Right hashtags also circulate widely in European Identitarian social media; for example, the epithet "cuck," an abbreviation of "cuckservative" and, more generally, a word of ridicule for someone who shows weakness and passivity, lacking self-worth and allowing himself to be taken advantage of or "owned" by others. Other Alt Right expressions that have made it into the wider Identitarian vocabulary include "normie/s," which basically describes people who "go with the flow," who adhere to mainstream, conventional views, and "Red Pill" (from the movie *The Matrix*), alluding to that moment in time when a "normie" is faced with the uncomfortable truths suppressed or hidden by the system and becomes "awakened."

Of Race and Identity 311

FIGURE 34. German Identitarian street campaign in the northern state of Mecklenburg-Vorpommern, with an activist dressed as Pepe the Frog distributing propaganda leaflets.

FIGURE 35. Meme in support of the summer 2017 Identitarian Defend Europe mission depicting Pepe the Frog as the C-Star ship.

It is not an exaggeration to say that the Alt Right "army" of meme warfare specialists and trolls has helped shape one of the strongest, most appealing to youth, and technologically trendy expressions of the transatlantic ties between the self-proclaimed defenders of European identity.

JQ—The "Jewish Question"

The path forward for "racially conscious Europeans" is, of course, not linear and is riddled with what they believe to be major obstacles and powerful antagonizing forces. What is described in white nationalist circles as the "Jewish Question" (JQ)—and the putative key role that influential Jews and the organized Jewish community played in promoting non-white immigration into Western countries, with "white genocide" as the endgame—is a topic of much internal debate—and dispute. A momentous episode came with the publication of Guillaume Faye's book *The New Jewish Question*, in which the French writer contended, to much outrage from certain racialist circles, both European and American, that the defenders of European identity should get rid of an obsessive and "chronic anti-Judaism" because the real danger is colonization from "the Third World and Islam."[162] This is a view shared by American Renaissance. Jared Taylor often says that prominent members of the Jewish community support that group's activities and that "a growing number of American Jews become aware that they belong to the Euro-American community and that it is their duty to contribute to its defense."[163]

In other sectors, Jewish "machinations" are still seen as the main enemy of whites. O'Meara, in his criticism of Faye, says that the Jewish Question *is* of "political interest to the struggle for white survival" owing to Jews' "pathologization of white identity" while instigating "genocidal" open-borders policies as a way of replacing the indigenous white communities.[164] "If we are going to name the principal enemy of whites," Greg Johnson says in one of his rebuttals to Faye, "in the dual sense of (1) who has done more to cause our present demographic and cultural decline and, more importantly, (2) who is the hard core of the opposition to fixing our problems, the answer has to be the organized Jewish community." Johnson writes, "My attitude toward Jews is exactly analogous to his views about Muslims." "There are good and bad Jews, but such distinctions should not distract us from the overriding necessity of freeing European lands from Jewish power, and that means separating ourselves from the whole community. I want good and moderate Jews to flourish, but in Israel, with the rest of their people."[165] This idea of a basic separation between Jews and whites is also part of the worldview of Identity Evropa's second leader, Eli Mosley, for whom "Jews are a fundamentally different group with often competing interests to our own."[166] Not surprisingly, one of the questions that prospective members have to answer in the process of application to Identity Evropa is "Are you of European, non-Semitic heritage?" Mosley's successor, Patrick Casey, downplays the importance of the "Jewish Question," saying, "The issue of Jewish identity and influence isn't one that's central or essential to our group," even if "it's impossible to ignore that virtually all Jewish organizations support mass immigration into the West (with many opposing the same in Israel)"—a predominant idea in WN as a whole.[167]

The hostility regarding the alleged evil menace of the Jews to European identity—and their insidious influence—is also salient in some racialist European groups, such as Terre et Peuple, and particularly heightened in the case of *Réfléchir & Agir*. "We know the reasons that make anti-racists advocate universal miscegenation (although for most of them, their religious tenets forbid them to mingle their blood with that of a foreigner)," read one of its editorials.[168] The magazine reviews and pays tribute to books that "reveal the influence and the power of Jews throughout history," from Edouard Drumont's *La France Juive* (Jewish France) to Douglas Reed's *The Controversy of Zion*. And when the former socialist foreign minister, Roland Dumas, declared that the French prime minister Manuel Valls was "probably" under "Jewish influence," the magazine briefly commented, "At last a free man."[169] *Réfléchir & Agir*—which in recent years has intensified its coverage of the US white nationalist movement, interviewing its figureheads, such as Jared Taylor and Greg Johnson—featured, for example, a dialogue between Eugène Krampon and the "herald/hero of white resistance in the United States," David Duke, about "the sense of his/our combat." A major theme of discussion was the role played by "Zionist lobbies" and "Judeo-American world domination" and their alleged vicious destruction of White identity.[170]

Too "Radical" for Europeans?

Writing in the same magazine about the metapolitical online combat of the Alt Right, Thierry Durolle noted that because of its role in electing Donald Trump, "it is not surprising that (((some))) wish to muzzle this last bastion [the Internet] of freedom."[171] Here Durolle was using the echo parentheses used by the Alt Right to identify Jewish-controlled institutions or Jewish individuals. This symbol, although employed by racialists, is one of the memes that is hardly found on the pragmatic front of European Identitarian activism. In fact, although, particularly after Donald Trump's rise to power in the United States, the Alt Right gained fame—or infamy—and it became common for mainstream media outlets to describe European Identitarians as "the European version of the Alt Right," the analogy, especially with regard to European youth activism, is not entirely accurate. Although, as shown in this chapter, there are many points of contact and influence between US and European Identitarians, there is also a distinction. Not only because European Identitarians are not a uniform group (with different views regarding the centrality of "race," for example) but also because in some instances there is open criticism of the Alt Right by European activists.

"I have spoken at length with several members of Generation Identity regarding whether or not they see their movement as similar to the Alt Right. They do not," notes Brittany Pettibone.[172] Talking about white nationalists (who constitute a very important, although not exclusive part, of the Alt Right), the American Budapest resident John Morgan—an enthusiast and promoter of the European Identitarian youth movement—says, "I can sympathize with them, provided that such people avoid the xenophobia, supremacism, and other such destructive qualities which afflict some strands of their movement."[173] In fact, the Austrian leader Martin Sellner, for example, who is an admirer of the subversive metapolitical activities of the Alt Right, says that in order for US activists to be truly Identitarian they have to "find a clear position against racism/racial supremacy and anti-Semitism." In like manner, the German Identitarian activist Robert Timm says that "we have a lot in common with the Alt-Right: we are patriots, we are against mass immigration, and we embrace the memetic culture," adding "but they are much more radical." Also, "if you listen to their leader Richard Spencer, who says that America must remain a country of White people, I as an Identitarian cannot accept this." Timm states, "Certainly people in Europe and in the United States are against certain tendencies in the developments of their countries, but the logic of the Alt Right, and their idea of white supremacy ('white domination') does not suit us at all."[174] And so it seems that the odds that not only the "Jewish Question" but the broader issue of "whiteness" will remain points of contention at least in some parts of the wider transatlantic Identitarian camps are, in fact, relatively high. This, of course, is not an issue in regard to the Alt Right franchise—umbilically tied with the Alt Right corporation—but it does complicate matters in the relationship with the European Identitarian youth movement.

The divide, however, is not just ideological. It is also strikingly present in terms of both the presentation and production of activism.[175] Identitarian youth groups—especially those that operate under the Lambda sign—have high levels of self-enforced discipline that rein in members around the need to focus and stay on message—meaning that, in the same way that there is an acceptable way of celebrating one's culture, roots, and ethnicity, there is an unacceptable way. A "European Charlottesville" would be unthinkable—not only because of the legal system, which often prohibits symbols from a damned past—but also due to the effort by Identitarian leaders to disassociate the Identitarian brand from the wrong kind of people and imagery. When Greg Johnson writes, "Instead of large, unity events open to all comers—including undisciplined clowns—we need smaller, more disciplined groups with more focused messaging," he sees it as *the* way to avoid PR disasters, taking a page from the Euro-style "Identitarian playbook,"[176] with the conviction that wrong optics from "undisciplined clowns" is the kiss of death for all WN ambitions to reach and influence the outside world. This warning was not limited to Johnson. Jared Taylor—speaking in the Netherlands at a conference organized by the Dutch group Erkenbrand—spoke of Charlottesville as a "black eye to the movement as a whole" while calling for a new, Generation Identity–like, approach to activism: "If we are to have public demonstrations of that kind they must be much better organized, much more along the lines of Generation Identity, for example—they do different things and their strategy is different."[177]

All of this does not mean that the scenario of adapting Alt Right activism should be outright excluded. In reality, after the Charlottesville debacle there were signs within the Alt Right populist movement of a change of modus operandi—one more aligned, in fact, with said "Identitarian playbook," even if with an American, white nationalist, twist. In their post-Charlottesville street activism against what for them is an ongoing war on white existence and heritage, members of the Alt Right adopted guerrilla-style tactics of protest, akin to flashmobs, in which organized and disciplined activists—overwhelmingly young men, often wearing white polos and khakis—led by Spencer and other leaders (like Eli Mosley), bullhorns in hand, momentarily occupied public spaces and expressed their pro-white views loud and clear before departing the scene to the surprise and shock (sometimes heckling) of onlookers. This tactic was tested both on the steps of the Jefferson Memorial in Washington, DC, and in Lee Park in Charlottesville, where they conducted another, albeit brief, torchlit demonstration with cries of "You Will Not Replace Us." "It shows that we can learn and evolve," noted Spencer. "The flashmob is a good model in its own right—that's why it's used by lots of different groups. In the sense that we can have a small amount of people highly motivated/highly coordinated—we make our statement—we get in, we get out, no confrontations, no one gets hurt."[178] Likewise, and shortly after these direct actions, Eli Mosley (while still leading Identity Evropa)—in a video interview with Identity Evropa supporter and YouTube Alt Right personality James Allsup—noted how "We're kind into this new wave of the Alt Right . . . where this is a complete new kind of idea. . . . Look, there's no 'how to run an American Identitarian organization for dummies' book," and added, "We're all going at this kinda blind. . . . We have to be willing to make mistakes, and we have to be willing to kinda learn from those mistakes."[179] While discussing the symbology that the Alt Right should adopt in order to increase its appeal, Spencer recognized the merits of the European Identitarian activist movement in creating a "new image," even if rejecting any sort of imitation, saying, "I don't think we should ape European Identitarians. . . . I think we're a lot bigger than they are, to be frank. . . . I'm not talking about Identitarianism as a philosophy [but] about Génération Identitaire, etc." At the same time, he added, "I do like the Spartan lambda as a flag, the gold, I think, is a powerful color. . . . I'm not against adopting that. . . . I don't know if we wanna steal that from them, I'm not sure how they would feel if we did that. . . . Maybe it should be a European flag [as our symbol] . . . that we should fly along[side] the American flag."[180]

All things considered, in the long run there is the possibility that Identity Evropa may fare better in terms of a rapprochement with European Lambda Identitarian activists, especially if its leadership decides to further realign its optics and ideology with Europeans and away from Spencer's brand of activism, which is viewed by some critics as unable to break away from "old" vices. "The European Identitarians are very cautious about associating with American groups—for good reason. GI has managed to create something new, while many American groups are under the impression that resurrecting National Socialism is the only way forward," says Casey. "With that said, I think in the future there is a potential for Identity Evropa to work with GI in some capacity—we'd love to!"[181] Unlike the first leaders of Identity Evropa, Casey—an anthropology major and collaborator with the white identity politics media network Red Ice (using the pseudonym Reinhard Wolff)—directed his group on a more autonomous path in regard to Spencer's shadow, veering its optics, street activism, and themes in a more European-Lambda way while maintaining the WN brand. Besides continuing its activism on US campuses and its banner-unfurling initiatives, IE activism started to include, for example, staging die-in protests, cleaning up public places, providing food relief for homeless people and needy families, emphasizing themes such as "ethnopluralism" and "remigration," and holding flash demonstrations aimed at spreading iconic images of activism. An example of this activism was the demonstration in Tennessee—after IE's first national conference (at which Jared Taylor, among others, was invited to speak) which was held in front of Nashville's Parthenon, where dozens of activists unfurled a forty-foot-long banner that read "European Roots/American Greatness," lighted flares, and waved IE and American flags.[182] Aesthetically, in fact, this event was an attempt to create an iconic image in the style of Génération Identitaire (at Poitiers) and Identitäre Bewegung (at Brandenburg).

Whether this sort of on-the-job learning of activism—with more or less imitation of European Identitarians, as well as the ability to develop the capacity for response and adaptation to a sociopolitical environment with plenty of hostile forces—will expand, or falter, is, and it could not be otherwise, an open-ended question.

A White Brotherhood?

In Canada, Rémi Tremblay, the leader of the North American Identitarian group Federation of the Quebecois of [Quebecois] Stock (FQS) and contributor to many publications, along with the site Alternative Right, has little doubt that "the future of white peoples is threatened, whether we name it soft genocide or great replacement, it is a fact demographically proved." Nevertheless, the FQS leader does not bill the group as "white nationalist" because "in a European context—Quebec being a homogeneous nation in the European sense and not like the American melting pot—identities are more ethnic, cultural and linguistic than racial." Therefore, "We are not White Nationalists, although we are in solidarity with the other peoples of European descent which today face the same migratory threat,"[183] Tremblay says, emphasizing the importance of this fellowship.

The "brotherhood of European peoples," in principle, extends beyond Europe, North America, South Africa, and Australasia. O'Meara's words about "our America" as a "nativist variant of European civilization"[184] could also be applied to the way that some Latin Americans of European descent, especially in the region's Southern Cone, aggregated around creolism, see themselves and their place in the world. The racialist Identitarians of Chile's Fuerza Nacional-Identitaria—for whom "an identitarianism that does not take into account the racial factor is doomed"[185]—believe that "it is not culture that generates identity, it is the Blood and Soil." Insisting on the primacy of their "blood ties" with our "European brothers," they nevertheless do not see themselves as identical to them, because their identity has been nurtured in a different territory: "We are no longer Europeans, we are Creoles, sons of European blood and American soil."[186] The Argentinian Identitarian Juan Pablo Vitali sees creolism as the transnational common destiny of European descent in America. He said in a poem dedicated to Venner, "Just like your Frenchmen in Indochina, I live in the mists of a distant estuary / Fulfilling my Creole destiny: The Overseas White Man."[187] Vitali believes that "every American white man, who is self-consciously

Creole, enriches us and can be our brother."[188] And, as written at the site of the Chilean Identitarians, "If Europeans encourage and achieve the destruction of Europe thanks to their pusillanimous attitude, it's up to them, we will not let our Blood be lost in these lands and we will fight to preserve it." But "if Europe decides to fight for its existence, there it will have us fighting at its side."[189] Creole or not, the Identitarian perception of a "common destiny" of the White European peoples triggers, in different lands, manifestations of solidarity against their submission in these new "perilous" times.

SIX

The Coming War?

> The simple neighbors meet and hold a feast, and sing thy praises, holy Terminus: "Thou dost set bounds to peoples and cities and vast kingdoms; without thee every field would be a root of wrangling."
> —Ovid, *Fasti*, Book 2

HISTORY AS TRAGEDY

Modern-day dissidents have no doubt: The cultists of Progress are wrong. History's path is not foreordained; it does not advance in a straight ascending line toward an ever-improving condition. Its path is nonlinear, an endless back-and-forth of reversals, metamorphoses, and resurgences. History's essence is not messianic but fundamentally tragic. So says the *Little Lexicon of the European Partisan*, a treatise prepared in the mid-1980s by Guillaume Faye, Pierre Freson, and Robert Steuckers. The *Little Lexicon* describes the "tragic" as a defining "sentiment" of a "pagan conception-of-the-world," apprehending life as "random, risky, threatened by death and devoid of any other finality than the one imprinted upon it, through combat and challenges faced, by human will." This "tragic sentiment" is not viewed as "pessimism" or any sort of "drama" but as a decal of the experience of life as it is.[1] This view of history as a tragedy is widely shared among Identitarians, irrespective of "'pagan' sympathies."

"Tragic" implies a *conflictual* perspective of history. Identitarians perceive idealistic and utopian views and usages of the political sphere—often described as suffering from "angelism" or as advocating an illusory, conflict-free society—as constituting a negation of its essence. In this Identitarians often draw from the political philosophy of Julien Freund, who was deeply influenced by Carl Schmitt. Freund was depicted in the pages of *Enquête sur l'Histoire* at the time of his passing as the "philosopher of reality, [because] it was from life itself that he extracted the substance of his reflection."[2] In his doctoral thesis, *The Essence of the Political*, he affirmed the foundational role of enmity in the political domain; unlike liberal conceptions that often reduce the political to a management and bureaucratic affair, what Freund postulated was that the focus of political power is on the defense of the community both *externally* (i.e., protection) and *internally* (i.e., civil peace) through the acknowledgment and designation of *the friend* and *the enemy*. This, Freund declared, is the essence of the political as a distinct and autonomous sphere of human action.[3] At the same time, he also views the idea that it is possible to purge violence from society—another manifestation of progressive ideology in terms of reaching a Kantian "perpetual peace"—as a consequence of the utopian denial of conflict. This is a recurring narrative, for example, among ND theorists.[4] The eradication of violence—etymologically derived from the Greek *bia*, or "vital *élan*" and broadly understood as an effervescence, a source of creation—is yet both another denial of reality (because the world *is* violent) and a misreading of human nature. It misinterprets or negates the role of human passions and aggressiveness and ultimately aims at an amorphous, devitalized, and anti-Faustian society. What is more, if this natural violence is repressed in such a way that it does not find an escape, a discharge, it may manifest itself—*explode*, really—in its most perverted, brutal, and barbarian fashion.

In consequence, in spite of the progressive hopes of a neutralization (or even erasure) of the tragic essence of history, war will not be evacuated, and its *possibility* forever looms. Ernst Jünger's claim in *War as an*

Inner Experience that "sometimes it may be asleep, but when the earth trembles, it erupts burning-hot from all volcanoes"[5] is understood to be a realistic and, in the case of the German conservative-revolutionary, a firsthand account of an unwritten law of history itself. Commenting, in an editorial of an issue of *Nouvelle Revue d'Histoire* dedicated to "Men and War" on Benjamin Constant's notion that the "age of commerce" would "necessarily replace that of war," Dominique Venner exclaimed, "Naïve Benjamin! He took up the very widespread idea of indefinite progress leading up to the advent of peace between men and nations."[6] An issue of the same magazine covering "the eternal return of war," this time after Venner's death, contained an editorial by Philippe Conrad that declared that "the peace dreamed by pacifists is not for tomorrow, and everyone familiar with long-term history cannot be surprised." Conrad then pointed to the explanation by "the great prehistoric historian Jean Guilaine [author of *The Origins of War: Violence in Prehistory*] . . . that 'war takes root in Paleolithic times.'"[7] "Why wouldn't there be more wars?" asked the writer Philippe Randa (the pseudonym of Philippe-André Duquesne). "The history of humanity is one long succession of peace, war, unrest, fears of impending conflicts, sometimes proven, sometimes avoided."[8] According to Adriano Scianca, a "dialectic confrontation" between peace and war is at the root of any Identitarian vision worthy of its name; contrary to a reductionist view of reality, an "organic, tragic and non-moralistic vision" excludes all possibility of "think[ing] about peace without thinking about war," because war itself constitutes the condition that makes peace possible. War is thus "the mother of peace [and] *Polemos* the father of all things."[9] The "father" that gives birth to peaceful landscapes as well as near and distant battlefields.

EUROPE AS A BATTLEFIELD

On Extremism and Violence

Through print, digital, and street activism and networking, Identitarians appeal for a radical change of society and acknowledge, to different degrees, the *possibility* of violence, which they understand as a legitimate reaction against ominous trends—especially, and only if they continue unabated—that imperil the very future of native Europeans. Ultimately, it is a question of ethnocultural survival. Even if, according to the academic canon, this is sufficient to categorize them as extremists,[10] Identitarians and those sympathetic to their cause for the most part outright reject the extremist label. Pierre Vial, for his part, sees it as a badge of honor: "If being an extremist is to only want the salvation of his own people by all means, then I consider the word 'extremist' to be a compliment of vice to the virtue!"[11] Often the label is turned back onto the accusers. This is done, for example, by Pierre Krebs, who says, "insofar as Identitarian consciousness derives initially from an instinct, to consider [this consciousness to be] a manifestation of extremism, it is the same to say—gross absurdity—that the very existence of races and the cultures that result from them is in itself an extremism!" For that reason, "To deny their existence and their fundamental right to have their differences respected stems from, by contrast, a dogmatic blindness that I do not hesitate to qualify as extremist!"[12] Or, Jared Taylor states, "To say someone is an 'extremist' is name-calling, and name-calling is the most graceless way of admitting you have lost the argument."[13] Other voices, however, see a positive, groundbreaking dimension to what is dubbed extremism. Such is the case of Colin Liddel, who thinks that "in its essence, extremism is the creation of new, untested ideas on the fringe of human experience. It is a form of innovation. Extremism can only ever be justified by novelty or success, and in the latter case success means that it is no longer extreme."[14] Similarly, Alex Kurtagic insists that "perspectives change. New or oppositional ideas are often extreme at first because they are on the edge, pushing accepted boundaries, calling into question the accepted absolutes. That is a healthy and necessary process."[15]

Finally, others believe that the "strange phenomenon" of labeling as "extremist" the healthy and necessary assertion of European identity is doomed to failure. It is coming to an end for the reason that the popular groundswell is moving toward Identitarian beliefs and attitudes. Such is the view of John Morgan: "I firmly believe that the ideas represented by Identitarianism are already spreading rapidly, and that when the Identitarian revolution comes, it won't be a revolution of violence, but rather a peaceful one that will be supported by the majority. What the Identitarians are saying already lies in the hearts and souls of the vast majority of Europeans." Because "extremism implies something unnatural," those who "oppose the Identitarians and the true Right are the extremists, because they want Europeans to deny their own natures and roots. This is not only unnatural, but wrong. Identitarianism is an attempt to counteract this strange phenomenon."[16] "Our ideas (about immigration, the role of Islam, etc.) are shared by a majority of French," argues Fabrice Robert. "Does that mean then that there are many extremists in our country?" At the end of the day, concludes Scianca, "the biggest extremists" are the "sorcerers of financial capitalism" or the "Left-wing opinion makers," who impose a multiracial society that "in reality is a denial of any true civilization." Scianca, the CasaPound head of cultural affairs, adds, "In the face of these fanaticisms the reaction of those who have at heart the fate of European peoples is only sheer common sense."[17]

It is true that, by and large, Identitarians—in all their heterogeneity, from theorists to street and political activists—do not constitute a force, as Morgan notes, that is unified in "seeking to overturn the present political order through violence." The Identitarian Lambda movement, in particular, lays a strong emphasis on the "nonviolent" dimension of their activism. From the get-go, their goal has been the metapolitical one of changing the system from within. Further, within the wider Identitarian movement, some groups have even participated, or participate, in the electoral process, and as a whole they accept the rules of the democratic constitutional state, even when under intense scrutiny and vigilance from authorities. But it is also true that, in the face of a society that they believe to be in a calamitous state, many Identitarians believe that Europe will go through a period of social convulsion and strife sometimes characterized as a "civil war" along cultural and ethnic lines. Again, for them, this is only the "natural" end result of the elite-driven imposition of multiculturalism and all its pathologies on the traditions, values, and ways of life of autochthonous Europeans. At the same time, this scenario is not viewed as a hypothetical; the stage is already set, the troubles have already started, and in one way or another, the "war" is already raging in many European cities. It is *this* reality (not the one promoted by the political-media establishment) that, in the eyes of Identitarians, justifies their belligerent discourse and calls for self-defense in preparation for a time when "true Europeans" will need to fight back.

FIGURE 36. Meme from the German Identitarian movement advertising the need to rekindle the "fighting spirit" of Europeans. It reads: "Identity needs defense."

FIGURE 37. Meme from the early incarnation of Génération Identitaire (Une Autre Jeunesse) depicting an ancient Spartan warrior with the message "We are the youth that chooses Thermopylae rather than softening and renunciation."

In fact, Identitarian Lambda movement training camps have sometimes been under the radar of the mainstream media, which has equated them to paramilitary-style boot camps where European youth prepare for the coming war, constituting a worrying development for the secret services. "The secret camp where an army of European Identitarians get ready for war," read the title of an article in the weekly French news magazine *L'Obs* about the summer gathering of the French (and other European) activists. Arnaud Delrieux reacted with a tweet: "Defamatory. *L'Obs* does not know what else to do to sell its rag. A secret camp with public videos and an official communication? Frauds."[18] When a similar article came out in the Italian press ("Extreme Right: The 'Identitarian' Youth That Prepares for War"), Generazione Identitaria posted on its Facebook page the comment that "we do not want to prepare the war, but prevent it."[19] Although the camps comprise a whole variety of activities (intellectual and physical) and the goal is to reinforce the esprit de corps of Identitarian activists, the idea of some kind of confrontation or war—country-wide or Europe-wide—*does* hang over these kinds of activities. But again, this is rationalized as a form of self-defense made necessary by the perilousness of the times. In the Identitarians' minds, if violence is unavoidable and predictable, it is not because they actively seek it but because it has been hurled at them by the "mad policies" of the establishment. Europe's self-destruction sanctions its Identitarian defense. And, in their view, the longer Europe's downfall continues, the likelier the possibility that its defense will be waged by all means necessary.

A Widespread Dread

It must be noted, as Europe heads toward the third decade of the twenty-first century, that this sense of dread is far from exclusive to ethnocultural Identitarian settings. Additionally, this malaise is more acute in some countries than in others, which is mostly explained by the salience of issues related to immigration and Islamization. In the Francophone world the alarm is certainly heightened, pervading many milieus. The journalist Éric Zemmour, author of the best seller *The French Suicide*, an indictment of the alleged dominant ideology that is waging a cultural war against the people and leading to the destruction of the country, sees

FIGURE 38. T-shirt reading "Europa calling and I must go" sold by the German Identitarian movement shop. The bubble reads, "Oh my God, he is in love with his homeland."

FIGURE 39. T-shirt reading "Defender of Europe" from the French Génération Identitaire online shop. It shows the Lambda sign and the image of the Spartan King Leonidas.

as a "serious possibility" the hypothesis of a civil war triggered by the "multiplication of Islamic Republics in the French suburbs."[20] In *The Coming Civil War*, the conservative Catholic journalist Ivan Rioufol explains that the people, abandoned by the "new multicultural Republic" and its elites, and under assault by "Islamic totalitarianism," is in a heightened state of "legitimate defense." The columnist for *Le Figaro* hopes that the "insurrectional dynamic" that pervades civil society may lead to a true popular government that is willing to launch the tough policies—free from the shackles of multiculturalism and self-loathing—that may avert the impending civil war.[21] These tales of coming warfare are not restricted to those who warn about the consequences of "deranged" public policies; those who vow to combat the ascension of the radical right in Europe use similar terms. Donald Tusk, the European Council president from 2014–19), for example, cautioned, "We need to be effective as possible in our campaign against radicalism because I feel that as a historian it is very similar to some very dangerous moments in our history." Tusk added further emphasis: "You know what I mean: it is like the day before World War One."[22] Identitarians may agree with the Polish politician. But if these times are, indeed, "like the day before World War One," then, in Identitarian minds, the blame lies squarely on the shoulders of a deluded caste of politicians, oligarchs, media types, and intellectuals. At the same time, if current societal dynamics *do* lead to civil wars in European countries, it will not be an utter shock, especially to the readers of Freund, who believes that "no state is permanently immune from civil war." This is because, "as soon as the internal rivalries evolve in the direction of the distinction between friend and enemy, a civil war arises that could destroy the political unity of the State."[23]

The Die Is Cast?

In any case, as the geostrategist Gérard Chaliand argues, we seem to be living in times of "verbal inflation" and in an "era of the adjective."[24] This is the least of concerns for Identitarians such as Guillaume Faye. This is not a time to mince words—especially because "we have long since passed the point of no return, the point where it's still possible to check the prevailing decadence through peaceful reform. In no case will the European revolution be a 'velvet revolution.'" What is more, "The coming century will be a century of iron."[25] In fact, particularly since the turn of the century, Faye has specialized in shedding light on the future of Europe, foretelling upcoming events and predicting scenarios that for the most part are somber and dire but always contain the seeds of European revival. Throughout the years he has never stopped voicing his prophecies about the continent. "Everything is in place for the opening of the Tragedy, all the ingredients of the explosion are present, [and they are] terribly archeofuturistic," Faye announced in late 2001, in the *Terre et Peuple* magazine, as part of the promotion of his book *Pre-War: Account of an Impending Cataclysm*. "The great awakening of Islam," he declared, "and the reprise of its world offensive that started 1300 years ago; the colonizing invasion of Europe by the peoples of color, marching towards an ethnic civil war; the insurmountable problems of an overpopulated planet; the Promethean possibilities offered by technoscience in terms of massive supremacies and destructions. All of this forms an explosive cocktail never before seen in history."[26] Faye often integrates his predictions into an analytic scheme that he calls a "convergence of catastrophes," which is also the title of a book that he first published in 2004 in France under the assumed name Guillaume Corvus (later published in English by Arktos, with a foreword by Jared Taylor). In this work Faye described the "lines of catastrophe" in Europe that are converging and getting worse by the day, such as demographic decline, economic bankruptcy, uncontrolled immigration from abroad, Islamic and ethnic civil war, the deep crisis of mentalities, and the predictable end of the European Union: "Of course, for the moment these predictions seem wildly exaggerated. . . . However, the interlocking of the disorders will proceed very rapidly." In typical tragic manner, Faye calls this process the "return of history, that is, the return of tempests." *Alea iacta est*—the die is cast. Faye also foretold a future development that has become (with the exception perhaps of the nuclear dimension) a mantra of many Identitarian narratives: "War is coming and announcing itself with unheard-of violence: war in the streets, civil war, widespread terrorist war, a generalized conflict with Islam and, very probably, nuclear conflicts. This will probably be the face of the first half of the twenty-first century."[27] More and more, this vision is embraced not as a prophecy but as an exercise in truth-telling.

In the face of what Faye calls the "Great Threat," the situation is even more critical, because European states have relinquished their primal function of defense of the community. In typical Freundian fashion, Venner affirms that "concrete historical thought reminds us that assuring the longevity of the group in the face of external perils, intrastate wars, and threats of internal entropy, is the first function of the state." If this is forgotten "in periods of peace, or if this is violated by an unworthy oligarchy, it leads to a perilous or illegitimate situation."[28] What is more, through their policies, the "princes that govern us" are actively fomenting the conditions that lead to internecine havoc, endangering in this way the prolonged existence of the group of which the state should be the shield. This idea is recurrent in all Identitarian accounts. "How can we pretend that we want to preserve peace if, at the same time, we are programming war by fomenting the cohabitation, in the interior of a society and territory, of different human groups that possess different or even contradictory conceptions of life, religion, values and law?" asked Pierre Krebs.[29] Markus Willinger is blunter: "He who drives all cultures and peoples together into one territory will cause the bloodiest wars, in the long term. . . . You [elites] will bear the guilt for these conflicts, not the combatants!"[30] On top of this, and in order to postpone the "inevitable" civil war, European governments have adopted a policy of laxity and concession toward communitarian aspirations that will only intensify the conflagration. "The more delayed the courageous decisions are, the more difficult they will be, and the more likely violent conflicts will be," wrote Jean-Yves Le Gallou about the French predicament. "For forty years, we enjoy a civil peace on credit, at the cost of small compromises increasingly expensive."[31] Maybe not an "all-out civil war," thinks Götz Kubitschek—who has co-written a book about rampant immigrant violence in Germany (*German Victims, Foreign Perpetrators*)—but what will happen instead will be a steady "general coarsening, and I think that we will have to get used to latent violence and should train ourselves to act in self-defense. We could only avert this denouement by systematically establishing immigration criteria regarding numbers, composition, and ethno-cultural origin, with the next steps being the repatriation of at least 2.5 millions of incompatible immigrants (from Germany alone) and a tight border security." But he admits: "It is almost too late indeed."[32] This sentiment is shared by Martin Sellner, who, regarding the situation in German-speaking countries and in the rest of Europe, says, "I couldn't really believe the predictions of a 'coming civil war' some years ago . . . but this danger can no longer be denied." He lays the blame at the feet of multiculturalism, which "has destroyed our social trust (as Robert Putnam has proved scientifically), fragmented our democracy and conquered the streets of every big city in Europe." He adds, "Almost none of those millions of foreigners who are living here have adopted a European identity and many of them are Welfare dependents," pointing to the danger (also invoked by Akif Pirinçci in *Umvolkung*) that "those angry and frustrated young men will not stay peaceful when this 'bribe' of welfare money ceases to flow into their pockets."[33] The collapse of European Welfare systems, then, and the dwindling of the European contributive middle classes, will only add fuel to the fire. Sellner, moreover, believes—as he said in a YouTube video conversation with Brittany Pettibone dedicated to the theme "Civil War in Europe?"—that the only way to avoid such a "war" is to use political power to reverse the policies that make such a scenario a probability. He believes that, without an immediate policy of "shutting down non-European immigration and remigration coupled with de-islamization," such a war will happen. In that case, "If the states actually break down then we'd be completely lost. Because we don't control any borders . . . the whole of Africa and the Middle East would just swamp Europe . . . and this would be an ethnic war situation . . . there would be no chance for us at all . . . it would be a South African scenario all across Europe."[34]

Europe's peace, then, for Identitarians, is "on credit," but Europe is visibly and painfully falling into default. The signs are everywhere, and they believe that, to an honest and discerning observer, these signs show themselves in many ways. Behind trends such as the formation of religious-ethnic communities (ghettoes, "lost territories," states formed within states), the outbreak of riots, the increase of criminal activity, the proliferation of gangs, and the rise of sexual assaults lies a larger, ominous meaning. Like pieces of a puzzle, they constitute symptoms of a civil war that is *ethnic* in character and scope. What this means is that the clash of civilizations, in Europe, is taking the form of an ethnic civil war. This is a mainstay of Faye's thought, and he says that "although the entire political class does not want to know about it, it is more than probable that the constant increase in crime taking place in Europe is a sign of the beginning of an ethnic civil war. . . . A number of these acts of delinquency are of an insurrectional and political nature."[35] Espousing a similar frame of mind, Polémia's *Dictionary of Newspeak* says that "insurrection" is the proper word to describe what the oligarchy calls "riots" in predominantly Afro-Maghrebin communities.[36] Accordingly, the violent clashes that shook France at the end of Ramadan 2005, for example, are described not as "senseless" or "nihilistic" but rather as exemplifying a clear ethnic dimension, as they were acts of the territorial assertiveness of foreign-born populations over the native-born. In their aftermath, *Terre et Peuple* dedicated an issue of its magazine to "We, the Gauls, and the Ethnic War." The "rioters from North Africa and Black Africa," Vial noted, have the "habit of designating the hated Europeans—ourselves—by the term 'Gauls.' They show a lot of contempt but, at the same time . . . they recognize and even proclaim the ethnic divide between them and us. . . . We accept, and claim, such a difference. Well yes, we are, we want to be, Gauls."[37] Whether in the form of riots or not, there are many different faces of the same phenomenon of ethnic war on the European continent. "Well, if mass immigration is about to continue as it does now, especially the huge and disproportional influx of young men mainly from Islamic cultures, this is a very likely scenario," says the Austrian Martin Lichtmesz, about the possibility of unconventional warfare. "Gang violence connected with ethnic tribalism will be a huge part of it. As I consider it, the urban riots, i.e., in Paris, Stockholm [2013], and many English cities in 2011 are already part of or a prelude to those wars, but also the increasing crime caused by multiculturalist policies, including the rape attacks, as in Cologne [on New Year's Eve 2016], are so to speak micro acts of war."[38] Similarly, Julian Langness, author of *Fistfights with Muslims in Europe: One Man's Journey through Modernity*, reached the conclusion that "the collision that events have been building toward is inevitable. All sober participants in the debate understand that civil war will soon reach Europe." Langness is of the opinion that "the burgeoning war in Europe will be/is ethnic for a variety of reasons. (I) our opponents act in explicitly ethnic ways. The Pakistanis in Britain [as in the town of Rotherham in what became a national scandal] gang-raped 1,400 little white girls because they were white and non-Muslim. (II) Our traitorous leaders are exemplars of an ideology of progressivism whose chief characteristic is white self-hatred. (III) Throughout all of human history, conflicts sort populations into ethnically organized groups."[39] Evidently, the "war of Islam against Europe" is playing a central role in the development of such ethnic war because, as Alain Cagnat explained, speaking at a Terre et Peuple roundtable, this is an "ethnic-religious war" with a "double enemy, the alien immigration and Islam, the second being directly induced by the first." For the most part, insists René Marchand, Islam's multifaceted war is still largely indirect, conducted through *taqiyyah*, or the deliberate dissimulation of the real intentions of Muslims (i.e., the destruction of European civilization through total Islamization). But this "soft phase" of conquest may evolve into a "hard phase," an "open, frontal war," if Muslim leaders "believe that Islam has reached such a level of power in Europe that armed Jihad will guarantee a rapid victory," or if "Europeans conclude that the presence of Islam on their soil is too disruptive and menacing, launching violent acts which, initially localized and sporadic, spread like wildfire." A scenario, in other words, of "permanent civil war."[40] What is certain, in the view of Cagnat, is that "the state of emergency in which we find ourselves will justify and authorize exceptional means to restore a situation that can be considered today as desperate." Only these draconian measures toward immigration and Islam will avert, or at least lessen the impact, of the "coming" all-out war.[41]

The Racialist's View

Dominant in Identitarian racialist circles is the notion that the coming war will pit race against race. The Great Replacement, in the words of Vial, is nothing but a "racial invasion of Europe," setting up "all the conditions of a racial war, which will be the war of the XXI century. A war that is under way." Vial adds that this will be "[a war] that we will wage in the name of a very simple reminder addressed at the invaders: the suitcase or the coffin." This reminder makes new use of the slogan of the Algerian National Liberation Front at the time of the Algerian War.[42] "Even in the interior of the same genetic pool, between peoples therefore ethnically close, the co-existence of cultures does not work," states Krebs. "When genetic otherness is added, in addition to cultural otherness, it is even obsolete to talk of a 'clash of civilizations,' as we went from a state of peace to a state of war." Thus "we are already in a war, a war that is infinitely more dangerous than classic wars. We are the witnesses of a change of population, the witnesses of a genetic war. The future will tell if Europeans know how to confront it. Requiem or Reconquista!"[43] The imperative of mounting a pan-European defense against an "open race war" aimed at European peoples is dominant in the writings and speeches of the Finnish revolutionary nationalist—in practice a true Identitarian racialist—and motivational speaker Kai Murros. Although he has never been involved in any political organization—"It is my policy not to join movements because I value my intellectual freedom too much"—Murros, who lives a quiet life and keeps a "low profile" in his native Finland, says that "indeed, my main reason to write/deliver speeches is that I worry about the survival of European people. I feel very strongly about them—even though they actually seem to be quite happy about committing an ethnic suicide." Murros's speeches always have a general feeling of a call to arms: "When I write a speech I try to come up with sentences, ideas, expressions, slogans, figures of speech, phrases etc. that are psychologically as powerful and empowering as possible."[44] His video lectures are widely shared on racialist platforms. In his 2004 address "National Revolution—Turn On, Tune In, Take Over," posted on YouTube, Murros outlined what kind of war Europe (we, the "Pan-Europeans"), are facing:

> This war is fought every day and it affects every aspect of our lives. This war is fought in the media, as our elite pollutes our minds with shameless lies, trying to make us accept unconditional surrender in the face of rampant masses swarming to Europe. This war is fought in the academic world, as the malicious, perverted intellectuals who preach self-hatred and guilt are seducing us to welcome death and extinction in order to make room for the ever-swelling masses of hostile aliens. This war is fought in the bloody confrontations in our streets and town squares, as our people are being attacked by gangs of predatory immigrants waging an open race war against us.

After making this statement, Murros declared, "I can assure you—we refuse to be at the receiving end of the stick anymore for very long. Soon Europe awakes, and when that day comes—then FINALLY—the storm breaks loose!"[45] And so the "war for the national liberation of Europe" will begin.

Of course the supposed "unity" of Europeans in the face of their racial nemesis has its own challenges. Georges Feltin-Tracol says that "civil war" is a misnomer, because "one of the parties is not specifically European." As a consequence, "if there will be 'civil wars' they will be primarily wars of national and continental liberation."[46] If "war" happens, Renaud Camus said at the founding of the European Council of European Resistance, it will "not have anything civil, despite the number of collaborators and traitors," adding that it will be "part of the great tradition of fighting for the right of peoples to self-determination, for the liberation of the territory and for decolonization."[47] Tomislav Sunić, crucially, sees no straightforward, clear-cut distinction along ethnic lines in the coming civil war. As the Croatia-born Identitarian told *Réfléchir & Agir*, "The civil war before us will be dirty. It will present no clear line of racial demarcation, no separate point of reference between friend and foe, between allogenous and autochthonous." It is important not to forget that "every European people has its own Ganelon," he says, in reference to the Frankish baron who, in the French epic *Song of Roland*, betrays Charlemagne's army to the Saracens. "An important number of white so-called antifascists will take the side of immigrants, whereas violent clashes between different tribes of immigrants will take center stage."[48] Alex Kurtagic takes a similar stand. In a social breakdown scenario, the notion that "*everybody* falls into line along ethnic or tribal lines" may happen "with the non-European demographic in our part of the world, but simple everyday observation suggests Europeans, and particularly Northwestern Europeans, will remain as divided as they are now, fractured along moral or morally justified ideological lines."[49] Many will be on the opposite side of their co-ethnics. In this sense, for example, the clashes between pro-refugee and anti-refugee protesters that have happened during the "migrant crisis" in European cities "announce" what the coming civil war will look like.[50]

Europe's Protracted Internal Conflict

This point is, of course, connected to the ongoing internecine conflict that rages across European lands between Identitarians of all sorts and an informal army of antifascists, or antifa. Throughout the years, Identitarian street rallies have been violently confronted by antifa and/or anti-racist protesters, and sometimes these clashes have become a part of the Identitarian folklore and are celebrated as such. That happened in Lyon in 2004, when a rally of Jeunesses Identitaires (the earliest incarnation of Génération Identitaire), in a protest against the entry of Turkey into the EU, was met by hundreds of antifascists with slogans such as "Racists, Nazis, no pasaran!" Today the French activists view the clashes that ensued as a sort of badge of honor in the history of the movement—as the "battle" of the square of Jacobins. Identitarians in France occasionally are the targets of antifascists (with attempted disruptions of Identitarian meeting places, for example, or attacks on Identitarian Houses), and antifa have also attacked the nascent Generation Identity movement in the United Kingdom. There were physical clashes, for example, at the end of the group's first "European Reunion" conference in the town of Sevenoaks, when participants were chased and confronted by black-clad antifascists. It is especially in German-speaking countries, though, that the Identitarian movement is a permanent focus of attack. Of course these antifascists combat all seeming manifestations of right-wing extremism, but for them, Identitarians are no different; in fact, Identitarians are widely viewed as veiled Nazis who have simply "rebranded" old ideas and prejudices to make them more palatable to present-day public opinion. As noted earlier in the book, Identitarians vehemently rebuff the Nazi link. Martin Lichtmesz calls the accusation little more than a trick, and an effective one. "Saying that IB [Identitäre Bewegung] is in fact a mimicry cover up of Nazism, or that we don't actually mean what we say, or talk in 'code language,' is one of [the antifa's] major tricks—that way you can neither refute nor prove your allegation, but just put everything under suspicion," says the Austrian theorist.[51] Regardless, in a report of the Identitarian movement published in the German version of Indymedia, its "dangerousness" is emphasized, not so much in terms of the "formation of an extreme-right mass movement," but rather in terms of the influence that a "small group" can have on "social discourse" by its diffusion of an "evident racial, ethnic and social-chauvinistic view of society."[52]

The anti-Identitarian campaign takes many forms. In social media anti-Identitarian activities are extensively disseminated, and the #noIB hashtag is conspicuous in the Germanophone antifa Twittersphere. Major or recurring initiatives have been the doxing of activists, as well as the "outing" of Identitarians in the neighborhoods where they live by putting up posters and flyers with their names and pictures and the caption "Attention! Neo-Nazi!" and distributing an open letter to residents warning them that "The IB is a nationalist, racist & xenophobic youth organization, which has been active since 2012 in the German-speaking world. No place for racists/nationalists . . . in [the name of the area] and elsewhere!"[53] Identitarians have denounced the consequences of such

FIGURE 40. Antifa sticker against Generation Identity. This is the German version. It reads "Hunt Nazi Hipsters—Smash the Identitarian Movement."

campaigns (for example, destruction of the property of those targeted) and in response have made their own stickers and flyers—in the same format as those of the antifa campaign—with each bearing the name of the Identitarian, who is referred to as "our activist" instead of a neo-Nazi, a higher-quality photo, and the caption below, "Loves his home." This response to the protest becomes in this way a marketing tool that promotes the movement.[54] When the apartment of Austrian Identitarians was vandalized with Nazi-related graffiti on the door, IBÖ asked for a PayPal donation to pay for the damages and made a meme out of it with the captions "Attempted Burglary at Christmas" and "Left-Wing Terror Targets Patriots." On other occasions, Martin Sellner, the IBÖ leader, as well as Robert Timm, the head of the Identitarians in Berlin, for example, have been physically assaulted. Sellner insists that although "in Halle, Paris, and Vienna Identitarians will always defend themselves when attacked," they will not engage in a vicious cycle of "retaliation," arguing that "successful activist actions, and with it media attention, rising membership numbers and growing structures, hurt the Antifa much more than any revenge."[55] And this notwithstanding the Identitarians' view that antifa "left-wing terrorism" runs amok in German-speaking countries—with the supposed "complicity" of the state and the "sympathy" of mainstream media. This accusation is a mainstay of Identitarian narratives. When the members of the Oldschool Society, a right-wing extremist group, were sentenced to jail for planning to use violence against immigrants, the German Identitarians manifested their gladness that they were "locked up before causing any damage" but immediately drew an analogy between those of the Oldschool Society and the antifa, which, for them, is *also* a terrorist group. "It is similar to the 'Oldschool Society,'" they proclaimed, "except that the term 'foreigners' is swapped with the term Nazi."[56] In Italy, which has its own traumatic history of right-wing and left-wing terrorism, there have also been violent incidents, especially in relation to CasaPound and its left-wing foes, with episodes of physical violence on both sides. As referred to in chapter 1, CasaPound also puts in its pantheon of "memorable" activism the Roman clashes in Piazza Navona against antifascists, and throughout its life span the group's properties, from headquarters to libraries, have also been the targets of politically motivated violence that has sometimes included the use of plastic explosives and incendiary devices. Like IB, CasaPound accuses the state of "turning a blind eye" to antifascist violence—to which [CasaPound activists] say that they react as a mechanism of "self-defense"—as if, from the point of view of the Italian state, political violence against "the Italians who do not surrender" is legitimate.[57]

Rule by Chaos?

In all, then, for many Identitarians the "liberation" of Europe will be a messier and more ambiguous affair, at least from an ethnic and racial standpoint. What is certain is that the handwriting is on the wall. At some stage Europeans—or at least those in regions and countries most affected by the multiculturalist immigrationist "madness"—will need to take upon themselves the physical defense of their territories, communities, and mores in what is widely seen as a war for survival. The chances of such an "inevitable" outcome have increased proportionally to the abdication by each European state of the defense of its own native-born populations. "They have explained it to us in many ways: the state was born to make us leave the state of nature in which lives the *homo homini lupus* [man as a wolf to man]. If the State ceases to exist or does not do its duty the state of Nature returns. And if man becomes a wolf to man, the blame is not certainly his," warned Scianca in typical Hobbesian manner.[58] Not that the renunciation by the state of its basic responsibilities has been necessarily "innocent," unintentional, or inexorable due to the force of the circumstances. Influenced by the social critic Alexander Zinoviev (1922–2006), an earlier Soviet dissident who also dissected the totalitarian dynamics of Western democracies,[59] the Geneva-born essayist and philosopher Eric Werner has put forth the thesis, especially since the turn of the century, that the European states and military and civilian powers have deliberately created the conditions for social chaos at the expense of the autochthonous population in order to preserve their rule. The strategy of the ruling powers has been one of divide and rule. In *The Pre–Civil War*—a popular essay in ND and Identitarian circles that Venner called "resounding" and of an "unusual lucidity"—Werner answered the question of why the European political class has favored non-European immigration by indicating the "profit" and benefits that they have gotten from it. "It must be recognized," Werner said, "particularly, that a multicultural balkanized State is much more easily manageable and controllable than a State non-balkanized and culturally homogenous. A people that is organically *one* (what was once the nation-state) is capable of facing and resisting its leaders."[60] In a new preface to the 2015 edition of the book, Werner further argued that the state is still very capable of waging war, "but the war that it wages, in fact, is no longer related to the one it formerly waged. It is an intrastate war (in the case of the State against its own citizens), with the focus (as forecast by Orwell in the past) on the establishment of a total power."[61] In the "new" multicultural societies—viewed as cauldrons of disruptive delinquency, antagonisms, hostilities, and conflicts—the ruling powers instrumentalize to their own benefit the "ingredients" of civil war. "The Prince plays with fire," Werner says.[62] In such a climate, the people, strangers in their own land, are in such a state of disorientation and fear that their fall into complete submission is inevitable—the state is seen as their "only" salvation. The disorder becomes *the* condition for order. In this way, Werner believes that in contemporary "democracies" not only is any sort of popular rebellion thus prevented but also the "total control" of society is reinforced, with repressive and intrusive legislation as well as widespread surveillance as facilitated by the digital revolution.

Georges Feltin-Tracol agrees: "I fully share the view that the oligarchies intend to rule crowds by chaos." The French Identitarian thinker argues, "Without getting into conspirationism, by simultaneously promoting an increase in insecurity among the poorest *and* large-scale non-European immigration, the 'elites' aim at generating instability in society in order, in a second stage, to allow the adoption of securitarian and liberticidal measures."[63] This "administration of fear"—an idea also invoked by Paul Virilio,[64] along with its orchestration and management as a way for a criminal oligarchy to guarantee and perpetuate its power—is viewed by many social critics (whether of Identitarian leanings or not) as the chief characteristic of contemporary "totalitarian" Western societies. According to this view, and until the situation runs completely out of control, the pyromaniacs are always ready and willing to become the firefighters of the "European battlefield."[65]

GENERATION WARFARE

The "Soft" Europeans

The Internet meme posted on the Facebook page of Generation Identity–Paris showed the image of armed black-clad terrorists, the Lambda sign, and the words "It is the enemy that chooses you." These words were taken from Freund's *The Essence of the Political*: "Even if you do not choose the enemy, the enemy chooses you. And if he wants you to be his enemy, you can show him the most beautiful acts of friendship. As long as he wants you to be the enemy, you are. And he will prevent you from tending your own garden."[66] According to this narrative, decades of pacifism and humanitarianism have made Europeans forget the central role that enmity plays in life and politics. It is only through a shock of reality—the living experience of a society causing itself to disintegrate into strife, tribalism, and barbarism—that Europeans will recover belligerence and the lost martial tradition. This is true even if, as stated by Werner in *L'Avant-Blog*, his own contribution to the blogosphere, anesthetized Europeans are not easily recoverable: "Some say that people will revolt, says the ethnologist. Personally I do not believe it. When you acquire a wildebeest's behavior, no matter what falls upon you, you will keep a wildebeest's behavior."[67] The "wildebeest theory" is indeed shared by others, such as the editorial staff of *Réfléchir & Agir*:

> Until the great comeback of the tragic, the indigenous peoples of Europe will be in a relative [state of] torpor instilled by the bludgeoning weapons of mass media stupidification. A generalized European revolt should not be expected. The great Swiss philosopher Eric Werner estimated [in his book *Ne vous approchez pas des fenêtres*] at 5% the share of resisters and other rebels in society. It will be they, and only they, that will make possible—or not!—the reversal of public opinion, and then a salutary revolution.

At any rate, "It is equally possible that the Europeans will be ultimately led as docile sheep to the slaughterhouse, halal or not,"[68] they conclude. In a context in which, for Identitarians, true intellectual and cultural dissidence is weak, to aggravate things, the vast majority of Europeans find themselves woefully prepared for a social environment within which the possibility of widespread low-level ethnic warfare is ever more a reality.

After all, Identitarians believe that Europeans—and Europeans from the West more than everyone else—live in a feminized society. A long-standing defender of this view, de Benoist says that in these "soft" times, "we love the maternal vocabulary: the dialogue, the understanding, the tolerance, the welcoming, the openness, to the point of only showing fierceness with those who do not commune according to this magma-like ideal."[69] This view is entwined with what Robert Redeker depicted, in *The Impossible Soldier*, as the coming of age, particularly in Western Europe, of the *civilisation de la femme*: feminine values, the cult of victimization, repentance, self-hatred, emotionalism, and denigration of the idea of sacrifice, as well as the idea of war and the figure of the soldier. Faye subsumes this process under the name "devirilization," whose hallmark is the "declining values of courage and virility for the sake of feminist, xenophile, homophile, and humanitarian values." This is an ironic development, because "devirilization has become a sign of civilization, of refined mores, the paradoxical discourse of a society, half of which is sinking into violence and primitivism."[70] Effeminate Euro men—or "nu-males"—are lacking warrior values precisely at a time when the "alien colonizers" exude virility and aggressiveness. Venner believes that, even if we are living in an age when, in fact, "the figure of the warrior [has been] dethroned" to the profit of the tradesman, the institution of the military still endures, and "weak though they may be, today's European armies constitute islands of order in a crumbling environment where fictions of states promote chaos."[71] Amid such "chaos," the threshold question for Identitarians is put by Jean-Yves Le Gallou: "Will we leave the civil war as a legacy to our children and grandchildren?" More than ever, "It is urgent to act. A great urgency. . . . We have ten years to save France and Europe. By deeds, not by mere words."[72]

It was Alexander Zinoviev who described "historical optimism" in the following way: "Whoever says that we are doomed and *that* is why we must fight to the end (as the Russians say, if we have to die, let it be done with music), that one is not a pessimist. That one is a historical optimist. The historical optimism means that we know the truth, cruel as it is, and we are determined to fight, whatever the cost."[73] By and large, instead of fatalism, it is *this* voluntarism and optimism of the will that pervades Identitarian accounts about the current state of Europe and "what is to be done" about it. In one of his presentations of Faye's *The Convergence of Catastrophes*, Robert Steuckers said that "the frightening events *ante portas* [before the gates] should not lead to pessimism of action." After all, Europe has always been capable of a reaction *in extremis*, of which the Flemish thinker mentioned episodes such as "the squads of Cantabrian Visigoths who beat the Moors and stop their progression, thereby initiating the Reconquista; the Spartans at Thermopylae; the defenders of Vienna [against the Ottomans] under [the leadership] of the Count Starhemberg; the hundred thirty-five English and Welsh soldiers in the Battle of Rorke's Drift [against Zulu warriors], etc." In order to accelerate such reaction, indigenous Europeans should remember "the strategic audacity of the Europeans, highlighted by the

American military historian [Victor David] Hanson in *Why the West Always Won*. This implies the knowledge of ancient and modern models of this fearless audacity and the creation of a warrior mythology, 'quiritarian' [Roman], based on real events, similar to what the *Iliad* did."[74]

The awareness of the need, at this critical juncture of European history, to fall back on warrior values is very much present among the younger French Identitarians. "Realistically, if tomorrow an ethnic conflict were to break out in France—which we want to avoid at all costs by pursuing the path of political engagement—obviously we would not sit down with our arms folded," warned Arnaud Delrieux in an interview. "We reject violence but we will use force if necessary. And if the French have fallen asleep from consumerism and been rendered docile by the need to earn their living, nevertheless, they remain a warlike people who, having long endured numerous outrages without reacting, have always ended by throwing off their tyrants in a way that serves as a lesson to all who might be tempted to chain us again."[75] Such an attitude of "not sitting down with arms folded" at a time when the state is alleged to have failed in its duty to protect its citizens is behind these Identitarians' tribute to self-defense in initiatives associated with Generation Anti-Rabble; in offers of self-defense, martial arts, and boxing training (prevalent, for example, in the annual Identitarian camps that gather activists); or in "security tours" in public places. At the same time, they defend the enlargement of the legal framework of self-defense in order to include homes and commercial enterprises, permanent targets of the "rabble."[76] Ultimately, a reversal of the mentality of self-abdication is what stands between Europeans and a reconquest of their lands. That, according to Kai Murros, is the "irony" of Europe's tragic hour: "The irony is that when we finally get Europeans to fight, we have already won the war. And this is because our biggest enemy, in the end, is not the alien mob occupying our streets, but our unwillingness to do anything about it."[77] The unwillingness, that is, to rise and stand up, asserting their primal condition as a warlike people.

A New Kind of Warfare

"There was something sublime about the fact that, as soon as we heard the signal to attack, hardly a person stayed behind," recalled Jünger about the World War I European battlefields. "Those who jumped out of the trenches were overcomers; hence also the equanimity and calm with which they walked through the fire."[78] For many Identitarians, the twenty-first-century European war, however, will be a new, irregular, hybrid kind of war, at the antipodes of the neatly separated trenches evoked by the German writer. This is connected to the way that war has fundamentally changed in character since the last decades of the previous century in a process that is ascribed, in many places, to the erosion of the state's monopoly of war and the ascension of all sorts of irregular warring actors. The belligerents of these "new wars" that are taking place in weak or failed states are not exclusively regular armed forces but a combination of state and nonstate actors—loose networks of fanatics, criminals, gangs, warlords, militias, and so on—in a situation in which it is increasingly difficult to distinguish between combatants and civilians and the boundaries between war and peace, as well as war and crime, are increasingly blurred.[79]

At the current stage of intensified globalization, so this narrative goes, what is happening is the gradual passage from interstate to intrastate chaotic wars in which the actors, weapons, strategies, goals, and rules of engagement have mutated and adapted to fit the new environment. In the mid-1990s the German writer Hans Magnus Enzensberger, with events such as the Los Angeles riots and the Yugoslavian collapse in mind, described the rise of "molecular civil wars" in the interiors of states, particularly in urban settings. "Civil wars have not yet infected the mass of the population; they are still molecular," he warns. "But we are deluding ourselves when we reason that the reason we are at peace is simply because we can still collect our bread from the baker's without being blown away by sniper fire. The reality is that civil wars have long since moved into the metropolis." Here, too, the withering away of the state is what allows the passage from molecular to full-scale civil war. The abrupt decline of civilized behavior, episodes of raging destruction and senseless violence, the proliferation of gangs and armed bands, lawless and no-go areas, heavily guarded residential areas, the growth of the security industry, soaring firearms sales, and rising vigilantism—all of these constitute signs of the march of the civil war toward its climax.[80]

Asked about whether there might be widespread civil wars in Europe, the Israeli military historian Martin van Creveld answered, "I am very much afraid so. Things seem to be moving in this direction, and I do not see that the old European parties, either right or left, have what it takes to stop them."[81] Van Creveld, a proponent of the "transformation" of war in recent decades—in the sense that war is no longer neatly based on the Clausewitzian trinity of state, military, and the people but it is a messier "non-trinitarian" affair—has insisted on the increasing role, in future wars, of intrastate low-intensity conflicts waged by networks of nonstate actors. Such a development is a central idea of what has come to be known—particularly through the writings and advocacy of the US analyst William S. Lind—as the theory of fourth-generation warfare (4GW).[82] Contrary to the tactics of the previous generations of warfare— particularly the first two, characterized by essentially linear tactics, while the third, initiated with the German blitzkrieg, gave more space to maneuver and consequently led to the use of nonlinear tactics—in the new generation of warfare indirect tactics aiming at "collapsing the enemy internally rather than physically destroying him" take center stage, says Lind.[83] This is the world of insurgents, where the battlefield is everywhere, low-tech weaponry predominates, and the goal is to disrupt the system, against which heavy, technologically advanced, conventional militaries are of little use. The operational environment is society as a whole, and a crucial part of the strategy is to wage moral and mental warfare, encouraging uncertainty and confusion in the enemy with the conviction that it is in the "moral and cognitive domains" that "wars are won and lost."[84] Fourth-generation warfare is not novel per se, but it constitutes a "return, specifically a return to the way war worked before the rise of the State," writes Lind. "Now, as then, many different entities, not just governments of states, will wage war. They will wage war for many different reasons, not just "the extension of politics by other means."[85] The unremitting weakening of the state is thus counterbalanced by the rise of alternative primary loyalties to nonstate actors (such as tribes, gangs, cartels, or terrorist groups), for which "a growing number of men are willing to fight." Lind is a self-described cultural conservative— sharing many of the hallmarks of the paleoconservative movement— whose belief system ties the "poisonous" ideology of multiculturalism and mass immigration to a rising 4GW of a "home-grown variety," on American and European soil, "which is by far the most dangerous kind." As he explains:

In 4GW, primary loyalties shift away from the state—someone's native state or one to which they have immigrated—to a wide variety of other things, including religions, races and ethnic groups, and cultures. Immigrants who do not acculturate are especially likely to become Fourth Generation threats, because they probably will not give their loyalty to a state whose culture is not their own (and to which they may be hostile). . . . If a population becomes a base for 4GW on a state's soil, that state may have to expel them. There may be no other way for the state to perform its primary duty, maintaining order. Any state that cannot maintain order—safety of persons and property—will disappear.

What is worse, for him, is that the dangerous delusions of "cultural Marxists" seem to have no end: "The degree to which the establishment has abandoned all grasp of reality was shown last week [December 2015] in *Time* magazine's choice of Angela Merkel as Person of the Year. Merkel will go down in history as Germany's poisoner, the person who flooded what was a safe, orderly country with carriers of the 4GW bacillus."[86] John Robb, a US counterterrorism planner and editor of the "Global Guerrillas" site (which investigates "Networked tribes, system disruption and the emerging bazaar of violence [and provides a] blog about the future of conflict"), predicts the intensification of a new style of warfare that he calls "open source" because it is based on networks and greatly dependent on information technology and the Internet, and it also empowers individuals and groups by providing them with all that is necessary to wage a do-it-yourself guerrilla war, as well as readily available platforms for exchanges. In the post "Germany just screwed Europe" Robb foretold, in typical 4GW fashion, what will happen after the country's 2015 decision to welcome more than a million Middle Eastern migrants:

> Almost all of these migrants were young, single men. . . . Insurgencies run on a fuel of young men. These young men are culturally incompatible with EU/US standards re: women, homosexuality, free speech, etc. . . . Most of these young men have recent combat experience earned on the killing fields of a fractured Syria. . . . Here's how I believe this will play out: Social disruption will rise. We are

already seeing this with recent attacks by roving gangs of immigrants in Cologne. Schengen will disintegrate as transborder attacks by radicals ramp up. . . . Over the medium term? Terrorist violence. This population, and those that soon follow, will soon become the main conduit for extremism in Europe. Its large size, antagonism and cohesiveness will make it impossible to police.

Finally, "Over the long term? As the demographics of these countries rapidly shift in favor of the new arrivals: *open source insurgency*. An insurgency that will spread far from the borders of Germany. An insurgency I'm not sure Germany, nor the EU, can win."[87]

Narratives such as these, even though for the most part European Identitarians do not explicitly place them under the umbrella of 4GW, fit to perfection the way that they sense the raging war in Europe. Following this logic, the neotribalism of "multiracist" societies provides a "perfect environment" for the development of insurgencies of all types; further, all the lost no-go zones (the Molenbeeks of this age) provide operational bases for crime and warfare, only accentuating the effective breakdown of many states and the aforementioned blurring of war, peace, order, and chaos on the "new" European continent. Faye sees the possibility of a steady increase of what he calls "low cost terrorism"—whose aim is to "provoke a psychosis and to terrify the European populations"—as ever more likely, especially because what distinguishes these kinds of "low cost" attacks is the fact that they "can be carried out by a large number of non-professional fanatic assassins recruited from immigrant populations."[88] Taken aback by the messiness, Camus tweeted, "Even war was better before, when there were ones on one side and others on the other side."[89] When in the summer of 2016 Éric Zemmour said that the French army had already drawn operational plans, with the help of the specialists for the Israeli army, to "re-conquer those regions that have become foreign on our own soil," the president of France's Generation Identity observed that "fifty years of uncontrolled immigration will result inevitably in Operation Ronces [Operation Brambles, the alleged name of the military campaign]." He added, "*That* is also the shock of History," bringing up an expression ("the shock of History") often used by Dominique Venner and also the title of one of his books.[90] In his defense of Identitarian "European-preservationism," Julian Langness is adamant about the fact that "we are in a violent conflict whether we wish to be or not, for our opponents are using massive levels of violence against us, through terrorist attacks, 4GW crime, physical assaults (especially upon the elderly), and of course the overwhelming epidemic of ethnically driven rape. With that said, the violence our side engages in MUST be congruent with our own cultural honor codes and morals."[91] All of this with the certitude that, as voiced by Fenek Solère, "no one within the right wing milieu wanted this confrontation. In fact, prominent speakers have, for the most part, consistently raised their voices to warn of the inevitable consequences of the ethnic confrontations we now face in our schools and streets. The voice of reason was ignored. So, now, if we want to avoid the sort of 4th generation warfare scenarios . . . we need to find a humanitarian way to remove millions of these undesirables from our communities."[92] This in tandem with the idea expressed by Lind that if a population becomes a home base for 4GW there is no easy solution short of expulsion.

"At the beginning of the summer, an author evoked the 'climate of a molecular civil war' currently in progress, says the student. It is the word 'molecular' that bothers me. With what has happened, can we still talk of war as molecular?" Thus started a blog entry by Eric Werner in the form of a dialogue between fictional characters shortly after the terrorist attacks that hit Paris in November 2015. It continued:

> "Schematically, we are in the presence of two wars," says the colonel. "The first merits, effectively, to be called 'civil molecular.' It is a product of planetarian mass immigration, as it was powered in Europe for forty years. . . . Molecular war, but also vaporous, stochastic, espousing diverse and varied forms of crime in the quotidian. . . . The other war is the global civil war, war initially centered on the Middle East, but today extended toward Europe at the initiative of Daesh. . . . Each of these two wars gears on the other, serves as an engine to the other."[93]

The "author" cited at the beginning of Werner's blog post was the Swiss strategist Bernard Wicht, who wrote *Europe Mad Max Tomorrow? Return to Citizenship Defense*—a book that Feltin-Tracol, writing in *Réfléchir & Agir*, says "opens new perspectives to all serious dissidents of the 'New world disorder.'"[94]

Wicht's message is clear: The end of the historical cycle of the nation-state and its institutions constitutes a watershed moment. We are thus living in a transitional period characterized by new political-military organizations and new types of warriors against which our citizens are for the most part disarmed and unprepared for the coming chaotic times, which will increasingly look like a "New Middle Ages." In these new times of the refeudalization of societies and anarchic conflicts "à la Mad Max," the elimination of national armies (and of citizen-soldiers) goes together with the rise of new "war machines," from autonomous armed groups to a typology of new combatants, such as terrorists, partisans, contractors, and shadow warriors. "With the return of anarchic violence," says Wicht, "with the displacement of the center of gravity of the war (from the war between states to the war inside the state), the citizen is left defenseless."[95] Against this background Wicht's proposed solution is the adaptation of citizens, their reempowerment, through the constitution of autonomous local communities, based on direct democracy, that will be in charge of their collective self-defense. This junction of group autonomy with the spirit of militias is termed *Swissbollah*, which is a model of citizenship defense geared no longer toward the protection of state sovereignty but aimed at shielding the population, its civilization, and its values—with the web 2.0, open sourcing, and crowdsourcing playing a pivotal role in the mobilization of citizens. In short, a return of the citizen-soldier but in a new, upgraded, 2.0 version. "Now, in a world where threats are now capillaries (raids, robberies, racketeering), the bottom-up formation of small, networked communities organized for the legitimate defense appears as a more appropriate response than the top-down recruitment of wholesale battalions," Wicht concludes.[96] According to Feltin-Tracol in a review of the book for the readers of the Polémia site, "Our near future belongs then to the communities, to their citizenship, to their identity, especially if the chaotic time of war returns."[97]

Such a return of "the chaotic time of war" is part of the civilizational "collapse" predicted by Swiss author Piero San Giorgio. As he makes clear in *Survive the Economic Collapse: A Practical Guide*—a book whose Italian version he presented at the headquarters of CasaPound in Rome, while the English version was released by Richard Spencer's NPI publisher—the combination of overpopulation, finite resources, ecological and agricultural failure, a rapacious and uncontrollable global economy of endless growth, and consumption will cause a major economic, political, and social collapse. As he argued in *éléments*, "Our world, as we knew it, a world of opulence and ease, is over. In the short term, and sooner or later, we enter—in fact we rediscover—a world of scarcity, shortage."[98] Social upheaval and "molecular civil wars" will follow, such as in Europe. "Not a civil war between 'natives' and 'immigrants,' but MANY civil wars between many groups, often between simple individuals stranded and with a multiplicity of small alliances based, most probably—as history shows—on ethnic and religious lines," San Giorgio said in an interview. "You could well have, say in France, a conflict between on one side radical Muslims, on another side the government and the radical left, on another side conservatives and Catholics, on yet another side blacks from the French Caribbean, and another with Identitarians, and another, and another . . . all fighting, forming alliances of convenience." In such a raw Darwinian context dominated by the competition to survive and natural selection, Europeans would find themselves at a disadvantage owing to cultural and social trends that have made them soft (mass consumerism, instant gratification, devirilization), aggravated by mass immigration from countries where tribalism and warrior values are very much alive. He continued:

> Of course, the survival instinct of people may wake some up and regroup them around the leadership of those who never changed and warned for decades of the perils of diversity and consumerism. [Yet] not all will change—many will suffer or be eliminated in the chaos that is coming—but many will regroup culturally and in their attitudes. Will that be enough? Will that be too late? And with what consequences? Impossible to say at this point as it could resolve fairly peaceful or it can, and I think that's more probable, [descend] into mass ethnic cleansing, civil wars, and even Rwanda-style genocides. It's not something to look forward to, but again, it IS natural selection.[99]

Says Murros, "They may preach leftism, liberalism, feminism, love and peace, reason and tolerance—but as our desperation and anger grows, the old instincts start working again. . . . You can fight Nature only so far, but once you have crossed the line, Nature strikes back."[100] In Spain, Ernesto

Milà also believes that the process is past the point of a peaceful return: "We have introduced on the continent the ferments of racial-social-religious civil war, which will grow and become increasingly violent in the coming years." However, the Identitarian Catalan still thinks that when a certain level of chaos and violence is reached, the European states will intervene: "Personally, I do not believe that 'armed groups' will emerge from the Identitarian universe" and that at some point in the future "it will be the Islamists themselves who will resort to force (in fact, now it is isolated jihadist attacks, but ten years ago there were already small ethnic revolts, setting fire to vehicles, violent acts by gangs of criminals, and the establishment of 'no-go zones')." In other words, Milà believes that the "inevitable" escalation of violence leading to a "widespread insurrection" will "generate an inevitable response on the part of what remains of the structures of government in Europe."[101]

Regardless of what the outcome will be, the notion that the harsh realities of a tumultuous and disorderly world will eventually tap into something deeper—the instinct for self-preservation of Europeans—fuels the literature of contemporary dissidence, whether of an explicit or an implicit, Identitarian nature.

A LITERATURE OF DOOM

The visions of Eurocalypse take many forms. They include several likely scenarios, awful outcomes, while also holding the promise, still, of a volte-face for the besieged native Europeans. Predictions, prophetic narratives, and hypothetical assessments circulate and intermingle. Authors who write of it do not need to be avowed Identitarians as long as the narratives fit the Identitarian belief that European civilization *may* collapse.

The Fall of Rome, Again

First, historical analogies abound. It is common to recuperate events from the past as cautionary tales regarding the impending fate of Europe. A favorite historic parallel is the fall of the Roman Empire in the fifth century AD. "The fall of the Roman empire is similar to the process now underway in Europe. Will we one day speak of the decline and fall of the West?" asked Willinger.[102] The events that preceded the Battle of Adrianople (AD 378), which was waged in what is today's northwestern Turkey—the defeat of the Roman Emperor Valens at the hands of a Gothic army, which precipitated the beginning of the end of the Roman Empire in the West—are viewed by Scianca as eerily reminiscent of today's European context. After all, for "humanitarian reasons" the Romans allowed the Goths, who were escaping war and persecution from the Huns and were consequently treated as "refugees," to cross the Danube River and settle in imperial territory. Once they were within the empire, the die was cast: Their numbers grew, Gothic pillage and criminality spread, the emperor was defeated and died in battle against them, they exacted a policy of further concessions from the Roman authorities, the integration (Romanization) of the barbarians failed, followed by communitarianism and the protracted downfall of the Empire. "The fate of civilizations that collapse often has the shape of the cyclical fatality. Sometimes it also happens on the same fault lines. Like the one that separates Europe from Turkey," Scianca stated.[103] According to Jean-Yves Le Gallou, "The current population flows towards Europe has no modern precedent. It is necessary to go back to what happened in the Roman Empire between the 2nd and 5th centuries AD to find a similar phenomenon. Similar but not identical." Not identical because the present influx is much greater than the barbarian invasions of the past: "The penetration of the Empire by non-indigenous peoples took three centuries; it did not reach, in all, 10% of the autochthonous population," while today, the proportion of "invaders" is far superior, and it has occurred in a much shorter period (roughly forty years).[104] In addition, as Faye has argued, the situation back then was "much less severe than today because the said barbarians were European, moreover converted to Christianity."[105] In fact, the ruin of Rome is often invoked by Faye to reinforce his argument about the catastrophe that hangs over Europe: "If nothing changes, in two generations, France will no longer have a European majority for the first time in its history. Germany, Italy, Spain, Belgium and Holland are following the same gloomy path, though some years behind. Since the fall of the Roman Empire, Europe has never known a similar historic disaster." A "disaster" that is happening with the "complicity of a blind and ethnically masochistic political class" and the "collaboration of the pro-immigration lobbyists."[106] Tellingly, then, from the point of view of Identitarians, it was an ancient Roman, the famous orator Cicero, who in a speech to the Roman Senate denouncing a plot by other Romans against the country, said, "There is no nation for us to fear—no king who can make war on the Roman people. All foreign affairs are tranquilized, by both land and sea, by the valour of one man. Domestic war alone remains." Then he added, "The only plots against us are within our own walls—the danger is within—the enemy is within."[107]

At the same time, it should be noted that the comparative exercise between Rome and the Europe of today is not exclusive to outright Identitarian theorists and activists. The German-speaking Belgian historian David Engels—the holder of the Roman History chair at the Free University in Brussels—rejects the historical comparison coming from the Identitarian camp between the current movement of populations toward contemporary Europe and the Barbarian invasions. For him, the correlation between "the contemporary, mostly Muslim, immigrants and the Germans of the 4th and 5th centuries AD" falls short. "The Germans were just as Christianized as the majority of the inhabitants of the Roman Empire (albeit Arian confession); they did not seek to transform the political structure of the empire, but rather to take it over; they did not strive to impose on the Romans any kind of 'culture' of their own, but used their own inheritance as much as they could.... They did not appear as petitioners who appealed to the humanitarian obligations of the host country, but were regarded as a 'service provider' due to their military qualifications." Moreover, "the late Roman empire was an authoritarian, bureaucratically centralist, militarized, culturally unified, collectivist, heavily depopulated and profoundly religious state. None of this corresponds to the present state."[108] Having said that, Engels sees as a much more fitting historical analogy the current situation of Europe and the late, decaying, phase of the Roman Republic in the first century BC—a chaotic period witnessed by, and written about, by the poet Virgil. Not only are the same sociocultural factors that were found in that Roman period present in today's Europe—"a crisis of political participation, the beginning of a massive globalization, the decline of the traditional religion, the tendency towards a demographic decline, a high [level of] unemployment, a strong individualism"—but also the migratory trends and dynamics of the two civilizations are eerily similar:

Just as today, [in Rome at that time] there was also an economic and poverty immigration from the Near East that led to the multiculturalization of the great metropolises and the desire for better livelihoods and participation in the state social welfare. And as today, many, though not all, of the new arrivals were characterized by a certain resentment towards the Roman-Hellenistic "Leitkultur [dominant culture]," which was regarded as materialistic, individualistic and decadent, so that, as happens now, it was the origin of numerous fundamentalist movements of faith, whose resistance to these developments resulted in martyrdom.

Engels further believes that, as happened at the end of the Roman Republic, a period of "war" will follow in the coming decades, not as militarized as in the times of the Republic but pitting ethnic groups with different cultural and religion models against each other, leading eventually to a full social and political reorganization of the European continent.[109] In the very near future "with suburbs slipping from state control, with landscapes dominated by paramilitary, ethnic or religious groups, with overwhelming criminality, with economic bankruptcy and complete political immobility"—amid such context—"the citizens of Europe will then gladly throw themselves into the arms of the first ruler who gives the continent a functioning social state, peace and order. A leader just like Emperor Augustus."[110] At such time, then, Europe will fulfill its "imperial destiny," Engels said to Alain de Benoist in an interview for *éléments pour la civilisation européenne*.[111]

Forecasts of Chaos, Submission, and Revolt

Political fictional works often serve as a platform for giving an account of, and a warning about, the calamities befalling Europe. They project readers into a uchronian period located not in a remote past but in the near future, a time to come that, driven by existing disturbing social and cultural trends, is invariably worse, and dystopian, at least for all those still clinging to the idea of a once splendid European civilization.

Many of these works, in simpler, shorter, or more complex form, attempt to be explicitly sober and predictive. Such as when Willinger outlined a future scenario by writing that after Europe was "devastated and weakened by the Second World War, allegedly clever European politicians sought help from outside. The borders were opened to millions of Muslims, intended to breathe new life into a Europe with a declining birth rate." In time, what happened was that "The number of Muslims continued to grow, and at a certain point, they began to dominate the state and civil society." At this stage the point of no return has been passed: "When the Europeans finally attempted to rise up against them, their rebellion was suppressed. The Europeans, having grown old and weak, had nothing with which they could oppose the young and strong Muslims. Western civilization dissolved, and new Muslim empires emerged on its former territory."[112]

In *Hamlet*, Shakespeare may have written that "something is rotten in the state of Denmark," but, according to Georges Feltin-Tracol, if he had lived today he would have noticed instead that "the rottenness is now settled in Sweden."[113] That Scandinavian country is viewed by Identitarians—and more widely by critics of immigration policies in Europe—as a paradigmatic example of the utter failure of multiculturalism on the continent—illustrated by the growth of the number of "vulnerable areas" (the term used by Swedish authorities to name what for critics are "no-go," lawless zones), rampant crime, gang violence, and a deterioration of women's safety as a result of harassment in public spaces (from swimming pools to music festivals), as well as a dramatic increase in reported sex crimes—incidents in which first- or second-generation immigrants are overrepresented.[114] It was with this state of affairs in mind that Julian Langness—who sees Faye's *The Colonization of Europe* as gaining in the future a similar status regarding "our own civilizational upheaval" as Edward Gibbon's book has today with respect to the fall of Rome[115]—picked the Swedish-Danish border, an area most approaching "Failed State" status (of which the city of Malmö is the utmost symbol), as a starting point for a conjectural scenario of 4GW that may lead to "Europe's war of liberation." Langness's forecast starts thus:

> Increased friction between the Swedish state and immigrants has enflamed tensions throughout the country. Malmö begins seeing increasing immigrant-on-native violence of a level previously unknown. . . . The police force in Malmö is on the brink of collapsing. Their operations are increasingly militarized as any form of regular

policing is impossible. . . . The justice system is collapsing and the judicial system has fully collapsed. The first hints of 4GW crime begin appearing, such as kidnappings and [the imposition of] tolls to travel through certain areas. Native Swedish vigilante violence begins as chaos escalates.

In the midst of the crumbling of the Swedish state, what follows is a full-scale conflict between "preservationist militias" and "Muslim gangs/organizations," until "eventually troops from neighboring European countries join fighting on behalf of Preservationist militias. The original Swedish government has ceased to exist. Numerous left-wing politicians have been executed as traitors." Even if "it is difficult to extrapolate beyond this point," it is "likely that with the huge numbers of Muslims now in Scandinavia, and in Europe as a whole, the occurrence of war would serve as a catalyst for both the massive movement of refugees (consider the sick irony), as well as a hardening of ethnic zones and Balkanization." At the same time, "as the conflict escalates, it is likely to attract passionate individuals from across the Occidental world, all sharing a drive to save Sweden, save Europe, and preserve our culture, heritage, and lands," which means that such war could prove beneficial for the reawakening of European peoples through a process of solidarity under fire.[116]

Not surprisingly, Faye has specialized in offering prognostications, suggesting outcomes, and alerting his readers to what he calls "political fiction." The French forecaster, for example, has hypothesized three scenarios for France, from a "tepid death" (a slow, gradual Islamization) to "territorial partition" (the "Lebanonization" of the country) and at the other extreme, the "Second French Revolution": "Later called by historians the Second French Revolution, it bursts around 2030. It is of great violence and surprises the entire world," he writes. It started because "Invading Islam made the mistake of not following its original strategy of mischief and moved too quickly to that of violence. . . . The native population, and those who followed it, eventually revolted, tired of being provoked without reacting. They rebelled also against a powerless, or accomplice, state." Amid the turbulence, a new party emerges from the civil society, reaches power, and launches a revolutionary process throughout the decade 2030–40, the "famous conservative revolution," and the "terror of the progressive intelligentsia." Faye continues, "As in the 1789–1794 period, France suffered an earthquake, because of its incapacity to reform smoothly, but only in emergency. The new Third Estate, that is to say, the indigenous people, regained power and chased away the new aristocracies and new clergies." Faye's foretelling even includes a condemnation by a *New York Times* editorialist, "Linda Linsay, muse of the trendy left of the East Coast," on April 9, 2039, with the title "New French Revolution: No!" Faye, however, believes that the first scenario, of a gradual submission, is more likely than the "terror" feared by progressives on both sides of the Atlantic.[117]

In any case, is a popular, even bloody, uprising inevitable? William S. Lind believes so: "At some point, enraged Frenchmen, Swedes, Belgians, and others will overthrow the cultural Marxists, take their countries back, and expel the Moors, at least those not hanging from lampposts." And, for dramatic effect, Lind adds, "Don't be surprised if it happens first in France. It's been a while since French mobs took to the streets crying, '*À la lanterne!*' [To the lamppost!], but I doubt they've forgotten how."[118] His is another version, more impressionistic, of the coming Second French Revolution.

Books of War and Survival

In fact, it is not a little surprising that France is taken as the favorite scenario of most dystopian tales about Europe's future—after all, it is widely seen as a microcosm of all of the trends and risks that endanger Europe as a whole. This focus also emerges in some of the full-blown novels that have emerged, which are usually built around the resistance of a number of native Europeans to a future of subjugation to the new alien forces that, in a not-so-distant tomorrow, will rule Europe. In this respect, Philippe Randa's *Poitiers Demain* (Poitiers Tomorrow), originally published in 1987, has a pioneering role.

In Randa's book, the twenty-first century, ravaged by a third world war, and with the French and other Europeans being enslaved and conquered by Muslim invaders, witnesses a guerrilla war launched against the enemy, led by Gautier, a Norman descendent of King Arthur. The conflict reaches its final climax in a "new battle of Poitiers" in 2032, or 1,100 years after the original battle in 932; although the African sheik vows not to become "a second Abd er-Rahman [the defeated emir of the original battle of Poitiers]," the last of the European warriors, using all sorts of ingenious tactical moves, triumph over a far superior Muslim army. At last, the "world of the hyperboreans" is saved, and Gautier is celebrated in the "Friedrich Nietzsche stadium" of Rouen, as Emperor of the New Europe.[119]

According to Randa, there is no such "happy ending" in sight in Europe. On the contrary, since at the time of writing the "invasion" has only accelerated and the imagined revolt of Europeans has not taken place:

> It is true that when I wrote *Poitiers Tomorrow*, I was convinced that the Europeans would soon rise up violently against the migratory invasion of the continent.... It was in 1986! Thirty years later, I see that it has not happened and that migratory invasions, far from having ceased or reverted, have even grown considerably, with a million invaders in 2015—in addition to the usual annual illegal arrivals—and another million is even planned in 2016.... True, so-called populist parties that oppose this invasion have progressed significantly in the polls, but so far without access to power in their respective nations. There is no more electoral uprising than that there is armed uprising.[120]

The French writer's view of the current state of the French, and of the native European population in general, is gloomy:

> They only shake off their torpor in order to gather in huge apathetic flocks bellowing that they are all "Charlie," before returning home, saying that the terrorist attacks are very unfortunate; their rulers are surely rascals; their future, very uncertain.... But that *they* are very brave not to let themselves be seduced by the extremists' sirens. That's what counts! And then they go back to sleep in peace, self-assured that they have properly discharged their duty of submission to political correctness.[121]

Submission, the title of the novel by Michel Houellebecq describing the gradual, and smooth, transformation of France into a new Islamic

State, is not a word cherished by the resisters of Fenek Solère's novel *The Partisan*. "I am very familiar with Houellebecq's oeuvre and admire his gifts as a writer," says Solère. "*Submission* offers a cogent but defeatist view of the future. It is a narrative that reflects the pathology of someone looking at the world through the bottom of a glass of absinthe." On the contrary, "My book is the polar opposite to the vision painted by faux rebels of the so-called avant garde like Houellebecq. Our people will not acquiesce to foreign over-lordship."[122] Houellebecq "underestimates" the "factor civil war," Faye once wrote, adding, "It is terrible to have to say and assume that in it [civil war] rests maybe the only chance of a revival and reconquest."[123]

Sabine La Pétroleuse, the leader of the anti-Eurabic dissidents of Solère's novel, embodies such an urge for reconquest against the invaders, with France standing as the front line. As she puts it, "We are Charles the Hammer's new phalanx, his second coming, a revolutionary vanguard, more determined, better trained, utterly resilient."[124] Against the "new

FIGURE 41. Covers of (*left*) Philippe Randa's book *Poitiers Demain* (orig. pub. 1986) and (*right*) Fenek Solère's *The Partisan* (orig. pub. 2014).

Berber overlords" and all their collaborators, the Resistance's political soldiers—irregular fighters well versed in Carl Schmitt's *Theory of the Partisan*—hit "at the heart of the Eurabic state in small commando units, organized on the principle of phantom cells, conducting a war of the flea upon the system." In the end, the martyred leader and her companions become inspiring examples for the wider European insurgency, composed of those "*kuffar*" that are willing to fight and die in the "Battle for Europe."[125] Set in the near future, *The Partisan*—reviewed in the Counter-Currents webzine as a "militant novel of the alt-Right struggle" that stands in comparison to Ernst von Salomon's *The Outlaws*[126]—is, in the view of its author "not wish fulfillment, rather a shrill cry of concern about what will occur unless positive steps are taken now."[127] In the first pages of the book, it is mentioned that the Eurabic authorities "had never anticipated such unprecedented terrorism. Questions were being asked at the highest levels. Would the docile French really fight back? Had years of brainwashing proved insufficient? . . . Could they have miscalculated?"[128] Such "miscalculation" is present throughout the literature of doom (and rebirth) that chronicles the near future of Europe. Or, as Murros professes, "Today the media claim that Europeans are sterile, aging, and tired—that Europeans are peace-loving—that Europeans are shy, weak, and always willing to step aside—that Europeans are too tired to build anything anymore, too lazy to produce anything anymore—that Europeans have lost their lust for life. We will show them!"[129]

The "League of the Old Habitants," an extraparliamentary group self-described as "the only movement of French resistance to Islamization" and a major protagonist of Modeste Lakrite's 2016 novel *L'Édit de Mantes* (The Edict of Mantes), certainly displays the fighting spirit invoked by Murros. They are, however, engaged in an uphill and, ultimately, desperate battle against an increasingly assertive enemy amid a resigned and submissive political class. Symbolic evidence of the strength of their opponents is provided by their intent to transform the Basilica of Saint-Denis into a mosque. As Modeste Lakrite (a pseudonym) writes in his 2016 novel, the political establishment is under pressure from a widespread insurrectional movement coming from the suburbs: "The France of 2027 is like Bosnia before the civil war," warned the Minister of the Interior. The political establishment saw appeasement and accommodation as the only way out, leading to the

FIGURE 42. Cover of Modeste Lakrite's *L'Édit de Mantes*, originally published in 2016.

signing of a concordat between the Republic and Islam, which represented a step further toward the official recognition of a Muslim state within the French state. "Today, we sold off our collective identity," lamented Geneviève Nisat, the League's *pasionaria*. In the end, after episodes of violence and terrorist acts from both sides, not even the compromise of a concordat worked; there was a de facto partition and the emergence of an "autonomous territory of Islamistan" ruled by Sharia Law and closely associated with the "separatist enclave of Belgistan." The editorial of a French newspaper published in 2028 glumly reads: "Europe Has Been Taken Over by the Fatal Contagion of Fragmentation."[130]

"The catastrophe, we anticipate it, we wait a long time for it, but when it is here we understand that nothing and nobody can go as fast as she," mulled a character of Laurent Obertone's disaster novel *Guerrilla: The Day When Everything Burns*, the chronicle of the collapse of France in three days.[131] As a sort of fictional follow-up to his *France, a Clockwork*

Orange, which was a report on the explosion of violence, crime, insecurity, and savagery in the country, *Guerrilla*, according to its author, is based on "leaks of French Intelligence" about probable future scenarios facing the French population.

"It will be understood by reading this book, that this gigantic Battle of France has nothing improbable, and it is already widely experienced both by our police and Intelligence services," says a French journalist and writer, born in 1984, who uses the pseudonym Obertone.[132] Called the "prophet of the apocalypse" by the conservative newsmagazine *Valeurs Actuelles*, he says instead that "I'm not a prophet, but the conditions for such a drama are in place."[133] What is needed is a "trigger." In the book, which reads like the script of a movie, the spark is a deadly encounter between police and Afro-Maghrebin youths in one of the no-go areas of the Paris region, which sets off simultaneous riots and attacks in cities and in the countryside by enraged hordes, armed gangs, and Islamic terrorists on the French state and on the autochthonous population—

FIGURE 43. Poster by the French Identitarians of Lyon advertising a book talk by *Guerrilla*'s author, Laurent Obertone, at their Identitarian house, La Traboule (November 2016).

which for the most part is unable to defend itself, bound up as they are in an incapacitating guilt-ridden morality. In a typical case of "chickens coming home to the roost," no one is spared in France's descent into chaos—intensified by the sabotage of critical infrastructures such as electricity and water supplies—as is the case with the apologists of multiculturalism and of "living together": do-gooders, pacifists, antifascist militants, anarchists, left-wing activists, trendy progressive bloggers, and pro-refugee types, who are all consumed in the flames of Fourth-Generation Warfare. In the end, "On the third day, the master was dead, and everywhere we screamed his names: State, government, emergency, police, support, security. . . . And everywhere we were answered by the same appalling silence. And citizens were crying like children. Nobody would come anymore for their rescue."[134] At the same time, this sense of abandonment, which the collapse of the electrical grid transformed into despair, elicits dynamics of self-defense and survivalism among the population, forced to adapt itself to the new, fear-infested world, where "reality," not "morality," reigns supreme. "A must-read,"[135] said Piero San Giorgio about *Guerrilla*, which offers a powerful glimpse of what may befall France and other European nations in a future that, as many Identitarians believe, is not so distant and far-fetched, but increasingly looks like the present that is unfolding under our noses.

Postscript

A longtime American friend, after reading the manuscript of *The Identitarians*, called it a "great book, but depressing," while an academic reviewer of an earlier draft noted that its ending should "appeal to students' humanism and tolerance in working to come to terms with the multicultural realities of the whole world." A sort of therapeutic, healing finale, however, would be antithetical to an endeavor that, from the opening pages, has described the realities and dynamics of groups and movements that truly see themselves engaged in the Identitarian battle for the future and the survival of Europe. And this, as much as possible, was done in order to capture their self-understanding in full, without holier-than-thou lecturing or toning down and softening what was said, done, or predicted, regardless of the potential unpleasantness felt by readers. As a result, and within the task that motivated this work, these concluding pages run through the articles of faith of Identitarian doctrine and the dynamics of its activism with an eye to modern-day trends and streams that help to fuel and shape the ongoing Identitarian rebellion.

The choice of words for these remaining pages, as an addendum rather than a set-in-stone conclusion, is in line with the open-ended metapolitical and activist struggle of a movement that, irrespective of internal variances and polemics, will not rest—at least that is the profession of faith of many of its theorists and activists—until the political and social order of Europe is upended. Backed up by the theoretical body of work provided by the Nouvelle Droite, this overturning of the current European order ultimately implies reverting what they see as the radical discontinuity, impermanence, and rootlessness brought about by liberal capitalist modernity in traditional European societies. Today, in times that Identitarians believe to be under the supreme rule of Western universalism and its homogenizing powers, in which liberalism runs wild both economically and socioculturally, erasing the fundamental differences between the Establishment Right and the Establishment Left, these self-proclaimed defenders of Europe do not proclaim allegiance to "tired" and "outdated" ideological categories but gather instead under the banner of Identity. This identity is ethnocultural and multilayered, with a nonexclusive attachment to its regional, national, and European dimensions, even if on the wider Identitarian spectrum some individuals and groups may favor one side over the other, while always retaining Europeism as crucial. "Civilizationism," indeed, is the key Identitarian word.[1]

While globalizing processes ultimately aim at the integration of societies and economies, expanding markets, and liberal democracy, they have also breathed into many communities an urgent sense of the need to defend their identity, their integrity, and their distinctiveness.[2] Ethnocentrism and ethnic resentment as defensive reactions have followed suit. As *The Identitarians* shows, this phenomenon is not exclusive to the non-Western part of the world.[3] The eruption of European Indigenism is part of this ethnic backlash. It should be viewed as a display of identity politics in which native, autochthonous Europeans present themselves as the marginalized ones, the ones who are oppressed, whose interests are ignored, and whose voice is stifled. Identitarians at large are the hardest-hitting gloves-off expression of this sentiment. What pervades their narratives is, as in the case of identity politics of every kind, the demand for respect—in this case for Europeans' ethnocultural diversity, for their authenticity as peoples who populate an equally authentic continent, for their historical and spatial memory, and for their own self-worth extricated from the self-flagellation imposed by a decades-long culture of guilt and repentance. What is more, all of this is topped off with the demand for self-determination, or emancipation from the establishment, which is seen as the source of oppression. In their view "establishment" means, basically, pro-globalist organized political, economic, and media powers, upholders of policies that are out of touch, misguided, deceptive, or outright criminal with regard to the safety, prosperity, welfare, and future of Europeans of European stock. Liberated from these ruling powers, the once-subjugated Europeans may then choose their own paths and recapture their nations and continent's own singularity as a community of descent and destiny. Logically, such a new path involves a geopolitical realignment, or the deliverance from the postwar US-global order. While the tendency is to look to the East as a preferable orientation—often to Russia, but not necessarily so—the overriding emphasis is on a sovereign Europe as a geopolitical force yet again, with its lost might at last salvaged after decades of drawn-out impotence. Finally, a media war is part and parcel of the identity politics of and for the original peoples of Europe. Identitarians have set up a full alternative media network—comprising sites of "re-information" reverberating all over social media and blogging platforms—that functions online as an advocacy media for indigenous Europeans against the globalist, corporate, and in practice anti-European, news media.

It has been observed, quite frequently, that because of the complexity of human beings, the ascription of a singular affiliation to individuals as a sort of one-and-all identity is a crude and false, impoverished vision; after all, individuals have many loyalties and allegiances of all kinds that define their life experience and humanity.[4] This commonsensical view, however, does not detract from the fact that, in the eyes of Identitarians, at a historical time when Europeans are well on their way to fading into ethnocultural oblivion, it is *this* affiliation, not any other, that takes precedence and overrides the rest. For Identitarians, Europe is living through such a state of emergency. If an Identitarian radar was ever built, its antennae would be made to detect and capture the dynamics of the defining event of our times: the Great Replacement. Hostile or skeptical observers may see what has become in recent years the flagship of the entire Identitarian movement—the substitution of a people, in this case those of European descent, by non-Europeans—as a case of overkill, or an exaggeration of reality. Identitarians, however, see the Great Replacement as a matter not of opinion, unsympathetic as it may be, but as a self-evident fact, in spite of what the watered-down and misleading official statistics say about the demographic trends. In fact, for them it is a truth available to anyone—anyone, that is, who is willing to open his or her eyes in the many neighborhoods, roads, streets, avenues, boulevards, parks, and playgrounds of contemporary European cities and their sprawling suburbs. Identitarian racialists in particular describe this development as the substitution of whites by non-whites. Most of all, what the recognition of this alleged European tragedy does is to raise the discourse of Identitarians to the level of survival, setting their sights on a threat that in the long run is an existential threat to native Europeans. The fear is not that Europe will not emerge unscathed from this development; the fear is that Europe will not emerge at all. It will be a new entity, a new people, and a new post-European civilization.

At this point in time—and because of the intensifying replacement of peoples in Europe—the issue, for Identitarians, is no longer one of adaptation to the new reality. Attempts at assimilation and integration of immigrants are not merely undesirable; the sheer number of non-European newcomers makes such policies unworkable. The multicultural model of society in European lands is a failed experiment that triggers fragmentation and all sort of social and cultural pathologies, including ethnic tribalism. In many countries and regions, it is leading to a "new normal" of daily violence and widespread insecurity. Eventually, widespread conflicts will ensue as well as the warlike scenarios already depicted in (as of yet) fictional works. The assertiveness of Islam in Europe—whether in the form of creeping Islamization or Jihadi terrorism—is at the forefront of many Identitarian battles. But ultimately the Islamic question is the tip of the iceberg called ethnocultural replacement. The clock is ticking. Europe is past the point of muddling through; Identitarians believe that it needs to be swept clean. The gravity of the Great Replacement rules out nuanced politics. If this phenomenon was brought about by political choice, political willpower must open the doors for the Great Unmixing. In some Identitarian quarters, this solution is called Remigration, the return to their original lands of those who do not belong in Europe, starting with illegal immigrants and eventually subsuming the majority of non-Europeans and their descendants living in Europe, regardless of citizenship status. This because, in their view, those who belong in Europe belong by right of blood and lineage, not on the basis of birth in any given European territory. Only when the mixing of culturally different populations stops, and the unmixing starts, will it be possible to reverse the Great Replacement and fire the first salvos of what some Identitarians call the new European *Reconquista*.

Identitarianism is only a part, a theoretically oriented part, for that matter, of the Identitarian offensive in Europe. The fact is that this offensive is galvanized by not just ideas but also by a new youthful activism that operates as a direct-action arm of the Identitarian frame of mind. Whether in the form of the Identitarian Lambda movement, particularly exuberant in Francophone and Germanophone lands, or the more nationalist variety of CasaPoundism, these high-energy groups share many grammars and repertoires of Identitarian contestation. The development of information technology and software has enabled the copying and pasting everywhere of many of the Identitarians' ideas, practices, even logos and graphics, sometimes giving rise to copycat movements. This embrace of "open-source ideology"—particularly striking in the case of the Lambda groups, leading to a sort of international franchise of sociopolitical activism—shows the primary role of the Internet in the diffusion and consolidation of the Identitarian movement.[5] What is more, Identitarians' knack for headline-grabbing activism in the public sphere—in the streets, in demonstrations, flashmobs, sit-ins, die-ins, occupations, or aesthetic interventions, often accomplished in unconventional and spectacular fashion—is always joined with incessant and savvy use of social media, video, blogging platforms, and Internet memes. The digital world magnifies their message to such an extent that there may be no necessary correspondence between the impact that their actions has in real life (the number of activists involved, the disruption caused, etc.) and the far greater inflated impact that these actions end up having. Not only do the national and sometimes international mainstream media cover many of their actions in a knee-jerk fashion—often mixing derogation and indignation—but across alternative media platforms and social media their bombastic activism resonates widely in the virtual sphere. Zealous attachment to the cause coupled with Internet know-how is often sufficient to give the impression—which is not inconsequential to activists and public opinion alike—that a coterie of activists is an unstoppable transformative force. In fact, although these groups have a much larger number of social media followers, the number of actual activists, although varying from country to country, is still in the lower thousands across Europe.

But the contemporaneousness of the Identitarians' activism does not stop here. It also shows itself in the ways that they use pop culture to combat the dominant culture with its own weapons while extending their pull and magnetism by adopting cultural references of youth at large. The goal is always to counteract the "cool" of the media, music, and entertainment industry—often hedonistic and self-indulgent—with the newer Identitarian version of cool, which is tradition-oriented and spreading nonbourgeois values of heroism, sacrifice, honor, and community. The Identitarian cool—its merchandise, images, videos, and memes—is archeofuturism packaged for millennials and postmillennials. Or a way for Generation Identity to reach further into the depths of Generation Z. Finally, and in the spirit of the old anarchist vow of planting the seeds of the new society "within the shell of the old," the cultural combat of young Identitarians also entails experiencing the counterculture that guides their activism. Hence the effort to create alternative communities as spaces of freedom from the dominant value system, whereby "total militancy" is sought in Identitarian houses of ideological formation and comradeship or in militant encampments devoted to physical, moral, and intellectual formation. As for many contemporary anti- and alter-globalists, another world is indeed possible for these Identitarians, and they, too, anticipate it.

With the partial exception of CasaPoundism—which is self-consciously and proudly bound with the older fascist/political/activist tradition—the youth-driven Identitarian movement presents itself as the "new activist kid in town" and as a modern-day, fresh, and hip defense of the ethnocultural roots of Europe. Critics and antifascists may view them as little more than "rebranded" extremists, but Identitarians persistently counteract this claim with a narrative that operates both externally and internally and emphasizes that they are "actually" regular, patriot-loving, Europe-caring, nonviolent youths. It is true that their political backgrounds vary; many are first-time political activists, while others—especially some who are, or have been, in leadership positions—have histories of engagement in extreme political milieus. Invariably, however, they all adhere to the idea that Identitarian activism is a sort of "safe space" for expressing ethnocultural views, one that is ideologically inoculated from damaging historical connotations, and that the decades-long stigma associated with defending one's own people, culture, country, territory, and civilization is a stigma no more. Because they have "nothing to hide" or "be ashamed of," in their recruitment campaigns activists, especially men but also women, "show" their faces in the hope that many more activists will join them in the "nonstigmatized" movement of patriotic and European youths. In short, their message is this: Join the Identitarians because the incapacitating spell of European self-effacement—at long last—has been broken.

"Faced with all the things that threaten our identity and our survival as Europeans, we have lost the safeguard of an Identitarian religion. There is little we can do about this," noted Dominique Venner in *The Shock of History*.[6] It is difficult, however, after coming into close contact with present-day Identitarian narratives, to brush off the feeling that Identity—their own understanding of European Identity—is invested with a quasi-religious sacredness. It is as if in an increasingly de-Christianized Europe, when the spiritual and immaterial nexus between peoples, territory, memory, and traditions is being attacked and lacerated by globalism and its evils, Identitarians crusade to rescue identity as a sacred form that justifies defense at any cost. Such transference of the sacred to identity—which also transpires from the high levels of commitment, emotion, and righteousness of Identitarian collective mobilization—adds further strength and legitimacy to Identitarians' setting up sacred boundaries between Europeans, the heirs of a perennial tradition and memory, and the "profane" non-European outsiders. In a way it is a summoning up, a recall, of the "safeguard" of an Identitarian religion that Venner supposed to be "lost."

Like any "religion," the Identitarian one has its own moral foundation. An important insight follows: The rejection of the current liberal democratic system is also—and crucially—a moral one. Identitarians are far from lacking a moral compass. In fact, what they have is a *different* notion of "good" and "evil" than the one that is promoted by the ruling liberal order and its Western elites. What Identitarians defend—although it is more forcefully expressed in some quadrants than in others—is a political system based on the criteria of territorial (i.e., continental European) belonging, historical and cultural inheritance, collective memory, hereditarianism, and ethnic ties (basically their "good"), while rejecting a political system that, from their perspective, is grounded in abstract human rights and on the celebration of the wrong kind of diversity (non-ethnic European), along with the wrong kind of identity politics (for all sort of minorities). It is the Identitarians' overwhelming perception that this diffusely all-inclusive system not only discriminates against natives (read Europeans of European stock) but—and dramatically so—endangers/threatens their future survival as a people (this, in short, is the Identitarian conception of "evil"). In the end, what they aim at is not just a recalibration of the liberal state but a fundamental change in the political landscape: the rise of a noncosmopolitan, anti-universalist democracy based—for the most part—on the fusion between demos and *ethnos*. This is a change that, in order to occur, requires a shift from the current moral order and—as I hope became clear in the pages of this book—is viewed not only from a regional and nation-state perspective but in continent-wide pan-European terms. Of course, and because they *are* seen as a threat to the standing order, Identitarian groups such as the ones presented in this volume and others that may appear in the near future have an uphill battle in front of them with the establishment's increasing vigilance and hostility. Prosecution by state judicial systems for violating laws against hateful speech, the imposition of travel bans upon Identitarian figures, anti-Identitarian campaigns by watch dogs, and increasing suppression of their online platforms by tech companies have recently and quickly arisen.

It is true that our times are easily given to melodrama and sensationalism. Especially because the liberal world order that has characterized much of the era since World War II seems to be "under deconstruction" by a variety of forces within and outside the Western world. Identitarians of all ages and provenances are certainly committed to this undermining—after all, their focus is on reaching deep into Europe's distinct tradition in order to flush out an alternative to Western-style liberal democracy. They view the anti-establishment mood and advance of political insurgencies across Western democracies as confirmation of the justice of their struggle, and they hope it intensifies in the coming decades. In general, they endorse anti-system movements dubbed as populist, specifically those with strong ethnocultural foundations. The rising popular call for roots, borders, cultural protection, and tradition—which they see as a deeper, unstoppable trend, even if politically and electorally characterized by advances and setbacks—confirms, in their eyes, that the accusations made against their immoderation and fanaticism are fundamentally baseless; in fact, they are the ones attuned to the pulse of the times, contrary to the increasingly "marginal" and "extreme" establishment. From this sentiment derives their self-image as warriors of a wider movement for the liberation of peoples from a globalist oligarchy. In the end, they sense that History is on their side. It is as if the pendulum of History, at least Europe's History, after swinging hard in the first half of the twentieth century toward the pinnacle of ethnocultural communities and veering violently to the other extreme of postethnoculturalism since then, is finally making its way back. The theorists and activists studied in this book hope that this way back leads to a new Identitarian beginning.

NOTES

INTRODUCTION

1. Venner 2011a, 11.
2. Murray 2017.

CHAPTER 1 Intellectual Foundations, Practices, and Networks

1. Lindholm and Zúquete 2010; Bar-On 2013; Casadio 2014.
2. Valla 2013, 96.
3. De Benoist and Champetier 2012, 28–30.
4. Steuckers 2015a.
5. De Benoist and Champetier 2012, 32.
6. De Herte 2004, 3.
7. See De Benoist 2006, 108–11.
8. De Benoist 2014, 160.
9. De Benoist 2015a, 5–6.
10. De Herte 2004, 3.
11. Isabel 2014, 60–71.
12. De Benoist 2013c, 37.
13. O'Meara 2015.
14. O'Meara 2013, 7.
15. Faye 1997, 38.
16. Krebs 2011, 23.
17. Faye 2011, 134.
18. De Benoist 2014, 159.
19. De Benoist 2004.

20. Marmim 2010, 39.
21. Faye 2011, 44, 214.
22. Steuckers 1999.
23. See Steuckers 2013; O'Meara 2013, 146–75; Tudor 2015b.
24. Vial 2016.
25. Vial 2010c, 24.
26. Vial 1999.
27. Vial 2010a, 3.
28. Vial 2010b, 23.
29. Arteault 2005, 17, 18, 21.
30. Valla 2013, 137.
31. Haudry 2010, 57, 58; Haudry 2015, 6–9.
32. Vial 2015c, 52.
33. *Réfléchir & Agir* 2016c, 4.
34. Krampon 2009a, 44.
35. Krampon 2015a, 3.
36. *Réfléchir & Agir* 2010b, 19.
37. Rix 2010, 48.
38. *Réfléchir & Agir* 2010a, 5.
39. Gillieth and Krampon 2010, 18.
40. Venner 2015a, 26.
41. Valla 2013, 83.
42. Dard 2015, 316–17.
43. Venner 2003c, 58.
44. Ibid., 59.
45. Venner 2005, 5.
46. Venner 2011a, 13.
47. Venner 2003b, 57.
48. Venner 2011b, 153–54.
49. Venner 2003c, 59.
50. Venner 2011a, 264.
51. Venner 2009a, 5.
52. See, for example, Venner 2011b, 34.
53. Venner 2015, 54.
54. Venner 2013a.
55. Venner 2016, 30, 177.
56. De Benoist 2013b, 31.
57. Krampon 2013b, 44.
58. EAS 2018.
59. Venner 2001, 17.

60. *Iliade* 2014; Conrad 2015a.
61. Polémia 2015.
62. *Paris Vox* 2017.
63. Jünger 2012.
64. Génération Identitaire 2012; see also Generation Identity 2013, 9–11.
65. Generation Identity 2013, 12–13.
66. *Identitaires* 2016a.
67. For a comprehensive review of the early network, see Casajus 2014.
68. See Cahuzac and François 2013, 279–83.
69. Bloc Identitaire n.d., 2.
70. Robert 2014, 7.
71. Robert 2010.
72. Robert 2012b, 12.
73. Vardon-Raybaud 2011, 279.
74. Ibid., 278.
75. Robert 2015b.
76. Vardon 2012, 7.
77. Robert 2014, 7.
78. Generation Identity 2013, 32.
79. *Identitaires* 2015, 2.
80. *Identitaires* 2013a, 2.
81. On this, see Albanese et al. 2014, 17–36; also Marchi 2015.
82. Scianca 2011.
83. Adinolfi 2015.
84. Blocco Studentesco 2006.
85. Adinolfi 2008, 10, 12, 14, 33.
86. Iannone 2010, 27–29.
87. Scianca 2011.
88. See Castriota and Feldman 2014, 241.
89. CasaPound Italia, n.d.
90. Iannone 2010, 28.
91. Scianca 2015a.
92. CasaPound Italia, n.d. F.A.Q.
93. *Espresso* 2012.
94. Scianca 2011, 362.
95. Albanese et al. 2014, 134.
96. Marchi 2015, 207.
97. Venner 2001, 17.
98. Vardon-Raybaud 2011, 12.
99. Faye 2011, 265.

100. Van Zee and Marly 2006, 3.
101. Iannone 2011.
102. Bérard 2009, 36.
103. Venner 2009b, 38.
104. See Iannone 2010, 29; Iannone 2011.
105. Adinolfi 2008, 24.
106. Iannone 2010, 28.
107. Iannone 2015b.
108. See Adinolfi 2013.
109. CasaPound Italia 2013.
110. Bobby Sands Trust 2010.
111. Bloc Identitaire 2005.
112. Vardon-Raybaud 2011, 22–23.
113. See Casajus 2014, 140; Projet Apache 2011.
114. Vardon-Raybaud 2011, 193.
115. Venner 2016, 5–6.
116. Iannone 2015c.
117. Generation Identity 2013, 31.
118. Iannone 2010, 28.
119. Cammelli 2015, 84.
120. Vardon-Raybaud 2011, 17, 157.
121. D'Her 2007, 2–3.
122. Vardon-Raybaud 2014.
123. Chatov 2007, 9.
124. Robert 2007, 12.
125. Iannone 2011.
126. Cammelli 2015, 75.
127. Albanese et al. 2014, 68.
128. Cammelli 2015, 77.
129. Albanese et al. 2014, 42.
130. Generation Identity 2013, 40.
131. Venner 2001, 17.
132. Generation Identity 2013, 11–13.
133. Castriota and Feldman 2014, 231.
134. Robert 2014, 5.
135. Generation Identity 2013, 9–10.
136. Albanaese et al. 2014, 65.
137. Willinger 2013, 16–19, 81.
138. Robert 2015b.
139. Generation Identity 2013, 32.

140. Willinger 2013, 18.
141. Iannone 2010, 28.
142. Tarchi 2010.
143. Iannone 2011.
144. Vardon-Raybaud 2011, 283.
145. Digital Crusades 2012.
146. Le Gallou et al. 2015, 11.
147. Geoffroy 2015b, 231.
148. Robert 2014, 5.
149. Steuckers 2015a.
150. Digital Crusades 2012.
151. See, for exemple, Casajus 2014, 122.
152. Cammelli 2015, 96–98; Albanese et al. 2014, 120–21.
153. Robert 2013b, 7.
154. Cahuzac and François 2013, 6.
155. Le Gallou 2008.
156. Geoffroy 2015a, 225–26.
157. Vardon-Raybaud 2011, 89–90, 182.
158. Casajus 2014, 116.
159. Venner 2013b, 298.
160. Iannone 2010, 28.
161. Scianca 2011, 52–53.
162. Zentropa 2012a.
163. Vardon 2013, 9–10.
164. *Cercle Non Conforme* 2015.
165. Faye 2011, 157.
166. *Identitaires* 2013b, 6.
167. Vardon-Raybaud 2011, 281.
168. Generation Identity 2013, 10.
169. *Identitaires* 2013a, 2.
170. Scianca 2011, 364.
171. Blocco Studentesco 2015.
172. Zentropa 2012b.
173. Casajus 2014, 139.
174. Circolo Futurista n.d.
175. Scianca 2011, 365.
176. Zentropa n.d.
177. Novak 2011, 169.
178. Zentropa n.d.b.
179. Digital Crusades 2012.

180. Generation Identity 2013, 45.
181. Faye 2011, 34.
182. Vardon-Raybaud 2011, 209.
183. Robert 2010.
184. *Identitaires* 2013c, 10–11.
185. *Identitaires* 2014a, 6–7.
186. Rieu 2014a.
187. Génération Identitaire 2017a.
188. *Identitaires* 2013c, 10–11.
189. *Identitaires* 2013b, 12.
190. Liddell 2015b.
191. Zentropa n.d.a.
192. *Identitaires* 2012, 6.
193. Génération Identitaire Flandre Artois Hainaut 2016.
194. *Identitaires* 2015, 11.
195. Digital Crusades 2012.
196. Generation Identity 2013, 34.
197. *Identità* 2011, 1.
198. Digital Crusades 2012.
199. *Identitaires* 2014c, 4–5; *Libération* 2015.
200. *Présent* 2015b.
201. *Monde* 2017.
202. Novopress 2012b.
203. Iannone 2015a.
204. Di Stefano 2015b.
205. Scianca 2015c.
206. Di Stefano 2016.
207. Tudor 2015a.
208. Scianca 2015b.
209. O'Meara 2015.
210. Krampon 2010, 25–26.
211. See, for example, Holloway 2005.
212. Faye 2011, 268.
213. Robert 2012a.
214. Vardon-Raybaud 2011, 243, 279.
215. De Benoist 2015b, 183.
216. Faye 2011, 269–70.
217. Morgan 2015.
218. Tudor 2015a.
219. Sunić 2015.

220. Liddell 2015.
221. *Europe-Identité* 2008.
222. *Terre et Peuple* 2007, 4.
223. Vial 2015b.
224. RésistanceS.be.
225. Martins 2016.
226. Marchi 2015.
227. *Pena e Espada* 2015.
228. SOM 2015.
229. Milà 2017.
230. Solère 2015.
231. Digital Crusades 2012.
232. Generation Identity 2013, 37.
233. *ID Magazine* 2006, 6.
234. Vardon-Raybaud 2011, 44.
235. The mock dialect was in the original.
236. Markovics 2017.
237. Markovics 2015.
238. YouTube 2016a.
239. Mayer and Sauer 2014.
240. Since 2017 Alexander Markovics has blogged at www.alexandermarkovics.at; "The New Right—A glimpse of Europe's Spiritual Future" is the title of a lecture given by Markovics in the German city of Aachen to the local section of the AfD. See Markovics 2018.
241. See the action at Youtube 2016c.
242. IBD 2016d.
243. Ibid.
244. Von Salomon 2013, 264.
245. IBD 2016a.
246. *Sezession* 2015.
247. Sellner 2015.
248. *PI-News* 2016; see also Salzborn 2016, 46–50.
249. Kubitschek 2016b.
250. *PI-News* 2016.
251. Lichtmesz 2016a.
252. Sellner 2016c.
253. Machiavelli 2006, 45.
254. IBD 2016b.
255. Sellner 2016c.
256. Phalanx Europa 2012.

257. Cuneus was founded in 2016. See their website at https://www.cuneus-culture.de.
258. Lüdtke 2017.
259. Sellner 2016c.
260. *Hannoversche Allgemeine* 2016.
261. YouTube 2018a.
262. IB Schwaben 2017a.
263. Ibid.
264. Sellner 2014.
265. *Guardian* 2017.
266. *Zeitfragen* 2016.
267. Belltower 2017.
268. Meinhart 2014.
269. *Metropolico* 2016.
270. Kubitschek 2016a.
271. verfassungsschuetzer.info 2017.
272. IBÖ 2018.
273. *Identitaires* 2016a, 3.
274. *Identitaires* 2014a, 12.
275. Berčík 2016.
276. Identitás Generáció 2014. Although the group was officially founded in 2016, from 2014 there was already online activity of some members under the "Identitarian" banner.
277. Kőrössy 2017.
278. pestisracok.hu 2017.
279. Generacija Identitete Slovenija 2013.
280. Perino 2016.
281. *Redacta* 2016.
282. Generazione Identitaria Sardegna 2017.
283. Generatie Identiteit 2017.
284. De Geyndt 2017.
285. Zetland 2018.
286. Generation Identity UK and Ireland 2017.
287. Dupré 2018.
288. McKenna 2017.
289. *Identitaires* 2013b, 7; *Identitaires* 2017, 20.
290. CasaPound Italia—International 2015.
291. Albanese et al. 2014, 109.
292. Robert 2016a.
293. Lichtmesz 2016a.

294. Sellner 2016c.
295. *Harfang* 2014, 13.
296. Iannone 2015c.
297. *Cercle Non Conforme* 2015.
298. CasaPound Italia 2015c.
299. CasaPound Italia 2015d.
300. *Réfléchir & Agir* 2010c, 32–34.
301. Bissuel 2017.
302. *Marea* 2014.
303. *Mundo* 2016.
304. *Publico* 2015.
305. CasaPound Italia 2015b.
306. Hogar Social Madrid 2016.
307. Tremblay 2016.
308. FQS 2015.
309. Tremblay 2015.
310. Breizh-Info 2017.
311. Morgan 2015.
312. Right On website. No longer available.
313. Friberg 2016c.
314. Friberg 2016b.
315. Morgan 2013.
316. Johnson 2015b.
317. Breitbart 2016b.
318. Rebel Media 2016.
319. YouTube 2017a.
320. Pettibone 2017.
321. Délský potápěč n.d.; Vejvodová 2014.
322. Délský potápěč 2017.
323. Franco 2017.

CHAPTER 2 Identity against Globalism

1. Faye 2011, 127, 257.
2. De Benoist and Champetier 2012, 15.
3. Faye 2011, 259.
4. Vial 2010b, 23.
5. Robert 2015b.
6. Le Gallou et al. 2015, 131.

7. Sunić 2015.
8. Ochsenreiter 2015.
9. *Identitaires* 2014c, 4–5.
10. CasaPound Italia n.d.
11. CasaPound Italia 2011, 2.
12. Steuckers 2012.
13. See, for example, Lindholm 2008, 100–101.
14. Valla 2013, 84.
15. Saint-Loup 2014.
16. *Réfléchir & Agir* 2009, 38.
17. Vial 2008, 2.
18. Smith 1991, 13–15.
19. Saint-Pierre 2004, 2.
20. Guillemot, 2006, 23–24.
21. *Terre et Peuple* 2014c, 9.
22. Cagnat 2014b, 13.
23. Vial 2001, 19.
24. *Terre et Peuple* 2014b, 16.
25. Krebs 2003, 33.
26. Steuckers 2015a.
27. Krampon 2009b, 38.
28. Krampon 2015b, 17.
29. Bloc Identitaire n.d.
30. *Réfléchir & Agir* 2014.
31. Faye 1981, 21–22.
32. Faye 1986, 15.
33. Venner 2009b, 38.
34. Cau 1974, 40.
35. Faye 1986, 14.
36. De Benoist 2015b, 158.
37. Le Gallou et al. 2015, 103.
38. Hauffen 2005a, 8.
39. Scianca 2003, 57.
40. Rix 2011, 11–15.
41. Steuckers, cited in Rix 2011, 15.
42. Krampon 2014a, 15.
43. Venner 2011a, 18.
44. Vial 1992, 110.
45. Hesse 1963, 170.
46. Scianca 2011, 191.

47. Bousquet 2015, 73.
48. *Figaro* 2014.
49. Virilio 2000, 38.
50. Fusaro 2015, 42–43.
51. *Secolo d'Italia* 2014.
52. Steuckers 1994.
53. *Réfléchir & Agir* 2013b, 32.
54. Ibid., 34.
55. Michéa 2013, 2014.
56. Robin 2015; Eysseric 2015.
57. Digital Crusades 2012.
58. L'Epée 2013, 41.
59. *Réfléchir & Agir* 2013b, 14.
60. Faye 2011, 222.
61. Fiorini 2013a.
62. Fiorini 2013b, 28.
63. Vardon-Raybaud 2011, 219.
64. *Identitaires* 2013a, 3.
65. Hauffen 2005b, 13–14.
66. *Identitaires* 2013c, 5.
67. *Identitaires* 2015, 4.
68. De Benoist 2013a, 35.
69. Scianca 2011, 344.
70. Iannone 2011.
71. Scianca 2011, 347–49.
72. Zentropa 2012b.
73. Gattinara et al., 2013, 254.
74. Scianca 2011, 350.
75. CasaPound Italia 2011, 1–3.
76. CasaPound Italia n.d.
77. CasaPound Italia Milano 2015.
78. *Giornale* 2017.
79. CasaPound Italia Facebook 2015a.
80. CasaPound Italia 2011, 3.
81. Branquinho 2016a.
82. De Benoist 2015b, 174.
83. Scianca 2015a.
84. Le Gallou et al. 2015, 58.
85. Faye 2011, 222.
86. *Terre et Peuple* 2014c, 3.

87. Robert 2010.
88. Coussedière 2012.
89. Markovics 2017.
90. Lambert, 2006, 19.
91. Fiorini 2013a.
92. Friberg 2017.
93. Dumont 2014, 11.
94. Chauprade 2006, 59–61.
95. Faye 2015, 289.
96. Scianca 2011, 367.
97. Scianca 2015c.
98. Robert 2015b.
99. Le Gallou et al. 2015, 105.
100. Faye 2011, 175.
101. Ibid., 94.
102. *Terre et Peuple* 2014c, 3.
103. Venner 2009b, 38.
104. Faye 2011, 136.
105. Raspail 2014, 38.
106. Willinger 2013, 14.
107. Faye 2011, 262.
108. Vardon-Raybaud 2011, 267.
109. Robert 2011, 218–19.
110. Osborne 2017, 107.
111. *J'ai Tout Compris* 2015b.
112. *Réfléchir & Agir* 2015b, 3.
113. *J'ai Tout Compris* 2015b.
114. Iliade 2015.
115. Virchow 2015, 185.
116. Di Stefano 2015a.
117. CasaPound Italia 2011, 4.
118. Iannone 2014.
119. Scianca 2017a.
120. CasaPound Italia Facebook 2015b.
121. Di Stefano 2017.
122. Scianca 2017d.
123. *Tempo di essere madri* n.d.
124. CasaPound Italia 2017a.
125. CasaPound Italia 2015.
126. Mattino 2017.

127. Scianca 2015f.
128. Kurtagic 2016.
129. Vardon 2013, 8.
130. Generation Identity 2013, 41.
131. Robert 2015b.
132. *Identitaires* 2015, 9.
133. Robert 2015a.
134. *Identitaires* 2015, 7.
135. *Identitaires* 2016a, 7–9.
136. Génération Identitaire 2015b.
137. *Local* 2015.
138. IBÖ video 2016.
139. Defend Europe 2017.
140. Mudde 2017.
141. Farage 2017.
142. Sellner 2017a.
143. Generazione Identitaria 2018.
144. See also Defend Europe 2018.
145. See Pettibone's report of Mission Alps at https://www.youtube.com/watch?v=UdF0wv_UYHI.
146. Raspail 2014, 286.
147. Chauprade 2006, 60.
148. Camus 2013a.
149. Camus 2013b.
150. Camus 2013c, 64.
151. CNRE 2017.
152. Camus 2015.
153. Camus 2014, 34.
154. Steuckers 2015c.
155. Fiorini 2013b, 28–29.
156. Gambier 2015, 11.
157. Camus 2015.
158. Novopress 2015b.
159. Delrieux 2016d.
160. De Benoist 2018.
161. See, for example, UN POP 2000.
162. *Journal du Dimanche* 2014.
163. Chauprade 2013b.
164. Vial 2016, 30.
165. Faye 2016g.

166. *Giornale* 2015b.
167. Barenaked Islam 2015.
168. Verlag & Antaios 2016.
169. IBD 2015.
170. Pirinçci 2016; Lichtmesz 2016a.
171. *Stern* 2016.
172. *Hannoversche Allgemeine* 2016.
173. Generation Identity Éire/Ireland and Northern Ireland 2018.
174. Novopress 2017.
175. Scianca 2016j, 15.
176. CasaPound Italia Facebook 2016.
177. Scianca 2015g.
178. CasaPound Italia Facebook 2015b.
179. Scianca 2016b.
180. Scianca 2015e.
181. Camus 2013c, 24.
182. Scianca 2016a.
183. *Primato Nazionale* 2015b.
184. *Giornale* 2015a.
185. *éléments pour la civilisation européenne* 2015, 48–55.
186. Willinger 2013, 88.
187. Bloc Identitaire 2014.
188. *Identitaires* 2014a, 14–15; Le Brun 2015.
189. Friberg 2016b.
190. Sellner 2017a.
191. Berčík 2017.
192. Franco 2014.
193. Franco 2017.
194. Scianca 2011, 108.
195. *Identitaires* 2014b, 4.
196. Le Gallou et al. 2015, 129.
197. Roberts 2018; *Sunday Times* 2018.
198. Generation Identity 2013, 33.
199. *Identitaires* 2012, 11.
200. Venner 2006, 29–32.
201. Timmermans 2015; Lichtmesz 2016b.
202. Sellner 2016c.
203. Vial 2005a, 3.
204. Rieu 2016.
205. Le Gallou et al. 2015, 40.

206. Venner 2003b, 7.
207. Chauprade 2013a, 8.
208. *Nouvelle Revue d'Histoire* 2003, 27.
209. Vial 2015b.
210. Chauprade 2013a, 11.
211. *Terre et Peuple* 2014a, 15.
212. *Terre et Peuple* 2014b, 16.
213. Robert 2015b.
214. *Réfléchir & Agir* 2003, 3, 5.
215. Randa 2015.
216. Ochsenreiter 2015.
217. Robert 2015b.
218. *Nouvelle Revue d'Histoire* 2003, 27.
219. *Terre et Peuple* 2015a, 22.
220. *Identitaires* 2015, 10.
221. Lenart 2017.
222. Faye 2015, 98.
223. De Benoist 2015b, 171.
224. Scianca 2015c.
225. Krampon 2013a, 14.
226. Sunić 2007, 44.
227. Venner 2009b, 38.
228. Venner 2015b.
229. Sunić n.d.
230. Valla 2013, 138.
231. Bardèche 1994.
232. Faye 2011, 178.
233. Generation Identity 2013, 31.

CHAPTER 3 Identity against Islam

1. Venner 1996, 10.
2. Walker 2008.
3. See, for example, Archer 2013.
4. Lane 2016.
5. Venner 2015a, 2–3.
6. Venner 2003a, 7.
7. Camus 2013c, 28.
8. De Benoist 2001, 54, 290.

9. Faye 2016a.
10. Faye 2011, 174.
11. CREA 2016, 32.
12. Dragan 2015, 27.
13. Rieu 2014b.
14. Sellner 2016c.
15. Gordon 2012.
16. *Novopress* 2013.
17. Marchand 2013, 7–8.
18. Marchand 2003, 47.
19. Faye 2011, 189.
20. Le Gallou 2016, 421, 425.
21. Marchand 2013, 198–99.
22. Faye 2015, 54–57.
23. Cagnat 2015b, 28–29.
24. Geoffroy 2015a, 216.
25. Faye 2015, 96.
26. Venner 1996, 11.
27. Marchand 2013, 164.
28. Iliade video 2015.
29. Conrad 2016b, 20–21.
30. Fanjul 2009.
31. Faye 2015, 145.
32. Radio Courtoisie 2017.
33. See, for example, Mirkovic 2016.
34. Vial 2005b, 33.
35. Duarte 1982, 93.
36. Vial 2005b, 34.
37. Gibbon 1782.
38. *éléments pour la civilisation européenne* 2016b, 95.
39. Gillieth 2016, 12.
40. Iliade video 2015.
41. Marchand 2013, 8.
42. Poitou-Info 2015.
43. Vial 2015d.
44. *Terre et Peuple* 2015b, 5.
45. See the calendar here: http://www.libertiesalliance.org/2010/02/06/october-2010-calendar/.
46. Faye 2012a, 58.
47. De Villiers 2016, 19.

48. Cagnat 2015a, 25.
49. Conrad 1996, 28.
50. Conrad 2016a, 5.
51. Generation Identity 2013, 18.
52. *Identitaires* 2014b, 12.
53. Generation Identity 2013, 22–23.
54. Génération Identitaire 2017b.
55. *Identitaires* 2016a, 15.
56. Robert 2012a.
57. Vardon-Raybaud 2011, 67.
58. Robert 2013a.
59. Generation Identity London 2018.
60. Vardon-Raybaud 2011, 177.
61. Robert 2010.
62. *Figaro* 2011.
63. Generation Identity 2013, 25.
64. Rebeyne 2010.
65. *Identitaires* 2018, 10.
66. *ID Magazine* 2006, 8.
67. *Identitaires* 2016a, 6.
68. Lignier 2016.
69. *Identitaires* 2016a, 6.
70. Larti 2016.
71. Rieu 2014b.
72. Robert 2011, 220–21.
73. Vardon-Raybaud 2011, 283.
74. See *Identitaires* 2013b, 3.
75. Veliocas 2016.
76. Ibid.
77. Cassen 2016.
78. Cassen and Tasin 2011, 111, 115, 238.
79. For a remarkable study of the EDL see Busher 2016.
80. Ibid., 2011, 255.
81. Robert 2015b.
82. *Le Figaro* 2016.
83. *Terre et Peuple* 2014c, 3.
84. Le Gallou and Ormain 2016, 55.
85. Sellner 2016a. See also *Identitaires* 2016b, 8–9.
86. Robinson 2017.
87. YouTube 2018b.

88. An Identitarian content producer who goes by the moniker Retro-Rebel made a music-video mixing Robinson's address with material from the Identitarian Lambda movement. This, too, is an example of the Identitarian "New Cool." See also RetroRebel 2018.
89. Sellner 2018.
90. IBÖ 2016b.
91. *Live Leak* 2016.
92. IBÖ 2016a.
93. Franziska 2017.
94. *Independent* 2017.
95. IBD 2017e.
96. IBÖ 2017c; Le Identitarie 2017.
97. #120dB 2018.
98. Morars 2018.
99. #120dB: The Documentary 2018.
100. Identitäre Bewegung Baden 2016.
101. Phalanx Europa 2012.
102. IBÖ 2017a.
103. Sunić 2016.
104. IBÖ 2017d.
105. IBS 2017.
106. IBÖ 2017b.
107. Marchand 2013, 111.
108. Faye 2015, 95.
109. Faye 2007a, 14.
110. Faye 2013.
111. Marchand 2013, 232.
112. Faye 2015, 74–75.
113. Venner 2005, 5.
114. Faye 2013.
115. *Terre et Peuple* 2015c, 34.
116. Faye 2016a.
117. Veliocas 2016.
118. Marchand 2013, 363.
119. Le Gallou et al. 2015, 149.
120. Cagnat 2015b, 29.
121. Faye 2015, 92–93, 118.
122. *Terre et Peuple* 2015c, 13.
123. *Boulevard Voltaire* 2016.
124. *Independent* 2017.

125. Conrad 2016a, 5.
126. *éléments* 2016a.
127. Vial 2015b.
128. Faye 2015, 95.
129. *Novopress* 2012a.
130. *Identitaires* 2014b, 3.
131. In France alone, from 2013 to 2018 there have been 78 terrorist plans: 50 were foiled, 17 failed, and 11 were successful, leaving 245 dead and more than 900 wounded. See *Monde*, 2018.
132. *Enquête & Débat* 2015.
133. Vial 2015a.
134. Bloc Identitaire 2015.
135. Génération Identitaire 2015c.
136. *Présent* 2015a.
137. *Réfléchir & Agir* 2015a, 23–26.
138. Génération Identitaire 2015a.
139. Ibid., November 15.
140. *Identitaires* 2016a, 11.
141. *Identitaires* 2016c.
142. Generation Identity 2016.
143. *Novopress* 2016.
144. Larti 2016.
145. IBN 2017.
146. IBD Berlin-Brandenburg 2017.
147. *New Observer* 2016.
148. IB Schwaben 2017b.
149. Breitbart 2016a; *Kleine Zeitung* 2016.
150. IBH 2016.
151. IBD 2016e.
152. See, for example, IBD 2016c.
153. See, for example, IBMV 2016.
154. IBÖ 2016c.
155. Generazione Identitaria 2016.
156. Sellner 2017b.
157. IBD 2016c.
158. IB Schwaben 2017c.
159. *Stampa* 2017.
160. *Novopress* 2014.
161. Cassen 2014.
162. Martin 2014, 7.

163. Génération Identitaire 2016.
164. Markovics 2016a.
165. Veliocas 2016.
166. Le Gallou 2016, 430.
167. Marchand 2013, 318, 385–89.
168. *Primato Nazionale* 2015e.
169. Di Stefano 2015c.
170. Scianca 2016e.
171. Scianca 2015c.
172. Scianca 2017c.
173. Morgan 2015.
174. Tudor 2015a.
175. *Primato Nazionale* 2015c.
176. Scianca, quoted by *Primato Nazionale* 2015d.
177. Steuckers 2014b.
178. *Primato Nazionale* 2015a.
179. CasaPound Italia 2017b.
180. Oppedisano 2015; EFSS 2013.
181. Oppedisano 2015.
182. Al-Ahed News 2016.
183. *Repubblica* 2015.
184. Oppedisano 2016.
185. De Benoist 2006, 113–14.
186. Ochsenreiter 2015.
187. Venner 2011a, 46.
188. Faye 2011, 180–82.
189. Randa 2015.
190. Conrad 2016c.
191. Delrieux 2016a.
192. Rebeyne—Génération Identitaire Lyon 2015.
193. Le Gallou et al. 2015, 57.
194. *Identitaires* 2015, 2.
195. Faye 2015, 154.
196. *Identitaires* 2013a, 8.
197. Sellner 2016b.
198. Langella 2013.
199. Langella 2016.
200. Ibid.
201. Ibid.
202. Sunić 2017.

203. Raspail 2014, 135.
204. Lichtmesz 2016c.
205. Langella 2016.
206. Faye 2016c.
207. Faye 2016d.
208. Scianca 2016g.
209. *Jihad Watch* 2016.
210. Raspail 2015.
211. Raspail 2014, 45, 317.

CHAPTER 4 For a New Geopolitics of Europe

1. Conrad 2014, 5.
2. Venner 2011a, 243.
3. Venner 2015a, 66.
4. La Rochelle 1931.
5. Valla 2013, 78.
6. De Herte 1980, 2.
7. Faye 1997, 41.
8. Valla 2013, 139–49.
9. De Herte 1980, 2.
10. De Benoist, 1992, 33.
11. De Herte 1991, 3.
12. For example, De Benoist 2007.
13. De Benoist 2014, 42.
14. De Benoist 1993, 204.
15. De Benoist 2014a, 42.
16. De Benoist 2014a.
17. De Herte 2010, 3.
18. *Finis Mundi—A Última Cultura* 2014, 166.
19. De Herte 2009, 3.
20. De Benoist 2008, 7–15.
21. See the cover of *éléments pour la civilisation européenne* 2009, n. 131 (April–June).
22. identitaere-generation.info. 2015.
23. De Benoist and Dugin 2014.
24. Rossman 2015.
25. Dugin 2012b.
26. Dugin 2016a.

27. Bassin and Aksenov 2006.
28. Dugin 2014.
29. "Color revolutions" refers to a series of street protests that from 2003 to 2005 toppled regimes in Georgia, Ukraine, and Kyrgyzstan. They were hailed in the West as democratic achievements. Putin, too, sees the "color revolutions" as part of a Western geopolitical strategy to transform the region. "In the modern world extremism is being used as a geopolitical instrument and for remaking spheres of influence. We see what tragic consequences the wave of so-called color revolutions led to," he said on one occasion. See Reuters, 2014.
30. *éléments* blog 2014.
31. De Herte 2009, 3.
32. *éléments* blog 2014.
33. *Polémia* 2014.
34. Venner 2011a, 27.
35. Von Salomon 2013, 266.
36. Monnet 1978.
37. *J'ai Tout Compris* 2016b.
38. *Terre et Peuple* 2014b, 22.
39. Krampon 2014b, 18.
40. Le Gallou et al. 2015, 191.
41. *Réfléchir & Agir* 2016a, 3.
42. Krampon 2014b, 17.
43. Friberg 2016a.
44. Branquinho 2016b, 138.
45. Feltin-Tracol 2016a.
46. *Primato Nazionale* 2016.
47. *J'ai Tout Compris* 2016b.
48. Génération Identitaire 2014.
49. IBD 2016a.
50. Tom Dupré 2018.
51. Sellner 2016c.
52. Generace Identity 2016.
53. The blog of Robert Steuckers is at http://robertsteuckers.blogspot.pt.
54. Steuckers 2017, 299–300.
55. Steuckers 2016, 209.
56. Brzezinski 1997, 30.
57. Steuckers 2016, 284; *Le Blanc et le Noir* 2016.
58. Ibid., 262.
59. Ravello 2005, 90.

60. Faye 2011, 141–42.
61. Cagnat 2014a, 20.
62. Cagnat 2009, 29.
63. Cagnat 2014a, 20.
64. Arteault 2014, 26.
65. Faye 2001, 8.
66. Steuckers 2014b.
67. Tulaev 2015.
68. Euro–Rus n.d.
69. *Réfléchir & Agir* 2016b, 28.
70. *Terre et Peuple* 2015d, 33.
71. Cagnat 2014a, 18.
72. LBTF 2013.
73. Dugin 2013.
74. Dugin 2012a.
75. Le Gallou 2016, 438.
76. Prilepin 2006, 244.
77. *Réfléchir & Agir* 2016b, 11.
78. *Real Politik* 2013.
79. Venner 1994, 11.
80. Venner 2012a, 5.
81. Arteault 2008, 52.
82. *Terre et Peuple* 2014a, 18.
83. *Terre et Peuple* 2014b, 16.
84. Faye 2012b.
85. Le Gallou et al. 2015, 172.
86. Steuckers 2016, 97.
87. *J'ai Tout Compris* 2015a.
88. *J'ai Tout Compris* 2016a.
89. Vial 2014a.
90. *Washington Post* 2016.
91. Steuckers 2014a.
92. Steuckers 2017, 270–72.
93. Steuckers 2018.
94. Friberg 2016a.
95. Almássy 2016; *Réfléchir & Agir* 2016b, 29.
96. YouTube 2017c.
97. Breitbart 2017a.
98. Breitbart 2017c.
99. Conrad 2016d.

100. *Réfléchir & Agir* 2017, 61.
101. Kaalep 2016a.
102. Kaalep 2016b.
103. Zeltīts 2016.
104. Kubitschek 2016b.
105. Feltin-Tracol 2016a.
106. Friberg 2016b.
107. Kaalep 2016a.
108. Feltin-Tracol 2016a.
109. Lichtmesz 2016a.
110. Sellner 2016c.
111. *Compact* 2016.
112. *Identitaires* 2016b.
113. Robert 2016a.
114. Delrieux 2016b.
115. Generation Identity 2013, 25.
116. Phalanx Europa 2012.
117. IBD 2017d.
118. Markovics 2016b.
119. identitaere-generation.info 2015.
120. Ochsenreiter 2016b.
121. Ochsenreiter 2016a.
122. CCC 2015.
123. CCC 2016a.
124. European Identity blog 2016.
125. Kofner 2017.
126. Suvorov Institute 2016.
127. CCC 2016b.
128. Poppel 2017.
129. Scianca 2016h.
130. CasaPound Italia 2014.
131. *IntelligoNews* 2014.
132. Scianca 2017b.
133. Sellner 2016d.
134. Trump 2016.
135. RT 2017.
136. Robert 2016b.
137. Sellner 2016c.
138. IBD 2017a.
139. Markovics 2016c.

140. Cattin 2016.
141. *Renaissance Européenne* 2016.
142. Faye 2016f.
143. Scianca 2016i.
144. Breizh-Info 2016b.
145. De Benoist 2017.
146. Dugin 2016b.
147. Markovics 2017.

CHAPTER 5 Of Race and Identity

1. Faulkner, cited in Hamblin and Peek 1999, 367.
2. Scianca 2016f.
3. Scianca 2016d.
4. Venner 2012b, 8.
5. Bousquet 2016.
6. De Benoist 2013c, 33–35.
7. Kubitschek 2016b.
8. Geoffroy 2015a, 215.
9. Le Gallou 2016, 371.
10. Ibid., 268.
11. Redecker 2014, 9.
12. Willinger 2013, 44.
13. Tudor 2014, 89–90.
14. Eibl-Eibesfeldt 2007.
15. This suitable distinction has been taken from Vick 2013.
16. Krebs 2012, 79.
17. De Benoist, cited in François 2014, 154.
18. See, for example, O'Danieli 2016.
19. De Benoist 2005, 21.
20. See, for example, Christen 2014, 56–58.
21. De Benoist 2016b, 3.
22. François 2014, 41–42.
23. Vial, cited in Faye 2011, 228.
24. *Terre et Peuple* 2014c, 9.
25. Krampon 2009, 38.
26. Krebs 2015.
27. Ibid.
28. Faye 2011, 148, 228.

29. *Rue 89* 2014.
30. François 2014, 177–89.
31. Cited in Haudry 2006, 30.
32. Venner 2011a, 67–68.
33. Favrit 2013, 4.
34. De Lamberterie 2014, 42.
35. Arteault 2006, 12.
36. Feltin-Tracol 2016a.
37. Vial 2009, 33–36.
38. *Terre et Peuple* 2014a, 9.
39. Faye 2011, 142.
40. *Terre et Peuple—La Revue* 2006, 9.
41. Tulaev 2006.
42. Vial 2009, 34.
43. Krampon 2003a, 35.
44. Krampon 2003b, 45.
45. *Terre et Peuple* 2007, 17.
46. Günther 2013.
47. Krampon 2003b, 48.
48. *Réfléchir & Agir* 2003, 17.
49. Michel 2008, 47–51.
50. See Dutton and Lynn 2015. *éléments pour la civilisation européenne* interviewed one of the co-authors of this study, Richard Lynn, an emeritus professor of psychology at the University of Ulster, who believes that the main reason for the drop in IQs in the twenty-first century, not just in France but in the rest of Western Europe, the United States, and Australia, is the fact that in recent decades women with higher IQs have had fewer children than those with lower IQs. Immigration from non-European countries has also been a factor, but to a lesser extent. See O'Danieli 2018, 75–76. Lynn's studies on intelligence have been criticized by some as "unsystematic." The watchdog group Southern Poverty Law Center calls him "one of the most unapologetic and raw 'scientific' racists operating today." In February 2018, Ulster University's student union called on the university to revoke his "emeritus" title.
51. *Réfléchir & Agir* 2003, 53.
52. Ibid.
53. Krampon 2017, 17.
54. Vial 2009, 33.
55. Cagnat 2014a, 16.
56. Faye 2011, 136.
57. Venner 2011a, 38.

58. Venner 2015a, 4.
59. Raspail 2014, 104.
60. *IdentidaD* 2006.
61. *Réfléchir & Agir* 2003, 17.
62. *Terre et Peuple* 2015a, 52.
63. Faye 2016e.
64. Krampon 2015c, 56.
65. Krebs 2012, 84.
66. Faye 2016b.
67. Lichtmesz 2016a.
68. Sellner 2016c.
69. Le Gallou 2015.
70. Gérard 2016.
71. Verhassel 2016.
72. Finkielkraut 2013.
73. Robert 2013a.
74. Vardon-Raybaud 2011, 228.
75. Bloc Identitaire 2011.
76. Lichtmesz 2016a.
77. Langella 2015a, 85–105.
78. Breitbart 2017b.
79. Le Gallou et al. 2015, 160.
80. Pichon 2013, 21, 89.
81. Langella 2015a, 135–36.
82. Langness 2016b.
83. Langness 2018.
84. Generation Identity 2013, 41.
85. Martins 2016.
86. Robert 2010.
87. Joly 2009, 13.
88. Langella 2015b, 34.
89. Le Gallou 2016, 151.
90. See *Libération* 2016.
91. Vardon 2010.
92. *Novopress* 2015a.
93. Pichon 2014.
94. Génération Identitaire 2018.
95. Beauregard 2016.
96. YouTube 2016b.
97. Scianca 2015c.

98. Iannone 2014.
99. Scianca 2011, 117.
100. *Espresso* 2012.
101. Scianca 2011, 140.
102. *IntelligoNews* 2015b.
103. *Spiegel* 2011.
104. *Vera Opposizione* 2011.
105. Scianca 2011, 198.
106. Scianca 2015h.
107. Scianca 2016c.
108. Taylor 2015a.
109. Ibid.
110. Taylor 2015c. On the issue of white nationalism versus white supremacy, see Hawley 2016, 246; see also George Michael (2017), who points out that "the overwhelming number of white nationalists eschew the term white supremacy" (*Washington Post* 2017).
111. *Huffington Post* 2016.
112. Johnson 2013, 9.
113. Kurtagic 2011.
114. O'Meara 2010, 29.
115. Zentropa 2015.
116. Spencer 2015a.
117. Johnson 2013, 192.
118. Kurtagic 2015b.
119. Spencer 2015a.
120. Radix 2013.
121. *American Renaissance* 2013.
122. Taylor 2015a.
123. Johnson 2013, 2.
124. O'Meara 2015.
125. Sunić 2011.
126. Lambton 2016.
127. Morgan 2015.
128. Morgan 2017.
129. Tudor 2015a.
130. Taylor 2015d.
131. Johnson 2013, 2.
132. Devlin 2013.
133. *Libération* 2017.
134. Spencer 2015a.

135. Liddell 2015a.
136. Spencer 2015b.
137. Taylor 2012a, 9.
138. Taylor 2012b.
139. Robert 2013a.
140. Lichtmesz 2017.
141. Taylor 2015a.
142. Taylor 2014.
143. Taylor 2015b.
144. O'Meara 2004, 45–46.
145. AltRight Radio 2017.
146. Nordic Frontier 2018.
147. Red Ice TV 2017.
148. Morgan 2017.
149. Spencer 2015a.
150. Ruben 2017.
151. Doxers are those who make the private information of citizens public.
152. Johnson 2017a.
153. Johnson 2015c.
154. Identity Forum 2014.
155. Dewitt 2015.
156. IE 2016.
157. Damigo assaulted a Muslim man, an episode he regrets and blames on PTSD.
158. *Mother Jones* 2017.
159. IE 2017.
160. Michael 2017.
161. *New Yorker* 2017.
162. Faye 2007b, 240–44.
163. Taylor 2012c.
164. O'Meara 2007.
165. Johnson 2015a.
166. Mosley 2017a.
167. Casey 2017.
168. *Réfléchir & Agir* 2003, 17.
169. *Réfléchir & Agir* 2015a, 5.
170. Duke 2015.
171. Durolle 2017, 31.
172. Pettibone 2017.

173. Morgan 2017.
174. 3ndscape 2017.
175. This issue is connected to what George Hawley (2017, 172) says about the lack of "seriousness" and "organization" of the Alt Right.
176. Johnson 2017b.
177. Erkenbrand 2017.
178. AltRight Radio 2017.
179. Mosley and Allsup 2017.
180. Spencer 2017.
181. Casey 2017.
182. IE 2018.
183. Tremblay 2016.
184. O'Meara 2010, 124.
185. *Fuerza Nacional-Identitaria* 2015.
186. Villena 2014.
187. Vitali 2014.
188. Vitali 2015.
189. Villena 2014.

CHAPTER 6 The Coming War?

1. Faye, Freson, and Steuckers 1985.
2. Mourreau 1994, 81.
3. Freund 2004; Rosenberg 2014.
4. See Isabel 2010, 44–51.
5. Jünger, cited in Kohns 2013, 143.
6. Venner 2011c, 5.
7. Conrad 2015b.
8. Randa 2015.
9. Scianca 2011, 185.
10. See, for example, Bourseiller 2012, 38.
11. Vial 2015b.
12. Krebs 2015.
13. Taylor 2015a.
14. Liddell 2015.
15. Kurtagic 2015b.
16. Morgan 2015.
17. Scianca 2015c.
18. Delrieux 2017.

19. Generazione Identitaria 2017.
20. *MYTF1 NEWS* 2014.
21. Rioufol 2016, 147–52.
22. *The Independent* 2016.
23. Freund 2004.
24. *Ballast*, 2015.
25. Faye 2011, 38, 239.
26. Faye 2001, 7.
27. Faye 2013, 91–94, 198.
28. Venner 2011b, 127.
29. Krebs 2006, 104.
30. Willinger 2013, 72.
31. Le Gallou 2016, 438.
32. Kubitschek 2016b.
33. Sellner 2016c.
34. YouTube 2017b.
35. Faye 2012a, 94.
36. Le Gallou et al. 2015, 70.
37. Vial 2005c, 19.
38. Lichtmesz 2016a.
39. Langness 2016b.
40. Marchand 2013, 173–74, 326–27.
41. Cagnat 2013.
42. *Terre et Peuple* 2014b, 16.
43. Krebs 2015.
44. Murros 2017.
45. Murros 2004.
46. Feltin-Tracol 2016a.
47. CNRE 2017.
48. *Réfléchir & Agir* 2016b, 29.
49. Kurtagic 2015a.
50. *Jazeera* 2016.
51. Lichtmesz 2017.
52. Exif—Recherche & Analyse 2017.
53. Indymedia 2017.
54. IBD 2017b.
55. *Sezession* 2016.
56. IBD 2017c.
57. *Il Primato Nazionale* 2017.
58. *IntelligoNews* 2015a.

59. Werner 2013; *Synergies Européennes* 2016.
60. Werner 2015a, 125.
61. Ibid., 17.
62. Ibid., 139.
63. Feltin-Tracol 2016a.
64. Virilio 2012.
65. Werner 2015a, 157.
66. Freund 2004.
67. Werner 2015b.
68. *Dissidence Française* 2015.
69. De Benoist 2016a, 3.
70. Faye 2011, 117.
71. Venner 2011c, 5.
72. Le Gallou 2016, 439.
73. Zinoviev 1981, cited in Boldyrev 1994, 64.
74. Steuckers 2006.
75. Generation Identity 2013, 39.
76. Vardon-Raybaud 2011, 27.
77. Murros 2004.
78. Kohns 2013, 144.
79. Kaldor 2013.
80. Enzensberger 1994, 19–20, 42–48.
81. Van Creveld 2016.
82. The first generation lasted from the Peace of Westphalia in 1648 until the American Civil War (1861–65) and is "identified through its tactics (line and column), technology (the smoothbore musket), and participants (nations)." The second was developed by the French during and after World War I and was based on changes in technology, which "produced heavy artillery, the rifled musket, and the machine gun, [which] gave some nations a profound military advantage." The third generation was developed by the Germans during and after the same World War. "It was a new era of maneuverability. For example, the introduction of the tank and the airplane shifted soldiers into non-linear, multidimensional battlefields . . . and . . . also facilitated the use of blitzkrieg, where the swiftness of an invasion gave a nation a decided advantage." See Pearlstein 2014.
83. Lind et al. 1989.
84. Freedman 2015, 226.
85. Lind 2004.
86. Lind 2015.
87. Robb 2016.

88. Faye 2017.
89. Camus 2016.
90. Delrieux 2016c.
91. Langness 2016a.
92. Solère 2016.
93. Werner 2015c.
94. Feltin-Tracol 2014, 58.
95. Wicht 2013, 64.
96. Ibid., 142.
97. Feltin-Tracol 2013.
98. San Giorgio 2013, 7.
99. San Giorgio 2016a.
100. Murros 2010.
101. Milà 2017.
102. Willinger 2013, 63.
103. *Primato Nazionale* 2016.
104. Le Gallou 2016, 14, 161.
105. Faye 2015, 81.
106. Faye 2012a, 95.
107. Cicero 1856.
108. Engels 2017.
109. Ibid.
110. *Huffington Post Deutschland* 2017.
111. Engels 2013.
112. Willinger 2013, 63–64.
113. Feltin-Tracol 2016b, 261.
114. See, for example, Neuding 2017. See also *New York Times* 2018.
115. Langness 2016c.
116. Langness 2016a.
117. Faye 2015, 294–306.
118. Lind 2016.
119. Randa 1987.
120. Randa 2016.
121. Ibid.
122. Solère 2016.
123. Faye 2015, 213–14.
124. Solère 2014, 41.
125. Ibid., 144, 236.
126. O'Meara 2015.
127. *Wermod & Wermod* 2014.

128. Solère 2014, 4–5.
129. Murros 2010.
130. Lakrite 2016, 188, 395, 494.
131. Obertone 2016, 391.
132. Breizh-Info 2016a.
133. Radio Notre Dame 2016.
134. Obertone 2016, 399.
135. San Giorgio 2016b.

POSTSCRIPT

1. On the idea of "civilizationism," see also Brubaker 2017.
2. Lindholm and Zúquete 2010.
3. Chua 2004.
4. For example, Sen 2006; Maalouf 2012.
5. Steiger 2014; Vejvodová 2014; Virchow 2015.
6. Venner 2015a, 85.

BIBLIOGRAPHY

#120dB. 2018. "German Women Speak Up against Migrants' Violence, Abuse and Terrorism." January 30. Available at https://www.facebook.com/identitaere/videos/2033249120026470/.

#120dB: *The Documentary*. 2018. "It Can Not Be Silenced." April 2. Available at https://www.youtube.com/watch?v=5QoO1KR634k.

3ndscape. 2017. "Identitarians—Who Are They?" June 17. Available at http://3ndscape.com/blog/2017/06/17/identitarians-not-radicals-europe-lost-common-sense/.

Adinolfi, Gabriele. 2008. *Sorpasso Neuronico: Il prolungato ómega della destra radicale e I vaghi bagliori dell' alfa*. May. Available at http://www.gabrieleadinolfi.it/Sorpassoneuronico.pdf.

———. 2013. "L'Intervista: Che Guevara, dallastellarossaallacamicianera." *Libero Quotidiano*, October 10. Available at http://www.liberoquotidiano.it/news/politica/1328351/Che-Guevara--dalla-stella-rossa-alla-camicia-nera--.html.

———. 2015. "Entretien avec Gabriele Adinolfi: Le Projet Lansquenet." *Terre et Peuple*, n. 66 (Solstice of Winter): 13–16.

Al-Ahed News. 2016. "Italian Delegation: Hizbullah Is the Best Answer against Terrorism!" May 28. Available at http://www.english.alahednews.com.lb/essaydetails.php?eid=33497&cid=269#.V39kKIQ03lI.

Albanese, M., G. Bulli, P. Castelli Gattinara, and C. Froio. 2014. *Fascisti di un altro millennio? Crisi e partecipazione in CasaPound Italia*. Rome: Bonano Editore.

Almássy, Ferenc. 2016. Email interview with the author, October 21.

AltRight Radio. 2017. "AltRight Now—1—The Beginning." January 18. Available at https://soundcloud.com/altright/altright-now-1-the-beginning.

American Renaissance. 2013. "The West Faces Many Crises, but the Greatest Is the Crisis of Race." January 7. Available at http://www.amren.com/news/2013/01/announcing-the-2013-american-renaissance-conference/.

Archer, Toby. 2013. "Breivik's Mindset: The Counterjihad and the New Transatlantic Anti-Muslim Right." In *Extreme Right-Wing Political Violence and Terrorism*, ed. Max Taylor, P. M., and Donald Holbrook Currie, 169–85. London: Bloomsbury.

Arteault, Jean-Patrick. 2005. "Guerre culturelle et combat Identitaire." *Terre et Peuple*, n. 25 (Equinox of Autumn): 17–21.

———. 2006. "Être gaulois à l'ère de la mondialisation," *Terre et Peuple*, n. 29 (Equinox of Autumn): 11–20.

———. 2008. "Comprendre le conflit entre la Russie et la Géorgie." *Terre et Peuple*, n. 37 (Equinox of Autumn): 43–52.

———. 2014. "Questions d'Europe." *Terre et Peuple*, n. 59 (Equinox of Spring): 21–26.

Ballast. 2015. "Gérard Chaliand: 'Nous ne sommes pas en guerre." December 22. Available at http://www.revue-ballast.fr/gerard-chaliand/.

Bardèche, Maurice. 1994. *Sparte et les sudistes*. Originally published in 1969. Reprint, Éditions Pythéas.

Barenaked Islam. 2015. "NO TO 'THE GREAT REPLACEMENT,' Says "Generation Identity" Representing the Youth of Europe against Massive Muslim Immigration and Islamization." August 6. Available at http://www.barenakedislam.com/2015/06/08/no-to-the-great-replacement-says-generation-identity-representing-the-youth-of-europe-against-massive-muslim-immigration-and-islamization/.

Bar-On, Tamir. 2013. *Rethinking the French New Right: Alternatives to Modernity*. London: Routledge.

Bassin, M., and K. E. Aksenov. 2006. "Mackinder and the Heartland Theory in Post-Soviet Geopolitical Discourse." *Geopolitics* no. 11, 99–118.

Bauer, Shane. 2017. "I Met the White Nationalist Who 'Falcon Punched' a 95-Pound Female Protester." *Mother Jones*, May 9. Available at http://www.motherjones.com/politics/2017/05/nathan-damigo-punching-woman-berkeley-white-nationalism/#.

Beauregard, Didier. 2016. "Racisme: C'est mon people qu'on assassine!" March 23. Available at http://www.polemia.com/racisme-cest-mon-peuple-quon-assassine/.

Bérard, Pierre. 2009. "La rebellion est-elle possible?" *éléments pour la civilisation européenne*, n. 132 (July–September), 30–36.

Berčík, Adam. 2017. Email interview with the author, April 9.
Bissuel, Steven. 2017. "Parla Bastion Social: Diventiamo movimento nazionale: Il Gud cambia pelle." August 30. Available at http://www.ilprimatonazionale.it/esteri/parla-bastion-social-diventiamo-movimento-nazionale-il-gud-cambia-pelle-71868/.
Bloc Identitaire. n.d. "Qu'est-ce que le Bloc Identitaire?" Available at http://www.bloc-identitaire.com/files/file/plaquette_bloc.pdf.
———. 2005. "Photos: Hommage à Louis Rossel." November 11. Available at http://www.bloc-identitaire.com/album/16/hommage-a-louis-rossel.
———. 2011. "Toulouse, 14 décembre 2011: Racisme anti-blanc; Les souchiens montrent les crocs." Available at http://www.bloc-identitaire.com/video/480/toulouse-14-decembre-proces-bouteldja-souchiens-montrent-crocs.
———. 2014. "Assises de la Remigration—infos pratiques sur le grand rendez-vous du 15 novembre à Paris." November 11. Available at http://www.bloc-identitaire.com/actualite/3198/assises-remigration-infos-pratiques-grand-rendez-vous-15-novembre-paris.
———. 2015. "Charlie Hebdo: Personne ne pourra prétendre lutter contre le djihadisme sans remettre en cause l'immigration massive et l'islamisation." January 7. Available at http://www.bloc-identitaire.com/actualite/3212/charlie-hebdo-personne-ne-pourra-pretendre-lutter-contre-djihadisme-sans-remettre-cause-immigration-massive-et-islamisation.
Blocco Studentesco. 2006. "Chi Siamo." Available at http://www.bloccostudentesco.org/blocco-studentesco/chi-siamo.html.
———. 2015. "Il simbolo." Available at http://bloccostudentesco.org/blocco-studentesco/simbolo.html.
Bobby Sands Trust. 2010. "Trust Condemns Italian Group." December 29. Available at http://www.bobbysandstrust.com/archives/1935.
Boldyrev, Boris. 1994. "Le feu sous la cendre: Les idées nationales en Russie." *Enquête Sur l'Histoire*, n. 9 (Winter): 63–66.
Boulevard Voltaire. 2016. "Jean-Yves le Gallou—Le grand remplacement? Un fantasme vous dis je." May 31. Available at http://www.bvoltaire.fr/jeanyveslegallou/le-grand-remplacement-un-fantasme-vous-dis-je,259874.
Bourseiller, Christophe. 2012. *L'Extrémisme: Une grande peur contemporaine*. Paris: CNRS Éditions.
Bousquet, François. 2015. "Michel Foucault: Notre siècle neoliberal porte son nom." *éléments pour la civilisation européenne*, n. 154 (January–March): 68–73.

———. 2016. "#ColloqueILIADE: L'idéologie Big Other, les autres avant les nôtres." April 17. Available at http://institut-iliade.com/colloqueiliade-lideologie-big-other-les-autres-avant-les-notres/.

Branquinho, Duarte. 2016a. Email interview with the author, February 1.

———. 2016b. *Ideias a Contracorrente*. Lisbon: IAEGCA.

Breitbart. 2016a. "Green Party Headquarters Bricked Up in Protest against Mass Migration Policies." August 2. Available at http://www.breitbart.com/london/2016/08/02/identitarians-brick-austrian-green-party-hq/.

———. 2016b. "Identitarians Occupy Brandenburg Gate, Slam Chancellor Merkel." August 27. Available at http://www.breitbart.com/london/2016/08/27/identitarians-occupy-brandenburg-gate-slam-chancellor-angela-merkel/.

———. 2017a. "Orban Easter Speech: 'Battlefield Europe . . . Stop Mass Migration. The Future of Europe Is at Stake.'" April 16. Available at http://www.breitbart.com/london/2017/04/16/battlefield-europe-stop-mass-migration-future-europe-viktor-orban/.

———. 2017b. "Exclusive: Paris Generation Identitaire Leader: 'This Is the Last Election We Have' to Make Powerful Solutions for France's Future.'" May 5. Available at http://www.breitbart.com/london/2017/05/05/paris-generation-identitaire-leader-mass-migration-islamisation-future-europe/.

———. 2017c. "Identitarian Activists Donate Goods to Hungarian Border Guards to Congratulate Their Success in Reducing Mass Migration." October 5. Available at http://www.breitbart.com/london/2017/10/05/identitarian-activists-donate-goods-hungarian-border-guards-reducing-mass-migration/.

Breizh-Info. 2016a. "Pourquoi écrire sur la guerre civile? Par Laurent Obertone." September 29. Available at http://www.breizh-info.com/2016/09/29/50513/guerre-civile-laurent-obertone-guerilla.

———. 2016b. "Entretien—Alain de Benoist." November 9. Available at http://www.breizh-info.com/2016/11/10/52839/alain-de-benoist-9-novembre-1989-chute-mur-de-berlin-9-novembre-2016-election-de-donald-trump-interview.

Breizh-Info. 2017. "Atalante Québec: 'L'Europe est pour nous une sorte de boule de cristal pour notre avenir.'" Interview, September 3. Available at https://www.breizh-info.com/2017/09/03/76820/atalante-quebec-europe-canada-boule-cristal#disqus_thread.

Brubaker, Rogers. 2017. "Between Nationalism and Civilizationism: The European Populist Moment in Comparative Perspective." *Ethnic and Racial Studies* 40, n. 8 (March): 1191–1226.

Brzezinski, Zbigniew. 1997. *The Great Chessboard: American Primacy and Its Geostrategic Imperatives*. New York: Basic Books.

Busher, Joel. 2016. *The Making of Anti-Muslim Protest: Grassroots Activism in the English Defence League*. London: Routledge.

Cagnat, Alain. 2009. "L'Europe et ses frontières." *Terre et Peuple*, n. 40 (Solstice of Summer): 16–29.

———. 2013. "Demain les guerres?" December 6. Available at http://euro-synergies.hautetfort.com/archive/2013/12/06/alain-cagnat-demain-les-guerres-5239568.html.

———. 2014a. "Europe, Eurasie, EuroSibérie, l'éclairage géopolitique." *Terre et Peuple*, n. 59 (Equinox of Spring): 14–20.

———. 2014b. "Deux hirondelles ne font pas le printemps." *Terre et Peuple*, n. 62 (Solstice of Winter): 10–13.

———. 2015a. "La fulgurante expansion Arabo-Musulmane." *Terre et Peuple*, n. 65 (Equinox of Autumn): 23–25.

———. 2015b. "Islam ou Islamisme?" *Terre et Peuple*, n. 65 (Equinox of Autumn): 26–29.

Cahuzac, Yannick, and Stéphane François. 2013. "Les stratégies de communication de la mouvance identitaire: Le cas du Bloc identitaire." *Questions de communication*, n. 23, 275–92.

Cammelli, Madalena Gretel. 2015. *Fascisti del terzo millennio: Per un'antropologia di CasaPound*. Verona: Ombre Corte.

Camus, Renaud. 2013a. "Discours de Notre-Dame du 31 mai 2013." May 31. Available at http://www.le-non.fr/textes/#Venner.

———. 2013b. "Discours de Renaud Camus du 8 décembre 2013." December 8. Available at http://www.le-non.fr/textes/#discours.

———. 2013c. *Le Changement de Peuple*. Self-published.

———. 2014. "Révoltez-vous, nom de Dieu!" *Réfléchir & Agir*, n. 46 (Winter): 30–34.

———. 2015. "European Politics and the Future: A Conversation with Renaud Camus, Part I." Right On. December 10. Available at https://www.righton.net/2015/12/10/the-great-replacement-part-i/.

———. 2016. "Même la guerre c'était mieux avant." July 20. Available at https://twitter.com/RenaudCamus/status/755714190606827520.

Casadio, Massimiliano Capra. 2014. "The New Right and Metapolitics in France and Italy." *Journal for the Study of Radicalism* 8, n. 1 (Spring): 45–86.

Casajus, Emmanuel. 2014. *Le Combat Culturel: Images et Actions chez les Identitaires*. Paris: L'Harmattan.

CasaPound Italia. n.d. "F.A.Q." Available at http://www.casapounditalia.org/p/le-faq-di-cpi.html.

———. 2011. "Una nazione: Il programma politico di CasaPound Italia." Available at http://94.23.251.8/~casapoun/images/unanazione.pdf.

———. 2013. "Chávez, CasaPound lo ricorda con striscioni in 50 città." March 11. Available at http://www.casapounditalia.org/2013/03/chavez-casapound-lo-ricorda-con.html.

———. 2014. "Ucraina, CasaPound: Sovranità riconquistata con sforzo eroico, ora attenti a sirene Ue e Nato." February 24. Available at http://www.casapounditalia.org/2014/02/ucraina-casapound-sovranita.html.

———. 2015a. "Roma, CasaPound há partecipato al corteo per la chiusura del Centro Enea." March 28. Available at http://www.casapounditalia.org/2015/03/roma-casapound-ha-partecipato-al-corteo.html.

———. 2015b. "CasaPound, striscioni di solidarietà in 60 città per Hogar Social Madrid." May. Available at http://casapounditalia.org/2015/05/casapound-striscioni-di-solidarieta-in.html.

———. 2015c. "Grecia: Delegazione CasaPound ad Atene consegna 10 tonnellate di aiuti umanitari e li distribuisce con Alba Dorata." September 2. Available at http://www.casapounditalia.org/2015/09/grecia-delegazione-casapound-ad-atene.html.

——— 2015d. "Alba Dorata: 'Manolis e Giorgos Immortali,' in 100 città italiane l'omaggio di CasaPound ai caduti di Atene." November 1. Available at http://www.casapounditalia.org/2015/11/alba-doratamanolis-e-giorgos-immortali.html.

———. 2017a. "CasaPound, banchetti in 100 città, al via la raccolta firme | per il Reddito Nazionale di Natalità nel giorno della festa del papà." March 19. Available at http://www.casapounditalia.org/2017/03/casapound-banchetti-in-100-citta-al-via.html.

CasaPound Italia. 2017b. "La bandiera della #Siria." April 7. Available at https://www.facebook.com/casapounditalia/photos/a.1943323 27841.12 7257.193902102841/10154636410212842/?type=3.

CasaPound Italia Facebook. 2015a. "Grecia: Delegazione CasaPound ad Atene consegna 10 tonnellate di aiuti umanitari e li distribuisce con Alba Dorata." September 2. Available at http://www.casapounditalia.org/2015/09/grecia-delegazione-casapound-ad-atene.html.

———. 2015b. "No Ius soli: La cittadinanza non si regala." October 17. Available at http://www.casapounditalia.org/2015/10/ius-soli-casapound-mette-striscioni-in.html.

———. 2016. "Un appuntamento imperdibile a CasaPound." February 17. Available at https://www.facebook.com/casapounditalia/photos/a.19433 2327841.127257.193902102841/10153529717582842/?type=3.

CasaPound Italia—International. 2015. "About." Available at https://www.facebook.com/CasaPound-International-882078118574002/.

CasaPound Italia Milano. 2015. "Sabato 17 Ottobre dale ora 15 raccolta alimentare per le famiglie Italiane in difficoltà." November 3. Available at http://www.casapoundlombardia.org/index.php/en/milano/618-milano-raccolta-alimentare-per-le-famiglie-italiane-in-difficolta.

Casey, Patrick. 2017. Email interview with the author, December 8.

Cassen, Pierre. 2014. "La remigration pour éviter l'islamisation." November 13. Available at http://www.bvoltaire.fr/pierrecassen/remigration-eviter-lislamisation,138384.

———. 2016. "Ce sont toujours des Kelkal, Merah, Nemmouche, Kouachi frères, Coulibaly, Abdeslam qui tuent des infidèles, au nom de leurs textes sacrés." June 15. *Boulevard Voltaire*, available at http://www.bvoltaire.fr/pierrecassen/entre-la-france-et-lislam-la-separation-devient-urgente,262795.

Cassen, Pierre, and Christine Tasin, eds. 2011. *18 décembre 2010: Assises internationales sur l'islamisation de nos pays*. Paris: Éditions Riposte Laïque.

Castriota, Anna, and Matthew Feldman. 2014. "'Fascism for the Third Millennium': An Overview of Language and Ideology in Italy's Casapound Movement." In *Doublespeak: The Rhetoric of the Far Right since 1945*, ed. Matthew Feldman and Paul Jackson, 223–46. Stuttgart: *ibidem*-Verlag.

Cattin, Jean-David. 2016. "Victoire de Donald Trump: Un tournant historique." November 9. Available at http://www.les-identitaires.com/2016/11/victoire-de-donald-trump-tournant-historique/.

Cau, Jean. 1974. "Marx et Coca Cola." *éléments pour la civilisation européenne*, nn. 8–9 (November): 40.

CCC (Center for Continental Cooperation). 2015. "About Us." available at http://greater-europe.org/about.

———. 2016a. "European Identitarianism and Russian Eurasianism: An Interview with Martin Sellner." April 12. Available at http://greater-europe.org/archives/800.

———. 2016b. "The Continental Center Discussed Europe's Liberation from Transatlanticism." July 21. Available at http://greater-europe.org/archives/1371.

Cercle Non Conforme. 2015. "Entrevue # 21: Adriano Scianca, responsible culturel de CasaPound Italia." July 20. Available at http://cerclenoncon

forme.hautetfort.com/archive/2015/07/20/entrevue-21-adriano-sciancn-responsable-ca-5659592.html.

Chatov, Pierre. 2007. "Vers un crepuscule des militants?" *ID Magazine*, n. 9 (Spring); 9.

Chauprade, Aymeric. 2006. "Ce que reserve l'avenir." *Nouvelle Revue d'Histoire*, n. 22 (January–February): 59–61.

———. 2013a. *Chronique du choc des civilisations*. Paris: Chronique Éditions.

———. 2013b. "Entretien exclusif—Aymeric Chauprade: 'Je crois que la France va s'en sortir.'" October 24. Available at http://fr.novopress.info/142732/aymeric-chauprade-grand-remplacement-ethnique-nest-donc-pas-illusion/.

Christen, Yves. 2014. "Les ambiguités du transhumanisme." *éléments pour la civilisation européenne*, n. 152 (July–September): 56–58.

Chua, Amy. 2004. *World on Fire: How Exporting Free Market Democracy Breeds Ethnic Hatred and Global Instability*. London: Arrow Books.

Cicero, Marcus Tullius. 1856. *The Orations of Marcus Tullius Cicero*. Literally translated by C. D. Yonge, B.A., London, and Henry G. Bohn. London: York Street, Covent Garden.

Circolo Futurista. n.d. *Circolo Futurista*. Available at http://www.circolofuturista.org/?page_id=4.

CNRE. 2017. "Conseil National de la Résistance Européenne.: Allocution de Renaud Camus Colombey-les-Deux-Églises." November 9. Available at https://www.cnre.eu/camus-colombey.

Compact magazine. 2016. "Der Konformisten-Schocker: Identitäre erklimmen Brandenburger Tor." August. Available at https://www.compact-online.de/identitaere-erklimmen-brandenburger-tor/.

Conrad, Philippe. 1996. "La Reconquista espagnole." *Enquête sur l'Histoire*, n. 15 (Winter): 25–28.

———. 2014. "L'Été tragique de 1914." *Nouvelle Revue d'Histoire*. Hors Série, n. 8, 5.

———. 2015a. "Discerner les continuités qui donnent au monde européen son identité." April 20. Available at http://www.lerougeetlenoir.org/opinions/les-inquisitoriales/philippe-conrad-discerner-les-continuites-qui-donnent-au-monde-europeen-son-identite.

———. 2015b. "Vers l'explosion de la poudrière mondiale." *Iliade*, June 23. Available at http://institut-iliade.com/vers-lexplosion-de-la-poudriere-mondiale/.

———. 2016a. "Éditorial—Une religion sûre d'elle et dominatrice." *Nouvelle Revue d'Histoire*, special issue, n. 12 (Spring–Summer): 5.

———. 2016b. "La dhimmitude, un statut d'infériorité." *Nouvelle Revue d'Histoire*, special issue, n. 12 (Spring–Summer): 20–21.

———. 2016c. "Une révolution culturelle pour renouer avec le fil de l'aventure européenne." April 7. Available at http://www.lerougeetlenoir.org/opinions/les-inquisitoriales/philippe-conrad-une-revolution-culturelle-pour-renouer-avec-le-fil-de-l-aventure-europeenne.

———. 2016d. "La longue et riche histoire de la Hongrie." *Nouvelle Revue d'Histoire*, n. 87 (November–December). Available at https://www.la-nrh.fr/2016/11/editorial-et-sommaire-du-n87-novembre-decembre-2016/.

Coussedière, Vincent. 2012. *Éloge du populisme*. Grenoble: Elya Editions.

CREA. 2016. "L'Islamisme, mais bien sur c'est l'extreme droite!" *Réfléchir & Agir*, n. 53 (Summer): 31–32.

Dard, Olivier. 2015. "De la 'Défense de l'Occident' à 'l'Occident comme déclin.'" In *Références et Thèmes des Droites radicales au XX Siècle Europe-Amériques*, ed. Olivier Dard, 304–19. Bern: Peter Lang.

De Benoist, Alain. 1992. "C'est encore loin, l'Amérique?" In *États-Unis: Danger*. Actes du XXV colloque national du GRECE. Paris: Éditions du Labyrinthe, 33–55.

———. 1993. "Three Interviews with Alain de Benoist." *Telos* 98–99 (December 1993–May 1994): 173–207.

———. 2001. *Dernière Année: Notes pour conclure le siècle*. Lausanne, Switzerland: L'Age d'Homme.

———. 2004. "Entretien paru dans le magazine 'Terre et Peuple,' 2004." Available at https://s3-eu-west-1.amazonaws.com/alaindebenoist/pdf/entretien_terre_et_peuple.pdf.

———. 2005. "European Son." *Occidental Quarterly* 5, n. 3 (Fall): 7–27. Available at https://www.toqonline.com/archives/v5n3/53-bs-debenoist.pdf.

———. 2006. *Nous et les autres: Problématique de l'identité*. Paris: Krisis.

———. 2007. *Carl Schmitt Actuel*. Paris: Éditions Krisis.

———. 2008. "L'Europa tra delusione e speranza." *Diorama Letterario* 287 (January–February): 1–15.

———. 2013a. "Lorsque le capital ne produit plus assez de valeur, c'est l'ensemble de la société qui peut être appelée à se revolter." *Réfléchir & Agir*, n. 44 (Summer): 33–37.

———. 2013b. "Les raisons de vivre et les raisons de mourir sont bient souvent les memes." *éléments pour la civilisation européenne*, n. 148 (July–September): 31.

———. 2013c. "En finir avec 'le racisme'?" *éléments pour la civilisation européenne*, n. 149 (October–December): 32–37.

———. 2014a. "Envers et contre tout l'Europe!" *éléments pour la civilisation européenne*, n. 151 (April–June), 38–42.

———. 2014b. "Alain de Benoist Answers Tamir Bar-On." *Journal for the Study of Radicalism* 8, n. 1 (Spring): 141–68.

———. 2015a. "L'Identité?" *Krisis, Revue d'Idées et de Débats*, n. 40 (March): 2–8.

———. 2015b. *On the Brink of the Abyss: The Imminent Bankruptcy of the Financial System*. London: Arktos.

———. 2016a. "Une société flottante." *éléments pour la civilisation européenne*, n. 160 (May–June): 3.

———. 2016b. "À l'Est, du nouveau." *éléments pour la civilisation européenne*, n. 163 (November–December): 3.

———. 2017. "Trois tigres et un canard sans tête." *éléments pour la civilisation européenne*, n. 165 (April–May): 3.

———. 2018. "Entretien avec Alain De Benoist—'La Grande Transformation, plutôt que le Grand Remplacement.'" February 28. Available at http://www.bvoltaire.fr/entretien-alain-de-benoist-grande-transformation-plutot-grand-remplacement/.

De Benoist, Alain, and Alexander Dugin. 2014. *Qué es el Eurasismo? Una conversación de Alain de Benoist con Alexander Dugin*. Tarragona, Spain: Ediciones Fides.

De Benoist, Alain, and Charles Champetier. 2012. *Manifesto for a European Renaissance*, trans. Isabel Martin Bendelow and Francis Greene. London: Arktos.

Defend Europe. 2017. "Our Mission." May 14. Available at http://defend-europe.org/en/the-mission_fr/.

Defend Europe. 2018. "Defend Europe Alps Mission: Generation Identity Makes the Government Capitulate on Massive Immigration." April 24. Available at https://www.facebook.com/DefendEuropeID/photos /a.158179831397278.1073741828.157953414753253/242573619624565 /?type=3.

De Geyndt, Bo. 2017. Email interview with the author, October 23.

De Herte, Robert. 1980. "Ni des esclaves, ni des robots." *éléments pour la civilisation européenne*, n. 34 (Spring): 2.

——— 1991. "L'Amérique, c'est Carthage." *éléments pour la civilisation européenne*, n. 70 (Spring): 3.

———. 2004. "Liberté, égalité, identité." *éléments pour la civilisation européenne*, n. 113 (Summer): 3.

———. 2009. "Russie, Europe, Même Combat!" *éléments pour la civilisation européenne*, n. 131 (April–June): 3.

———. 2010. "La quatrieme dimension." *éléments pour la civilisation européenne*, n. 136 (July–September): 3.
De Lamberterie, Nicolas. 2014. "Entretien: Márton Gyöngyösi." *Réfléchir & Agir*, n. 46 (Winter): 39–43.
Delrieux, Arnaud. 2016a. "Génération Identitaire: 'Ce combat pour l'identité est une question de survie.'" March 16. Available at http://fr.novopress.info/199660/arnaud-delrieux-generation-identitaire-ce-combat-lidentite-question-survie/.
———. 2016b. "'Le danger N1 pour l'Europe c'est la Russie pas le terrorisme.'" July 20. Available at https://twitter.com/ArnaudDelrieux/status/755792568198234112.
———. 2016c. "50 années d'immigration incontrôlée." September 7. Available at https://twitter.com/ArnaudDelrieux/status/773566966024003584.
———. 2016d. "Le sujet de la présidentielle ce doit être celui la." September 23. Available at https://twitter.com/ArnaudDelrieux/status/779535256164638720.
———. 2017. "Diffamatoire: L'Obs ne sait plus quoi faire pour vendre son torchon." March 12. Available at https://twitter.com/ArnaudDelrieux/status/840983507694411776.
Délský potápěč. n.d. "Proč název, Délský potápěč?" Available at https://www.facebook.com/delian.diver/about/?entry_point=page_nav_about_item&tab=page_info.
Délský potápěč. 2017. Email interview with Jiri, October 19.
De Villiers, Philippe. 2016. "On sait que là où l'Islam s'est installé, la Reconquista a pris six siècles." *France*, n. 2 (June): 16–25.
Devlin, Roger. 2013. "Generation Identity Introduces Itself." December 13. Available at http://www.counter-currents.com/2013/12/generation-identity-introduces-itself/.
Dewitt, Bain. 2015. "The Erasure and Subsequent Re-emergence of Racial Consciousness amongst White Europeans." March 11. Facebook post.
D'Her, Pierre. 2007. "'Au commencement était l'action.'" *ID Magazine*, n. 9 (Spring): 2–3.
Digital Crusades. 2012. "Permanent Media War: The Strategic Provocation of Bloc Identitaire & an Interview with Fabrice Robert." March 29. Available at http://www.bloc-identitaire.com/files/file/Digital_Crusades_29mars2012.pdf.
Dissidence Française. 2015. "Entrétien avec Réfléchir & Agir." October 7. Available at https://la-dissidence.org/2015/10/07/entretien-avec-reflechir-agir/.

Di Stefano, Simone. 2015a. "Io sono fiero di essere una bestia." September 7. Available at https://it-it.facebook.com/distefanocasapound/posts/728505640586662?fref=nf.

———. 2015b. "A Bologna con Salvini, Di Stefano CP: 'Ecco come andremo nella cità rossa.'" *IntelligoNews*, October 20. Available at http://www.intelligonews.it/articoli/20-ottobre-2015/31942/a-bologna-con-salvini-di-stefano-cp-ecco-come-andremo-nella-citt-rossa.

———. 2015c. "Parigi, Casapound: 'E' il fallimento dell'Europa: Leggasi Salah; Culturalmente impreparati per l'emergenza.'" November 23. Available at http://www.intelligonews.it/articoli/23-novembre-2015/33503/parigi-casapound-e-il-fallimento-dell-europa-leggasi-salah-culturalmente-impreparati-per-l-emergenza.

———. 2016. "Di Stefano: 'No al Referendum è anche vittoria di CasaPound: Ora elezioni súbito.'" December 5. Available at http://www.ilprimatonazionale.it/politica/di-stefano-no-al-referendum-e-anche-vittoria-di-casapound-ora-elezioni-subito-54009/.

———. 2017. "Erdogan invita I turchi che vivono in Europa fare almeno 5 figli 'perché cosi fra poco l'Europa sarà vostra'!" March 18. Available at https://www.facebook.com/distefanocasapound/posts/1070297509740805.

Dragan, Robert. 2015. "Faux Drapeau." *Terre et Peuple*, n. 63 (Equinox of Spring): 23–27.

Duarte, D. 1982. *O Leal Conselheiro*. Ed. João Morais Barbosa. Lisbon: IN-CM.

Dugin, Alexander. 2012a. "Interview with Alexander Dugin." July 27. Available at http://www.counter-currents.com/2012/07/interview-with-alexander-dugin/.

———. 2012b. "Eurasian Keys to the Future." August. Available at http://www.geopolitika.ru/en/article/eurasian-keys-future#.U63CdVTD_0M.

———. 2013. "Alexander Dugin on 'White Nationalism' & Other Potential Allies in the Global Revolution." Counter-Currents Publishing, June. Available at http://www.counter-currents.com/2013/06/alexander-dugin-on-white-nationalism/.

———. 2014. "The Multipolar World and the Postmodern." *Journal of Eurasian Affairs*. May 14. Available at http://www.eurasianaffairs.net/the-multipolar-world-and-the-postmodern/.

———. 2016a. "Europe vs. The West." August 2. Available at http://katehon.com/article/europe-vs-west.

———. 2016b. "Donald Trump's Victory." November 10. Available at http://katehon.com/article/donald-trumps-victory.
Duke, David. 2015. "J'appelle à la libération des peuples Européens." *Réfléchir & Agir*, n. 51 (Autumn): 38–42.
Dumont, Gérard-François. 2014. "Histoire et démographie—Propos recueillis par Pauline Lecomte." *Nouvelle Revue d'Histoire*, n. 72 (May–June): 10–15.
Dupré, Tom. 2018. Email interview with the author, April 4.
Durolle, Thierry. 2017. "À la découverte de l'Alt Right." *Réfléchir & Agir*, n. 55 (Winter): 31–32.
Dutton, Edward, and Richard Lynn. 2015. "A Negative Flynn Effect in France, 1999 to 2008–9." *Intelligence*, n. 51: 67–70.
EAS. 2018. *Dominique Venner: El enviado de Homero*. Torrevieja (Alicante): Editorial EAS.
Eibl-Eibesfeldt, Irenäus. 2007. "Us and the Others." In *Ethnic Conflict and Indoctrination: Altruism and Identity in Evolutionary Perspective*, ed. Irenäus Eibl-Eibesfeldt and Frank K. Salter, 35–52. New York: Berghahn Books.
EFSS (European Front of Solidarity with Syria). 2013. "Chi Siamo." Available at http://www.frontesiria.org/?page_id=60.
éléments blog. 2014. "De Benoist—Ukraine: La fin de la guerre froid n'a jamais eu lieu." March 23. Available at http://blogelements.typepad.fr/blog/2014/03/laffaire-ukrainienne-est-une-affaire-complexe-et-aussi-une-affaire-grave-à-une-autre-époque-et-en-dautres-circonstan.html.
éléments pour la civilisation européenne. 2009. Cover. n. 131 (April–June).
———. 2015. "Les ambiguïtés du 'multiculturalisme.'" n. 155 (April–June), 58–62.
———. 2016a. "Entretien avec Jean-Yves le Gallou 'Non à l'immigration! Propos recueillis par Pascal Eysseric.'" n. 159 (March–April): 32–33.
———. 2016b. "Juin éphémérides." n. 160 (May–June): 95.
Engels, David. 2013. "L'Europe ne peut pas echapper a son destin imperial." *éléments pour la civilisation européenne*, n. 148 (July–September): 6–9.
———. 2017. Email interview with the author, October 9.
Enquête & Débat. 2015. "Guillaume Faye: 'La convergence des catastrophes est en train d'arriver.'" February 20. Available at http://www.enquete-debat.fr/archives/guillaume-faye-la-convergence-des-catastrophes-est-en-train-darriver-61535.
Enzensberger, Hans Magnus. 1994. *Civil Wars: From L.A. to Bosnia*. New York: The New Press.
Erkenbrand. 2017. "Erkenbrand: Towards a New Golden Age." October 14. Available at https://www.youtube.com/watch?v=JrmoBJdbTHw.

Espresso. 2012. "Roma, Casapound spiazza tutti." February 8. Available at http://espresso.repubblica.it/palazzo/2012/02/08/news/roma-casapound-spiazza-tutti-1.40175.

Europe-Identité. 2008. "Qui-sommes-nous?" n.d. Previously available at http://www.europe-identite.com/. Site no longer available.

European Identity blog. "About us." Available at http://europe-identity.tumblr.com/about.

Euro-Rus. n.d. "About." Available at https://www.facebook.com/paneuropeism/about/.

Exif—Recherche & Analyse. 2017. "Die 'Identitäre bewegung' in Norddeutschland." February 3. Available at https://exif-recherche.org/?p=577.

Eysseric, Pascal. 2015. "Les deux faces du libéralisme." *éléments pour la civilisation européenne*, n. 154 (January–March): 52–53.

Fanjul, Serafín. 2009. "Uses of a Myth: Al-Andalus." *Studies in 20th & 21st Century Literature* 33, n. 2, article 3. Available at http://dx.doi.org/10.4148/2334-4415.1700.

Farage, Nigel. 2017. "This Says a Lot . . . ." August 14. Available at https://www.facebook.com/nigelfarageofficial/posts/1434271503287115.

Favrit, Bruno. 2013 "L'Éternel retour du soleil invaincu." *Jean Mabire: Magazine des Amis de Jean Mabire*, n. 39 (Solstice of Summer): 4.

Faye, Guillaume. 1981. *Le Système à tuer les peuples*. Paris: Copernic.

———. 1986. "Panem et Circenses: A Critique of 'The West.'" *The Scorpion*, n. 9 (Spring): 4–5.

———. 1997. "Exclusif: Guillaume Faye; L'Anti-Pape de la Nouvelle Droite." *Réfléchir & Agir*, n. 2 (1st trimester): 38–41.

———. 2001. "La Pensée Délinquante: La Guerre Nécessaire." *Terre et Peuple—La Revue*, n. 10 (Solstice of Winter): 7–8.

———. 2007a. "Le bloc-notes de Guillaume Faye." *Terre et Peuple*, n. 32 (Summer): 12–14.

———. 2007b. *La Nouvelle Question Juive*. Paris: Les Editions du Lore.

———. 2011. *Why We Fight: Manifesto of the European Resistance*, trans. and intro. by Michael O'Meara. London: Arktos.

———. 2012a. *Convergence of Catastrophes*, trans. E. Christian Kopff. London: Arktos.

———. 2012b. "La Russie sauvera l'Europe." November 9. Available at http://french.ruvr.ru/radio_broadcast/5646129/93663540/.

———. 2013. "Islamisation de la France: Prophétie." *J'ai Tout Compris—Blog de Guillaume Faye*. Available at http://www.gfaye.com/islamisation-de-la-france-prophetie/.

———. 2015. *Comprendre l'Islam*. Paris: Tatamis.

———. 2016a. *The Colonization of Europe*. Originally published in 2000. Reprint, London: Arktos.

———. 2016b. "The Intentional Genocide of European Peoples?" March 1. Available at http://www.counter-currents.com/2016/03/the-intentional-genocide-of-european-peoples/.

———. 2016c. "Who Is Pope Francis Really?," trans. Hannibal Bateman. April 29. Available at https://www.righton.net/2016/04/29/who-is-pope-francis-really/.

———. 2016d. "Le Pape François et la soumission à l'islam." *J'ai Tout Compris—Blog de Guillaume Faye*. June 6. Available at http://www.gfaye.com/le-pape-francois-et-la-soumission-a-lislam/.

———. 2016e. "Racisme islamique et complicite d'Etat." August 4. Available at http://www.gfaye.com/racisme-islamique-et-complicite-detat/.

———. 2016f. "Trump, révolution ou simulacre? 3 Risque d'échec ou d'explosion." November 21. Available at http://www.gfaye.com/trump-revolution-ou-simulacre-3-risque-dechec-ou-dexplosion/.

———. 2016g. "Fillon contre Marine: Qui choisir? Marion." December 18. Available at https://www.gfaye.com/fillon-contre-marine-qui-choisir-marion/.

———. 2017. "Terrorisme musulman 'low cost': La contagion." April 5. Available at https://www.gfaye.com/terrorisme-musulman-low-cost-la-contagion/.

Faye, Guillaume, Pierre Freson, and Robert Steuckers. 1985. *Le Petit Lexique du partisan européen*. Vouloir archives.

Feltin-Tracol, Georges. 2013. "Europe Mad Max demain? Retour à la defense citoyenne, de Bernard Witch." September 9. Available at http://www.polemia.com/europe-mad-max-demain-retour-a-la-defense-citoyenne-de-bernard-wicht/.

———. 2014. Notes de lecture *Réfléchir & Agir*, n. 46 (Winter): p. 58.

———. 2016a. Email interview with the author, August 12.

———. 2016b. *Éléments pour une pensée extrême*. Les Éditions du Lore.

Ferrier, Thomas. 2013. "Guillaume Faye et la Russie." *Le Blog Thomas Ferrier*, November 30. Available at http://thomasferrier.hautetfort.com/guillaume-faye/.

Figaro. 2011. "Le Bloc identitaire s'en prend à une ville." November 4. Available at http://www.lefigaro.fr/flash-actu/2011/11/04/97001-20111104 FILWWW00463-le-bloc-identitaire-s-en-prend-a-une-ville.php.

———. 2014. "Le malheur identitaire est plus grave que le malheur économique." July 4. Available at http://www.lefigaro.fr/vox/monde/2014 /07

/04/31002-20140704ARTFIG00161-herve-juvin-le-malheur-identi taire-est-plus-grave-que-le-malheur-economique-22.php.

———. 2016. "En France, des associations et groupuscules veulent copier Pegida." February 6. Available at http://www.lefigaro.fr/politique/2016/02/06/01002-20160206ARTFIG00005-en-france-des-associations-et-groupuscules-veulent-copier-pegida.php.

Finis Mundi—A Última Cultura. 2014. "De Benoist—A Geopolítica Hoje." n. 7: 159–66.

Finkielkraut, Alain. 2013. *L'Identité malheureuse*. Paris: Gallimard.

Fiorini, Roberto. 2013a. "Capitalisme et immigration." *fdesouche*, July 21. Available at http://www.fdesouche.com/312937-roberto-fiorini-capitalisme-et-immigration.

———. 2013b. "Entretien avec un syndicaliste nationaliste-révolutionnaire." *Réfléchir & Agir*, n. 44 (Summer): 25–29.

FQS (Fédération des Québécois de Souche). 2015. "Compte-rendu: Conférence de CasaPound et du Blocco Studentesco à Montreal." March 7. Available at http://quebecoisdesouche.info/conference-de-casapound-et-du-blocco-studentesco/.

Franco, João. 2014. *Fundamentos Identitários para a pós-modernidade*. Lisbon: Contra-Corrente.

———. 2017. Email interview with the author, March 25.

François, Stéphane. 2014. *Au-delà des vents du nord: L'Extrême droite française, le pôle Nord et les Indo-Européens*. Lyon: Presses universitaires de Lyon.

Franziska, Benita. 2017. "Brittany Pettibone Interviews Young German Identitarian." October 18. Available at https://www.facebook.com/giEIRE/videos/125110004782740/.

Freedman, Lawrence. 2015. *Strategy: A History*. New York: Oxford University Press.

Freund, Julien. 2004. *L'Essence du politique*. Paris: Dalloz.

Friberg, Daniel. 2016a. "Interview with Daniel Friberg by Vlaams Belang." August 13. Available at https://www.righton.net/2016/08/13/interview-with-daniel-friberg-by-vlaams-belang/.

———. 2016b. Email interview with the author, September 15.

———. 2016c. "Europe Rises—Speech at Identitarian Ideas." October 10. Available at https://www.youtube.com/watch?v=TkZp-xyeh8A.

———. 2017. "Entering the New Paradigm." January 17. Available at https://altright.com/2017/01/17/entering-the-new-paradigm/.

Froio, Caterina, and Pietro Castelli Gattinara. 2015. "Neo-fascist Mobilization in Contemporary Italy: Ideology and Repertoire of Action of CasaPound Italia." *Journal for Deradicalization* 15, n. 2 (Spring): 86–118.

Fuerza Nacional-Identitaria. 2015. Email interview with the author, March 10.
Fusaro, Diego. 2015. "Entretien avec Diego Fusaro: À la droite de Marx, à la gauche du capital." *éléments pour la civilisation européenne*, n. 156 (July–September): 42–45.
Gambier, Grégoire. 2015. "L'Institut Iliade met à l'honneur 'l'univers esthétique des Européens." *Éléments le magazine des idées*, n. 155 (April–June), 11.
Gattinara, P., Caterina Froio, and Matteo Albanese. 2013. "The Appeal of Neo-fascism in Times of Crisis: The Experience of CasaPound Italia." *Fascism*, n. 2 (2): 234–58.
Generace Identity. 2016. "Pohřbili jsme Evropskou unii." September 28. Available at http://generace-identity.cz/pohrbili-jsme-evropskou-unii/.
Generacija Identitete Slovenija. 2013. "About." Available at https://www.facebook.com/GeneracijaIdentiteteSLO/about/.
Generatie Identiteit. 2017. "Wij zijn een politieke beweging die jongeren bewust wensen te maken van hun Europese culturele identiteit." Available at https://www.facebook.com/GeneratieIdentiteit/.
Génération Identitaire. 2012. "An Open Declaration of War from The Youth of France—English Subtitles." Available at https://www.youtube.com/watch?v=H-qUx9ydFeU.
———. 2014. "Notre Europe n'est pas votre UE." Available at https://www.generation-identitaire.com/vienne-manifestation-notre-europe-nest-pas-votre-ue/.
———. 2015a. "Le gouvernement socialiste n'expulse pas les islamistes mais il place en garde à vue ceux qui le réclament!" August 29. Available at https://www.generation-identitaire.com/le-gouvernement-socialiste-nexpulse-pas-les-islamistes-mais-il-place-en-garde-a-vue-ceux-qui-le-reclament/.
———. 2015b. "Communiqué de Génération Identitaire: Génération Identitaire lance la grande campagne 'On est chez nous'!" September 15. Available at https://www.facebook.com/GenerationIdentitaire/posts/74794745198 0733.
———. 2015c. "Pleurer, mais ne pas plier: Jeunesse lève toi!" November 15. Available at https://www.generation-identitaire.com/pleurer-mais-ne-pas-plier-jeunesse-leve-toi/.
———. 2016. "Berlin: L'Immigration tue à nouveau!" December 21. Available at https://www.facebook.com/GenerationIdentitaire/photos/a.28 6547528120730.61908.203085803133570/1029560040486138/?type =3&permPage=1.

———. 2017a. "Des militants de Generation identitaire securisent le centre ville de Rouen." April 3. Available at https://www.facebook.com/ginormandie/videos/1889167474698388/?hc_ref=PAGES_TIMELINE.

———. 2017b. "SCANDALE: Génération Identitaire condamné à plus de 40 000 euros d'amende pour l'occupation du chantier de la mosquée islamiste de Poitiers." December 7. Available at https://www.facebook.com/GenerationIdentitaire/posts/1337472823028190.

———. 2018. "Scandale des viols collectifs à Telford—L'antiracisme responsable, des musulmans coupables!" March 19. Available at https://generationidentitaire.org/2018/03/19/scandale-des-viols-collectifs-a-telford-lantiracisme-responsable-des-musulmans-coupables/.

Génération Identitaire Flandre Artois Hainaut. 2016. "Bar identitaire à Lille." October 6. Available at https://www.facebook.com/GIFlandreArtoisHainaut/posts/846775868791769.

Generation Identity. 2013. *We Are Generation Identity*, trans. Roger Devlin. London: Arktos.

———. 2016. "Interdiction de la manifestation à Molenbeek." March 30. Available at https://www.facebook.com/GenerationIdentitaire/videos/836248613150616/.

Generation Identity Éire/Ireland and Northern Ireland. 2018. "They Can't Pull the Wool over our Eyes." March 4. Available at https://www.facebook.com/giEIRE/photos/a.107593893201018.1073741828.101837350443339/152415558718851/?type=3.

Generation Identity London. 2018. "London Activists Were Back Out on the Streets Tonight Handing Out Warm Pork Suppers to the Homeless." March 21. Available at https://www.facebook.com/GenerationIdentityLondon/posts/162997057849678.

Generation Identity UK and Ireland. 2017. Offical site. Available at https://identitarian-movement.org/generation-identity-faqs/.

Generazione Identitaria. 2016. "Islamizzazione non sarà il nostro future." December 23. Available at https://www.facebook.com/GenerazioneIdentitaria/posts/1165592280202649.

———. 2017. "Ai ragazzi de 'L'Indro.'" April 5. Available at https://www.facebook.com/GenerazioneIdentitaria/posts/1257750604320149.

———. 2018. "Bruxelles: Generazione Identitaria intervenuta al Parlamento Europeo." February 22. Available at https://generazione-identitaria.com/2018/02/bruxelles-generazione-identitaria-intervenuta-al-parlamento-europeo/.

Generazione Identitaria Sardegna. 2017. "About." Available at https://www.facebook.com/GenerazioneIdentitariaSardegna/.

Geoffroy, Michel. 2015a. "La bataille du vocabulaire." In *Dictionnaire de Novlangue: Ces 1000 mots qui vous manipulent*, ed. Jean-Yves Le Gallou, Michel Geoffroy, and Polémia, 207–26. Versailles: Via Romana.

———. 2015b. "La novlangue, vision du monde de l'oligarchie." In *Dictionnaire de Novlangue: Ces 1000 mots qui vous manipulent*, ed. Jean-Yves Le Gallou, Michel Geoffroy, and Polémia, 227–31. Versailles: Via Romana.

Gérard, Christopher. 2016. "#ColloqueILIADE: A propos du Camp des saints." April 17. Available at http://institut-iliade.com/colloqueiliade-a-propos-du-camp-des-saints-par-christopher-gerard/.

Gibbon, Edward. 1782. *The History of The Decline and Fall of the Roman Empire*, vol. 5 Project Gutenberg EBook.

Gillieth, Pierre. 2016. "Charles Martel, un héros pour notre temps." *Réfléchir & Agir*, n. 52 (Winter): 12–14.

Gillieth, Pierre, and Eugène Krampon. 2010. "Ou en est notre presse?" *Réfléchir & Agir*, n. 34 (Winter): 17–21.

Giornale. 2015a. "Salvini a Radio Padania: 'Italiani vittime di pulizia etnica.'" February 17. Available at http://www.ilgiornale.it/news/politica/salvini-radio-padania-italiani-vittime-pulizia-etnica-1095227.html.

———. 2015b. "Fermi immigrati ed islam, oppure l'eu esploderà come l'Urss." April 15. Available at http://www.ilgiornale.it/news/pegida-1115459.html.

———. 2017. "CasaPound aiuta i poveri italiani: 'Fascisti?' Ci danno da mangiare." February 20. Available at http://www.ilgiornale.it/news/cronache/casapound-aiuta-poveri-i-italiani-fascisti-ci-danno-mangiare-1366697.html.

Gordon, Jerry. 2012. *The West Speaks*. Nashville, TN: New English Review Press.

Guardian. 2012. "Ezra Pound's Daughter Fights to Wrest the Renegade Poet's Legacy from Fascists." January 14. Available at http://www.theguardian.com/world/2012/jan/14/ezra-pound-daughter-fascism.

———. 2017. "Germany's Top Court Rules against Ban on Far-Right NDP." January 17. Available at https://www.theguardian.com/world/2017/jan/17/germany-s-top-court-rules-against-ban-on-far-right-ndp.

Guillemot, Xavier. 2006. "L'Europe des patries charnelles." *Terre et Peuple*, n. 28 (Solstice of Summer): 23–24.

Günther, Hans. 2013. *Religiosité Indo-Européenne*. Trans. Robert Steuckers. Éditions BIOS.

Hamblin, Robert W., and Charles A. Peek, eds. 1999. *A William Faulkner Encyclopedia*. London: Greenwood.

Hannoversche Allgemeine. 2016. "Jung, hip, rechtsextrem." July 12. Available at http://www.haz.de/Nachrichten/Politik/Deutschland-Welt/Die-Identi taere-Bewegung-hat-Kontakt-zu-AfD-und-NPD.

Harfang—Magazine de la Fédération des Québécois de Souche. 2014. Vol. 2, n. 5 (June–July): 12–13.

Haudry, Jean. 2006. "Thulé, le soleil retrouvé des Hyperboréens." *Terre et Peuple*, n. 28 (Solstice of Summer): 28–30.

———. 2010. "Regards sur les Indo-Européens." *Terre et Peuple*, n. 43 (Equinox of Spring): 55–58.

———. 2015. "Les Indo-Européns, victims posthumes du politiquement correct." *éléments: Le magazine des idées*, n. 155 (April–June): 6–9.

Hauffen, Karl. 2005a. "Porquoi nous sommes Identitaires." *ID Magazine*, n. 1 (Spring): 8–10.

———. 2005b. "Une économie identitaire pour dépasser le libéralisme." *ID Magazine*, n. 1 (Spring): 13–14.

Hawley, George. 2016. *Right-Wing Critics of American Conservatism*. Lawrence: University Press of Kansas.

———. 2017. *Making Sense of the Alt Right*. New York: Columbia University Press.

Hesse, Hermann. 1963. *Steppenwolf.* New York: Modern Library.

Hogar Social Madrid. 2016. "Imágenes de la manifestación." May 23. Available at https://www.youtube.com/watch?v=ViwqeKZ6b54.

Holloway, John. 2005. *Change the World without Taking Power*. London: Pluto Press.

Homer. 1998. *The Iliad*, trans. Samuel Butler. Orange Street Press Classics.

Huffington Post. 2016. "Emails Show How White Nationalists Are Rebranding to Help Donald Trump." April 4. Available at http://www.huffington post.com/entry/donald-trump-american-freedom-party-emails_us_5 702 b470e4b0a06d580659c7.

Huffington Post Deutschland. 2017. "Historiker David Engels: 'Wir haben keine Chance, einen Bürgerkrieg zu vermeiden' by susanne-klaiber." February 1. Available at http://www.huffingtonpost.de/2017/02/01/david -engels-buergerkrieg_n_14546506.html.

Iannone, Gianluca. 2010. "Casapound l'avant-garde italienne." *Réfléchir & Agir*, n. 34 (Winter): 27–29.

———. 2011. "In the House of Pound: An Interview with Gianluca Iannone." *Alternative Right*. Available at http://alternative-right.blogspot.com/2015 /03/in-house-of-pound-interview-with.html.

———. n.d. "Interview." Available at http://zentropaville.tumblr.com/post /61853752321/interview-gianluca-iannone.

---. 2014. "Intervista a Gianluca Iannone, fondatore di CasaPound Italia." *Secolo Trentino*. November 9. Available at http://www.secolo-trentino.com/15526/politica/intervista-gianluca-iannone-fondatore-casa-pound-italia.html.

---. 2015a. "Exclusiva, Iannone CasaPound: 'Con Salvini convergenza su tre temi, no patto di sangue.'" *Intelligonews*, March 5. Available at http://www.atuttadestra.net/index.php/archives/278193.

---. 2015b. "Il lato pop di CasaPound: 'Playboy' intervista Iannone." *Secolo d'Italia*, October 12. Available at http://www.secoloditalia.it/2015/10/lato-pop-casa pound-playboy-intervista-iannone/.

---. 2015c. "Une manifestation pour dire aux ennemis de l'Europe: Nous sommes là!" *Zentropa*, November 16. Available at http://zentropaville.tumblr.com/post/13 3787617768/iannone-une-manifestation-pour-dire-aux-ennemis.

IBD (Identitäre Bewegung Deutschland). 2015. "Der große Austausch! #derAu stausch." May 2. Available at https://www.facebook.com/identitaere/photos/a.58 3269085024488.1073741828.581482171869846/995464920471567/?type=3 &theater.

---. 2016a. "Briten verlassen EU!" June 24. Available at https://www.facebook.com/identitaere/posts/1168780089806715.

---. 2016b. "Wir stehen in der ersten Reihe—Wir sind die patriotische Phalanx!" July 22. Available at https://www.facebook.com/identitaere/photos/a.583269050 24488.1073741828.581482171869846/1280 042595347130/?type=3&theater.

---. 2016c. "Stellungnahme der IB Hamburg zur Beobachtung durch den Verfassungsschutz." August 17. Available at http://www.identitaere-bewegung.de/presse/.

---. 2016d. "Weitere kleine Bildeindrücke von der gestrigen Aktion auf dem Brandenburger Tor." August 28. Available at https://www.facebook.com/identi taere/posts/1315118398506216.

---. 2016e. "Blockade der CDU." December 22. Available at https://www.face book.com/identitaere/posts/1461458033872251.

---. 2017a. "Wir bauen die Mauer!" January 26. Available at https://www.face book.com/identitaere/photos/a.583269085024488.107374182 8.5814821718698 46/1523176281033759/?type=3.

---. 2017b. "Nazi-Methoden mit prominenter Unterstützung." March 24. Available at https://www.facebook.com/identitaere/posts/1592808440737209.

---. 2017c. "Der neue Terror von links." March 25. Available at https://www.face book.com/identitaere/posts/1594181383933248.

---. 2017d. "Russland-Bashing nach Terrorakt." April 3. Available at https://www .facebook.com/identitaere/posts/1606790346005685.

---. 2017e. "Präsident Österreichs: Frauen sollten alle Kopftuch tragen—aus Solidarität!" April 26. Available at https://www.facebook.com/identitaere/posts/163 9965579354828.

IBD Berlin-Brandenburg. 2017. "Warum wir Aktivisten von der Identitären Bewegung unter dem Motto: 'GRENZEN SCHÜTZEN—LEBEN RETTEN' die Stadthalle in Cottbus besetzt haben?" October 21. Available at https://www.facebook.com/identitaere/posts/1888791447805572.

IBH (Identitäre Bewegung Hessen). 2016. "#Nizza, #Würzburg, #München, #Reutlingen, #Ansbach und #Rouen—die Ereignisse häufen sich in den letzten Wochen." July 28. Available at https://www.facebook.com/IdentitareBewegungHessen/posts/920899974689114.

IBMV (Identitäre Bewegung Mecklenburg-Vorpommern). 2016. "Symbolischer Protest auf dem Neuen Markt in Rostock." July 28. Available at https://www.facebook.com/IBmeckuvp/posts/1889065781320892.

IBN (Identitäre Bewegung Niedersachsen). 2017. "Identitäre Aktivisten gedenken der Opfer islamischen Terrors." April 8. Available at https://www.facebook.com/IdentitaereNiedersachsen/posts/1141275332662058.

IBÖ (Identitäre Bewegung Österreich). 2016a. "Identitäre stürmen Veranstaltung." June 9. Available at https://www.youtube.com/watch?v=h14tgF6XIoI.

———. 2016b. "Zum dritten Mal demonstrierten wir unter dem Motto 'Europa verteidigen.'" June 11. Available at https://www.facebook.com/identitaeroesterreich/posts/899162536861742.

———. 2016c. "Wenn wir nichts tun ist das unsere Zukunft!" November 29. Available at https://www.facebook.com/identitaeroesterreich/photos/a.331848393593162.72982.287774531333882/1032093296901998/?type=3&permPage=1.

———. 2017a. "Prinz Eugen price." January 29. Available at https://www.facebook.com/identitaeroesterreich/posts/1086405241470803.

———. 2017b. "Erdogan—hol deine türken ham!" Video, March 23. Available at https://www.facebook.com/identitaeroesterreich/videos/1132804876830839/.

———. 2017c. "NICHT MIT UNS!" April 28. Available at https://www.facebook.com/identitaeroesterreich/posts/1170625556382104.

———. 2017d. "VIDEO ZUM EGDENKZUG AM KAHLENBER!" September 11. Available at https://www.facebook.com/identitaeroesterreich/videos/1294608833983775/.

———. 2018. "Aktivismus ist weder kriminell noch verhetzend." May 3. Available at https://twitter.com/Identitaere_B/status/992072955554422787.

IBÖ video. 2016. "Aktionsvideo Audimax—14.4.2016." April 14. Available at https://www.youtube.com/watch?v=S2B8lDve1EE.

IB Schwaben. 2017a. "Ihr lügt dass sich die Balken biegen!" January 12. Available at https://www.facebook.com/IdentitaereSchwaben/photos/a.1430 270763894008.1073741828.1430266453894439/1800008886920192/?type=3&permPage=1.

———. 2017b. "Aktivisten machten auf die Folgen von Multikulti aufmerksam." March 19. Available at https://twitter.com/IBSchwaben/status/843706891326906368.

———. 2017c. "#Europa—#Jugend—#Reconquista." March 14. Available at https://twitter.com/IBSchwaben/status/841691435611103233.

IBS (Identitäre Bewegung Steiermark). 2017. "Mit Erdo sind wir on Tour." March 20. Available at https://www.facebook.com/ib.stmk/posts/1468 824859825198.

IdentidaD. 2006. "Pierre Krebs, o el arte de señalar los problemas de fondo." 384–89.

Identità: Journal de la résistance niçoise. 2011. n. 6 (March).

identitaere-generation.info. 2015. "Interview—Alexander Dugin." April 4. Available at http://www.identitaere-generation.info/interview-alexander-dugin/.

———Identitaires. 2016a. "Communique officiel: Le Bloc Identitaire devient Les Identitaires." July 20. Available at https://www.bloc-identitaire.com/actualite/3251/bloc-identitaire-devient-identitaires.

———. 2016b. "Les Mots." Available at http://www.les-identitaires.com/en-mots-2/.

———. 2016c. "10 Mesures d'Urgence pour defender la sécurité et l'identité de la France." Available at https://www.les-identitaires.com/2016/12/10-mesures-durgence-proteger-lidentite-securite-de-france/.

Identitaires—Actualités de la résistance enracinée. 2012. n. 12 (December).

———. 2013a. n. 15 (July).

———. 2013b. n. 16 (October).

———. 2013c. n. 17 (December).

———. 2014a. n. 18 (May).

———. 2014b. n. 19 (July).

———. 2014c. n. 20 (October).

———. 2015. n. 22 (May–June).

———. 2016a. n. 23 (May–June).

———. 2016b. n. 24 (July–August).

———. 2017. n. 25 (November–December).

———. 2018. n. 26 (January–February).

Identitäre Bewegung Baden. 2016. "Aktiv in Karlsruhe." July 17. Available at https://www.facebook.com/permalink.php?story_fbid=11004736100181 30&id=516327785099385.

Identitás Generáció. 2014. "Generation Identity Hungary." November. Available at http://generacio.eu/generation-identity/.
Identity Forum. 2014. "Introducing the Identity Forum." Available at http://identityforum.org.uk/2014/03/metapolitics/introducing-the-identity-forum/.
ID Magazine. 2006. "Campagne Jeunesse Identitaires." n. 5 (Spring): 6–8.
IE (Identity Evropa). 2016. Official site. www.identityevropa.com.
———. 2017. "Identity Evropa Calls for an End to Immigration." Press release, Atlanta, June 20. Available at https://www.identityevropa.com/action-report/2017/6/20/press-release-atlanta-identity-evropa-calls-for-an-end-to-immigration.
———. 2018. "European Roots, American Greatness!" March 11. Available at https://twitter.com/IdentityEvropa/status/972897038483492864.
Iliade. 2014. "Œuvrer à la réappropriation de leur identité par les Européens—Présentation—Iliade—Institut pour la longue mémoire européenne." Available at http://institut-iliade.com/presentation.
Iliade. 2015. "Europe Is Not Lampedusa." June 20. Available at https://www.youtube.com/watch?v=02nLxNzIA9g.
Independent. 2016. "'It's Like the Day before World War One': European Chief's Stark Warning over Scale of Refugee Crisis.'" February 10. Available at http://www.independent.co.uk/news/uk/politics/migrants-heading-for-eu-could-boost-support-for-brexit-warns-donald-tusk-a6866151.html.
———. 2017. "Austrian President Calls on All Women to Wear Headscarves in Solidarity with Muslims to Fight 'Rampant Islamophobia.'" April 28. Available at http://www.independent.co.uk/news/world/europe/austrian-president-alexander-van-der-bellen-all-women-headscarves-hijab-veils-burqa-muslim-a7707166.html#commentsDiv.
Indymedia. 2017. "Antifaschistische Aktion Bad Oldesloe & Umland: Stefan Lüdtke geoutet." February 9. Available at https://linksunten.indymedia.org/en/node/203477.
IntelligoNews. 2014. "Di Stefano CPI: 'Ucraina, bene gli sforzi di Putin per mondo mutipolare.'" March 3. Available at http://www.intelligonews.it/articoli/3-marzo-2014/15335/di-stefano-cpi-ucraina-bene-gli-sforzi-di-putin-per-mondo-multipolare-caso-cremona-conferma-nostre-idee-oscar-e-renzi.
———. 2015a. "Dopo il muro anche I profughi 'marchiati': Colpa delle indecisioni Europee." September 3. Available at http://www.intelligonews.it/articoli/3-settembre-2015/29990/dopo-il-muro-anche-i-profughi-marchiati-colpa-delle-indecisioni-europee.

———. 2015b. "Visto negato a Salvini, CasaPound replica: Tirati in ballo, non siamo antisemiti." November 13. Available at http://www.intelligo news.it/articoli/13-novembre-2015/33042/visto-negato-a-salvini-casa pound-replica-tirati-in-ballo-non-siamo-antisemiti-un-errore-le-leggi-razziali.

Isabel, Thibault. 2010. "La violence civilisée et celle qui ne l'est pas." *éléments pour la civilisation européenne*, n. 137 (October–December): 44–51.

———. 2014. *Le parti de la tolérance: Critique du monologisme contemporain*. Lille: La Méduse.

J'ai Tout Compris—Blog de Guillaume Faye, Essayiste Patriote Français et Européen. 2015a. "La machination américaine contre la Russie—et l'Europe." May 20. Available at http://www.gfaye.com/la-machination-ameri caine-contre-la-russie-et-leurope/.

———. 2015b. "Invasion migratoire, 1: L'Effrayant diagnostic." September 6. Available at http://www.gfaye.com/invasion-migratoire-1-leffrayant-diagnostic/.

———. 2016a. "Kaliningrad: Retenez ce nom; Danger de guerre en Europe." May 3. Available at http://www.gfaye.com/kaliningrad-retenez-ce-nom-danger-de-guerre-en-europe/.

———. 2016b "Brexit: Pétard mouillé ou séisme?" July 12. Available at http://www.gfaye.com/brexit-petard-mouille-ou-seisme/.

Jazeera. 2016. "Pro- and Anti-refugee Protests Staged in Berlin." May 7. Available at http://www.aljazeera.com/news/2016/05/pro-anti-refugee-protests-staged-berlin-160507162824154.html.

Jihad Watch. 2016. "Pope Francis: 'We Can Speak Today of an Invasion' of Europe.'" March 2. Available at https://www.jihadwatch.org/2016/03/pope-francis-we-can-speak-today-of-an-arab-invasion-of-europe.

Johnson, Greg. 2013. *New Right versus Old Right & Other Essays*. San Francisco: Counter-Currents Publishing.

———. 2015a. "The Muslim Problem." January 27. Available at http://www.counter-currents.com/2015/01/the-muslim-problem/.

———. 2015b. "Three Questions on Identitarianism." March 10. Available at http://www.counter-currents.com/2015/03/three-questions-on-identi tarianism/.

———. 2015c. Email interview with the author, May 16.

———. 2017a. Email interview with the author, July 8.

———. 2017b. "Unite the Right Did nothing Wrong but There's Still Room for Improvement. August 19. Available at https://www.counter-currents .com/2017/08/unite-the-right-did-nothing-wrong/.

Joly, Joseph-Marie. 2009. "Notre combat est amour et liberté." *ID Magazine*, n. 16 (Autumn): 13.

Journal du Dimanche. 2014. "Le FN a-t-il un problème avec le 'grand remplacement'?" November 2. Available at http://www.lejdd.fr/Politique/Le-FN-a-t-il-un-probleme-avec-le-grand-remplacement-698644.

Jünger, Ernst. 2012. *The Adventurous Heart: Figures and Capriccios*. Trans. Thomas Friese. Candor, NY: Telos Press.

Kaalep, Ruuben. 2016a. Email interview with the author, July 8.

———. 2016b. "Safe East European Home." September 8. Available at http://www.counter-currents.com/2016/09/safe-east-european-home/.

Kaldor, Mary. 2013. "In Defence of New Wars." *Stability* 2, n. 1, art. 4: 1–16.

Kleine Zeitung. 2016. "Makabre Aktion: Kartonsärge vor Parteizentrale auf gestellt." August 23. Available at http://www.kleinezeitung.at/steiermark/graz/5073311/Makabre-Aktion_Kartonsaerge-vor-Parteizentrale-auf gestellt.

Kofner, Jurij. 2017. Email interview with the author, October 9.

Kohns, Oliver. 2013. "An Aesthetics of the Unbearable: The Cult of Masculinity and the Sublime in Ernst Jünger's 'Der Kampf als inneres Erlebnis,' (Battle as an Inner Experience.)" *Image & Narrative* 14, n, 3: 141–50.

Kőrössy, Gergely. 2017. Email interview with the author, September 27.

Krampon, Eugène. 2003a. "Les races d'Europe: A quelle race appartenez-vous?" *Réfléchir & Agir*, n. 14 (Spring): 33–35.

———. 2003b, "Arthur, Georges, René, Jacques . . . et les autres 'théoriciens du racisme.'" *Réfléchir & Agir*, n. 14 (Spring): 45–48.

———. 2009a. "Les sept familles de l'extrême-droite française." *Réfléchir & Agir* n. 31 (Winter): 42–44.

———. 2009b. "Vers la Grande Europe des ethnies." *Réfléchir & Agir*, n. 33 (Autumn): 38–39.

———. 2010. "Qu' est-ce que la rupture?" *Réfléchir & Agir*, n. 34 (Winter): 25–26.

———. 2013a. "Face à la gauche et à la droite du capital, notre socialisme IDENTITAIRE." *Réfléchir & Agir*, n. 44 (Summer): 14.

———. 2013b. "Hommage, Dominique Venner, 1935–2013." *Réfléchir & Agir*, n. 44 (Summer): 44.

———. 2014a. "Les jumeaux divins du monde moderne: L'Argent et le marché." *Réfléchir & Agir*, n. 46 (Winter): 15–16.

———. 2014b. "Le traité transatlantique: L'Europe vassale des Américains." *Réfléchir & Agir*, n. 46 (Winter): 17–18.

———. 2015a. "Le Front National peut-il prendre le pouvoir?" *Réfléchir & Agir*, n. 50 (Summer): 3.
———. 2015b. "La révolution française: La matrice du totalitarisme républicain." *Réfléchir & Agir*, n. 50 (Summer): 16–17.
———. 2015c. "Notes de Lecture." *Réfléchir & Agir*, n. 50 (Summer): 56.
———. 2017. "Plaidoyer pour un ethno-nationalisme blanc." *Réfléchir & Agir*, n. 55 (Winter): 15–17.
Krebs, Pierre. 2003. "L'Europe à l'avant-garde de l'Ethnos . . . ." *Terre et Peuple*, n. 16 (Solstice of Summer): 33–34.
———. 2006. *La lucha por lo esencial*. Valencia, Spain: Kontinent Europa.
———. 2011. "It's about the Primordial Fire." In *Why We Fight: Manifesto of the European Resistance*, by Guillaume Faye, trans. and intro. by Michael O'Meara, 19–25. London: Arktos.
———. 2012. *Fighting for the Essence*. London: Arktos.
———. 2015. Email interview with the author, March 6.
Kubitschek, Götz. 2016a. "Die Identitären unterstützen, denn: Der beste Verfassungsschutz ist eine sichere Grenze." August 28. Available at https://sezession.de/55129.
——— 2016b. Email interview with the author, October 26.
Kurtagic, Alex. 2011. "Masters of the Universe." September 23. Available at http://www.counter-currents.com/2011/09/masters-of-the-universe/.
———. 2015a. "Interview with Fenek Solère by Alex Kurtagic." June 29. Available at https://neweuropeanconservative.wordpress.com/2015/06/29/interview-with-fenek-solere-kurtagic/.
———. 2015b. Email interview with author, July 29.
———. 2016. Email interview with author, February 18.
Lakrite, Modeste. 2016. *L'Édit de Mantes*. Paris: Éditions Diffusia.
Lambert, Pierre. 2006. "Les Scythes: L'Empire eurasiatique des cavaliers blancs." *ID Magazine*, n. 7 (Autumn): 18–19.
Lambton, John. 2016. Email interview with the author, March 16.
Lane, M. K. 2016. "After Brussels: The Trap of Counter-Jihad." March 28. Available at http://www.counter-currents.com/2016/03/the-trap-of-counter-jihad/.
Langella, Julien. 2013. "Jeunes catholiques, engagez-vous jusqu'au bout!" September 8. Available at http://www.lerougeetlenoir.org/opinions/les-opinantes/jeunes-catholiques-engagez-vous-jusqu-au-bout.
———. 2015a. *La Jeunesse au Pouvoir*. Paris: Les Éditions du Rubicon.
———. 2015b. "La Jeunesse au pouvoir!" *Réfléchir & Agir*, n. 51 (Autumn): 32–34.
———. 2016. Email interview with the author, June 13.

Langness, Julian. 2016a. "How Europe's War of Liberation Could Begin." *European Civil War*, March 10. Available at http://www.europeancivilwar.com/how-the-war-could-begin/.
———. 2016b. Email interview with the author, March 23.
———. 2016c. "Desired Storms: Guillaume Faye's *The Colonisation of Europe*." July 12. Available at www.counter-currents.com/2016/07/fayes-the-colonisation-of-europe/print.
———. 2018. *Identity Rising: How Nationalist Millenials Will Retake Europe, Save America, and Become the New "Greatest Generation."* Self-published.
La Rochelle, Pierre Drieu. 1931. *L'Europe contre les Patries*. Paris: Gallimard.
Larti, Pierre. 2016. *"On est chez nous! demo."* Speech organized by Génération Identitaire in Paris, May 28. Available at https://www.youtube.com/watch?v=brLWEBre2P8.
LBTF (*Le Blog Thomas Ferrier*). 2013. "Guillaume Faye et la Russie." November 30. Available at http://thomasferrier.hautetfort.com/guillaume-faye/.
Le Blanc et le Noir. 2016. "Fronts du Donbass et de Syrie: deux théâtres d'une même guerre," Robert Steuckers, July 7. Available at www.leblancetlenoir.com/2016/07/fronts-du-donbass-et-de-syrie-deux-theatres-d-une-meme-guerre.html.
Le Blog de Robert Steuckers. 2015. October. Available at http://robertsteuckers.blogspot.pt/2015/10/crise-syrienne-paysage-intellectuel.html.
L'Epée, David. 2013. "Édouard Berth et les enfants terribles du syndicalisme." *éléments pour la civilisation européenne*, n. 148 (July–September): 38–41.
Le Identitarie—gruppo identitario femminile. 2017. May 2. Available at https://www.facebook.com/LeIdentitarie/posts/209739062864234.
Le Brun, Patrick. 2015. "The Best Nationalist Pamphlet Ever: *26 Concrete Legal Measures for Remigration*." September 25. Available at http://www.counter-currents.com/2015/09/26-concrete-legal-measures-for-remigration/print/.
Le Gallou, Jean-Yves. 2008. "Douze thèses pour un gramscisme technologique." November 1. Available at http://archives.polemia.com/article.php?id=1763.
———. 2015. "Forum de la dissidence—Entretien." November 18. Available at http://www.polemia.com/forum-de-la-dissidence-entretien-avec-jean-yves-le-gallou-president-de-polemia/.
———. 2016. *Immigration: La catastrophe; Que faire?* Versailles: Via Romana.
Le Gallou, Jean-Yves, and Antoine Ormain. 2016. "Le retour de l'Histoire." *France*, n. 1: 54–55.
Le Gallou, Jean-Yves, Michel Geoffroy, and Polémia. 2015. *Dictionnaire de Novlangue: Ces 1000 mots qui vous manipulent*. Versailles: Via Romana.

Lenart, Patrick. 2017. "Samuel P. Huntington: Kampf der kulturen." November 30. Available at http://www.patrick-lenart.eu/samuel-p-huntington-kampf-der-kulturen/.
Libération. 2015. "Philippe Vardon, rassemblement brun Marion." July 10. Available at http://www.liberation.fr/france/2015/07/10/philippe-vardon-rassemblement-brun-marion_1346028.
———. 2016. "Le racisme 'anti-blanc' n'est 'pas une expérience de masse' par Sylvain Mouillard." January 8. Available at http://www.liberation.fr/france/2016/01/08/le-racisme-anti-blanc-n-est-pas-une-experience-de-masse_1425131.
———. 2017. "La culture Alt-Right: De l'extreme droite francaise a 'Fight Club.'" January 17. Available at https://oeilsurlefront.liberation.fr/les-idees/2017/01/17/la-culture-alt-right-de-l-extreme-droite-francaise-a-fight-club_1542075.
Lichtmesz, Martin. 2016a. Email interviews with the author, March 15, April 26, July 29, August 18, and October 27.
———. 2016b. "Frans Timmermans: Der Große Austausch als 'Manifest Destiny.'" April 7. Available at http://www.sezession.de/53702/frans-timmermans-der-grosse-austausch-als-manifest-destiny.html.
———. 2016c. "Kardinal Woelkis Hommage an das Heerlager der Heiligen." May 30. Available at http://www.sezession.de/54168/kardinal-woelkis-hommage-an-das-heerlager-der-heiligen.html/2.
———. 2017. AmRen 2017, Tennessee, July 29. Available at https://www.youtube.com/watch?v=3zg1z5i2ycs.
Liddell, Colin. 2015a. Email interview with the author, May 31.
———. 2015b. "Sound as a Pound." November 12. Available at https://www.counter-currents.com/2015/11/sound-as-a-pound/.
Lignier, Anaïs. 2016. "*On est chez nous! demo.*" May 28. Available at https://www.youtube.com/watch?v=BxPTUX-BYRg.
Lind, William S. 2004. "Understanding Fourth Generation War." Available at http://www.antiwar.com/lind/?articleid=1702.
———. 2015. "The View from Olympus: Donald Trump and Fourth Generation War." December 16. Available at https://www.traditionalright.com/the-view-from-olympus-donald-trump-and-fourth-generation-war/.
———. 2016. "The View from Olympus: Stopping the Truck Threat." July 18. Available at https://www.traditionalright.com/the-view-from-olympus-stopping-the-truck-threat/.
Lind, William S., Keith Nightengale, John F. Schmitt, Joseph W. Sutton, and Gary I. Wilson. 1989. "The Changing Face of War: Into the Fourth Generation." *Marine Corps Gazette*, October: 22–26.

Lindholm, Charles. 2008. *Culture and Authenticity*. Malden, MA: Blackwell.
Lindholm, Charles, and José Pedro Zúquete. 2010. *The Struggle for the World: Liberation Movements for the 21st Century*. Palo Alto, CA: Stanford University Press.
Live Leak. 2016. "ISIS Beheading in Center of Vienna." December 21. Available at http://www.liveleak.com/view?i=e7b_1450789131&comments=1.
Local. 2015. "Identitarian Activists Block Border Crossing." September 29. Available at http://www.thelocal.at/20150929/identitarian-activists-block-border-crossing-in-immigration-protest.
Lüdtke, Stephan. 2017. "Linke outings und andere Peinlichkeiten." April. Available at https://www.identitaere-bewegung.de/blog/linke-outings-und-andere-peinlichkeiten/.
Maalouf, Amin. 2012. *In the Name of Identity: Violence and the Need to Belong*. New York: Arcade Publishing.
Machiavelli, Niccolo. 2006. *The Art of War*. New York: Dover.
Marchand, René. 2003. "Les Européens, ces enemis." *Nouvelle Revue d'Histoire*, n. 4 (January–February): 47.

———. 2013. *Reconquista ou Mort de l'Europe—L'Enjeu de la guerre islamique—Pour une stratégie de contre-offensive*. Paris: Éditions Riposte Laïque.
Marchi, Riccardo. 2015. "Book Review: Fascisti di un altro millennio? Crisi e partecipazione in CasaPound Italia." *Análise Social*, n. 214: 205–8.

———. 2016. "La réutilisation de symboles, références et actions par les groupes Identitaires portugais." In *Internationalisation des droites radicales: Europe Amériques; Réferénces e thèmes des droites radicales*, edited by Olivier Dard, 153–76. Bern: Peter Lang.
Marea. 2014. "Okupando en nombre de Ledesma y Pound." September 13. Available at http://www.lamarea.com/2014/09/13/okupando-en-nombre-de-ledesma-y-pound/.
Markovics, Alexander. 2015. "Taking Action to Preserve the Future of Austrian Identity—Right On." November 22. Available at https://www.righton.net/2015/11/22/taking-action-to-preserve-the-future-of-austrian-identity.

———. 2016a. "Die Folgen von Brüssel." March 22. Available at http://www.identitaere-generation.info/die-folgen-von-bruessel/.

———. 2016b. "Europäischer Kontinentalismus, 2014–2016: Ein geopolitisches Déjà-vu in Osteuropa?" June 24. Available at http://www.identitaere-generation.info/europaeischer-kontinentalismus/.

———. 2016c. "Donald Trump—Chance für Europa?" November 12. Available at http://greater-europe.org/archives/1958.

———. 2017. Email interview with author, September 19.

———. 2018. "Vortrag bei der AfD Aachen zum Thema 'Die Neue Rechte—Ein Ausblick auf Europas geistige Zukunft.'" February 27. Available at https://twitter.com/AlexanderMarko8/status/968502362439671814.

Marmin, Michel. 2010. "La Nouvelle Droite entre quat'z'yeux." *éléments pour la civilisation européenne*, n. 136 (July–September): 28–41.

Martin, Clément. 2014. "Du Djihad à la remigration." *Identitaires*, n. 19 (July): 7.

Martins, João. 2016. Email interview with the author, March 28.

Mattino. 2017. "Emergenza stupri, a Napoli CasaPound offre corsi di autodifesa per donne." October 8. Available at https://www.ilmattino.it/napoli/cronaca/emergenza_stupri_a_napoli_casapound-3288896.html.

Mayer, Stephanie, and Birgit Sauer. 2014. "A European Youth against Europe? Identity and Europeanness in the Austrian 'Identitarian' Discourse.'" Paper presented at the conference Digital Populism and the Young: Populism, Young People and the World Wide Web in Theory and Practice, September 8, University of Leicester, UK.

McKenna, Damhnait. 2017. "Meeting Damhnait of Generation Identity Ireland." October 25. Available at https://www.youtube.com/watch?v=5IVwu6QXpAU&t=63s.

Meinhart, Edith. 2014. "Das verquere Weltbild der Identitären." May 20. Available at http://www.profil.at/oesterreich/das-weltbild-identitaeren-353357.

Metropolico. 2016. "Interview mit der IBB." November 13. Available at http://www.metropolico.org/2016/11/13/metropolico-interview-mit-der-ibb/.

Michael, George. 2017. "The Rise of the Alt-Right and the Politics of Polarization in America." *Skeptic* 22, n. 2 (June 26): 9–17.

Michéa, Jean-Claude. 2013. *Les mystères de la gauche: De l'idéal des Lumières au triomphe du capitalisme absolu*. Paris: Climats.

———. 2014. "Michéa face à la stratégie Godwin." January 4. Available at http://www.marianne.net/Michea-face-a-la-strategie-Godwin_a234731.html.

Michel, Alain. 2008. "Races et intelligence." *Terre et Peuple*, n. 35 (Equinox of Spring): 47–51.

Milà, Ernesto. 2017. Email interview with the author, September 19.

Mirkovic, Nikola. 2016. "Les Balkans sous le joug ottoman." *Nouvelle Revue d'Histoire*, special issue, n. 12 (Spring): 32–35.

Monde. 2017. "Les Identitaires investissent le Front national." January 2. Available at http://www.lemonde.fr/politique/article/2017/01/02/les

-identitaires-investissent-le-front-national_5056584_823448.html#axq 146JDlkSDJOO5.99.

———. 2018. "De 2013 à 2018, la France au rythme des attentats." March, 30. Available at http://www.lemonde.fr/societe/article/2018/03/30/de-2013-a-2018-la-france-au-rythme-des-attentats_5278453_3224.html#liste_reactions.

Monnet, Jean. 1978. *Memoirs*, trans. Richard Mayne. New York: Doubleday.

Morars, Aline. 2018. "FLA Birmingham Aline from #120db Germany full speech." March 24. Available at https://www.youtube.com/watch?v=MpGn2IvLqZM&feature=youtu.be.

Morgan, John. 2013. "Identity vs. Globalism in Stockholm." July 5. Available at http://www.counter-currents.com/2013/07/identity-vs-globalism-in-stockholm-identitarian-ideas-5/.

———. 2015. Email interview with the author, May 18.

———. 2017. Email interview with the author, March 21, September 20.

Mosley, Eli. 2017. Email interview with the author, August 28.

Mosley, Eli, and James Allsup. 2017. "Charlottesville 3.0." October 11. Available at https://www.youtube.com/watch?time_continue=12&v=cydize_kPug.

Mother Jones. 2017. "I Met the White Nationalist Who "Falcon Punched" a 95-Pound Female Protester—by Shane Bauer." May 9. Available at http://www.motherjones.com/politics/2017/05/nathan-damigo-punching-woman-berkeley-white-nationalism/#.

Mourreau, Jean-Jacques. 1994. "La disparation d'un maître." *Enquête sur l'Histoire*, n. 10 (Spring): 81–82.

Mudde, Cas. 2017. "Given That Key Objective of 'Identitarians'. . . ." July 26. Available at https://twitter.com/CasMudde.

Mundo. 2016. "Melisa, el amanecer rubio de la ultraderecha española." October 24. Available at http://www.elmundo.es/papel/historias/2016/10/24/5808c1ccca4741d30e8b4674.html.

Murray, Douglas. 2017. "Douglas Murray on Europe's Problems with Immigration, Identity, and Islam." *Rubin Report*, September 22. Available at https://art19.com/shows/the-rubin-report/episodes/596c5bac-fdb4-414a-9682-5fe5bdec5a76.

Murros, Kai. 2004. "National Revolution—Turn On, Tune In, Take Over." April 4. Available at https://www.youtube.com/watch?v=ok-XnmfLLyY.

———. 2010. "The Voice of Europe." Moscow. Available at https://www.youtube.com/watch?v=wlmMhQtND2c.

———. 2017. Email interview with the author, April 21 and 24.

MYTF1 NEWS. 2014. "Class sur LCI, Éric Zemmour menace de quitter le plateau." November 24. Available at http://lci.tf1.fr/politique/eric-zem mour-clashe-une-journaliste-de-lci-et-ses-questions-stupides-8523381 .html.

Neuding, Paulina. 2017. "Sweden's Sexual Assault Crisis Presents a Feminist Paradox." October 10. Available at http://quillette.com/2017/10/10 /swedens-sexual-assault-crisis-presents-feminist-paradox/.

New Observer. 2016. "Austrians: 'Reds, It's Your Fault.'" March 24. Available at http://newobserveronline.com/austrians-reds-fault/.

New Yorker. 2017. "The Alt-Right Branding War Has Torn the Movement in Two." July 6. Available at http://www.newyorker.com/news/news-desk /the-alt-right-branding-war-has-torn-the-movement-in-two.

New York Times. 2018. "Hand Grenades and Gang Violence Rattle Sweden's Middle Class." March 3. Available at https://www.nytimes.com/2018/03 /03/world/europe/sweden-crime-immigration-hand-grenades.

Nordic Frontier. 2018. "Nordic Frontier # 55 Cristoffer Dulny." February 27. Available at https://www.spreaker.com/episode/14157817?utm_medium =widget&utm_term=episode_title&utm_source=user%3A9256352.

Nouvelle Revue d'Histoire. 2003. "Dossier—Le choc des civilisations." n. 7 (July–August): 27.

Novak, Zvonimir. 2011. *Tricolores: Une histoire visuelle de la droite et de l'extrême droite*. Montreuil: Éditions l'Échappée.

Novopress. 2012a. "Les islamistes de *Forsane Alizza* visaient le Bloc Identitaire et *Libération*." April 13. Available at http://fr.novopress.info/111250/les -islamistes-de-forsane-alizza-visaient-le-bloc-identitaire-et-liberation/.

———. 2012b. "Italie: Entrevue avec Gianluca Iannone, Président de Casa-Pound." November 20. Available at http://fr.novopress.info/126244/italie -entrevue-avec-gianluca-iannone-president-de-casapound/.

———. 2013. "Un jour un livre: Reconquista ou mort de l'Europe, l'enjeux de la guerre islamique." December 29. Available at http://fr.novopress.info /150205/jour-livre-reconquista-mort-leurope-lenjeux-guerre-islamique/.

———. 2014. "René Marchand participerá aux assises de la remigration." November 12. Available at http://www.bloc-identitaire.com/actualite/3197 /rene-marchand-participera-aux-assises-remigration-15-novembre -2014-paris.

———. 2015a. "Délit de facies, arme politique de l'anti-France?" July 7. Available at http://fr.novopress.info/189872/delit-facies-arme-politique-lanti -france-fabrice-robert/.

———. 2015b. "Le Grand Remplacement en Suisse." October 6. Available at http://fr.novopress.info/193277/grand-remplacement-en-suisse/.

———. 2016. "Les Identitaires décernent à Trappes le label 'Molenbeek Français.'" May 3. Available at http://fr.novopress.info/200774/les-identi taires-decernent-trappes-label-molenbeek-francais/.

———. 2017. "Le Grand Remplacement, une réalité implicitement reconnue par l'INSEE." March 3. Available at https://fr.novopress.info/203994/le -grand-remplacement-une-realite-implicitement-reconnue-par-linsee/.

Obertone, Laurent. 2016. *Guerilla: Le jour où tout s'embrasa*. Editions Ring.

Ochsenreiter, Manuel. 2015. Email interview with the author, April 4.

———. 20. "Why the New Europe Is a Chance for Our Continent and the Middle East." July 1. Available at http://germancenter.net/2016/07/01 /new-europe-chance-continent-middle-east/.

———. 2016b. Email communication with the author, July 28.

O'Danieli, Bastien. 2016. "Les origines de l'homme: Le mythe du berceau unique." *éléments pour la civilisation européenne*, n. 159 (March–April): 71–77.

———. 2018. "Entretien avec Richard Lynn: L'homme qui a mesuré la baisse du QI des Français." *éléments pour la civilisation européenne*, n. 170 (January–February): 75–76.

O'Meara, James J. 2015. "An Iconography for the Alt-Right: Fenek Solère's *The Partisan*." January 28. Available at http://www.counter-currents.com /2015/01/fenek-solere-the-partisan/.

O'Meara, Michael. 2004. "Boreas Rising: White Nationalism and the Geopolitics of the Paris-Berlin-Moscow Axis." *Occidental Quarterly* 4, n. 4 (Winter): 28–52.

———. 2007. "The New Jewish Question of Guillaume Faye." *Occidental Quarterly* 7, n. 3 (Fall): 71–83.

———. 2010. *Toward the White Republic and Other Essays*. San Francisco: Counter-Currents.

———. 2013. *New Culture, New Right: Anti-Liberalism in Postmodern Europe*. London: Arktos.

———. 2015. Email interview with the author, February 5.

Oppedisano, Ada. 2015. "Mediterraneo solidale: Il volontariato identitario a convegno." September 10. Available at http://www.ilprimatonazionale.it /cultura/mediterraneo-solidale-il-volontariato-identitario-a-convegno -30256/.

———. 2016. "*Esteri: La missione non conforme di 'Sol.Id.,' onlus solidarista tra Siria e Mediterraneo*." October 7. Available at http://www.barbadillo.it /48280-esteri-missione-non-conforme-di-sol-id-onlus-solidarista/.

Osborne, Lawrence. 2017. *Beautiful Animals*. London: Hogarth.
Ovid. 1931. *Fasti—Book 2*, trans. James G. Frazer. Available at http://www.theoi.com/Text/OvidFasti2.html.
Paris Vox. 2017. "Les 'Bobards d'Or' font le plein!" February 7. Available at https://www.parisvox.info/2017/02/07/bobards-dor-plein/.
Pearlstein, Mitch. 2014. "Fourth Generation Warfare." Available at https://www.americanexperiment.org/article/fourth-generation-warfare/.
Pena e Espada. 2015. "Pelo renascimento da cultura europeia." May 6. Available at http://penaeespada.blogspot.pt/2015/05/pelo-renascimento-da-cultura-europeia.html.
Perino, Umberto Actis. 2016. Email interview with the author, December 21.
pestisracok.hu. 2017. "Identitáriusok vallomása: Orbán példát mutatott, Magyarországon a baloldal nem győzhet többé." October 22. Available at http://pestisracok.hu/identitarianusok-vallomasa-orban-peldat-mutatott-magyarorszagon-baloldal-nem-gyozhet-tobbe/#comments.
Pettibone, Brittany. 2017. Email interview with the author, August 27.
Phalanx Europa. 2012. Page of goods offered. Available at https://www.phalanx-europa.com.
Pichon, Gérald. 2013. *Sale Blanc! Chronique d'u Scianca ne haine qui n'existe pas*.... Nice: Éditions IDées.
———. 2014. "Gérald Pichon: 'Ce sont les visages pales qui sont prioritairement pris pour cible.'" February 4. Available at http://fr.novopress.info/155130/gerald-pichon-ce-les-visages-pales-prioritairement-pris-cible/.
PI-News (*Politically Incorrect*). 2016. "Götz Kubitschek—der Che Guevara von Rechts." August 31. Available at http://www.pi-news.net/2016/08/goetz-kubitschek-der-che-guevara-von-rechts/.
Pirinçci, Akif. 2016. *Umvolkung: Wie die Deutschen still und leise ausgetauscht warden*. Verlag Antaios.
Poitou-Info. 2015. "Rencontres-Charles-Martel 2015: Une première édition réussie + vidéos." June 11. Available at http://poitou-info.fr/463/politique/rencontres-charles-martel-2015-une-premiere-edition-reussie-videos/.
Polémia. 2014. "De Benoist—Misère de l'Union européenne, besoin d'une Europe unie." April 26. Available at http://www.polemia.com/misere-de-lunion-europeenne-besoin-dune-europe-unie/.
———. 2015. "Pourquoi *Polémia*?" Available at http://www.polemia.com/mentions-legales/.
Poppel, Patrick. 2017. "'Putinversteher'—Warum wir Putin lieben!" September 26. Available at https://bachheimer.com/artikelarchiv/229-putinversteher.

Présent. 2015a. "Fabrice Robert: 'Les islamistes n'ont pas gagné.'" January 15. Available at http://www.bloc-identitaire.com/actualite/3213/fabrice-robert-islamistes-n-ont-pas-gagne.

———. 2015b. "Entretien avec Philippe Vardon: 'Les racines contre le village global.'" December, 25.

Prilepin, Zakhar. 2006. *Sankya.* London: Glagoslav.

Primato Nazionale. 2015a. "Con I terroristi abbiamo sbagliato tutto: L'Única salvezza è Assad." January 8. Available at http://www.ilprimatonazionale.it/cronaca/con-terroristi-abbiamo-sbagliato-tutto-lunica-salvezza-e-assad-13273/.

———. 2015b. "Immigrazione: Salvini sposa la tesi della 'Grande Sostituzione.'" February 13. Available at http://www.ilprimatonazionale.it/politica/matteo-salvini-tesi-immigrazione-grande-sostituzione-16842/.

———. 2015c. "Siamo in Guerra: Ma sappiamo contro qui?" February 15. Available at http://www.ilprimatonazionale.it/esteri/siamo-guerra-ma-sappiamo-contro-chi-16976/.

———. 2015d. "Perché è giusto dire: 'Basta com la Fallaci'; Sopratutto oggi." November 14. Available at http://www.ilprimatonazionale.it/politica/basta-fallaci-34188/.

———. 2015e. "La forza dei tuoi hashtag: Le 10 reazioni occidentali alle stragi." November 15. Available at http://www.ilprimatonazionale.it/cronaca/la-forza-dei-tuoi-hashtag-34237/#zTvIlf82M6hrE1FW.99.

———. 2016. "Perche tifiamo brexit fra tanti pero." June 23. Available at http://www.ilprimatonazionale.it/prima/perche-tifiamo-brexit-fra-tanti-pero-46817/.

———. 2017. "'Antifascismo' e 'CasaPound': Due parole che nessuno pronuncia sulla bomba di Firenze." January 2. Available at http://www.ilprimatonazionale.it/politica/antifascismo-e-casapound-due-parole-che-nessuno-pronuncia-sulla-bomba-di-firenze-55364/.

Projet Apache. 2011. "1871–2011—Hommage du Projet Apache aux communards." March 23. Available at https://www.youtube.com/watch?v=XPXx85Jqt5g.

Publico. 2015. "Ultras del 'Hogar Social Madrid': 'No somos nazis, somos socialistas.'" May 7. Available at http://www.publico.es/espana/ultras-del-hogar-social-madrid.html.

Radix. 2013. "Radical Identity." Available at http://www.radixjournal.com/about/.

Radio Courtoisie. 2017. "Révélations sur l'esclavage des européens par les musulmans en terre d'islam." May 24. Available at https://reinformation1

.wordpress.com/2017/05/24/revelations-sur-lesclavage-des-europeens-par-les-musulmans-en-terre-dislam/.
Radio Notre Dame. 2016. "3 octobre 2016: Laurent OBERTONE, écrivain, journaliste et essayiste. Publie Guérilla—le jour où tout s'embrasa Ring," October 3. Available at https://radionotredame.net/emissions/legrandtemoin/03-10-2016/.
Randa, Philippe. 1987. *Poitiers Demain*. Vent du Nord.
———. 2015. Email interview with the author, May 7.
Raspail, Jean. 2014. *The Camp of the Saints*, translated from the French by Norman Shapiro. Petoskey, MI: Social Contract Press.
———. 2015. "Jean Raspail: 'Que les migrants se débrouillent.'" *Point*, September 29. Available at http://www.lepoint.fr/politique/jean-raspail-que-les-migrants-se-debrouillent-29-09-2015-1968909_20.php.
Ravello, Enrique. 2005. "Pedro I el Grande, el Zar que miró a Europa." *Nihil ObstAt Revista de Ideas, Cultura y Metapolítica*, n. 6: 83–92.
Real Politik. 2013. "L'Appel de Moscou d'Aymeric Chauprade." *Blog Realpolitik*, June 13. Available at http://blog.realpolitik.tv/2013/06/lappel-de-moscou-daymeric-chauprade-le-13-juin-2013/.
Rebel Media. 2016. "Lauren Southern: Europe's Culture; Is It Dying? Is the 'Identitarian' Movement the Cure?" June 21. Available at https://www.therebel.media/lauren_southern_show_june_21_2016.
Rebeyne. 2010. "Rebeyne! vs Quick Halal." March 7. Available at https://www.youtube.com/watch?v=y-WffENxK6U.
Rebeyne—Génération Identitaire Lyon. 2015. "Personne n'interdira à la jeunesse lyonnaise d'honorer Marie!" December 4. Available at http://www.lyonlemelhor.org/2015/12/personne-ninterdira-a-la-jeunesse-lyonnaise-dhonorer-marie/.
Redacta. 2016. "Generazione Identitaria, intervista ad Umberto Actis." November 29. Available at http://redacta6.webnode.it/l/generazione-identitaria-intervista-ad-umberto-actis/.
Redeker, Robert. 2014. "La guerre seule peut ressusciter la politique." *éléments pour la civilisation européenne*, n. 151 (April–June): 6–9.
Red Ice TV. 2017. "Christoffer Dulny—From Sweden Democrat to Alt-Right: The Metapolitical Struggle." July. 2017. Available at https://www.youtube.com/watch?v=Um5PwiMIooc.
Réfléchir & Agir—Revue Autonome de Désintoxication Idéologique. 2003. "Choc des civilisations: Attention aux mots." n. 14 (Spring): 4.
———. 2009. "Vers la Grande Europe des Ethnies." n. 33 (Autumn): 38–39.
———. 2010a. "Sarkozy et l'identité nationale: L'Imposture comme politique d'état." n. 34 (Winter): 5.

———. 2010b. "Où en est notre presse?" n. 34 (Winter): 17–19.
———. 2010c. "Le Mouvement d'Action Sociale: Étude d'un petit groupe militant qui pratique la rupture." n. 34 (Winter): 32–4.
———. 2013a. "Face a la gauche et a la droite du capital, notre socialisme Identitaire." n. 44 (Summer): 14.
———. 2013b. "Peut-on encore se dire 'socialiste'?" n. 44 (Summer): 32.
———. 2014. Cover. n. 48 (Autumn).
———. 2015a. n. 50 (Summer).
———. 2015b. n. 51 (Autumn).
———. 2016a. n. 53 (Summer).
———. 2016b. n. 52 (Winter).
———. 2016c. n. 54 (Autumn): 4.
———. 2017. n. 55 (Winter).

Renaissance Européenne. 2016. n. 109 (October/November/December).

Repubblica. 2015. "Roma, la strana coppia Hezbollah-Casapound insieme al convegno." September 20. Available at http://roma.repubblica.it/cronaca/2015/09/20/news/roma_convegno_mediterraneo_solidale_iniziativa_fascio-islamica-123310960/.

RésistanceS.be. Web page. Available at http://www.resistances.be/actioneurop.html.

RetroRebel. 2018. "RetroRebel—Speakers Corner." March 20. Available at https://www.youtube.com/watch?v=Z5ZDMcUT9o8.

Reuters. 2014. "Putin Says Russia Must Prevent 'Color Revolution.'" November 20.

Rieu, Damien. 2014a. "Les seuls qui ont le droit d'être armés dans ce pays, ce sont les racailles! Entretien réalisé par Charlotte d'Ornellas." May 11. Available at http://www.bvoltaire.fr/damienrieu/generation-identitaire-ressusciter-civisme,59505.

———. 2014b. "Remarquable discours de Damien Rieu sur l'islam: Bravo Génération Identitaire!" November 4. Available at http://resistancerepublicaine.eu/2014/11/04/remarquable-discours-de-damien-rieu-sur-lislam-bravo-generation-identitaire/.

———. 2016. July 8. Available at https://twitter.com/damienrieu/status/751373104706949120.

Rioufol, Ivan. 2016. *La guerre civile qui vient.* Paris: Pierre-Guillaume de Roux.

Rix, Edouard. 2010. "Immigration, de la dénonciation à l'acceptation." *Réfléchir & Agir*, n. 34 (Winter): 46–48.

———. 2011. "Généalogie de l'individualisme modern." *Terre et Peuple*, n. 48 (Solstice of Summer): 11–15.

Robb, John. 2016. "Germany Just Screwed Europe." *Global Guerrillas*, January 11. Available at http://globalguerrillas.typepad.com/globalguerrillas/2016/01/germany-just-screwed-europe-for-the-third-time.html.

Robert, Fabrice. 2007. "Qu'est-ce qu'un militant?" *ID Magazine*, n. 9 (Spring): 12.

———. 2010. "Fabrice Robert, president du Bloc identitaire: Être populiste, c'est défendre son peuple." *Riposte Laïque*, October 11. Available at http://ripostelaique.com/Fabrice-Robert-president-du-Bloc.html.

———. 2011. "Pour s'opposer à l'islamisation, il faut réactiver nos anti-corps Identitaires." In *Assises Internationales sur l'Islamisation de nos pays*, ed. Pierre Cassen and Christine Tasin, 215–21. Paris: Éditions Riposte Laique.

———. 2012a. "The 'Identitaire' Have a Historical Role to Play." February 2. Available at http://www.bloc-identitaire.com/actualite/2284/english-interview-fabrice-robert-bloc-identitaire-historical-role-to-play. Since the Bloc changed its name in 2017, this link has no longer worked.

———. 2012b. "10 ans: un bilan et un horizon." *Identitaires*, n. 12 (December): 10–12.

———. 2013a. "Europe Awakes." April 5–7. Available at http://www.bloc-identtaire.com/actualite/3096/europe-awakes.

———. 2013b. "Novopress media incontournable de la réinformation." *Identitaires*, n. 17 (December): 6–7.

———. 2014. "Victoires patriotiques, victoires identitaires: Envisager l'avenir." *Identitaires*, n. 20 (October): 5–7.

———. 2015a. "Aylan Kurdi est mort." Facebook entry, September 3. Available at https://www.facebook.com/fabrice.robert.blocidentitaire/posts/894648357278200?fref=nf.

———. 2015b. Interview with the author, November 26.

———. 2016a. Email interview with the author, February 12.

———. 2016b. "L'election de Donald #Trump." November 9. Available from https://twitter.com/.

Roberts, Charlie. 2018. "Proof That." Twitter posting. April 1. Available at https://twitter.com/CRobertsGI/status/980371821957664768.

Robin, Charles. 2015. "L'Extrême-gauche a un role crucial dans le modèle du citoyen-consommateur liberal." *Réfléchir & Agir*, n. 51 (Autumn): 18–21.

Robinson, Tommy. 2017. " We Are Walking Into Oblivion—With Brittany Pettibone." October 28. Available at https://www.youtube.com/watch?v=T189gOGGf9U.

Rosenberg, Daniel. 2014. "War and Peace in the Political Philosophy of Julien Freund." *Peace Review: A Journal of Social Justice*, 26, n. 3: 334–41.

Rossman, Vadim. 2015. "Moscow State University's Department of Sociology and the Climate of Opinion in post-Soviet Russia." In *Eurasianism and the European Far Right*, ed. Marlene Laruelle, 55–76. Lanham, MD.

RT (*Russia Today*). 2017. "Trump Taking Office Spells End to World Order of 20th Century—German FM Steinmeier." January 22. Available at https://www.rt.com/news/374688-steinmeier-trump-end-era/.

Ruben. 2017. Twitter posting. August 20. Available at https://twitter.com/675 324676423d/status/899113934954930176.

Rue 89. 2014. "Oubliez 'Game of Thrones': Les Identitaires ont des théories plus folles." November 5. Available at http://rue89.nouvelobs.com/2014 /05/11/oubliez-game-of-thrones-les-identitaires-ont-theories-bien -plus-folles-252022.

Saint-Loup. 2014. "Toward a Europe of Carnal Fatherlands." Originally published in 1976, translated by Greg Johnson. Available at http://www .counter-currents.com/2014/10/toward-a-europe-of-carnal-fatherlands/.

Saint-Pierre, Jacques. 2004. "Jean Mabire et les combattants de la cause irlandaise." *Les Amis de Jean Mabire*, n. 9 (September): 1–2.

Saint-Exupéry, Antoine. 1965. *A Sense of Life*. New York: Funk and Wagnalls.

Salzborn, Samuel. 2016. "Renaissance of the New Right in Germany?" *German Politics and Society* 34, n. 2 (Summer): 36–63.

San Giorgio, Piero. 2013. "Nous allons redécouvrir un monde de manqué et de pénurie." *éléments pour la civilisation européenne*, n. 147 (April–June): 6–8.

———. 2016a. Email interview with the author, May 10.

———. 2016b. "Piero San Giorgio—Revue de 'Guerilla' de Laurent Obertone." September 19. Available at https://www.youtube.com/watch?v=Q2 _5SUDnd1E.

Scianca, Adriano. 2003. "La imposture liberal." *Elementos de Metapolítica para una Civilización Europea*, n. 28: 55–58.

———. 2011. *Riprendersi tutto: Le parole di CasaPound; 40 concetti per una rivoluzione in atto*. Cusano Milanino: Società Editrice Barbarossa.

———. 2015a. "Ecco perché le elite ci odiano." *Il Primato Nazionale*, March 26. Available at http://www.ilprimatonazionale.it/cultura/recensione-libro -le-mepris-du-peuple-jack-dion-19844/.

———. 2015b. "Ecco perché l'Italia non puo dimenticare Benito Mussolini." *Il Primato Nazionale*, April 28. Available at http://www.ilprimatonazio nale.it/cultura/perche-l-italia-non-puo-dimenticare-benito-mussolini -22096/.

———. 2015c. Email interview with the author, May 8.

———. 2015d. "Salvini? Una rivoluzione conservatrice che i media non hanno capito." *Il Primato Nazionale*, May 15. Available at http://www.ilprimato nazionale.it/cultura/matteo-salvini-saggio-antonio-rapisarda-23438/.

———. 2015e. "'Repubblica' vuole 250 milioni di immigrati: Noi lo dicevamo che erano pazzi . . . .'" *Il Primato Nazionale*, September 9. Available at http://www.ilprimatonazionale.it/politica/repubblica-vuole-250-milioni-di-immigrati-30200/.

———. 2015f. "Il paradosso di un'epoca che si commuove solo per gli stranieri." *Il Primato Nazionale*, September 11. Available at http://www.ilprimatonazionale.it/cultura/il-paradosso-di-unepoca-che-si-commuove-solo-per-gli-stranieri-30310/.

———. 2015g. "La Grande Sostituzione e la battaglia per l'essenziale." *Il Primato Nazionale*, October 20. Available at http://www.ilprimatonazionale.it/cultura/grande-sostituzione-32682/.

———. 2015h. "Via il dottorato honoris causa a Konrad Lorenz: 'Era nazista.'" *Il Primato Nazionale*, December 18. Available at http://www.ilprimatonazionale.it/cultura/konrad-lorenz-nazista-36565/.

———. 2016a. "'Il nuovo comunismo è venuto per sostituire i popoli': Parla Renaud Camus." *Primato Nazionale*, February 6. Available at http://www.ilprimatonazionale.it/cultura/renaud-camus-39456/.

———. 2016b. "Se la sostituzione di popolo si chiama "rinascita": Il caso Sutera." *Primato Nazionale*, February 12. Available at http://www.ilprimatonazionale.it/cronaca/sostituzione-di-popolo-sutera-39846/.

———. 2016c. "Come la natura ci fa rifiutare l'invasione: L'Imperativo territorial è genético." *Primato Nazionale*, February 22. Available at http://www.ilprimatonazionale.it/cultura/imperativo-territoriale-40466/.

———. 2016d. "Anche oggi è la giornata mondiale contro il razzismo." *Primato Nazionale*, March 21. Available at http://www.ilprimatonazionale.it/cronaca/giornata-contro-razzismo-42073/.

———. 2016e. "Bruxelles: L'Inferno lo avete evocato voi, com le vostre 'migliori intenzioni.'" *Primato Nazionale*, March 22. Available at http://www.ilprimatonazionale.it/esteri/bruxelles-42134/.

———. 2016f. "Il ministro Boschi e il feticismo dell'immigrazione." *Primato Nazionale*, March 23. Available at http://www.ilprimatonazionale.it/politica/boschi-immigrazione-42235/.

———. 2016g. "Papa Francesco è il nemico numero uno dell'Europa?" *Primato Nazionale*, April 19. Available at http://www.ilprimatonazionale.it/cronaca/papa-francesco-nemico-europa-43688/.

———. 2016h. "Essere non anti, ma alter-europeisti: In che modo?" *Primato Nazionale*, May 6. Available at http://www.ilprimatonazionale.it/approfondimenti/alter-europeisti-44656/.

———. 2016i. "Le oligarchie lo normalizzeranno presto: Ma, per or, Trump ci strappa un sorriso." *Primato Nazionale*, November 9. Available at http

://www.ilprimatonazionale.it/esteri/le-oligarchie-lo-normalizzeranno-presto-ma-per-ora-trump-ci-strappa-un-sorriso-52605/.

———. 2016j. *L'Identita Sacra: Dei, popoli e luoghi al tempo della Grande Sostituzione*. Milan: Aga Editrice.

———. 2017a. "Il piano ONU per l'invasione: andiamoli a prendere tutti." *Primato Nazionale*, January 26. Available at http://www.ilprimatonazionale.it/cronaca/il-piano-onu-per-linvasione-andiamoli-a-prendere-tutti-56455/#eWOsTF6eh5kQCzh7.99.

———. 2017b. "L'Europa, no, gli altri: Quattro tesi per superare le allucinazioni." *Primato Nazionale*, February 28. Available at http://www.ilprimatonazionale.it/cultura/leuropa-noi-gli-altri-quattro-tesi-per-superare-le-allucinazioni-58282/.

———. 2017c. "L'Immigrazione? È conquista demográfica, non religiosa; La trappola fallaciana." *Primato Nazionale*, May 3. Available at http://www.ilprimatonazionale.it/cronaca/limmigrazione-e-conquista-demografica-non-religiosa-la-trappola-fallaciana-63506/.

———. 2017d. "Manifesto contro lo ius soli: 10 ragioni per evitare il suicidio." *Primato Nazionale*, June 13. Available at http://www.ilprimatonazionale.it/politica/manifesto-contro-lo-ius-soli-10-ragioni-per-evitare-il-suicidio-67040/#.

Secolo d'Italia. 2014. "Minacciato il filosofo Fusaro che doveva parlare di Marx a CasaPound: 'Clima intollerabile, rinuncio al dibattito.'" February 14. Available at http://www.secoloditalia.it/2014/02/minacciato-il-filosofo-fusaro-che-doveva-parlare-di-marx-a-casapound-clima-intollerabile-rinuncio-al-dibattito/.

Sellner, Martin. 2014. "Gestaendnis einer maske teil 2." Available at http://www.identitaere-generation.info/gestaendnis-einer-maske-teil-2/.

———. 2015. "Warum wir auf die strase gehen?" May 31. Available at http://www.sezession.de/49893/warum-wir-auf-die-strasse-gehen.html.

———. 2016a. "Speech at '*On est chez nous!*' Demo." May 28. Available at https://www.youtube.com/watch?v=eZa6tslMXU8.

———. 2016b. "An alle Christen." July 26. Available at https://twitter.com/Martin_Sellner/status/757983467422511104.

———. 2016c. Email interviews with the author, August 2–6, September 15, October 27, and December 2.

———. 2016d. "We Are Making History Folks." November 9. Available at https://www.instagram.com/p/BPe4VXKhc0y/.

———. 2017a. Email interviews with the author, March 24 and September 21.

———. Sellner, Martin. 2017b. "Westminster Bridge—UK Starting to Fight Back against Islamization." October 23. Available at https://www.instagram.com/p/BalRPvTFfRD/.

———. 2018. "Please Support @TRobinsonNewEra in His Work and Projects." March 12. Available at https://twitter.com/Martin_Sellner/status/973137672645632000.

Sen, Amartya. 2007. *Identity and Violence: The Illusion of Destiny*. New York: W. W. Norton.

Sezession. 2015. "Wiener #deraustausch-Demonstration, bundesrepublikanisch gesehen." June 9. Available at http://www.sezession.de/49996/wiener-deraustausch-demonstration-bundesrepublikanisch-gesehen.html.

Sezession. 2016. "Linke Gewalteskalation—Was tun, Martin Sellner?" October 13. Available at https://sezession.de/56090/linke-gewalteskalation-was-tun-martin-sellner.

Smith, Anthony D. 1991. *National Identity*. London: Penguin.

Solère, Fenek. 2014. *The Partisan—Les enfants de la nouvelle école*. London: Iron Sky.

———. 2015. "Identitarianism, a Catalyst for Ethnogenesis in Europe." *New European Conservative*, August 20. Available at https://neweuropeanconservative.wordpress.com/2015/08/20/identitarianism-a-catalyst-for-ethnogenesis-in-europe-solere/.

———. 2016. Email interview with author, April 29.

SOM. 2015. Web page. Available at http://www.somcat.cat.

Spencer, Richard. 2015a. Email interview with the author, March 31.

———. 2015b. "Guillaume Faye's Speech—'Become Who We Are,'" October 31. Available at https://www.youtube.com/watch?v=Ss-QNSiN2oY.

———. 2017. Alt Right Politics, November 1. Available at https://altright.com/2017/11/03/alt-right-politics-november-1-2017-ich-kann-nicht-anders/.

Spengler, Oswald. 1934. *The Hour of Decision*, trans. Charles Francis Atkinson: New York: Alfred A. Knopf.

Spiegel. 2011. "Italy Killings Underscore European Extremism Problem." December 15. Available at http://www.spiegel.de/international/europe/a-big-leap-in-right-wing-currents-italy-killings-underscore-european-extremism-problem-a-803938.html.

Stampa. 2017. "Otto giovani denunciati dopo il blitz anti-Islam." January 17. Available at http://www.lastampa.it/2017/01/17/edizioni/vercelli/otto-giovani-denunciati-dopo-il-blitz-antiislam-55Bz7noY6NWreIqfrOLJ2O/pagina.html.

Steiger, Florian. 2014. "Die Identitäre Bewegung—Open-Source—Ideologie aus dem Internet." Available at http://www.belltower.news/artikel/die-"identitäre-bewegung"-open-source-ideologie-aus-dem-internet-9343.

Stern. 2016. "Die neuen Rechten—hip und völkisch." December 18. Available at http://www.stern.de/panorama/gesellschaft/identitaere-bewegung—die-neuen-rechten—hip-und-voelkisch-7238900.html.

Steuckers, Robert. 1994. "Faux socialisme et vraie socialisme." November. Available at http://robertsteuckers.blogspot.pt/2012/03/faux-socialisme-et-vrai-socialisme.html.

———. 1999. "La redecouverte des facteurs 'Russie,' 'siberie,' et ' Eurasie' dans la 'nouvelle droite' en France." *Vouloir: Revue Culturelle Pluridisciplinaire*, n. 146–8 (Autumn): 3–8. Avaliable at http://www.evrazia.org/modules.php?name=News&file=article&sid=257.

———. 2006. "Introduction par Robert Steuckers à la présentation par Guillaume Faye du livre 'La convergence des catastrophes, signé Guillaume Corvus, Bruxelles, Ravensteinhof.'" January 21. Available at http://euro-synergies.hautetfort.com/archive/2010/01/27/64a10782cb9b97ce5ea9f041f9b1724d.html.

———. 2012. "Causerie à bâtons rompus sur la notion de patrie charnelle—Conférence prononcée à Nancy, à la tribune de 'Terre et Peuple Lorraine.'" March 10. Available at http://robertsteuckers.blogspot.pt/2013/03/sur-la-notion-de-patrie-charnelle_8.html.

———. 2013. "Europe, Globalization and Metapolitics." *Euro-Synergies—Forum des résistants européens*, June 13. Available at http://euro-synergies.hautetfort.com/archive/2013/06/13/europe-globalization-and-metapolitics.html.

———. 2014a. "L'Europe espionnée par la NSA." April 10. Available at http://robertsteuckers.blogspot.pt/2014/09/leurope-espionnee-par-la-nsa.html.

———. 2014b. Email interview with the author, October 5.

———. 2015a. Email interview with the author, April 4.

———. 2015b. "Syrian Crisis, French Intellectual Landscape and 'Grand Remplacement.'" October. Available at http://robertsteuckers.blogspot.pt/2015/10/crise-syrienne-paysage-intellectuel.html.

———. 2015c. Le Blog de Robert Steuckers. October. Available at http://robertsteuckers.blogspot.pt/2015/10/crise-syrienne-paysage-intellectuel.html.

———. 2016. *The European Enterprise: Geopolitical Essays*, trans. Alexander Jacob. Melbourne, Victoria, Australia: Manticore Press.

———. 2017. *Europa*, vol. 1: *Valeurs et racines profondes de l'Europe*. Éditions BIOS.

———. 2018. Email interview with the author, February 18.

Sunday Times. 2018. "London Murder Rate Beats New York as Stabbings Surge." April 1. Available at https://www.thetimes.co.uk/edition/news/london-murder-rate-beats-new-york-as-stabbings-surge-f59w0xqs0.

Sunić, Tomislav. n.d. Interview on *Réfléchir & Agir*. Available at http://tomsunic.com/?p=390.

———. 2007. "Homo Americanus: The Dissolution of American materialism." *Occidental Quarterly* 7, n. 1 (Spring): 43–57. Available at https://www.toqonline.com/archives/v7n1/Sunic.pdf.

———. 2011. "Which Way White Man? Part 1." March 22. Available at http://theoccidentalobserver.net/2011/03/which-way-white-man-part-1/.

———. 2015. Email interview with the author, February 2.

———. 2016. "Where Is Prince Eugene? Multicultural Madness and the End of Europe." February 27. Available at http://www.theoccidentalobserver.net/2016/02/where-is-prince-eugene-multicultural-madness-and-the-end-of-europe/.

———. 2017. "Non-White Migrants and the Catholic Church: The Politics of Penitence." April 29. Available at http://www.theoccidentalobserver.net/2017/04/non-white-migrants-and-the-catholic-church-the-politics-of-penitence/.

Suvorov Institute. 2016. "Unser Auftrag." Available at http://www.suworow.at/wir-ueber-uns/.

Synergies Européennes. 2016. "La tyrannie mondialiste et le totalitarisme démocratique—Entretien réalisé par Victor Loupan, Munich, Juin 1999." Available at www.euro-synergies.hautetfort.com/entretiens.

Tarchi, Marco. 2010. *La Rivoluzione Impossibile: Dai Campi Hobbit alla Nuova destra*. Florence: Vallecchi.

Taylor, Jared. 2012a. "Foreword." In *Convergence of Catastrophes*, by Guillaume Faye, trans. E. Christian Kopff, 9–11. London: Arktos.

———. 2012b. "Why We Fight: Review of Guillaume Faye, *Why We Fight: Manifesto of the European Resistance*." *American Renaissance*, February 17. Available at http://www.amren.com/features/2012/02/why-we-fight/.

———. 2012c. "Autopsie d'une malveillance: La parole à Jared Taylor, orateur des assises 'La France en Danger?' [Entretien]," February 21. Available at http://fr.novopress.info/108478/autopsie-dune-malveillance-la-parole-a-jared-taylor-orateur-des-assises-la-france-en-danger-entretien/.

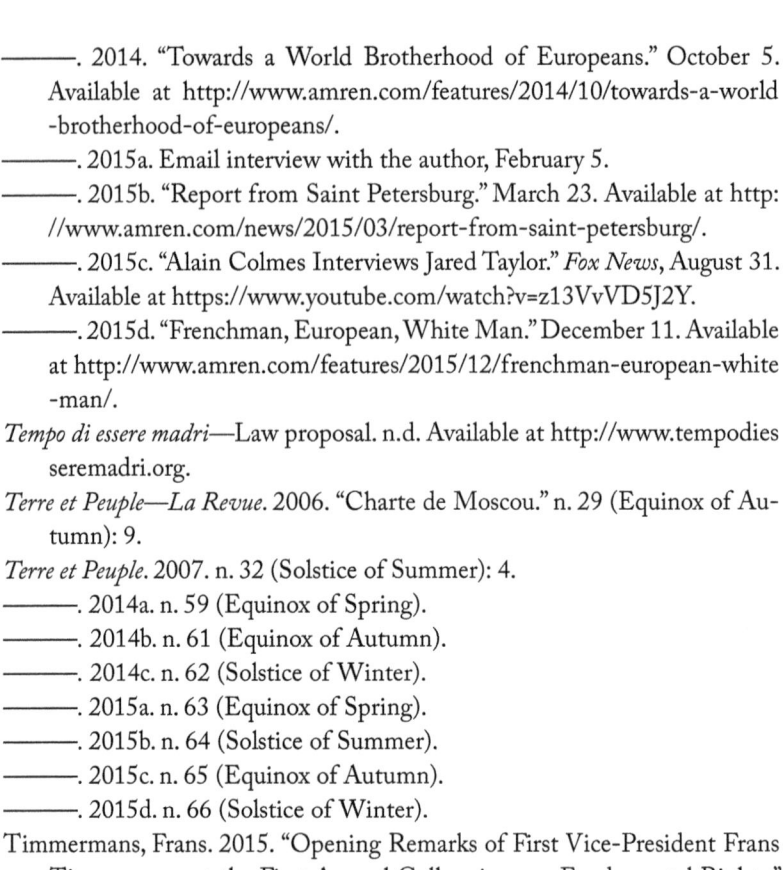

———. 2014. "Towards a World Brotherhood of Europeans." October 5. Available at http://www.amren.com/features/2014/10/towards-a-world-brotherhood-of-europeans/.

———. 2015a. Email interview with the author, February 5.

———. 2015b. "Report from Saint Petersburg." March 23. Available at http://www.amren.com/news/2015/03/report-from-saint-petersburg/.

———. 2015c. "Alain Colmes Interviews Jared Taylor." *Fox News*, August 31. Available at https://www.youtube.com/watch?v=z13VvVD5J2Y.

———. 2015d. "Frenchman, European, White Man." December 11. Available at http://www.amren.com/features/2015/12/frenchman-european-white-man/.

Tempo di essere madri—Law proposal. n.d. Available at http://www.tempodieseremadri.org.

Terre et Peuple—La Revue. 2006. "Charte de Moscou." n. 29 (Equinox of Autumn): 9.

Terre et Peuple. 2007. n. 32 (Solstice of Summer): 4.

———. 2014a. n. 59 (Equinox of Spring).

———. 2014b. n. 61 (Equinox of Autumn).

———. 2014c. n. 62 (Solstice of Winter).

———. 2015a. n. 63 (Equinox of Spring).

———. 2015b. n. 64 (Solstice of Summer).

———. 2015c. n. 65 (Equinox of Autumn).

———. 2015d. n. 66 (Solstice of Winter).

Timmermans, Frans. 2015. "Opening Remarks of First Vice-President Frans Timmermans at the First Annual Colloquium on Fundamental Rights." October 1. Available at http://europa.eu/rapid/press-release_SPEECH-15-5754_en.htm.

Tremblay, Rémi. 2015. "Casapound's Recipe for Success." *Alternative Right*, March 7. Available at http://alternative-right.blogspot.com/2015/03/casapounds-recipe-for-success.html.

———. 2016. Email interview with the author, October 31.

Trump, Donald J. 2016. "Donald J. Trump Foreign Policy Speech," April 27. Available at https://www.donaldjtrump.com/press-releases/donald-j-trump-foreign-policy-speech.

Torga, Miguel. 1993. *Diário XVI*. Coimbra, Portugal.

Tudor, Lucian. 2014. "The Philosophy of Identity: Ethnicity, Culture, and Race in Identitarian Thought." *Occidental Quarterly* 14, n. 3 (Fall): 83–112.

———. 2015a. Email interview with the author, January 31.

———. 2015b. *From the German Conservative Revolution to the New Right.* Chile: Identitas/Círculo de Investigaciones PanCriollistas.
Tulaev, Pavel. 2006. "Euro-Russia in the context of World War IV." June 8. Available at http://www.ateney.ru/old/eng/eng010.htm#c.
———. 2015. Email interview with the author, September 8.
UN POP. 2000. "Press Release DEV/2234 POP/735." March 17. Available at http://www.un.org/esa/population/unpop.htm.
Valla, Jean-Claude. 2013. *Engagements pour la civilisation européenne.* Billère: Alexipharmaque.
Van Creveld, Martin. 2016. Email communication with the author, May 6.
Van Zee, Jean-Charles, and Charles Marly. 2006. "Culture: La loi du pognon règne" *ID Magazine*, n. 6 (Summer): 2–3.
Vardon, Philippe. 2010. "A Béziers Philippe Vardon revendique l'autonomie, l'autogestion, l'autodefense." November 23. Available at http://www.bloc-identitaire.com/actualite/1608/beziers-philippe-vardon-revendique-autonomie-autogestion-autodefense.
———. 2012. "Direction Reconquête!" *Identitaires*, n. 12 (December): 5–7.
———. 2013. "Foreword: The Front Line." In *Generation Identity: A Declaration of War against the '68ers*, by Markus Willinger, 7–10. London: Arktos.
Vardon-Raybaud, Philippe. 2011. *Éléments pour une Contre-Culture identitaire.* Nice: Idées.
———. 2014. *Militants: 14 histoires qui sentient la colle et le gaz lacrymo.* Nice: Idées.
Vejvodová, Petra. 2014. "The Identitarian Movement—Renewed Idea of Alternative Europe." Paper presented at the ECPR General Conference, Glasgow, September 3–6.
Veliocas, Joachim. 2016. Email interview with the author, June 13.
Venner, Dominique. 1994. "Quand la Russie s'éveillera . . . ." *Enquête sur l'Histoire*, n. 9 (Winter): 10–11.
———. 1996. "Nostalgies d'Europe." *Enquête sur l'Histoire*, n. 15 (Winter): 10–11.
———. 2001. "Comment peut-on ne pas être rebelle?" *éléments pour la civilisation européenne*, n. 101 (May): 16–17.
———. 2003a. "Le défi des civilisations." *Nouvelle Revue d'Histoire*, n. 4: (January–February), 7.
———. 2003b. "Éternité des civilisations." *Nouvelle Revue d'Histoire*, n. 7 (July–August): 7.
———. 2003c. "Les Européens sous le choc." *Nouvelle Revue d'Histoire*, n. 7 (July–August): 57–59.

———. 2005. "Infidèles Européens." *Nouvelle Revue d'Histoire*, n. 20 (September–October): 5.

———. 2006. "Les vingt jours qui ont ébranlée la France." *La Nouvelle Revue d'Histoire*, n. 22 (January–February): 29–32.

———. 2009a. "Vous avez dit autochtone?" *Nouvelle Revue d'Histoire*, n. 44 (September–October), 5.

———. 2009b. "Violence et 'doux commerce.'" *Nouvelle Revue d'Histoire*, n. 44 (September–October): 35–38.

———. 2011a. *Histoire et Tradition des Européens: 30 000 ans d'identité*. Monaco: Éditions du Rocher.

———. 2011b. *Le Choc de l'Histoire: Religion, mémoire, identité*. Versailles: Éditions Via Romana.

———. 2011c. "L'homme de la guerre et la cité." *Nouvelle Revue d'Histoire*, n. 52 (January–February), 5.

———. 2012a. "Trois campagnes de Russie." *Nouvelle Revue d'Histoire*, n. 60 (May–June): 5.

———. 2012b. "Ce que valent les civilisations . . . ." *Nouvelle Revue d'Histoire*, n. 60 (May–June): 8.

———. 2013a. "Suicide Note." May 21. Available at https://occamsrazormag.wordpress.com/2013/05/22/translation-of-dominique-venners-suicide-note/.

———. 2013b. *Un samouraï d'Occident, Le bréviaire des insoumis*. Paris: Éditions Pierre-Guillaume de Roux.

———. 2015a. *The Shock of History: Religion, Memory, Identity*, trans. Charlie Wilson. London: Arktos.

———. 2015b. "Le Blanc Soleil des vaincus—Nouvelle préface d'Alain de Benoist." December 9. Available at http://www.dominiquevenner.fr/2015/12/le-blanc-soleil-des-vaincus-nouvelle-preface-dalain-de-benoist/.

———. 2016. *Un Samurai d'Occidente: Il breviario dei ribelli*, organized by Andrea Lombardi and Adriano Scianca. Rome: Edizioni Settimo Sigillo.

Vera Opposizione. 2011. "Simone Di Stefano a Pomeriggio 5: CasaPound non è identitaria razziale." December 17. Available at https://veraopposizione.wordpress.com/tag/simone-di-stefano/.

verfassungsschuetzer.info. 2017. "Vorwürfe und Widerlegungen der Identitären Bewegung." Available at http://verfassungsschuetzer.info/vorwuerfe-und-widerlegungen-der-identitaeren-bewegung/.

Verhassel, Aurélien. 2016. "Même si ça va sans dire, c'est plus clair en le disant!" Twitter posting, September 5. https://twitter.com/A_Verhassel/status/772756092564676608.

Verlag & Antaios. 2016. "Renaud Camus—Revolte gegen den Großen Austausch." Available at http://antaios.de/gesamtverzeichnis-antaios/einzel titel/14322/revolte-gegen-den-grossen-austausch.

Vial, Pierre. 1992. "Le mondialisme destructeur de l'identité des peuples." In *Le Mondialisme: Mythe et réalité*, ed. Jacques Robichez et al., 107–12. Paris: Éditions Nationales.

———. 1999. "Editorial—Plantons notre drapeau." *Terre et Peuple*, n. 1 (Autumn): 3.

———. 2001. "Ni Jihad, ni Mc World: Europe Liberté." *Terre et Peuple*, n. 10 (Solstice of Winter): 17–19.

———. 2005a. "Le colosse aux pieds d'argile." *Terre et Peuple*, n. 25 (Equinox of Autumn): 3.

———. 2005b. "Croisade, Résistance, Reconquête." *Terre et Peuple*, n. 25 (Equinox of Autumn): 28–34.

———. 2005c. "Nous les Gaulois et la guerre ethnique." *Terre et Peuple—La Revue*, n. 26 (Solstice of Winter): 19.

———. 2008. "Jean Mabire, ethnologue?" *Jean Mabire: Magazine des Amis de Jean Mabire*, n. 39 (Solstice of Summer): 2.

———. 2009. "Europe Blanche." *Terre et Peuple*, n. 40 (Solstice of Summer): 33–36.

———. 2010a. "Oui, nous avons raison." *Terre et Peuple*, n. 43 (Equinox of Spring): 3.

———. 2010b. "Identités: La Révolution du XXI Siècle." *Terre et Peuple*, n. 43 (Equinox of Spring), 23.

———. 2010c. "Identité, Identitaire." *Terre et Peuple*, n. 43 (Equinox of Spring): 24–25.

———. 2014a. "La Grande Russie." March 22. Available at http://www.terreetpeuple.com/chroniques-par-pierre-vial/1058-la-grande-russie.html.

———. 2014b. "Le réveil des patries charnelles." *Terre et Peuple*, n. 62 (Solstice of Winter): 9.

———. 2015a. "'If This Isn't War . . .': The *Charlie Hebdo* Massacre," trans. Patrick Le Brun. Counter-Currents, January 7. Available at http://www.counter-currents.com/2015/01/if-this-isnt-war-the-charlie-hebdo-massacre/.

———. 2015b. Email interview with the author, March 17.

———. 2015c. "Choc des Civilisations: Une vieille histoire." *Terre et Peuple*, n. 63 (Equinox of Spring): 51–52.

———. 2015d. "Poitou-Info—Rencontres-Charles-Martel 2015: Pierre Vial." June 11. Available at https://www.youtube.com/watch?v=L4YH-PV-D80.

———. 2016. "Le Populisme, une tradition française." *Terre et Peuple*, n. 68 (Solstice of Summer): 26–30.

Vick, Alexandre. 2013. "Les Identitaires se réorganisent pour la survie de la 'race blanche.'" February 28. Available at http://www.resistances.be/actioneurop.html.

Villena, Patricio. 2014. "Qué es ser criollo?" March 1. Available at https://pancriollismo.com/2014/03/01/que-es-ser-criollo/.

Virchow, Fabian. 2015. "The 'Identitarian Movement': What Kind of Identity? Is It Really a Movement?" In *Digital Media Strategies of the Far Right in Europe and the United States*, ed. Patricia Anne Simpson and Helga Druxes, 177–90. Lanham, MD: Lexington Books.

Virilio, Paul. 2000. *From Modernism to Hypermodernism and Beyond*, ed. John Armitage, London: Sage.

———. 2012. *The Administration of Fear*. Cambridge, MA: MIT Press.

Vitali, Juan Pablo. 2014. "To Dominique Venner," trans. Francisco Albanese. June 11. Available at http://www.counter-currents.com/2014/06/to-dominique-venner/.

———. 2015. "El pan-Criollismo como destino del hombre blanco americano." January 11. Available at http://fni.cl/csm/el-pan-criollismo-como-destino-del-hombre-blanco-americano.

Von Salomon, Ernst. 2013. *The Outlaws*. London: Arktos.

Walker, Michael Francis. 2008. Email interview with the author, April 13.

Washington Post. 2016. "National Security: As Russia Reasserts Itself, U.S. Intelligence Agencies Focus Anew on the Kremlin." September 14. Available at https://www.washingtonpost.com/world/national-security/as-russia-reasserts-itself-us-intelligence-agencies-focus-anew-on-the-kremlin/2016/09/14/cc212c62-78f0-11e6-ac8e-cf8e0dd91dc7_story.html.

———. 2017. "From Idea to Action: White supremacy's New Visibility—Interview with George Michael." August 24. Available at https://www.washingtonpost.com/news/post-nation/wp/2017/08/24/from-idea-to-action-white-supremacys-new-visibility/?utm_term=.af3976a20dc7.

Wermod & Wermod. 2014. "Interview with Fenek Solère—by Alex Kurtagic." October 31. Available at http://www.wermodandwermod.com/newsitems/news311020140001.html.

Werner, Eric. 2013. "Eric Werner: De la démocratie à la 'mafiocratie.'" *Nouvelle Revue d'Histoire*, n. 65 (March–April): 21–22.

———. 2015a. *L'Avant-guerre civile: Le chaos sauvera-t-il le système?* Sion, Switzerland: Éditions Xenia.

———. 2015b. "Risques." *L'Avant-Blog, Chronique de la modernité tardive*, September 5. Available at http://ericwerner.blogspot.pt/2015/09/risques.html.

———. 2015c. "Climat." *L'Avant-Blog, Chronique de la modernité tardive.* November 19. Available at http://ericwerner.blogspot.pt/2015/11/climat.html.

Wicht, Bernard. 2013. *Europe Mad Max Demain? Retour à la défense citoyenne.* Lausanne, Switzerland: Éditions Favre.

Willinger, Markus. 2013. *Generation Identity: A Declaration of War against the '68ers*, trans. David Schreiber. London: Arktos.

YouTube. 2016a. "Zukunft für Europa—Identitäre Bewegung." January 21. Available at https://www.youtube.com/watch?v=rPXI6tA31yI.xYouTube.2016b. "Tous unis contre le racism anti-blanc." March 25. Available at https://www.youtube.com/watch?v=_JNxUz5i4Bk.

———. 2016c. "Besetzung Brandenburger Tor—Sichere Grenzen—Sichere Zukunft." August 29. Available at https://www.youtube.com/watch?v=smRj9Erq8Y4&feature=youtu.be.

YouTube. 2017a. "Generation Identity: Europe's Youth Reconquista." May 11. Available at https://www.youtube.com/watch?v=QbbSv0m8CGI.

YouTube. 2017b. "Civil War in Europe?" October 8. Available at https://www.youtube.com/watch?v=-0M1NoZ8Njo.

YouTube. 2017c. "Generation Identity Hungary—Ábel Bódi." October 22. Available at https://www.youtube.com/watch?v=SuuVNsYxokw&feature=youtu.be.

YouTube. 2018a. "Austria Decides to Grow a Spine." January 12. Available at https://www.youtube.com/watch?v=GPuqGwQoXyE.

YouTube. 2018b. "Breaking: Tommy Robinson Removed from Speakers Corner Hyde Park." March 14. Available at https://www.youtube.com/watch?v=ybauuaAj0fI.

Zeitfragen. 2016. "Die 'Identitäre Bewegung' Gegen alles, was anders ist." August 15. Available at http://www.deutschlandradiokultur.de/die-identitaere-bewegung-gegen-alles-was-anders-ist.976.de.html?dram:article_id=363174.

Zeltīts, Raivis. 2016. Email interview with the author, November 9.

Zentropa. n.d.a. "Interview: Gianluca Iannone." Available at http://zentropaville.tumblr.com/post/61853752321/interview-gianluca-iannone.

Zentropa. n.d.b. "Zentropa est l'expression politique." Available at http://zentropaville.tumblr.com/post/167832742418/zentropa-est-lexpression-politique-dune.

Zentropa. 2012a. "Turbodynamism." Available at http://zentropaville.tumblr.com/post/26969144436/amour-absinthe-revolution-the-manifesto-of.

———. 2012b. "Why Is the Casapound Symbol the Tortoise?" Available at http://sexorcismo.tumblr.com/post/36211671184/zentropista-why-is-the-casapound-symbol-the.

———. 2015. "Who Are We?" Available at http://zentropaville.tumblr.com/post/135253108798.

Zetland. 2018. "De er unge og dannede: Danmarks nye højreradikale citerer Oehlenschläger og rekrutterer med Instagram-lækre actioner." January 5. Available at https://www.zetland.dk/historie/sevMmg3z-aOZj67pz-91915.

Zinoviev, Alexander. 1981. *Nous et l'Occident*. Lausanne: L'Âge d'homme.

INDEX

aesthetics, 24, 50–57, 100. *See* Identitarian New Cool
agitprop, 48
al-Assad, Bashar, 215–17, 264
Almássy, Ferenc, 248–49
Alter-Europe, 234–39, 251–52
Alt Right, 295, 299, 302–7; European Identitarians and, 309–11, 314–18
America. *See* United States, the
anarchism, 67–68, 369
anti-elitist and anti-Establishment expressions, 2–3, 47–48, 75, 111, 126–27, 132, 161, 204, 279, 281, 330, 340, 370
antifa, 78, 94, 96, 118, 191, 304, 306, 335–38
anti-Semitism, 290–91, 314. *See also* Jewish Question, the
anti-white racism, 282–89, 300
archeofuturism, 14, 295, 329, 369
Arteault, Jean-Patrick, 16, 244, 274
Atalante Québec, 97–98
autochthonous Europeans, 61, 136, 192, 276, 280, 283, 286, 296, 365, 370–71

Bannon, Stephen, 303
Bastion Social, 95–97
battles, historic, 177–82, 194–96
Berčík, Adam, 87, 159
Big Other, 137, 267

Bloc Identitaire: change of name, 28; history of, 28–31
Borghezio, Mario, 73, 144
Bousquet, François, 117, 267
Bradbury, Ray, 32
Branquinho, Duarte, 71–72, 236, 275
Brazilization, 160–61
Brexit, 236–39, 262, 302

Cagnat, Alain, 112, 163, 165, 174, 181, 201, 236, 242, 245, 279, 332–33
The Camp of the Saints, 131, 137, 145–46, 225, 279–80, 283
Camus, Renaud, 146–52, 153, 155–56, 171, 184, 189–90, 202, 212, 267, 309, 334, 347
capitalism, 11, 32, 35, 113–16, 118–23, 164, 231, 243, 324
CasaPound: alliance with Lega Nord, 65–66; history of, 32–37; Islam and, 213–18; network of, 93–98; racialism and, 289–92; social question and, 123–26; violence and, 36, 51, 55–56
CasaPoundism. *See* CasaPound: network of
Casey, Patrick, 308–9, 313, 317
Cattin, Jean-David, 74, 87–89, 102, 145, 165, 262
chaos, governance of, 338–40

459

Charlottesville, 304–6, 315–16
Chatov, Pierre, 43, 56
Christianity: critique of, 105–6, 219; Identitarian dimension of, 220–26
clash of civilizations, 25, 162–67, 187, 280, 285, 290, 331, 333
collaboration: elites and, 132, 165, 200–201; ethnicity and, 335, 352–53, 360
combat sports, 47, 59, 62, 82, 98. *See also* self-defense
Conservative Revolution (Germany), 8, 10, 27, 35, 84, 208, 291, 294, 322
consumerism, 52, 77, 116–17, 224, 248, 343, 350
continentalism, 233, 255–57
Counter-Currents (publisher-website), 101–2, 170, 293, 296, 298–99, 303, 306–7, 360
counter-jihadism, 169–70, 180, 215, 219, 307
crowdfunding, 86, 98, 142

De Benoist, Alain: Alt Right and, 299; the Great Replacement and, 150; identity and, 10–11
Defend Europe (mission), 142–45
Delrieux, Arnaud, 31, 63, 73, 137, 150, 182, 201, 220, 222, 287, 343
demography, 128–31
deplatforming (social media), 305
dhimmitude, 176–77, 180–81
Dictionary of Newspeak, 25, 47, 108, 115, 127, 131, 160, 162, 174, 200–201, 236, 245, 285, 331
Di Stefano, Simone, 33, 65, 66, 134–36, 214, 258, 291
doxing, 306, 336
Dugin, Alexandr: criticism by Identitarians of, 243, 252, 275; Eurasianism and, 232–34; *The Fourth Political Theory*, 255–56; praise for Donald Trump, 263–64

Dupré, Tom, 90, 237–38
Durden, Tyler, 54–55
Durolle, Thierry, 314

Engels, David, 353–54
ethnoculturalism, 12, 14, 70, 77, 107, 132, 270, 291, 323, 365–66
ethnodifferentialism: Bloc Identitaire (Les Identitaires) and, 30; Casa-Pound and, 35, 289–90; German New Right and, 268; the ND and, 9–10
ethnomasochism, 131–37, 279
ethnopluralism, 255, 268, 317
Eugene, Prince, 195–97
Eurasianism: Dugin and, 232–34; Identitarian rejection of, 242–43, 252
European civilization, 1, 162; demise of, 138, 167; demographic crisis of, 129; Identitarian Lambda movement and, 91; Islam and threat to, 173, 175; Venner and, 20–21
Europeanism: background of, 228–29; identity and, 4, 30, 365; rejection of the EU and, 234, 260
Europeans of stock. *See* autochthonous Europeans
Evola, Julius, 93, 98, 113, 275
extremism: accusation of, 83, 153, 336–37; Identitarian denial of, 84–86, 322–26

fascism: CasaPound and, 34–36, 43, 92–93, 109, 124–25, 290–91; Hogar Social and, 96
Faye, Guillaume: combat against Islam, 173–74, 181, 199, 201–2; critique of globalism, 105–7, 114–16; defense of a bellicose Christianity, 219–20; defense of metapolitics, 38, 52; and European ethnic wars, 280–81, 331, 347, 359; immigration as invasion/

colonization, 131–33, 200, 355; the Jewish Question and, 312; need for geopolitical shift, 241–42, 245–46; prophecies and, 151, 198, 328–29, 352, 356–57; "revolt of doing" and, 67–68; role in Identitarianism, 13–15; Donald Trump victory, 262–63; *Why We Fight*, 13, 103, 300, 308
Fédération des Québécois de Souche [Federation of the Quebecois of Stock], 97, 121, 318
Feltin-Tracol, Georges, 119, 236–37, 251–52, 275, 334, 340, 348–49, 355
feminization, 129, 340–42; and nu-males, 342
Fiorini, Roberto, 121, 128, 148
Fiß, Daniel, 82, 85, 154
food drives, 94, 98, 123, 125
Fourth-Generation Warfare (4GW), 343–51, 355
Fourth Political Theory, 232, 255–56
Francis (pope), 156, 224–26
Franco, João, 103, 159–60
Freund, Julien, 321, 328–29, 340
Friberg, Daniel, 99–100, 128, 158, 236, 243, 248, 251, 302–3, 306
Fuerza Nacional-Identitaria, 318

Game of Thrones (TV series), 96, 273
Gauls, the, 79, 180, 287, 332
Generation Identity (GI): Austria, 74–86; Czech Republic, 87; Denmark, 89–90; Flanders and, 88–89; France, 27–32, 37–66; Germany, 74–86; Hungary, 87–88; Ireland, 90–91; Italy, 88; Slovenia, 88; United Kingdom, 90–91
Generation Z, 369
Geoffroy, Michel, 174, 268
geopolitics: defense of an independent Europe, 251–52, 258–60; paradigm shift toward the East, 239–51; rejection of the European Union, 234–36
Gibbon, Edward, 168, 179, 355
globalism, Identitarian stance against, 2, 105–7, 113–18, 170. *See* immigration; liberalism
Great Replacement, the: Renaud Camus and, 146–48; CasaPound and, 155–57; Identitarian Lambda movement and, 148–55; as key idea of Identitarians, 201–2, 253, 366–67; racialists and, 333–35
Greenpeace, as model of activism, 48, 82, 183

Heidegger, Martin, 15, 34
Holloway, John, 67
Houellebecq, Michel, 179, 358–59
Hyperboreans, 273–77, 358

Iannone, Gianluca, 33–36, 39–40, 42, 44, 46–47, 51, 55, 57, 61, 65–66, 92–94, 124, 134, 216, 290
Identitarian houses, 61–62, 68, 81, 187, 336, 369
Identitarianism: diffusion of, 98–104; as direct-action, 31, 46, 77–78, 80, 367–68; as school of thought, 3, 12, 27, 31, 67, 69, 239, 250
Identitarian Lambda movement. *See* Bloc Identitaire; Generation Identity
Identitarian New Cool, 52, 56, 79–80, 211, 256, 368–69, 389n88
identity: biology and, 14, 269, 272, 275, 279, 292, 318; defense of, 12–13, 30–31, 57, 75, 365; endangered, 2–3, 235; sacred, 370; semantics and, 47, 70, 108; three levels of, 2, 113, 365
Identity Evropa, 308–9, 313, 316–17

immigration: the Great Replacement and, 146–47, 150, 152, 154–56; as invasion/colonization, 2–3, 129, 131, 134, 212, 278; as root cause of Islamization, 4, 61, 171, 222, 332; the Western liberal order and, 166, 215, 257
Indo-Europeans, 17–18, 20–21, 112–13, 273–74, 277
Islam: the conquest of Europe by, 2, 197–213; as the eternal enemy of Europe, 175–82, 329; Identitarian activism against, 182–97, 209–10
Islamization, 4, 25, 48, 61, 72–73, 75, 137, 139, 150, 155, 253, 307, 171–97; as the gravest threat to Europe, 197–202
Islamophobia, 193, 201

Jewish Question, the, 312–13
jihad, 112, 174, 190, 195, 202–3, 205, 207, 212, 333, 351, 367
Johnson, Greg, 101–2, 293, 295, 298, 303, 306–7, 312–13, 315
Jünger, Ernst, 8, 27, 79, 321–22, 343–44
Jus Soli (birthright citizenship), Identitarian stance against, 135, 137, 157, 214

Kaalep, Ruuben, 250–51
Kofner, Jurij, 256–57
Krampon, Eugène, 18, 22, 67, 113, 119, 121, 133, 236, 242, 250, 272, 276–79, 313
Krebs, Pierre, 13, 71–72, 113, 242, 270, 272–73, 275, 280–81, 323, 330, 333
Kubitschek, Götz, 77–78, 86, 191, 251, 268, 330
Kurtagic, Alex, 137, 293, 295, 323, 335

Lambda, meaning and use of, as symbol, 53

Langella, Julien, 222, 224–25, 285–86, 288
Langness, Julian, 286, 332, 347–48, 355–56
Le Gallou, Jean-Yves, 24–26, 50, 70, 151, 158, 173, 190, 202, 213, 268, 282, 288, 330, 342, 352
Lenart, Patrick, 74, 79, 165
Les Identitaires. *See* Bloc Identitaire
liberal democracy: backlash against, 365; criticism of, 127, 170; overhaul of, 66, 371
liberalism: counter-jihadism and, 170; Dugin and, 232–33, 255; modernity and, 9, 106; new humans and, 268–69; rejection of, 18, 24, 115–16, 120, 127, 350, 365; Western Europe eroded by, 236, 243, 248–49
Lichtmesz, Martin, 78, 92–93, 102, 153, 161, 225, 252, 285, 300, 332, 336
Liddell, Colin, 60, 69, 157, 299
Lignier, Anaïs, 58, 186
literature of doom, 351–63
Locchi, Giorgio, 34–35, 229–30

Mabire, Jean, 110–13, 274
Macron, Emmanuel, 151, 185
Marchand, René, 172–73, 180, 183, 189, 197, 199–200, 211, 213, 332
Maréchal-Le Pen, Marion, 64, 151
Markovics, Alexander, 74, 76, 85, 101, 128, 141, 152, 212, 255, 257, 261–62, 264, 378n240
Martel, Charles, 179–83, 186–87, 204, 294
memes, 49, 80–81, 141, 209, 310, 314, 368–69
metapolitics: Identitarian youth movements and, 37–39; Metapolitics 2.0 and, 310–11; the ND and, 7–8
Milà, Ernesto, 72, 350–51
millennials, 369

miscegenation: globalism and, 16, 18, 268, 287; Jews and, 313; new humans and, 287–88; as threat to white identity, 279–81
Mohler, Armin, 8, 35
morality, change of paradigm and, 132, 137, 225, 322, 370–71
Morgan, John, 69, 99, 101, 215, 243, 297, 303, 314, 323–24
movies, 54–56, 119
multipolarism, 232–33
Murros, Kai, 333–34, 343, 350, 360
music, 29, 32, 38, 45, 47, 61–62, 73, 369
Muslims. *See* Islam

nationalism: CasaPoundism and, 94; overcoming of, 29, 37, 107–9, 228, 274; pan-Europeanism and, 30, 90, 241, 333, 371; transnationalism and, 20, 91
Nazism/neo-Nazism, 83–85, 336
new beginnings, identity and, 14–15, 34–35
Newspeak, 25–26, 47–48, 174
Nietzsche, Friedrich, 7, 15, 35, 79, 113, 116–17, 295, 358
nonconformism, 3, 24, 34, 39, 55, 61, 118

occupations, Identitarian activism and, 3, 32, 67, 95–96, 192
Ochsenreiter, Manuel, 164, 219, 255
O'Meara, Michael, 12–13, 67, 294, 296, 300, 301–2, 312, 318
120 Decibels (#120db) campaign, 193–94
open source, Identitarian activism and, 368
Oppedisano, Ada, 217–18
Orbán, Viktor, 249–50
origins. *See* new beginnings, identity and
Osborne, Lawrence, 132

Ottoman Empire, 177, 180–81, 194–96, 252, 342

paganism, 17–18, 282; Christianity and, 22, 219–20
patriot, as word of choice of Identitarians, 4, 61, 80, 84, 87, 86, 96, 108, 228, 244, 253, 314, 337
PEGIDA (Patriotic Europeans against the Islamization of the Occident), 190–91
Pepe the Frog, 310–11
Perino, Umberto Actis, 88, 92
Pettibone, Brittany, 102–3, 143, 145, 191, 314
Phalanx Europa, 79, 194–95, 254
Pirinçci, Akif, 153, 331
Poitiers: Battle of, 179–80, 196, 204, 206, 301, 357–58; occupation of mosque in, 182–83, 188, 190
Polémia, 25–26; and Forum of Dissidence, 26, 249
political correctness, rejection of, 18, 25, 31, 34, 47–48, 104, 127, 204, 260, 262, 282, 295, 359
political parties, 5, 34, 42; Identitarian ideological entry into, 63–65
Pope Francis. *See* Francis (pope)
Poppel, Patrick, 257
populism, Identitarian support of, 5, 86, 126–28, 151, 190, 371
postgenderism, 77
posthumanism, 271
Pound, Ezra, 32, 39, 40, 124
Powell, Enoch, 301
Prilepin, Zakhar, 243
progress: criticism of, 107–8, 161, 322; modernity and, 10, 106, 320
publishing houses, 77, 99–101, 122, 189, 248, 277
Putin, Vladimir, 231, 234, 242, 244, 246, 248, 254, 257, 259, 264, 393n29

Rabelais, 48, 309
race, as taboo, 201, 268, 272, 281
racialism, Identitarianism and, 270–81
racism, 11, 14, 137, 290, 296, 299, 314; anti-racism and, 130, 132, 148, 266–70, 288–90. *See also* anti-white racism
radicalism, 2, 18, 94, 328; right-wing, 4, 46
Randa, Philippe, 164, 220, 322, 357–58, 359
rape, 185–86; grooming gangs and, 289
Raspail, Jean, 131, 137, 145–46, 225–26, 279, 283
Ravello, Enrique, 72, 241, 275
rebellion, 1, 25, 33, 39–42, 61, 340, 355, 364; aesthetics and, 50–57
Rebel Media, 102, 191
rebranding, ideological and political, 369
Reconquista, 57, 79, 102, 163, 172, 177–78, 181, 188–89, 194–95; remigration as, 211–13
Redeker, Robert, 14, 268, 341
refugees, 132–36, 141–42, 156, 183, 192, 209, 212, 224, 225, 352
regionalism: carnal homelands and, 109–13; identity and, 2, 365, 371
re-information, alternative media and, 24–27, 47–50, 366
religion: Identitarian Catholicism, 222–26; Islam as, 172–75, 184
remigration, 157–60, 192, 196, 211–13, 222, 280, 317, 331, 367
revolution, 66–68
Rieu, Damien, 59, 64, 162, 171, 181, 186
Robert, Fabrice, 29–32, 44, 92, 138, 203–4, 260; failure of multiculturalism, 160, 288, 324; Identitarian activism and, 57–58, 61, 63–64, 68, 183, 190, 284; Identitarian networking and, 73, 300; identity and, 46–47, 107–8, 127, 132, 164; Russia and, 253–54
Robinson, Tommy, 189–92, 194, 389n88
Ruiz, Melisa, 96–97
Russia: as last best hope of Identitarians, 241–48; the ND and, 231–32, 234; skepticism of, 251–52
Russophilia, 239, 246
Russophobia, 246, 254–55

sacredness, 17, 21, 155, 220, 274, 370
Salvini, Matteo, 65–66, 157, 291
San Giorgio, Piero, 349–50, 363
Schmitt, Carl, 165, 230, 321, 360
Scianca, Adriano, 33–54, 66, 93–97, 115, 118, 124–25, 128, 166, 216, 237, 263, 292; anti-immigration and, 130, 134–35, 290; demographic crisis and, 129; European civil war and, 329, 352; Europeanism and, 259–60; the Great Replacement and, 155–56; identity and, 34, 52, 66, 117, 291; moral sentimentalism and, 137, 213–14; multiculturalism failure and, 160, 214–15, 266–67, 324; the papacy and, 225–26; populism and, 126; tragedy and, 322
self-defense, 36, 59–60, 136, 186, 192–93, 343, 349; coming war and, 324, 330, 363
Sellner, Martin, 74–93, 102, 122, 143–44, 191–92, 210, 222, 249, 256, 337–38; the Alt Right and, 314; Brexit and, 238; election of Donald Trump and, 260–61; European civil war and, 330–31; the Great Replacement and, 253; race and, 281; remigration and, 159, 161

"Show Your Face" campaigns, 58, 80–81, 369–70
socialism, Identitarian version of, 118–22, 148
social media: Alt Right and, 309–10; anti-Identitarian activism and, 336–37; Identitarian activism and, 48–50, 75, 88, 193–94, 197, 204, 206–7, 366, 368
social work, 38, 98, 123. *See also* solidarity, Identitarian activism and
Solère, Fenek, 72, 348, 359–60
solidarity, Identitarian activism and, 94, 98, 122–23, 125, 216–17, 317
Sorel, George, 120–21, 125, 294
Soros, George, 224, 250
Southern, Lauren, 102, 143, 145
Sparta (ancient): Battle of Thermopylae and the 300, 53–54, 180, 325, 342; as model, 53–54, 59–60, 70, 79, 112, 254
Spencer, Richard, 294–95, 299, 300–306, 308, 310, 315–17, 349
Steuckers, Robert: defense of real socialism, 119; geopolitical contribution, 216, 239–42, 246–47; historical optimism and, 342–43; identity and, 10, 14, 109, 113; metapolitical combat, 24; tragic philosophy of history, 320–21
stoicism, 21–23, 42
street theater, 48, 192, 207, 284
summer camps: CasaPound and, 47; Identitarian Lambda movement and, 45, 53, 60, 81–82, 89, 91, 187–88, 326, 343
Sunić, Tomislav, 69, 101, 108, 166, 195, 297, 335
surveillance society, 247, 340
survivalism, 338–39, 350, 363
Syria, 203, 207, 216–18, 240

Taqiyyah, 198, 201–2, 332
Taylor, Jared, 292–93, 296–98, 300–301, 312–13, 315, 317, 323, 329
terrorism: as companion to Islamization, 202–11; Identitarian condemnation of left-wing terrorism, 94, 338
Thule, 71, 113, 272–74
Timm, Robert, 82, 314–15, 338
tradition: reinvention of, 5, 8, 14–15, 20–21, 35, 51–52, 66, 295, 371. *See also* archeofuturism
tragedy: Identitarian philosophy of history and, 320–22, 329, 341
treason, 119, 124, 127, 138, 195, 201. *See also* collaboration
Tremblay, Rémi, 97, 318
"True Right": Alt Right as, 295; Identitarians as, 4, 100, 128
Trump, Donald: criticism of 264–65; support of, 261–64; white nationalism and, 297, 302–4, 306, 309, 314
Tudor, Lucian, 66, 69, 104, 215, 269, 298
Turkey, 196–97, 241, 335. *See* Ottoman Empire

Union of Islamic Organizations of France (UOIF), 188, 205–6, 212
United States, the: clash of civilizations and, 163–67; continentalism opposed to, 255–57; failure of multiculturalism and, 151–52, 288; globalism and, 105–7, 113–18, 170–71; imperialism and, 227–32, 239–41, 247; independence of Europe from, 233–34

van den Bruck, Moeller, 8, 15, 35, 246–47

Vardon, Philippe, 30–31, 38, 41, 43, 47, 52, 54, 57, 61, 63–65, 68, 73, 79, 85, 87, 101, 132, 137, 184, 284, 288
Veliocas, Joachim, 188, 200
Venner, Dominique: the civilizational crisis of Europe and, 1, 21, 114, 116, 131, 161–62, 199, 227–28, 279; Islam as the Other, 168–69, 175; rebellion and, 19, 22–23, 37, 39, 45, 146; rebirth/revival of Europe and, 20–21, 31, 35, 50–51, 228; as role model, 19, 22–23, 41–42, 258, 298
Vial, Pierre: clash of civilizations and, 163, 280; postnationalism and, 110–12; racialism and 270–71, 275–76, 279; *Reconquista* and, 178, 180; role in Identitarianism, 15–18, 70–72; Russophilia and, 245–46; war and, 333
violence: multiculturalism and, 160–61, 193–94, 208, 284–85, 289, 326, 330; tragedy and, 321–22
Vitali, Juan Pablo, 318–19
Vlaams Belang, 70, 73, 143, 183
von Salomon, Ernst, 8, 19, 76, 95, 235, 360

war, non-Europeans and/or Muslims against Europeans, 173, 177–78, 198–99, 203–4, 329, 332–33. *See also* Fourth-Generation Warfare (4GW)
Werner, Eric, 339–41, 348
white nationalism, 292–96
Wicht, Bernard, 348–49
Willinger, Markus, 45–46, 100–101, 137, 157, 269, 330, 352, 354
women: activists, 44–45, 75, 185–86, 192–94, 369; defense of, 59, 136, 185–86, 192, 286, 289, 355. *See also* 120 Decibels (#120db) campaign

youth: cult of, 27, 45–46; Identitarian activism and, 5, 28, 39, 52, 57–59, 61, 64, 75–77, 91, 103, 191, 211, 301, 325, 369–70

Zeltīts, Raivis, 250–51
Zentropa, 56, 93, 222, 294
ZetaZeroAlfa (band), 32, 33, 55, 92, 216
Zinoviev, Alexander, 339, 342
zombies, 55, 114, 184

JOSÉ PEDRO ZÚQUETE is a research fellow at the Social Sciences Institute of the University of Lisbon. He is the author of *Missionary Politics in Contemporary Europe* and co-author of *The Struggle for the World*.